The Bloomsbury Handbook of Popular Music Video Analysis

The Bloomsbury Handbook of Popular Music Video Analysis

Edited by Lori A. Burns and Stan Hawkins

BLOOMSBURY ACADEMIC
NEW YORK • LONDON • OXFORD • NEW DELHI • SYDNEY

BLOOMSBURY ACADEMIC
Bloomsbury Publishing Inc
1385 Broadway, New York, NY 10018, USA
50 Bedford Square, London, WC1B 3DP, UK

First published in the United States of America 2019

Cover design: Louise Dugdale
Cover image © iStock images/BrianAJackson

Library of Congress Cataloging-in-Publication Data
Names: Burns, Lori, editor. | Hawkins, Stan, editor.
Title: The Bloomsbury handbook of popular music video analysis / edited by
Lori A. Burns and Stan Hawkins.
Description: New York, NY : Bloomsbury Academic, 2019. | Includes
bibliographical references and index. | Summary: "Music videos promote
popular artists in cultural forms that circulate widely across social
media networks. With the advent of YouTube in 2005 and the proliferation
of handheld technologies and social networking sites, the music video
has become available to millions worldwide and it continues to serve as
a fertile platform for the debate of issues and themes in popular
culture. This volume of essays serves as a foundational handbook for the
study and interpretation of the popular music video, with the specific
aim of examining the industry contexts, cultural concepts, and aesthetic
materials that videos rely upon in order to be both intelligible and
meaningful. This study develops a deeper understanding of the
intersecting and interdisciplinary approaches that are invoked in the
analysis of this popular and influential musical form"– Provided by publisher.
Identifiers: LCCN 2019015845 | ISBN 9781501342332 (hardback) |
ISBN 9781501342356 (pdf) | ISBN 9781501342349 (epub)
Subjects: LCSH: Music videos–History and criticism. |
Popular music–History and criticism.
Classification: LCC PN1992.8.M87 B58 2019 | DDC 780.26/7–dc23
LC record available at https://lccn.loc.gov/2019015845

ISBN: HB: 978-1-5013-4233-2
         ePDF: 978-1-5013-4235-6
         eBook: 978-1-5013-4234-9

Typeset by Integra Software Services Pvt. Ltd.
Printed and bound in the United States of America

Contents

Figures

Tables

Examples

Contributors

Philip Auslander is Professor in the School of Literature, Media, and Communication at the Georgia Institute of Technology, Atlanta, United States. His primary research interest is in performance, especially in relation to art, music, media, and technology. His books include *Liveness: Performance in a Mediatized Culture* (1999, 2008), *Performing Glam Rock: Gender and Theatricality in Popular Music* (2006), and *Reactivations: Essays on Performance and Its Documentation* (2018).

Lori Burns is Professor of Music at the University of Ottawa, Canada. Her work on popular music has been published in leading journals, edited collections, and in monograph form. Recent publications include *The Pop Palimpsest: Intertextuality in Recorded Popular Music* (co-edited with Serge Lacasse) and chapters in *The Routledge Research Companion to Popular Music and Gender* and *The Routledge Handbook to Popular Music Analysis*. She is co-editor of the *Ashgate Popular Music and Folk Series* and her recent research project on genre in popular music video was supported by the Social Sciences and Humanities Research Council of Canada (2013–2018).

Norma Coates is Associate Professor at Western University, Canada. Her research on popular music and identity, and popular music and television, has been published in several leading anthologies and journals of popular music topics and taught internationally. She is a former co-chair of the Sound Studies Special Interest Group of the Society for Cinema and Media Studies, and was a visiting fellow at the International Institute of Popular Culture at the University of Turku, Finland in 2015.

Robert Michael Edwards is Lecturer at the University of Ottawa, Canada, in the areas of ancient Judaism, early Christianity, apocalypticism, and Western religions. He has researched extensively in the field of Nag Hammadi studies and early Christian martyrdom narratives. Edwards' work has been published in the journal *Henoch*, as well as in the edited collections, *La croisée des chemins révisitée: quand l'Église et la Synagogue se sont-elles distinguées?* and *La littérature des questions et réponses dans l'Antiquité profane et chrétienne: de l'enseignement à l'exégèse.*

Karen Fournier is Associate Professor of Music Theory at the University of Michigan, USA, where she teaches classes in music theory, analysis, and popular music. Her work has been published widely in the area of popular music and she has contributed a volume entitled *The Words and Music of Alanis Morissette* to the Praeger singer-songwriter series.

She is also completing a book on gender in British punk entitled *Punk and Disorderly: Acting Out Gender and Class in Early British Punk*.

Stan Hawkins is Professor of Musicology at the University of Oslo and Adjunct Professor at the University of Agder, Norway. He is author of *Settling the Pop Score* (2002), *The British Pop Dandy* (2009), *Prince: The Making of a Pop Music Phenomenon* (co-author Sarah Niblock, 2011), and *Queerness in Pop Music* (2016). Edited volumes include *Music, Space and Place* (co-editors Sheila Whiteley and Andy Bennett, 2005), *Essays on Sound and Vision* (co-editor John Richardson, 2007), *Pop Music & Easy Listening* (2011), *Critical Musicological Reflections* (2012), and *The Routledge Research Companion to Popular Music and Gender* (2017).

Christofer Jost works as a lecturer at the Center for Popular Culture and Music at the University of Freiburg, Germany; he is also associate professor (*Privatdozent*) in the Department of Media and Cultural Studies at the University of Freiburg. From 2003 to 2009 he was a performing and recording artist in the field of popular music, which included extensive touring in countries such as Australia, the United States, China, and the United Kingdom, as well as joint performances with the former Kraftwerk member Wolfgang Flür.

Jem Kelly is Senior Lecturer in Performing Arts (Film, TV, and Stage), Programme Leader for the MA in Performing Arts, and Research Co-ordinator in the Department of Performance and Dance at Buckinghamshire New University, United Kingdom. He is a practice-led researcher interrogating intermediality and memory in film, video, and live performance, and has performed and published extensively in this field. He is also an international musician writing and performing with The Lotus Eaters and The Wild Swans.

Mathias Bonde Korsgaard is Assistant Professor of film and media studies at Aarhus University, Denmark. His work focuses on music video, audiovisual studies, and audiovisual remixing. He has published several pieces on music video, film, and other audiovisual media in international journals and anthologies. He is the author of *Music Video After MTV* (Routledge, 2017) and co-editor of the online film journal *16:9*.

Marc Lafrance is an Associate Professor of Sociology at Concordia University, Canada. Informed by an intersectional approach, his research on popular music explores issues of self, body, and society and how they are bound up with the cultural politics of gender, sexuality, race, class, and ability. His work has been published in a variety of peer-reviewed journals such as *Popular Music and Society, Music Theory Online*, and *Twentieth-Century Music*, as well as edited collections such as *The Music and Culture Reader, The Routledge Research Companion to Popular Music and Gender*, and *The Cambridge Companion to the Singer-Songwriter*.

John McGrath is a Lecturer in Music at the University of Surrey, United Kingdom. He has published a monograph with Routledge entitled *Samuel Beckett, Repetition and Modern Music* (2018), which explores the writer's extensive use of repetition alongside the responses to his work by composers such as Morton Feldman and Scott Fields.

Laura McLaren is a PhD student of musicology at the University of Toronto, Canada. Her research interests are popular music, feminist theory, music video, and digital media. She completed her MA with a specialization in women's studies at the University of Ottawa.

Tiffany Naiman is a scholar of popular music, temporality, disability studies, and the voice, and holds a PhD in Musicology from the University of California, Los Angeles, United States. Her work considers musical and cultural responses to illness, disability, and dying, while contributing to the understanding of the social significance of popular music in regard to these areas. She has also successfully built a recognized specialization in the work of David Bowie; her research on him has been published in four edited collections, and outlets such as the *Washington Post* have asked her for her expert commentary. She is also a DJ, electronic musician, film festival programmer, and award-winning documentary film producer.

Anna-Elena Pääkkölä is Lecturer in Musicology at the University of Turku, Finland, a cultural musicologist, and a performing musician with eclectic interests in music research, audiovisual studies, and performance studies. Her dissertation (2016) discussed themes of gender, sexuality, and embodiment in various music genres and her work has been published on film music and sound, Finnish popular music, and musicals and opera. As a musician, she performs in several bands and is currently working on a songwriting project.

Lisa Perrott is Senior Lecturer at the University of Waikato, New Zealand. Her research traverses popular music, audiovisual aesthetics, music video, animation, cultural studies, and audience and fan studies. Her current publications examine the intersections between popular music, avant-garde subversive strategies, audiovisual media, and animation. She is co-editor of the Bloomsbury book series *New Approaches to Sound, Music and Media* and the forthcoming book *Transmedia Directors: Artistry, Industry, and New Audiovisual Aesthetics*. She is also co-editor of the Celebrity Studies journal special issue *Navigating With the Blackstar: The Mediation of David Bowie* (2019). Lisa is currently completing her monograph entitled *David Bowie: Music Video, Transmedia and Collaborative Process* (Bloomsbury, 2019 [forthcoming]).

John Richardson is Professor of Musicology at the University of Turku, Finland. He is the author of *An Eye for Music: Popular Music and the Audiovisual Surreal* (Oxford University Press, 2012) and *Singing Archaeology: Philip Glass's Akhnaten* (Wesleyan University Press, 1999). He is also co-editor of *The Oxford Handbook of New Audiovisual Aesthetics* (with Claudia Gorbman and Carol Vernallis, 2013), *The Oxford Handbook of Sound and Image in Digital Media* (with Carol Vernallis and Amy Herzog, 2013), and *Memory, Space, Sound* (with Johannes Brusila and Bruce Johnson, 2016). He is an active songwriter and musician. His first solo album, *The Fold*, was released in 2017.

Jamie Sexton is Senior Lecturer in Film and Television Studies at Northumbria University, Newcastle, United Kingdom. His publications include *Stranger Than Paradise* (Columbia University Press, 2018), *Cult Cinema: An Introduction* (Wiley-Blackwell, 2013, co-authored with Ernest Mathijs), and the edited collection *Music, Sound and Multimedia: From the Live to the Virtual* (Edinburgh University Press, 2007). He is currently working on a monograph on the intersections between American indie film and indie music, due to be published by Edinburgh University Press in 2019.

Robert Strachan is based in the School of Music at the University of Liverpool, United Kingdom. He has published numerous articles on a variety of aspects of popular music culture including DIY music cultures, electronic music and creativity, sound art, the history of British black music, and music and audiovisual media. He is author of *Sonic Technologies: Popular Music, Digital Culture and the Creative Process* (Bloomsbury, 2017).

Tore Størvold is a PhD student in the Department of Musicology, University of Oslo, Norway. His doctoral research project is titled "Sounding Northern Environments" and applies ecocritical perspectives to contemporary musical practices in Iceland. He has published articles in the journals *Popular Music* and *Popular Music and Society*.

Carol Vernallis teaches at Stanford University, United States. Her books include *Experiencing Music Video: Aesthetics and Cultural Context* (Columbia University Press, 2004) and *Unruly Media: YouTube, Music Video, and the New Digital Cinema* (Oxford University Press, 2013), as well as two co-edited handbooks on contemporary audiovisual aesthetics: *The Oxford Handbook of New Audiovisual Aesthetics* and *The Oxford Handbook of Sound and Image in Digital Media* (Oxford University Press, 2013). Her articles have appeared in *American Music, Cinema Journal, The Journal of Popular Music Studies, Journal of the Society for American Music, Music, Sound, and the Moving Image, Popular Music, Quarterly Review of Film and Video*, and *Screen*.

Jada Watson holds a PhD in Musicology from Université Laval and a Master of Information Studies from the University of Ottawa, Canada. She is currently Adjunct Professor at the University of Ottawa, where she teaches music, information studies, and digital humanities. She is also the Co-ordinator of Digital Humanities for the Faculty of Arts. Her SSHRC-funded research uses computational techniques to pose musicological queries about the geo-cultural origins of the country music genre. Her research has been published in the *Journal of the Society for American Music, American Music, Popular Music & Society, Popular Music*, and *Music, Sound, and the Moving Image*. She also has written chapters for *The Oxford Handbook to Country Music* and *The Cambridge Companion to the Singer-Songwriter*.

Alyssa Woods is Assistant Professor of Music at the University of Guelph, Canada, where she teaches popular music, music history, and theory. In her research, she adopts an interdisciplinary approach to musical theoretical and socio-cultural analysis, focusing on gender and race in popular music, particularly hip-hop. She has published articles in the journals *Music Theory Online* and *Twentieth-Century Music*, as well as the edited collections *Pop-Culture Pedagogy in the Music Classroom, The Cambridge Companion to the Singer-Songwriter, The Ashgate Companion to Popular Music and Gender*, and *The Pop Palimpsest: Intertextuality in Recorded Popular Music*.

Acknowledgments

As editors, all we can claim is to have pieced together a rich tapestry of ideas and perspectives from a group of inspiring scholars at different stages in their careers. It is first and foremost our authors that we thank, for their dedication and commitment to this collection from the word go. Their work makes and defines this collection.

As two editors working at different music institutions on two different continents, our thanks go to our respective departments: Burns's School of Music at the University of Ottawa and Hawkins's Musicology Department at the University of Oslo and Popular Music Section at the University of Agder. It is their support of our work that has made this project and the research allocations required for any such venture possible. We also want to thank friends and colleagues for their efforts and support, as well as the cohorts of students we have both had the privilege of working with throughout the decades that we have been engaged as academics. In particular, thanks go to Kjetil Hallaråker, research assistant to Stan Hawkins, who assisted with a number of the tasks. We would like to thank Leah Babb-Rosenfeld and Amy Martin at Bloomsbury, who have shown tremendous support in the production of the volume.

As the reader will quickly discover upon entering the chapters of this volume, our authors have been inspired by the work of a vast range of artists, producers, directors, and genres. We have all entered into this project for the love of music video—a cultural form that offers artistic creativity, technological innovation, as well as social, cultural, and political commentary.

Introduction: Undertaking Music Video Analysis

Lori Burns and Stan Hawkins

As a ubiquitous cultural form, popular music videos permeate our lives and are experienced in many contexts through a vast array of technologies. Over the past several decades, they have emerged as one of the most powerful sources for mediating music and musician, contributing to new social, political, and cultural patterns. While the first videos arguably can be traced back to the beginning of the last century, they really came into their own during the 1980s due to the launch of MTV—an American cable and satellite channel—with its headquarters in New York City. From the outset, MTV's mission was to broadcast music videos selected by video jockeys (VJs) and target primarily teenagers and young adults. MTV was conceived in 1977 when Warner Cable started its interactive two-way cable-television system, QUBE. This included a variety of channels, such as *Sight on Sound*, a music outlet that featured music-oriented television shows and live-concert footage. The interactive nature of QUBE meant that viewers could vote for their favorite artists and the music they loved. At 12:01 a.m. (Eastern Time) on Saturday, August 1, 1981, John Lack uttered the words: "Ladies and gentlemen, rock and roll," launching MTV, with footage of the first Space Shuttle launch countdown of *Columbia* earlier that year and a montage of the *Apollo 11* moon landing. Symbolically, it was the clip "Video Killed the Radio Star" by The Buggles (produced by Trevor Horn) that ushered in MTV, followed by "You Better Run" by Pat Benatar. Marking the beginning of twenty-four-hours-a-day music television viewing, MTV's slogan, in Mark Goodman's words—one of the first five MTV VJs—would be: "Starting right now, you'll never look at music the same way again … We'll be doing for TV what FM did for radio."[1]

From that moment on, the music video developed in exciting directions, with the spectacle of performance reaching new heights. Pop and rock artists became more glamorized due to technological innovation, while editing equipment and video recorders became more accessible—a new generation of high-profile color recorders and cameras now enabled pop artists to churn out their promotional material at increasingly faster rates. The term "promo" (for promotional video) was coined in the United Kingdom to describe videos or concert clips that record companies commissioned. Among the first artists and groups to be played on MTV were Adam Ant, Blondie, Eurythmics, Culture Club, Mötley

Crüe, Duran Duran, Ultravox, Van Halen, Def Leppard, Bon Jovi, The Cars, and The Police. In addition to the coverage of numerous rock, pop, new wave, and heavy metal acts, mainstream dance trends gained high levels of audiovisual exposure. It was not long before dance would dominate mainstream popular music, evident in the performances of the1980s mega-stars Madonna, Michael Jackson, and Prince, all of whom drew on lavish choreography. MTV would now broadcast musical acts on a global scale never witnessed before, featuring the legendary coverage of live global benefit concerts, including the Live Aid concerts in London and Philadelphia in July 1985, organized by Bob Geldof and Midge Ure (fundraising for famine relief in Ethiopia), and, in 2005, together with VH1, the Live 8 concerts from the G8 countries and South Africa.

The advent and subsequent growth of the internet as a vibrant, global, and user-generated arena would later have a tumultuous impact on the dissemination of music videos. In particular, the internet ushered in the viral video, which could be dispatched through an email from a friend or colleague, posted on a Facebook timeline, or shared through a blog. Today, viral videos—often containing music—traverse social media at lightning speed, closing the gap between radio, television, and the internet. Michael Gregory, a Brooklyn musician, released his first viral music video in 2008. Entitled "Debate Highlights," it included footage from the first US presidential debate during that same year, featuring Barack Obama and John McCain. Notably, Gregory formed a band, "The Gregory Brothers," that made videos using Auto-Tune (an audio processor that adjusts and rectifies vocal and instrumental pitch). Subsequently, the band began to create its "Auto-Tune the News" series of YouTube videos, now known as "Songify the News," which were distributed through their website and YouTube channel, "Schmoyoho." Here the viral video demonstrates the convergence of a networked society, offset by fragmentation, sharing, and digitization.

Music videos in all their forms remain powerful cultural artifacts that circulate widely across social media platforms to promote music and musicians. Undergoing a seismic shift in the twenty-first century, the music industry has witnessed the mushrooming of new communication networks, such as the portals of Myspace (founded in 2003), Facebook (2004), YouTube (2005), Twitter (2006), and Instagram (2010), and the evolving assemblages of music technology such as mp3 sound files, mp3 players, smartphones, and tablets. The proliferation of social networking sites and handheld technologies has changed the course and format of the video and its modes of screening music. In stark contrast to MTV's global twenty-four-hour music video era with a "dual functionality" to listen and to watch, social media sites would facilitate twenty-four-hour multi-functionality: to listen, to watch, to read, to blog, and to actively or passively interact.

Over the course of this volume, we seek to *analyze* the intriguing artistic, cultural, social, and political synergies that emerge in and through the remarkable audiovisual form that is the music video. More specifically, we set out to lay the groundwork for new approaches to analyzing music videos by linking the performances that characterize them to the power relations that pervade music production on and off the stage. Since audiovisual performance representations typically glamorize structures of social subordination, they consequently relay elaborate forms of social and cultural values and ideologies. As music videos animate our social and cultural spaces, they shape significant representations of gendered, sexualized, raced, and classed identities. One of our aims is to explore the connections between these representations of cultural identity and the musical genres from which they arise. In this regard, we understand the musical contexts of genre and style to comprise a driving force in the shaping of cultural identities.

That music videos are predicated upon advances in digital media means that human performance is not only influenced but also altered by an extraordinary range of aesthetic manipulations. The sight of the performing body invites intensified reflexivity on the part of the viewer, characterized by embodiment, simulation, cognition, and agency. By identifying the materiality of the music video, the video spectator engages in a process of distinguishing the expressive parameters that negotiate significant social and cultural issues. When bodies function musically, they provide recourse for understanding how cultures function, especially in relation to the agency of subjectivities. Significantly, the digitized body on display is an intricate compound of gendered, sexual, racial, and ethnic embodiment, the specific configurations of which discipline the materiality of the body. Simultaneously, videos are outlets for creativity, entertainment, and contemplation. In this way, they call for an investigation of musical composition itself, which leads, in turn, to the critical appraisal of cultural practices and the processes of mediation.

As multimodal forms, music videos reside at the crossroads of musical genres and styles, visual genres and styles, lyrical narratives and messages, artistic subjectivities and cultural representations, new media technologies, as well as participatory culture and social media. In an attempt to understand the workings of the music video, scholars grapple with interpretive approaches, issues of transmediality, and theoretical principles. These writings emanate from the fields of popular music studies, media studies, film theory, cultural studies, gender studies, critical discourse analysis, and sociology. The formulation of an appropriate analytic and interpretive method is dependent upon, and arises from, the selected object of inquiry, hence the diversity of approaches exemplified in this collection and the broad spectrum of music discussed. While a musical artist or band is often presented as the primary object of inquiry, we also recognize the collaborative process of production that exists behind every video—involving performers, writers, producers, directors, and technicians—and the fact that each of these participants has a profound impact upon the content and expression of the music video is never in doubt.

The field of music video analysis owes a major debt to E. Ann Kaplan's seminal work, *Rocking Around the Clock* (1987). Kaplan was the first scholar to adopt a postmodern approach for the analysis of MTV video types and styles. On the heels of her work, the study of music and image has burgeoned, with methods and theories devised for analyzing audiovisuality, where both audio and visual properties are scrutinized. Scholars from the fields of music, languages and literatures, media and communication, digital humanities, gender studies, and sociology, to name just a few, draw upon the contents of the popular music video in order to illustrate not only musical and artistic expressions, but also social, political, and cultural concerns and ideologies. Lisa Lewis, following in E. Ann Kaplan's footsteps, explored gendered address in her *Gender Politics and MTV* (1990), while

Andrew Goodwin proposed a blend of musicological and sociological perspectives in his *Dancing in the Distraction Factory: Music Television and Popular Culture* (1992).[2] In this groundbreaking study, Goodwin outlined a taxonomy of music video narrative structures, offering a critical reflection on how the dynamics of stardom and the social variables of fandom relate to video reception. His work ushered in the next generation of scholars, who continued to provide valuable insights into how specific musical and visual codes are used in specific musical genres. The first collection published on music videos, *Sound and Vision: The Music Video Reader* (1993), edited by Frith, Goodwin, and Grossberg, presented a set of essays that continued the scholarly reflection on postmodernism and MTV, with a clear motivation to examine the implications of the music video for the communication of genre values and gendered subjectivities.[3] On a broader scale, the scholarly writings on audiovisuality took a theoretical turn with Nicholas Cook's *Analysing Musical Multimedia* (1998), which pinpointed the intersections between and among the individual multimedia layers of music video, as well as other musical media (opera on film, Disney animation of classical music, and so on).[4] At the dawn of the new millennium, Carol Vernallis's book *Experiencing Music Video* (2004) established new directions for the analysis of the music video form, which she later expounded upon in *Unruly Media* (2013). Film theorist Michel Chion's work on audiovisual aesthetics would be one of many incentives for Vernallis to explore visual processes in relation to sonic processes, ranging from the deliberate coordination of musical and visual events to the communication of a gesture both in the images and in the sounds.[5] Simultaneously, a great number of edited collections and books on audiovisuality have been forthcoming that have directly influenced the shape of this collection.[6] And while the field of music video studies has established itself as a serious scholarly discipline, there is also clear evidence of an increasing interest in music videos in the public domain.[7]

In the interest of responding to Douglas Kellner's (2011) call for "critical media literacy,"[8] the chapters in this volume explore the dynamic workings of the multifaceted music video across a range of analytic perspectives and examples. With this mandate in mind, the assembled chapters address issues such as: the impact of recent developments in music video production and distribution upon music consumption and reception;[9] the significance of audiovisual expression for cultural and political identities and lifestyles; the influence of multimedia technologies and aesthetics upon the worldbuilding strategies of popular music artists; and the application of theoretical approaches from a range of disciplinary perspectives for the critical analysis of audiovisual discourses. Accordingly, the analytic materials on offer derive from observations, interviews, and creative involvement, with a prime method being textual analysis, a method contingent on rigorous interpretation, close reading, and the rigorous assessment of audiovisual details. Intended to serve as a foundational handbook for the study and interpretation of the popular music video, the ensuing chapters examine the industry and its contexts, cultural concepts, modes of mediation, aesthetic materials, performance stagings, and representations of human subjectivities. In their entirety, the studies reveal a deep understanding of the intersecting and interdisciplinary approaches that are engaged in the analysis of this popular and influential musical form.

To date, music videos have prompted much audiovisual theorization. To explore the subject further and advance the scholarly dialogue, we have drawn together a wide range of examples and innovative approaches. The chapters are gathered into five parts in order to illuminate several key factors that we understand influence, inform, and shape music video expression: Part I examines music video from its point of creation through the concepts of *Authorship, Production, and Distribution*; Part II explores a range of *Cultural Codes, Representations, and Genres* as these are mobilized in the communication of genres, styles, and performances; Part III offers critical reflections on the processes of *Mediation*, revealing multifaceted aspects of music videos as multimodal, intermedia, and transmedia texts; Part IV takes up the concept of *Aesthetics*, with consideration of the parameters of space, place, time, and a range of sensorial perceptions invoked by audiovisual texts; and Part V undertakes the challenging topic of *Subjectivities and Discourses*, to reveal the significant commentaries on social and cultural identities, such as gender, sexuality, race, and religion.

The chapters in *Authorship, Production, and Distribution* by Mathias Bonde Korsgaard, Jamie Sexton, Lisa Perrott, and John Richardson explore a series of important questions: who is creating these cultural forms and how are they doing so? What impact does the producer's own artistic vision have upon the music video work? And what happens when the consumers (fans) themselves receive and even manipulate the work of musical artists? **Mathias Bonde Korsgaard** studies the degree to which the music video has diversified in its distribution, taking the extreme example of videos that are "not safe for work" (NSFW). Through their content, Korsgaard argues, these videos push against the boundaries of the hegemonic mainstream. **Jamie Sexton** explores the work of indie video directors who also produce feature films, revealing features that point to the influence of music videos on filmmaking, an influence that is manifest in identifiable indie music aesthetics. **Lisa Perrott** also considers the creative agency of the video director; in her chapter, that role is adopted by a fan who creates complex video treatments as fan-made videos, which, she argues, contribute to the transmedia worldbuilding efforts of the band in question. The final reflection on authorship and production is offered by **John Richardson** who, in the direction and production of his own music videos, translates his knowledge of music video analysis into the practice of research creation.

In *Cultural Codes, Representations, and Genres*, the chapters by Philip Auslander, Norma Coates, Karen Fournier, Rob Strachan, and Laura McLaren address the intersections of visual and musical genres to examine how music videos reflect societal norms and shape cultural understanding. Music videos operate within the traditions of popular music genres as well as visual genres; however, the interpretive literature on the music video has not yet robustly probed the question of how these genres are juxtaposed. Scholars in media studies have developed ways of classifying music video genres around narrative forms and rhetorical types. For instance, Kaplan's (1987) classificatory scheme includes the romantic genre, the socially conscious genre, the modernist genre, the oppositional genre, and the nihilist genre;[10] however, video genre classification has yet to be queried in relation to musical genre categories (pop, R&B, rock, punk, metal, country, indie, alternative, etc.). Centering his study on the performers, **Philip Auslander** examines the music video as a performance space for the enactment of musical personae. Contemplating videos that cross genre boundaries, his analytic nuances help us to understand the complex set of factors, including the representation of gender and race, which cultivate a musical persona. **Norma Coates** takes us back to the 1960s to consider *Hullabaloo*—a rock and roll program—for its contribution to television genre and style, revealing that it was among the first programs that reflected changing norms about gender and race. From 1960s television we move into the 1970s with **Karen Fournier**'s analysis of punk subculture, to interpret how embodied aspects of the moving image are *détournés* by punk artists, and specifically by female punks in order to contest gender norms. Equally compelled by historical video treatments, **Robert Strachan** provides a study of contemporary applications of older technologies (e.g., Super 8 and VHS) to produce music videos, arguing that such technologies leave traces of significance on the very surfaces of music videos, thus marking the videos within the genre practices of indie rock. To close this part, **Laura McLaren** establishes the genre parameters of the lyric video, a music video category that has gained traction during the first part of the twenty-first century. With an analysis grounded in genre theory, she argues that lyric videos follow specific parameters while simultaneously participating in musical genre ideologies and conveying artistic personae.

Inevitably, issues of *Mediation* abound in the creation, design, and distribution of a cultural form that comprises the intersection of word, music, and image in a myriad of mediated styles and approaches. Authors Lori Burns, Christofer Jost, Jem Kelly, and John McGrath address the theme of mediality in order to illustrate multimodal, intermedia, and transmedia narratives and aesthetics. As music videos are usually released in connection with a popular music album, and as artists more and more frequently present their music videos in relation to additional materials (e.g., artwork, clothing, books, comic books, internet materials, etc.) and the live concert spectacle, the interpretation of the music video is now linked with and dependent upon cross-platform media and materials. To begin this part, **Lori Burns** considers dynamic multimodal expression, offering both a reflection on the theories relevant to multimodal analysis and a close reading of an extreme metal performance video. **Christofer Jost** examines transmedia practice in popular music, revealing the music video to be central in the creative approaches to popular music production; he identifies three common manifestations of transmediality: aesthetics, artification, and virtual stardom. Analyzing the popular music video as an instance of the "pop palimpsest," **Jem Kelly** applies theories of intermediality and hypermediality to the analysis of popular music video, showing how music videos produce new meanings through their palimpsestic practices. The final chapter in this part, by **John McGrath**, strives toward a theory of audiovisual repetition for the close reading of transmedia relations in a selected music video from the 1980s, raising questions about the development and cohesion of narratives across fragmented media texts.

From mediality, we next turn to the topic of music video *Aesthetics*, to examine how the themes of space, place, time, and the senses are configured in the multimodal contexts of music video aesthetics. In the larger field of popular musicology, these spaces and places have emerged as formative elements in the creation and communication of cultural meanings.[11] The three chapters in this part—by Carol Vernallis, Jada Watson, and Tiffany Naiman—explore a range of theoretical and artistic/technical assumptions for aesthetic analysis, illustrating the application of theoretical tools and approaches to selected video examples. Asking "how to analyze music videos," **Carol Vernallis** adopts an empirical approach to the gathering of aesthetic attributes in lyrics, music, and images, placing these expressive modalities into dialogue in a close reading of a popular video. Adopting an ecocritical approach to the analysis of place and space in country music video, **Jada Watson** explores how rural and urban contexts are significant for the identity of a country songwriter's artistic persona. Closing this part, **Tiffany Naiman** considers the modernist aesthetics of an art rock video that utilize symbols of life and death to articulate a message about memory and legacy.

In the final part of the volume, we build upon the foregoing examinations of production contexts, cultural codes, modes of mediation, and aesthetics in order to interpret the important function of music videos to convey powerful messages about the human condition. The range of social messages and cultural interventions that intersect in the music video corpus provides us with an opportunity to develop a more comprehensive approach to the analysis of this form. Arguing that music videos contribute to the crafting of artistic personae and that spectators connect to musical artists in and through their music videos, this part concentrates on *Subjectivities and Discourses*: how do music videos communicate narratives, what stories are told through this medium, whose stories are told, and how do videos shape the subjectivity of the one who is doing the telling? Four chapters, by Stan Hawkins and Tore Størvold, Alyssa Woods and Robert Edwards, Anna-Elena Pääkkölä, and Marc Lafrance, offer compelling analyses of music video storytelling, drawing upon tools from discourse analysis, gender theory, and religious studies as these are applied to popular music video expression. Taking an ecomusicological and gendered intertextual approach, **Stan Hawkins** and **Tore Størvold** theorize masculine lumbersexuality in the work of a mainstream pop artist with a highly influential star persona. Another co-authorial team, **Alyssa Woods** and **Robert Edwards** address the recent hip-hop phenomenon of "finding God," studying a selected male rapper whose struggle with faith emerges in his music, lyrics, and images. Staying with the genre of hip-hop, **Anna-Elena Pääkkölä** selects a female rap artist who grapples with historical misogyny by asserting her gendered, sexualized, and racialized agency in a highly controversial music video. And, to close the volume, **Marc Lafrance** studies a video that "flips the script," so to speak, in a representation of intimate partner violence in which a woman enacts violence upon her male partner. In his critical analysis, Lafrance grapples with how the video represents dominant norms of masculinity, femininity, heterosexuality, and disability.

As editors of this exciting collection, it is our sincere hope that the reader will derive as much satisfaction from this journey as we have when compiling these chapters from start to finish. If anything, it is the diversity of approaches and the case studies themselves that verify the need for ongoing research in the burgeoning field of music video studies. The sheer breadth and magnitude of our scope is evident through a simple (but extensive) list of directors, artists, bands, producers, visual artists, engineers, and programmers who are studied throughout this volume: Childish Gambino's NSFW-video "This Is America"; Steve Hanft's lo-fi videos and Danny Perez's experimental low-budget videos and films; visual artist Gastón Viñas and Chris Hopewell's development of Radiohead's "Burn the Witch"; The Fold's "Dawnsong" and "Birdman of Bognor"; "Walk This Way" by Run-DMC featuring Aerosmith; Darius Rucker's country performance of "Wagon Wheel"; prime-time television's *Hullabaloo* as a hallmark of mid-1960s music programming; early British punk and "Rule Britannia" from Derek Jarman's *Jubilee*; indie rock and post-digital music video in Alvvays's 2014 track "Archie, Marry Me"; Kate Perry's lyric video "Wide Awake"; director Peter Ullaeus's extreme metal video performance capture for Dark Tranquillity's "Uniformity"; The Who's feature movie, *Quadrophenia* (directed by Franc Roddam); the pioneering role of Kraftwerk in design aesthetics; virtual stardom in Daft Punk, Gorillaz, and the artificial singer, Hatsune Miku; U2's video "The Fly"; The Lotus Eaters' video for "It Hurts"; Michel Gondry's treatment of "The Hardest Button to Button" by The White Stripes and "Bachelorette" by Björk; Laurie Anderson's transmedia work, "O Superman" and her documentary *Heart of a Dog*; Beyoncé's "Pretty Hurts", directed by Melina Matsoukas; country artist Corb Lund's "September"; David Bowie's epic "Blackstar"; Justin Timberlake's "Man of the Woods"; religious rap and hip-hop videos by Kendrick Lamar, DMX, NAS, and The Game; Nicki Minaj's controversial "Anaconda"; and Pink's "Please Don't Leave Me." Thus, through the analysis of this vast array of music videos, new concepts are born and it is envisaged that the range of musical genres, artists, and conceptual frameworks on offer will pave the way for a better understanding of the industry, its media structures, and the roles people play in the name of entertainment. Ultimately, our mission is to draw special attention to the ways in which music videos operate, the range of mediation strategies that are available, their cultural impact, aspects of the creative production process, and the aesthetic materials that shape their complex narratives, subjectivities, and social identities.

Notes

1   Casey Phillips, "Bringing It Back: MTV, VH1, CMT Feature 12 Hours of All-Music Programming Today," *Times Free Press*, July 4, 2013, https://www.timesfreepress.com/news/life/entertainment/story/2013/jul/04/bringing-it-back-mtv-vh1-cmt-feature-12/112397.

2   Lisa Lewis, *Gender Politics and MTV: Voicing the Difference* (Philadelphia, PA: Temple University Press, 1990); E. Ann Kaplan, *Rocking Around the Clock: Music Television, Postmodernism, and Consumer Culture* (London and New York: Routledge, 1987); and Andrew Goodwin, *Dancing in the Distraction Factory: Music Television and Popular Culture* (Minneapolis, MN: University of Minnesota Press, 1992).

3   Simon Frith, Andrew Goodwin, and Lawrence Grossberg, eds., *Sound and Vision: The Music Video Reader* (London: Routledge, 1993).

4   Nicholas Cook, *Analysing Musical Multimedia* (New York: Oxford University Press, 1998).

5   Carol Vernallis, *Experiencing Music Video: Aesthetics and Cultural Context* (New York: Columbia University Press, 2004).

6   On the heels of Vernallis's influential text, several edited collections emerged: Roger Beebe and Jason Middleton, eds., *Medium Cool: Music Videos from Soundies to Cellphones* (Durham, NC: Duke University Press, 2007); Jamie Sexton, ed., *Music, Sound and*

Multimedia: From the Live to the Virtual (Edinburgh: Edinburgh University Press, 2007); John Richardson and Stan Hawkins, *Essays on Sound and Vision* (Helsinki: Helsinki University Press, 2007); Graeme Harper, Ruth Doughty, and Jochen Eisentraut, eds., *Sound and Music in Film and Visual Media* (New York: Continuum, 2009); Henry Keazor and Thorsten Wübenna, eds., *Rewind, Play, Fast Forward: The Past, Present and Future of the Music Video* (Bielefeld: Transcript Verlag, 2010); Julie McQuinn, ed., *Popular Music and Multimedia* (Burlington, VT: Ashgate, 2011); John Richardson, *An Eye for Music: Popular Music and the Audiovisual Surreal* (New York: Oxford University Press, 2012); John Richardson, Claudia Gorbman, and Carol Vernallis, eds., *The Oxford Handbook of New Audiovisual Aesthetics* (Oxford and New York: Oxford University Press, 2013); Carol Vernallis, Amy Herzog, and John Richardson, eds., *Oxford Handbook of Sound and Image in Digital Media* (Oxford: Oxford University Press, 2013); Enrique Encabo, ed., *Reinventing Sound: Music and Audiovisual Culture* (Newcastle upon Tyne: Cambridge Scholars Publishing, 2015); and Lyndon Way and Simon McKerrell, eds., *Music as Multimodal Discourse: Semiotics, Power, and Protest* (London and New York: Bloomsbury, 2017). In another recent collection, *Music/Video: Histories, Aesthetics, Media*, edited by Gina Arnold, Daniel Cookley, Kirsty Fairclough-Isaacs, and Michael Goddard (New York: Bloomsbury, 2017), the music video is interpreted by scholars from the fields of media studies, communications, film, and visual arts. In 2017, the journal *Volume!* included a special issue, edited by Marc Kaiser, on music video cultures. Marc Kaiser, ed. "Watching Music: Music Video Cultures," special issue of *Volume! The French Journal of Popular Music Studies* 14, no. 2 (2017): 1–6.

7   For instance, Saul Austerlitz's *Money for Nothing: A History of the Music Video from the Beatles to the White Stripes* (London and New York: Continuum, 2007) offers a valuable overview of music video development that is intended for the general audience and also serves as an indicator of the popular readership that exists for the topic. Steve Reiss and Neil Feineman's *Thirty Frames Per Second: The Visionary Art of the Music Video* (New York: Abrams, 2001) is a beautiful coffee-table book that celebrates the visual styling of several leading videographers.

8   Douglas Kellner, "Cultural Studies, Multiculturalism, and Media Culture," in *Gender, Race, and Class in Media: A Critical Reader*, edited by Gail Dines and Jean M. Humez (London: Sage, 2011), 7–19.

9   In her *Unruly Media: YouTube, Music Video, and the New Digital Cinema* (Oxford and New York: Oxford University Press, 2013), Carol Vernallis defines what she refers to as the music video's intensified aesthetics, but also extends beyond the music video to explore recent cinematic techniques and web media. Also valuable to the scholarly community is Mathias Bonde Korsgaard's *Music Video After MTV: Audiovisual Studies, New Media, and Popular Music* (London and New York: Routledge, 2017), which offers an in-depth study of the technologies, production, and distribution aspects of the music video. In a similar line of inquiry, Steven Shaviro's *Digital Music Videos* (New Brunswick, NJ: Rutgers University Press, 2017) considers recent developments in music video technology.

10   Kaplan, *Rocking Around the Clock*.

11   See John Connell and Chris Gibson, *Sound Tracks: Popular Music, Identity and Place* (New York: Routledge, 2003); and Adam Krims, *Music and Urban Geography* (New York: Routledge, 2007).

Part I

Authorship, Production, and Distribution

1

Changing Dynamics and Diversity in Music Video Production and Distribution

Mathias Bonde Korsgaard

At this moment, as I commence writing this chapter, the music video *de jour* is without a doubt Childish Gambino's "This Is America,"[1] directed by accomplished music video director Hiro Murai.[2] The video premiered on May 5, 2018, and, in approximately a week, it had received more than 100 million YouTube views (a figure that has likely multiplied several times as you are reading these words). Along the way the music video has sparked a lot of debate, think pieces, and social media discussion, and the song went on to debut at the top spot of the Billboard *Hot 100*, arguably largely on the basis of the popularity and ubiquity of the video. The video is first and foremost characterized by sudden shifts in tone, both musically and visually. Musically, the track mostly alternates between a section led by choir singing and acoustic guitar that is of a somewhat cheerful nature and then another, more beat-heavy, section featuring Donald Glover's rap and an ominous bass. Visually, we are presented with sudden and surprising moments of murderous gun violence at both times when the track transitions from the first musical section to the second—and generally the visuals are dominated by sharply irreconcilable contrasts between acts of violence and mayhem on one hand and blissfully ignorant dancing and singing on the other (Figure 1.1).

It is not hard to understand why such a video is able to draw massive attention and generate debate, thereby becoming one of the most talked-about cultural objects of its moment;[3] however, this is not the only way in which this video is "of its moment." Had it been made back when music videos were mostly seen on television, it probably would not have been seen (or perhaps even made) at all. There are several reasons why a video like this would *never ever* have made it onto MTV—and, in a sense, this is what this chapter is about. What separates a music video of the bygone MTV days from a contemporary music video on YouTube? And why are they different? In this chapter I will suggest that part of the answer to these questions lies in the historically changing dynamics of music video distribution. Approaching music videos from the point of view of their means of distribution will allow

Figure 1.1 Childish Gambino, "This Is America," directed by Hiro Murai, 2018 (0:52).

us to better understand how institutional and technical factors tie in with and have an effect on aesthetic practices and reception contexts. What is more, this focus on distribution would also seem to address a general deficiency in the study of music videos, given that the distribution perspective is implicit at best and entirely lacking at worst.[4]

Given that this approach has been largely neglected, the study of music video distribution clearly holds the potential to offer new perspectives. Examining music video distribution can help to make visible and explain some of the main differences between music videos of the televisual past and those of the post-televisual present. Here, I will pursue the main argument that the shift from television to the internet as the music video's primary site of distribution is key to grasping the fact that the contemporary music video (or, music video online) is a comparatively more *diverse* phenomenon than the music video used to be in the MTV days. This increased diversity is manifested on several different levels. First, there is the fact that music videos are now made for a wider spectrum of musical genres. Second, there is a gradual expansion of audiovisual styles and aesthetics—if there ever was a *single* music video aesthetic, then surely this is no longer the case with the plurality of available styles. Third, there is also the tendency to experiment more wildly with the formal characteristics of the music video.[5] Fourth, there has been a general broadening of the limits of representation and the possible types of content and identity politics on display in music videos, allowing for more diverse and transgressive types of imagery. And fifth, music videos are now accessed and seen in a widened array of different reception contexts. Surely, the fact that music videos are met with far fewer institutional and technical constraints in the digital age, when compared to the televisual past, is one of the main reasons behind why this cultural form has become a progressively more and more heterogeneous phenomenon. As I draw to my conclusion, I will corroborate this fact by examining the phenomenon known as the NSFW music video (NSFW stands for "not safe for work"), arguing that these clips, with their graphic content, clearly demonstrate the increasing diversity of music videos—and thus the extent to which the boundaries of the music video have broadened as a consequence of the shift from television to online distribution.

Three phases of the music video's (distribution) history

Looking back at the development of the music video as a cultural form, it seems reasonable to divide its history into three distinct phases relating to the means of distribution: a pre-televisual, a televisual, and a post-televisual phase.[6] In other words, music videos existed well before MTV, and now that MTV has largely turned its back on music videos with its focus on reality television, music videos have found a new home online. These changing forms of distribution should also have an impact on the study of the cultural phenomenon, because, if it is indeed true that "music video's association with television may well turn out to be a pre-historical anomaly,"[7] then the music video itself should not necessarily be studied as a form of television.

As with all historical periodization, there is, of course, some overlap or some transitionary moments between the main phases—or even some parallel histories involving, for instance, the distribution of music videos on VHS and DVD. Other such fissures would include the period of time leading up to the launch of MTV (i.e., the last half of the 1970s) and the time in-between the waning of the music video on MTV[8] and its rise online (i.e., the time around the turn of the millennium), while another possible objection to this division is how one even defines "television" in the digital age.[9] But even as such modifications are highly relevant, the general division into these three phases should still provide some clarity. This should also help make it clear to what extent these historical changes in distribution have led to corresponding changes in music video production and user engagement.

As Henry Keazor and Thorsten Wübbena have noted on the history of the music video, it "has not one, but several histories."[10] Depending on how one defines what a music video even is, it has a complex and multifaceted lineage. Perhaps contrary to popular belief, music videos have a rather rich pre-televisual history.[11] Those pre-televisual phenomena that can be considered music videos *avant la lettre* were of course not called music videos, they were not institutionalized as such, and they did not necessarily serve the same purposes as modern-day music videos, but even so the roots of the music video arguably stretch back more than a century. Some of the most obvious precursors to the music video proper include the so-called visual jukeboxes, like the 1940s' Panoram Soundies and the 1960s' Scopitones. Also in the 1960s, another format that saw the light of day comprised the so-called "promos" that were in effect music videos, even though their promotional use was not yet fully determined.

But if we were to travel back in time to the 1960s and ask what people would consider to be the first ever music video, we would most likely be met by confusion. While we can trace this lineage in historical hindsight, phenomena such as these were not considered music videos in their own time. As noted by Craig Marks and Rob Tannenbaum in their history of the "golden age of MTV," it was not until MTV provided a steady delivery system that the music video became formalized and thereby came to connote "a specific set of qualities" including "aggressive directorship, contemporary editing and FX, sexuality, vivid colors, urgent movement, nonsensical juxtapositions, provocation, frolic" aimed for "maximum impact on the small screen."[12] Therefore, they are also right to claim that the search for the origins of the music video is necessarily a futile task, seeing that there "is no such thing as 'the first music video'"[13]—or, put the other way around, there are in fact *too many* contenders for "the first ever music video."

This also offers a possible explanation as to why the pre-televisual music video appears to be less standardized than its televisual successor. For one thing, if they were not thought of as music videos in the first place, there were not yet any codified aesthetic norms to adhere to, and as a result experimentation was the order of the day. It was also not yet clear what kind of reception context or usage such products were aimed at—and the differences between jukebox films, promos, and for instance some of the early television formats that somewhat resembled music videos, are quite clear and also clearly a result of their different means of distribution that all entail different institutional and technical constraints. Accordingly, the pre-televisual music video is quite hard to pin down precisely because it was still quite a dispersed phenomenon.

Exactly when the music video entered its televisual phase is of course debatable. If it had not already fully found a home on television before, then it certainly did with the launch of MTV in the United States in 1981. By many accounts, the place of MTV in the history of the music video is so fundamental that the two have even become synonymous sometimes—and the history of MTV has certainly been studied more often than that of the music video in and of itself.[14] Studying music videos and music television started in the 1980s and, for some, MTV offered the perfect illustration of the postmodern condition— not only because of what characterized MTV as a television network, but also because of the particular aesthetics of the music video of the MTV era. This would lead John Fiske— in a well-known article that is highly emblematic of the research on music videos of that era—to conclude that "MTV is TV at its most typical, most televisual."[15] Even if we accept the validity of this statement (and I would suggest that there are, in fact, sound reasons not to, for instance when considering the changes MTV has undergone since the article was published in 1986), the same is decidedly *not* true of the music video in and of itself. The music video is not and never was "TV at its most televisual," since the music video was never restricted to distribution on television in the first place.

This non-restriction is also recognizable in some of the second-wave writings on the music video, beginning around the turn of the millennium. Here, the relation between the music video and television is problematized and not considered a natural given,[16] and, when looked at from the present moment, it is certainly clear that music videos were never specifically a form of television. Rather, as this short distribution history has already demonstrated, they existed well before television, and they continue to exist *after* television as well. At the same time, MTV has changed quite a lot since its early days of 24-hour music video transmission. To the extent that music videos are shown on MTV at all, they are most often relegated to being shown at night time when most people do not watch television. Along these lines, one might argue that music videos appear to have been tailor-made for online distribution (even though this is obviously not the case).[17] There are several reasons why music videos have transferred so well to an online environment. For one thing, in the early days of YouTube the large back catalog of music videos provided a great resource of materials at a time when content was in high demand. Also, the brevity of music videos was a particularly important feature in this period when technical restraints called for short videos. Moreover, their musical basis and their promotional nature generally make for media texts with a large appeal on any imaginable platform. And finally, the fact that they have always been aimed at "small screens" (from video jukeboxes to television sets) has made them suitable for consumption on the computer and phone screens. In fact, this nature of being a small-screen media form may turn out to be the one feature that ties all the historically different incarnations of music videos together (even as music videos have also occasionally been shown on large screens in museums and film theaters).

In particular, it is the shift from the second to the third phase—with the relocation of music videos from the television screen to several other screens—that has most significantly altered how music videos are made and enjoyed. It is clear that this change in distribution has changed many other facets of the music video—some more obvious than others. In terms of the reception of music videos, they are now accessed and seen through a greater variety of technical media than ever before and thus are also seen in a much greater variety of contexts and viewing modes. There is also the seemingly simple fact that we get to choose which videos to watch. In other words, where music videos were once mostly restricted to being seen in private or public spaces that had a television set, now they can be seen pretty much anywhere at any time.

There are also several new types of music videos that are incompatible with the technology of television, as a result of their uniquely digital features. This would include for instance interactive music videos or the music video–like apps in Björk's *Biophilia* project.[18] The 360-degree music video and the VR music video are also inherently digital phenomena. Another music video project that ties in with experiments in distribution would be Death Cab for Cutie's "You Are a Tourist" (2011), a one-take video that was streamed live at the same time as it was made. There is also a more recent phenomenon that is directly shaped by the technologies we now use to watch music videos, namely the so-called vertical music video, referring to the fact that the orientation of the screen is vertical instead of horizontal. Because it is increasingly common to watch music videos on a phone—and because the natural orientation of your phone screen is vertical—music videos are now being tailor-made for this particular mode of viewing. Vertical music videos have become gradually more popular since at least 2015, for example, for such popular artists as Selena Gomez, Taylor Swift, Ariana Grande, and Nicki Minaj (Figure 1.2). In the context of this chapter, Nicki Minaj's "Chun-Li"[19] is a fitting example, seeing that, apart from being a vertical video,

Figure 1.2 Nicki Minaj, "Chun-Li," directed by Nicki Minaj, 2018 (1:53).

it is also somewhat NSFW in its presentation of Minaj. Like many other vertical videos, the video is mostly shot by the performer, who is filming herself with her cellphone camera in hand (although a little bit of the video's footage is also shot by someone else). Throughout the video, Minaj is posing for the camera, often realigning the framing to ensure that we see her famous behind which is also just barely covered by her clothes. Literally, this is the first thing that happens in the video: Minaj moving her cellphone so that it films her *derrière* instead of her face. The same thing goes for the frame-grab from the video included here: at the 1:53 minute mark, Minaj consciously readjusts not the position of the camera but rather her head in order to clear the line of sight between the viewer and her rear. Thus, the video is quite sexually suggestive; however, whereas this might have seemed unduly provocative in the days of MTV, nowadays the video presumably comes off as being only mildly NSFW—at least in comparison with some of the videos discussed later in this chapter.

If we were instead to consider the music video as a kind of "visual radio,"[20] could we then understand its transmigration from media platform to media platform as perhaps all the more natural? Many people probably use YouTube in the way that they used to use MTV—namely as a (visual) jukebox, mostly for the consumption of music, with the image being a kind of surplus value that is not necessarily given any attention. Depending on which markets we are discussing, there are also places on the globe where YouTube has the largest number of users of all music streaming services ahead of Spotify, Apple Music, Tidal, and others. In terms of distribution, the music video is also certainly more closely associated with the world of music than with that of film or television, which can be confirmed by the recent practice of tying music videos to the promotion of these music streaming services. Some of the above-mentioned vertical videos premiered on Spotify, just as Beyoncé's famed visual album *Lemonade* (2016) was initially only offered as an exclusive release on Tidal. At the same time, music videos have also been used to promote feature films, and directors have frequently moved back and forth between directing music videos, television, commercials, and feature films.[21] With these new contexts, the music video is not only located at the intersection between different aesthetic and sensory registers, but also between different industries and economies.

Yet another example of a music video type that has only come into being after music videos became an online phenomenon is the so-called lyric video, which, in a more or less simple fashion, shows the lyrics to the song as the video progresses (even as, again, there are some televisual forebears, including Prince's "Sign o' the Times" [1987] and the Gondry-directed video for Jean François Coen's "La Tour de Pise" [1993]). Initially, lyric videos were made mostly by users, although it has recently become more and more common for these to be made professionally. But why did these videos—that are often aesthetically unsophisticated due to their origin as user-generated content—suddenly become popular? One might imagine that the lyric video came about as an indirect result of the fact that, when listening to music today, it is no longer all that common to have physical album covers containing the song lyrics readily at hand. In this sense, the lyric video was initially nothing more than a practical solution to those people who wanted to either sing along or just simply decode the lyrics, i.e., a way to overcome the physical dematerialization of the album cover.[22]

Another important change in music video distribution is the rise not only of user-generated content, such as the aforementioned lyric video, but also of user distribution. While there are many examples of users and fans making their own music videos—and also a pre-digital lineage connecting this to the culture of "vidding"[23]—the role of the user is quite often only that of a distributor—and not necessarily a creator—of content. By liking, sharing, and commenting on—and sometimes also uploading or even ultimately creating—music videos, the practices of everyday media users are more active and more visible than was the case in the era of the music video on satellite services. But even as the shift to digital distribution seems to be generally favorable to the user due to the user's increased access to and free choice of content in the digital age, there are also other aspects that pull in a different direction. For one thing, perhaps the most important role played by the user is one that is both invisible and mostly unheeded: it is neither that of creating nor of disseminating music videos, but that of providing data. Our viewing habits are constantly monitored and the insights into this monitoring forms a large part of what enables sites such as YouTube and Vevo to generate revenue—by establishing links between certain musical genres, certain types of content, and certain kinds of consumer behavior. Viewed in this light, the real value added by users is that of "generating metadata on the social behaviour of a profitable consumer segment."[24] Even if we may sometimes not feel this way, due to the fact that music videos are apparently offered to us "for free" online, the viewer still solidly remains a commercially targetable consumer in the digital age.

The NSFW music video

Finally, I will consider a music video phenomenon that is indicative of several of the changes addressed above—namely the NSFW video, or the "not safe for work" video. NSFW is a term that came into existence around the turn of the millennium and it refers to any kind of content that you, for one reason or another, would prefer not to be caught watching while working—most often due to its sexual and/or violent nature. In terms of the *changing reception contexts* of music videos, the very implication that you even *can* watch music videos while working is in itself telling in terms of the variety of different viewing contexts of today.

These videos are also symptomatic of the *aesthetic and formal changes* that music videos have undergone due to the change in distribution methods. Transgressive content in music videos has certainly become much more common, even if we can name several NSFW videos from the MTV days, for instance, the videos from Nine Inch Nails' long-form video-EP *Broken* (1993) that were considered so offensive they were almost exclusively limited to bootlegged VHS tapes in the 1990s (although today most of the videos on the EP can be easily found online). Other early NSFW classics would include the collaborations between Aphex Twin and Chris Cunningham or some of the videos directed by Jonas Åkerlund, perhaps most infamously his video for The Prodigy's "Smack My Bitch Up" (1997).[25] But for most of these NSFW videos to be shown on television, they would often have to be edited, censored, or shown only at night time. In a notable case, MTV Europe was fined by Ofcom in 2008 for airing Aphex Twin's "Windowlicker"[26] (1999) before 9:00 p.m. (Figure 1.3). Stan Hawkins was the first to analyze this particular video in a reading that served to demonstrate how "Windowlicker," for its time, challenged more or less everything that was expected of music videos—particularly in its destabilization of gender norms, sexuality, race, and promulgation of IDM (intelligent dance music). Hawkins also observed how, unsurprisingly, "US MTV would not show it,"[27] which was certainly not the first instance of MTV steering clear of a particular video. Madonna's "Justify My Love" (1990), for which Hawkins provided another musicological reading in his book *Settling the Pop Score*,[28] also exemplifies this: controversial for its time, MTV famously refused to air the video due to its images of sadomasochism and bisexuality. Even as music videos on MTV were in no way devoid of sexual content, it was ostensibly a delicate balance to decide when the line had been crossed. Or in the humorous words of one of the founding fathers of MTV, Tom Freston: "There's a lot of grey stuff. Is that too much or too little of Cher's ass? Somebody has to decide."[29] Tellingly, if the Nicki Minaj video mentioned earlier had been made in the MTV days, that might have been too much of her rear for MTV to handle!

Faced with such decisions, MTV developed a two-stage process for determining the fate of a music video. In order for it to be shown, it had to first pass a primary sorting by the so-called Acquisition Committee that would assess whether or not it lived up to the channel's general standards. If accepted at that stage, it would then pass on to MTV's Program Standards and Public Responsibility Department that would either fully refuse or suggest changes to those clips that were deemed in any way offensive (mostly in their depiction of sex, drugs, and/or violence). Only about 20 percent of the video submissions would eventually go on to get airtime.[30]

Figure 1.3 Aphex Twin, "Windowlicker," directed by Chris Cunningham, 1999 (7:49).

While a platform such as YouTube obviously does not allow all content to pass,[31] there are fewer constraints today, and accordingly music videos are far less limited in content. Before, directors had to attend to the official constraints once imposed by MTV, while simultaneously trying to live up to constraints of a more implicit nature—that is, trying to figure out what the committees would approve of and what would fall outside of their tastes. Even if directors did not always have the committees in mind when making their videos, it is quite likely that they felt some indirect influence from the videos that had already made their way onto MTV, shaping their videos to match what was already acceptable, thereby making the favored aesthetic of the channel implicitly self-reinforcing. Carol Vernallis notes the same, stating that consciously or unconsciously "directors and artists tailored their work for these committees," noting that the consequence of this was "a high degree of uniformity."[32] With a general decrease in vetting and controls, NSFW videos have become much more common. One of the most adventurously transgressive music videos is the video for Peaches' 2015 track "Rub."[33] Herein we witness not only much nudity, sexually explicit content, and images of women urinating while standing up, but also a scene where—and there is no delicate way to put it—Peaches is "dick-slapped" in the face, much in keeping with Peaches' tendency to aesthetically assault heteronormative values. Whatever one may think of this, by comparison it makes Madonna seem mild. And certainly, had this video been made before the turn of the millennium, it is difficult to imagine where it could have even been shown. While there may have always been an audience for these kinds of subversive videos that broaden the kinds of sexuality on display, before music videos migrated online there was no viable way of actually reaching this audience.

Returning to Childish Gambino's "This Is America," there are several reasons why this video would never have made it onto MTV (or at least not without first being changed beyond recognition). First, there is the NSFW aspect, the explicit murderous violence and politically-loaded messages about racism, gun violence, and police brutality, to all of which the spectator is presumed to turn a blind eye while escaping into the safety of dance, music, and entertainment. The very fact that the video occupies itself with real-life political issues would probably also have made it too controversial for television airtime. The most intriguing aspect of the video perhaps is how it seems to be aware of the way in which it is itself paradoxically caught up in what it aims to criticize: even if the video suggests that we turn to entertainment as an escapist means of not having to deal with actual serious issues, it is simultaneously also entertaining in itself. Apart from the blissfully joyous dancing, the video's *mise en scène* is packed with elements and references that also constantly threaten to divert the viewer's attention away from the mayhem going on in the video (and in real life). Accordingly, much of what was written on "This Is America" immediately in its wake was devoted to unpacking all of these symbols and references[34]—to name but a few of these: the physical likeness between the guitarist and Trayvon Martin's father; the intertextual reference to the horror film *Get Out* (2017) and its so-called "sunken place" near the end of the video (possibly, this film's director, Jordan Peele, is also seen in the video as one of the singers in the choir); the puzzling cameo by SZA; the biblical reference to Death riding a pale horse; the origins of the many different dancing moves and styles; the fact that the music of the video goes silent for exactly seventeen seconds, interpreted as paying respect to the seventeen victims of the Parkland shooting. The four minutes of the video thus have been scrutinized in careful detail by journalists and fans alike on the lookout for its hidden meanings—thereby both confirming *and* drawing attention away from its message that we become so absorbed watching music videos that we forget the brutal things happening in both the video and the real world. This constant fusion between delightful entertainment and troubling violence is also evident in the music. If the section with acoustic guitar and singing represents the pleasant aspects of the video, then the beat-heavy section featuring bass and rapping represents grim reality. But in the final chorus before the video's coda, the two are seemingly fused as the beat and bass suddenly infiltrate the more joyous section of the music (at the 3:16 mark in the video). Lyrically, the song likewise moves from "just wanting to party" or "just wanting the money" to "guns in my area."

It is highly doubtful that an institution such as MTV would have approved this message: that their particular brand of entertainment actually serves to obfuscate pressing societal issues. Another possible obstacle, had the video been made in the 1980s, is the simple fact that the artist in question is black. As is well known, in the early 1980s MTV had a reputation of generally omitting music videos by black artists. The station denied that this was racially motivated by claiming that its omission of black artists was grounded in demographic targeting and modelling of AOR (album-oriented-rock) radio, for which genre it declared a dearth of black artists—and to be fair, the policy also changed somewhat along the way. But by comparison, the music videos of today—representing a far wider spectrum of musical genres *and* a far wider spectrum of musical performer identities of many a different race and sexuality—are thus more diverse than ever before:

the reception contexts have multiplied, the ways in which music videos circulate in media culture are ever-more multifaceted, the types of music heard are much more diverse, the audiovisual aesthetic is increasingly heterogeneous, the form of music videos is also much less restricted, and there is a broader range of representations.

In response to this argument for an increased "diversity," one might also raise some obvious and weighty counterarguments. First, the algorithms of YouTube arguably constrain which videos a user will accidentally stumble upon, both in terms of personalized recommendations, and also in terms of which videos are trending and which are not. Since YouTube recommends—and even auto-plays—videos on the basis of general viewing trends and one's personal viewing history, viewers consequently receive less exposure to videos that are outside their musical comfort zone and thereby become more easily enclosed in an echo chamber of their own musical tastes. In addition, YouTube and Vevo are commercial enterprises through and through, and even if you can find outliers, such as "This Is America," the top 100 most played music videos on YouTube are generally more conservative in approach and in their identity politics. These videos almost never push the envelope—neither visually nor musically. Furthermore, even while a video such as "This Is America" suggests a more progressive and subversive approach, it must be considered that it is distributed by the label mcDJ, under license to RCA Records as a division of Sony Music Entertainment—in other words, one of the Big Three that own Vevo together with Abu Dhabi Media and Alphabet/Google. A less benign approach might stress the fact that music videos are still big business and fully commercial in nature. Viewed from this perspective, "This Is America" points to the role of controversial content as a commercial attribute within the infinite stream of music videos online. At the same time, it is also probable that the arguably "controversial" nature of such a video is highly calculated as a strategy for speaking to and for a fan base that is attuned to the political values on display. It is probably naive to think otherwise, as the commercial goal of any video—however admirable or problematic its values may be—is always to attract rather than to deter fans.

Acknowledgment

This work was supported by the Independent Research Fund Denmark under Grant number DFF-4089–00149 ("Audiovisual Literacy and New Audiovisual Short-Forms").

Notes

1   Childish Gambino, "Childish Gambino—This Is America (Official Video)," YouTube video (4:05), official music video, directed by Hiro Murai, posted by "Donald Glover," May 5, 2018, https://www.youtube.com/watch?v=VYOjWnS4cMY.

2   Murai has directed music videos since the mid-2000s and, even though it is not my aim here, I wish to emphasize that he is certainly one of those directors who is deserving

of more academic attention (particularly his work of the 2010s)—as I also noted near the very end of my book, *Music Video After MTV: Audiovisual Studies, New Media, and Popular Music* (London and New York: Routledge, 2017), 200.

3   For example, the *New York Times* has collected eight of the most relevant pieces on "This Is America" produced immediately after the video's release, but obviously a lot more than this has also been written about the video. See Judy Berman, "'This Is America': 8 Things to Read About Childish Gambino's New Music Video," *New York Times*, May 8, 2018, https://www.nytimes.com/2018/05/08/arts/music/childish-gambino-this-is-america-roundup.html.

4   To me, it is not only a general but also a personal lack, seeing that the same largely holds true of my own book on the music video: the distribution perspective is implicit at best and entirely lacking at worst. Of course, this is not to say that music video distribution has not been studied at all, but more often than not aesthetic or cultural matters have been the main focus of music video studies. Notable exceptions include parts of Carol Vernallis's *Unruly Media: YouTube, Music Video, and the New Digital Cinema* (Oxford and New York: Oxford University Press, 2013); some of Heather McIntosh's work, for instance, "Vevo and the Business of Online Music Video Distribution," *Popular Music and Society* 39, no. 5 (2016): 487–500; or Maura Edmond's "Here We Go Again: Music Videos after YouTube," *Television and New Media* 15, no. 4 (2014): 305–320. Indeed, it also seems to be true of media studies in general that distribution is often neglected when compared to production and reception studies—as also suggested by Alisa Perren, "Rethinking Distribution for the Future of Media Industry Studies," *Cinema Journal* 52, no. 3 (2013): 165–171.

5   I have addressed such formal developments in "Music Video Transformed," in *The Oxford Handbook of New Audiovisual Aesthetics*, edited by John Richardson, Claudia Gorbman, and Carol Vernallis (Oxford and New York: Oxford University Press, 2013), 501–521.

6   As I also propose in my book in one of the few passages where the distribution perspective actually *is* present. See Korsgaard, *Music Video After MTV*, 17.

7   Diane Railton and Paul Watson, *Music and the Moving Image: Music Video and the Politics of Representation* (Edinburgh: Edinburgh University Press, 2011), 142.

8   There does not seem to be general consensus on the exact time of MTV's decline. The movement away from 24/7 music video content and the first significant ratings drop allegedly happened as early as 1985. See Edmond, "Here We Go Again," 307; R. Serge Denisoff, *Inside MTV* (New Brunswick, NJ and Oxford: Transaction Books, 1988), 317; and Jack Banks, *Monopoly Television: MTV's Quest to Control the Music* (Boulder, CO and Oxford: Westview Press, 1996), 122. Craig Marks and Rob Tannenbaum suggest that 1992 marks the end of what they term "MTV's Golden Era." See Craig Marks and Rob Tannenbaum, *I Want My MTV: The Uncensored Story of the Music Video Revolution* (New York: Dutton, 2011), 18.

9   See, for instance, Amanda Lotz, *The Television Will Be Revolutionized* (New York: New York University Press, 2007) for a discussion of television in the post-network era.

10   Henry Keazor and Thorsten Wübbena, eds., *Rewind, Play, Fast Forward: The Past, Present and Future of the Music Video* (Bielefeld: Transcript Verlag, 2010), 21.

11   I have delved into this prehistory at greater length in the first chapter of *Music Video After MTV*.

12   Marks and Tannenbaum, *I Want My MTV*, 21–22.

13 Ibid., 22.

14 To my knowledge, there are only two books that focus specifically on the history of music videos—namely Saul Austerlitz's *Money for Nothing: A History of the Music Video from the Beatles to the White Stripes* (London and New York: Continuum, 2007) and Michael Shore's *The Rolling Stone Book of Rock Video. The Definitive Look at Visual Music from Elvis Presley—and Before—to Michael Jackson—and Beyond* (London: Sidgwick & Jackson, 1985). Compared to these, there are more than a handful of books that deal (at least in part) with the history of MTV—namely Denisoff's *Inside MTV*; Tom McGrath's *MTV: The Making of a Revolution* (Philadelphia, PA and London: Running Press, 1996); Marks and Tannenbaum's *I Want My MTV*; Klaus Neumann-Braun's *Viva MTV! Popmusik im Fernsehen* (Frankfurt am Main: Suhrkamp Verlag, 1999); Kip Pegley's *Coming to You Wherever You Are: MuchMusic, MTV, and Youth Audiences* (Middletown, CT: Wesleyan University Press, 2008); and Ray Paul Temporal's *The Branding of MTV: Will Internet Kill the Video Star?* (New York: John Wiley & Sons, 2008).

15 John Fiske, "MTV: Post-Structural, Post-Modern," *Journal of Communication Enquiry* 10, no. 1 (1986): 77.

16 See, for instance, Antti-Ville Kärjä, "Arty Adverts, Puffy Pictures? Finnish Music Videos in Cinema," *Musiikin Suunta: Special Issue in English on Music Videos* 21, no. 2 (1999): 34; Roger Beebe and Jason Middleton, eds., *Medium Cool: Music Videos from Soundies to Cellphones* (Durham, NC: Duke University Press, 2007), 8.

17 I suggest this in *Music Video After MTV*, 174; so does Maura Edmond in "Here We Go Again," 316.

18 I have addressed both of these before in Korsgaard, "Music Video Transformed," 501–521.

19 Nicki Minaj, "Nicki Minaj—Chun-Li (Vertical Video)," YouTube video, vertical music video, directed by Nicki Minaj, posted by "Nicki Minaj," April 13, 2018, https://www.youtube.com/watch?v=SCq8n_hOcN8.

20 As does Michel Chion who has given the title "Image-radio" to his brief section on music videos in *Audio-Vision: Sound on Screen*, edited and translated by Claudia Gorbman (New York: Columbia University Press, 1994), 165–168.

21 As also addressed in a forthcoming volume on "transmedia directors." See *Transmedia Directors: Artistry, Industry, and New Audiovisual Aesthetics*, edited by Carol Vernallis, Holly Rogers, and Lisa Perrott (New York and London: Bloomsbury Academic, 2019).

22 Laura McLaren considers the genre implications for the lyric video in Chapter 9 of this volume.

23 "Vidding" is a practice where users and fans make their own music videos by editing footage from a film or television series—thereby providing a sort of "double-reading" in which the music provides new perspectives on the footage and vice versa.

24 José Van Dijck, "Users Like You? Theorizing Agency in User-Generated Content," *Media Culture Society* 31, no. 1 (2009): 49.

25 When it comes to NSFW videos, there are certain musical artists and certain music video directors that seem bent on pushing the boundaries (or simply provoking the audience)—musicians ranging from Madonna to Nine Inch Nails, Marilyn Manson, Rammstein, Lady Gaga, or even Arca, and directors ranging from Jonas Åkerlund to Chris Cunningham, Romain Gavras, and maybe even to some extent Hiro Murai.

26   Aphex Twin, "Aphex Twin—Windowlicker (Director's Version)," YouTube video, official music video, directed by Chris Cunningham, posted by "Aphex Twin," November 24, 2018, https://www.youtube.com/watch?v=5ZT3gTu4Sjw.

27   Stan Hawkins, "Aphex Twin: Monstrous Hermaphrodites, Madness and the Strain of Independent Dance Music," in *Essays on Sound and Vision*, edited by John Richardson and Stan Hawkins (Helsinki: Helsinki University Press, 2007), 28.

28   Stan Hawkins, *Settling the Pop Score: Pop Texts and Identity Politics* (London and New York: Routledge, 2002), 48–52.

29   Quoted in Axel Schmidt, "Sound and Vision Go MTV—die Geschichte des Musiksenders bis heute," in *Viva MTV! Popmusik im Fernsehen*, edited by Klaus Neumann-Braun (Frankfurt am Main: Suhrkamp Verlag, 1999), 123.

30   According to Banks, *Monopoly Television*, 176.

31   A fairly recent example of a music video being banned from YouTube is the video for the track "Shitshow" (2018) made by the experimental noise-rap trio Death Grips. Quite the NSFW video, among other things it graphically depicts the drummer Zach Hill wiping his own ass and images of a woman peeing. Considering the fact that Death Grips are somewhat renowned for their promotional antics, it seems like a reasonable assumption that it was in fact the band's intention to make a video that was designed to get banned—and thereby probably generate more publicity than it otherwise would have had.

32   Vernallis, *Unruly Media*, 208.

33   Peaches, "Peaches—Rub (Uncensored Music Video)," YouTube video, official music video, directed by Peaches, A. L. Steiner, and Lex Vaughn, posted by "Trax Magazine," December 2, 2015, https://www.youtube.com/watch?v=WyL5ABXltW8.

34   As already mentioned, the amount of commentary that the video sparked is vast, but two representative examples include Jacob Shamsian, "24 Things You May Have Missed in Childish Gambino's 'This Is America' Music Video," *Insider*, May 9, 2018, https://www.thisisinsider.com/this-is-america-music-video-meaning-references-childish-gambino-donald-glover-2018-5 and Candice Nembhard, "8 Things You May Have Missed in Childish Gambino's 'This Is America' Video," *Highsnobiety*, May 7, 2018, https://www.highsnobiety.com/p/childish-gambino-this-is-america-recap.

2

Low-Budget Audiovisual Aesthetics in Indie Music Video and Feature Filmmaking: The Works of Steve Hanft and Danny Perez

Jamie Sexton

In this chapter I explore the interactions between music videos and feature films within the category of low-budget indie productions. I do so through the lens of authorship and focus on two particular directors who have moved between music video and feature film direction: Steve Hanft and Danny Perez. My focus on these directors aims to broaden the general points made about the music video's influence on indie feature filmmaking which have, up until now, largely explored more commercially-oriented and higher-budgeted feature films. Within the broad indie sphere, there are a number of directors who have made features and music videos, including Sofia Coppola, Jonathan Dayton and Valerie Faris, Michel Gondry, Spike Jonze, Floria Sigismondi, and Tarsem Singh. Work on how Coppola, Gondry, and Jonze move between music video and feature filmmaking, and how such works inform one another, have been subject to previous analyses.[1] Directors who work across music video and feature filmmaking can provide a good place to start thinking concretely about the influences of music video on feature filmmaking. Indeed, John Richardson has argued that the "large number of film directors with a background in music videos … constitutes a compelling case for arguing how they have influenced new approaches to film."[2] In this chapter I extend this authorial focus beyond the more commercial, privileged examples, which tend to operate within the "Indiewood" sphere, where Hollywood studio production merges with elements more associated with independent production.[3] Indie is, however, a broad category that also includes lower-budgeted, underground productions, and this is the area of indie production that I will explore through these two authorial case studies.

Hanft and Perez, who have both worked closely with a range of indie music artists through directing music videos and films, display a strong authorial signature across a number of their productions. Focusing on their work will enable me to identify some prominent traits of innovative directors and to interrogate whether general points made about music videos influencing feature films apply to these low-budget examples. Carol Vernallis argues that music video is a particularly important influence on contemporary cinema, which is marked by "intensified audiovisual aesthetics."[4] In particular, a heightened "musicalization of the image" is evident: post-classical films "may be able to hold on to the traditional five-act structure, but within that all formal constraints become changed, and they approach a condition of music … this aesthetic makes the image, sound, and form more fluid."[5] Mathias Bonde Korsgaard has detailed the main aesthetic ways in which cinema has incorporated the "MTV aesthetic" as follows:

> the increasing use and importance of popular music alongside moving images; an often closer framing; freer camera movements; a faster and more rhythmical editing; the use of loose, modular and fragmented narratives; the highlighting of visual spectacle; a glitzy look and color palette; and the use of non-representational imagery and visual effects.[6]

While acknowledging these techniques, Korsgaard stresses how difficult it is to definitively prove that they are influenced by MTV because of the array of other factors that might have influenced their increased adoption into feature filmmaking. Despite such doubts, Korsgaard still argues that the music video has influenced cinema even though it is "difficult to move beyond the level of assumption when it comes to tracing the influence of one medium upon another."[7]

Korsgaard makes an important point about assuming influences, but by focusing on particular interrelations between two directors' work across music videos and feature films, such influences can be more concretely identified. General patterns and tendencies across categories of aesthetic production are important and necessary to catalog, but in practice they will always be inflected by more particular factors, including key production personnel, budgets, and adopted technologies. This chapter therefore looks at two lesser-known directors who have worked across music videos and feature films, and who have tended to work in the indie area across both forms. The focus enables me to explore whether broader points about music video and feature film interactions are applicable to lower-budgeted indie productions, in addition to my analysis of the work of two interesting, yet largely overlooked, directors, who span these forms and who have worked with evolving technologies that have impacted on the evolution of both music video and feature film production.

Lo-fi audio-visions: Steve Hanft

At the time of writing this chapter, Steve Hanft has directed three feature films, a few short films, and a number of music videos.[8] His films are often saturated with musical cues and references, and he was also an indie musician in the band Loser, which featured future breakout star Beck. In many ways, it is Hanft's association with Beck that has resulted in greater interest circulating around his movies, although they are still very niche. *Kill the*

Moonlight was actually made in 1991, having started when Hanft was enrolled in CalArts Film, but he did not have the money to release the film.[9] It was only after Beck's song "Loser" became a surprise hit, following Beck being signed to a major label (Geffen), that Hanft managed to gather funds to release the film. Hanft, whose first music video was "Loser," did not enter feature filmmaking following an apprenticeship in music video production, but gravitated from feature production to music videos (and then moved between these forms and short films). Nevertheless, *Kill the Moonlight* does include a few sequences that feel inspired by some forms of music video production, which is unsurprising considering that Hanft was steeped in music culture. Such influences intermingle with a number of other influences, the most striking of which seems to be New Hollywood filmmaking and underground/experimental filmmaking.

Kill the Moonlight, the story of aspiring stock-car racing driver Chance (played by Thomas Hendrix), fits the mold of a slow-paced, narratively aimless 1970s film such as *Two Lane Blacktop* (Hellman, 1971). And, like the latter, it offers a critique of the car race film. Both movies downplay the thrill of the car race and instead focus more on existential matters. In *Kill the Moonlight*, Chance attempts to gain money to enter a stock-car race but never actually does so. The only car racing footage we witness in *Kill the Moonlight* takes place during the opening credits. The bulk of the film is concerned with the drifting Chance's attempts to seek out funds so he can fix up his own car and enter a race. The ending of the film also echoes *Two Lane Blacktop*, which concluded abruptly with a representation of the film being burned in the projector. *Kill the Moonlight* ends suddenly when Chance crashes his car, depicted abstractly via a montage of fleeting images and accompanied by grating music (1:15:05). Hanft's incorporation of experimental techniques is no surprise considering he was taught by James Benning—who even briefly features in the film as Chance's landscaping boss—at CalArts. Hanft has himself discussed the abstract nature of *Kill the Moonlight*, noting how he was influenced by Benning, as well as other avant-garde filmmakers such as Warhol.[10] His interest in the abstract manifests itself in a fascination with texture, composition, and acting. At various moments in the film concrete representation is abstracted—for example, faces are sometimes blurred, occasional snippets of abstract film are flashed, and the camera motion becomes jerky for no apparent reason.

Kill the Moonlight features a number of indie rock artists from the Los Angeles area, as Hanft drew on people he already knew, including Beck. Although Beck (as an independent artist) was trading mostly in lo-fi folk and rock music at the time, the soundtrack (available commercially) is mostly dominated by what Hanft terms "garage rock."[11] Most of the bands were, and remain, little known and include The Pussywillows, Delta Garage, and The Dynamics. The bands on the soundtrack are nevertheless far from unified in their influences and various generic traces, including country rock, rockabilly and surf rock, are detectable in different artists' contributions. The use of songs in the film is frequent, although some are foregrounded to a greater extent than others. A few music tracks are briefly used as low-volume source background (playing on a car radio or in a bar, for example), and in these contexts the music does not influence the image flow in any discernible way. When the music is foregrounded on the soundtrack, to the extent that it dominates, then it more obviously impacts on the arrangement of images. This includes the presentation of musical performances—for example, when Chance visits a contact and The Dynamics are rehearsing in preparation to shoot a video, or when Beck performs/records songs in his recording shed. At other times, musical montages—moments when music comes to the fore and drowns out dialogue and ambient sound—are used. These montages in the film—such as when Chance goes out driving with Sandra just after she has told him she will lend him money to enter the car race (44:25), or when he gets mad with Dennis over money and goes out driving to vent his anger (55:35)—function as intensive interludes. Reasonably compacted and hectic in contrast to the film's predominantly slow pace, these montages reflect rare, emotionally heightened states in a largely lackadaisical film. Chance's romantically-tinged sense of excitement and anger are depicted within the music, which functions to heighten such emotional tension.

The influence of music videos therefore can be detected in *Kill the Moonlight* to a certain extent; Hanft was in a band himself and involved in the LA music scene, which suggests he would have been familiar with music videos. Such an influence, however, is not as marked as the independent and new Hollywood influences on the film, and co-exists with additional touchstones such as experimental filmmaking and other types of music-focused filmmaking (e.g., direct cinema or punk cinema). It was only after making this film that Hanft actually began to make music videos. In fact, he claims that he was asked to direct music videos before this moment, but was never interested in them as he was more focused on directing shorts and making a feature; however, he has expressed that he enjoyed the experience of directing his first music video because he realized there was a lot of freedom to experiment and "do what you like" within the form.[12] This comment supports Steven Shaviro's contention that music videos enjoy a privileged position in terms of allowing freedom to experiment "with new modes of visual expression," because their "sonic content already comes ready-made and because they are usually of such short length."[13]

Hanft's video for Beck's "Loser" not only made reference to *Kill the Moonlight*, but also stirred further interest in the film, enabling Hanft to afford its release costs.[14] It was also a lucrative endeavor for Beck. Although "Loser" was made when he was an independent artist, it gained a lot of airplay and became an unexpected success, leading to a major label contract with Geffen. While initially released as a limited independent 12-inch single in 1993 on Bong Load records, it became a commercial hit when it was re-released by Geffen subsidiary DGC in 1994. The video itself refers to *Kill the Moonlight*, most explicitly through Beck's incorporation of a dialogue sample from the film: Chance's comment, "I'm a driver, I'm a Winner. Things are gonna change, I can feel it." The video features a brief flash of the film character Chance when this sample is heard, creating a visual match with the sound source (2:56). There is a further reference to *Kill the Moonlight* when Beck wields a leaf blower in the video, a contraption that Chance uses in the film when carrying out one of his many menial jobs. More generally, the "Loser" music video recalls the aesthetic style of the film in its loose formal arrangement, its lo-fi quality, and its playful abstraction. The music video format, however, led Hanft to increase the abstract elements that fed into *Kill the Moonlight*; in particular, he experimented with the image quite frequently, incorporating negative and solarized images, superimpositions, video feedback effects, black and white footage, as well as some stop-motion animation (as when a coffin starts moving around, which is another reference to Hanft and Beck's past musical history as Hanft had previously built a coffin for Beck to emerge out of when the band Loser played gigs).[15] The result is a playful video that comprises an abstract assemblage of footage featuring Beck in various situations (sometimes performing the vocals, at other times goofing around or just strolling), two women dancing, a coffin moving through different spaces, and other performers (such as the guitarist on the roof), as well as previously shot footage of Beck actually performing live and footage from *Kill the Moonlight* (although not extensive, there are a couple of stock-car racing shots from the film in addition to Chance uttering the sampled dialogue). Ultimately, the "Loser" music video is a goofy, self-deprecating, lo-fi surrealist collage, characterized by some of the broader aesthetic tendencies evident across indie music videos from the late 1980s to the early 1990s. Austerlitz, for example, has noted that many indie rock music videos in this period could commonly be distinguished from the more glossy, mainstream music videos that received heavy rotation on MTV. Austerlitz argues that many college rock bands had "constricted budgets" but often created interesting, minimalist videos: "Groups like R.E.M., the Cure, Depeche Mode, Black Flag, Hüsker Dü, and Sonic Youth turned a constraint into an aesthetic, crafting clips that were small, clever and cool."[16] The "Loser" video continued this lo-fi, low-budget trend but moved away from minimalism. Receiving heavy rotation on MTV, it became a key music video related to the "slacker" generation and an important music video touchstone. Demopoulos, for example, has noted its innovative use of mixing different stock and argues that such experimental techniques found their way into feature films such as *Natural Born Killers* (Stone, 1994) and *He Got Game* (Lee, 1998).[17]

After directing Beck's "Loser," Hanft directed three more of the artist's music videos: the singles "Beercan" and "Pay No Mind (Snoozer)"—both of which, like "Loser," were from Beck's *Mellow Gold* (1994) album[18]—and "Where It's At," which was the first single from his next album, *Odelay* (1996).[19] The first two of these continued the lo-fi, playful aesthetic of "Loser," thus nudging Beck into the alternative music category (or indie as it would more commonly be labelled over time), despite his major label contract. "Where It's At" was slightly more polished than the earlier videos Hanft had made for Beck, although still quite modest in terms of budget and concept. Hanft also directed a number of other music videos between 1994 and the release of his second feature, *Southlander: Diary of a Desperate Musician* (2001), by acts including The Cure, Elliott Smith, Insane Clown Posse, Jon Spencer Blues Explosion, L7, and Primal Scream.[20] While many stylistic elements differentiate these videos, they also reveal some connecting threads that typify Hanft's style. These include the following traits: his play with different image textures; his use of different film and video formats; his combination of color and monochrome footage; and his frequent abstraction of the image, in particular the creation of abstract images via image manipulation and layering, brief flash edits of abstract film, or even simulating film slipping in the projector (as in Primal Scream's "Kowalski"). On a structural level, the music videos are characterized by thin narrative elements and/or surreal segments, usually mixed with performance footage from the music artist(s) involved. This, in itself, is quite common within the form; as Vernallis has argued, the form of the music video tends to work against the employment of detailed narratives that are rarely developed, even when they are employed.[21] In some of Hanft's videos, he uses other films as a touchstone. Jon Spencer Blues Explosion's "Dang" (1994) recalls *Plan 9 From Outer Space* (Wood Jr., 1959) through its cheap models of UFOs, resulting in a kind of thrift-shop sci-fi video.[22] Primal Scream's "Kowalski," which references the main character from the film *Vanishing Point* (Sarafian, 1971), inevitably recalls that film through its lyrics.[23] Hanft creates a video around car chases and crime that recalls aspects of the film, but also injects it with a gender twist as models Kate Moss and Devon Aoki drive around in a Dodge Challenger (also used in the film although the color of the car is different) beating up men. Primal Scream would have likely chosen Hanft to direct a video based on an existentialist 1970s road movie because he had directed a film harking back to 1970s New Hollywood/independent road films. While still relatively low budget, Hanft's music videos became more structurally ordered and less fragmented, moving toward a more polished aesthetic. While he certainly did not gain the prominence of directors such as Spike Jonze, Mark Romanek, and Michel Gondry, he nevertheless forged a distinctive style that would further influence his second feature, *Southlander*.

Southlander is informed by music culture to an even greater extent than *Kill the Moonlight*, including moments that seem heavily influenced by music videos. This is far from surprising considering that Hanft had not directed a music video prior to *Kill the Moonlight*, but had made a number before making *Southlander*. Like his first feature, the narrative of *Southlander* is quite slight and loose, but feels less indebted to the more arty, existentialist New Hollywood features. It is shot on video rather than film so that the surface of the screen looks different when compared to *Kill the Moonlight* (and many other independent and low-budget Hollywood pictures), and closer to music videos that were shot on video. The musical dimensions of his debut feature are extended in *Southlander*: the narrative actually concerns a musician, again named Chance (Rory Cochrane), attempting to obtain a "Moletron" synthesizer in order to join a band. Music artists—mostly indie musicians based in Los Angeles—are again present on the soundtrack and within the film. The band in the film, Future Pigeon, is a fictional version of a real LA dub reggae band (the real Future Pigeon provided music for the film); this fictional version includes singer Rocket, who is played by British indie folk singer Beth Orton. The film also features cameos from music artists: Jennifer Herema, from Royal Trux and later of RTX and Black Bananas, portrays a record-store clerk who chases Chance's friend Ross after he steals an item, all the while accompanied sonically by Royal Trux's "End of the Century"; Elliott Smith briefly appears as a bus driver, and two of his tracks—"Snowbunny's Serenade" and "Splitzville"—appear on the soundtrack; and Hank Williams III appears as a character who steals Chance's keyboard and is filmed performing "Alone and Dying" in his mobile home. The performer with the highest profile in the film is Beck, who at this time had become an established music artist, albeit one still often positioned as an alternative/indie artist. Beck plays "Bek," who sings a couple of tracks in the film, including a performance at Lane's (Gregg Henry) party. The film also features a performance by skate punk band Union 13, who perform in a mobile home when trying out an amp they are considering buying. The choice of Richard Edson as an actor in the film—he plays Thomas, friend of music artist Motherchild (Lawrence Hilton-Jacobs, who is also a recording artist)—further links to music, as Edson was a member of post-punk bands Sonic Youth and KONK in the 1980s. That he made his name as an actor in Jim Jarmusch's seminal independent feature *Stranger Than Paradise* (1984) would have also been relevant as Hanft's features belong to a tradition of low-budget, DIY feature filmmaking based around a loose narrative.

In addition to featuring a number of musical artists in the film, as well as musical performances of acts rehearsing or playing live, *Southlander* contains a couple of sequences which seem to be simulations of music videos. The first of these shows Ross—who states he cannot drink alcohol—being plied with booze by Motherchild (36:22). After Ross initially attempts to turn down the offer, he is confronted by an asserted threat to "drink." There follows a brief montage of doubly exposed street-scene imagery filmed from the front of a moving vehicle and shot with a fish-eye lens, bordered by the windscreen (which creates a kind of iris effect, something Hanft often uses in his music videos) and set to a slow, dub track featuring a swirling glockenspiel motif and heavily echoed guitar stabs, which match the rather hazy nature of the images. This montage reflects both visually and sonically the addled nature of Ross's mental state while also marking the passing of the night, as the passage concludes with images at sunrise.

After another brief scene of Chance visiting an electronics store, we are then presented with a dream-like fantasy sequence of Ross in a diner. We first see Ross at the bar of the diner with his face down in a plate of food, flanked by Thomas and Motherchild who are laughing at him. Raising his face from the plate in a dazed state, he suddenly starts to get onto the diner bar to dance and mime to the music being played, a pop-inflected piece ("Piano Drop" by Ross Harris) (37:45). The waitresses then start to dance and Thomas picks up a guitar—which seems to have magically appeared—from a table and throws it to Ross, who then continues to mime the instrument (Figure 2.1). When Ross jumps there is a match cut of him landing, but now the background has changed (38:00), thus

Figure 2.1 Ross jumps onto the bar with a guitar and starts to sing.

emphasizing the dream-like nature of the clip. He is now placed against an obviously artificial composited backdrop of setting sun, sky, and clouds, while continuing to mime guitar and lip-sync, although adopting an exaggerated performance pose. In this clip, Ross's body multiplies into three (echoing Hanft's video for Beck's "Where It's At"), while he also appears playing drums; other characters from the film—including Motherchild playing the Moletron synth—are also present at moments in the clip (Figure 2.2).

The second "music video moment" occurs when, following the theft of his Moletron, Chance is filmed sitting by Lane's poolside having a drink with his friends. We see Chance preoccupied with his internal thoughts, separated from others at the table and accompanied by the sound of waves lapping on the shore. A slow dissolve into the water follows, briefly succeeded by a silhouetted shot of Chance and Rocket on the beach. The next cut (54:51) brings us to another sequence in which two layers are obviously composited. Chance is now dressed in a suit and playing a grand piano, while the back projection consists of abstract water patterns flecked by shimmering light. Rocket also appears and is lip-syncing Beth Orton's own "Sweetest Decline" while swimming. This (day) dream sequence reflects Chance's state of mind: he desires to play in the band and to be with Rocket, both of which might disappear if he cannot access the Moletron.

These two sequences feature a number of characteristics associated with music video. First, there is a sense of "polyvalent play" at work in these clips. Vernallis has written how "the editing in music videos loosens the representational functions that filmed images traditionally perform, opening them up to a sense of polyvalent play."[24] This is evident in these clips through the ways in which artificial elements come to the fore in a heightened manner and transform rapidly, transcending any realist rules in the process. This nudges the clips toward surrealism in that objects, such as the guitar on the table, appear as if by magic at the same time that the environment fluidly changes in reaction to emotions.

Figure 2.2 The landscape suddenly transforms and Ross multiplies into three figures.

Both of these musical dream sequences relate to the film narrative to some extent—Ross's addled state and Chance's romantic feelings for Rocket—but also seem to pull away from the narrative in order to explore emotions in a musically heightened manner. The presence of characters miming instruments, lip-syncing, and other deliberately artificial elements, such as the obvious compositing in these video-esque segments, strengthen this musical dimension. As such, these sequences encapsulate the idea of the "musical moment" in narrative films, as outlined by Korsgaard (drawing on the work of Amy Herzog):

> [T]he concept of the musical moment refers to those instants [*sic.*] in feature films where music takes on an independent role, liberating itself from its usual function of supporting the visuals and the narrative. In these cases music is actively foregrounded and assumes precedence over the images, sometimes also affecting the editing rhythm of the images.[25]

While many of the previous musically influenced elements of Hanft's features can be considered musical moments, these two sequences in *Southlander* are especially heightened examples.

Hanft's music videos made for Beck are important contributions to the indie rock music video of the 1990s. His low-budget collages for Beck's early singles drew on the amateurish lo-fi videos that characterized the 1980s, but inched them into more playful, surreal directions through imaginative scenarios and an innovative approach to mixing different stock. Importantly, he drew on some of the techniques when directing his second feature film, *Southlander*, demonstrating the influence that music video production had on his filmmaking. While Hanft continues to direct music videos, he does not do so to the same extent that he once did. My next focus is on a music video director who is more representative of the shifts in music video and film production during the 2000s, in particular, the turn to digital production technologies.

Digital delirium: Danny Perez

As with Hanft, Danny Perez is a filmmaker who has made low-budget music videos and independent films, but emerged at a later period than Hanft and is representative of a newer generation of music video and film directors. Both directors, however, have formed close alliances with particular musicians in their work, and have a penchant for abstract imagery, rooting their work in a tradition of experimental media. Perez himself is most closely associated with the musical acts Animal Collective and Black Dice. He started his visual work by performing live visuals for Black Dice and also created some of that band's music videos, while he has made music videos for Animal Collective and collaborated with that band on a visual album, *ODDSAC* (2010).[26] He has also directed music videos for other artists including Blood on the Wall, Hot Chip, Kurt Vile, and Unknown Mortal Orchestra. Coming from a video jockey (VJ) background, his early work in music video was characterized by free-flowing, abstract digital imagery, which, like Hanft's work, bore influential traces of previous experimental forms of filmmaking.

Whereas Hanft's work harks back to the slow drift of the more radical New Hollywood features and diaristic avant-garde shorts, many of Perez's music videos draw on visual music films, particularly the more psychedelic variety. Flowing digital abstractions—sometimes mixed with filmed imagery—characterized his visual accompaniments for videos such as Black Dice's "Luveas" and Panda Bear's "You Can Count On Me" and "Alsatian Darn."[27] These videos were very much extensions of the live visuals that he created for the respective artists (Panda Bear himself is a solo artist and also a member of Animal Collective). They recall the light shows associated with certain psychedelic acts of the late 1960s, which utilized slide projections, film and liquid effects (and later, in the 1970s, would use abstract video imagery). Examples include the Joshua Light Show's abstract live visuals for artists such as Frank Zappa and Janis Joplin, or Mark Boyle and Joan Hills's light shows for Pink Floyd and Soft Machine.[28] Such abstract visual displays were often inspired by innovative filmmakers such as John and James Whitney, and Jordan Belson; both Whitney and Belson had works shown as part of the Vortex Concerts—live events which combined abstract film with music in live spaces at a series of performances at the Planetarium in San Francisco.[29] These filmmakers created films that were often termed psychedelic, or "visionary," in that some of their films were linked to altered states and spiritual experiences.[30] Whitney's *Lapis* (1966), for example, features constantly evolving mandala patterns accompanied by a sitar raga, which invoked alternative forms of non-Western spirituality in vogue among psychedelic elements of the counterculture. The fluid, evolving patterns of the film would also have been conducive to viewing under the influence of hallucinogenic drugs, which were popular with the 1960s counterculture and often used to access non-normative states. The Whitney brothers, along with artists such as Stan Vanderbeek, were also important early adopters of computers and were pioneers in computer animation. Perez can be linked to these precedents through his focus on largely abstract moving imagery, his syncing of such visuals to music in an attempt to create immersive, synesthetic audiovisual spectacles, and his creation of "psychedelic" imagery. His interest in the genre of horror, however, shifts the positive spirituality marking the 1960s' abstract filmmakers onto a darker level. Perez's films do not feel so imbued with such spiritual urges, and are more likely to revel in disconcerting, sometimes grotesque, images.

Perez's earlier work largely dealt with completely abstract imagery which, in addition to drawing on previous abstract work, fitted in some ways into broader trends in low-budget music videos and other content posted on YouTube. Vernallis, for example, mentions how many recent indie music videos and YouTube video clips parade "technologically showy devices" such as "trails, kaleidoscopes, sinusoidal waves," while Korsgaard also mentions "morphing, kaleidoscopic effects" as one common way in which digital music videos have amplified a sense of visual polyphony.[31] While Perez continued to create colorful, abstract forms of digital animation, he also began to incorporate more live footage as well as elements of narrative in his music videos. The earliest example is his video for Animal Collective's "Who Could Win a Rabbit" (2004), which is a take on the tortoise and hare fable, featuring members of the band dressed in a rabbit and tortoise costume, respectively.[32] In the video, the rabbit and tortoise compete in a cycle race that descends into violence as the rabbit attempts to foil the tortoise by attacking him and burying him. It concludes with the tortoise eating the rabbit. The video image is low resolution, linking it to a broader tradition of lo-fi indie music and visuals, and incorporates abstract imagery, stop-motion footage, jump cuts, and superimpositions. So, while the broad framing story is a linear, concrete narrative, this is interrupted and overlaid with abstract effects. At one point in the video, following a scene in which the tortoise falls from his bicycle, colorful hexagonal shapes (the same as on the tortoise's shell) are partially superimposed over the footage of the tortoise on the floor and reaction shots of the rabbit laughing (0:49). This method of abstracting more concrete images would become a key trait of Perez's later work. "Who Could Win a Rabbit" also includes a number of elements that would become frequent staples of Perez's work: use of costumes and body paint, horror-influenced imagery, and vibrant colors. This not only became a trait of Perez's video work but also a key component of many Animal Collective (and related acts) videos.

Animal Collective's music often mixes child-like wonder with psychedelic and, occasionally, horrific vibes, and it is this component of the band's identity that has been particularly evident across a number of its videos. In addition to horror tropes that occasionally feature in the band's music videos, it also shares with Perez a penchant for psychedelic imagery and a tendency to adopt costumes and masks. Perez's music videos for Animal Collective's "Summertime Clothes" (2009) and "Today's Supernatural" (2012) both contain masked figures, a very colorful, psychedelic palette, and combine these with visual movements that frequently interlock with musical rhythms.[33] "Summertime Clothes" features dance troupe FLEX in a choreographed routine, with some dancers dressed in face-obscuring robes and others dancing inside plastic balls. This choreography, in tandem with editing, flashing lights, and fire and ice imagery, amounts to a very busy video in which physical movement, colorful *mise en scène*, and pulsing lights create a synesthetic display. Here Perez has created a video very different from his purely abstract digital animations, while still using more concrete elements in an abstract manner, and thereby continuing his interest in psychedelic and synesthetic audio-vision.

Perez's increasing incorporation of filmed, as opposed to animated, imagery moved his music videos away from being "absolute" in their abstraction. They remained, however, imbued with abstract elements, such as psychedelic animation, increasingly sophisticated lighting designs, and the tendency for a number of his videos to feature masked and/ or costumed performers. Some of these videos feature brief scenes that exist outside of established narrative contexts. An example is his video for Hot Chip's "Look At Where We Are" (2012), which portrays a surgeon operating on a female robot juxtaposed with a fragment from a film rehearsal.[34] The robot's face is opened to reveal shifting, digitally-rendered patterns (1:47), giving the surgery a surreal effect, before it segues into the scene of an actress under stress (2:05). The story itself is far from straightforward, as testified by a number of confused responses from people on YouTube. In many ways, Perez's non-linearity serves to cognitively disrupt viewers' minds; in this case, it is mostly dependent on rendering a narrative situation oblique, rather than relying on psychedelic visual effects.

ODDSAC, Perez's collaboration with Animal Collective, was a visual album and his longest film to date at just under an hour. Its main difference from a typical music video, apart from its length, is that Perez and Animal Collective produced the visual and musical aspects of the film in collaboration (while there was no corresponding music-only release). This allowed for musical ideas to influence moving images and vice versa, enabling a greater conceptual fit between the two tracks. Following Perez's previous video work, the film once again works to produce an immersive, synesthetic audiovisual experience. It also continues his (and Animal Collective's) interest in horror tropes, as well as having an emphasis on natural landscapes and psychedelic imagery.[35] The narrative elements are more developed in this film than in his previous music videos, but this is largely because of the greater length of the piece, which produces more room for development. In terms of narrative clarity, it is still very obtuse. The film comprises a series of loosely connected sections that contain elements of narrative progression—recurring figures and environments can be mapped out—but these are very "open" in their signification. While all narratives are open to an extent (in that even a simple and concretely straightforward narrative can be subject to differing interpretations), *ODDSAC* exists at the further end of such openness. It is a narrative that requires active decoding by an audience, one that may require re-viewing. As argued by Sean Matharoo, the film "warrants multiple viewings, encouraging an enthusiastic audience to revisit it, read it closely and thus develop a personalized attachment to it."[36] Narrative comprehension of *ODDSAC* also may be thwarted by its affective dimensions, resulting from its synesthetic, psychedelic nature (Figures 2.3 and 2.4). Matharoo stresses how its "non-representational assemblage of competing elements ... operate to disorient and challenge spectators."[37]

Perez's first feature film, *Antibirth*, while featuring many stylistic and thematic tropes evident in his previous work, is structured more conventionally.[38] It is a narrative feature film, even though the narrative is not always easy to follow. This is partly because we experience the narrative via the subjective disorientation of the main character, Lou (Natasha Lyonne), who imbibes prodigious quantities of drugs and alcohol. Her self-medicated delirium is further heightened as the film progresses and is accompanied by strange physical transformations such as flaking pieces of flesh and an unaccounted-for pregnancy (Figure 2.5). The film can be placed in the category of "body horror" as it focuses on the horrific, unwanted transmogrification of subjective flesh. *Antibirth* continues Perez's interest in horror, especially in grotesque imagery, and also incorporates aspects prevalent across his previous work, such as heavy use of neon colors and surrealist sequences. Surrealist sequences, however, are used reasonably sparingly and are partially subordinated to the predominant, linear narrative. They are also linked to the narrative in the sense that they are often composed of Lou's distorted, mangled memory flashbacks. They do not, however, form into complete, meaningful flashbacks that offer total explanations, remaining too indistinct and vague.

Continuities between Perez's music video work and this feature film are also evident on the soundtrack to *Antibirth*. The soundtrack features a throbbing electronic score by Eric Copeland (of Black Dice) and Jonathan J.K. Kanakis, and also includes Black Dice and other Copeland tracks. In addition, it comprises a specially recorded interlude by Avey Tare (of Animal Collective) and a range of post-punk and indie music by acts such as Suicide and Black Lips. Not only does the soundtrack feature musicians that Perez had

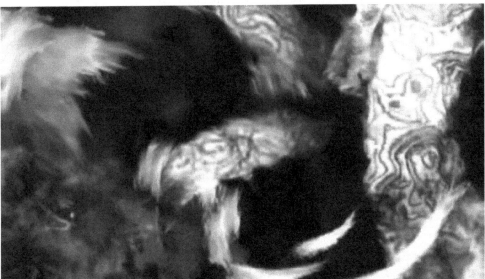

Figures 2.3 and 2.4 A masked character ("Mr. Fingers") produces delirious abstractions with fire (6:36).

previously worked with, but also it remains a very persistent presence. While the film does not feature simulations of music video clips in the way *Southlander* does, music nevertheless is present—often as underscore—for a large duration of the film and on many occasions comes to the fore more powerfully. Further stylistic and thematic connections between this film and some of Perez's previous work are apparent, including his use of a vibrantly colorful palette. Even though most of the film is set at night time, darkness is illuminated by neon lighting and images being transmitted from television sets. Other elements found in his music videos, such as masks and grotesque bodies, also appear in *Antibirth*.

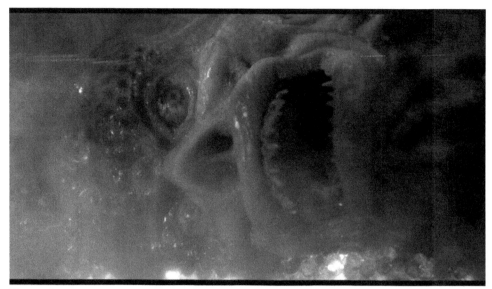

Figure 2.5 Lou gives birth to an alien head in *Antibirth* (1:20:06).

Grotesquerie is obviously a key part of a film that belongs to the body horror genre—for instance, *Antibirth* features a woman with a caved in mouth and a major character who undergoes severe bodily transformations, eventually birthing an alien monster. Masks and costumes also make an appearance in the film through the location of the Funhouse, a children's entertainment center and eatery where staff are dressed in furry outfits that include slightly creepy facial masks.

The narrative of *Antibirth* is partly difficult to fully comprehend because the film proceeds through a series of scenes that often seem disconnected. Even though most scenes *are* connected, the narration contains gaps that audioviewers are likely to have to struggle to actively piece together. This strategy may be considered—as it often was in the frequent negative reviews of the film—as a music video director struggling to adapt to the demands and conventions of a narrative feature. There may be some truth in this, but it also could be related to how Perez wants us to share Lou's often confused and addled state. The film does, after all, commence with a scene of disorientation, showing Lou at a party and eventually being dragged away by a man. The use of slow motion and flash-frame edits toward the end of the scene (accompanied by glitch-like sound fragments) indicates that something has gone wrong, but what has happened is not at all clear. The segmented narration is related to Lou's hazy mental state—it is sometimes interrupted by a hallucinogenic dream sequence or splintered memories, but even when it is not, its development feels somewhat fragmented.

The musical moments of *Antibirth* are most evident in the flashback and hallucinatory scenes when music dominates the soundtrack and Perez plays around with fragmented, often horrific, images, in which neon colors are heightened to produce a delirious, nightmarish atmosphere. Yet a musical rhythm also runs through the film and, in the absence of a strong, coherent narrative structure, provides a degree of fluidity. In particular, scenes are often connected through music-heavy interludes. Most commonly, this is achieved through recurring shots of Lou driving in a car, usually with her friend Sadie (Chloë Sevigny), although there are occasions when close-ups of television imagery also act as transitional segue points. Both driving and televisual transitions are given abstract treatments. The driving scenes are usually accompanied by an overlaid series of geometric globules slowly raining down the screen, while the television images are distorted through quite heavy reception interference. Such abstractions lend a warped perspective to the scenes, reflecting not only Lou's disoriented subjectivity but also the general environment in which she exists, peopled as it is by drug addicts, crooks, and crazed experiments.

Indie, technology, and history

These two case studies have outlined the main stylistic traits of Hanft and Perez, as well as the connections between their music video work and feature films. I now want to consider how their work relates to broader trends. First, to what extent does their work reflect some of the typical traits that recur across indie music videos? Providing a straightforward answer to this question is difficult because of a number of factors, including the sheer scope of music that has been referred to as "indie," encompassing a number of sub-generic categories, music made on varying budgets, and changes—technological, cultural, and social—over time.

Hanft's music videos represent a resolutely lo-fi aesthetic that is found in many indie videos, particularly low-budget ones from the late 1980s and 1990s. Drawing on home movies, avant-garde films and independent feature films, they often attract attention to their own artificiality through a range of techniques, including frequent changes of image (e.g., use of solarized, negative, and monochrome images), use of irises, shifts to slow-motion, and stop-motion animation. They are frequently playfully experimental and range from surrealist-like collages of seemingly unrelated situations (e.g., "Loser") to thin, oblique narratives harking back to previous cinematic touchstones (e.g., "Vanishing Point").

Perez started to produce music videos during a slightly later period, in the 2000s, and his work partially reflects the contextual shifts that have occurred since the turn of the millennium, which include the increased consumption of music videos on the web and the rise of affordable, digital technologies. His work also connects to some general shifts within indie cultures over the years. In particular, the status of the horror genre as an "illegitimate genre" has softened, as well as a broadening of the range and types of music associated with indie—especially a greater sense of generic openness within indie cultures (partly related to the sheer wealth of music available to people so that they can freely explore other genres) and a more enthusiastic embrace of electronic sounds. Hanft's work, however, already demonstrated an eclectic palette in *Southlander*, which featured a range of different generic styles of music that were linked together by artists who were independent (with the exception of Beck, who was nevertheless generally still appealing to indie audiences around this stage). Harking back to previous examples of "visual music," much of Perez's earlier music video work was marked by digital abstraction, in which patterned shapes transform and evolve as if in response to musical rhythm and texture. Generally, digital technologies are importantly linked to the rise of animated work, having enabled the automation of many laborious aspects of animation production and making it easier to synchronize images and sounds with more precision. Combined with the decreasing prices of computers and associated software, this has led to a greater array of people dabbling creatively in animation techniques.

These case studies also can be linked to questions around the influence of music video on feature filmmaking more broadly, and within the indie film sector more specifically. On a more general level, these two case studies certainly indicate such an influence; however, it does seem that we need to take account of Korsgaard's caution about making any definitive statements about such influences. Certainly, elements of Hanft's and Perez's features demonstrate such an influence through the prominence music assumes on the respective soundtracks of their features, including frequent musical moments, as well as stylistic continuities between their music videos and features. But there are influences evident from other works apparent in these, including other feature films, experimental shorts, documentaries, YouTube videos, and advertisements, to name just a few. And such influences might be prominent in some films, but partial or non-existent in others. In my case studies, Hanft's *Southlander* is most influenced by music video aesthetics. The fact that it evidences more of a music video aesthetic than his previous film, *Kill the Moonlight*, may be explained by Hanft becoming involved in music video production after releasing his first film. A further possible factor is that Hanft made his second feature on digital video rather than film, which would have enabled him to create the composite music video images with more ease.

Not all music video directors incorporate such aesthetics into their feature films to this extent. While Perez, as demonstrated, displays elements of his music video work in his first feature *Antibirth*, he also tones down many of the more *outré* elements that characterized such work. At the higher budget end of indie feature film production, the work of Jonathan Dayton and Valerie Faris demonstrates that directors who have come from music video (and, in Dayton's and Faris's cases, advertisements and music television) may not evidence any particularly perceptible influence. Other directors at the higher end of indie feature filmmaking might veer between making features which demonstrate a substantial music video influence and films that do not. An example is Sofia Coppola, whose *Lost in Translation* (2003) and *Marie Antoinette* (2006) seem infused with music video influences but whose most recent feature, *The Beguiled* (2017), does not.

Finally, these case studies can be linked more specifically to overlaps between indie music and indie film, which have been increasing in recent years.[39] Indie music has been featuring more in filmmaking generally, although it is within indie filmmaking, both in lower-budgeted varieties and higher-budgeted, studio-backed examples, that indie music has become licensed more frequently. One explanation for this trend is the commercial, marketing value of indie. In an age where there is so much choice in terms of available media, indie becomes more important as a strategy to target particular audiences, as testified by its use as a genre-like category on numerous film and music streaming sites. Indie artists are now more likely to use film—in addition to other media—as a means to earn extra revenue in an age of dwindling sales of music releases and to expose their music to new audiences.[40] Another reason fueling this trend is the idea of cultural congruence. Directors and other creative personnel who make indie films are often likely to have tastes in other indie media, and may also be committed to an indie ethos. Hence the many film directors who have also been involved in other types of indie media, particularly evident in the area of music videos, but also apparent in other forms of production. Indie film director Mike Mills, for example, has not only directed music videos, but also has designed record covers for indie bands, such as Buffalo Daughter, Jon Spencer Blues Explosion, and Sonic Youth among others.[41] As mentioned, Faris and Dayton have been involved not just in directing music videos and advertisements, but also in music television, having directed on MTV's seminal indie/alternative slot *The Cutting Edge* (1983–1987). Many indie filmmakers, including Mills, are also involved in producing and/or directing live music films and/or music documentaries and Hanft himself directed a documentary on Elliott Smith, *Strange Parallel* (1998). This is not to claim that such directors will limit themselves to working in and with different forms of indie media, but rather indicates that it might well be a dominant factor of a director's profile.

Conclusion

The above-mentioned factors should alert us to significant trends and developments. The rise of music's (moving) visualization—for example, its increased documentation, both official and unofficial, its continuing importance within filmmaking, and renaissance of music videos, including user-generated music videos—has inevitably impacted on the realms of indie/alternative music. Fabian Holt has noted an increased visualization of music generally, which he also considers to be particularly evident within indie music.[42] While there has always been a visual dimension to aspects of indie music cultures, as noted, there was a reluctance among some indie artists to engage in music videos in the 1980s. This situation has now certainly changed, not only are indie music videos prevalent on indie-oriented websites, but indie music is increasingly sourced to accompany moving images whether feature films, television, or web-based videos. Documentation of indie live gigs and the number of documentaries on indie music have also increased. By considering a number of such moving visuals, we can begin to chart conventions and tropes associated with indie music's audiovisual dimensions, some of which I have identified within the two case studies covered in this chapter. Any generalized points must, however, be tempered in the knowledge that they can only partially illuminate the whole picture, for they are always inflected by other factors including specific filmmakers' and music artists' style and temperament, and contexts of production.

Notes

1   See Tim Anderson, "The Melodramatic Mode of Sofia Coppola," in *Popular Music and the New Auteur: Visionary Filmmakers After MTV*, edited by Arved Ashby (New York: Oxford University Press, 2013), 63–83; James Annesley, "Being Spike Jonze: Intertextuality and Convergence in Film, Music Video and Advertising," *New Cinemas: Journal of Contemporary Film* 11, no. 1 (2013): 23–37; and Carol Vernallis, *Unruly Media: YouTube, Music Video, and the New Digital Cinema* (Oxford and New York: Oxford University Press, 2013).

2   John Richardson, *An Eye for Music: Popular Music and the Audiovisual Surreal* (New York: Oxford University Press, 2011), 58.

3   Geoff King, *Indiewood USA: Where Hollywood Meets Independent Cinema* (London: I.B. Tauris, 2009).

4   Vernallis, *Unruly Media*, 36.

5   Ibid., 40. John Richardson has also reflected on the music video's influence on a range of films, contending that its influence has led to new aesthetic traits such as greater attention to audiovisual flow (implying repetition), narrative fragmentation, micro-rhythmic and micro-visual detail, and surrealist juxtapositions. Richardson, *An Eye for Music*, 92.

6   Mathias Bonde Korsgaard, *Music Video After MTV: Audiovisual Studies, New Media, and Popular Music* (London and New York: Routledge, 2017), 150.

7   Ibid., 145.

8   I will not focus on his third feature, *Averageman* (2012), as it has been difficult to locate a copy of the film.

9   *Kill the Moonlight*, directed by Steve Hanft, 1994 (Plexifilm DVD, 2006).

10   In Steve Hanft interview, *Kill the Moonlight* (Plexifilm DVD, 2006).

11   Ibid.

12   Ibid.

13   Steven Shaviro, *Digital Music Videos* (New Brunswick, NJ: Rutgers University Press, 2017), 8.

14   Beck, "Loser," YouTube video (3:53), official music video, directed by Steve Hanft, posted by "Beck," October 7, 2009, https://www.youtube.com/watch?v=YgSPaXgAdzE.

15   Steve Hanft, liner notes, *Kill the Moonlight*. I should note that, in the liner notes, Hanft refers to the band he was in with Beck as Loser, but in the interview with Hanft on the DVD extras he refers to the band's name as Liquor Cabinet. I have not been able to ascertain which was correct (or whether they changed names) as information is scarce and the band did not officially release any records.

16   Saul Austerlitz, *Money for Nothing: A History of the Music Video from the Beatles to the White Stripes* (London and New York: Continuum, 2007), 70. "College rock" was a term used frequently in the 1980s in the United States but gradually fell out of use. Much of the music would have been called indie in the United Kingdom at the time.

17   Maria Demopoulos, "Blink of an Eye: Filmmaking in the Age of Bullet Time," *Film Comment* 36, no. 3 (May/June, 2000): 34–39.

18   Beck, "Beercan," YouTube video (3:58), official music video, directed by Steve Hanft, posted by "Beck," October 7, 2009, https://www.youtube.com/watch?v=zVay-RfNGv8; Beck, "Pay No Mind (Snoozer)," YouTube video (3:13), official music video, directed

by Steve Hanft, posted by "Beck," October 7, 2009, https://www.youtube.com/watch?v=yHjjqYQpBQg.

19 Beck, "Where It's At," YouTube video (3:31), official music video, directed by Steve Hanft, posted by "Beck," October 6, 2009, https://www.youtube.com/watch?v=EPfmNxKLDG4.

20 *Southlander: Diary of a Desperate Musician*, directed by Steve Hanft, 2001 (Eclectic DVD, 2003).

21 Carol Vernallis, *Experiencing Music Video: Aesthetics and Cultural Context* (New York: Columbia University Press, 2004), 13–20.

22 Jon Spencer Blues Explosion, "Dang," YouTube video (1:56), official music video, directed by Steve Hanft, posted by "In Style and Out of Print!," January 23, 2018, https://www.youtube.com/watch?v=3fQY7uFTfVI.

23 Primal Scream, "Kowalski," YouTube video (4:18), official music video, directed by Steve Hanft, posted by "Primal Scream," January 16, 2011, https://www.youtube.com/watch?v=0xBzYsE4y1k.

24 Carol Vernallis, "Strange People, Weird Objects: The Nature of Narrativity, Character and Editing in Music Videos," in *Medium Cool: Music Videos From Soundies to Cellphones*, edited by Jason Middleton and Roger Beebe (Durham, NC and London: Duke University Press, 2007), 111–151.

25 Korsgaard, *Music Video After MTV*, 154.

26 *ODDSAC*, directed by Danny Perez, 2010 (Plexifilm DVD, 2010).

27 Panda Bear, "You Can Count On Me," YouTube video (2:23), official music video, directed by Danny Perez, posted by "Paw Tracks Records," December 19, 2011, https://www.youtube.com/watch?v=eoOv1tyWHe0. Black Dice's "Luveas" music video is not currently on YouTube.

28 Kerry Brougher, "Visual-Music Culture," in *Visual Music: Synaesthesia in Art and Music Since 1900*, edited by Kerry Brougher, Jeremy Strick, Ari Wiseman, and Judith Zilcer (London: Thames & Hudson, 2007), 88–179.

29 Aimee Mollaghan, *The Visual Music Film* (Basingstoke: Palgrave Macmillan, 2015), 73.

30 P. Adams Sitney, *Visionary Film: The American Avant-Garde* (New York: Oxford University Press, 1974).

31 Vernallis, *Unruly Media*, 36; Korsgaard, *Music Video After MTV*, 92.

32 Animal Collective, "Who Could Win a Rabbit?," YouTube video (2:25), official music video, directed by Danny Perez, posted by "Fat Cat Records," November 29, 2006, https://www.youtube.com/watch?v=UTbd0Ncsyus.

33 Animal Collective, "Summertime Clothes," YouTube video (4:30), official music video, directed by Danny Perez, posted by "Domino Recording Company," June 10, 2009, https://www.youtube.com/watch?v=GxhaRgJUMl8; Animal Collective, "Today's Supernatural," YouTube video (3:47), official music video, directed by Danny Perez, posted by "Domino Recording Company," August 15, 2012, https://www.youtube.com/watch?v=47xbkT3calM.

34 Hot Chip, "Look At Where We Are," YouTube video (4:09), official music video, directed by Danny Perez, posted by "Creators," July 17, 2012, https://www.youtube.com/watch?v=sZgUOiwOuC0.

35 While Animal Collective's horror influences aren't hugely marked in the band's music, its music does occasionally explore, or refer to, discomfort and dread, as in the track "Panic" (from the 2003 album *Here Comes the Indian*). It is more explicitly referenced

through the band's videos (not only those directed by Perez, but also in other videos such as "Peacebone," which features a romance between a monstrous creature and a young woman) and other references. Avey Tare, the band's main singer, named his spin-off group Avey Tare's Slasher Flicks, for example, while he programmed a film day for the AV club (Dowd, 2014), which included horror films such as *Deranged* (Gillen, Ormsby, 1974), *Halloween* (Carpenter, 1978), *Possession* (Zulawski, 1981), and *Dead Ringers* (Cronenberg, 1988). See Animal Collective, "Peacebone," YouTube video (5:13), official music video, directed by Timothy Saccenti, posted by "Domino Music," August 21, 2007, https://www.youtube.com/watch?v=fxvGHQHiY70.

36   Sean Matharoo, "'A Weird Creature That's Operating in the Theater': Cult, Synaesthesia and the Ethico-Politics of Horror in Danny Perez and Animal Collective's *ODDSAC*," *Horror Studies* 7, no. 2 (2016): 275–291.

37   Ibid., 279.

38   *Antibirth*, directed by Danny Perez, 2016 (Matchbox DVD, 2017).

39   Jamie Sexton, "Independent Intersections: Indie Music Cultures and Independent Cinema," in *A Companion to American Independent Film*, edited by Geoff King (Malden, MA: Wiley-Blackwell, 2016), 106–128.

40   See Bethany Klein, *As Heard on TV: Popular Music in Advertising* (Farnham: Ashgate, 2009).

41   Danny Perez has recently added album design to his own portfolio, having created the cover design for Panda Bear's album *Buoys* (2019).

42   Fabian Holt, "Is Music Becoming More Visual? Online Video Content in the Music Industry," *Visual Studies* 26, no. 1 (2011): 51.

3

The Animated Music Videos of Radiohead, Chris Hopewell, and Gastón Viñas: Fan Participation, Collaborative Authorship, and Dialogic Worldbuilding

Lisa Perrott

Introduction

A pig's head stuck on a stake, a man cradling a fizzing time bomb while his head explodes, a line-up of anthropomorphized cats clapping in unison, a wolf and pig at electioneering podiums addressing a queue of miniature children, a hybrid cow-human crucified on a red cross: these images adorn the website of Radiohead fan and visual artist Gastón Viñas.[1] Collectively they exhibit themes of authoritarianism, animal–human power relations, a distinctive visual aesthetic, and a subversive tone, all of which build upon a sense of entering into an imaginary world with original dimensions. But a closer examination reveals that many elements of this world are derived from the lyrics, songs, and music videos of the band Radiohead.

This chapter examines the fan-made music videos created by Gastón Viñas, and their close relationship to Radiohead's "official" music videos and associated "world" components. Framing my analysis of these videos with the concepts of dialogism and intertextuality,[2] I argue that fan-made music videos can play a generative role within a reciprocal process of "dialogic worldbuilding." As a synthesis of old and new concepts developed across the fields of media studies, linguistics, and narratology, this term describes the unofficial collaborative authorship and intertextual dialogue involved in the process of building imaginary worlds, along with their components and texts. Forming an interconnected web, my analyses of differently authored videos demonstrate that a transmedia and transauthorial approach can enable a holistic impression of the establishment, appropriation, and regeneration of "storyworlds."[3]

The forms and functions of music videos have diversified in many ways since the birth of MTV.[4] New digital technologies, along with networking and file-sharing capabilities, have enabled previously unconsidered means of collaboration and new production practices. These developments have also formed ideal conditions for participatory cultures to proliferate and activate. The production of music video is now complicated by alternative models of authorship, and increased participation in the production process by fans and uncommissioned video artists, who produce an abundance of "non-official" and "fan-made" music videos. New types of collaborative authorship have emerged, engaging fans in acts of cultural participation and producing new forms that challenge expectations about the codes, conventions, and functions of music videos. When analyzing fan-made music videos, we cannot assume that these videos function primarily as commercial or marketing strategies for musicians. On the other hand, we cannot assume that they are entirely disconnected from the creative and marketing pursuits of musicians. Scholars express differing perspectives about the functions of these videos and the authorial status of their creators. They provoke a range of perspectives about auteurism, collaborative authorship, participatory culture, assemblage, and intertextuality.[5] These issues of fan participation and dispersed authorship have also been explored by Henry Jenkins, who asserts that "Fans are poachers who get to keep what they take and use their plundered goods as the foundations for the construction of an alternative cultural community."[6] Emphasizing the creative processes involved in cultural borrowing, he argues that fan-generated texts:

> cannot simply be interpreted as the material traces of interpretive acts but need to be understood within their own terms as cultural artifacts. They are aesthetic objects which draw on the artistic traditions of the fan community as well as on the personal creativity and insights of individual consumers/artists. If there is an *art* of "making do" … that art lies in transforming "borrowed materials" from mass culture into new texts. A fan aesthetic centers on the selection, inflection, juxtaposition, and recirculation of ready-made images and discourses. In short, a poached culture requires a conception of aesthetics emphasizing borrowing and recombination as much or more as original creation and artistic innovation.[7]

While Jenkins's examination of fan-made music videos provokes a useful consideration of the creative process and assemblage, he focuses here on a particular subset of fan-video artists: those who re-fashion the "ready-made images and discourses" of television series. Assuming that the source of the fan's admiration lies within the television series, Jenkins's approach barely touches on how a fan might borrow from the ready-made sonic forms, images, and discourses of a musician or band, who may in many instances serve as the primary object of a fan's admiration. Since Jenkins extrapolates from his study a number of generalized observations about the form and function of fan-made music video, I have used the strengths and limitations of his study as a springboard from which to explore the forms and functions of another subset of fans: visual artists who draw primarily upon the storyworlds of musicians. Rather than utilizing "ready-made" screen footage and television characters, like the video artists in Jenkins's study, the fan/music video artist discussed in my study uses their skills in visual art and editing along with strategies of intertextuality and assemblage to create original fan-made music video.

Analysis of fan-made videos created by visual artists can draw out insights about processes of collaborative assemblage: how fans respond creatively and collaboratively to music; and how and why they might tap into or mimic the distinctive codes, branding, and storyworlds already established by musicians. My use of the term "world" implies a type of imaginary vessel that is both a creative assemblage and a dynamic "system of relationships between individual existents."[8] Considering the representational function of this vessel in relation to authorship, a world is a useful signifying system as it contains various components, described by Marie-Laure Ryan as "the social and historical setting typical of the author's works ... the major themes and recurrent images of this work ... and the author's general ideas and philosophy of life," what we might informally understand as a "worldview."[9] While a world might represent the essential qualities, philosophies, and aesthetic attributes associated with an artist, it differs from a storyworld, which requires the components of a world to be narrativized and imaginatively interpreted by authors and audiences. Lori Burns's framework for multimodal analysis provides a sense of how narrative elements bind stories to worlds. Borrowing from David Herman, Burns examines how a transmedia storyworld is materialized in and through the following narrative elements: "discursive context and situatedness," "time course of specific events," "events that disrupt the storyworld," and the subjective experience of the disruptive experience.[10] In conjunction with these elements, the concepts of storyworld and worldbuilding are intended to frame my analyses and help to elucidate the authorial role of fan-video makers in relation to musicians. Do the texts created by these fans modify, estrange, or subvert existing storyworlds? If fan-made videos draw on existing worlds as a means of elaboration, do these new entities function as satellite storyworlds that orbit the officially created world? Or do they function as independent storyworlds, perhaps generating their own orbit of fan worlds? Similar questions are discussed by Mark Wolf, who observes that: "Imaginary worlds are often not only transmedial and transnarrative, but transauthorial as well."[11] Extending upon Jenkins's assertion that transmedia storytelling generates an incentive for fans to engage in "gap filling" activities,[12] Wolf suggests that fans are like "elaborationists" as they "go beyond the unconscious filling of gaps to consciously devising stories and world material that elaborate upon and extend the narratives and characters of a world."[13]

Viewing the situation as more complex than either Jenkins or Wolf suggest, I draw upon Mikhail Bakhtin's interrelated concepts of intertextuality, dialogism, and heteroglossia to further develop a theoretical framework that I will return to in my concluding discussion. By sketching the different components of this framework, I aim to emphasize the way in which each of these concepts relies semantically on their interrelationship.[14] Julia Kristeva drew extensively from Bakhtin to argue that a text is "a permutation of texts, an intertextuality in the space of a given text" within which "several utterances, taken from other texts, intersect and neutralize one another."[15] In this sense, rather than studying a text as an isolated, stand-alone object, a more holistic understanding can be gained by considering a text as a "compilation of cultural textuality."[16] This idea can be metaphorically illustrated by building upon Roland Barthes's definition of a text as "a tissue, a woven fabric,"[17] from which the concept of intertextuality can be represented by the figure of the weave. If we consider a text to be like a reconstituted garment, woven from the threads of prior garments that have been created and worn by others, each garment (text) and thread (word/utterance) is inflected with the fray and residue of other times, cultures, and experiences. As strands of signification, these threads connect texts to antecedent and subsequent texts. Such a metaphorical conception of intertextuality can assist an examination of the complex relationships and signifying systems within, between, and across intertexts.

Contributing a distinctly social dimension to this concept of intertextuality, Bakhtin argues that, as "living utterances," all texts are to some extent constantly in dialogue: "having taken shape at a particular historical moment in a socially specific environment," they thus "cannot fail to brush up against thousands of living dialogic threads, woven by socio-cultural consciousness and around the given object of an utterance."[18] In other words, just as living organisms undergo change when they brush up against each other, all texts alter their form in relation to other texts, accents, discourses, and socio-cultural affordances. Bakhtin defined heteroglossia as "another's speech in another's language, serving to express authorial intentions, but in a refracted way. Such speech constitutes a special type of double-voiced discourse."[19] As we shall see, this refracted authorship and "double-voiced discourse" form the dynamic interstices of the collaboratively authored intertexts discussed in this chapter. Emphasizing the suitability of a Bakhtinian framework for analyzing song and related forms, Caroline Ardrey argues that the nature of "heteroglossia is altered and enriched when collaboration crosses the boundaries between art forms and, in the case of song, the plethora of languages contained within each word is further refracted through the filter of music."[20] In this respect, intertextual collaborations that cross the boundaries of sonic, lyrical, and visual media (such as song, music video, film, and written novel) produce an enrichment of voices and layered refraction of authorship, thus providing a useful example of how intertextuality works within audiovisuality. In order to fully explicate this audiovisual enrichment, scholars have developed particular analytical tools that enable the analyst to discern the different layers of intertextuality within sonic, lyrical, and visual domains so that the "analysis not only distinguishes the layers but also illustrates how they intersect to create a complex multidimensional artistic expression."[21] Having followed a similar analytical approach, my analysis seeks to discover how dialogic authorship and intertextuality operate within audiovisual media. Building upon recent scholarship on fan authorship in relation to intertextuality,[22] it is anticipated that exploring this audiovisual dimension will provide a fresh perspective on the idea that fan creators go beyond the simple act of filling in the gaps and elaborating a "mothership" storyworld.

Radiohead as a vanguard of fan participation

Radiohead is distinctive for its experimental approach to sonic and audiovisual composition, its active engagement with visual art, and its role as a vanguard in inciting fan participation as a new means of collaborative authorship.[23] The band has been selective in working with innovative music video directors who have experimented with new technology and audiovisual aesthetics, where the manipulation of time and space has been a prominent feature. Many of the band's music videos utilize a variety of animation methods that add further tonal complexity to the musical compositions. This interest in the innovative capacity of animation is also evinced by the band's provocative engagement with participatory culture via social media platforms, where they have invited fans to produce animated music videos and visual vignettes that respond to their music. In 2008 Radiohead partnered with the online animation studio *Aniboom* to promote a competition seeking animated video responses to its album *In Rainbows*.[24] After receiving at least 1,000 entries to this competition, thirteen of these fan-made videos were screened on the music-sharing platform Myspace, after which four videos were then selected and exhibited as the winners of the competition.[25] In 2016 Radiohead invited fans to "match the creativity" of the album *A Moon Shaped Pool* by creating vignettes for its song "Daydreaming."[26] Several of these fan-made vignettes were shared via Instagram.[27] While these fan-participant experiments have resulted in diverse responses and a broad array of production values, the selected videos share some similar characteristics with Radiohead's official videos. Many of their creators had, like the official directors, used animation and digital technologies to manipulate time and space and to engage in acts of defamiliarization. Fan video creators operating outside the framework of these two experiments use similar strategies to emulate the experimental nature of Radiohead's music. Just as Radiohead has experimented with sonic composition along with the tonal clash of vocal harmonies and discordant string arrangements, several of the band's fans have experimented with animation techniques and digital technologies in order to manipulate temporal, spatial, and kinetic elements. While these fan participants indulge in the creative freedom and opportunity to assert their authorial vision, many also attempt to mimic the themes, motifs, and aesthetics that belong to a vaguely discernible alt world defined by Radiohead, along with the band's musical paratexts and fans.[28] Collectively, these fan-made videos reveal alternative approaches to collaborative process, along with assemblage strategies that appear more aligned to agit-pop[29] and experimental art practice than to the music video as a promotional tool or marketing enterprise.

Intertextual, transmedial, and transauthorial analytical methods

Fan-made music videos have seldom been subjected to close audiovisual analysis or rigorous examination of their production processes. Yet such close examination has the potential to unearth valuable insights about collaborations between musicians and their fans. With this aim in mind, I combine audiovisual and semiotic methods of analysis to examine two videos created to accompany Radiohead songs.[30] To establish a benchmark example of a Radiohead storyworld, I begin with my analysis of Chris Hopewell's video for "Burn the Witch,"[31] which was officially commissioned by Radiohead and released in 2016 as a teaser announcing the release of the band's album *A Moon Shaped Pool*. My analysis of this video will then form a backdrop for my examination of the storyworlds drawn upon and created by Gastón Viñas, and subsequently for my analysis of the unofficial video created by Viñas to accompany the song "2+2=5"[32] from Radiohead's album *Hail to the Thief*.[33]

In order to examine the shared sign systems and intertextual flow of storyworld aesthetics[34] at play between officially released music videos and fan-made videos, I have adopted audiovisual and semiotic analysis for their capacity to reveal the relationships, affects, and broader meanings generated by the composition of sonic and visual signifiers.[35] Hoping to uncover broader insights about this transmedia flow across media and authors' worlds, Viñas's fan-made videos are examined in relation to my analysis of "There There,"[36] "Burn the Witch," and "Paranoid Android";[37] three animated music videos that were officially commissioned by Radiohead, and which provide storyworld components utilized by Viñas and other visual artists.

Given the extensive use of animation by fan creators and interpreters of Radiohead's music and videos, the following section draws on my prior research into Radiohead's officially released music videos, which examines the use of animation as part of a broader audiovisual strategy of subversion.[38] Since Radiohead has actively provoked fan participation in constructing innovative visual responses to its music, I explore how the band's subversive strategies have helped to shape Viñas's music video storyworlds. Although his fan-made videos were not officially commissioned by Radiohead, his oeuvre draws on many elements found in Radiohead's official videos, particularly those directed by Chris Hopewell.

In his direction of the music video for Radiohead's song "There There," Hopewell used pixilation to "puppetize" and "objectify" Thom Yorke's body.[39] As a kinetic counterpoint to the robotic illusion created by this method, he used stop-motion animation to anthropomorphize puppets closely resembling birds, cats, and rodents. Performing the human rituals associated with tea parties and wedding ceremonies, their animated sentient gestures imbue these animals with a paradoxical sense of human agency. As an unwelcome puppetized giant intruding into this animistic miniature eco world, Yorke's dehumanized motion and lack of agency intensifies the sense of audiovisual tonal paradox produced by this music video. As we shall see, this construction of an imaginary world depicting inverse power relations between animals and humans is a distinctive trait reiterated throughout Viñas's oeuvre, and a central theme of his video for Radiohead's song "Wolf at the Door."[40] Since these connections between the work of Viñas and that of Hopewell were already apparent in 2003, it makes sense to investigate this dialogic relationship further by analyzing Hopewell's music video for "Burn the Witch."

"Burn the Witch"

As with his treatment of "There There," for "Burn the Witch," Hopewell uses stop-motion animation as a means to achieve audiovisual tonal paradox. But for this video a distinctly childlike aesthetic accompanies beautifully disturbing sonic arrangements to achieve a different type of tonal subversion. Hopewell's innocent stop-motion figurines work paradoxically with the music and lyrics of "Burn the Witch," creating a tonally complex and subversive political allegory. Strongly referencing the storyworld of the film *The Wicker Man*,[41] the video tells the story of an official inspector who pays an investigative visit to a small isolated village. The village mayor greets the inspector and shows him around, revealing dubious rituals suggesting associations with paganism or fundamentalism. Although shocked by what he sees, the inspector follows the mayor's lead and is drawn into an elaborate wooden trap. As a sacrificial ritual witnessed by the townsfolk, this "Wicker Man" trap is set on fire with the inspector locked inside. While the events of this story produce the affective conditions associated with the horror genre, further tonal complexity is achieved by the interplay of visual, sonic, and kinetic signifiers.

"Burn the Witch" opens with a shot of a bird puppet emitting a sweet chirping sound (Figure 3.1). Having established a sense of tranquility and harmony, this tone carries through the following shots, where the simplistic setting and doll-like puppets bear a strong resemblance to those of the BBC *Trumptonshire Trilogy* series.[42] An innocuous visual tone is established by the setting, style, and movement of the puppets, which refer intertextually to the playful innocence of children's stop-motion animations of the *Trumptonshire Trilogy* and *Postman Pat* ilk.[43] The sense of innocence and harmony associated with this animation style is quickly destabilized by the staccato sound of the string instruments,

Figure 3.1 Radiohead, "Burn the Witch," directed by Chris Hopewell, 2016, screenshot (0:01).

which sets up a state of absolute tension as soon as we see the protagonist driving into town. Although barely audible in competition with the strings, an electric bass sound introduces a menacing tone, appearing as short syncopated phrases alongside the drums, and establishing the minimalistic rhythmic bedrock of the song. This menacing tone is reinforced visually as we see a red cross being painted on the door of a surprised villager (Figure 3.2). Accompanied by Yorke singing "this is a low flying panic attack," this ominous audio-visual-lyrical combination foreshadows the verse "red crosses on wooden doors" (1:38), which is possibly intended to signify the way in which houses were marked to identify plague carriers.

This section of portentous imagery and taut instrumentation then changes when the inspector sets his gaze on a miniaturized model village (1:05). As though to reinforce the sense of paradox we may feel in identifying with his expanding vision of the miniature village, the addition of reverb expands the sense of acoustic space and builds intensity by suggesting a full orchestral resonance. As we shall see, the sense of irony produced by couplings of paradoxical and inverted scale and miniaturized worlds can be identified as an intertextual and dialogic thread weaving through the music video worlds of Radiohead, Hopewell, and Viñas.

Just as the inspector is ushered into the next disturbing scene, the staccato strings move up in pitch (1:25), sonically adding a sense of urgency to the video's ceremonial precursors

Figure 3.2 Radiohead, "Burn the Witch," directed by Chris Hopewell, 2016, screenshot (0:57).

to the witch-burning ritual. Perhaps alluding to the real-world rise in fundamentalist intolerance, the Trumpton-esque dolls are adorned with goat-like head masks, pagan robes, and swords pointing to a woman tied to a tree. These visual implications of sacrificial ritual combine with the sonic tension of the strings to compound the tonal paradox we might experience as we watch these powerless figurines move in harmless stop-motion.

Yorke's vocal reference to "red crosses" is marked by another acoustic change (1:38). Although returning to the initial verse structure, the violin strings are no longer the short sharp staccato that set up the state of tension, but rather now are long lyrical legato notes. While smooth and beautiful, this harmonious content works in counterpoint to its visual companions: two foreboding scenes delivering sinister warnings about the inspector's fate. The first depicts a bakery stall laden with communal food, the salient feature being a pie. A close-up reveals this pie is stuffed with a sacrificial goat, with protruding limbs and blood leaking from its pastry encasement. The accompanying rare moment of acoustic harmony continues into the next scene, where the inspector comes across gallows being adorned with flowers, in preparation for his sacrificial death (2:00). Both of these scenes produce a sense of irony, since they draw the viewer into the charming communal spirit of the village, while also pushing us away with the foreboding signs of sacrificial ritual.

When the song returns to the string staccato (2:02), a second layer of higher-pitched staccato plays over the top of the lower-register staccato. Much like the urgent swirling sound of wasps swarming in multidirectional unison, this sound conjures the Penderecki-like[44] discordant string sounds that provide the creepy iconic tone to horror films such as *The Exorcist* and *The Shining*.[45] Initially appearing as an undercurrent, this beautifully creepy sound builds to a climax at the song's end, contributing its own distinctive layer of complexity to the tone of audiovisual paradox. In conjunction with the unsettling tone conjured by string instruments, the lyrics play a part in alluding to discomforting allegorical messages. As though to confirm the political intent of the song, on November 9, 2016, Yorke responded to the election of Donald Trump by tweeting lyrics from "Burn the Witch."[46] The anxiety generated by this music video's lyrical-sonic-visual complexity escapes the borders of its storyworld, thus resonating with the disaffected sentiment of the current zeitgeist.

Along with the allegorical propensity of the lyrics, the style of animation used for this video provides further resonance to musical arrangements that are already tonally complex. My analysis of "Burn the Witch" highlights the power of music video to produce tonal complexity and to subvert audience expectations. While this music video draws on *The Wicker Man* and *Trumptonshire Trilogy* to create its own complex storyworld, we shall now see how the sonic, lyrical, visual, and philosophical components that comprise the world of Radiohead have provided one of the band's most ardent fans with material for the creation of similarly subversive and allegorical storyworlds.

The entangled storyworlds of Gastón Viñas and Radiohead

Gastón Viñas has utilized his fandom for Radiohead as inspiration for his entire body of artwork, including the officially commissioned music videos he has created for other musicians. However, his music videos for Radiohead's songs are identified on media platforms as fan-made videos. Viñas has developed a distinctive visual aesthetic that travels across his graphic artwork, animated vignettes, exhibitions, and music videos. Beyond aesthetics, he has created his own imaginary world, which is populated by anthropomorphized alienated characters and is recognizable by a consistently dark aesthetic and subversive tone. Despite being created for a range of different musicians and musical styles, most of his music videos feature reiterated motifs such as birds, pigs, cats, rodents, wolves, and cows, many of which are anthropomorphized using similarly subversive strategies to those used in "There There." Other repeated motifs include exploding heads and a table setting with two characters seated, engaging in activities such as drinking tea, discussing business, or playing a game. Appearing repeatedly in Viñas's videos for ELI's "Something Happens,"[47] Peter Adams's "Bending Sky,"[48] Second Person's "Demons Die,"[49] and Radiohead's "Wolf at the Door," this two-person-at-a-table motif is similar to an image depicted in Oskar Fischinger's animated 1927 film *Seelische Konstruktionen*.[50] Other references to animation history, aesthetics, and techniques are dotted throughout Viñas's work. For example, intertextual references to Walt Disney's animated film *Skeleton Dance* can be found in Viñas's video for Radiohead's song "2+2=5" and in his 30-second vignette *Clock*.[51] Viñas's video for "Wolf at the Door" references the animated "bouncing ball" technique originally used by Max Fleischer in 1924 for the "Ko Ko" *Song Car-Tunes*,[52] which subsequently became iconic for its capacity to represent the visual rhythm of a song.[53] Viñas's use of this technique indicates his interest in the rhythmic interplay between music and animated visual imagery. His capacity for achieving such rhythmic interplay has become a distinctive characteristic of his music videos.

Revealing a magpie approach to assemblage,[54] Viñas's music videos weave together multiple intertextual references to cinema, animation history, literature, mythology, and music. His video for "Wolf at the Door" begins and ends with archaic-looking title frames, much like those used during the silent era of cinema to indicate the start and end of a story. These italicized titles are etched into the time-worn emulsion of black film leader, calling up the haptic materiality of bygone media. In keeping with this archaic aesthetic, Viñas draws heavily from the mythology and storybook aesthetics associated with the children's fairy tale *Little Red Riding Hood* to establish the setting and characters for the "Wolf at the Door" storyworld. This audiovisual coupling of children's storybook aesthetics with sinister lyrical and musical evocations creates a tonal paradox akin to that of "Burn the Witch." In "Wolf at the Door," Viñas uses additional subversive strategies to generate this tone of sinister irony. Reminiscent of Hopewell's video for "There There" and the artwork of Barbara Daniels,[55] Viñas's drawings depict reversals of the normalized power relations in which humans are usually understood to be in control of animals. These include ironic scenarios such as wolves tucked up in bed while gazing at miniature children trapped inside a bird cage, and wolves walking in a park controlling tiny children using leashes and dog collars. Characteristic of much of Viñas's graphic imagery, his detourned mythical world of *Red Riding Hood* is rendered using ironic hand-drawn images and a monochromatic color palette, punctuated with salient pops of red color. Just as this purposeful use of red serves as a trademark unifying his body of work, we shall see how red is used with pronounced semiotic purpose in his video for "2+2=5."

While Viñas's storyworlds embody his own reiterated motifs and a distinct signature style, this has also become entangled with the worlds that have been created around the songs and artwork of Radiohead, including several of the band's officially released music videos. Because of this entanglement of themes, aesthetics, and motifs, the more one delves into the storyworlds of Viñas, the more difficult it becomes to pry them apart from those of Radiohead. While the titles published on Viñas's website explicitly appropriate the song and album titles from artists such as Nick Cave (*Push the Sky Away*,[56] "O Children") and Pulp ("The Day After the Revolution"), he makes extensive use of Radiohead song titles and lyrics as titles for his graphic artworks. These include: "Exit Music," "The Tourist," "We Suck Young Blood," "Fitter Happier," "How to Disappear Completely," "The Lukewarm," "Life in a Glasshouse," "Talk Show Host," "Decks Dark," and "Squeal to the Cops."[57] Radiohead's lyrics are also embedded within layers and frames of his music videos, along with intertextual references to Radiohead's official videos. One such visual motif directly plucked from the world of Radiohead is that of birds, whether they be flying, trapped in a cage, or perched on a tree branch, a motif which has been used to bookend Radiohead's animated music videos for "Paranoid Android," "There There," and "Burn the Witch" (Figure 3.1). Almost all of Viñas's videos include birds, often also used as bookends, and often signifying pertinent ideas within the videos.

Viñas's graphic artwork titled *Burn the Witch* depicts a monochromatic drawing of two rodent-headed soldiers with weapons drawn. The salient feature of the image is a red cross painted on a flag that is hanging between the rodent-humanoid soldiers.[58] A similar red cross appears on the cats' heads used by Viñas as branding for his Facebook page and YouTube channel.[59] Presumably Viñas derived this red cross from the official video for "Burn the Witch." As with other visual motifs derived from Radiohead's storyworlds, the painted red cross travels across internet platforms as a Viñas branding stamp, and also across his still and moving image works. In his music video for "Something Happens," a framed picture of a professor-capped cat becomes painted over with a red cross (2:13). Near the end of the video (3:36–3:38), Viñas's still artwork *Burn the Witch* emerges, followed by his visual interpretation of "red crosses on wooden doors" (Figure 3.3), which then subtly transforms into an image of red crosses over the faces of cats. To understand the holistic significance of this travelling transmedial motif, it helps to be familiar with the storyworlds associated with Hopewell's video for "Burn the Witch." Providing a graphic interpretation of the witch-burning scene from this video, Viñas's still artwork *The Day After the Revolution* depicts a pig's head stuck on a stake, surrounded by six spear-wielding, bowler-hatted men closely resembling the ill-fated inspector from "Burn the Witch."[60] There are many other examples of Viñas's intertextual references to Radiohead, some of which occur in music videos made for other musicians. In Viñas's video for "Something Happens," the typewriter text "2+2=4"

Figure 3.3 ELI, "Something Happens," directed by Gastón Viñas, 2018, screenshot (3:39).

(1:19) intertextually references the Radiohead song "2+2=5," as well as referencing Viñas's own video for this song. Through his reiterated and recontextualized use of motifs derived from Radiohead's music videos and paratexts, Viñas enforces a sense of shared authorship of these motifs, thus blurring the act of intertextuality with that of self-referentiality, and creating further entanglements between storyworlds.

"2+2=5"

As of 2018, Radiohead had not commissioned an official music video to accompany its song "2+2=5 (The Lukewarm)," which was released as part of the album *Hail to the Thief* (2003). In an interview by David Fricke for *Rolling Stone*, Yorke confirmed the pointed reference to the phrase "hail to the chief," explaining "the whole album is about thinly veiled anger … the BBC was running stories about how the Florida vote had been rigged and how Bush was being called a thief. That line threw a switch in my head."[61] The song title refers to the symbolic term that appeared in George Orwell's novel *Nineteen Eighty-Four*,[62] where it was used to indicate the ideological transmission of a false dogma, particularly associated with totalitarian societies. Along with the song's subtitle, the lyrics also reinforce this Orwellian theme, evoking the ideologically "interpellated" plight of "the lukewarm" from Canto three of Dante's *Inferno*.[63] According to Dante, "the lukewarm" are morally neutral souls who are damned to suffer in eternal limbo, tormented by wasps, flies, and worms.

Mirroring Yorke's lyrical expression of anger, misused authority, interpellated and tormented souls, Viñas draws upon the storyworlds of Orwell and Dante to build his own world of eternal suffering. Viñas's visual accompaniment to the song takes its cue from the title, building on the idea of false dogma, and blending the key themes of *Nineteen Eighty-Four* with the characters and setting of Orwell's novel *Animal Farm*.[64] The visual framework of this video storyworld is initially rendered with rudimentary white line drawings animated in two dimensions on a minimalist black background. While evoking a childlike quality, these white line drawings refer back to the early history of animation by referencing the chalkboard aesthetic of Émile Cohl's animated film *Fantasmagorie* (1908).[65] But while Cohl's pioneering film demonstrates how line drawing can achieve fluid transitioning between frames and mobility of forms within frames, Viñas emphasizes the abrupt transition between frames and frequently uses images where characters and forms remain mostly static within the frame. This established style of animation, where movement occurs primarily *between* rather than within frames, continues until the video's first turning point (2:05), where a noticeable shift in the pace of the music is accompanied by intensified cynicism in Yorke's vocal tone, frantic cutting, and increased movement within the frames.

The initial prelude for the video introduces hand-drawn pictorial symbols representing "cow" + "pig" =. Introduced incrementally across a sequence of frames, these symbols are animated to match the musical click track (metronomic beat), thereby positioning the animator like a member of the band, collaboratively aligning his metronomic "instrument" with the time signature of the song. Following this prelude, Viñas coheres to Radiohead's coded bookends by initiating his video with an animated bird, flying among the clouds and then perched in a tree (0:32), in keeping with the familiar Radiohead motif (Figure 3.1). This mid-shot transitions into an establishing shot, revealing cows grazing in a farmyard. Setting the scene for an *Animal Farm*-esque psychodrama, these first few shots of the video play out in time with an establishing rhythm-and-bass riff. Perfectly synchronized, a head-and-shoulders shot of a cow directly addressing the audience accompanies the first note of Yorke's characteristically angelic voice. As Yorke sings "are you such a dreamer to put the world to rights?" we see a sequence of wider shots depicting anthropomorphized cows using a range of tools, potentially signifying the activity of the working class. These cows are at work building their own "storyworld set" for the music video they are acting in, a world replete with many codified signs of domestic stability. A childlike drawn house wafts smoke from its chimney and a flag blows gently in the breeze. Branded with the symbol of a cow's head, this flag on a pole signifies ownership and affirms the cows as the protagonists of this storyworld. These are the characters we are meant to identify with and feel empathy for when this stable storyworld is thrown into turmoil by the intrusion of fascist pigs enforcing their capitalist regime in unison with rampant musical shifts.

An inciting incident alters this established scene of domestic stability, when a pig turns up at the door of a cow's house, adorned with only a briefcase, collar, and tie (1:07). These signs operate together to signify the entry of capitalism and consumerism, a signification that is reinforced in the frames that follow. We see the pig pointing to a television set, followed by a close-up shot of the television screen, broadcasting an image of a cow shaking its human breasts (1:12), an image that intertextually references the crass aesthetics of the objectified breast imagery dotted throughout Radiohead's music video for "Paranoid Android" (0:06; 2:47; 5:41; 6:03). While cohering to the codified aesthetics of Radiohead's world, this image suggests that the cows are being exploited as commodified sexual objects while also being seduced and ideologically interpellated by mass media.[66] This idea is further reinforced in the next image, where it is inferred that the cow seated on a couch is watching this exploitative objectification of cows on a freshly purchased television set.

In the shots that follow, we are introduced to further signifiers of capitalism and consumerism, and an environmental message emerging from the juxtaposition of images. The domestic calm signified by the childlike drawing of a house reassuringly emitting smoke from its chimney is juxtaposed with images depicting multiple factories, each branded with a symbol of a pig's head, and each billowing massive plumes of smoke from multiple chimneys. A simple example of Sergei Eisentein's theory of montage,[67] these images create new meaning through the juxtaposition of opposing visual signifiers. Eisensteinian montage is also suggested by the song's title "2+2=5," and the variety of ways in which this is used symbolically throughout the music video. As a visual accompaniment to the angelic voice of Yorke singing "two and two always makes a five," we see a sequence of drawings cut in unison to the tempo of Yorke's voice (1:22–1:30). This sequence animates a pictorial sequence signifying a Marxist dialectical critique of the idea that "cows" (working class/productive lactators) + "pigs" (capitalists) = "cogs turning" (industrial productivity).[68] As Yorke extends out the octave shift with the word "fi_ive" (1:28), his angelic vocal tone is complicated by the sinister tone implied by the accompanying visual sequence. We see a train being driven along a track by a pig, with cows crammed, like concentration camp victims, into the carriages. Perhaps a reference to trains heading to Auschwitz, in a point of view shot the train disappears into a dark tunnel, taking us along for the ride into the sinister underbelly of this oppressive world. Then, to reinforce our sense of the metaphorical entrapment of this dark tunnel, we are given another simple exemplar of Eisensteinian montage. A drawing of a bird flying freely is juxtaposed with a drawing of a bird trapped in a cage, thus referencing the animated signification of the proto-cinematic "thaumatrope."[69] Lyrically emphasizing this sense of entrapment, Yorke sings, over a layer of harpsichord plucking: "It's the devil's way now, there is no way out." Viñas then visually transports the idea of entrapment back to the establishing shot of the farmyard setting, where the initially established harmony has been destabilized due to this new authoritarian regime. Instead of flying freely or perching in a tree, the bird overlooks the farmyard from inside its cage, and the lactating cows leak streams of milk across the farmyard (1:39). Referring again to concentration camp victims, the cows turn into skeletal udder-leaking machines, servicing the capitalist pigs who fatten themselves up on milk. Yorke's lyrics, "You can scream and you can shout, it is too late now," are accompanied by drawings of skeletal cows protesting with placards and megaphones, only to be over-shouted by a gnashing dog on the leash of a Stasi pig. In a state of despair, the skeletal cows resort to alcohol as an opiate for their Dantean plight.

In the following sequence, prior shots are repeated and visually reverberated, thus "re-animating space" and signaling the upcoming shift in the music (2:05).[70] The previously established melodic time signature of 7/8 changes into a more aggressive rock beat of 4/4. This musical gear-shift is instigated by a cow's head blowing up like a balloon until it bursts, releasing an explosive gush of red that engulfs the screen. Accompanying this visual explosion is a sudden outburst of sonic aggression, with Yorke's voice appearing to release a bottle-neck of repressed anger by singing "because you have not been, payin' attention, payin' attention, payin' attention, payin' attention." Given the angelic, sympathetically victimized vocal tone previously established, this sonic tonal shift comes as a shock, which Viñas matches with equally shocking visual imagery. A sequence of crash-zooms frantically flashes an onslaught of almost subliminal images: a skeletal cow crucified on a red cross (2:06) and a pig at a red podium gnashing its teeth while looking down upon a uniform row of dogs with red collars (2:18). This image is reminiscent of a high-angle shot of Hitler looking down upon uniform rows of Nazi militia in Leni Riefenstahl's film *Triumph of the Will*.[71] Following a shot of teeth-baring copulating pigs, a teacher pig wearing a red tie points to the writing "2+2=5" on a chalkboard. Intertextually, the uniform rows of cow pupils seated at red school desks refer to similar images from *Pink Floyd—The Wall*,[72] a film that also deals with themes of authoritarianism and Orwellian power and control. This sequence concludes by inferring the sad plight of a cow family under the spell of their television: a red pig trough full of bones (2:34).

After the first explosive turning point, red is used sparingly but saliently throughout the second half of the video. Established as a signifier of evil, red becomes a thread of continuity between shots, indicating the transference of evil from one animal to another, and one regime to another. For instance, we see a pig gorging from a red dog bowl filled with baby cows, expanding like a balloon until it bursts, repeating the explosion motif and filling the frame with red (2:36). As though giving birth to a messiah, emerging from this red explosion is a Jesus-like cow crucified on a red cross adorned with flashing white lights (Figure 3.4). The camera pans up the length of the crucifix and then down to a throng of opiated deifying

Figure 3.4 Radiohead, "2+2=5," directed by Gastón Viñas, 2003, screenshot (2:47).

cows, suggesting the establishment of a new regime. Visually reinforcing this transition of regime and reversal of power, the background shifts from black to white, and the drawing style changes from white chalk on a blackboard to black line drawings on white paper. The camera pans down to reveal three small cows limply hanging from nooses, followed by an image of a hybrid cow-human with a slender hour-glass figure, red nipples, whip, and high heels. The camera then pans up to reveal three pigs with red studded dog collars hanging from chains. Stripped of agency, these pigs resemble ceramic piggy banks: mere vessels used to amass wealth. In the next shot these objectified pigs are ridden, whipped, and eventually smashed by the cow in red high heels, now wielding a wrecking-ball (2:53). There's no sense of comfort in this inversion of power relations in which the cows have become corrupted by consumerism, religious deification, and sexual power games.

This fast onslaught of disturbing imagery is difficult to comprehend, yet the intensity of its affective resonance is perplexing and discomforting. While these images are simplistically drawn, they are comprised of a complex repertoire of signs, operating together as a sophisticated animated sign system. This sign system communicates the internal logic of the "2+2=5" storyworld, the metaphorical role of the key characters and the inciting incident that catalyzes a chain of events: stability is disrupted, power relations are overturned, capitalism, patriarchy, and consumerism become the prevailing world order, ideologically interpellating, controlling, and exploiting the working (lactating) class. But when the proponents of this order over-indulge, they explode, giving rise to a self-perpetuating cycle of authoritarian abuse of power. Eschewing any expectation of a neatly tied-up "classical narrative" resolution, Viñas perplexes his audience with a frantic montage of images repeated from earlier in the video. In true Radiohead form, the end of the song follows with a coda depicting a bird. The sole survivor of this sorry tale, this vulture plucks at the skeletal remains of a cow carcass (Figure 3.5).

Conclusion

My analyses have shown how officially commissioned and fan-made music videos have the capacity to build complex social and political allegories that are connected by multiple intertextual threads, which speak to each other dialogically. Audiovisual and semiotic analysis form a particularly useful combination for a comparative examination of fan-made music videos in relation to officially commissioned music videos. On a broader level, a transmedial and transauthorial analytical approach has enabled a picture to emerge about the ways in which signs, codes, aesthetics, themes, and subversive strategies transfer across the sonic, visual, still, and moving imagery that form the building blocks of storyworlds. These methods of analysis are also ideal for examining the ways in which fan-made music videos create new meaning from the re-mediation of multiple intertextual references.

My analyses of the videos for "Burn the Witch," "There There," "Wolf at the Door," and "2+2=5" show how Viñas has utilized similar strategies to the directors of Radiohead's official music videos. In the same way as "Burn the Witch," Viñas's "2+2=5" employs a

Figure 3.5 Radiohead, "2+2=5," directed by Gastón Viñas, 2003, screenshot (3:32).

simplistic childlike animation style along with references to classic literature and cinema to create an allegorical work of art operating as subversive political commentary. Viñas goes beyond stylistic mimicry or occasional intertextual referencing of Radiohead songs and videos. He overtly engages with themes depicted in Radiohead songs and videos, such as authoritarianism, the rise of right-wing political power, thought control, animal-human power relations, consumerism, and the opiating function of screen media in everyday life. "2+2=5" constitutes a hand-drawn Orwellian world in which its occupants are represented as being enslaved by consumerism, industrial processes, and the control mechanisms of mass media. In its visual expression of these themes, this video also shares a similarly crass aesthetic and cynical tone with the animated video for Radiohead's song "Paranoid Android," which also utilizes audiovisual tonal complexity to make a subversive statement about capitalism, objectification, and social and moral decline. In these ways, Viñas coheres closely to Radiohead's political concerns and subversive strategies while simultaneously pillaging from the band's music video storyworlds in order to furnish his own. By utilizing Radiohead's music and world components to promote his own art, Viñas unashamedly overturns the established relationship whereby musicians use the work of visual artists to promote their music. But this is not a simple inversion. As indicated by the extensive comments on Viñas's YouTube channel, viewers perceive the worlds of Radiohead and Viñas as overlapping in mutually symbiotic ways that generate new layers of meaning. While both Viñas and Radiohead benefit from their shared fan base and revitalized fan engagement with their work, their fans are also beneficiaries of the enriched aesthetics and new meanings generated by overlapping worlds and unofficially shared authorship.

What, then, does my examination of the overlapping worlds of Radiohead and Viñas suggest about worldbuilding? In order to answer my preliminary questions about the relationship between officially created worlds and fan-made worlds, I refer to Wolf's conception of authorship as a series of concentric circles:

> extending out from the world's originator (or originators), with each circle of delegated authority being further removed from the world's origination and involving diminishing authorial contributions, from the originator and main author to estates, heirs and torchbearers; employees and freelancers; the makers of approved, derivative and ancillary products that are based on a world; and finally to the noncanonical additions of elaborationists and fan productions.[73]

If we accept such a conception of authorship as a series of concentric circles, how then can we situate the worlds of Viñas in relation to the worlds created by Radiohead and their officially commissioned music video directors? Such a model would position Viñas on the very outer circle at some distance from the "mothership" author, and thus render his authorial contribution as diminished. This would seem to underplay his authorial contribution to a wider universe made up of the intersecting worlds of Radiohead, music video directors, and fans. It follows that, while fan authorship can be conceived of in terms of proximal relations to an originary author or "mothership" project, such a conception might eclipse the less obvious ways in which musicians and fans engage in collaborative authorship without officially sanctioning the activities of intertextuality and dialogic world-sharing. Elaborating on his theorization of dialogism and intertextuality, Bakhtin wrote that: "The artistic act … lives and moves not in a vacuum but in an intense axiological atmosphere of responsible interdetermination,"[74] thus suggesting that texts influence each other in multiple directions, in ways that are not solely determined by a singular author. This emphasis upon the dialogic interdetermination between texts provides an organic and dynamic view of authorship, which extends upon those conceptions of fans as fulfilling a gap-filling function, or of existing in a peripheral orbit with no reciprocal influence upon the authors of antecedent intertexts. A true test of this theory would require a more extensive empirical study involving interviews with the musicians and artists who created the videos discussed here. Perhaps such a study might provoke a more explicit dialogic process between Radiohead, Hopewell, and Viñas. But it would be a shame if the determination produced by official dialogue were to eclipse the experimental nature generated by the "axiological atmosphere of responsible interdetermination,"[75] for a world without such unpredictable collaboration would be devoid of creative life force.

Notes

1   See https://www.gastonvinas.com.
2   Mikhail Bakhtin, "Discourse in the Novel," in *The Dialogic Imagination: Four Essays*, edited by Michael Holquist, translated by Caryl Emerson and Michael Holquist (Austin, TX: University of Texas Press, 1981).

3 Marie-Laure Ryan, "Story/Worlds/Media: Tuning the Instruments of a Media-Conscious Narratology," in *Storyworlds Across Media: Toward a Media-Conscious Narratology*, edited by Marie-Laure Ryan and Jan-Noël Thon (Lincoln, NE: University of Nebraska Press, 2014), 25–49.

4 Mathias Bonde Korsgaard, *Music Video After MTV: Audiovisual Studies, New Media, and Popular Music* (London and New York: Routledge, 2017); Mathias Bonde Korsgaard and Tomáš Jirsa, "The Music Video in Transformation," *Music, Sound, and the Moving Image* 13, no. 2 (2019) (forthcoming special issue); Steven Shaviro, *Digital Music Videos* (New Brunswick, NJ: Rutgers University Press, 2017); Carol Vernallis, *Unruly Media: YouTube, Music Video, and the New Digital Cinema* (Oxford and New York: Oxford University Press, 2013).

5 Angelina Karpovich, "Reframing Fan Videos," in *Music Sound and Multimedia*, edited by Jamie Sexton (Edinburgh: Edinburgh University Press, 2007), 17–28; Louisa Stein and Kristina Busse, "Limit Play: Fan Authorship between Source Text, Intertext, and Context," *Popular Communication* 7, no. 4 (2009): 192–207; Iain Smith, ed. "Cultural Borrowings: Appropriation, Reworking, Transformation," *Scope: An Online Journal of Film and Television Studies* 15 (2009): 1–224; Emily Caston, "Not Another Article on the Author! God and Auteurs in Moving Image Analysis: Last Call for a Long Overdue Paradigm Shift," *Music, Sound, and the Moving Image* 9, no. 2 (2015): 145–162.

6 Henry Jenkins, "'Layers of Meaning': Fan Music Videos and the Poetics of Poaching," in *Textual Poachers: Television Fans and Participatory Culture* (New York: Routledge, 2012), 223.

7 Ibid., 223–224.

8 Ryan, "Story/Worlds/Media," 30.

9 Ibid., 30.

10 Lori Burns, "Interpreting Transmedia and Multimodal Narratives: Steven Wilson's 'The Raven That Refused to Sing,'" in *The Routledge Companion to Popular Music Analysis: Expanding Approaches*, edited by Ciro Scotto, Kenneth Smith, and John Brackett (London and New York: Routledge, 2018), 97; David Herman, *Basic Elements of Narrative* (Hoboken, NJ: Wiley, 2009), 9.

11 Mark Wolf, *Building Imaginary Worlds: The Theory and History of Subcreation* (New York: Routledge, 2012), 269.

12 Henry Jenkins, "Transmedia Storytelling 101," *Henry Jenkins: Confessions of an Aca-fan*, March 22, 2007, http://henryjenkins.org/blog/2007/03/transmedia_storytelling_101.html.

13 Wolf, *Building Imaginary Worlds*, 279.

14 Graham Allen, *Intertextuality: The New Critical Idiom* (London: Routledge, 2000), 27.

15 Julia Kristeva, "The Bounded Text," in *Desire in Language*, edited by Leon Roudiez (New York: Columbia University Press, 1980), 36–63.

16 Allen, *Intertextuality*, 36.

17 Roland Barthes, *Image-Music-Text* (London: Fontana, 1977), 159.

18 Bakhtin, "Discourse in the Novel," 276.

19 Ibid., 324.

20 Caroline Ardrey, "Dialogism and Song: Intertextuality, Heteroglossia and Collaboration in Augusta Holmès's Setting of Catulle Mendès's 'Chanson,'" *Australian Journal of French Studies* 54, no. 2–3 (2017): 238.

21 Lori Burns and Alyssa Woods, "Rap Gods and Monsters: Words, Music and Images in the Hip-Hop Intertexts of Eminem, Jay-Z, and Kanye West," in *The Pop Palimpsest: Intertextuality and Recorded Popular Music*, edited by Lori Burns and Serge Lacasse (Ann Arbor, MI: University of Michigan Press, 2018), 218.

22 Stein and Busse, "Limit Play."

23 Some musicians actively generate fan participation and collaboration in worldbuilding activities, resulting in innovative projects that challenge prior notions of authorship. See, for instance, Gareth Schott and Karen Barbour, "Filmic Resonance and Dispersed Authorship in Sigur Rós' Transmedial *Valtari Mystery Film Experiment*," in *Transmedia Directors: Artistry, Industry, and New Audiovisual Aesthetics*, edited by Carol Vernallis, Holly Rogers, and Lisa Perrott (New York: Bloomsbury, forthcoming); Ioana Literat, "The Work of Art in the Age of Mediated Participation: Crowdsourced Art and Collective Creativity," *International Journal of Communication* 6 (2012): 2962–2984.

24 Radiohead [studio album], *In Rainbows*, XLCD324 (XL Recordings CD, 2007).

25 Sean Michaels, "Radiohead Quadruple Aniboom Winners," *Guardian*, August 12, 2008, https://www.theguardian.com/music/2008/aug/12/radiohead.animation.pop.rock.news.

26 Radiohead [studio album], *A Moon Shaped Pool*, XLLP790X (XL Recordings CD, 2016).

27 Chris Riotta, "Radiohead Just Chose an Extraordinary Winner for Their 'Daydreaming' Short Film Contest," *Mic*, September 12, 2016, https://mic.com/articles/153936/radiohead-just-chose-an-extraordinary-winner-for-their-daydreaming-short-film-contest#.srM2wyQNA.

28 Joseph Tate, *The Music and Art of Radiohead* (Aldershot and Burlington, VT: Ashgate, 2012).

29 Agit-pop is the use of popular music along with artistic strategies to engage with political ideas.

30 While semiotic analysis has been used to determine the codified meanings of visual and sonic signs, this method tends to focus analysts' attention on signs and sign systems. Thus, a more holistic insight can be achieved by combining semiotic methods with other methods such as audiovisual analysis, discourse analysis, and affect analysis. These combined methods are outlined in Gillian Rose, *Visual Methodologies: An Introduction to Researching with Visual Materials* (Los Angeles, CA: Sage, 2016).

31 Radiohead, "Radiohead—Burn the Witch," YouTube video (3:59), official music video, directed by Chris Hopewell, posted by "Radiohead," May 3, 2016, https://www.youtube.com/watch?v=yI2oS2hoL0k.

32 Radiohead, "Radiohead—2+2=5/A Wolf at the Door—Subtitulos Español," YouTube video (7:00), unofficial music video, directed by Gastón Viñas, posted by "Callampa Producciones," April 5, 2015, https://www.youtube.com/watch?v=UFjtHyf1FQI.

33 Radiohead [studio album], *Hail to the Thief*, 7243 5 84543 2 1 (Parlophone CD, 2003).

34 Geoffrey Long, "Creating Worlds in Which to Play: Using Transmedia Aesthetics to Grow Stories into Storyworlds," in *The Rise of Transtexts: Challenges and Opportunities*, edited by Benjamin Derhy Kurtz and Mélanie Bourdaa (New York: Routledge, 2016), 139–152.

35 Rose, *Visual Methodologies*.

36 Radiohead, "Radiohead—There, There," YouTube video (4:57), official music video, directed by Chris Hopewell, posted by "Radiohead," July 18, 2008, https://www.youtube.com/watch?v=7AQSLozK7aA.

37 Radiohead, "Radiohead—Paranoid Android," YouTube video (6:38), official music video, directed by Magnus Carlsson, posted by "Radiohead," January 23, 2015, https://www.youtube.com/watch?v=fHiGbolFFGw.

38 Lisa Perrott, "Radiohead's Tonal Complexity: Animation: Creeping the Pop Out of Popular Music," paper presented at *Mixing Pop & Politics: Subversion, Resistance and Reconciliation in Popular Music* (Wellington, New Zealand: IASPM-ANZ Conference, 2017).

39 Lisa Perrott, "Music Video's Performing Bodies: Floria Sigismondi as Gestural Animator and Puppeteer," *Animation: An Interdisciplinary Journal* 10, no. 2 (2015): 124–126.

40 Radiohead, "Radiohead—2+2=5/A Wolf at the Door—Subtitulos Español," YouTube video (7:00), unofficial music video, directed by Gastón Viñas, posted by "Callampa Producciones," April 5, 2015, https://www.youtube.com/watch?v=UFjtHyf1FQI.

41 *The Wicker Man* [film], directed by Robin Hardy (United Kingdom, 1973).

42 *Trumptonshire Trilogy* [television series], BBC (United Kingdom, 1966–1986).

43 *Postman Pat* [television series], BBC, Woodland Animations (United Kingdom, 1981–1996).

44 Tom Service, "When Poles Collide: Jonny Greenwood's Collaboration with Krzysztof Penderecki," *Guardian*, February 23, 2012, https://www.theguardian.com/music/2012/feb/23/poles-collide-jonny-greenwood-penderecki.

45 *The Exorcist* [film], directed by William Friedkin (United States, 1973); *The Shining* [film], directed by Stanley Kubrick (United States, 1980).

46 Michelle Geslani, "Thom Yorke Uses Radiohead's 'Burn the Witch' to Comment on the Ill-fated 2016 election," *CoS News*, November 10, 2016, https://consequenceofsound.net/2016/11/thom-yorke-uses-radioheads-burn-the-witch-to-comment-on-the-ill-fated-2016-election.

47 ELI, "Something Happens," YouTube video (5:57), official music video, directed by Gastón Viñas, posted by "Gastón Viñas," March 1, 2018, https://www.youtube.com/watch?v=Wi8rikJfgFk.

48 Peter Adams, "Bending Sky," YouTube video (2:33), official music video, directed by Gastón Viñas, posted by "Gastón Viñas," March 5, 2010, https://www.youtube.com/watch?v=TUjYS4bKV88.

49 Second Person, "Demons Die," YouTube video (3:02), official music video, directed by Gastón Viñas, posted by "Gastón Viñas," August 27, 2007, https://www.youtube.com/watch?v=pF_8nnSzCxI.

50 *Seelische Konstruktionen* [animated film], directed by Oskar Fischinger (Germany, 1927).

51 *Skeleton Dance* [animated film], directed by Walt Disney (United States, 1929); *Clock* [vignette], directed by Gastón Viñas, using extract from song *The Clock* by Thom Yorke (2007), https://www.youtube.com/watch?v=o4BtCRGOXdM.

52 *Song Car-Tunes* [animated film], directed by Max Fleischer (United States, 1924).

53 Daniel Goldmark, "Before *Willie*: Reconsidering Music and the Animated Cartoon of the 1920s," in *Beyond the Soundtrack: Representing Music in Cinema*, edited by Daniel Goldmark, Lawrence Kramer, and Richard Leppert (Oakland, CA: University of California Press, 2017), 232–234.

54 The magpie approach of David Bowie (which has inspired my own magpie approach to scholarship) is explained in Kathryn Johnson, "David Bowie Is," in *David Bowie: Critical Perspectives*, edited by Eoin Devereux, Aileen Dillane, and Martin Power (New York: Routledge, 2015), 11.

55   See: http://www.barbaradanielsart.com.

56   Nick Cave and the Bad Seeds [studio album], *Push the Sky Away*, catalogue # BS001CD (Bad Seed Ltd. CD, 2013).

57   "Squeal to the cops" are lyrics from Radiohead's song "A Wolf at the Door."

58   See this image at: https://www.gastonvinas.com/projects/dawn-patrol.

59   See Viñas's branding image at: https://www.youtube.com/gastonvinas and https://www.facebook.com/GastonVinas.

60   See this image at: https://www.gastonvinas.com/projects/the-day-after-the-revolution.

61   David Fricke, "Bitter Prophet: Thom Yorke on 'Hail to the Thief,'" *Rolling Stone*, June 26, 2003, https://www.rollingstone.com/music/music-news/bitter-prophet-thom-yorke-on-hail-to-the-thief-87869.

62   George Orwell, *Nineteen Eighty-Four* (London: Secker & Warburg, 1949).

63   Renee Jarre, "Louis Althusser: Hailing, Interpellation and the Subject of Mass Media," *Ezine@rticles*, June 27, 2007, http://ezinearticles.com/?Louis-Althusser:-Hailing,-Interpellation,-and-the-Subject-of-Mass-Media&id=614657; Louis Althusser, "Ideology and Ideological State Apparatuses," in *Lenin and Philosophy and Other Essays*, translated by Ben Brewster (New York: Monthly Review Press, 1971); Alighieri Dante, *The Divine Comedy of Dante Alighieri: Inferno, Purgatory, Paradise* (New York: Union Library Association, 1935), 1265–1321.

64   George Orwell, *Animal Farm* (Harcourt, NY: Brace and Co., 1946).

65   *Fantasmagorie* [animated film], directed by Émile Cohl (France, 1908).

66   Althusser, "Ideology"; Jarre, "Louis Althusser."

67   Sergei Eisenstein, *Towards a Theory of Montage: Sergei Eisenstein Selected Works*, vol. 2, edited by Michael Glenny and Richard Taylor, translated by Michael Glenny (New York: I.B. Tauris, 1991).

68   Adam Schaff, "Marxist Dialectics and the Principle of Contradiction," *The Journal of Philosophy* 57, no. 7 (1960): 241–250.

69   The thaumatrope is an optical toy typically depicting a bird on one side of a disc and a cage on the other. Due to "persistence of vision," when the disc is set in motion, we see the two images as blended, thus producing the visual image of a caged bird.

70   Aylish Wood, "Re-animating Space," *Animation: An Interdisciplinary Journal* 1, no. 2 (2006): 133–152.

71   *Triumph of the Will* [film], directed by Leni Riefenstahl (Germany, 1926).

72   *Pink Floyd—The Wall* [film], directed by Alan Parker (United Kingdom, 1982).

73   Wolf, *Building Imaginary Worlds*, 269.

74   Mikhail Bakhtin, *Art and Answerability: Early Philosophical Essays*, edited by Michael Holquist and Vadim Liapunov (Austin, TX: University of Texas Press, 1990), 275.

75   Ibid.

4

From Music Video Analysis to Practice: A Research-Creation Perspective on Music Videos

John Richardson

Behind the writing of this chapter are some two decades of experience researching and teaching music video analysis and audiovisual analysis to students of musicology and related disciplines.[1] Alongside this are my experiences as a musician and creative artist, latent for much of my academic career, but emerging more strongly of late. The project discussed in this chapter has given me license to explore these artistic leanings by combining them with questions arising from the field of research creation, an emerging field that extends traditional ideas about academic research and the existing domain of practice-based research of the arts,[2] offering methods and outcomes that meet stringent academic criteria while producing high-level creative outcomes that are clearly informed by academic research. The approach goes beyond simply reporting creative work undertaken in parallel to academic work, or reflecting on creation in academic writing after the fact. An essential premise of research creation is namely the close-knit interdependency of its constituent creative and academic components.[3] The research-creation project in this case includes all the work that went into the composition, recording, promotion, and performance of my first solo album and song cycle, *The Fold*, released by one of Finland's largest independent labels in 2017.[4] The combination of research and creation was justified here by my experience as a researcher in relevant fields and the level of ambition in the artistic work: the scope of the project, the fact that its end products were professionally produced and widely distributed, and that it had some impact in terms of critical and audience reception.

Since work in research creation involves artistic as well as scholarly pursuits, it is by its nature experimental and interdisciplinary. A background in musicology and audiovisual studies was undoubtedly an advantage when it came to reflecting on the subject of this chapter: the music videos produced in connection with *The Fold* project. More broadly, this study connects to questions of interdisciplinary cultural analysis and inter-arts approaches to close reading.[5] My understanding of close reading encompasses a wide range of activities that fall under the category of analysis, but within an arts-centered interdisciplinary context in which the readings are open-ended and developed with reference to cultural context, implying shifting frames of reference. This emphasis brings my work into alignment with some earlier theorists working in interdisciplinary contexts.[6] In tandem with close reading, I also draw freely on the cluster of approaches that in recent research have been called autoethnography.[7] Typical of autoethnography is the use of personal experiences to critique cultural beliefs and practices; recognition of the relational nature of the work one is caught up in; probing reflection on the interactions between oneself and others, including the individual and society, the personal and the political; a micro-level concern with mundane activities and processes, and how these contribute to forming meanings and larger actions; the combination of intellectual activities with emotions and creativity; and a concern with bringing about social change through activist engagement.[8] The relevance of these concerns to research creation will be immediately apparent, especially in the context of a project where the agencies of researcher and creator coalesce in the same person.

One final theoretical area from which this research has undoubtedly benefitted is that of research on intertextuality. My interest in intertextuality owes more to the post-structuralist theories of Julia Kristeva, Mikhail Bakhtin, and Linda Hutcheon, and their descendants in critical musicology, than to the more rigorous semiotic approaches of Gerard Genette and music semioticians like Raymond Monelle, Philip Tagg, and Robert Hatten. Readers wishing to delve deeper into the conceptual complexities of current intertextual theory should look up the recently published volume on the subject edited by Lori Burns and Serge Lacasse.[9] Here I have chosen not to theorize intertextuality extensively, as this would distract from the primary aims of this study. Rather, I am generally referring to clearly observable and intentional inclusions and influences, which are abundant in the video that I will discuss here. I am not thinking of questions of stylistic affinity or broader cultural tendencies, which might also be included under the umbrella of intertextual theory.

In addition to the approaches listed above, my work draws on conceptual foundations from cultural studies, literature, and philosophy. Ideas and concepts from these academic domains spilled over onto the artistic content itself, including the idea of "the fold," which was informed by the theories of Maurice Merleau-Ponty and Gilles Deleuze. The notion of the fold implies an interest in points of transition, where one thing becomes another, and where oppositions are dismantled or brought into correspondence with one another. Two principle sources informed the intellectual or conceptual background to the project, but they did not in any sense tangibly direct *how* I was working. It is more that they seemed to explain the mode in which I had chosen to work even before I was able to conceptualize it, and this realization perhaps encouraged me to see how far the general principles that undergirded this *modus operandi* could be extended. I do not consider myself a Deleuzean thinker in any strict sense, but the idea of *the fold* as it is set forth in the book *The Fold: Leibniz and the Baroque*[10] interested me primarily because of the explanatory power it seemed to possess with respect to phenomena that interest me. The core of the book is the chapter "What is Baroque?" wherein Deleuze enumerates six features of relevance to his understanding of Baroque aesthetic style and thinking:

i)   an interest in work and process that is eternal, where one ending in a sense signifies only another beginning or extension;

ii) a movement between insides or outsides, whether this refers to architecture, clothing, or bodies;

iii) a folding in of high and low, where movement from one to the other is implied through the use of pleated, cleaved or embedded forms (a maze is one such form) that are simultaneously monadic and at the same time make reference to another level or space, their extension;

iv) the implication that what folds can also *unfold* or *unravel*, implying that fullness or plenitude must give way to emptiness;

v)   the notion that enfolded forms are manneristic, preoccupied by style more than being heterogenous; concerned with the energies put into producing them and the materials that constitute them rather than expressing an underlying organic unity comprising traditional peaks and troughs;

vi) the idea that the choice of materials is fundamental but that "the composite materials of the fold (texture) must not conceal the formal element or form of expression."[11]

In other words, structure and form should be immediately apparent on the level of musical and visual surfaces, such as they are in minimalist music, for example, or recent forms of popular music ranging from intelligent dance music (IDM) to experimental indie-folk.[12]

I did not follow these ideas slavishly, but rather felt an affinity that became self-reflexive. They allowed me to reflect on what I was doing: working in a processual way; using embedded structures that have the capacity to generate new structures; dealing with absence or loss through presence; representing the hustle and bustle of noise and movement; and doing all of the above in a highly stylized or manneristic way that deflected attention away from content toward the unfolding moment and reflexive consciousness—pointing out connections between now and then, here and elsewhere, past and present, largely through a process that was referential of other works, times, and places (intertextuality). Such intertextual references were enfolded into the textures of what I was creating, producing resonances and sometimes poignant dissonances that cry out for interpretation.

A second writer whose work interested me was Merleau-Ponty, who employs "the fold" in his book *The Invisible and the Invisible*, emphasizing the concept of "flesh" and some notion that, from a perceptual standpoint, tactile contact always implies a mingling of subject and object, an enfolding of sorts.[13] Touching necessitates being touched, in a certain sense, by the object one touches, with reference to which the toucher becomes an object as well as a subject. The crux of this theory is a reflexivity that is most apparent when Merleau-Ponty discusses the visual sphere, where he argues that the act of seeing implies the possibility of being seen by another. This takes place at a distance, which is not present in tactile encounters, but the repercussions are similar: the duality of observer and observed can be reversed in an instant, folded in on itself. Even a painter capturing inanimate objects such as a landscape is part of the field of vision *of* the landscape: the seer can always be transformed into the seen. The implications for this in terms of cultural theory, gender studies, and ecological theory might be self-evident. Reflexivity challenges the solitary heroic subject of Romantic aesthetics, making that subject part of the universe of things—both touching and touched by them, ultimately continuous with them. In the music video I will discuss here, I played with questions of point of view and "the gaze" in a quite deliberate way, which bears a direct relation to Merleau-Ponty's notion of the fold.[14]

My experiences researching the surreal in popular music were also brought to bear quite directly on the creative work in question.[15] Specifically, I related the notion of the fold to the surrealist practice of exquisite corpse drawings, where one person starts to draw a picture, folds over the section they have drawn, allowing someone else to continue the creative process where the previous artist had left off. On an individual level, I attempted something similar when working on the musical composition. Although the record was conceived as a collection of individual songs, a process akin to automatic writing resulted in songs that would progress one to the next simply by following the musical flow that had arisen as a tangent or deviation within a preceding song. These tangents became folding points. I similarly explored the notion of memory as something malleable by employing flashbacks, flashes forwards, and temporal elisions as structural principles, both within songs and across the song cycle as a whole. These themes, a free-flowing or emerging aesthetic, and the idea of the plasticity of memory became the conceptual keystones that would hold the project together.

While working on this project, my academic orientation was virtually impossible to suppress. In the analysis that follows, I will reveal ways in which my creative decisions were informed by my research knowledge. Things I had learned in music research and audiovisual analysis inevitably resurfaced as part of the creative process and these influenced creative outcomes to a significant degree. The process began for me in 2016, when I started working on a cycle of thematically interrelated songs that would become the song cycle *The Fold* (which is also the title of the first song). I had no knowledge of this until the largely self-funded project was completed, but the song cycle comprised eight songs that would eventually end up being released by the independent label Svart Records. While I will touch here to some extent on the compositional and song-writing processes, the chapter focuses on the music videos that I produced, primarily as a means of promoting the album, but with an undeniable sense of curiosity about what I was capable of achieving in this—in terms of practical experience—unfamiliar sphere.

Producing the videos myself became a necessity, if they were to be produced at all, since resources that had initially been promised by the label for producing a video for the first single release ("The Fold") failed to materialize once the album release was imminent. "Plan A" had been to storyboard ideas myself based loosely around song content, mood, and lyrics, which I did. I even filmed some iPhone footage while working on the songs, as well as making field recordings when recording sounds as a part of the album's sound design. Additionally, I had several hours of video footage from the recording of the album, originally intended as video ethnography. My aim had been to cooperate with a trained video producer or video artist late in the creative process. Given the aforementioned budgetary constraints, I contacted a colleague at the Turku Arts Academy involved in the audiovisual program there to ask for assistance, hoping that a student might be interested in producing a video for an assignment or final project. No one expressed interest, but he told me, as an aside, that I should not be offended; apparently a similar request had been received a few years earlier for a project involving Radiohead and no one had expressed interest in that project either. If I wanted music videos for my album, it seemed that I would have to make them myself.

In total, I produced three "teaser" videos about work in progress, which were posted on my music Facebook page,[16] three music videos for the songs "The Fold,"[17] "Open Page (Journey to Enceladus),"[18] and, in extended form, for the songs "Dawnsong" and "Birdman of Bognor." The main focus here will be on the creative processes behind the last of these projects, the extended music video "Dawnsong and Birdman of Bognor,"[19] combined with a reflexive analysis of the video itself. I should premise this discussion by pointing out that these were my first experiments in music video production. These were low-budget, DIY videos, made by an inexperienced director with limited training in video production.[20] I did, however, learn some things when working on the videos: "tricks of the trade" and perspectives that are not easily encountered when reading the academic or practical literature on the subject. The value of the work *as such* is not the main point here but, rather, what I learned about audiovisual production in the context of a research-creation project. My objective here is to explore how my experience as a researcher influenced my artistic decisions and how the experience of making videos concretely influenced my analysis. My purpose, therefore, is to reflect on what went into producing these videos and relate to readers what lessons I have learnt as a result of this process. I will attempt to bring these findings to bear to some extent on the existing knowledge and theory of the form.

Narrativity of song and lyrics vs. visual message

A debate that has repeatedly resurfaced since the early days of research on music videos is whether they have any "content" or "substance" to speak of: whether they function first and foremost as promotional devices for the star performer, and whether any meanings they might convey are coherent or specific given the constraints of the form. More generally, the following question has often been raised: are videos worthy of serious critical attention? Along similar lines, but not implying a pejorative value judgment, E. Ann Kaplan argued in the 1980s that the primary modality of videos was "postmodern pastiche."[21] This might have been true for a while, and I will argue below that postmodernism is in some important respects interchangeable with surrealism. Jameson famously called postmodernism "surrealism without the unconscious";[22] but this lineage has been overlooked in much of the subsequent theory. Research on the subject, however, at least since Andrew Goodwin's *Dancing in the Distraction Factory: Music Television and Popular Culture*,[23] has shown that there are a wide range of video styles, wherein traditional narrative coherence or "content" is only one option among many, and in some respects is atypical.

The conceptual foundation of "the fold" is relatively loose, mainly commenting reflexively on the nature of the creative process itself. I did include a few literary allusions in the lyrics of some songs, but those will not be the main focus of this discussion. In "Dawnsong," these include references to the myth of Aurora and Tithonus, especially Tennyson's poem *Tithonus*. Aurora is essentially the regenerative power of the rising sun, invented anew each day while Tithonus, her spouse, ages irrevocably, but without dying. Some of the lyrics draw directly from this poem, as well as from a novel by the Icelandic surrealist writer Sjón entitled *The Blue Fox*. At the time of this project, I conducted fieldwork in Iceland on three occasions for a different line of research, which had an impact both in terms of musical influences and some of the textual references included in the songs; for example, the dark beaches mentioned in "Dawnsong." These allusions are generally a subtext more than being connected to an explicit narrative. As for the broader meaning of the two songs for me, I did not see Aurora and Tithonus as separate entities, but rather more as archetypes. Arguably not a tragic figure, Tithonus mourned the loss of (feminine) regenerative power in his consciousness; he became prematurely infirm by living in a box of others' design. There are other possible interpretations, and although it was foremost in my mind, I did not intend for this narrative background to determine audience experiences.

Regarding audiovisual narrativity, two extremes are arguably found in the production of music videos: the first resembles a video like Peter Gabriel's "Sledgehammer," for which the musician himself was involved in the conceptualization.[24] The videographer Stephen Johnson punctuated every detail of the lyrics with corresponding visual images, resulting in what he has called "thought beats."[25] So tightly are the music and lyrics stitched together that the constantly morphing imagery takes on an ironic character. The ubiquitous visual movement, produced through stop animation and Claymation, results in the presence of visual micro-rhythms, which in turn reflect back on the music: the complexity of the groove and its rough-hewn and glistening sonic and multisensory textures. Concept albums and the videos that arise from them (e.g., Pink Floyd's "Just Another Brick in the Wall") err toward a different kind of narrative specificity, not cleaving to the lyrics through the level of sensory detail present in "Sledgehammer"—something that is more typical of video art—but instead conveying embeddedness within a plot. My approach was closer to the former than the latter: it had more to do with sensory playfulness and the juxtaposition of materials and imagery in unexpected ways, although there is a powerful "political" subtext to the second half of the video, the song "Birdman of Bognor," to be discussed presently. From the beginning of the project, however, I was thinking of the album more as a song cycle bound together by sound design, common thematic elements, and tonal and textural elements. These priorities extended also to the corresponding visual materials.

At the opposite end of the scale to the kinds of narrative specificity discussed above are the more abstract and less illustrative approaches of directors like Anton Corbijn, whose music videos are quite straightforward, although narratively oblique, atmospheric more than discursively specific, often with a Super-8 grainy quality. Such videos don't typically simulate performance, unlike Gabriel's. I was aiming for something between these extremes. The music industry does not always expect or *welcome* visual imagination in a popular music artist. Auteur artists in the mold of Peter Gabriel, David Bowie, or Frank

Zappa are exceptions to this rule, although success brings at least the possibility of greater artistic control. This type of control is possible at the independent end of the spectrum, for accomplished auteur artists such as those discussed above, and artists with proven commercial worth and standing, such as Beyoncé with *Lemonade*. Some of the skepticism of video producers and label marketing staff might be justified, however, when it comes to artist participation. Do songwriting artists always know best how to get their music across visually? Perhaps not. I would happily have collaborated with video professionals and had no fixed ideas about how the songs should be rendered visually. My lyrics are mainly concerned with producing evocative imagery that supports and channels musical atmospheres. Add supporting visual imagery to this and the risk of overdetermination grows. In retrospect, this might have happened to some extent in this particular music video.

Intertextuality and allusion vs. direct affective involvement

One reviewer has commented of *The Fold* that you can tell it was the brainchild of an academic, as the project is densely packed with allusions—tastefully, in this reviewer's opinion, but still enough to mention.[26] If the reviewer had seen the videos as well, their visual imagery would probably have reinforced this impression. The opening line of "Dawnsong"—"the silence of the sheets" (0:27)—is wordplay, referring to the film *The Silence of the Lambs* via "silence of the *sheep*"—a near homonym with *sheets* and a pun. I tried to emphasize the wordplay audiovisually, by bringing in visual allusions to the film *The Silence of the Lambs*. When posing for the early lip-synced headshots close to the beginning of the video and in the second verse (Figure 4.1), the idea was to mimic Anthony Hopkins in a straightjacket, confronting the camera directly with his gaze rather than milking the song's emotion. Because of the dreamy and epic quality of "Dawnsong," I wanted to bring in the work of the French experimental director Jean Cocteau. In addition, there's something of a queer agenda in both of the songs, which I wanted to bring forward. I viewed Cocteau's aesthetic sensibility as suitable for conveying such a mood. Furthermore, the word "sheets" made me think of a scene in Jean Cocteau's *La Belle et la Bête* (1946), which I studied some years ago in connection with Glass's cinematic operatic adaptation.[27] There's a scene in *La Belle* where the characters meet among sheets that have been hung out to dry. Characters wander in and out of the sheets (which are *folded* in an accelerated motion sequence found at the end of the song) as though through a labyrinth. I attempted something similar, creating passageways of hanging sheets through which characters wandered as if shut off from the surrounding world. This becomes a metaphor for cinematic drapes, implying the constructedness of the storyworld (a Brechtian gesture). In addition, the sheets are used for partially concealing characters and as props for shadow play. By superimposing images over the sheets in some shots, I wanted to make it appear as though they were projected onto them—projected also in the psychoanalytical sense: reflections of the singer's internal world. Moreover, I recalled a scene in Gondry's *Be Kind Rewind* (2008) involving projection, which had a glitchy, detached, and nostalgic mood to it, and wanted to achieve something similar.[28] The Cocteau influence carried across

Figure 4.1 Close-up headshot of the author and lead singer of "Dawnsong."

to other aspects, too. The dancing scene and the mirroring of the dancers in the choruses of both "Dawnsong" and "Birdman" have a distinct neoclassical mood that resembles the cinematic imagination of Cocteau. The movements of the dancers (Lilli Heberg and Jutta Pääkkölä) in "Dawnsong" are highly stylized and their white attire corresponds with the white backdrop of the sheets in the verses (1:46; 3:42). Superimposed over this, the woman from the opening lines (Alana, the artist name of the backing singer and pianist in the song, Anna-Elena Pääkkölä) scribbles indecipherable hieroglyphs (2:21). I had the opening titles of director Jean Cocteau's *Orpheé* (1950) in mind here. Likewise, the use of reverse motion in both the dancing and writing (2:21: 3:35) was partly inspired by a sequence from the film *Orpheé* (also David Lynch's *Twin Peaks*). Alana wears black in the footage (in contrast to the dancers), much like The Princess—Death in *Orpheé* (0:28), who becomes a kind of Jungian Anima archetype (I made this video before Arcade Fire released "Reflector," which invokes the Orpheus myth in a similar way). Another allusion is found in the "swing scene" in verse 2 (1:36), an ironic tip of the hat to Fragonard's painting (1767), again raising issues reflexively about observer and observed. One could say that subverting such iconic images was an agenda throughout the video, and this can be related to the conceptual background of the album: "the fold" as theorized by Merleau-Ponty in this instance.[29]

"Birdman of Bognor" also contains a fair number of sonic and visual allusions. As part of the album's sound design, I incorporated a number of concrete sounds. One of these was recorded on a train at Gatwick Airport station (5:32), which later divided into two parts at Haywards Heath station, one bound for Eastbourne, the other for Bognor Regis.[30] I treated sounds from the public address announcement in much the same way as Steve Reich did in his tape compositions, *Come Out* (1966), *It's Gonna Rain* (1965), and *Different Trains* (1988). To make my indebtedness more obvious, I mimicked the cover art of a recording of Reich's *Different Trains*, which shows three parallel railway tracks (5:45). The initial motivation for the inclusion of the railway tracks was more pragmatic, however: the images of the lip-syncing singers in the first and second verses of Birdman were simply too static to be audiovisually involving. Through a process of trial and error, I gradually superimposed the shots of the railway tracks over the top of the lip-syncing singers (Tuuli Kristola and Maija Lindroos) following the loop sequence at the beginning of the song (see Figure 4.2). Immediately, the rhythms of the music seemed more vivid. My intention was not originally to use the footage in this way; however, the static headshots following the train announcement seemed to demand something more dynamic in order to match up with the music. The use of two lip-synced, gender-fluid singers was otherwise important to me conceptually, stemming from gendered themes in the lyrics, so I used more of the footage I had collected of railway tracks, and filmed yet more still. This temporally animated the images nicely,[31] while not stealing too much attention away from the actors. A fortuitous coincidence was the fact that, during some of the filming, my own reflected image became visible in the train window, along with the iPhone I was using to film (creating a strange cyborgian effect of the phone being attached to my head; 5:43). I synced this up with the lyrics, "you hold my attention," at the beginning of the song, and this again brought a level of critical reflexivity, seeming to comment on my dual positions as both observer and observed, author and subject, and reflecting back on some of the gender positioning in "Dawnsong."

In parallel with the presence of gender non-conformist lip-syncing actors, "Birdman" includes various allusions to 1970s gender bending and glam rock: principally, David Bowie, Suzie Quatro, ABBA, and Queen. Bowie's "Changes" and "Fame" are invoked in the repeated and pitch-shifted line "change, change, change" in the bridge of "Birdman" (9:16). Quatro is quoted in the line "Can the Can when you can" (6:53). Following this, the final verse contains the pun, "what counts is *trans*-actions, this dye that's unset" (10:00). Using these and other allusions as audiovisual anchors, I elevated the political content of the video

Figure 4.2 Lip-syncing actor Tuuli Kristola superimposed over railway tracks.

by having Tuuli and Maija lip-sync most of the vocals, and additionally, filming symbols of gender-neutral lavatories in the final verse (10:00). The figure of the Birdman in the song represents (for me) the courage to spread your wings in a metaphorical sense, to have the courage to be who you feel you are, but more specifically to embrace gender fluidity in much the same way as the 1970s artists I have mentioned. Furthermore, I couldn't resist reinforcing this message by performing sections of both "The Fold" and "Birdman" in partial drag (9:24)—as if to somehow counterbalance the bearded (Tithonus) character from the beginning of "Dawnsong." Had I been braver, I could have gone further than this, but I did not want to steal too much attention from the song's primary actors.

I wrote the song "Birdman of Bognor" before the death of David Bowie, although the "changes" sequence of that song was intended as direct homage to the (at the time) living Bowie. In a similar way, the filtered dark imagery of the winged Isis dancer (Noora) walking on a jetty against a blackened sky was a deliberate reference to Bowie's "Ashes to Ashes," a video he storyboarded himself (8:14). I endeavored to create a science-fiction mood in parts of "Birdman," and the scene reminiscent of "Ashes to Ashes" was in keeping with this goal, alongside other imagery borrowed from the film *Interstellar* (2014; 8:00). Science-fiction would come out also in the work of my collaborator, Alana, in her steam-punk character Jade, who is seen in the final verse of "Birdman" (9:39; 10:48). In a sense, this character has internalized society's prejudices and is locked in a dystopic prison of her own making. This character, who moves partially in uncanny reverse motion, is an indirect allusion to *Blade Runner* (1982). Images of barbed wire and Turku's former prison building Kakola in "Birdman" (see Figure 4.2 background; 5.58; 7:50) similarly refer to the dystopian societal restraints of closet culture, from which the characters in the video strive to break free. My intention here is not to map out every single allusion of this type, but there are some subtle ones, like the filming of Tuuli and Maija head to head (7:38), which invoke the

Figure 4.3 Lip-syncing actors Tuuli Kristola and Maija Lindroos in head-to-head profile.

cinematography of ABBA's music videos, such as "Knowing Me, Knowing You";[32] and the presence of a chess board (Figure 4.3), pointing to Benny Andersson and Björn Ulvaeus's post-ABBA career (arguably this refers also to Ingmar Bergman, a likely influence on the ABBA videos, who was keen on silhouetted profiles). I definitely had a queer agenda in mind in my use of ABBA, due to the band's status as LGBTQ icons of sorts, but also the repetitive patterning of the board itself—one of many such textural images in the video— and the notion of a puzzle to be solved involving struggle and loss in order to achieve self-realization, were motivating factors behind my creative choices.

Timing and synchronization

I will return now to questions of lip-syncing and, more generally, issues of timing and synchronization. I chose to lip-sync substantial parts of these videos or to get others to do so. In my view there were at least three options in this regard: not to lip-sync or synchronize performances at all, which is becoming increasingly common in videos at the independent end of the spectrum; to synchronize them non-reflexively, as happens in much mainstream pop; or to synchronize sound and vision reflexively, acknowledging the constructed nature of the audiovisual contract and the fact that the music precedes corresponding visual representations. I chose the third of these alternatives.

But why lip-sync performers in the first place? First, the most obvious rationale is to elevate the agency of the performer, an approach that interested me little (I was not initially keen on pushing myself to the fore; it was only at the insistence of the record label that I used my own name for the project). A second is that lip-syncing can divert attention away from low-budget production values and add interest to the visuals; this was a consideration. A third is to emphasize the haptic and cross-modal sensations of performing and producing sound from bodies and instruments, by anchoring or "source-bonding" the auditory sources to corresponding images, to borrow Dennis Smalley's term.[33] A fourth rationale was very much in my mind: in music where lyrics matter, visual synchronization makes them more intelligible. The video I had made immediately before this one, "Open Page (Journey to Enceladus)," was a lyric video, which is a more obvious way of foregrounding the song's lyric, but this approach seemed either too banal or too ironic, detracting from both the music and the lyrics. I wanted people to attend to the lyrics, so I opted to include more lip-syncing passages. But if one is aware of the cultural baggage connected to traditional approaches, one might wish to demonstrate reflexive awareness, so I chose to destabilize lip-syncing conventions by having different and incongruous-looking actors synchronize with my singing voice. This served the additional end of communicating the video's gender politics.

With similar goals in mind, I made the first shot in "Dawnsong" not of me but of "backing singer" Alana (0:27), to keep audioviewers guessing about the main subject of the song. Rather than adding depth, my hope was that lip-syncing and misleading embodiment through synchronization would draw attention to the *surfaces* of the audiovisual entity.

When asking Tuuli, the blue-haired actor in the video (also a talented sound technician and drummer) to play my part, I had in mind the charismatic performance of Robert Downey Jr. in Elton John's "I Want Love."[34] I asked Tuuli to watch this video as well as the lip-syncing montage sequence in the song "Wise Up" from *Magnolia* (1999). These served as the primary inspiration for my approach.

What about instrumental performance? Here I chose not to deconstruct. In fact, in the three videos I have produced so far, the studio footage was taken at the time of the music recording. Here the only such recording is the e-bow guitar played by Kimi Kärki in the choruses of "Dawnsong" (2:11). This was originally intended to be ethnographic field footage from the recording of the album. Elsewhere, my motivation for reconstructing instrumental footage was twofold: first, the inclusion of movement temporalizes the images and, second, by including shots of performed instruments, I could draw attention to specific musical parts (even make them seem more prominent in the mix). An example is Alana's singing at the beginning of "Dawnsong" (0:27) and the performative agency of her character in the song (as Aurora/Anima/death/projection). Elsewhere, I brought out specific electric, acoustic, and piano parts (e.g., the rhythmic accents in the choruses of "Birdman," 7:02), which might not otherwise have been so easily perceived.

One of my preferred shots in the extended video is the aerial drone footage (Figure 4.4) in "Dawnsong" (filmed and operated by Kristian Heberg), which serves the function of illustrating the protagonist's detachment (0:58; 2:28). It is pleasingly abstract but brings a sense of constant movement. The landscape in the shot is ambiguous: it is a beach, a theme in the first song. While the dark beaches in the song actually refer to Icelandic beaches, these were filmed at Nallikari beach in Oulu, Finland, but they could equally have been shots of another planet, since there is no visible vegetation and few signs of life initially. For this reason, there's something otherworldly about the footage; I delayed the re-entry of

Figure 4.4 Superimposed images of piano and walking dancers.

other filmed footage—a fleeting shot of a safety information video on a flight—to suggest preoccupation on the part of the protagonist, and used visual repetition of the flight safety demonstration to emphasize the rhythmic patterns or *folds* of the music (1:20). There's no strict logic dictating how the drone footage was synchronized with the song structure; it changes with each instance, which for me accentuates the sense of dreamlike distraction.

I was not present at the filming of the dance sequences, which were filmed in Oulu by my collaborator, Alana, together with Kristian Heberg. Editing these sequences in post-production was one of the most challenging and time-consuming tasks of producing the video. The "Dawnsong" dance sequences were filmed using three cameras (extending a technique we had used when filming "Birdman" a few weeks earlier): a hand-held iPhone, for low-angle close-ups, providing a sense of movement and corporeality; a locked-down medium shot filmed with a Canon digital camera, which gave a sense of the classical form of the dance and provided stability; and an aerial shot filmed with the drone. I read up on this type of editing in advance and wanted to enhance the sense of movement in the dancing and conceal some of the lo-fi values of the equipment, while adding a sense of modern angularity and some degree of glitch to the visuals. The shots were filmed in sync with the music, although Alana had to shout out the beats as numbers because the music was hard to hear on a windy day. I wanted to add to the floating, dreamlike quality of the video. The ideal way to do this was to speed up the music when filming and resynchronize with everything slowed down to the video footage in postproduction. Spike Jones did something similar in his award-winning video for Björk's "It's Oh So Quiet."[35] The Finnish director Tommi Pietiläinen has worked in a similar way in his videos for the indie band The Crash.[36] To achieve similar ends, I slowed down many shots in the dance sequence (by 55 percent, 70 percent, and 95 percent), especially jumps and twirls, and added some visual repetition—in fact mirroring a pre-echo added in the production of the lead vocal in the bridge sections of the song (2:09; 3:41). This took a tremendous amount of work, including several days of editing in Final Cut Pro for the dance sequence alone (see Figure 4.5). Twirling is a theme in the lyrics, and I re-edited the second bridge section of the song in order to place an emphasis on twirling movement. I also intentionally left in some Brechtian moments when the dancers stopped dancing altogether (2:25), in this way stepping out of character. The same is true of the aerial walking shots at the end of the song where the two dancers start to turn around and walk back along the beach (4:44). The accelerated motion of folding up sheets at the end of "Dawnsong" is similarly deconstructive, in effect disassembling the props of the first section and also the fourth wall (5:30), more so because of the reference to the conceptual foundations of the album.

I am especially pleased with one subtle audiovisual effect in "Birdman" that gives the illusion of the visuals motivating or steering the music rather than the other way around, which was actually the case. In videos the sound *always* comes first; but is it possible to create the reverse impression, that the sound cleaves to the actions of the filmed characters? The visual flourishes where the dancer flaps her wings at the beginning of the second chorus and the end of the last verse was edited in such a way that the flapping seems to instigate the arrival of the following section, coming a few seconds earlier rather than being synchronous with the song section transitions (8:43; 10:15). This non-synchronization or

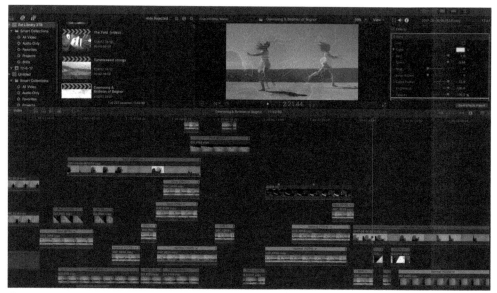

Figure 4.5 Final Cut Pro screenshot of the first dance sequence in "Dawnsong."

pre-synchronization, to impart agency to characters, was a matter of trial and error. I was following no model when doing this, at least none of which I was consciously aware.

Editing principles: Toward surrealism and psychedelia

In comparison to my earlier two attempts at producing videos, "The Fold" and "Open Page (Journey to Enceladus)," I paid greater attention to color and light balance, as well as to issues such as visual continuity between and within scenes, and balancing different elements within the frame. I learned a fair amount from film editor and writer Walter Murch (2001) in this regard. Where I used split shots, such as the lip-synced verses of "Dawnsong" (0:41; 1:25), I could make the audioviewer concentrate more on the face and lips by making these brighter (I used a spotlight plug-in for the headshots; see Figure 4.1) or larger, and by increasing the transparency or lowering the brightness of background images. The images of Alana walking through the sheets in the background were intended to be distracting at times. The sense of distraction was accomplished by her movements and my use of abrupt, glitchy editing and flashing light effects in postproduction. The main focus would remain on the singing subject, due largely to lighting, position in the frame, and audiovisual synchronization (lip-syncing).

This video was almost certainly informed by my research on surrealism and psychedelia. I will not theorize much about this here, but recommend my book *An Eye for Music: Popular Music and the Audiovisual Surreal* to those wishing to find out more.[37] In brief, my theory of surrealism is informed less by the unconscious, which is commonly, and in my view mistakenly, assumed to be the primary defining feature of surrealism, than by an oneiric quality combined with the idea of superimposing two formally similar images. This comes close also to Fisher's definition of the "weird,"[38] implying recombination and an uncanny sense of re-animation or superseding the laws that govern the natural world. But when things become weird they can also become complicated, resulting in attention overload; in order to place constraints on the audioviewer and thereby improve legibility, I partitioned the screen into sections (as might be familiar from the directing style of Peter Greenaway), ensured where possible that no more than two images would be present at the same time, and, in cases where more than one image was present, one of them should be made dominant and the other(s) secondary. Again, there is no rule book for this sort of editing, just intuition and trial and error, although tips about making some visual information prominent and other material secondary by the likes of Walter Murch can be useful.[39] Where two superimposed images are found, they are generally transitional and the intention is to signify flux or confusion. One example that works quite well is the image of the two dancers walking on a beach on top of an upright piano (see Figure 4.4). This image is surrealist in a fairly obvious way: the dancers are made to look like miniature characters standing on top of the instrument rather than on the beach. In the choruses, the winged Isis dancer stretches her wings in mirrored motion. Between her images a piano keyboard appears, which momentarily takes on the semblance of a keyboard stairway to heaven (7:23). Another compound form is the kaleidoscopic image of the dystopic sci-fi beach, which transforms into the eye of the character Jade (the eye was a popular image for the surrealists) and then a purple disco ball (8:31). These transitions were achieved through the formal similarity of the three objects, a technique the surrealists would have recognized. A third similar sequence is the image of a hang-glider superimposed over the steam-punk Jade character, both of which transform into the winged Isis dancer—the song's Bird-*woman*—through the action of flapping her wings (10:14), which, as we have seen, ushers in the final chorus. Finally, close to the end of the extended video, the image of Jade transforms into a Da Vinci-like Vetruvian character by the superimposition of a circular figure inside a grand piano, perhaps another example of gender destabilization (10:57). It could be said that the ambiguity of the images provides folds in the audiovisual surface, functioning as portals to different but formally similar domains, where the whole becomes more than the sum of its parts; but this technique also reflexively indicates the artifactual nature of the presented images. In the end, perhaps what we are seeing is images floating in a dreamlike manner, one into another, forming patterns in a design we cannot exhaustively decode.

The psychedelic is another aspect I wished to emphasize in the visuals. Scholars who have written on the psychedelic include Sheila Whiteley,[40] William Echard,[41] and myself on Icelandic music.[42] I wanted to produce an effect of disorientation inferring escapism, stepping outside of normality, including oppressive social structures. To those ends, I used visual effects, including a kaleidoscope effect, glitch techniques, and exaggeratedly bright, shimmering, and shifting colors. These psychedelic effects complement electronic effects used in the music, such as the use of exaggerated delay on the horns in the second bridge section (3:50), a flanger on the acoustic guitar also in the bridges, and hippy-era multipart harmonies in the drop-out section of "Dawnsong" (3:52). This was a conscious choice, almost a joke, but with a subtext of calling conventional truths into question.

Artistic open-endedness vs. (thematically specific) activism

The narrative content of my original songs is intended to be fairly oblique, thereby allowing greater scope for ambiguity and active decoding; however, I did include some content in the video to address questions of transgender rights and gender fluidity. I consciously steered the video in this direction, more than the original song, where it is nothing more than a subtext, in response to hearing of an increased number of reports of violence against sexual minorities and transgendered people in Russia, the United States, and elsewhere. When this music video was released, I included a short statement in which I clarified the political content of the video. This (and perhaps also the video still of gender non-conformist Tuuli as the main framing shot for the video) might have encouraged some audioviewers to press the thumbs-down button on the label's official YouTube site. The first video release from the album "The Fold," at the time of writing, has been viewed more than three times as much and received a far greater number of likes; however, the video I'm discussing here also attracted some positive attention internationally; for example, a review on SWIT (Super World Indie Tunes).[43] There's a risk of narrowing the message when directly attaching a song or video to a political cause, and of people assuming this is all they are about, but it was probably worth the risk. The risk is compounded when one considers the profile of Svart Records as a label and a certain subgroup within its user demographic. In Finland, Svart Records is known largely for republishing classic Finnish rock (and other genres) on vinyl, but internationally the label is primarily known for niche releases in metal genres and, to some extent, also hardcore punk. The audience demographic for these genres, and for rock in general, traditionally has not been as progressive or inclusive when it comes to gender politics as has been the case with genres like acoustic indie, synthpop, singer-songwriter, electronic dance music, and disco. In comparison to the video for "The Fold" (the subversive character of which can easily be overlooked), the extended video "Dawnsong and Birdman of Bognor" is quite obviously politically provocative and likely to upset an audience subset committed to traditional gender binaries. Gestures such as shaving half a beard, a sequence that I performed in drag, and intentionally confusing the audioviewer by having a song lip-synced by gender-queering actors, might well have fallen short of reaching the label's ideal target audience, creating gender trouble but having only limited influence. On a superficial level, "Dawnsong" might seem stable in terms of gender politics, even stereotyped (if you overlook the stylized irony of the representations), but a deeper level knowingly shakes up these very conventions. One might even say that an act of betrayal is staged, a dramatic twist that might confound an investment that audioviewers have already made.

Reflections

Research creation should imply a different approach to traditional arts-based research. When it comes to these videos, I certainly benefitted from insights I had gained through academic research. And perhaps what I learned from practice, on questions such as synchronization, the complexities of editing visual movement, and the experience of learning and using professional editing software, will inform how I undertake audiovisual analysis in the future. I am more acutely aware than ever before of the pressures artists are subjected to in the music business, particularly those, like myself, who end up having to do much of the work themselves, including the financial investments. I did the best I could in the circumstances, the emphasis being on artistic vision more than technical realization, although I would certainly like to move toward more polished realizations in the future. At the time of writing, I am uncertain if I will make more videos. Music video production can be extremely time-consuming and I enjoy making music more than producing videos. Some independent performers, whose creative identity is closely bound up with their intermodal creative work, continue to do both, but the amount of time and labor involved in producing credible end results is considerable.[44] This speaks to the economics of contemporary audiovisual production in an obvious way: artistic production in an age of digital streaming is precarious, with the amount of revenue returning to both artists and labels decreasing markedly, and the resulting pressures to do everything yourself result in a level of multitasking and overload that is easily transmitted to the audiovisual products.[45]

While I have presented some critical views on these videos, and audience reception of this particular video has been mixed, some positive feedback has found its way to me, both when teaching and in other contexts, such as reviews and random comments from people who follow my music. Given the low budget of this video and the fact that I was inexperienced in video production, I am not entirely dissatisfied with how some things turned out, and the experience has taught me a few practical lessons about the minutiae of audiovisual production, which could be of benefit when teaching and conducting research. Undoubtedly, I would not have been able to do what I did without some experience of analyzing music videos, as might be apparent from some of the examples I have provided. In this work, I attempted to turn DIY aesthetics (the queer art of failure, to borrow from Halberstam)[46] into a virtue, including elements of documentary aesthetics, the use of studio footage, regional and biographical materials, and self-reflexive performativity. But I created a huge challenge by making an extended music video for two songs, thus flouting the conventions of the form, and by packing the video so densely with different audiovisual materials and intertextual points of reference. The somewhat simpler approach in "The Fold" was ultimately more successful (in my estimation and in terms of the number of hits it has received on social media), incorporating more elements of simulated performance; visual trickery such as the use of extreme close-up cameras attached to the bodies of performers and instruments; the visceral movement this approach implied; a longer sequence of live studio footage for the guitar solo in that song; the successful use of effects and filters; a more upbeat and shorter song; and a short video art/montage sequence at the end, including diegetic sounds from the location, after the song had finished. All of this came together to form a more artistically cohesive video that seems to have had a greater impact on audiences. But this video remains an important research-creation exercise, becoming a record of how I was thinking at the time. Both the song and the video walk a fine line between surrealist refraction and intertextual overdetermination. If at times the implied authorial subject behind the video falters and teeters on the brink of failure in attempting such a balancing act, I am learning to dissociate myself from this authorial subject (and, admittedly, that of my collaborators), while focusing (after writing this chapter) on the challenges ahead.

Notes

1   John Richardson, "Double-Voiced Discourse and Bodily Pleasures in Contemporary Finnish Rock: The Case of Maija Vilkkumaa," in *Essays on Sound and Vision*, edited by John Richardson and Stan Hawkins (Helsinki: Helsinki University Press, 2007), 401–441; John Richardson, "Plasticine Music: Surrealism in Peter Gabriel's, 'Sledgehammer,'" in *Peter Gabriel, From Genesis to Growing Up*, edited by Michael Drewett, Sarah Hill, and Kimi Kärki (Farnham: Ashgate, 2010), 195–210; John Richardson, *An Eye for Music: Popular Music and the Audiovisual Surreal* (New York: Oxford University Press, 2012); John Richardson, "Music Videos" [revised from an original text by Alf Björnberg], in *The Grove Dictionary of American Music*, 2nd ed., edited by H. Wiley Hitchcock and Stanley Sadie (New York: Oxford University Press, 2013); Stan Hawkins and John Richardson, "Remodeling Britney Spears: Matters of Intoxication and Mediation," *Popular Music and Society* 30, no. 5 (2007): 605–629.
2   Annette Arlander, "Artistic Research and/as Interdisciplinarity," in *Artistic Research Does #1*, edited by Catarina Almeida and André Alves (Porto: i2ADS, 2016), 1–27. Linda Candy, "Practice Based Research: A Guide," *CCS Report* 1.0 (November 2006): 1–19.
3   Natalie Loveless, "Introduction, Short Statements on Research-Creation," *Polemics* 1 (2015): 41–54; Sophie Stévance and Serge Lacasse, "Research-Creation in Music as a Collaborative Space," *Journal of the New Media Caucus* (2015), http://median.newmediacaucus.org/research-creation-explorations/research-creation-in-music-as-a-collaborative-space.
4   John Richardson, *The Fold*, Svart Records, Svart064 (vinyl); Svart064CD (CD). Also available via all major digital streaming services.
5   John Richardson, "Closer Reading and Framing in Ecocritical Music Research," in *Music Moves: Musical Dynamics of Relation, Knowledge and Transformation*, edited by Charissa Granger, Friedlind Riedel, Eva-Maria van Straaten, and Gerlinde Feller, *Göttingen Studies in Musicology*, vol. 7 (Hildesheim: Olms, 2016), 157–193; John Richardson, "Ecological Close Reading of Music in Digital Culture," in *Embracing Restlessness: Cultural Musicology*, edited by Birgit Abels, *Göttingen Studies in Musicology*, vol. 6 (Hildesheim: Olms, 2016), 111–142.

6   Erving Goffman, *Frame Analysis: An Essay on the Organization of Experience* (Boston, MA: Northeastern University Press, 1974); Mieke Bal, *Traveling Concepts in the Humanities: A Rough Guide* (Toronto, ON: University of Toronto Press, 2002); Gregory Bateson, *Steps to an Ecology of Mind* (Northvale, NJ: Jason Aronson, 1972); for more on "ecological close reading," see Richardson, "Closer Reading" and "Ecological Close Reading."

7   Tony E. Adams, Stacy Holman Jones, and Carolyn Ellis, *Autoethnography: Understanding Qualitative Research* (New York: Oxford University Press, 2015); Heewon Chang, *Autoethnography as Method* (Walnut Creek, CA: Left Coast Press, 2008); Heewon Chang, Faith Ngunjiri, and Kathy-Ann C. Hernandez, *Collaborative Autoethnography* (London: Routledge, 2013); Carolyn Ellis, *Music Autoethnographies: Making Autoethnography Sing/ Making Music Personal* (Bowen Hills: Australian Academic Press, 2009).

8   Adams, Jones, and Ellis, *Autoethnography*.

9   Lori Burns and Serge Lacasse, eds., *The Pop Palimpsest: Intertextuality in Recorded Popular Music* (Ann Arbor, MI: University of Michigan Press, 2018).

10 Gilles Deleuze, *The Fold: Leibniz and the Baroque*, translated by Tom Conley (London and New York: Continuum, 2006).

11 Ibid., 42.

12 Ibid.

13 Maurice Merleau-Ponty, *The Invisible and the Invisible*, translated by Alphonso Lingis (Evanston, IL: Northwestern University Press, 1968).

14 Ibid.

15 See Richardson, *An Eye for Music.*

16 See www.facebook.com/songwriterJohnRichardson.

17 John Richardson, "The Fold," YouTube video, official music video, Svart Records, directed by John Richardson, Slow Floe Productions, 2017, https://www.youtube.com/watch?v=SG0O47F7tiA.

18 John Richardson, "Open Page (Journey to Enceladus)," YouTube video, official music video, Svart Records, directed by John Richardson, Slow Floe Productions, 2017, https://www.youtube.com/watch?v=AdCZaVJ_PHc.

19 John Richardson, "Dawnsong and Birdman of Bognor," YouTube video, official music video, Svart Records, directed by John Richardson with Alana, Slow Floe Productions, 2017, https://www.youtube.com/watch?v=2zZB2hRkLoE.

20 As an undergraduate student, I had taken a course in video ethnography, but this was some two decades earlier.

21 E. Ann Kaplan, *Rocking Around the Clock: Music Television, Postmodernism, and Consumer Culture* (London and New York: Routledge, 1987).

22 See Richardson, *An Eye for Music*, 34.

23 Andrew Goodwin, *Dancing in the Distraction Factory: Music Television and Popular Culture* (Minneapolis, MN: University of Minnesota Press, 1992).

24 See Richardson, "Plasticine Music."

25 Johnson quoted in Goodwin, *Dancing in the Distraction Factory*, 62.

26 Mikko Malki wrote in *Inferno* magazine (May 27, 2017, no page reference available): "Influences and references are manifold, but all done with impeccable taste; shades of psychedelic rock, 90s alternative rock, soul and jazz [my translation]." "Vaikutteita ja referenssejä tarjoillaan vähän joka suunnalta, onneksi kuitenkin hyvällä maulla.

Mukana on vivahteita niin psykefolkista, 90-luvun alternativerockista, soulista kuin kappakkajazzista."

27   John Richardson, "Resisting the Sublime: Loose Synchronisation in *La Belle et la Bête* and *The Dark Side of Oz*," in *Musicological Identities: Essays in Honour of Susan McClary*, edited by Steven Baur, Raymond Knapp, and Jacqueline Warwick (Aldershot: Ashgate, 2008), 135–148.

28   See Richardson, *An Eye for Music* for an analysis of this film.

29   For a nuanced discussion of the gender implications of the conventional positions of the observer and the observed in a music video, see Lori Burns and Marc Lafrance, "Gender, Sexuality and the Politics of Looking in Beyoncé's 'Video Phone' (featuring Lady Gaga)," in *The Routledge Research Companion to Popular Music and Gender*, edited by Stan Hawkins (London and New York: Routledge, 2017), 102–116.

30   On personal note, Bognor Regis is a town where my now deceased mother lived and spent some of the happiest and most professionally fulfilling years of her life, working as a theatrical costume designer.

31   See Michel Chion, *Audio-Vision: Sound on Screen*, edited and translated by Claudia Gorbman (New York: Columbia University Press, 1990), 13–14.

32   ABBA, "Knowing Me, Knowing You," YouTube video, directed by Lasse Hallström, https://www.youtube.com/watch?v=iUrzicaiRLU.

33   Dennis Smalley, "Spectromorphology: Explaining Sound-Shapes," *Organized Sound* 2, no. 2 (1997): 110–111.

34   Elton John, "I Want Love," YouTube video, directed by Sam Taylor-Wood, https://www.youtube.com/watch?v=ufbexgPyeJQ.

35   See Stan Hawkins, "Musical Excess and Postmodern Identity in Björk's Video 'It's Oh So Quiet'," *Musiikin Suunta* 2 (1999): 43–54.

36   See John Richardson, "Intertextuality and Pop Camp Identity Politics in Finland: The Crash's Music Video 'Still Alive'," *Popular Musicology Online* 2 (2006), http://www.popular-musicology-online.com/issues/02/richardson-01.html.

37   Richardson, *An Eye for Music*.

38   Mark Fisher, *The Weird and the Eerie* (London: Repeater Books, 2016).

39   Walter Murch, *In the Blink of an Eye: A Perspective on Editing*, 2nd ed. (Hollywood, CA: Silman James Press, 2001).

40   Sheila Whiteley, "Progressive Rock and Psychedelic Coding in the Work of Jimi Hendrix," *Popular Music* 9, no. 1 (1990): 37–60.

41   William Echard, "Psychedelia, Musical Semiotics, and Environmental Unconscious," *Green Letters: Studies in Ecocriticism* 15, no. 1 (2011): 61–75.

42   John Richardson, "Surrealism in Icelandic Popular Music," in *Sounds Icelandic: Essays on Icelandic Music in the 20th and 21st Centuries*, edited by Þorbjörg Daphne Hall, Nicola Dibben, Árni Heimir Ingólfsson, and Tony Mitchell (Sheffield: Equinox, 2019), 172–193.

43   Posted by SWIT on September 13, 2017, https://superworldindietunes.com/2017/09/13/john-richardson/?fbclid=IwAR0pXuugWQiROHefIUQ2OLR4HeK2NSIS507Wg-ZsOrdAdtbqAyWK8clyHE4.

44   An example is the Icelandic musician and performance artist Dj. flugvél og geimskip, whose work I have discussed elsewhere. See Richardson, "Surrealism."

45   For more on the concept of the zany, see Sianne Ngai, *Our Aesthetic Categories: Zany, Cute, Interesting* (Cambridge, MA: Harvard University Press, 2012); and Richardson, "Surrealism."

46   Judith Halberstam, *The Queer Art of Failure* (Durham, NC: Duke University Press, 2011).

Part II

Cultural Codes, Representations, and Genres

5

Framing Personae in Music Videos

Philip Auslander

I first developed the concept of the musical persona to enable a discussion of musicians as performers in their own right, rather than just as vehicles for the realization of musical works.[1] "Persona" is a flexible term that I (and others) have used in other contexts to suggest a performed role that is somewhere between a person's simply behaving as themselves and an actor's presentation of a fictional character.[2] For the most part, musicians in performance do not portray fictional entities: they portray themselves as musicians. Although this is the normative case, there certainly are instances in which musicians do portray fictional characters as part of their normal stage routine—think of the members of the rock band KISS, for example. A schema for the analysis of musicians as performers must be able to account for the entire range of cases. Since 2004, I have defined the musical persona as a version of the musician designed for public performance, i.e., the identity a musician presents to audiences. In this chapter I suggest taking musicians' personae as central objects in the analysis of music videos. I begin by defining musical personae with regard to elements of musical performance, including musical genre, and the relationship of performance to socio-cultural discourses, including discourses of race—which I emphasize in my examples here—gender, and other dimensions of identity. I then refine the definition by reference to Erving Goffman's concept of self-presentation and identify specific constituents of musical personae that can be analyzed fruitfully. Finally, I discuss the question of the relationship between musical genre and genres of music video. I suggest that, compared with live performance, the music video is in some ways an ideal space for the performance of musical personae because of the greater degree of control over expressive means that video affords performers.

Musical personae

Michael Jackson dramatized the process of persona construction in a routine he would perform frequently in concert before launching into the song "Billie Jean." Jackson, dressed in a billowy white T-shirt, athletic pants, and tap shoes, would walk on stage—sometimes meanderingly, sometimes purposefully—carrying an old valise. After placing the valise on a high stool, he opened it and started removing items from it, beginning with a sequined black shirt, which he put on, followed by a single sequined white glove, which he wriggled onto his hand. Finally, he removed from the valise a black Fred Astaire-style fedora. He would adjust the brim, dust it off, walk around with it, but not put it on his head until he had walked across the stage to a microphone on a stand in a single spotlight. The moment when he put the hat on his head and struck the pose that begins the "Billie Jean" choreography was the moment when his transformation from Michael Jackson, the human being, into "Michael Jackson," the musical persona was complete and the concert could begin.[3]

When I originally proposed the concept of the musical persona in the context of popular music studies—an appropriate context for a discussion of music video—I turned initially to Simon Frith's analysis of performance in that realm. Frith helpfully identifies three different strata in popular musicians' performances, all of which may be present simultaneously. Frith proposes that we hear pop singers as "personally expressive," that is, as singing in their own persons, from their own experience. But two other layers are imposed on that first one because popular musicians are "involved in a process of double enactment: they enact both a star personality (their image) and a song personality, the role that each lyric requires, and the pop star's art is to keep both acts in play at once."[4] Drawing on Frith's insights, I identified the three layers of performance in which popular musicians engage as: the real person (the performer as human being), the performance persona (which corresponds to Frith's star personality or image), and the character (Frith's song personality).[5]

Since *character* refers to entities defined through the music and lyrics of songs but not all musicians are singers, and we generally do not have access to the musicians we see perform as *real people*, the *musical persona* is the most important of the three layers because it is the primary interface between musicians and their audiences. The persona is also an identity that musicians generally perform whenever they are publicly visible, whether onstage or offstage (although there have been cases in which the musician seeks to make a clear distinction between person and persona—Vincent Furnier's insistence that he and Alice Cooper are completely distinct individuals is an example). Admittedly, the line between persona and character is not always clear. For example, Ziggy Stardust was both a character in some of David Bowie's songs and the persona he assumed while performing those and other songs, creating complexity and ambiguity. It is also true that the line between the real person and the musical persona is not always clear, especially in musical contexts such as the singer-songwriter genre as exemplified by James Taylor and Joni Mitchell, where there is a desire to believe that the person we see on stage is identical with the artist as a private person and that the songs are in some measure autobiographical or confessional.[6] All of this notwithstanding, the vocabulary of real person, musical persona, and song character provides a way of describing and analyzing multiple elements of performed musical identities and their interrelationships in both clear-cut and more ambiguous cases.[7]

Framing musical performance: Performance, genre, identity, and society

I have suggested that musical performances, as events, are thrice framed.[8] I borrowed the term "frame" from sociologist Erving Goffman, who defines frames as the "principles of organization which govern events—at least social ones—and our subjective involvement in them."[9] The way in which an event is framed allows us, as social actors, to understand what is going on in a particular situation and what our options for interaction are. For example, the New York City based performance group Improv Everywhere staged an event in Grand Central Station in 2008 called "Frozen Grand Central."[10] The performance itself was simple: at a specific time during a rush hour, over 200 ordinary-looking people suddenly and simultaneously froze in place and remained frozen for five minutes, then resumed their previous activities as if nothing had happened. The video of this event documents the reaction of those witnessing these actions. At first, they are mystified and ask each other questions about what is going on. Then, they start to offer hypotheses as to the nature of the event, suggesting that it could be a protest or an acting class. Once the performers start to move again, the bystanders applaud. The video clearly shows that, in order to understand how to interact with what was going on around them, the bystanders first had to understand the frame. Eventually, they determined that the event in question was framed as a performance. They then could conclude that the people frozen in position were performers and they, the bystanders, were in an audience role. Once they understood the frame and their role within it, they performed the audience role by applauding.[11]

I see musical performance as framed by three nested frames. The innermost frame, the one that most immediately defines the event, is the frame that allows us to understand that an event is a musical performance such as a concert, a recital, or an open rehearsal (each of which is a musical event of a somewhat different kind that entails different behavioral conventions). This frame has to do with the basic expectations as to what is going to happen and what social roles, including but not limited to those of performer and audience, are available. The frame defines a shared understanding among all those involved as to what is going on, particularly concerning the interaction between and among performers and audience.

Expectations about what will and will not occur in the performance frame are highly influenced by the second frame, which is that of musical genre. Genre can be defined in many ways, especially in popular music. Genre labels are used differently by the music industry to market its products, by broadcasters to program, by professional organizations to grant awards, by fans and music lovers to identify their tastes, by musicians to describe specific styles of playing, and so on. In all cases, genre labels distinguish forms of musical experience from one another, erecting boundaries between them with various degrees of porousness. As Fabian Holt puts it: "Genre is a fundamental structuring force in musical life. It has implications for how, where, and with whom people make and experience music

… There is no such thing as 'general music,' only particular musics. Music comes into being when individuals make it happen, and their concepts of music are deeply social."[12]

In describing genres as frames in Goffman's sense, like Holt I am emphasizing the social dimension of genres, the ways whereby they serve as "principles of organization" that define the contexts in which—and the terms under which—people come together to make music. Genres define norms for performance by both musicians and audiences and the ways in which these two groups interact to constitute the performance of a specific kind of music. Certain musical personae and audience roles are deemed to be appropriate to particular genre contexts, and all performances within a particular genre context take these norms as reference points. Performers and audiences can assume a variety of relationships with genre norms and the personae and roles they entail. A performer can construct a persona that adheres to the norms of the genre, or use a persona to critique those norms or even to undermine them. It is clear that some genres impose more restrictive limits on a performance than others. For example, a member of a rock band has far more flexibility with respect to appearance and attitude than does a member of a symphony orchestra or a marching band. Nevertheless, all genres place limits on what is considered a valid performance in its context, no matter how generous the boundaries may appear to be.

The third frame around the performance of popular music is that of the socio-cultural conventions defined outside the context of musical performance and genre by society at large. There is a line of inquiry in performance theory that posits performance as a social context framed in such a way as to distinguish it from the flow of everyday life in which behaviors that would not be acceptable in other social contexts can be enacted. Goffman points out, for instance, that it is perfectly acceptable to subject other human beings to a kind of close scrutiny in events framed as theater that would be unacceptable in other social contexts.[13] This line of inquiry is traceable to Johan H. Huizinga's *Homo Ludens*, first published in 1944, in which Huizinga describes sites of play and ritual as "play-grounds, i.e. forbidden spots, isolated, hedged round, hallowed, within which special rules obtain. All are temporary worlds within the ordinary world, dedicated to the performance of an act apart."[14] For Victor Turner, these temporary worlds are liminal spaces in which the status quo can be queried and critiqued and "new ways of modeling or framing social reality may actually be proposed and sometimes legitimated in the very heat of performance."[15] Despite performance's status as a liminal context in which different realities may be explored and even enacted, transgressing against socio-cultural norms is risky, and at times can result in sanctions, such as those imposed on Jim Morrison of The Doors for alleged indecency and profanity during a 1969 performance in Miami or on Pussy Riot for its performance in a Russian Orthodox cathedral in 2012. Musical performance, as a liminal practice, acquires social or political meaning through its conformity or resistance to social and cultural norms. The personae enacted by British glam rockers of the early 1970s, to name but one example, placed into the public sphere queer gender performances that conformed neither to conventional behavioral codes nor to the genre conventions of the rock music that had preceded them in the late 1960s, which had had little use for such heterodox gender identities as those performed by Marc Bolan, David Bowie, and Suzi Quatro.[16] In the analyses that follow, I will be attentive to the functioning of all three of these frames and the relationship of musical personae to them in music videos. I will be particularly attentive to the ways in which the videos enact tensions between musical genre and racial identity through the performance of musical personae.

Musical personae as self-presentation

To refine my definition of the musical persona and to enable its analysis, I address musical performance using ideas developed by Goffman for the analysis of interactions in everyday life, which he calls self-presentation.[17] The playing of music is one of the routines, to use Goffman's term, that musicians perform in the course of their lives. As Goffman suggests, we present ourselves differently in the different routines we perform for our various audiences (I do not present myself in the same way to my students in the classroom as I do to my departmental colleagues at meetings, for instance). For Goffman, presentation of self is a matter of "impression management."[18] We seek to create a specific impression on a particular audience, one that we believe will cause that audience to perceive us in the way we wish that audience to perceive us, and we actively adjust our self-presentation in response to audience reaction. Therefore, there is no reason to suppose that musicians present the same identity when playing music as when they perform their other life routines. The version of self that a musician presents qua musician is what I am calling the musical persona.

Goffman's concepts work well in relation to the range of identities musicians may perform because his theory allows for the possibility that any given self-presentation in a social interaction can be a sincere presentation of a person's real feelings at the time or partly or wholly fictional. For example, if a student greets me on campus and asks how I am, I may respond that I am fine even when I am not feeling that way. I thus present myself as a fictional character, at least at this moment of the interaction. Unlike theories of acting that focus on how a real person may assume the identity of a fictional character, Goffman's concept of self-presentation applies equally well to fictional and non-fictional representations. From this perspective, the seemingly sincere demeanor of a singer-songwriter like James Taylor and the overtly stylized and artificial lounge-lizard persona of Bryan Ferry with Roxy Music are equally self-presentations. Whether real, fictional, or some combination of both, they are identities designed to create an impression of who the musician is in relation to a specific audience that both define and adhere to the norms for a genre of music.

Goffman initiates his discussion of self-presentation by considering the fronts presented by individuals;[19] however, he quickly makes it clear that he considers the team to be the basic unit of the performance of identity and individuals to be teams with only one member.[20] He goes on to analyze in detail the roles and interactions entailed in the performance of group identity. Although I have implied to this point that a musical persona is a matter of individual self-presentation, it is equally true that musical groups of any kind have collective personae. For example, during the era of Beatlemania in the mid-1960s, The Beatles had a collective identity of a cheerful, user-friendly, slightly irreverent boy band. Each Beatle had his own individual persona, but all of their personae had to harmonize with this group affect. By 1967, however, The Beatles' group persona had morphed into that of a psychedelic rock band plugged into the countercultural ethos of the time. At both moments, each individual Beatle's persona was articulated to the group persona. Whereas, in the mid-1960s, fans dubbed Paul McCartney the Cute Beatle, John Lennon the Smart Beatle, George Harrison the Quiet Beatle, and Ringo Starr the Funny Beatle, their individual identities shifted in relation to the group's overall persona. In Richard Avedon's canonicical portrait photographs of 1967—originally published in *LOOK Magazine* in the United States and other magazines in the United Kingdom and Europe, then disseminated widely as posters—Ringo is shown with a dove on his hand, suggesting his commitment to the "Peace and Love" dimension of the counterculture, while John Lennon is presented with spirals for eyes, perhaps indicating his engagement with psychedelia and the drug culture. Paul appears as a flower child in pastel blues, surrounded by blooms, and the portrait of George emphasizes his mysticism.[21]

The vocabulary Goffman uses to discuss the means people employ in self-presentation is readily applicable to musical performance. Goffman uses the word "front," which he defines as "expressive equipment of a standard kind," to describe the self-image one presents to others.[22] Front is made up of two elements: setting and personal front, which in turn consists of two aspects, appearance and manner.[23] Setting refers to the physical location where a performance takes place, which can be used to further the impression one wishes to create on an audience—the display of credentials on the walls of a doctor's office is an example. Jimmy Buffett is a good example of a musician who makes use of setting in his performances. To reinforce the persona he has built around the idea of a sybaritic lifestyle in the Florida Keys, Buffett has performed against backdrops depicting the ocean as seen from the beach, potted palms, Easter Island heads, Tiki bars, and other kitsch representations of a semi-tropical existence devoted to leisure. Appearance has to do with the visual dimensions of self-presentation, while manner has to do with the behavioral dimensions. In the context of musical performance, these are the basic units from which genre-specific personae are constructed and through which they are communicated to audiences. Their deployment is always context-specific or, to use a sociological term, situated. Musicians often perform their personae both onstage and offstage, through interviews and public statements as well as in live performances and music videos.

Performing genre, persona, and race: "Walk This Way" by Run-DMC featuring Aerosmith

The 1986 video for "Walk This Way" by Run-DMC featuring Aerosmith entertainingly narrativizes the ways in which musicians construct their performance personae within the terms of different musical genres.[24] The setting is two adjacent rehearsal studios divided by a wall. On one side, the rock band Aerosmith is jamming while, on the other side, the members of the hip-hop group Run-DMC bang on the wall and demand that Aerosmith turn down the volume (Figure 5.1). Each studio contains elements that make it an appropriate environment for performance within a specific genre and with its attendant personae. Aerosmith's studio, to the viewer's left, shows the band jamming in a hazy ambience with gigantic Marshall amplifiers against one wall and a messy array of cups, water bottles, and what appear to be full trash bags stacked against another wall that also features a number of posters. Run-DMC's side presents an environment that is both more spartan than Aerosmith's side and neater. The space is dominated by Jam-Master Jay's turntable setup and is lit primarily by a single bulb dangling from the ceiling by a cord. There are also some album covers on the wall, a gigantic sign with the group's name on it, and a couch on which a young woman sits. The contrast in settings clearly juxtaposes rock band nonchalance with hip-hop cool.

In the second half of the video, the setting switches to a concert venue. We see Perry and Tyler performing side-by-side until Run and DMC appear in silhouette on a screen at the top of a staircase behind them. Bursting through the screen, the two MCs descend the staircase and commandeer the show. The setting is generic and unremarkable, as Carol Vernallis suggests is typical for music video settings, except for one thing: the audience.[25] The few glimpses we have of the audience suggest that it is made up overwhelmingly of young white people dressed and coiffed in ways that indicate they are hair metal fans.

Figure 5.1 The split rehearsal studio with Aerosmith on one side and Run-DMC on the other (0:22).

This audience becomes a piece of expressive equipment; its presence indicates that we are seeing an Aerosmith concert into which Run DMC intrudes (although their intrusion is not resisted and is perhaps even welcomed by Perry and Tyler given that they turn to look at the staircase before Run and DMC venture down). Since the video is for "Walk This Way," a song Run-DMC acquired from Aerosmith, the implicit message is that hip-hop artists are impinging on turf traditionally occupied by rock artists.

The appearance of each set of musicians also contrasts sharply along genre lines. To begin, all of the members of Aerosmith appear to be white and all of the members of Run-DMC appear to be African-American. Considering the general paucity of black rockers and white rappers, this dimension of the performers' appearance adheres to genre norms, as does their apparel. Joe Perry, Aerosmith's guitarist, wears a sports jacket over a T-shirt, while singer Steven Tyler wears a black suit-cut leather jacket over his bare chest, which is adorned with necklaces and pendants, and skinny jeans. His trademark silk and chiffon scarves are tied around his microphone stand. By contrast, all of the members of Run-DMC dress identically in black slacks, jackets, T-shirts, and fedoras with unlaced white Adidas athletic shoes. While it is the case that hip-hop crews do not necessarily dress identically, and Run-DMC did not do so all of the time, it is inconceivable that the members of a traditional rock band such as Aerosmith would do so at all. Perry's and

Figure 5.2 Run, DMC, and Steven Tyler dance together during the climax of the concert sequence in the music video for Run-DMC featuring Aerosmith, "Walk This Way" (1986), directed by Jon Small (4:03).

Tyler's respective appearances underline the individualism and do-your-own-thing ethos of rock since the 1960s. Run-DMC projects a much stronger sense of collective identity than does Aerosmith.

The contrast between the more individualistic behavior of Aerosmith's principals and the more collectivistic behavior of Run-DMC is furthered at the level of what Goffman calls manner. In both halves of the video, Perry and Tyler enact their version of the relationship between lead guitarist and non-playing vocalist that is at the heart of the dynamics of many rock bands (think of Jimmy Page and Robert Plant of Led Zeppelin, Pete Townshend and Roger Daltrey of the Who, and Keith Richards and Mick Jagger of the Rolling Stones). Perry and Tyler stand near each other and interact through the music, but they don't look at or coordinate with each other. Perry's focus is on his guitar, while Tyler dances and performs acrobatics with his microphone stand. By contrast, the members of Run-DMC, in the first half of the video, interact extensively with one another, looking directly at each other, egging each other on and, in the case of the two MCs, dancing together. Representatives of both groups replicate this kind of interaction in the second half, as Run and DMC flank Tyler and provide responsive raps while he sings the lyrics. At the end, the three men form a chorus line and dance together (Figure 5.2), a notable show of unity between rappers and rockers in a scenario that began with the two groups at odds with each other. This overcoming of differences does not take place on neutral ground, but through Run-DMC's incursion into Aerosmith's territory.

Music video and genre

Pat Aufderheide, writing in 1986, relatively early in the history of music video in the United States, observed that the musicians in videos do not portray fictional characters but present themselves as "bold and connotative icons," further noting: "a bold image is crucial to video and, now, to recording artist celebrity." Aufderheide takes a dim view of music videos, arguing that with them "personal 'identity' has become a central element of commodity production" and that they contribute to "a betrayal of an authentic expression of talent."[26] Aufderheide's claim that music videos brought about the need for musical artists to present bold images is historically inaccurate, since modern popular musicians have been doing so since at least the 1920s; Fats Waller is but one of many examples of popular musicians who presented bold and connotative celebrity images in the 1920s and 1930s. Aufderheide's tone betrays the anti-ocular prejudice present in much discourse on music that I have addressed elsewhere, in which the visual dimensions of musical performance are seen as distracting from or undermining the music.[27] Leaving aside the negative aspects of Aufderheide's analysis, her emphasis on the way the music video calls upon musicians to construct their identities visually and through dimensions of performance other than those that directly involve the production of sound can be taken to suggest that the music video is an ideal venue for the performance of musical personae. I have made a related point in defense of lip-synced performances and music videos, which "provide performers with good opportunities to define and extend their personae. With no obligation to sing or play, musicians are unencumbered and free to focus on performing their personae."[28] Whether or not they involve lip-syncing, performances in music videos are produced under controlled conditions that arguably provide musicians with better opportunities to present their personae in exactly the ways they wish than do live performances.[29]

This is particularly true with respect to setting. Except in those cases where musicians perform in purpose-built spaces designed to serve as expressive equipment appropriate to performances within specific genres (symphony halls and the Grand Ole Opry in Nashville are examples), or those in which musicians are in a position to travel with stage sets that express their personae (such as the sets used by Jimmy Buffett that I mentioned earlier), musicians have relatively little control over the settings in which they perform. In music videos, by contrast, they have complete control, at least in principle, and can ensure that the setting is coherent with the persona they seek to communicate.

Carol Vernallis devotes an entire chapter of *Experiencing Music Video* (2004) to the question of how setting is used in music videos. She finds setting to be a function of genre: "each musical genre develops a repertoire of settings."[30] Whereas the action of rap videos frequently takes place on the street, contemporary R&B videos emphasize the studios where the music is made or performance venues that showcase the performers' professionalism. Heavy metal videos, by contrast, "are often situated in abandoned industrial sites, with exposed pipes and debris on the floor."[31] Since Vernallis bases these observations on her review of a great many videos, the trends she indicates are surely accurate. My approach, however, configures the question a bit differently. Consistent with my performer-centered perspective, I see setting as one of the items of expressive equipment that performers use to communicate their personae, which, in turn, are defined in large part through identification with a certain genre. The relationship between genre and setting thus is not a direct connection but runs through the performer's persona, which I place at the center of musical performance. Vernallis's approach and mine converge, however, when she discusses uses of setting designed to make a performer appeal to a specific audience. She notes, for example, "the black British singer Seal sells records primarily to white audiences; placing him in an empty environment, apart from black culture, distances him from other black artists."[32] This suggests that the empty setting is not just a function of Seal's genre identification but is also a piece of expressive equipment intended to convey a self-presentation to a particular audience.

Because performers construct their musical personae in relation to musical genres, it is important to consider the connections between the music video and genre in relation to the idea of personae. For one thing, the music video arguably should be seen as a genre unto itself rather than as a subgenre of film, television, or advertisement. The question of how musical genres map onto the music video genre has been the matter of a debate that centers on the question of whether there is such a thing as a "rock music video," a "country music video," etc. Diane Railton and Paul Watson, for instance, argue that "genres of music neither map onto genres of music video nor … necessarily govern the look of any given video."[33] They argue instead for a taxonomy of music videos constructed through combinations and permutations of two independent variables: musical genre and video style, the latter including "pseudo-documentary, art music video, narrative video, and staged performance."[34]

This approach is more flexible than one that argues for defining video style entirely in terms of musical genre, but aspects of Railton and Watson's argument are seriously flawed. They argue that, since both hip-hop and country music videos can contain similar elements—"the club, the beach, a pool and plenty of scantily clad women"—one cannot claim that these form part of the typical iconography of any one genre's videos.[35] To take the most obvious point, it may be simply that the elements they identify are present in the iconography of both genres. The mere fact that similar imagery can appear in videos associated with different genres does not in itself mean that the imagery is not a defining characteristic of each genre. The overlap could equally well suggest an orientation shared by the two genres. More important, however, is that the iconography Railton and Watson mention is much more specific than they allow. For one thing, honky tonks and strip clubs, the two kinds of establishments featured in the videos they mention, are both clubs, but they are hardly the same kind of club. For another, all of the women featured in the two country music videos they cite—Trace Adkins's "Honky Tonk Badonkadonk" (2005) and Travis Tritt's "The Girl's Gone Wild" (2004)—seem to be white, which is typically not the case in hip-hop videos.[36] It is observable, for instance, that when Snoop Dogg is performing in his rap persona, the women who surround him in his videos appear to be women of color, as in the video for "Drop It Like It's Hot" (2004). When Snoop Dogg repositions his persona in relation to the country genre in the video for "My Medicine" (2008), he wears cowboy attire, performs with Willie Nelson, and the women around him all look white. Railton and Watson argue for similarity by ignoring culturally significant aspects of the imagery they examine, aspects that are basic to analyzing the construction of a musician's persona in music videos in relation to genre norms and their socio-cultural implications.

In his discussion of country music videos, Mark Fenster argues that the country music video should be understood as a response to the rise of music videos in the context of rock music and, ultimately, as an instance in which one genre takes over a form associated with another to make something new.[37] He also posits that the typical visual style of country music videos is directly related to the content of the songs:

> [T]he development of a country video aesthetic includes the successful establishment of a classical narrative style that suits the genre's lyrical content. Unlike the more disjointed, fragmented narratives of pop/rock videos, which owe more to experimental films and advertising, most country video narratives are more directly descended from the classical Hollywood style. In fact, the tendency of country lyrics toward a character-centered, personal/psychological narrative can be traced back further than cinema, to their folk and blues roots.[38]

From this perspective, the term "country music video" is meaningful because there is a direct connection between the typical form, style, and iconography of the videos and the genre-specific content of the songs.

Performing personae, race, and genre: "Wagon Wheel" by Darius Rucker

The music video for Darius Rucker's performance of "Wagon Wheel" (2013) provides an opportunity to examine the performance of a musical persona in the context of both the genre and socio-cultural frames, in this case the framing of race in the context of country music.[39] As a genre, country music strongly emphasizes authenticity, meaning that its practitioners must appear to possess "appropriate backgrounds and proper cultural credentials [to be] carriers of a cultural tradition" rooted in the rural American South.[40] Rucker, who was born, raised, and still lives in South Carolina and experienced poverty in his childhood, clearly has a biography that includes some of the background of an authentic country musician. But, as an African-American, he faces what Michael Hughes describes as "a significant problem in dramatically realizing the role of a country music artist, because country music has been so strongly identified with whites and white Southern culture from the beginning."[41] Hughes is slightly mistaken; in fact, DeFord Bailey, an African-American harmonica player, was present at the inception of the Grand Ole Opry in 1927. Between Bailey and Rucker, however, although other African-American musicians recorded and performed in the country idiom, only Charley Pride has been accepted by the country music establishment as a full-fledged country musician, an acceptance achieved partly by his backers having hidden his racial identity when he was first introduced to the country music audience and industry. As Charles Hughes notes: "country music never had much room for black artists" even though "since the 1950s heyday of the Nashville sound, the genre's studio musicians, songwriters, and producers had included black-identified music styles, including soul, as part of country's musical mix."[42] This mix has a much longer history. As John S. Otto and Augustus M. Burns show, interaction between black and white musicians in the early part of the twentieth century, and especially in the 1920s and 1930s—country music's formative years—is traceable in both "black" music such as the blues and "white" music such as country (the so-called "hillbilly music").[43] Drawing on John Mowitt's concept of "musical interpellation," Geoff Mann argues that historically, formally, and culturally there is nothing inherently "white" about country music, and "that it has taken a great deal of ideological work both to make country the sound of American whiteness, and, at least as importantly, to make it continue to 'call' to white people to make country music seem not only something that only white people make, but also something that only white people 'hear' something that recruits white people to their 'whiteness.'"[44]

Given this context, the video for "Wagon Wheel" needed to construct Rucker's musical persona in a way that would establish his authenticity as an African-American country artist, especially since country music videos are usually among the discourses that do the ideological work to which Mann refers. The video opens with several shots that establish a rural Southern setting (it was shot in Watertown, Tennessee) belonging more to the past than the present. These shots depict, among other things, a railroad crossing, exteriors of small-town businesses with old-fashioned signs, rain on the pavement, and a hand turning back a clock. The first glimpse we have of Rucker in the main part of the video is of his hand, clutching a black and white photograph of a blonde woman. We also see her in intercut shots, applying lipstick and looking at a similar photograph of Rucker. Rucker's persona is that of an itinerant musician, traveling with guitar case in hand. In the song's lyrics, the protagonist tells the story of hitchhiking southward from New England along the East Coast of the United States to reunite with a loved one in Raleigh, North Carolina. The primary elements of Rucker's appearance are items of clothing that, while contemporary, evoke the Depression era. His clothes look lived-in; he wears a vest as well as a gray wool coat and a fedora, all in subdued colors. The guitar he plays is either a 1930s model Gibson archtop or resembles one very closely. His preferred modes of travel, walking railroad tracks and hitchhiking, also evoke the Depression.

Mann argues that country music asserts its whiteness through nostalgia not just "for an era when white supremacy operated more explicitly" but more so for a nonspecific "white 'used to,'" a nostalgia for "an authentic, stable whiteness" that is always already slipping away as the present becomes the past (hence the image in the video of literally turning back the hands of time).[45] If so, constructing Rucker's persona in a way that links him to the period in which country music as we know it today was evolving, partly through the contributions of legendary traveling musicians like Woody Guthrie, is a subtly subversive challenge to the country music imaginary. Rucker's persona as an itinerant Depression-era country musician not only implies that he is a legitimate bearer of its cultural heritage, but also that he (or someone like him) was there at the origins of the genre. The video thus suggests the outline of what Mann calls an "alternative history" of country music that "trouble[s] the white-country coupling."[46]

Michael Hughes argues that a typical country musician attempts to project a persona of "a sincere, down-to-earth average person," and Rucker's manner in the video suggests precisely this.[47] As he plays guitar and sings directly to the camera (and therefore directly and intimately to the audience watching the video) on the railroad tracks (Figure 5.3) and inside of old stores, he seems friendly, unpretentious, and approachable. He smiles genially while performing and seems to be truly enjoying himself. At one moment when the lyrics of the song refer to his having shared a toke of marijuana with a trucker, he shrugs apologetically and seems a bit abashed. Scenes in which he shivers and draws his coat in closer to himself while sitting in the back of a truck in which he is getting a lift contrast with scenes in which he is clearly enjoying playing and singing, as if to suggest the adversity he endures for the sake of his audience.

Another strategy of impression management at work in this video is what might be called "authenticity by association" (the same strategy Snoop Dogg employed by including Willie Nelson in a video for "My Medicine," a song in which he flirted with country style). Characters who offer Rucker rides in vintage pick-up trucks are played by members of the Louisiana-based Robertson family whose life was chronicled on the reality television program *Duck Dynasty*. Their presence as media-certified, iconic "rednecks" confers rural white Southern authenticity on Rucker by association. This effect is furthered by the appearance of Charles Kelley, a well-known country musician and member of Lady Antebellum, winner of Country Music Association awards and the group that backed Rucker on the track. The end of Rucker's journey is a club where he apparently is to

Figure 5.3 Darius Rucker performing on railroad tracks in the music video for "Wagon Wheel" (2013), directed by Jim Wright (1:00).

perform. His last ride is from Kelley, driving a vintage Buick convertible with a young woman at his side. If the Robertsons represent ostensibly ordinary white Southern folk in this video, Kelley represents the flashier Nashville country music establishment placing its stamp of approval on Rucker as it delivers him to the venue where he is to perform. A sign outside the club reads: "Appearing Tonight … Darius Rucker and Friends."

At this point, one of the most interesting moments in the video occurs as a bearded man working the door of the club, played by Jase Robertson, tries to prevent Rucker from coming inside (Figure 5.4). They scuffle slightly until Rucker is rescued by the female bartender who assures the doorman that Rucker is in the right place and ushers him to the stage where he joins a band and plays out the rest of the song. (To return momentarily to Railton and Watson's taxonomy, one could say that, although the video for "Wagon Wheel" falls squarely into the narrative category, at this point it arguably shifts from narrative to staged performance.) Although no explanation for the doorman's behavior is proffered, it seems probable that he denies Rucker entry because he cannot imagine that a black man could be the night's featured country music artist.[48] (It may be a coincidence that, in a wide shot in which we see the doorman trying to keep Rucker from reaching the stage, there is a poster on the wall behind them advertising a bluegrass festival at the White Farmers Market.) This is the only moment in the video that refers directly to Rucker's racial identity and the possibility of its being stigmatized in the context of country music. Juxtaposed with the earlier image of Rucker as a peripatetic musician who participated in the origins of country music, this scene suddenly jolts the video away from an imagined alternative history of the genre to remind the viewer of the reality of how race works in country music.

The way in which "Wagon Wheel" is framed offers a further wrinkle. The video actually begins with a shot of four bearded male members of the Robertson family walking from

Figure 5.4 The club doorman, played by Jase Robertson, tries to keep Darius Rucker from entering in the music video for "Wagon Wheel" (2013), directed by Jim Wright (3:41).

a black stretch limo toward a trailer, as seen through a window from the interior of the trailer. Inside, Darius Rucker is sleeping. His pillow features the emblem of the University of South Carolina's football team. Following the club performance, the video returns to the framing narrative with a low-angle close-up of Charles Kelley telling Rucker that it is time to wake up and do a show. As he leaves the bedroom, Rucker encounters four members of the Robertson family; he greets and hugs all of them, then says: "Y'all, I just had a crazy dream," although he seems to decide not to tell them what it was about. This narrative frame is intriguing but highly ambiguous. Through the narrative of Rucker's life as a quasi-Depression-era itinerant musician, and the racial tension he encounters at the club, the video constructs Rucker simultaneously as a historical figure in the evolution of country music and a contemporary figure who has to negotiate the situation of being an African-American artist in a genre that has not been hospitable to black musicians. The narrative claim that this whole story was a dream enables the video to have it both ways: to serve as a kind of historical parable of race relations and authenticity in country music while simultaneously disavowing any idea that race is a serious issue in contemporary country music. In this respect, it ultimately falls in line with the Nashville establishment's repeated assertion that "country music [is] color blind."[49]

Conclusion

I have argued here for an approach to analyzing music videos that centers on musical personae enacted by the performers. In some ways, the music video is an ideal context in which to examine musical personae. Although my initial formulation of the idea of musical personae assumed that a persona was developed primarily in the context of live performance with co-present performers and spectators, I would now argue that video is a performance space that lends itself even better to the definition of a persona than does live performance. Music videos allow artists to construct their personae exactly as they wish without having to consider the contingencies of live performance. This is particularly clear with regard to setting, since the juxtaposition of settings that establish the genre-related differences of personae between Run-DMC and Aerosmith in "Walk This Way" would be difficult to achieve in live performance, especially for the performance of a single song, as would the montage of location shots through which the setting of the first part of Darius Rucker's "Wagon Wheel" is created. Collaborations such as those between Run-DMC and Aerosmith as well as others I have mentioned, such as Willie Nelson's presence in a video by Snoop Dogg, can be replicated on stage, of course, but are logistically far easier to achieve in the space of music videos.

I understand the musical persona to be a specific kind of social self-presentation, in Goffman's sense, in which musicians engage when appearing before their audiences in any medium. The constituent parts of a musical persona can be described using Goffman's vocabulary for the elements of self-presentation: setting, appearance, and manner. These elements appear in performances framed in three ways: as musical performances, as performances in and of a specific genre of music, and as events taking place within a particular socio-cultural context. A musical persona is always constructed in relation to the norms of a musical genre, which, as we have seen in the case of country music's racial politics, can be reflective of larger socio-cultural formations. This does not mean that any musician's persona must adhere to these norms, only that they are inevitably a point of reference. The tensions among acknowledging, critiquing, and acquiescing to the status of African-American musicians in country music, which can be detected in different moments of the video for Darius Rucker's "Wagon Wheel," exemplify some of the positions an artist may assume toward established norms through the performance of a persona. Examining artists' musical personae through their music video readily opens discussion of the performance's implications in social terms, including representations of gender and race, by situating the persona in the interrelated contexts of genre and society.

Notes

1   Philip Auslander, "Musical Personae," *The Drama Review* 50, no. 1 (2006): 100–119. Previously, I had always taken live performance and live interaction with an audience as the primary context in which musical personae are enacted. This chapter is the first work in which I take recorded performance as the primary site of persona creation.

2   Philip Auslander, "On the Concept of Persona in Performance," *Kunstlicht* 36, no. 3 (2015): 62–79.

3   Michael Jackson, "'Billie Jean' Brunei 1996," YouTube video (9:49), October 1, 2016, https://www.youtube.com/watch?v=KjxRY7HCAMo.

4   Simon Frith, *Performing Rites: On the Value of Popular Music* (Cambridge, MA: Harvard University Press, 1996), 186, 212.

5   Philip Auslander, "Performance Analysis and Popular Music: A Manifesto," *Contemporary Theatre Review* 14, no. 1 (2004): 6.

6   David R. Shumway, *Rock Star: The Making of Musical Icons from Elvis to Springsteen* (Baltimore, MD: Johns Hopkins University Press, 2014), 154–160.

7   Philip Auslander, "'Musical Personae' Revisited," in *Investigating Musical Performance: Theoretical Models and Intersection*, edited by Gianmario Borio, Alessandro Cecchi, Giovanni Giuriati, and Marco Lutzu (London: Routledge, forthcoming 2019). Whereas it is possible to interpret my original formulation of the musical persona as a monolithic entity, in this chapter I treat the musical persona as a multivocal entity made up of different elements that are not necessarily in harmony with one another and therefore can produce tensions and ambiguities within the persona.

8   Auslander, "Performance Analysis," 10–11.

9   Erving Goffman, *Frame Analysis: An Essay on the Organization of Experience* (Boston, MA: Northeastern University Press, 1986), 10–11.

10 Improv Everywhere, "Frozen Grand Central," 2008, improveverywhere.com.

11 My interpretation of "Frozen Grand Central" in relation to framing is different from, but compatible with, that of an anonymous author on *The Sociological Cinema* blog who considers it to be "a typical example of an ethnomethodological breaching experiment" in which conventional expectations are intentionally breached to see how subjects will respond: June 23, 2011, https://www.thesociologicalcinema.com/videos/frozen-grand-central.

12 Fabian Holt, *Genre in Popular Music* (Chicago, IL: University of Chicago Press, 2007), 2.

13 Goffman, *Frame Analysis*, 123.

14 Johan H. Huizinga, *Homo Ludens: A Study of the Play-Element in Culture* (London: Routledge & Kegan Paul, 1949), 10.

15 Victor Turner, "Frame, Flow, and Reflection: Ritual and Drama as Public Liminality," *Japanese Journal of Religious Studies* 6, no. 4 (December 1979): 474.

16 Philip Auslander, *Performing Glam Rock: Gender and Theatricality in Popular Music* (Ann Arbor, MI: University of Michigan Press, 2006).

17 In a series of essays, I have developed an interactionist approach to musical performance based on Goffman's work. The heart of the interactionist perspective is that social reality is not a priori but is both enacted and produced through human interactions that reflect the social conventions and underlying assumptions of the particular context in which they occur. In the first of these essays, "Musical Personae," I broached the idea that musical performance could be understood on the model of self-presentation and coined the term "musical persona" to identify the specific kind of self-presentation in which musicians engage when performing. It is important to assert that, from an interactionist perspective, this persona is not something that is created by a musician then presented to an audience. Rather, it is something that comes into being through the mutually constituting interaction of performers and audience within a mutually understood frame.

18 Erving Goffman, *The Presentation of Self in Everyday Life* (New York: Anchor, 1959), 80.

19 Ibid., 17–76.

20 Ibid., 77–105.

21 Avedon's photographs are in the collection of the Museum of Modern Art, New York City. See https://www.moma.org/artists/248?locale=en.

22 Goffman, *Presentation*, 22.

23 Ibid., 22–26.

24 Run-DMC, "Walk This Way (Video)," YouTube video (4:03), October 25, 2009, https://www.youtube.com/watch?v=4B_UYYPb-Gk.

25 Carol Vernallis, *Experiencing Music Video: Aesthetics and Cultural Context* (New York: Columbia University Press, 2004), 75.

26 Pat Aufderheide, "Music Videos: The Look of the Sound," *Journal of Communication* 36, no. 1 (1986): 67–68.

27 Philip Auslander, "Music as Performance: The Disciplinary Dilemma Revisited," in *Sound und Performance*, edited by Wolf-Dieter Ernst (Würzburg: Verlag Königshausen & Neumann, 2015), 527–540.

28 Auslander, "Performance Analysis," 12.

29 Ian Inglis and I argue that a number of the filmed and televised performances by the Beatles, just before and after they stopped touring because they were unhappy with the conditions under which they performed, reflect a desire to create ideal performance conditions that could only take place in the studio. Philip Auslander and Ian Inglis, "Nothing is Real: The Beatles as Virtual Performers," in *The Oxford Handbook of Music and Virtuality*, edited by Sheila Whiteley and Shara Rambarran (Oxford: Oxford University Press, 2016), 42–45, 48–49.

30 Vernallis, *Experiencing Music Video*, 87.

31 Ibid., 79.

32 Ibid., 80. Arguably, Vernallis overemphasizes setting in her reading of Seal's relationship to black music and audiences. Although it is true that the setting for "Crazy" (1991), the video she discusses, is an empty white space, Seal's appearance, which includes a large gold medallion over his bare chest and other conspicuous bling as well as hair in beaded braids, clearly links him to contemporary African-American fashion and performance practices in black music. Additionally, the only musician other than Seal to appear in the video is an infrequently glimpsed bass guitarist who appears to be black and may be there to connect Seal with the funk music that emerged in the late 1960s and early 1970s to which a particular style of bass playing was central. Finally, the black-and-white video for Seal's version of Sam Cooke's "A Change Is Gonna Come" (2008) also takes place in an empty space (this time a dark one). Seal's appearance in this video is clearly meant to evoke Cooke: he is dressed in a tuxedo, seems to be in a spotlight, and sings into an old-fashioned looking microphone. In this case, it is quite clear that the emptiness of the setting in no way divorces Seal from black music, a connection that is strongly asserted through his evocation of Cooke.

33 Diane Railton and Paul Watson, *Music and the Moving Image: Music Video and the Politics of Representation* (Edinburgh: Edinburgh University Press, 2011), 45.

34 Ibid., 48.

35 Ibid., 46.

36 In a related vein, Railton and Watson do not address the fact that the term "badonkadonk" is a specifically African-American slang term referring to a part of the female anatomy that the songwriters knowingly appropriated for the country genre.

37 Mark Fenster, "Genre and Form: The Development of the Country Music Video," in *Sound and Vision: The Music Video Reader*, edited by Simon Frith, Andrew Goodwin, and Lawrence Grossberg (London and New York: Routledge, 1993), 94, 109.

38 Ibid., 99.

39 Darius Rucker, "Wagon Wheel," YouTube video (5:46), March 21, 2013, https://www.youtube.com/watch?v=hvKyBcCDOB4.

40 Michael Hughes, "Country Music as Impression Management: A Meditation on Fabricating Authenticity," *Poetics* 28 (2000): 197.

41 Ibid.

42 Charles L. Hughes, *Country Soul: Making Music and Making Race in the American South* (Chapel Hill, NC: University of North Carolina Press, 2015), 133–134.

43 John S. Otto and Augustus M. Burns, "Black and White Cultural Interaction in the Early Twentieth Century South: Race and Hillbilly Music," *Phylon* 35, no. 4 (1974): 407–417. The song "Wagon Wheel" is itself a product of black and white cultural interaction in a modest and somewhat indirect way. The song originated as a work Bob Dylan recorded in an unfinished form during the sessions for the soundtrack to *Pat Garrett and Billy the Kid* in 1973. Ketch Secor of The Old Crow Medicine Show heard "Wagon Wheel" on a Dylan bootleg and wrote his own verses for it. The song became a staple of the group's repertoire long before they recorded it in 2003. Dylan has acknowledged that key phrases in the chorus derive from older blues songs by black artists, particularly "Rock Me, Mama" by Arthur "Big Boy" Crudup, inspired by Big Bill Broonzy's "Rock Me Baby." As Edward Mack points out, other blues songs by Curtis Jones and Melvin "Lil Son" Jackson have related lyrics that may also have found their way into "Wagon Wheel." Edward Mack, "The Surprising Origins of 'Wagon Wheel,' One of the Most Popular Country Songs Ever," 2015, https://www.wideopencountry.com/song-day-wagon-wheel. The interaction among musicians of different colors that ultimately produced the song took place across at least three generations, across the genres of blues, country, and rock, and was mediated by the technology of sound recording.

44 Geoff Mann, "Why Does Country Music Sound White? Race and the Voice of Nostalgia," *Ethnic and Racial Studies* 31, no. 1 (2008): 83.

45 Ibid., 88, 91.

46 Ibid., 82.

47 M. Hughes, "Country Music," 196.

48 There is a very similar moment in the film *Cadillac Records* (2008)—a fictionalized account of the legendary Chicago blues label Chess Records—in which Chuck Berry (played by Mos Def) is denied entry to a club where he is to perform because the club doorman and manager believe Chuck Berry to be a country music artist and cannot fathom that the black man before them could be Chuck Berry. Berry seeks to demonstrate his identity by playing a Johnny Cash-like country rhythm on his guitar.

49 C.L. Hughes, *Country Soul*, 129.

6

Hullabaloo: Rocking the Variety Show in the Mid-1960s

Norma Coates

Shindig! and *Hullabaloo* were short-lived mid-1960s American prime-time television music programs that followed in the wake of the British Invasion. ABC's *Shindig!* premiered on September 9, 1964, followed by NBC's *Hullabaloo*, a mid-season replacement, on January 12, 1965. Both were cancelled before the 1966–1967 television season. The brief runs are too easily attributed to a desire to take advantage of what many cultural influencers, critics, and parents of baby-boom youth hoped was a fad. Yet *Shindig!* and *Hullabaloo* were not exploitative throwaways, but representative of and responsive to social and cultural changes affecting the entertainment industry, tensions between two industries that were in the midst of structural changes and internal tensions, and changing audience demographics and marketing practices.[1] Neither program broke with existing television practices but remained on a continuum with experimentation and programming that occurred earlier in the decade.[2] *Shindig!* employed visual techniques developed outside of the American television industry, but *Hullabaloo* was an earnest experiment by experienced television production personnel to update an aging genre.

Hullabaloo and *Shindig!*, American television's first prime-time rock and roll programs, are almost forgotten today except by those who were old enough to remember them, music obsessives, and those who encounter out-of-context performance clips on YouTube and other internet spaces. Rock and academic critics, writing years after the programs aired, tend to view them through a lens distorted by rock ideology, pitting rock's authenticity and integrity against television's artifice and commercial motivation.[3] Mentions of the programs, if any, had disappeared into footnotes or were thrown onto the scrapheap of cultural detritus not worth recovering or even thinking about. That *Hullabaloo* and *Shindig!* might have represented more than feeble attempts by big American television networks to exploit the craze set off by the British Invasion was not only silenced but unthinkable.[4]

This chapter situates *Hullabaloo* in rock and roll and television history. *Shindig!* demonstrated that rock and roll, and later genres of popular music, actively required the visual as well as the musical to communicate their affective messages, and that excitement was the key to rock and roll's power. *Shindig!* is accorded some respect from rock critics; for example, television music historian Marc Weingarten's opinion that: "[W]atching *Shindig!* was like flipping the radio dial in a great music city—R&B greats and soul divas shared the stage with pop poseurs and earnest folkies."[5]

Weingarten devoted several pages to *Shindig!* in his history of popular music on American television, but only two paragraphs to *Hullabaloo*, describing it as a misguided attempt to legitimate rock and roll with tame go-go dancers, a theme song that "sounded like a commercial jingle for aftershave lotion," and a "revolving door" of hosts who "dispatched stiffs like Frankie Avalon and Annette Funicello."[6] *Hullabaloo*'s direct impact upon rock music culture is admittedly less palpable but important.[7] The program offered a glimpse of the future of popular music and the variety genre during the era when three networks—CBS, NBC, and ABC—had an oligopoly over American television production. Its contribution was primarily in the area of television genre and style, and the influence and impact of its producers, dancers, and creative personnel on television award shows and Broadway dance has only just begun to wane. Its innovations and emphasis upon updating the variety show for a younger audience provided the aging genre with another decade and a half of performance life. *Hullabaloo* attempted to build continuity between old and new entertainment regimes, using rock and roll music to bridge, not divide, generations.

Updating the variety show for a younger generation

Rock historian Jake Austen called *Hullabaloo*'s combination of parent-generation (or older) stars and rock and roll musicians "pathetic," especially when compared to *Shindig!*[8] Even so, Austen admitted that *Hullabaloo* was good television, but it wasn't good rock and roll television because the "producers had no real respect for the music," a comment belying the naive idealism of a particular type of rock fan or critic who believes that rock and roll's "exceptionalism" should be obvious to all.[9] *Hullabaloo*, according to its creators, was a genre experiment, an attempt to update the variety show in line with NBC's branding as the network for young urban sophisticates, the audience that the network most hoped to capture and sell to its sponsors.

A January 1965 network research report that compiled data from the ARB ratings service indicated that NBC maintained its leadership as the number one adult network. As an April/May 1965 research report spun it: "NBC has sizeable leads over the other networks in every category except older people (50+), teens and children. CBS is the clear victor among old people (as it has been for the past several years) while 'youth-oriented' ABC wins *only* among teens and children."[10] NBC was the best network for advertisers interested in reaching adults aged under 50: "attracting over half-a-million more young adults per quarter hour than ABC" and, overall, reached two million more young adults than CBS, and half a million more than ABC.[11] The network staked its claim on the young adult audience, who had come of age with rock and roll. *Hullabaloo*, as conceived, fit that strategy well. It did not rest on its appeal to teenagers, but it was an attempt to make the variety show more youthful, even if it meant booking and promoting rock and roll acts.

Hullabaloo was also consistent with NBC's response to an industry dynamic. "Television's Accent on Youth as New Faces Pop Up Everywhere" announced a July 28, 1965 headline in *Variety*, the entertainment industry "bible." Reporter Jack Hellman observed that: "The youth movement is in full cry. Target of the sponsor is the young marrieds, who consume most of the plugged merchandise."[12] Additionally, some of the attraction of youthful programming was "girl-watching," as the ratings for beauty pageants and the like were rising. That is, more older men—a coveted prime-time audience—were tuning in to watch nubile young women on television. The older generation could not ignore the new sounds and the network's focus on younger adults. Nevertheless, television genres like the variety show were not going to disappear overnight. Accordingly, NBC assembled a production team of young television veterans with variety show experience to create *Hullabaloo*. All began their careers in television in the 1950s, and none had pre-television network radio experience. They were television professionals who knew production processes, and their limitations and opportunities, inside out.

Producer Gary Smith began his show-business career as a "paint boy" for a studio in New York City while still in high school, painting scenery for Broadway shows including *Guys and Dolls*. He attended Carnegie Tech, now Carnegie Mellon, to study scenic design. After college, he returned to New York City, took and passed the test to join the United Scenic Artists Guild Union, and, for his first job, designed a giant Geritol bottle for a CBS commercial. After a few years of dues-paying on television series, he was named art director of a summer replacement series starring singer Andy Williams in 1958. Smith became known for his spare and clean style, and before long was hired by his future long-time business partner, Dwight Hemion, to help refresh the design of Perry Como's television variety show. Hemion encouraged Smith to add depth to the set, a departure from the conventional way of visualizing television on a horizontal plane from left to right. Smith encouraged the production team to let visuals drive the program, not music.[13] Smith won an Emmy for his art direction but was anxious to move up in the industry and moved to California to do so. In 1963, Smith accepted a job as art director and co-producer for *The Judy Garland Show* and made producer after the network fired his predecessor after five episodes. Smith proved as good as anyone at managing the temperamental and unreliable Garland, and also created the memorable look of her show titles and finale, using lightbulbs to spell her name at the start, and to line the runway during the concert segment that concluded each episode. Lightbulbs were a Smith design hallmark; they were used liberally on *Hullabaloo* (see Figure 6.1). After a difficult stint with Garland, Smith, no longer content with being a designer, produced a few episodes for the *Bell Telephone Hour* and a six-week summer replacement series, *Ford Presents the New Christy Minstrels*.

In his 2001 interview for the Television Academy's oral history archive, Smith recalls meeting with his agent from GAC, Lester Gottlieb, and NBC vice-president Mort Werner to pitch the variety show that became *Hullabaloo*.[14] Gottlieb recounted the sequence of events differently, asserting that he pitched it and received "a stack of development dollars" for it.[15] The British Invasion was underway at the time, and Gottlieb asserts: "it was time

Figure 6.1 The *Hullabaloo* set.

that the kids stopped getting cheap lip synch shows."[16] Both recollections, neither of which may be entirely factual, indicate that established industry insiders were treating the British Invasion and the musical changes that it represented not as a fluke but as a sign of things to come. The television industry, as much as the music industry, had to change in order to remain relevant to the coming generation of viewers.

Gottlieb's perspective was published in a contemporary *TV Guide* cover article to promote *Hullabaloo*, and Smith's was provided almost forty years after the program aired for a subjective and therefore culturally politicized industrial archive, but it is clear that the idea of an updated variety show was attractive to NBC, and to Smith, its eventual producer. According to Smith, NBC executives believed that the Beatles brought credibility to youthful pop music and that, by 1964, the new musical style could draw a sizeable audience in prime time. Smith's task, of course, was how to imagine, capture, and keep that audience. Smith deployed distinctions between "stars"—experienced and known musicians, night club acts, and film and television actors who could attract and hold an audience—and "record acts" known primarily for radio play and lack of performance polish or experience. *Shindig!*, in his estimation, relied on record acts from the West Coast, and *Hullabaloo*, based in New York, would mix touring artists with stars, resulting in a more urbane production with appeal beyond the teen audience.

Smith and NBC likely anticipated that more viewers would tune in for "record acts" than for "stars." They approached Steve Binder to help launch the show. Binder, too, worked on television variety and talk shows in the 1950s. He began his television career in the mail room at LA local TV affiliate, KABC. After some time as operations manager for that station, and a short stint directing *The Soupy Sales Show* for ABC, he was approached by variety and talk show host Steve Allen about directing a syndicated jazz show, *Jazz Scene USA*.[17] Allen then hired him to produce his new syndicated talk show for Westinghouse. Binder learned how to produce and direct music for television and how to express its intimacy via extreme close-ups and montages.[18] According to Binder:

> Somehow in my mind I saw video with music. Traditionally, everyone would tend to "play it safe" and they would shoot music shows from a distance. I felt jazz music was so intimate that it needed to be shot extremely close, and I started to montage close-up to close-up to close-up. I wasn't going for the usual master shot, medium shot, close-up, but rather for something that reflected the intimacy of the artist on the instrument. I used close-ups of their fingers, the sweat on their brow.[19]

In 1964 Binder was asked by entrepreneur Bill Sargent to direct a closed-circuit rock and roll movie using a new video format he had co-invented—Electronovision[20]—in the first of what he hoped would be an annual event held in movie theatres.[21] Binder, at age 23, hadn't heard of most of the acts booked. A new to the US band, the Rolling Stones, was part of a package with Billy J. Kramer and Gerry and the Pacemakers. Sargent also booked some of the leading American acts of the era, including the Supremes, Marvin Gaye, Smokey Robinson and the Miracles, the Beach Boys, and James Brown. The surf music duo Jan and Dean served as hosts and performed in interstitial segments that Binder shot "guerrilla style," showing up at locations and shooting without a permit. Acts were filmed at the Santa Monica Civic Auditorium. Binder claims that the teenage audience in the arena set the template for the screaming and behavior that would follow: "[*T.A.M.I.*] was before teenage audiences knew how they were supposed to react in front of rock stars," but more likely, the *T.A.M.I. Show* reinforced behavior already modeled in news reports about Beatlemania and the response to British Invasion groups on television variety programs, particularly the *Ed Sullivan Show*.[22]

The filmed *T.A.M.I. Show* captured the growing excitement generated by rock and roll. Using the team he worked with on the most recent incarnation of *The Steve Allen Show*, Binder employed a principle that he had learned while working on that and other prime-time variety programs: "follow the action." He also did not care if cameras or other equipment entered the frame, believing that leaving them in the shot made the scene more dynamic and authentic. He rehearsed camera movements and shots with each band except one before the program. James Brown refused to rehearse, so Binder relied on patterns and his gut to call the shots on the fly. Just 23 years old at the time of the shoot, Binder had an affinity for the affective properties of the music and, crucially, the visuality of performances. With his variety show and *T.A.M.I. Show* experience, Binder was an appropriate intermediary who could strike a balance between stars and record acts, and who could marry music and visuals and deliver them with high television production value.[23]

That NBC went to the trouble of assembling a quality core creative team for *Hullabaloo*, including some with rock and roll experience, provides evidence that the network was not just trying to compete with ABC's *Shindig!* for the teen audience. Program and network executives were careful to differentiate *Hullabaloo* from *Shindig!*, to position it as a program for young adults as much as for teenagers, and to deny that it was a rock and roll program. *Hullabaloo* was an attempt to both retain the existing variety show audience and bring enough new viewers to the fold to assure the genre's ongoing relevance and, hopefully, the program's success.

In a promotional interview with the Chicago Tribune just after *Hullabaloo*'s premiere, producer Gary Smith asserted that: "There's nothing new about *Hullabaloo*'s format. The two-a-day, fast-paced vaudeville format is as old as time."[24] In a similar interview published just ahead of *Hullabaloo*'s premiere on January 12, 1965, Smith clearly differentiated it from *Shindig!* for a wary interviewer:

> You think it's a rock 'n' roll show! You think it's like *Shindig!* But it isn't. It's a vaudeville show. It has many acts. It's fast paced. We are presenting young entertainers in all categories. In place of Finks' Mules, we'll have a college marching band or a drill team.[25] We'll have rock 'n' roll, but we'll also have some of the good young comics. It's the whole spectrum of young entertainers with appeal not just to young people, but to everyone who's young in heart or young in mind.[26]

GAC agent Lester Gottlieb also pushed the "young vaudeville" angle: "It's a good vaudeville show, sure, but it's more than that. It has a style and a look. We at GAC felt the next step was an extension of vaudeville, but why not for a young audience this time instead of an adult audience? A young vaudeville show."[27] Rather than trying to actively contain or tame rock and roll, NBC was trying to widen the vaudeville format and, with it, what was appropriate for the mainstream. Television conventions could not immediately change in order to accommodate a very popular yet comparatively new musical style whose audience was still consolidating. In hindsight it is clear to see that post-British Invasion music, abetted by the baby boom and the social and cultural unrest of the era, would be more than a fad. In 1964 and 1965, that clarity was not yet discernible.

A rock and roll show ... with stars

Hullabaloo presented a particular televisual inflection of sophistication, one that was perhaps too mature for teenage audiences. Like other variety shows but unlike *Shindig!*, *Hullabaloo* was hosted by a rotating master of ceremonies (emcee), usually a younger singer or film or television actor from a current hit television series or film. Singer/hosts included Frankie Avalon, The Righteous Brothers, Paul Anka, George Harrison, Leslie Uggams, George Maharis, Petula Clark, Annette Funicello (with Frankie Avalon), David McCallum, Peter Noone, Barry McGuire, and Chad and Jeremy, among others. They were culled from the less raucous end of the musical spectrum of the era. Occasionally a host came from the entertainment generation that was quickly losing its hegemony to younger artists and audiences, such as Sammy Davis Jr., Soupy Sales, and Jerry Lewis, who co-hosted with his son Gary, of rock and roll group Gary and the Playboys.

Episodes usually opened with the *Hullabaloo* theme song backing the *Hullabaloo* Dancers as they danced from offstage to a white set, devoid of any scenery or prop besides a large 3D rendition of the program's logo. The host then sang a song or did a routine before the evening's sponsors were announced, their logos superscripted over the on-screen action. *Hullabaloo* was sponsored primarily by manufacturers of household products including Johnson Wax, Arrid Deodorant, Betty Crocker Cake Mix, and Carnation Instant Milk, who were hoping to capture the young wives watching the program. Other sponsors included purveyors of products that appealed to teenage girls as well as young adult women, such as Jergens Face Cream and Clearasil. After a commercial break the emcee returned to act or sing, then retired to a room lined with record covers to introduce the program and the next act. Acts, including rock and roll groups, were sometimes given scripted jokes or other routines to perform.

Hullabaloo abandoned the conventional proscenium style of variety show presentation. Its sets were minimal, consisting of often bold shapes and graphics on a clean white background, the scenery providing depth that was explored as the dancers, who frequently added visual interest while performers sang, moved around them, abandoning the tightly choreographed lines and movements of the previous generation. *Hullabaloo*'s directors had no qualms about including production apparatus, exposing the work and artifice that went into producing "entertainment." To that end, sets were sometimes rolled out on wheels by the *Hullabaloo* Dancers during transitions between acts. Camerawork was fluid and unobtrusive, relying upon the inherent showmanship of the performers, combined with the minimal sets, to carry numbers. That strategy worked well for stars and current pop singers who shared episodes with rock and rollers, such as Dionne Warwick, Lesley Uggams, Paul Anka, and Frankie Avalon, but often left rock and roll groups looking uncomfortable and out of place. *Hullabaloo*'s experiments in infusing rock and roll with style did not always work, but the attempts indicated that the production team took the genre and its artists as seriously as they did more conventional artists and musical genres.

Hullabaloo hosted many popular bands from most parts of the 1965–1966 rock and roll spectrum. Eight episodes during the first season featured a segment called "Hullabaloo London," hosted by Beatles manager Brian Epstein, who would introduce a British act who performed a number or two. Marianne Faithfull, Gerry and the Pacemakers, Freddie and the Dreamers, and The Searchers all appeared on this segment. Epstein interviewed Andrew Loog Oldham during one of them. The band Oldham managed, the Rolling Stones, appeared "live" on *Hullabaloo* during its second season, Mick Jagger providing live vocals to a pre-recorded backing track. The Beatles appeared once, during season two, via promotional videos for "Day Tripper" and "We Can Work It Out." A few folk artists associated with the commercial part of the genre appeared, but none of the big names of the folk revival. Motown artists and "girl singers," such as Petula Clark and Lesley Gore, were frequent guests, as were performers whose sound was already adult friendly, including Trini Lopez and Nancy Ames.[28] Bob Dylan never appeared, but his songs did.

Bold graphics sometimes rescued an unsuccessful concept, including an orchestrated medley of Dylan's songs performed on November 11, 1965. *Hullabaloo* featured production numbers, often medleys of songs by well-known songwriters, such as an homage to the work of Bert Bachrach and Hal David, as soundtracks for performances by the *Hullabaloo* Dancers or as a showcase for the emcee. By making medleys out of songs written by John Lennon and Paul McCartney, and those of Bob Dylan, *Hullabaloo* elevated their work for an audience that did not place the younger songwriters on the same level as their elders. The orchestral arrangements did not capture the bite of Dylan's pre-1965 work, turning them into something that had a greater resemblance to easy listening than to folk music.[29] Set design saved the day. It consisted of a blow-up of the cover of *The Times They Are A-Changing*, and two large photos of Dylan with his increasingly hip 1965 look. Yet by highlighting Dylan's compositions rather than the public version of his politics or affinity with a growing youth culture, the medley implied that Dylan's work was worth taking seriously as music, if not as message.

Hullabaloo's choreography brought modern Broadway dance to the television screen. Choreographer David Winters borrowed liberally from his experience as one of the dancers in the Jerome Robbins-choreographed stage and screen versions of *West Side Story*. Before joining *Hullabaloo*, Winters choreographed the *T.A.M.I. Show* and a few *Shindig!* episodes. His studio was popular with young television and film dancers. Winters's style had more in common with the Broadway choreography of Jerome Robbins than with television dance conventions. Winters choreographed moves that combined balletic leaps and jumps with the isolations and contractions of modern dance as translated into jazz dance.[30] In a feature article in *Dance Magazine*, a forum not overly friendly to dance on television variety shows, Winters described his specialty as "jazz-ballet," and described why he liked that combination: "The dancing I like best is dancing where there's real emotional involvement. Good jazz always has that, although lately I notice that some jazz dancing I see lacks strength. So many jazz students don't seem to have the sharpness and staccato excitement that makes jazz so satisfying."[31] Winters's choreography for the *T.A.M.I. Show* epitomized what he thought good jazz dancing should be, according to *Variety*'s review of the program: "David Winters' choreography has added considerably to the show's solid punch. His wild and abandoned terpsichore, like most of the dances, of course, complement the musical styles of the singers."[32] Jazz dance, by the early 1960s, had picked up elements of modern dance and was increasingly becoming synonymous with musical theater style. *Hullabaloo* was, through Winters and some of the dancers, part of a two-way exchange between Broadway and Hollywood. *Hullabaloo* Dancer Michael Bennett went on to choreograph one of the major Broadway shows of the 1970s, *A Chorus Line*. His ex-wife and fellow *Hullabaloo* Dancer Donna McKechnie played the lead female role in the show.

Gender and racial representation

Hullabaloo is most remembered for its images of pert girls in go-go boots, dancing frantically by themselves while isolated in glass cages above the action on stage. Media critic Susan J. Douglas characterized *Hullabaloo*'s girl in a cage as "one of the sicker, yet more apt, metaphors for the teen female condition during this era."[33] Douglas's point is decidedly valid, but she does not contextualize the source of the original "girl in the cage," the Whisky-a-Go-Go, or the stylistic message that it was meant to convey. That is, she does not consider it against the gender politics or gendered culture of the era. This is not to excuse the sexist aspects of the girl in the cage, but to assert that there are different readings that take its social, cultural, industrial, and stylistic context into account.

In her study of *Honey West*—a detective program with a female protagonist—television historian Julie D'Acci argues that Anne Francis's portrayal of a "sexy sleuth" was a network response to the sexual revolution. The character Honey West constituted a rupture in traditional female representations on television and a break with conventions of television femininity, aligning her instead with a new culture of "swinging singles" and the growing sexual freedom of women expressed elsewhere in popular culture.[34] D'Acci attributes this new representational style, introduced at the apex of the three-network oligopoly over television production, licensing, and advertising revenue, to NBC's, CBS's, and ABC's desire to retain their control over American television entertainment.[35] Television scholar Moya Luckett notes that thirteen programs in the 1965–1966 television season featured female protagonists, a decade high. Several of them, including *Honey West*, introduced what Luckett calls a "mobile femininity," their active bodies introducing a "new model of feminine possibility."[36] Nevertheless, the traditionally conservative networks sought to tame *Honey West*'s representation of a sexualized "new woman" by including a male character to serve as the detective's protector, and an older female to play her aunt/chaperone. D'Acci observes that "Honey's status as a conventional sex object was heavily played upon— flagging the new woman's sexuality but reinscribing it in traditional patriarchal terms" and that the character was "relentlessly depicted as stereotypically and safely feminine—high fashion, slim, blonde, glamorous and heterosexually paired."[37]

Hullabaloo's producers clearly adopted similar representational strategies. Prime time was the day part that drew the most male viewers. Although most of the program's advertisements were for products targeted to housewives and female teenagers, aspects of its visual style appealed to heterosexual men. Those aspects usually involved young women, some gyrating frenetically, others objectified as mannequins or trophies. For example, while dance routines and solo artists used the entire space of the white stage when performing, rock and roll groups were placed on accessorized sets intended to reflect the name of the group or aspects of the song that they were singing. Sometimes the relation between the set and the music was unclear. The set for the Kinks, who performed "You Really Got Me" on an early episode, looked like an alley between tenement houses, complete with live cats sitting on top of garbage cans (see Figure 6.2). Other sets scattered "human mannequins"—female models in static poses, sometimes holding props—around the stage while rock and roll bands performed. Binder took credit for this concept, claiming that this use of beautiful female models from the Ford Agency made "an adult statement about contemporary rock and roll."[38] He elaborated upon this in his online interview for the Emmy organization, describing the models as zombies who were observing the action on stage. They were intended as stand-ins, not only for the at-home audience, but for adults in general who were pondering what to think about the social changes signaled by resurgent rock and roll and the generation that it assembled and spoke for.

Figure 6.2 The Kinks' set.

The idea was innovative and interesting but the execution, in hindsight, was misguided and often misogynistic. The Animals' performance of "It's My Life" on the November 11, 1965 episode was staged in a hunting/ski lodge, complete with trophy heads of beautiful girls on the wall. More (unintentionally) ambiguously, a performance of LA folk-rock band the Byrds clothed the models in hunting outfits and gave them rifles to aim and hold. One model seemed to have hers pointed at lead singer Roger McGuinn's crotch (see Figure 6.3). Gary Smith claims that the "female mannequins" wore the latest clothing styles in order to attract the youth audience.[39] Smith and Binder may have been prescient in their association of rock and roll with high fashion, but their mode of articulating the two was not successful, reading as more of a misguided adult response to rock and roll than astute social commentary.

Smith and Binder were particularly proud of "*Hullabaloo*-a-Go-Go." During this regular segment, one of the featured groups, usually a rock band, played while the *Hullabaloo* Dancers danced with each other, often in interracial pairs, and other participants on that week's program sat at tables. The name of the "club" was spelled out in the electric light bulbs used so prominently in the program (see Figure 6.4). This was arguably the most youthful segment of the show, and one that highlighted the excitement generated from live rock and roll, absent the lighting and camera tricks employed on *Shindig!* Steve Binder claims to have come up with the idea of replicating the go-go cages inside LA Whisky-a-Go-Go,

Figure 6.3 The Byrds' set.

Figure 6.4 The *Hullabaloo*-a-Go-Go set.

whose owner, Elmer Valentine, appropriated the idea from European clubs.[40] According to a *Variety* article about LA discotheques, none of them truly followed the European model of playing records for dancing. At the Whisky-a-Go-Go, however, the girls in the go-go cages doubled as disc jockeys (DJs), spinning records for the dancers below in-between live sets.[41] *Hullabaloo*'s cage dancers were not permitted this agency, yet do not exactly conform to Susan Douglas's characterization of them as "sick."[42]

One of the dancers, Lada Edmund Jr., became a minor celebrity in her own right, gracing a cover of *TV Guide* and being featured in articles in several mainstream magazines and newspapers.[43] Edmund Jr. may have been caged, but she used her perch above the stage to draw attention to herself, especially sexualized attention, in a way normally not permissible on television for young women of the era. She was not a sick symbol of the era, but a sign of what was still to come.[44] More simply, the girls in the cage were to represent European sophistication. From a stylistic point of view, this segment, and the girls in the cage—there were usually at least two, often four, of them—brought the glamour and the energy of discotheque dancing to an audience too young for or too geographically remote from big city dance venues.[45] The girls in the cage wore tight, fringed white dresses that stopped at the knee, and white go-go boots. Dancers on the floor—both male and female—usually wore "mod" sweaters and skirts or pants, accented with go-go boots on the women. Dancing during this segment was not choreographed but reflected and tried to create popular dances. The dancers arguably were a bit too successful, especially Edmund Jr. Journalist Bob Lardine of the *New York Daily News* asked if *Hullabaloo*'s dances were a bit too indecent. Edmund Jr. claimed that the criticism was unfair, and that what she did in her cage was no more physical than the waltz or the foxtrot. She revealed that: "The network is very strict about what we do on the show. Their censors watch us closely."[46] The censors would not let her do the jerk, a very popular teen dance of the moment, and producer Gary Smith made sure that her skirts (and those of the other dancers) always reached her knees. Nevertheless, Edmund Jr. and other female cage dancers (up to four in some episodes), one of whom was African-American, danced with an erotic frenzy previously unseen from women on network television.

Hullabaloo, like *Shindig!*, was a progressive site for racial representation. African-Americans were rarely seen on television outside of variety programs and—as the civil rights movement grew in intensity—newscasts until the mid-1960s, and then in sparse guest or supporting roles in socially conscious programs such as CBS's *East Side West Side* in the 1963–1964 television season.[47] Media historian Aniko Bodroghkozy characterizes television's "embrace of the civil rights movement" as provisional.[48] Yet, by 1965, after the passage of the Civil Rights Act in 1964, television networks sought to include more African-Americans in their programming, although not in program conception, writing, or production. Smith recalls that he went out of his way to make *Hullabaloo* diverse. Motown artists, especially, fit Smith's vision of sophisticated variety and, indeed, Smith brought more of what he called "R&B" artists onto the program as the series progressed.[49] The *Hullabaloo* Dancers were racially and ethnically mixed, and included a rare African-American woman, Barbara Alston. Filipino-American male dancer Patrick Adiarte was featured in stand-alone dance performance spots and his ethnicity was highlighted in promotional stills. *Hullabaloo*-a-Go-Go segments featured the troupe dancing with each other, sometimes resulting in racially-mixed pairs. Sammy Davis Jr. and Trini Lopez each hosted several times, and Leslie Uggams, known to prime-time viewers from her stint on *Sing Along with Mitch*, emceed an episode. Smith does not recall network complaints about the racial or ethnic backgrounds of his hosts, dancers, or performers, remembering that they were more concerned with the ratings, and that NBC's Standards and Practices called for the occasional change of a lyric.[50] *Hullabaloo* also drew upon the long-held tradition of variety programming as the only accepted space for African-American appearances on prime-time television. Coincidentally, the 1965–1966 television season saw the premiere of *I Spy*, the first show with an African-American co-star, Bill Cosby.[51]

Conclusion

Hullabaloo was ultimately a transitional program, one that attempted to bridge two show-business generations and, correspondingly, two audience cohorts. Unfortunately, its timing was poor. Most daily newspapers and popular magazines that bothered to write about the program expressed disdain for it, as they did for *Shindig!*, more because of *Hullabaloo's* presentation of rock and roll music than for its formal tele-musical qualities. Critics appeared to pre-judge *Hullabaloo* and *Shindig!*, damning them because of their audience, not because of their production. Leo Mishkin, writing in the *New York Morning Telegraph*, fumed that: "Whatever claims the TV networks have had to adult programming are now being deliberately relinquished in favor of direct, forthright appeal to the tastes of millions of potential customers still well below voting age."[52] Producer Smith made several major changes for *Hullabaloo's* second season, including more rhythm and blues music—specifically Motown acts—more mature hosts, and banning screaming.[53] Smith, although only 30 years old, also belied his musical prejudices in his description of R&B as "good" music in comparison to rock and roll.[54] *Hullabaloo* was cut to a half hour for its second and last season.

Hullabaloo was cancelled after its second season but its rock and roll inflected production innovations and style went on to define network tele-musical programming for three decades. Smith went on to form Smith-Hemion Productions with his boss from the Perry Como Show, Dwight Hemion. Smith-Hemion Productions was the primary producer of television events, including the Tony Award broadcast and several Democratic National Conventions, until the firm broke up upon Hemion's retirement in the mid-2000s. David Winters went on to produce, direct, and choreograph specials for Nancy Sinatra and Raquel Welch, among others. Steve Binder, already known to rock and roll fans for his direction of the *T.A.M.I. Show*—for years a lost artifact until its DVD reissue in 2010—made television and rock history as producer/director of Elvis Presley's 1968 "Comeback" Special, which single-handedly revived the career of the faded star.[55]

Hullabaloo had a subtler and hitherto unrecognized influence on the acceptance of rock and roll in the mainstream and its ultimate hegemony over American popular music. Peter

Matz's orchestrations of rock and roll songs, such as the Dylan songs discussed earlier, jarred the ears of the Dylan fan but at the same time presented the songs in a musical setting familiar to fans of adult pop. With *Hullabaloo*, NBC consciously courted the young adult audience who were teenagers when Elvis Presley first appeared on television, as well as those who were fans of American Bandstand and teen idols in the pre-Beatles years.[56] This was not a British Invasion audience but nor was it an audience for the adult pop that preceded and was parallel to Elvis Presley. Consequently, when the variety genre entered its last decade in the 1970s, it was with what was then known as a soft rock soundtrack: pop music with a mild rock beat, often orchestrated, and performed by singers and groups who were gentler on the eyes and minds of now older ex-1950s rock and roll fans than the rock groups and stars who appealed to younger audiences.

Hullabaloo was a traditional variety show that presented some popular rock and roll acts. It delivered exactly what producer Gary Smith promised in interviews at the time of its run, and what he and Steve Binder remembered for posterity for the Television Academy. As a rock and roll show, *Hullabaloo* failed, especially when compared to the much more spirited and youthful *Shindig!*—whose producer, Jack Good, was considerably older than both Smith and Binder. If *Hullabaloo* is considered in terms of Smith's vision for it—an updated variety show that mixed stars from the parent generation or those who were familiar from film and television with new "record acts"—it was important for the future direction of the television music and variety genres.[57] *Hullabaloo*'s emphasis on visuals and dance was mirrored in the pop genre that developed along with, and arguably because of, MTV in the 1980s.[58] Regrettably, one *Hullabaloo* hallmark found its way onto MTV in heavy metal music videos of the 1980s, but alas, those caged girls were not dancing.

Notes

1   I have published work on *Shindig!* elsewhere. See Norma Coates, "Excitement Is Made, Not Born: Jack Good, Television, and Rock and Roll," *Journal of Popular Music Studies* 25, no. 3 (September 2013), 301–325.

2   In the early 1960s, networks began to freshen, and even experiment with, new concepts for variety programs. Dancers in kick-lines were replaced, on some programs, with moves seen on the Broadway stage, and sets became cleaner and more modern. ABC's *Hootenanny*, broadcast during 1963–1964, presented folk artists in concert at several universities and colleges.

3   See, for example, Kevin J.H. Dettmar, *Is Rock Dead?* (New York: Routledge, 2006); Jack Banks, *Monopoly Television: MTV's Quest to Control the Music* (Boulder, CO and Oxford: Westview Press, 1996); Jake Austen, *TV-a-Go-Go: Rock on TV from American Bandstand to American Idol* (Chicago, IL: Chicago Review Press, 2005); Marc Weingarten, *Station to Station: The History of Rock 'n' Roll on Television* (New York: Pocket Books, 2000).

4   Historian Michel-Rolph Trouillot argues that some historical events are silenced because they are not thinkable in hegemonic discursive formations. See Michel-Rolph Trouillot, *Silencing the Past: Power and the Production of History* (Boston, MA: Beacon Press, 1995).

5 Weingarten, *Station to Station*, 127.

6 Ibid., 130.

7 I refer here to Simon Frith's assertion that television was never part of rock and its culture. See Simon Frith, "Look! Hear! The Uneasy Relationship of Music and Television," *Popular Music* 21, no. 3 (October 2002): 288.

8 Austen, *TV-a-Go-Go*, 39.

9 Ibid.

10 NBC Research Highlights, US Mss. 17AF, Box 185, Folder 3 (Madison, WI: Wisconsin Historical Society, April/May 1965).

11 Ibid.

12 Jack Hellman, "Television's Accent on Youth as New Faces Pop Up Everywhere," *Variety*, July 28, 1965, ProQuest Entertainment Industry Magazine Archive.

13 Malcolm Macfarlane and Ken Crossland, *Perry Como: A Biography and Complete Career Record* (Jefferson, NC: McFarland and Company, Inc., 1999).

14 "Gary Smith Interview," Television Academy, July 9, 2001, https://interviews.televisionacademy.com/interviews/gary-smith#interview-clips.

15 David Newman and Robert Benton, "*Hullabaloo*—It's Real GONE," *TV Guide*, June 26, 1965: 26.

16 Ibid.

17 Allen was a television polymath, moving between variety, talk, and musical programs. It was on his program that Elvis Presley appeared in a tux and tails to sing "(You Ain't Nothing But a) Hound Dog" to an actual basset hound on July 1, 1956.

18 "Steve Binder Interview, Part 1," Television Academy, March 4, 2004, https://interviews.televisionacademy.com/interviews/steve-binder#interview-clips.

19 Brian G. Rose, *Directing for Television: Conversations with American TV Directors* (Lanham, MD: Scarecrow Press, 1999), 209.

20 A higher resolution video format, increasing the standard US National Television System Committee (NTSC) video image from 525 to 1,100 lines or more.

21 Steve Binder, dir. [DVD], *T.A.M.I. Show—Collector's Edition* (Los Angeles, CA: Dick Clark Productions, 2009). Sargent had worked with Binder when the latter filmed the West Coast segment of an all-star benefit commemorating the tenth anniversary of the Brown vs. Board of Education decision, a closed-circuit broadcast that aired on May 14, 1964.

22 "Steve Binder Interview, Part 2," Television Academy, March 4, 2004, https://interviews.televisionacademy.com/interviews/steve-binder#interview-clips. Given that the performances were shot between October 28 and 29, 1964, Binder's recollection may be exaggerated. The Beatles had been on US shores for several months, as was news and other footage of fan reactions to them. Moreover, *Shindig!* was already on the air, and audience screams were audible on its soundtrack. More accurately, the *T.A.M.I. Show* may have been among the first to present a sustained image of the fervent teen audience as is, without artificially arousing it or without exhortations to "quiet down" or otherwise pathologize the behavior. Accordingly, audience shots do not focus upon individual girls in extreme cases of feminized "hysteria," but roam the audience, sometimes focusing on male youths who are physically reacting to the music. Binder's visual treatment of *T.A.M.I.*'s audience provided it, especially teenage girls, with subjectivity. He did not objectivize, or worse pathologize, them.

23 Binder would achieve his greatest and, until the re-release of the *T.A.M.I. Show* in 2009, most-lasting fame as the producer-director of the 1968 Elvis "Comeback" special.

24 Monique Mariet, "*Hullabaloo* Producer Calls a Challenge," *Chicago Tribune*, February 14, 1965, ProQuest Historical Newspapers.

25 In his Television Academy interview, Binder reveals that he persuaded Smith not to book marching bands for future programs.

26 Harold Stern, "Producer Thinks Young, Hopes for '*Hullabaloo*,'" *Hartford Courant*, January 10, 1965, ProQuest Entertainment Industry Magazine Archive.

27 Newman and Benton, "'*Hullabaloo*'—It's Real GONE," 25.

28 For a complete list of performers from both seasons see http://www.tv.com/shows/hullabaloo/episodes.

29 In his late career, Bob Dylan recorded two albums of old standards.

30 Jazz dance is a rhythmic dance style that grew out of popular dance of the early twentieth century and spread to nightclubs, the Broadway stage, films, and television. Broadway choreographer Jerome Robbins's version of jazz dance—first introduced in *On the Town* in 1945 and most recognized in 1957's *West Side Story*—blended classic dance technique, jive, and tap. *Hullabaloo*'s choreographer, David Winters, was in the film and West Coast stage production of *West Side Story*. His choreography evinces a debt to Robbins. See Billie Mahoney, "Jazz Dance," in *The International Encyclopedia of Dance*, edited by Selma Jeanne Cohen and Dance Perspectives Foundation, ebook (New York: Oxford University Press, 2005).

31 Jack Anderson, "Don't Say You're a Dancer: Choreographer David Winters Won't Settle for Typecasting," *Dance Magazine*, November 1965: 14–15.

32 "The T.A.M.I. Show," *Variety*, November 18, 1964, ProQuest Entertainment Industry Magazine Archive.

33 See Susan J. Douglas, *Where the Girls Are: Growing Up Female with the Mass Media* (New York: Times Books, 1994).

34 Julie D'Acci, "Nobody's Woman? *Honey West* and the New Sexuality," in *The Revolution Wasn't Televised: Sixties Television and Social Conflict*, edited by Lynn Spigel and Michael Curtin (New York: Routledge, 1997), 74–78.

35 Ibid., 80.

36 Moya Luckett, "Sensuous Women and Single Girls: Reclaiming the Female Body on 1960s Television," in *Swinging Single: Representing Sexuality in the 1960s*, edited by Hilary Radner and Moya Luckett (Minneapolis, MN: University of Minnesota Press, 1999), 285.

37 D'Acci, "Nobody's Woman?," 85.

38 "Steve Binder Interview, Part 2."

39 Mariet, "*Hullabaloo* Producer Calls a Challenge."

40 David Kamp, "Live at the Whisky," *Vanity Fair*, November 2000, https://www.vanityfair.com/culture/2000/11/live-at-the-whisky-david-kamp.

41 John Hoggatt, "Go-Go Finds New Twists to Keep Fad Go-Ing," *Variety*, October 16, 1965, ProQuest Entertainment Industry Magazine Archive.

42 Douglas, *Where the Girls Are*, 98.

43 See, for example, Robert Higgins, "Kicking Up Her Own *Hullabaloo*," *TV Guide*, January 15, 1966: 22–24.

44 Edmund Jr. now goes by the name Lada St. Edmund. After *Hullabaloo* she pursued a stage and screen career for a while. At the time of writing, she was on the nostalgia circuit, and

working as a personal trainer and an "ambassador against obesity in children." See http://www.ladastedmund.com/about.

45 The Scholastic Book Service published a branded *Hullabaloo* instructional book in its catalog provided to classrooms in the United States and Canada. See *The Hullabaloo Discotheque Dance Book* (New York: Scholastic Book Services, 1967).

46 Bob Lardine, "Teen Dances: Are They Indecent?," *New York Daily News*, June 27, 1965.

47 See Aniko Bodroghkozy, *Equal Time: Television and the Civil Rights Movement* (Urbana, IL: University of Illinois Press, 2012), 155–179.

48 Ibid., 7.

49 "Quick Change Artist, Gary Smith Credits Tape with 'Hullabaloo' Nod," *Variety*, April 28, 1965: 42, ProQuest Entertainment Industry Magazine Archive.

50 Gary Smith, in discussion with the author, August 17, 2007.

51 Michele Hilmes, *Only Connect: A Cultural History of American Broadcasting* (Belmont, CA: Wadsworth Publishing, 2002), 230.

52 Leo Mishkin, "Those Teen-Agers Must Be Served—*Hullabaloo*," *New York Morning Telegraph*, January 15, 1965.

53 "Quick Change Artist."

54 Ibid.

55 See Gillian Gaar, *Return of the King: Elvis Presley's Great Comeback* (London: Jawbone Press, 2010); Ian Inglis, "The Road Not Taken. Elvis Presley: Comeback Special, NBC TV Studios, Hollywood, December 3, 1968," in *Performance and Popular Music: History, Place and Time*, edited by Ian Inglis (Aldershot: Ashgate, 2006), 41–51; Peter Guralnick, *Careless Love: The Unmaking of Elvis Presley* (Boston, MA: Little, Brown and Co., 1997), 293–315.

56 That NBC was hoping to assemble a young female adult audience is clear from the products advertised on the program, which included Top Job Floor Cleaner, Maclean Toothpaste, Bayer Aspirin, Mennen's Baby Powder, and Pond's Cold Cream.

57 The term "variety genres" as I use it here refers not only to musical variety shows, but also comedy variety, awards shows, and even the more recent incarnations, reality singing and dance contests.

58 For a more detailed discussion of television music after *Hullabaloo* and before MTV, see Norma Coates, "Television Music," in *A Companion to the History of American Broadcasting*, edited by Aniko Bodroghkozy (Hoboken, NJ: John Wiley & Sons, 2018), 321–345.

7

Détournement and the Moving Image: The Politics of Representation in an Early British Punk Music Video

Karen Fournier

As one of the last pop cultural movements before MTV, early British punk may seem like an odd place to forage for examples of music videos. When early punk was in its heyday in the decade that preceded MTV, the scene was chronicled primarily by a body of still imagery comprised largely of photographs taken from within clubs or on the streets of cities like New York, Los Angeles, and London, where punks tended to congregate in the early days of the scene. Punk's still imagery fulfills the purposes proposed by the film theorist Noel Carroll, who explains that photographs of a given subject (for our purposes, a punk subject) "might be said to represent [that subject]—photos, in our culture are generally used to document."[1] In this role, punk photographs capture the essence of the scene through raw, uncensored, still images of its participants and their various interactions with each other and with those outside the subculture. Compared to later musical genres that were promoted on MTV, punk was less commonly represented through moving imagery, and many of the examples that exist reinforce the documentary purpose of photographs: that is, they represent certain visual aspects of the subculture through such records as live musical performances, interviews, or film footage of punks as they move through various urban spaces. Like snapshots brought to life, documentary films like Don Letts's *The Punk Rock Movie* (1978) or Penelope Spheeris's *The Decline of Western Civilization* (1980) seek to capture the spontaneous embodiment of punk, in this case as a live practice without the intervention of staging or direction and frequently without the knowledge or consent of their subjects. But while documentary films serve as important "true-to-life" representations of punk, they are very different in kind from the (comparatively fewer examples of) staged imagery that was created by punk film *auteurs* who used film as a calculated and deliberate mode of artistic expression. Carroll explains that cinematic narratives, or what he calls "feature films," add an important dimension to the visual field by using live images to create "fiction [which] is surely the most visible purpose for which film is used in our culture."[2] If punk documentaries find their parallel in the photographic record of punk, then punk cinema takes this one step further by crafting characters from punk subjects that populate the scene's photographic record and placing them into situations where they can act out punk's social critique. Directors like Julien Temple (*The Great Rock 'n' Roll Swindle*, 1980) and Derek Jarman (*Jubilee*, 1978) illustrate this process when they situate recognizable punk icons (like Malcolm McLaren or Jordan) into "fictions" designed to critique the music industry, in the case of the former film, and the British Monarchy, in the case of the latter.

For the purposes of this study, one important, but undertheorized, aspect of punk critique lies in the area of embodied gesture, whose contributions to that critique are overshadowed in scholarly study by discussions of the more plentiful still imagery that emerged from the scene. As a complement to existing studies of punk's photographic record by scholars like Dick Hebdige and Simon Frith, this chapter will offer an analytical template of punk gesture through a close reading of a music vignette drawn from Jarman's *Jubilee*: specifically, a punk performance of "Hail Britannia" that marks a pivotal moment in the film.[3] Borrowing and expanding upon the concept of *détournement* from studies of punk art and iconography, this chapter will seek to address how movement and gesture are enlisted by Jarman to challenge mainstream social values, mores, and behaviors. Given the oppositional nature of punk and its artwork, we need to determine what constitutes "value" in the punk subculture and to determine how punk "value" originated in the up-ending (or *détournement*) of the values of the dominant culture against which punk positioned itself.

Defining value in punk's subculture

The term "subculture" is rife with connotations of value, social position, and cultural power. It suggests a minority group embedded within a broader cultural group that finds itself at odds with the interests and values that mark the more established and privileged culture. It implies a culture that is both concealed below the surface of the larger culture and less valued by those in positions of power and authority. The seminal British punk scholar Dick Hebdige associates the term with a set of "expressive forms and rituals" performed by subordinate groups "who are … treated at different times as threats to public order and as harmless buffoons" by those who observe from within their privileged place in the dominant culture.[4] Written in 1979, this definition finds an illustration in the punk subculture for which it was proposed, whose perceived "threat to public order" famously inspired Bernard Brook Partridge (member of the Greater London Council) to pronounce, in 1976, that most punk bands "would be vastly improved by sudden death" since, in his view, "they are the antithesis of humankind."[5] Partridge viewed the punk subculture as a menace to a social order that provided him with power and prestige, and the "moral panic" that infuses his assessment of punk is precisely the reaction that any subculture would hope to engender in the dominant social group. If, as Hebdige's writings assert, a "subculture" defines itself in opposition to the interests of any individual or group that controls the means of cultural production, then the success of a subculture will be measured by the extent to which it interrogates the values of the dominant group. But this requires the subculture to be aware of, and then to expose, the mechanisms through which its members are oppressed. The problem, Hebdige explains, is that "subordinate groups are, if not controlled, then at least contained within an ideological space that does not seem at all 'ideological': which appears instead to be permanent and 'natural,' to lie outside history, to be beyond particular interests."[6] The tastes, interests, and values of the dominant group are idealized to such an extent by that group that they come to represent a worldview to which *all* members of a community or a society should "naturally" aspire and subscribe. While they are excluded from any role in the creation of this idealized culture, members of subordinate groups are given the illusion of participation in cultural production by their roles as consumers of what subcultural theorist Ross Haenfler describes as "prefabricated, shallow, homogenizing, lowest-common-denominator cultural forms [that] pacify people into complacency or even submission, reinforcing the hegemony."[7] The power of the dominant group therefore lies in its ability to reframe the passivity of the consumer role as an active ingredient in cultural production. Practically speaking, the dominant class hoodwinks the consumer into believing that the marketplace responds to their desires and conceals the more honest picture of a marketplace that manipulates those desires for profit. As Hebdige implies, the success of a subculture will be measured by its ability to identify—and uncover the biases inherent within—the ideological space that restrains it and to disrupt the authority of the group controlling that space. By contrast, an unsuccessful subculture will be one that is easily dismissed by the dominant social group as "buffoonish" and either erased or absorbed into the dominant culture, where any signifiers of resistance will be stripped of their subcultural meaning to reduce the subculture to an impotent, marketable caricature of itself.

Firmly rooted in Marxist ideology, Hebdige's early study of British punk helps to situate the topic of subculture within the broader discourse about social class and power that was a central concern of British punk. In dialogue with Hebdige's writings, Pierre Bourdieu's concept of "cultural capital" explains how dominant groups define, accumulate, command, and confer social status and power, and his study helps to frame the workings of the hegemonic group against which punks positioned themselves. Bourdieu argues that a dominant social group marks itself not only by its monopoly on the markers of power and prestige, but also by its trade in the symbolic goods that represent "cultural capital." This type of capital manifests as "a form of knowledge, an internalized code, or a cognitive acquisition which equips the social agent with empathy toward, appreciation for, or competence in deciphering cultural relations and cultural artifacts."[8] Bourdieu explains that cultural capital can be embodied "in the form of long-lasting dispositions of mind and body," objectified "in the form of cultural goods," or institutionalized as "educational qualifications."[9] Brook Partridge's status, relative to the subordinate social group that he hopes to silence, provides an illustration. His membership of the dominant group is cued in his television appearance by various signifiers of his social rank: his accent, his outward attire, his political title and the education and social networking that this implies, the bookcase and desk that are used to set the scene, and his access to television as a conduit for his message. Also implicit in his comments are other forms of cultural capital whose absence in punk performances renders the subculture ripe for his criticisms: the expectations about "proper" social behavior and respect for authority that are lacking in punk, judgments about taste and aesthetics that reflect a predisposition toward music and art preferred by the dominant class, and so on. Taken together, these signifiers grant him authority to speak about punks in the way that he does. As Bourdieu argues: "nothing classifies somebody more than the way that he or she [self-]classifies."[10]

While Bourdieu focuses principally on the structure and workings of hegemony, many of his statements prove useful in subcultural theory. If subcultures conceive themselves to be oppositional, as Hebdige asserts, then we might expect them to trade in a subterranean economy of "rejected" symbolic goods. In her study of club cultures, Sarah Thornton suggests that its antithetical up-ending of cultural values prompts a subculture to trade in a currency of "subcultural capital," comprised of knowledge, competence, and dispositions that emerge through a process of subcultural production circulated through subcultural enculturation. As the term suggests, subcultural capital can be understood as the converse of the cultural capital held by the dominant group. Where that group sees value, a subculture will see its lack, and vice versa. Similarly, the dominant group will brand the markers of subcultural "taste" as distasteful, and hegemonic tastes will be ridiculed by the subculture. In Thornton's study of club cultures, the two forms of capital are often mapped onto generational difference. She argues that club-going youth navigate between the domestic trappings (parental capital) of family life and their own subcultural capital. She explains that:

> [J]ust as books and paintings display cultural capital in the family home, so subcultural capital is objectified in the form of fashionable haircuts and well-assembled record-collections … just as cultural capital is personified in "good" manners and urbane conversation, so subcultural capital is embodied in the form of being "in the know," using (but not over-using) current slang and looking as if you were born to perform the latest dance styles.[11]

This example describes youth resistance to the parent culture in a typically middle-class environment. For members of the punk subculture, by contrast, generational identity is compounded, and perhaps even overshadowed, by class identity, while for female punks who seek to resist a patriarchy that subjugates them as women, the subculture surfaces at the intersection of generation, class, and gender. Subcultural capital in punk is therefore constructed to contest the authority of a patriarchy that disempowers, and thereby emasculates, working-class males and silences and infantilizes their female counterparts.

Making subcultural capital from cultural capital

For Thornton, subcultural capital is constructed in opposition to, and is therefore seemingly different in kind from, the cultural capital held in esteem by the parent culture. Given the different artifacts that they value (books versus records) or dispositions that they embrace (urbane conversation versus slang), the parent and youth groups that she describes inhabit entirely different social spheres that appear, at least on their surface, to have few meaningful points of intersection. By contrast to Thornton's youth club cultures, the punk subculture does not eschew the cultural capital of the dominant group. Instead, punk's subcultural capital often emerges from incursions into the dominant space, from a place where tokens of power and prestige are strategically identified, hijacked, and turned against the culture from which they were stolen in the process called *détournement*. Greil Marcus explains that the *détourned* artifacts and dispositions for which punk has become known reflect the aims of the subculture as "a politics of subversive quotation, of cutting the vocal cords of every empowered speaker, social symbols yanked through the looking glass, misappropriated words and pictures diverted into familiar scripts and blowing them up."[12]

The origins of *détournement* and its practice of symbolic violence can be traced to the French situationist movement that influenced such key punk figures as the Sex Pistols' erstwhile manager Malcolm McLaren, the punk artist Jamie Reid, and the fashion designer Vivienne Westwood, to name just three. Situationist discussions of *détournement* help to explain how punk found multivalence in cultural artifacts whose meanings might have seemed unequivocal to those in the dominant culture and how punk embraced these artifacts as tokens of subcultural resistance to class and, for some, to gender oppression.

Founded in 1957, but more commonly connected to the May 1968 uprisings in France, Situationist International (or SI) was a radical movement whose central concept of "the society of the spectacle" is encapsulated in a treatise of the same name written and published by Guy Debord in 1967.[13] Although it dissolved in 1972, the SI movement made prescient and seemingly timeless observations about what it perceived to be the emptiness of a consumer culture in which power and influence are consolidated at the top of the economic ladder and where the "masses" are placated by the illusion of power doled out to them in the form of consumer choice. Situationists argue that the dominant group imposes value on objects and ideas (and, by implication, determines what has no value) and that these beliefs filter down to the masses through the mass media. In "the society of the spectacle," the state of "being" has been replaced by the state of "having," and subjective experience is suppressed and replaced by a life driven by the accumulation of goods whose meanings and value have been objectively determined by those in positions of power. Those at the bottom of the economic ladder find themselves distracted from the imbalances in power by the pursuit of "valued" commodities and by the futile quest to replicate the ever-changing and unattainable lifestyle touted by the ruling class. The situationists maintain that modern life has been reduced to a spectacle for the masses, whose everyday lives are constructed for, and not by, them. Debord explains that:

[W]hen images chosen and constructed by *someone else* have everywhere become the individual's principal connection to the world he formerly observed for himself, it has certainly not been forgotten that these imagines can tolerate anything and everything; because within the same image all things can be juxtaposed without contradiction. The flow of images carries everything before it, and it is similarly someone else who controls at will this simplified *summary of the sensible world*; who decides where the flow will lead as well as the rhythm of what should be shown, leaving no time for reflection, and entirely independent of what the spectator might understand or think of it.[14]

To regain control over the "summary of the sensible world" requires situationists to remove any barriers between the viewer and "the images" that represent the world, and to relocate the subjectivity of the spectator at the center of any search for meaning and value. In place of a mediated experience in which the value of cultural capital is decided by those in power, Debord imagines a world in which value is determined by whatever "the spectator might understand or think of it." He urges his reader to rethink the potential of tokens of cultural capital to signify in ways that may or may not be sanctioned by those whose interests they represent, and to consider how the meanings and values that might be attached to these tokens can change according to the unique social and cultural perspective of the individual viewer. By seizing control of the evaluation of hegemonic capital, situationism thereby blurs the line between cultural and subcultural capital and invites the incorporation of the former into the realm of the latter for the purposes of social critique and, ideally, social change. When this incorporation exposes the bias inherent in the meanings assigned by the dominant group through the "subversive quotation" of images, as it often does in punk, we find examples of *détournement* at work.

The semiotic landscape of the British punk subculture provides fertile ground for illustrations of *détournement*, but given that my purpose is to focus on the under-theorized realm of punk *détournement* in the moving image, I will illustrate the subcultural contexts of situationist theory with only one familiar example: punk's (mis)use of the Queen's personal Royal Stewart tartan. To appreciate the "subversive" quality of this appropriation, one has to understand the meanings that have been attached to the image by the dominant culture. The fabric represents the Queen and traces its history back to the founding of the House of Stewart in 1371. Because of its historical association with the Monarchy, the tacit understanding among mainstream designers has been that the tartan should only be used with her permission, although the design also has been embraced by the Scottish Register of Tartans as a "universal tartan" that can be used by anyone who has no personal clan tartan. Given its significance to members of the dominant class, the appearance of the Royal Stewart tartan in punk is an artful example of a subversive quotation and a powerful symbol of subcultural capital. When Vivienne Westwood appropriated the tartan for her famous bondage trousers, it exposed the subservience and oppression experienced by the Queen's working-class subjects, and the confined nature of the bondage trousers, themselves, brought other meanings to bear on the fabric. Legs strapped together suggest the imprisonment of the working-class wearer within the British class system, while zippers and safety pins imply their fruitless attempts to escape. The safety pin also can be read as a commentary on the perception of a fragile and eroding British Empire whose remaining territories are precariously "pinned together" beneath the banner of the Monarch. Finally, the tartan's authorized use by those who have no clan affiliation contributes to its subcultural cachet as the signifier of the British-born outsider who finds no clan within their home country. In his history of the tartan, Jonathan Faiers probes deeper when he claims that punk's use of the tartan points to an earlier time when Scotland was a credible military threat to England. He explains that "the history of tartan as a fabric expressive of revolt and opposition, its remarkable status as a cloth outlawed by the English and its association with royalty made it the perfect textile for a range of clothing that aimed to make anarchy, alienation, and indeed sedition wearable."[15]

The "spectacle" of the moving image

In most studies of punk, examples of *détournement* emerge from a catalogue of still images that chronicle the visual history of the subculture. By comparison, the moving image has been overlooked as a means of "subversive quotation" in punk. This oversight is surprising because of the centrality of film (and later, video) to what situationists describe as the "spectator culture" governed by those who "used cinema as a means of regulation and control—a repackaging of the spectacle that prevents meaningful exploration, interaction or critique within the spectacularized world."[16] The moving image therefore holds enormous potential for a critique of the dominant culture whose values and perspectives it reflects. Indeed, situationists such as Guy Debord and René Viénet often turned to the medium of film to illustrate their doctrine. Given punk's appeal to situationist philosophy in other facets of its visual field, it seems logical to assume that these practices also inform the subculture's moving image. If we take this hypothesis to be true, then films produced by Debord and Viénet, and their musings on the potential of film to serve as cultural critique, provide a preliminary conceptual framework for an analysis of *détournement* in the moving image.

In his study of the films produced within the SI movement, the historian Thomas Levin identifies three *détournement* strategies that emerge from the appropriation and reinterpretation of structural components of a film: (1) the insertion of new text or dialogue into or onto an existing film; (2) the creation of hybridized object, or *bricolage*, from appropriated visual imagery; and (3) the inversion of values touted by the film industry.[17] In instances where they employ *détournement*, punk videos tend to make use of the last two of these strategies, and examples from situationist film show how this might work in punk.

In the case of *bricolage*, Viénet encourages the filmmaker to "appropriate [the cinema's] most accomplished and modern examples, those that have escaped the ideology of art to an even greater extent than American B-movies: I mean, of course, newsreels, trailers, and most of all filmed advertisements," since each of these represents a form of coercion that can be isolated, deconstructed, and turned against its capitalist producer.[18] As an illustration, Debord's situationist film *The Society of the Spectacle* (1973) constructs its critique of mass culture from an assemblage of contemporary television advertisements, Hollywood movie clips, historical news footage, and still photographs, all of which accompany a script comprised of political slogans and quotations from authors like Marx, Machiavelli, and Debord. As I apply this analytic lens to moving clips that feature punk performance, I see the bricolage concept transferring to the assemblage of stylistic and performative elements that play out on the body of the performer. For instance, the clothing and outward appearance personifies the act of *bricolage*, and when the punk body is inserted into a video and therefore set in motion in a narrative, elements like the setting, characters and identities, dialogue, gesture, vocalizations, diegetic and non-diegetic sounds, and plot contribute to the act of *détournement*. For the purposes of my transfer of the concept to the domain of punk, however, sources of *détournement* are found beyond the propaganda films identified by Viénet. While he counsels the filmmaker to turn examples of these films against the dominant culture, punks see "propaganda" in *any* token of that culture. An example of this is the aforementioned appropriation of the tartan, which punks view as a form of "advertisement" for, and thereby a representation of the hegemony of, the Monarch and the ruling class that she symbolizes; in this regard, the tartan functions as a form of punk propaganda.

Analysis of *bricolage* in video is similar to its interpretation in the still image, with a few notable exceptions. Plucked out of its original context and fused to unrelated imagery, each element of a visual collage relies on the viewer to posit meanings from its relationship to its exterior source and to any other unmoored imagery with which it coexists in the image, and this is true both of still and moving images. In the case of film, however, the *détourned* artifact is placed in a dynamic relationship with other artifacts that move in and out of its orbit and contribute dynamically to its meanings. As an example, the appearance of the Royal Stewart tartan in a punk film or video retains any meanings that are attached to its portrayal in still imagery, but the moving image also allows the tartan to be subjected to movement (it can be torn, frayed, or otherwise mutilated in unfolding time by a particular character, in a specific space, to highlight an aspect of an unfolding narrative). A host of new, and additional, meanings come to be attached to the *détourned* artifact when it becomes a prop that is manipulated by a character in a punk narrative.

Levin's third category also proposes that situationist film can interrogate the hegemony within the film industry, and the concomitant passivity that it imposes on the spectator, by rejecting anything that evokes the cinema produced by the dominant culture. He suggests that situationist film would "let the heroes be some more or less historical people who are close to us, connect the events of the inept scenario to the real reasons which we understand are behind the actions, and connect them also to the events of the current week. Here you have an acceptable collective distraction."[19] To uncover cinematic bias toward the dominant culture, this approach would rely on an artistic inversion of dominant aesthetic values in film, so that "stars" are replaced by "anti-stars," images and situations that are typically hidden from view become foregrounded, narratives that idealize or romanticize mainstream life are exchanged for candid and uncensored depictions of everyday life, ugliness is embraced over beauty, and so on. Additionally, the punk music video also prompts us to examine who performs the song, how aspects of the song are underscored kinetically by the body or highlighted by the voice, and how resistance to the dominant culture emerges from this embodiment and performance. Finally, the plot or storyline of the video can also contribute to punk's *détournement* of the dominant culture in cases where punk hijacks or lampoons a narrative from that culture to uncover dominant preconceptions and to challenge a dominant gaze that would dismiss punk as "freakish" or not worthy of the spectator.

The moving image as cultural critique

In her ground-breaking work on music video analysis, Carol Vernallis advises the analyst of video narrative to examine "the dynamic relation between the song and the image as they unfold in time."[20] In the context of punk, I argue here that the relation between song and image is embedded within a deeper social relationship between an occupying and a vanquished class. As the voice and embodiment of the music video, the vanquished class speaks and gestures through the appropriated and repurposed cultural capital. This process finds its dramatic expression in film, which I will now illustrate in an analysis of the video "Rule Britannia," from Derek Jarman's *Jubilee* (1978).[21]

Filmed partially on location in areas of London that still bore the scars of the Blitz, the film from which this video originates paints a bleak picture of the country's future through a story that peers backwards in time to the "golden age" of Elizabethan England. This glorified era is invoked as a counter-pose to England's pockmarked present as the country struggles to rebuild its poorer neighborhoods thirty years after they were scarred or destroyed in the Blitz. The dystopian narrative exposes the hidden perspective of the British working-class youths who populate the film and for whom there was little to celebrate during England's 1977 Jubilee year. Since its release, the film has been embraced as a cult masterpiece whose critique of the royal family is enacted by such punk artists as Adam Ant, Wayne County, and Jordan (née Pamela Rooke, whose association with Vivienne Westwood and Malcolm McLaren's SEX boutique placed her squarely in the middle of the London punk scene).

The film opens onto a scene in which Queen Elizabeth I is transported into present-day England by her court alchemist and the angel Ariel. Once there, she is dismayed to witness an unraveling Empire inhabited by violent punk gangs, paramilitary groups, and vapid television executives who vie against each other for power after Queen Elizabeth II has been murdered in a mugging gone awry. The punks are represented by a group of females who coalesce around the Queen's murderer—a cunning and vicious female character named "Bod"—and who are instructed in the ways of life by a thoughtful philosopher, "Amyl Nitrate" (played by the punk icon Jordan). In the first "lesson" delivered to her gang, Amyl encapsulates the central thesis of the film when she reflects back on the time of the 1977 Jubilee and explains that "in those days, desires weren't allowed to become reality, so fantasy was substituted for them. Films, books, pictures. They called it 'art.' But when your desires become reality, you don't need fantasy any longer. Or art."[22] With its reference to the passive spectator of an idealized life constructed and portrayed in "films, books, and pictures" and its claim that in freedom resides the rejection of the imposed spectacle in favor of an active engagement with subjective desires, Amyl's rhetoric echoes that of Debord's *The Society of the Spectacle*. But the influence of situationism does not end there.

The film alternates between scripted scenes and musical vignettes, the former of which propel the story forward while the latter provide moments of reflection on the dystopian tale that frames them. Some of these vignettes exist for posterity as stand-alone music videos, of which "Rule Britannia" is likely the most famous. In the context of the film, this musical number occurs just before the midway point of the movie, once the struggle for power and control has been clearly defined and the characters engaged in the struggle have been delineated. The video places Amyl on a stage before a trio of judges, one of whom contextualizes the scene when he exclaims "She's England's entry for the Eurovision contest. She's my number-one!" (0:11). Meeting these media executives on their own turf, Amyl aims to undermine their bid for authority in a performance that lampoons a contest that is closely aligned with the production of their cultural capital. Her performance, which is simultaneously serious and silly, underscores the inherent spectatorship of the Eurovision enterprise, but, perhaps more importantly, helps her to reclaim the stage as a space endowed with power and to relegate the vacuous judges to the role of the spectator in a spectacle that she creates for them. The Eurovision setting is thereby turned against the dominant culture that finds its representation in the film's "media executives." Along with this inversion of power roles, Amyl also inverts the role that she plays in the narrative. As the antithesis of anything that might be deemed "acceptable" or "tasteful" by the dominant culture that controls the Eurovision contest, this "anti-star" nonetheless claims the role of "England's entry." Her clothing, make up, vocal style, and performance gestures are intended to parody her appropriated popular music counterparts and to offend the sensibilities of the dominant culture. In the context of a film that pits punks against their judges, "Rule Britannia" suggests a punk victory over a dominant culture that is portrayed as vapid and uncritical.

While the appropriation of the Eurovision contest as the central conceit of the video serves as an artful example of a *détourned* cultural event, the music and vocal performance practices enlisted by Amyl to highlight her "talents" to the judges are similarly hijacked from the dominant culture. "Rule Britannia" is a patriot song that was written by Thomas Arne in 1740 and has strong associations with the Royal Navy. Like the film's reference to Elizabethan England, the song hearkens back to a "golden era" in British military history when the country "ruled the waves." But this rendition of the song quickly sours as the singer edits the self-aggrandizing lyrics to a mere two lines before giving way to the familiar chorus. Like the torn Union Jack that has become emblematic of punk, the drastic cuts to the text drain it of any "pomp and circumstance," instead pointing to an Empire whose military triumphs have dwindled. Further, the lyrics of the second verse are replaced by the non-diegetic sound of a Nazi rally energized by the fanatical voice of Adolf Hitler. The freedom from tyranny seemingly enjoyed by post-war Britons and referenced in that verse (and in the chorus) is *détourned* by this sonic reference to a war whose economic effects continued to be felt by the British underclass well into the 1970s. Finally, those unfamiliar with the lyrics of the opening verse might have trouble comprehending the text because of certain performance decisions made by Jordan. Like an ill-trained operatic singer, the character Amyl embellishes her performance with an exaggerated and grating coloratura that satirizes a genre of music that is valued by the dominant culture and the opera divas who bring that genre to life. From an aural standpoint, the video "yanks" a patriotic song through the "looking glass" of faux-opera in the service of an embodied critique of the dominant culture that both represent.

Jordan's personification of the text through the Amyl Nitrate character is also an important feature of this dynamic illustration of *détournement*. She appears on a smoke-filled stage clad in a dress constructed from two faded Union Jacks that are stitched together at the shoulder. Open on both sides, the dress reveals black lingerie and a garter belt that attaches to a pair of lurid electric-green sheers. Amyl accessorizes this with pink gloves, a red fan, an ancient Roman *galea*, and a trident. This visual *bricolage* equates modern-day Britain with the failed Roman Empire, while the red cross that is foregrounded on Amyl Nitrate's tunic also recalls another failed military power, the Knights Templar. The smoky evocation of war coupled with the mirrored "strip club" vibe of the stage suggests that Britain has sold itself for an illusion of political power. A deeper interpretation of the visuals of the video emerges from the synergy between the costume, the stage, and the moving image, and the video invites us to examine how gesture might contribute to cultural critique through *détournement*.

In the interests of space, I would like to focus on what the film-music theorist Claudia Gorbman has termed "mutual implication" between the song, the setting, and a selection of gestures in the video that seem important either because of their recurrence or their placement within the narrative.[23] These gestures include what I describe as the "pole dance/trident thrust," the "ballet extension" and "fan flutter," the "goose-step," the "lip-sync," and the "farewell bum wiggle."

When she appears in the video for the first time, Amyl's actions appear to signify defiance and patriotic pride as she emphasizes the word "Britannia" with the wave of her fan and the rap of her trident on the floor (0:14). The pink fan, as a token of female sexuality, and trident, as a symbol of male military power, become important props in the performance to come. The opening defiance represented by the trident quickly gives way to a scene that resembles a "pole dance," as Amyl strokes her body with the fan, kicks one leg high in the air to expose her black panties, and gyrates around that object. At this point in the narrative, her gestures reinforce the meanings attached to a stage name redolent with suggestions of drug abuse, club cultures, and cheap sexual encounters. More importantly, the trident begins to lose its militaristic connotation and, instead, becomes a mere prop. As the verse ends, Amyl places the trident between her legs in a move to parody, and seizes control over the phallic masculine power embodied by the military that is referenced in the song (0:59). She emasculates the British Navy with this gesture, and by extension the dominant culture that it symbolizes, and simultaneously weaponizes her own sexuality—a sexuality that is meant to be silent and submissive in the eyes of the dominant culture. After being drained of its power, the "trident thrust" that subsequently accompanies the first chorus (and its kinetic enactment of the phrase "Britons never will be slaves") seems drained of any real power (1:26). Indeed, even before she can complete that gesture and set the trident back on the floor of the stage, the song has moved on to the second verse and the non-diegetic soundtrack that is superimposed on it (1:33).

Before turning to this verse, however, it is also important to highlight some smaller gestures that are *détourned* during the performance's opening verse. In the same way that the faux-coloratura vocal style serves to challenge the tastes of the dominant class, a couple of gestures within this portion of the video similarly critique that class. One of these is the "leg extension" gesture, performed twice and both times with obvious difficulty, which yanks a familiar gesture out of the ballet world and places it into a scene that is more reminiscent of a strip club (0:44). The appearance of this gesture in a foreign context challenges the idealized female form in dance while it also exposes the irony that lies behind the commodification of art. (Since we pay to see ballet, just as we pay to see a strip show, who determines what is art?) Another gesture that is appropriated from the dominant culture is the "fan wave," performed several times during the first verse and evocative of a demure, coy lady of the Royal Court who conceals her sexual desires behind a shield of feathers (e.g., at 1:20). Mapped against other features that mark the performer's look and attitude, the gesture can only be read as a satirical critique of conventional norms that dictate and constrain female behavior.

The second verse of the British patriotic song is overdubbed by an audio clip from a speech by Adolf Hitler (at 1:32). The clip begins with the sound of the cheering crowd that was heard in the opening moments of the video, but which is finally provided with its context here. Amyl's seeming defiance in the face of potential enslavement by a conquering power now seems impotent as she performs a robot-like "goose-step" march to the speech in her *bricolage* attire. Her reaction implies that the speaker has emerged as victorious over her, despite the resistance to enslavement uttered in the chorus of the song and in the description of freedom that comprises the missing lyrics of this second verse. Through its sonic and gestural references to the Third Reich, combined with signifiers of a crumbling British Empire, the video draws an admittedly ham-fisted parallel between the losing Axis powers and those among the Allied powers on the "winning" side whose lives had not improved despite the outcome of the war. We might go so far as to suggest a punk identification with the earlier Weimar Republic, whose crushing defeat and subsequent humiliation in 1918 was the basis for the Nazi party (with the further implication that any type of humiliation—e.g., of the British working class—potentially can lead to similarly disastrous consequences). If one aim of *détournement* is to challenge and critique the values of the dominant culture by foregrounding and re-enacting a forbidden narrative (and thereby exposing the cultural perspective inherent in any determination of "good" versus "bad" taste), this moment provides an illustration.

With a short hop, shoulder shimmy, and a flip of the fan (1:51), Amyl abandons the goose-step to resume the chorus, but this is short lived and is interrupted once again by overdubbed cheers from the Nazi rally. The strategic placement of cheers in the video—as she enters the stage or as she completes the defiant words and "trident thrust" of each chorus—finds its parallel in the cheers of the mainstream audience who show their appreciation at a Eurovision contest. Entertainment and politics become conflated through a sonic signifier of the passive and uncritical consumption of a reality constructed for the spectator by an all-powerful authority.

Where we might expect a third verse, the song reiterates the lyrical hook while it cuts to a close-up of Jordan's face. Lyrics that express resistance to enslavement are replaced by the sound of the Blitz. From a gestural point of view, the viewer is made keenly aware that the performance in this passage is lip-synced when sound and image fail to line up (2:31). The lack of attention to detail in the editing is doubtless intentional here and parodies the careful editing that lies behind the artifice of mainstream filmed performances (that are, in the case of many musical acts, also lip-synced). The chorus thereby performs a *détournement* of slick mainstream production values and exposes the inherent deceit of any spectacularized scene fed to the masses. Additionally, the association between the "lip-sync" gaffe and the sound of the air-raid siren interrogates the willful use of entertainment as an escape from, or a way to ignore, chaos and crisis. The closing scene therefore conflates the Blitz with the "social panic" engendered by punk in observers like Brook Partridge, and appropriates the well-known history of the former as a warning about the future.

In Ken Puckett's interpretation of the film, "*Jubilee* is … a comment on a mode of political sovereignty that directly links the violence of the past, present, and future."[24] This violence is signified, sung, and embodied in a narrative that turns tokens of the dominant culture against itself as if to say "what goes around, comes around." In the end, this dystopian narrative concludes with a gesture that, while surprising, should not be totally unexpected. In place of a thankful and hopeful Eurovision contestant, we are left with the closing image of a rear end clothed in see-through black panties (2:44). As a farewell gesture, the "bum wiggle," coupled with a dismissive wave of the fan, reiterates many of the tropes that comprise the video but, ultimately, stands as a parting token of resistance to judgment.

Few studies of punk and the moving image exist in scholarly literature, which is not surprising given that punk's visual record is overwhelmingly populated by still imagery. Despite its comparative absence in the scholarship about punk, the moving image provides missing details about the use of gesture in social critique. As "Britannia" illustrates, issues of class and gender coalesce into a critique of the British ruling class that uses gesture as a mode of resistance. In some instances, this critique involves a parody of the ruling class through the punk *détournement* of embodied gestures that mark that class (the wave of a fan or the thrust of a trident). In other cases, critique is constructed from brazen appropriations of forbidden gestures (like the Nazi goose-step) or from engagement with behaviors that would be deemed elicit in the "polite company" of the ruling class (like overtly sexual gestures). In the end, "Rule Britannia" provides a compelling illustration of how the moving image adds a new critical dimension to a visual record that is already rife with signifiers of resistance.

Notes

1   Noel Carroll, *Theorizing the Moving Image* (Cambridge: Cambridge University Press, 1996), 45.
2   Ibid., 46–47.
3   Early examples of studies that engage with punk's still iconography include Simon Frith and Howard Horne, *Art into Pop* (London: Methuen, 1987) and Dick Hebdige, *Subculture: The Meaning of Style* (London: Methuen, 1979).
4   Hebdige, *Subculture*, 2.
5   From a 1976 televised speech by Bernard Brooke-Partridge (Greater London Council). Quoted in David Huxley, "Ever Get the Feeling You've Been Cheated?: Anarchy and Control in the Great Rock 'n' Roll Swindle," in *Punk Rock, So What? The Cultural Legacy of Punk*, edited by Roger Sabin (London: Routledge, 1999), 95.

6   Hebdige, *Subculture*, 16.

7   Ross Haenfler, *Subcultures: The Basics* (London: Routledge, 2014), 8.

8   Pierre Bourdieu, *The Field of Cultural Production: Essays on Art and Literature*, translated and edited by Randal Johnson (New York: Columbia University Press, 1993), 8.

9   Pierre Bourdieu, "The Forms of Capital," reprinted in *Handbook of Theory and Research for the Sociology of Education*, edited by John G. Richardson (Westport, CT: Greenwood, 1986), 242.

10   Pierre Bourdieu, *In Other Words: Essays Towards a Reflexive Sociology*, translated by Matthew Adamson (Stanford, CA: Stanford University Press, 1990), 132.

11   Sarah Thornton, *Club Cultures: Music, Media, and Subcultural Capital* (Hanover, NH: Wesleyan University Press, 1996), 11–12.

12   Greil Marcus, *Lipstick Traces: A Secret History of the Twentieth Century* (Cambridge, MA: Harvard University Press, 1989), 179.

13   Guy Debord, *The Society of the Spectacle*, translated and annotated by Ken Knabb (Berkeley, CA: Bureau of Public Secrets, 2014 [originally published as *La Société du Spéctacle*, Paris: Buchet-Chastel, 1967]).

14   Guy Debord, *Comments on the Society of the Spectacle*, translated by Malcolm Imrie (London: Verso, 1998 [originally published in French by Editions Gérard Lébovici, 1988]), 27–28.

15   Jonathan Faiers, *Tartan: Textiles that Changed the World* (Oxford: Berg Publishers, 2008), 98.

16   Deron Albright, "Tales of the City: Applying Situationist Practices to the Analysis of the Urban Drama," *Criticism* 45, no. 1 (2003): 95.

17   Thomas Y. Levin, "Dismantling the Spectacle: The Cinema of Guy Debord," in *On the Passage of a Few People through a Rather Brief Moment in Time: The Situationist International 1957–1972*, edited by Elizabeth Sussman (Cambridge, MA: MIT Press, 1989), 76–81.

18   René Viénet, "The Situationists and the New Forms of Action against Politics and Art," in *Guy Debord and the Situationist International: Texts and Documents*, edited by Tom McDonough (Cambridge, MA: MIT Press, 2002), 184.

19   Levin, "Dismantling the Spectacle," 77.

20   Carol Vernallis, *Experiencing Music Video: Aesthetics and Cultural Context* (New York: Columbia University Press, 2004), 4.

21   *Jubilee* [film], directed by Derek Jarman (London: Whaley-Main Productions/ Megalovision, 1978), available on YouTube, https://www.youtube.com/ watch?v=aFRg5pLD9EI&list=RDaFRg5pLD9EI&start_radio=1.

22   Derek Jarman, "Part 1: Beyond the Endless City," ibid.

23   Claudia Gorbman, *Unheard Melodies: Narrative Film Music* (Bloomington, IN: Indiana University Press, 1987).

24   Kent Puckett, *War Pictures: Cinema, History, and Violence in Britain, 1939–1945* (New York: Fordham University Press, 2017), 196.

8

Post-Digital Music Video and Genre: Indie Rock, Nostalgia, Digitization, and Technological Materiality

Robert Strachan

Digitization has had a profound effect upon the ways in which music videos are created and viewed. Various stylistic trends such as the integration of handheld footage and improvised street scenes drawn from amateur YouTube videos;[1] the move from a fragmented aesthetic toward clearly understandable concepts and visual "hooks";[2] the rise of new music video styles such as interactive video, mash-ups, and user-generated video;[3] a turn toward risk-taking, "edgier" images and subject matter,[4] and the increased hyper-sexualizing of female artists as "clickbait"[5] have been read as indicative of post-digital aesthetics. The digital turn also has seen the rise of prosumer technologies (such as digital camcorders and editing apps), which have brought High Definition (HD) images and professional-level production values to an unprecedented swathe of the consumer market. The development and adoption of these technologies has somewhat levelled the playing field within music video production. As the HD image becomes ubiquitous, user-friendly editing packages allow for the visual language of music video to be instinctively replicated and progressed. As a result, the perceptible differences between videos commissioned by multinational music companies, DIY musicians, and amateurs have become increasingly blurred. Simultaneously, the reduction of the costs of bringing new products to the market has led to an over-saturated digital landscape in which thousands of new music videos are uploaded daily.

Yet, for all the digital push afforded by the emergence of new technologies of production and cultures of consumption, there is also an identifiable analog pull within post-millennial music video. A significant tranche of music video makers have turned to older, outmoded formats and technologies in their work. A broad strain of contemporary music video production regularly uses technologies such as 8 millimeter, 16 millimeter, and 35 millimeter analog film, video formats such as Betacam and Vertical Helical Scan (VHS), and broadcast analog cameras. Such is the attraction of these pre-digital technologies that a concomitant strain in contemporary video production is the use of digital post-production techniques to simulate their visual feel and surface textures. Both of these trends indicate that the aesthetic values and visual affordances of differing historical eras of audiovisual representation hold important signifying power in contemporary popular music culture. It is this appropriation of the technologies of the past that forms the core of this chapter.[6] Drawing on examples from contemporary indie rock and indie pop, the chapter examines the generic coding of music video through its technological materiality. Using case-study videos shot employing Super 8 and VHS, it examines how music videos in the post-digital era draw upon interwoven histories of popular music and visual cultures, and broader mediated discourses related to memory in their production of authenticity.

Technological materiality

The central assertion of this chapter is that the visual surfaces of contemporary music videos have a tremendous impact upon their semiotic and affective purchase. In order to unpack this analytical line of enquiry, a key theoretical concept is technological materiality. More specifically, I will argue that the technologies used to produce music and video leave textual traces that have significant experiential and symbolic power, and are key in situating individual music videos within nuanced systems of signification. In a general sense we can think of materiality as it is formulated by Katherine Hayles as a "selective focus on certain physical aspects of an instantiated text that are foregrounded by a work's construction, operation, and content."[7] What I am particularly interested in here is that a central aspect of technological materiality is its marking and signification of time and historical sense. This marking is both literal and metaphorical in that the signification of time is often achieved through the material patterning of the surface of the text, layered onto the image beneath. As Giuliana Bruno notes: "a visual text is also textural for the ways in which it can show the patterns of history, in the form of a coating, a film or a stain. One can say that a visual text can even wear its own history, inscribed as an imprint onto its textural surface."[8] This process is inherently bound up with the specific technologies used in a text's realization. Given the rapid turnover of media technologies, material properties form a key part in the way we apprehend historical periodization in media texts. Thus, as Brian Larkin points out in a discussion of Nigerian cinema: "media technologies do not just store time, they represent it,"[9] and further, "the materiality of media creates the physical details and the quotidian sensory uses through which these experiences [of historical place] are formed."[10] In other words, surfaces signify time and place, and have sensory qualities that evoke emotional responses linked to personal and collective memory. Further, media surfaces are simultaneously intertextual in that they draw upon a vast store of historical works, which share their means of production, and bring to mind the personal and social contexts in which the given media was consumed.

This idea of a material representation of time is crucial in understanding the use of outmoded technologies in contemporary music video. A key suggestion of this chapter is that technological materiality provides a primary point of entry into the generic coding of a text and is bound up with relevant genre discourses and meanings. Reading music video in this way aligns with Carmela Garritano's analysis of Ghanaian film, which she suggests "foregrounds the technological materiality and experiential dimensions of genre" through a reading of "the electronic signals scored onto analog [media] … or converted into digital data and then translated onto the screen as aural and visual effects."[11] While the concept of technological materiality has begun to be explored in art theory[12] and (especially post-colonial) film studies,[13] its application to music video necessitates an interrogation of the audiovisual that can be fruitful for expanding the analytical possibilities of the term. In film, sound accompanies, underpins, or supports on-screen action, thereby assisting in the communication of mood, emotion, characterization, etc. Music video differs in that the sonic is always foregrounded and the decisions made by the video maker are self-consciously constructed in relation to musical structure, genre, and other associative conventions. Music video therefore foregrounds the way in which technological materiality is inherently multi-discursive in audiovisual texts in that sonic and visual affordances simultaneously signify, and can interact, harmonize, and clash, in ways that are meaningful and nuanced. In music video, particular types of film and video stock, editing techniques, visual effects, and post-production all signify historical filmic eras but also draw upon the specificities of their historical use within the mediation and cultural documentation of popular music. As I explore below, the technologically mediated surface texture of an image—such as the graininess of Super 8, VHS tracking lines, drop-outs, common types of image distortion, and coloration—is semiotically charged with nuanced and specific historical trajectories related to particular musical forms. At the same time, that surface texture maintains a more conceptual relationship to genre related to aesthetics, ideologies, and political economies, articulated through its interaction with the sonic affordances of a text.

Materiality and multi-discursive affordance

A deeper analytic concentration on the material aspects of music videos is also highly pertinent as this approach has the potential to unpack an aspect of popular music culture that has been hitherto understudied: that is, the importance of technological materiality in popular music culture more generally. Given the domination of recorded sound from the beginnings of the twentieth century, the histories, aesthetics, and meanings of popular music have been connected to its physical capturing. In an age when the recording had become popular music's "autographic work,"[14] its textual articulations, conventions, and progressions have been bound up with recording and playback technologies.[15] In this sense, recorded popular music has always constituted a materialist culture in which the physical attributes and surfaces of sound carriers *mean something*. The tangible textures of music's means of capture and the physical limitations of its listening technologies constitute major ways in which we experience music, understand its historical periodization, and attribute value to it. This century of foregrounded materiality is entwined with the DNA of popular music culture and remains a spectral force in a post-physical sound-carrier era. Indeed, the continuing presence and importance of material culture within the consumption, meanings, and identity play associated with popular music are perpetuated in a dialectic with "music's newfound 'thin air' cloud-based intangibility."[16]

Technological materiality also transfers to audiovisual representations. Popular music has always been a multi-discursive form with dispersed textual sites that contribute to its meanings.[17] As the consumption of music becomes more audiovisual, this relationship is becoming even more imbricated. In this regard, I address the pressing need to examine both the sonic and visual surfaces of popular music in relation to each other. As I have argued elsewhere,[18] many post-millennial music genres reflect a cultural turn facilitated by digitization in which past styles and aesthetics are appropriated and adapted using material sourced through video-sharing sites. Sites such as YouTube act as seemingly infinite archives of source materials in which videos carry with them the signifying power of their surfaces. For example, electronic music genres—such as hauntology, vaporwave, and lo-fi (low-fidelity) house—not only utilize the instrumentation and technological materiality of past musical eras (analog and frequency modulation synthesis [FM synth], drum machines, and samplers), but also draw upon samples culled from films and VHS cassettes, and include the textural grain and surface noise of the mediated past (vinyl crackle, VHS-style drop-outs, the muffling caused by the limited frequency range of cassette tapes). Within these genres, the properties of visual technologies and the way they carry signification are in some ways as important as audio in terms of their function as post-digital textual resources. Their musical aesthetics are informed by a simultaneous appropriation of the sonic and visual past that is indicative of an increasing audiovisuality in the consumption of music in the post-digital era.

The multi-discursive affordances of the infinite audiovisual archive are highly significant. Alexander Jensenius, for example, notes that it is now normative for listeners to experience music as "a multimodal experience through audio-visual integration in various multimedia devices,"[19] arguing that music should be studied as a "multimodal phenomenon," which includes an acknowledgment of the visual as well as the sonic.[20] For Michael Webb, these multimodal engagements with music are part of a wider "clip culture"[21] in which particular modes of engagement are facilitated by YouTube and other video-sharing sites. Clip culture also enables a grazing across historical periods in which audiovisual textures appear next to each other, calling attention to the contrasts in their visual and sonic properties. All such historical surface textures are simultaneously available and accessible, forming a set of textual (and textural) resources to be mined and simulated in the creation of new works. As Carol Vernallis argues, YouTube is a space of "reanimation" which transcends time and death, where decades-old clips can garner new cultural significance and where users constantly create new texts out of old ones.[22] In order to provide a clearer focus upon such textural articulations, the chapter turns to two case studies of contemporary usage of analog technologies: Super 8 film and analog video. Each section below traces the historical trajectories of these technologies within popular music culture and analyses how their material legacies intersect with the broader aesthetics of genre and wider cultural associations.

Super 8

Super 8 footage presents us with an immediate set of material affordances. The physical (handheld portable) and material (frame rate, photographic granularity) qualities of Super 8 produce recognizable visual effects. Film stock quality, the propensity of dust and damage directly upon the film's surface, distinctive sun flares, and shaky camera shots constitute textural and textual markers that explicitly reveal the technology used in their production. In turn, these material aspects signify a specific marking of time linked to the format's historical use. Super 8 was launched in 1965 by the Kodak Eastman company as a format specifically targeted at the home-movie market. Although 8 millimeter moving film had been widely available prior to this date, the introduction to the market of small handheld cameras, which required little technical knowledge (cartridge loading made them extremely user friendly), served to move home-movie making out of the realms of the hobbyist to a truly mass market. In this way the format is inherently linked with the capturing of the quotidian and the intimate. As a format specifically aimed at home-movie usage, the specificities of its film grain and surface textures have become associated with intimate domestic moments, holidays, and family occasions in our collective memory of media formats. Its surface qualities not only signify the past (the 1960s and 1970s, when Super 8 was the dominant domestic format), but also take us into the realms of the personal and the hidden. Super 8 footage from this period often draws us in to moments that would be otherwise concealed and private, even inconsequential. In addition, true to its original purpose, the playback of Super 8 primarily took place in the domestic setting as part of collective social remembrance in the context of the family, friendship, or community networks. This is significant, as once home movies are removed from such contexts they become detached from the intimacies of their original meanings and take on a broader and more abstract signification bound up in ideas about memory, affect, and nostalgia rather than the personalized individual memories themselves.

In the context of the music video, a residue of musical genre can be seen in the lo-fi nature of Super 8 footage congruent with indie rock's discursive past. Entwined with indie rock was the inherited idea of DIY from punk in which a lo-fi and make-do culture, which utilized cheap technologies, became a central part of its critique of the political economies and aesthetics of a perceived hegemonic mainstream. Indeed, Super 8 itself was congruent with the DIY aesthetic of punk and was widely utilized at the time. The most well-known documentation of the London punk scene was Don Letts' *Punk Rock the Movie*, which was one of a number of underground films using Super 8 that documented the rise of the punk subculture in London. Other examples include Phil Munnoch's (Captain Zip's) series of anthropological films of differing aspects of the scene and John Maybury and Cerith Wyn Evans's surreal art films, which cast various members of the London club scene.[23]

These early punk films were evoked a decade later in Dave Markey's *The Year Punk Broke* (1991), a highly influential film that documented the emergence into the mainstream of a number of US indie rock bands (such as Sonic Youth, Nirvana, and Dinosaur Jr.). By the time Markey's film was released, 8 millimeter had been superseded as a format and the choice to make the film using Super 8 was demonstrably made as an aesthetic rather than a pragmatic decision, echoing and reinforcing the lo-fi aesthetic that had been a continuum in indie rock from punk throughout the 1980s.

Alvvays, "Archie, Marry Me"

It is through this entwined audiovisual history that contemporary indie music videos are situated within a culture with retro-appropriations of past textual articulations at its heart. In order to explore this further I will now use a case study to examine how the technological materiality of Super 8 is commonly exploited in indie rock music videos as a complex articulation of genre. The video for the Canadian band Alvvays's 2014 track "Archie, Marry Me"[24] utilizes differing modes of Super 8 filmmaking.[25] The clip is rooted in the nostalgic, domestic associations of the format and in a very literal manner plays with the type of events and images we would associate with home movies. The first verse of the song is accompanied by lead singer, Molly Rankin, who is shown to be walking down steps in a white dress surrounded by swirling confetti (0:21). Other sections have beach scenes, images of the aquarium (0:38), the freak show (1:51), and seafront at Coney Island Brooklyn, while the chorus sections show the band on a boat trip. These shots of travel and romance are self-consciously introduced by a short initial shot of what appears to be the keyboardist Kerri MacLellan pointing a Super 8 camera into a mirror (0:36). The materiality of the format is foregrounded throughout. The video is full of unstable handheld shots, discoloration, over-exposure, and dust marks, which further reinforce the appearance of the video as being homemade. Such sections replicate both the feel and subject matter of the home movie and are rooted in an understanding of the Super 8 format as a family/social medium that might be culturally bound up with personal/family memory practices.

The congruence between the audio and visual aesthetics of the track is discernible in the surface materiality of the audio recording itself. Timbral elements and production effects constitute analogous musical content to the visual affordances of the video. The song was recorded as part of the sessions for the band's eponymously titled debut album in producer Chad VanGaalen's Calgary home studio. VanGaalen became critically acclaimed for his solo albums recorded in his basement and released by the Sub Pop label, as well as for his production work for the lo-fi experimental band Women. The production of the Alvvays track retains the generic traits of this previous sound. It is topped and tailed with sonic markers of lo-fi production: field recording of the calling of doves and other birdsong (0:00 to 0:19) and a small snippet of what sounds like a cheap drum machine as the video fades out (3:09). In addition, the track's materiality is firmly rooted in other sonic affordances drawn from indie rock's canon. The strumming of slightly distorted open chords on dual offset Fender guitars producing a "jangly" sound, which accentuates the top end of the guitars' frequency range, places the track within a core sonic continuum stretching from 1960s pop through to various types of independent music of the 1980s and beyond. As Blake notes, timbral elements, and in particular guitar tones, constitute "the primary musical parameter[s] for comprehending strategies of differentiation omnipresent in indie music."[26] In other words, timbre marks out the discursive terrain of indie rock against a perceived hegemonic mainstream through sonic differentiation.

Likewise, recording technologies and effects are foregrounded in the track to produce a generically coherent technological materiality. The chorus sections include a second vocal line processed through analog delay fed through an unnaturally large reverb, which weaves itself into the sonic architecture of the track at this point (0:55–1:10). This serves to place the chorus in a soundworld associated with dream pop and shoegaze whereby a textural abstraction or "wall of sound" is produced in which "many interwoven sounds are present at the same time, not easy to separate spatially in the densely produced 'sound-box.'"[27] This generic association is reinforced in the second verse (1:09–1:29) when guitarist Alec O'Hanley plays a heavily fuzzed and reverbed counter melody to the vocal line utilizing the Fender Jazzmaster tremolo arm to pitch shift, a (widely copied) signature sound of Kevin Shields in his work with My Bloody Valentine.

This particular combination of sonic affordances serves to firmly root the text within an understandable set of aesthetics and discursive practices. The timbral and recording based elements of the text are part of a "process-oriented aesthetics" common to "self-consciously alternative, independent, or underground genres" in which core musical characteristics reside in "the recorded subtleties of timbre, ambiance, articulation, or layers of noise or distortion."[28] As Brian Jones points out, by aurally "showing the seams" of their production process, records from these genres emphasize the "doing" in "do-it-yourself."[29] In a similar way, the specific material effects of the Super 8 technology used in the video work as analogous textual parameters to the surface materiality of the recording by showing the seams of their technological mediation.

As I have noted elsewhere,[30] British record labels of the 1980s and 1990s, such as Sarah, the Subway Organisation, 53rd and 3rd, and Creation, were important because their releases assisted in defining a tight generic codification of indie pop (as opposed to the looser term indie). In many ways "Archie, Marry Me" constitutes an aural checklist of these generic markers; the "jangly" guitar sound, a "deliberately understated, fey … vocal line" and "a studied lyrical *naiveté* and a thematic preoccupation with an innocent approach to love and romance."[31] Both the verse and the chorus consist of a simple four-chord trick (I, V, II, IV) in the key of A major moving from the tonic chord (A) to the dominant (E), supertonic (B minor), before ending on the subdominant (D). Such a simplicity in chord sequence is one of the pillars of indie pop codification where variations on the tonic, dominant, and subdominant template are ubiquitous in song construction. In terms of vocal melody, the track follows a "basic diatonicism with frequent repetition, and use of 'primitive' melodic devices,"[32] which again are further key characteristics of indie.

Within the text, musical simplicity, timbral association, and the technological materiality of the visual media and imagery combine to form a tight generic coding. Each of these factors chimes with the way in which Simon Reynolds,[33] writing at the end of the 1980s, characterized the "pure" and "innocent" musical structures and sounds of indie pop as being related to a self-conscious, often child-like *naiveté* and softer representations of gender. For Reynolds this purity is set against the dominant sexualized thrust within mainstream rock music through a denial of the body and a rejection of the physicality of youth. For Marion Leonard these gendered articulations are vital in informing an alternative set of cultural values within indie culture set against a perceived cultural mainstream.[34] Indeed, alongside its engagement with the political economies of popular music,[35] indie's deconstructive approach to the gender norms of existing rock culture have been at the heart of its discursive practice.[36] Matthew Bannister points out that indie is a cultural space in which hegemonic modes of masculinity have been critiqued and alternative modes of masculinity played out.[37] Simon Reynolds argues that this has been articulated through a "flirtation with androgyny and camp, the prevalence of love songs with genderless objects and free of fixed sexual protocol, the defense of 'sensitivity' and the wimp, [and] the refusal of performance-orientated sex."[38] As Reynolds notes from the emergence of indie as a genre in the 1980s, these specific gender articulations were in themselves inherently nostalgic for an idealized childhood bereft of adult responsibility and sexuality. Here an incipient androgyny was articulated through a deliberately child-like aesthetic in terms of the genre's subject matter, studied instrumental *naiveté*, vocal delivery, fashion conventions, and visual image.

Within the Alvvays video, sonic affordances and image convey a studied *naiveté* that is entirely congruent with the histories, generic practices, and aesthetics of the indie genre. It is an almost *clichéd* articulation of generic signifiers that are immediately apprehensible by its perceived target audience. The choice of images and the grain of the footage itself evokes the nostalgic longing, innocence, and purity pervasive within indie rock's musical and visual representations. Travel/holiday-style Super 8 footage is something of a trope that can be found across various types of contemporary indie rock video. Like "Archie, Marry Me," locations sometimes can be recognizable tourist destinations. For example, the music video by Bad Suns, "We Move Like the Ocean" (2015), is shot at Venice Beach in Los Angeles, the Moloch's "You & Me" (2016) rests on typically touristy images of Niagara Falls, while Dodie's "You" (2017) offers a documentation of well-known Paris landmarks. More often, there is a more generic suggestion of the places and spaces of leisure and enjoyment. A key element of indie videos is their use of place as an evocation of memory and nostalgia, which tends to be restricted to a fairly limited set of location types, each with their own set of semiotic associations. The use of beach/coastal imagery is rooted in a collective memory of seaside holidays as a space of childhood innocence and escape (i.e., Laura Veirs, "Lost at Seaflower Cove" [2003]; Pinkshinyultrablast, "Umi" [2014]; and Fazerdaze, "Lucky Girl" [2017]). All of these videos offer familiar representations of idyllic sunlit locations, playful interaction, leisure, and escape, and all are scored with the recognizable surface qualities of Super 8. A similar trope of *naiveté* can be found in Super 8-shot videos that are based in rural locations. These videos often have very specific intertextual reference points such as countercultural escapes of the late 1960s (i.e., Julie Doiron, "Me and My Friend" [2006]; Edward Sharpe & The Magnetic Zeros, "Home" [2010]; and Allah Las, "Tell Me (What's On Your Mind)" [2012]) and echoes of performance films of the 1950s and 1960s (FUR's

"If You Know That I'm Lonely" [2017]). Urban/suburban located Super 8 videos are more inclined toward depictions of everyday leisure practices. Videos such as The Pains of Being Pure at Heart's "Everything With You" (2008), Toro Y Moi's "Still Sound" (2011), Coldplay's "A Head Full of Dreams" (2016), and The Clientelle's "Everyone You Meet" (2017) offer similar wistful evocations of place alongside a montage of play, travel, and movement.

While these videos obviously tap into well-worn tropes (youthful vitality and escape) that have been part of the visual representation of popular music more widely, their use of technology and materiality solidifies their particular staging of authenticity and adds an extra layer of signification. Efrén Cuevas argues that home movies themselves escape the structures of traditional representation and leave "aside the stereotypes of the mainstream media."[39] They are non-narrative and collage-like in the way they are shot and thus play back and document otherwise undocumented quotidian moments that form a "site of resistance against the standardization promoted by … institutional powers."[40] The use of Super 8 also provides a clear experiential quality. Its surface qualities imbue a spectrality, an almost dreamlike longing for the past.

As well as the primary associations of Super 8 pertaining to nostalgia and memory, many contemporary music videos shot with Super 8 also utilize techniques drawn from the secondary history of the format as a media within experimental film. Because of its ubiquity and relative cheapness, Super 8 took on something of a second life away from the domestic use that had been conceived as the format's primary commercial selling point. Almost immediately it began to be used across a variety of underground and experimental film movements across various international locations.[41] In particular, the format chimed with the structural/materialist approach to filmmaking that emerged in the 1960s and 1970s, a deconstructive strain in experimental film that sought to explore viewer/film relations and demystify the filmic process.[42] It was in this context that influential experimental filmmakers, such as Derek Jarman, Saul Levine, Stan Brakhage, and Joseph Bernard, took Super 8 to the heart of their practice. This served to cement Super 8 within the avant-garde, whereby the qualities and affordances of its surfaces became part of its visual language. Both Jarman and Bernard used the form with techniques that would later become widely utilized in the 1980s' MTV era: fast editing, superimpositions of film on film, close-up shots, blurring in which the image becomes abstracted, documented "parts of images that are greater than the whole,"[43] and tight angles on objects in motion rendering them nonrepresentational. This exploration of color, texture, and abstraction was a distinguishable feature of experimental film in this period and went on to have a tangible influence on the conventions of music video in subsequent decades. William Fowler, for example, traces the explicit crossover between the aesthetics and techniques of British underground film and the emergence of music video in the 1980s.[44] He traces how popular culture and popular music became subject material for a generation of experimental filmmakers and the subsequent career trajectories into the music video industry itself in the 1980s. The echoes of this crossover can still be ascertained in abstract/conceptual Super 8-shot videos such as Laura Marling's "My Manic & I" (2012), Noah and the Whale's "2 Bodies 1 Heart" (2012), and Barn Owl's "Void Redux" (2015), which self-consciously use the format to evoke the aesthetic qualities of underground film. But the pictorial and editing conventions of experimental film are also applied more widely across differing modes, often echoing the structural components of the music itself.

Let us take the case of the selected music video, "Archie, Marry Me," as an example. It begins with blocks of rotating colors (perhaps a tight shot of a carousel) gradually over-layered with short edits of tightly framed shots (a heart printed on a fairground banner [0:06], a neon sign saying "Wonder" [0:10], and the use of driftwood and a wedding cake to spell out the song's title [0:19]). These images perform an episodic function as the soundtrack of the musical introduction before the vocal takes over, but they also immediately introduce a level of abstraction that takes the video out of the realms of the purely documentary. These non-figurative moments continue throughout the song with elements, such as heavily overexposed film (0:24), abstracted light flares (1:00), and rotating painted spirals being edited in (usually for under a second, see for example, 3:13), briefly interrupting the overall realist aesthetic. While these elements are in keeping with the structural strategies of music video, the fact that they are shot on Super 8 gives them a material intertextuality with a broad history of experimental film. This in turn echoes the historical appropriation of artistic and literary avant-gardes that has been a feature of indie's creative practice since the post-punk era. More specifically, this particular facet of the video's technological materiality echoes the textural abstraction and is facilitated by recording techniques and timbre in the track (unnatural delays, reverbs, and distortion), which place the sound recording within its particular generic heritage (indie pop, shoegaze, and dream pop). These sonic elements form part of a codified experimentalism in which the "constant use of particular recording techniques across various types of independent rock suggests that rather than being truly 'experimental' or even new, they concur with an aesthetic ideal of experimentalism."[45] Thus, this mixed use of Super 8 techniques in this context serves to simultaneously connote both culturally constructed signifiers of nostalgia and an historical avant-garde, both of which have been major discursive strains within indie music since the post-punk era. As such, the materiality of the text has multiple layers of meaning but is firmly rooted in the audiovisual conventions and discourses of genre. It draws upon generic visual conventions, but also connotes aspects of identity, gender, and the political economies of indie music.

Video/VCR/VHS

What the discussion so far illustrates is that the technological materiality of a given medium and the surface textures it produces have defined affective and semiotic purchase. Each use of technology carries with it a sense of time, history, and cultural memory that is distinct. By way of further example, I now turn to the use of VHS and Video Cassette Recorder (VCR) technologies in contemporary indie music video in order to tease out the nuanced differences that can be discerned *between* differing types of retro technology.

The use of magnetic tape in capturing images emerged in the 1950s and during the first two decades of its use became synonymous with particular types of television such as outside and studio broadcasts (television drama at this point still tended to be shot on film). As such, its surface textures mark a very specific time and usage of media. The marking of time in indie music video's technological materiality often draws on this history of television in tandem with a reclamation of the sonic elements of 1980s' technology. From the early 2000s synth-based genres of the 1980s began to be reincorporated into indie music's canonic reference points (from which they had been hitherto largely proscribed). In these instances, sonic textures related to FM synth, vocal production, drum machines, and particular guitar tones became widely used within an emergent strain of indie music. The use of analog videotape within music videos used to promote this music often provides a direct echo of these incorporations of particular facets of popular music's history. Roosevelt's (2013) "Montreal", Ella Thompson's "Arcade" (2015), Olympia's "Smoke Signals" (2016), and Jakuzi's "Koca Bir Saçmalık" (2016), for example, are all performance videos shot on vintage analog video television cameras, which use blue-screen and post-production effects such as extreme color replacement, trace phase image trails, and kaleidoscopic mirroring. These visual elements (redolent of common effects used in 1980s' music television shows and videos) serve to reinforce these artists' use of retro technologies and musical signifiers within their work. Their specific material properties thus provide a close generic coding that ties them to particular strands in popular music's history. Unlike the use of Super 8 described above, the techniques and effects used in these videos tend to be those that were at the cutting edge of professional practice in the 1980s and related to industry standard technologies such as professional VCR cameras and early digital editing systems such as Vital Industries' Squeezoom and the Ampex ADO. The use and simulation of such technologies serve to prime the viewer through a perhaps unconscious decoding of key signifiers of visual style. They draw upon an imported set of semiotic codes that are readily accessible through the historical browsing of materiality afforded through post-digital clip culture. Thus, by giving the feel of "classic" video through these technologies, these artists are placing themselves within a tradition, which is understandable and canonic, visually inserting themselves into well-worn narratives of popular music's history and mediation. The surface of the text visually announces itself as a shorthand, which assists in giving it credibility, moving it away from dominant modes of contemporary marketing and into the more "authentic" frame of the past.

The use of VHS footage in contemporary indie music video offers a linked audiovisual generic coding in a slightly different way. Developed by the Japanese corporation JVC, VHS became the defining home-media technology enabling the home recording of broadcast television and the consumption of recent cinema releases in the home. As a domestic technology it became a mainstay of television consumption from the late 1970s until the latter half of the 1990s. The year 1983 saw the parallel introduction of both VHS and Betamax camcorders aimed at the domestic market, which quickly superseded 8 millimeter and 16 millimeter film as the medium for home movies. These developments provided a semantic shift in the meaning of the term video itself, "denoting an alternative to conventional television transmission and reception."[46] At this point, consumer-based VCR camcorder footage almost immediately took on connotations of authenticity in which its material qualities stood in contrast to professionally produced television.[47] VHS is thus dually tied to domestic consumption in terms of the capturing of personal movies and as a playback technology for officially produced media. As such, VHS produces a different set of material qualities and identifiable surfaces to analog film, which in turn has specific cultural associations. Present-day use of VHS plays upon these historical associations and can be linked to a core connection between materiality and memory in and through the explicit references to the format's deficiencies as a recording and playback medium. For example, Mac DeMarco's "Ode to Viceroy" (2012) has the appearance of an extremely degraded VHS tape; Arctic Monkeys' Cornerstone (2009) is a single-shot lo-fi VHS video; Late of the Pier's "Focker" (2009), Tennis's "Origin" (2012), and White Lung's "Face Down" (2015) all have an overly pronounced, washed out VHS coloration and color bleed; and the Raveonettes' "She Owns the Streets" (2012) and Otherkin's "Feel It" (2015) both have vertical tracking lines, signal noise, and a 4.3 aspect ratio that was conventional for VHS. All of these videos play upon a cultural memory of domestic leisure through graphic use of the common markers of deterioration of playback technologies (demagnetization, worn heads, poor tracking, and limitations in color) and, through their imperfections, inscribe and echo ongoing discursive strands relating to popular music and authenticity. As I have argued elsewhere, such "purposeful imprecision" in instrumental and vocal styles and the rejection of "mainstream" production values are at the heart of the stylistic conventions of indie.[48]

Hockey Dad, "I Need a Woman"

The individual combination of images, music, and surface within these texts leads to specificities and nuances in the way technological materiality can signify. To take one brief example in more detail, the video "I Need a Woman," by Australian band Hockey Dad (2014),[49] begins with five seconds of silence accompanied by angled horizontal interference immediately recognizable as a VHS surface texture (0:00–0:05). The effect is reminiscent of a VHS "drop-out" in which aging or damage on the surface of the tape leads to momentary losses in replay resulting in "holes" in the image. This interference is overlaid with the song title and band name in a standard camcorder font, establishing the text as self-consciously reflective of its means of production. When the track itself begins, the video is a montage of the band members skateboarding and cycling in recognizably suburban Australian settings (0:05–1:00) and beach footage filmed around their hometown of Windang, New South Wales. Other sections show the band in everyday suburban spaces such as a fast-food outlet (1:02–1:26), suburban residential streets, a pub with "pokies" (slot machines) (3:26–3:40), and a liquor store (1:40–2:00). The footage is shot using handheld equipment evident by numerous shaky camera images and unstable zoom shots. The overall visual style of the video is determined by its use of VHS camcorder technology. There are several moments of tracking flickers across the screen and slight jumps in the image, both of which are primary affordances of VHS technology. The overall coloration is also unmistakably a VHS product. Home VCRs had bandwidth limitations that meant that the composite video signal took on a certain degradation and distortion in playback. For example, the frequency band (5 kilohertz) needed to represent realistic colors is compressed in playback to 3.5 kilohertz, resulting in a "washed-out" appearance and a slight fuzziness of definition due to color bleed.

The video's technological materiality signifies on a number of differing levels, with its meanings tied up in overlapping fields of association. As well as overall generic connotations, VHS materiality in this context has extra-musical subcultural associations. As Sean Dinces notes, the circulation of VHS tapes produced from within the skateboarding scene became a key part of subcultural practice within skateboarding culture from the 1980s, becoming central in constructing a cultural identity for the practice.[50] The material qualities of VHS have subsequently become part of the foundational narratives of skateboard culture and its visual language. VHS-shot footage is also used widely in contemporary documentary representations of the skateboard culture, such as *Bones Brigade* (2012)—which uses stylized graphic representations of VHS interference within the graphic design of its title sequence—and the portrait of the Australian champion skating brothers Tas and Ben Pappas' *All This Mayhem* (2014). "I Need a Woman" taps into both these historical and contemporaneous representations, re-enforcing the mediated public image as a self-declared "surf rock" band whose members play up their ties to their Australian suburban roots in their music and interviews. Surfing and skateboarding are entwined historical cultures as evidenced by the 2001 film *Dogtown and Z-Boys*, perhaps the most well-known and influential skate documentary. Surf culture has long enjoyed a place as a "privileged site in Australian society,"[51] and also has been linked with "casual, anti-establishment [but at the same time] introverted" forms of masculinity.[52]

The video offers a very specific take on the gender conventions of indie rock, which are also inflected by particular representations of national culture. Its skate/surf references offer an alternative take on physicality and masculinity, which have been central to mainstream representations of Australian identity. The textual patina of nostalgia also chimes with the lyrical themes of unrequited teenage love and longing within the song (which have, of course, long been strains within popular songs). Similarly, the representation of banal vernacular locations is redolent with a concurrent theme of boredom and aimlessness of suburban life that has been present within wider representations of youth culture and the band's constructed public image.[53] Thus, the experiential feel afforded by the technological materiality is again anchored in a sense of authenticity and nostalgia.

Given the youthful age of the producers and target audience for such a text, the nostalgia effects can only be received as a vicarious expression instead of being generated from having actually experienced the quotidian use of particular media forms (as a central playback technology in the domestic space or a tool for capturing significant moments). This sense of nostalgia is mediated through the availability of endless texts of the past contained in the seemingly ever-expanding archive that is the web. The textual materiality of differing eras of media is simultaneously available, compressed into digital form, freely accessible, and easily replicable through virtual simulation technologies. Their very degradation (or appearance of degradation) is key to their signification. As Stephen Bull argues in a discussion of online "retro" photography apps, the decomposition of the image not only comes to be associated with particular eras, but also stands for the passage of time itself. He notes: "these images do not simulate the look of photographs as they were in the past, they simulate the look of aged photographs as they appear to us in the present."[54]

It is within this context that the self-conscious amateurism of the camera angles and the surface noise of the VHS tape constitute a recapturing of technological innocence. The materiality and production values hark back to a pre-digital age when the perceivable gap in quality between home-made and industry-produced media was significantly more pronounced. Changes in digital technologies from the 1990s onwards, through the development and marketing of "prosumer technologies" both in film and audio, have led to a flattening of boundaries between "professional" and "amateur" equipment and the media produced by such technologies.[55] The inscription upon the surface of the text that the use of outmoded technologies necessarily produces reinstates the dialectic between amateur and professional, between mainstream and DIY media texts, and between the slickly produced and the personal. This visual coding echoes authenticity discourses that have been a major strain within popular music culture for more than half a century.

Conclusion

The technological materiality of formats such as Super 8 and analog video must be considered within its immediate context of digital replication and dissemination. Despite being filmed using obsolete technologies, these texts are designed to be hosted, viewed, and disseminated through digital channels. As such, their meanings derive from a dialectic with contemporary aesthetics, media surfaces, and production values. As Ryszard Dabek comments, with regard to its contemporary usage in visual art, "the uniquely primitive aesthetic palette of … [a] medium (low image resolution, pronounced grain, unstable image registration) can be read as a direct counterpoint to the seamless perfection of the contemporary digital image."[56] As such, the marking out of the surface in these videos serves to reinscribe the physical in an intangible culture and, in turn, must also be considered in relation to wider issues about nostalgia in the post-digital context.

Barbara Stern makes the distinction between personal and historical nostalgia, indicating that nostalgia operates as a form of collective as well as personal memory, and that nostalgia can be felt for something that the individual has not necessarily personally experienced: a "received nostalgia."[57] Materially marked media forms are centrally complicit in constructing a vicarious nostalgia—they become the "vehicles of memory"[58] through which ideas about the past are linked to personal and collective identity. Both audio and visual recording and playback devices, then, are powerfully bound up with *ideas* of memory. For Douwe Draaisma, the phonograph is one of the key "metaphors of memory" of the modern age, that is, an external technology that is simultaneously used to recall and conceptualize memory itself.[59] Jonathan Sterne takes this idea further, arguing that "thanks to recording, sound exists in the memories of machines and surfaces as well as the memories of people" and that "this is one of the almost magical powers of recording."[60] It is perhaps unsurprising, given the importance of the materiality of recording within popular music cultures, that its articulations of nostalgia are often explicitly bound up with technology. Various scholars have identified a "technostalgia" within popular music culture in which the use of particular musical equipment,[61] recording techniques,[62] or thematic and aesthetic trends[63] is complicit in a process whereby "new technologies ... generate nostalgia for superseded formats."[64]

The inscription of a received nostalgia through the marking of the surface in the music videos described above, then, constitutes textual realizations in keeping with a culture in which technology and memory are historically entwined as part of its core aesthetic. In the context of the post-digital, the key characteristic of contemporary rock derived music is its replication and appropriation of textual and thematic elements from its seventy-year history. In comparison to its emergent and dominant historical epochs, rock music finds itself holding a diminishing cultural centrality in a highly fractured media landscape in which retro appropriations have become increasingly dominant. Simon Reynolds argues that the contemporary era of popular music is dominated by a "retro" aesthetic in which true creativity and innovation are sidelined in pursuit of homage to and quotation of a perceived "golden age" of pop music driven by a heightened commercial imperative.[65] Similarly, for Maël Guesdon and Philippe Le Guem, contemporary popular music is in itself inherently "spectral,"[66] with a nostalgic thrust that constantly drives itself to use more and more of its own reference points. They argue that contemporary popular music is in a constant process of "staging authenticity,"[67] which is in turn integral to its affective power. What the case studies presented here illustrate is that, in an age of increasing audiovisuality, technological materiality melds image to sound in a dual staging of authenticity. The visual representations outlined here are inherently tied to the position of their genre *in* time and *through* time. Indie rock is a generic grouping with its own specific historical trajectories, having a perceived golden age from which its emergent acts are now canonized and used as stylistic templates for further creative action. Contemporary articulations of indie music can never escape this history. To work within its generic codes necessitates a reiteration and re-uttering of its musical past. The type of visual codification and use of obsolete technology outlined in this chapter serve to frame this musical reiteration with the "authentic" surfaces of its mediated past. In an increasingly fractured media landscape in which narrowcasting and social media are omnipresent, independent music has splintered into increasingly more niche markets. The semiotic summoning of perceived golden eras of rock music connotes a time when the reach of independent rock music was much broader and was first tied more intrinsically to the perceived zeitgeist or the supposed generational characteristics of youth cultures in particular areas (e.g., the counter-culture and the rise of rock in the 1960s, independent rock, grunge, and Generation X in the late 1980s).

The use of obsolete technologies outlined in this chapter at once recalls and references this history and serves to further the nostalgic thrust of indie rock's genre aesthetics. This use lends a semiotic coding that is immediately apprehensible in a culture in which a retro materiality forms a significant part of the current visual language through the endless availability of film, television, and web video, and the way in which apps such as

Hipstermatic and Instagram create a "nostalgia for the present"[68] in the documenting of our daily lives. The materiality of these videos lends them an immediacy, in terms of their associative purchase, and ultimately their surfaces are not just a patina *upon* the text, but an integral part of the texts themselves, text and texture are inextricable.

Notes

1   Fabian Holt, "Is Music Becoming More Visual? Online Video Content in the Music Industry," *Visual Studies* 26, no. 1 (2011): 50–61.

2   Maura Edmond, "Here We Go Again: Music Videos after YouTube," *Television and New Media* 15, no. 4 (2014): 305–320.

3   Mathias Bonde Korsgaard, *Music Video After MTV: Audiovisual Studies, New Media, and Popular Music* (London and New York: Routledge, 2017).

4   Carol Vernallis, *Unruly Media: YouTube, Music Video, and the New Digital Cinema* (Oxford and New York: Oxford University Press, 2013).

5   Kristin Leib, *Gender, Branding, and the Modern Music Industry* (London: Routledge, 2017).

6   Due to space limitations, the videos under discussion here in this chapter are specifically those that use "outmoded" technologies themselves. The simulation of the surface textures of past media is a closely related aspect of music video aesthetics that has slightly different implications for analysis and is an area requiring further research.

7   Lisa Gitelman, "'Materiality Has Always Been in Play': An Interview with N. Katherine Hayles," *Iowa Journal of Cultural Studies* 2 (2002): 9.

8   Giuliana Bruno, *Surface: Matters of Aesthetics, Materiality, and Media* (Chicago, IL: University of Chicago Press, 2014), 5.

9   Brian Larkin, *Signal and Noise: Media, Infrastructure, and Urban Culture in Nigeria* (Durham, NC: Duke University Press, 2008), 233.

10 Ibid.

11 Carmela Garritano, "The Materiality of Genre: Analog and Digital Ghosts in Video Movies from Ghana," *Cambridge Journal of Postcolonial Literary Inquiry* 4, no. 2 (2017): 192.

12 See Bruno, *Surface*; Ryszard Dabek, "Immaterial/Materiality," *Journal of Asia-Pacific Pop Culture* 2, no. 2 (2017): 220–237; and Christopher Hauke, "'A Cinema of Small Gestures': Derek Jarman's Super 8—Image, Alchemy, Individuation," *International Journal of Jungian Studies* 6, no. 2 (May 2014): 159–164.

13 See Garritano, "The Materiality of Genre"; Kenneth W. Harrow, *Trash: African Cinema from Below* (Bloomington, IN: University of Indiana Press, 2013); and Larkin, *Signal and Noise*.

14 Theodore Gracyk, *Rhythm and Noise: An Aesthetics of Rock* (London: I.B. Tauris, 1996), 31.

15 See Albin Zak, *The Poetics of Rock: Cutting Tracks, Making Records* (Berkeley, CA: University of California Press, 2001); Mark Katz, *Capturing Sound: How Technology Has Changed Music* (Berkeley, CA: University of California Press, 2004); Jonathan Sterne, *The Audible Past: Cultural Origins of Sound Production* (London: Duke University Press, 2006); and Simon Frith, *Taking Popular Music Seriously: Selected Essays* (Aldershot: Ashgate, 2007).

16 Andy Bennett and Ian Rogers, "Popular Music and Materiality: Memorabilia and Memory Traces," *Popular Music and Society* 23 (2015): 34.

17 Andrew Goodwin, *Dancing in the Distraction Factory: Music Television and Popular Culture* (Minneapolis, MN: University of Minnesota Press, 1992), 3.

18 Robert Strachan, *Sonic Technologies: Popular Music, Digital Culture and the Creative Process* (New York: Bloomsbury, 2017), 135–151.

19 Alexander Jensenius, "Action-Sound: Developing Methods and Tools to Study Music-Related Body Movement," PhD dissertation (University of Oslo, 2007), 14.

20 Ibid.

21 Michael Webb, "Re Viewing Listening: 'Clip Culture' and Cross-Modal Learning in the Music Classroom," *International Journal of Music Education* 28, no. 4 (2010): 313.

22 Vernallis, *Unruly Media*, 138.

23 See Jo Comino, "Underground Film-Making: British Super 8 in the 1980s," in *The Routledge Companion to British Cinema History*, edited by I.Q. Hunter, Laraine Porter, and Justin Smith (London: Routledge, 2017), 309.

24 Alvvays, "Alvvays—Archie, Marry Me," YouTube video (3:14), official music video, directed by Gavin Keen and Allison Johnston, posted by "Alvvays A," July 30, 2014, https://www.youtube.com/watch?v=ZAn3JdtSrnY&list=RDZAn3JdtSrnY&start_radio=1&t=6.

25 Specifically, retro technological materiality is a running theme of the band's video work. "Adult Diversion" (2013) is filmed in Super 8; "Next of Kin" (2014) uses a lo-fi stop-motion animation technique; "In Undertow" (2017) uses the type of 1970s broadcast video technologies and effects discussed later in the chapter; and "Dreams Tonite" (2017) digitally superimposes footage of the band onto 16 millimeter footage of the Montreal World Fair Expo '67.

26 David Blake, "Timbre as Differentiation in Indie Music," *Music Theory Online* 18, no. 2 (2012): 11.

27 Torben Sangild, "Noise: Three Musical Gestures—Expressionist, Introvert and Minimal Noise," *Journal of Music and Meaning* 2, no. 1 (2004): 6.

28 Brian Jones, "Signifying DIY: Process-Orientated Aesthetics in 1990s Alternative Rock and Hip-Hop," PhD dissertation (University of North Carolina at Chapel Hill, 2014), 5.

29 Ibid.

30 Robert Strachan, "Do-It-Yourself: Industry, Ideology, Aesthetics and Micro Independent Record Labels in the UK," PhD dissertation (University of Liverpool, 2003), 39.

31 Ibid.

32 Matthew Bannister, *White Boys, White Noise: Masculinities and 1980s Indie Guitar Rock* (Aldershot: Ashgate, 2006), 70.

33 Simon Reynolds, *Blissed Out: The Raptures of Rock* (London: Serpent's Tail, 1990), 247.

34 Marion Leonard, *Gender in the Music Industry: Rock, Discourse and Girl Power* (Aldershot: Ashgate, 2007), 43–48.

35 See David Hesmondhalgh, "Indie: The Institutional Politics and Aesthetics of a Popular Music Genre," *Cultural Studies* 13, no. 1 (1999): 34–61; and Ryan Hibbett, "What Is Indie Rock?," *Popular Music and Society* 28, no. 1 (2005): 55–77.

36 Larissa Wodtke makes an explicit connection between these two pillars of indie pop discourse: "The apparent freedom offered by this adoption of childlike innocence and refusal to mature is also related to … [the] adoption of the do-it-yourself, amateur

aesthetic espoused in the 1970s by punk, which attempted to operate outside the mainstream capitalist market." Larissa Wodtke, "The Child's Place in Pop Music," *Jeunesse: Young People, Texts, Cultures* 10, no. 2 (2018): 181.

37 Bannister, *White Boys*, 138–146.

38 Simon Reynolds, *Bring the Noise: 20 Years of Writing about Hip Rock and Hip-Hop* (London: Faber & Faber, 2007), 16.

39 Efrén Cuevas, "Change of Scale: Home Movies as Microhistory in Documentary Films," in *Amateur Filmmaking: The Home Movie, the Archive, the Web*, edited by Laura Rascaroli, Gwenda Young, and Barry Monahan (New York and London: Bloomsbury, 2014), 141.

40 Ibid.

41 See Comino, "Underground Film-Making," 309.

42 See Peter Gildal, *Structural Film Anthology* (London: BFI, 1976).

43 Hauke, "A Cinema of Small Gestures," 160.

44 William Fowler, "The Occult Roots of MTV: British Music Video and Underground Film-Making in the 1980s," *Music, Sound, and the Moving Image* 11, no. 1 (2017): 63–77.

45 Strachan, "Do-It-Yourself," 318.

46 Michael Z. Newman, *Video Revolutions: On the History of a Medium* (New York: Columbia University Press, 2014), 16.

47 Ibid., 69.

48 Strachan, "Do-It-Yourself," 320.

49 Hockey Dad, "Hockey Dad—I Need a Woman," YouTube video (4:28), official music video, directed by Brett Randall, posted by "Farmer & The Owl," June 26, 2014, https://www.youtube.com/watch?v=dKCpPWEvZJ0.

50 Emily Yochim Chivers, *Skate Life: Re-imagining White Masculinity* (Ann Arbor, MI: University of Michigan Press, 2010).

51 Clifton Evers, "'The Point': Surfing, Geography and a Sensual Life of Men and Masculinity on the Gold Coast, Australia," *Social & Cultural Geography* 10, no. 8 (2009): 893.

52 Kent Pearson, "Conflict, Stereotypes and Masculinity in Australian and New Zealand Surfing," *Australia and New Zealand Journal of Sociology* 18, no. 2 (1982): 121.

53 As evidenced by the fact that the pair met in school and are from a suburban background, which forms a key part of their press profile.

54 Stephen Bull, "'Digital Photography Never Looked So Analogue': Retro Camera Apps, Nostalgia and the Hauntological Photograph," *Photoworks* 18 (Spring/Summer 2012): 25.

55 See Paul Théberge, "'The End of the World as We Know It': The Changing Role of the Studio in the Age of the Internet," in *The Art of Record Production*, edited by Simon Zagorski-Thomas and Simon Frith (Farnham: Ashgate, 2012), 83; and Strachan, *Sonic Technologies*, 19–21.

56 Dabek, "Immaterial/Materiality," 230.

57 Barbara B. Stern, "Historical and Personal Nostalgia in Advertising Text: The Fin de Siècle Effect," *Journal of Advertising* 21, no. 4 (1992): 13.

58 Alon Confino, "Collective Memory and Cultural History," *The American Historical Review* 102, no. 5 (1997): 1386.

59 Douwe Draaisma, *Metaphors of Memory: A History of Ideas about the Mind* (Cambridge: Cambridge University Press, 2000), 85.

60 Jonathan Sterne, "The Preservation Paradox in Digital Audio," in *Sound Souvenirs: Audio Technologies, Memory and Cultural Practices*, edited by Karin Bijsterveld and José van Dijck (Amsterdam: University of Amsterdam Press, 2009), 57.

61 Trevor Pinch and David Reinecke, "Technostalgia: How Old Gear Lives on in New Music," in *Sound Souvenirs: Audio Technologies, Memory and Cultural Practices*, edited by Karin Bijsterveld and José van Dijck (Amsterdam: University of Amsterdam Press, 2009), 156–160.

62 Michael Holland and Oli Wilson, "Technostalgia in New Recording Projects by the 1980s 'Dunedin Sound' Band The Chills," *Journal on the Art of Record Production*, no. 9 (April 2015), https://www.arpjournal.com/asarpwp/technostalgia-in-new-recording-projects-by-the-1980s-dunedin-sound-band-the-chills.

63 Timothy D. Taylor, *Strange Sounds: Music, Technology and Culture* (London: Routledge, 2001), 96–114.

64 Carolyn Birdsall, "Earwitnessing: Sound Memories of the Nazi Period," in *Sound Souvenirs: Audio Technologies, Memory and Cultural Practices*, edited by Karin Bijsterveld and José van Dijck (Amsterdam: University of Amsterdam Press, 2009), 169.

65 Simon Reynolds, *Retromania: Pop Culture's Addiction to Its Own Past* (London: Faber & Faber, 2011), 410.

66 Maël Guesdon and Philippe Le Guem, "Retromania: Crisis of the Progressive Ideal and Pop Music Spectrality," in *Media and Nostalgia*, edited by Katharina Niemeyer (London: Palgrave Macmillan, 2014), 73–75.

67 Ibid.

68 For a discussion of this term, see Mike Chopra-Gant, "Pictures or It Didn't Happen: Photo-nostalgia, iPhoneography and the Representation of Everyday Life," *Photography & Culture* 9, no. 2 (July 2016): 121–128.

9

Katy Perry's "Wide Awake": The Lyric Video as Genre

Laura McLaren

In 2014, the MTV Video Music Awards (VMAs) introduced a new category for "Best Lyric Video,"[1] with the decision regarding its introduction being associated with the seemingly sudden appearance of such videos and the attention that they were receiving at the time. Popular journalistic articles at the time questioned the value of these videos, asking "Why are we giving them awards?" and "What's the point?"[2] Evidently there were others, like the VMAs, who thought that the emerging genre deserved recognition; however, the "Best Lyric Video" award only appeared for a single year and the genre has not received much media attention since. Lyric videos themselves have not disappeared since 2014; in fact, they have become more and more common as mainstream artists frequently release lyric videos on YouTube in conjunction with new singles. In this chapter I employ genre theory to establish the lyric video as a subgenre of music video. I analyze the lyric video for "Wide Awake" by Katy Perry,[3] an early adopter of the genre, to show how this version of the video offers a unique perspective on the lyrical content and Perry's artistic persona, and even comments on larger cultural trends.

Lyric videos by definition offer a visual treatment of a song's lyrics, presented in synchronization with the recorded music. At present, they are typically released in conjunction with their associated single or album release, and are followed shortly thereafter by an official music video. In order to maintain focus on the lyrics, there is little dynamic change in the images or background that accompanies the words, and, although they are still sonically present, the artist is not always visually present, so as not to distract from the lyrics. Lyric videos are typically quick and inexpensive to create in comparison to official music videos, yet, as they have developed and gained popularity, they have become more sophisticated, innovative, and attuned to the mood or style of the tracks they promote.

While it would be easy to overlook lyric videos due to their apparent simplicity, or to dismiss them as merely a placeholder for the official music video, I believe that there is more to discover in the deceptively simple format of words on a screen accompanying a song, and in this chapter I ask the following questions:

- How do these videos function as a visual genre, distinct from official music videos or audio videos,[4] and, more specifically, what kinds of codes and conventions are present in these videos that allow them to be identified as lyric videos?
- How does the lyric video shape the lyrics of the song through animation and cinematography, and how does the aesthetic treatment of the words intersect with the musical content?
- How do these videos serve to promote the artist, and what do we learn about their identity or persona through the images?

By raising the question of how the artist is represented in and through the lyric video, I open my analytic investigation to the consideration of artistic personae, which are tied strongly to musical genres. Drawing from Simon Frith's and Philip Auslander's concepts of star personality and persona, intertwined with genre studies, I demonstrate how lyric videos offer complex meanings that are intricately linked to artistic personae and musical genres.[5] Building on these foundational questions about lyric videos, my objectives are to examine, first, how the lyric video has emerged and evolved throughout its recent development, and second, how lyric videos offer new ways of presenting an artist's work and persona through a particularly constrained visual genre.

In *Unruly Media*, Carol Vernallis examines how music videos have undergone "shifts in technologies and platforms, periods of intense cross-pollination with other media, financial booms and busts, and changing levels of audience engagement."[6] The lyric video is evidence of one of these "shifts." As I will outline, it was highly influenced by two types of video: (1) official music videos that included the lyrics; and (2) prosumer lyric videos.[7]

The first branch stems from the history of music video and consists of a few artists who chose to heavily feature their lyrics in some of their videos. The first video popularly considered to be a lyric video is Bob Dylan's 1965 "Subterranean Homesick Blues." In this black and white film segment, Dylan stands at a street corner with a stack of cue cards, each containing one handwritten word or short phrase. As the song continues, he drops each cue card as the word on it is sung until he is left empty handed and walks off screen. While the rest of the action on-screen is fairly static, the constantly changing cue cards are the focus of the video. Although not all the song's lyrics are included or entirely accurate, the viewer gets a better sense of the lyrical content of the song, which was likely Dylan's intention. Another example of a "proto" lyric video is Prince's 1987 single "Sign o' the Times." Directed by Bill Konersman, the lyrics of the song are creatively displayed through colorful graphics and pulsing text. Guilia Gabrielli suggests that this format was chosen in this video to "facilitate the comprehension of the lyrics," which deal with significant themes of AIDS, gang violence, natural disasters, and space exploration.[8] During the 1980s and 1990s, every music video that featured the lyrics accompanied songs which included important lyrical messages that the artist wanted to emphasize and ensure that their audiences understood.[9]

Perhaps more influential than these "proto" lyric videos described above is the "prosumer" lyric video.[10] These videos were very simply created using basic movie-making software and featured the lyrics of a song over a blank background and a photo of the artist, album cover, or any image that the artist decided to pair with the song.[11] Some even featured video homages to other texts such as movies or television shows where the song had been featured. These videos had several flaws. Often, they misspelled or mistranscribed the lyrics, or even misrepresented the artist in some way.[12] Other times, to avoid copyright infringement, they would use unofficial audio, either by using a cover version or modifying the audio in another way to avoid copyright infringement issues.[13] Likely in response to these unofficial videos, some artists like Katy Perry and Cee Lo Green began to release their own lyric videos in 2010, and the practice continues to gain popularity among mainstream artists. While they have not stopped prosumer lyric videos from appearing—dozens are still being released every day on YouTube—these official lyric videos have taken the forefront and draw much more attention, as evidenced by the fact that they routinely have more views than any prosumer lyric videos of the same song.[14]

Through the interaction between the recent emergence of prosumer videos and older official videos such as "Subterranean Homesick Blues," lyric videos have developed within a site "where old and new media collide … where the power of the media producer and the power of the media consumer interact in unpredictable ways."[15] This is how Henry Jenkins defines "convergence culture" and, although his seminal monograph was written before YouTube was well established, it is easy to see how this concept could be applicable to the YouTube community, where viewer comments, ratings, and popularity (view count) of videos have a direct impact on the content of the later videos.[16] Many lyric videos rely on the three concepts of convergence culture: "media convergence," "participatory culture," and "collective intelligence,"[17] as they are often promoted by the artist on various social media sites and their success depends on the active engagement of viewers, as well as their ability to recognize and understand codes and references. Transtextuality is another framework through which to productively consider the convergent nature of lyric videos, because they are often linked to the music videos for the same songs, other lyric videos from the same artist or album, the larger lyric video genre, and even cultural or other trends that they may reference.[18]

Theories of genre in media can help to situate the emergent genre of lyric videos. Through my readings of scholarly writings on genre in literature, film, television, and popular music, I have identified seven elements that I believe offer a comprehensive digest of genre theory that is applicable to genres in any field. My summary of these writings is organized around these seven elements, which I then apply as a basis for my own theoretical framework. Since the lyric video has only recently emerged, the literature upon which I draw does not address the lyric video specifically; however, the discussion below provides a foundation for understanding the lyric video as a distinct visual genre. The seven elements are summarized here, then discussed in more detail below:

1 genre is universal, in that every text participates in genre in some way;
2 genres have no definitive point of origin or conclusion but rather emerge gradually and develop in complex ways;
3 genres are maintained through both repetition and development of convention;
4 genres shape fictional worlds;

5 genres have both industrial contexts and cultural contexts, based on how they are produced, which is not always the same as how they are received or used;

6 genres function as part of a system through which they interact with other genres;

7 genres reveal the cultural assumptions and subjectivities of those participating in them.

The most basic understanding of genre relies on its universality—no text, whether it be a film, book, song, or email, is free of genre conventions. Therefore, no matter the medium, each text participates in genre by adhering to a genre's conventions, while also participating in the shaping of that genre by developing different attributes that deviate from the genre's conventions.

When confronted with a text, most readers will have expectations based on their previous encounters with other texts in that genre. Jason Mittell encourages the questioning of these assumed categories, and invites deeper analysis to see how genres participate in culture and are shaped by media practices.[19] Meanwhile, Christine Gledhill argues that genres, especially the naming of genres, are utilized as a way of communication by various groups of people for their own purposes, such as audiences recommending films to their friends, critics writing about them, or producers promoting a film as a particular genre.[20] Through labelling an unknown text in a specific genre, a comparison is being made and an expectation shaped.[21]

Similarly, just as every book, film, and television show participates and contributes to a given genre, so too does every song that is written and performed. The difficulty in the domain of popular music is that the output is much greater. Books take years to get written and published, films and television shows are constrained by budgets, schedules, and large production teams, but a single musician can record, mix, and release an album or single in a very short amount of time with much more freedom to promote and distribute it over the internet. Furthermore, each track that is released can change or transform the genre slightly, leading to a faster pace of musical genre evolution.[22] David Brackett calls the "issue of genre in the historical study of popular music … unavoidable"[23] and, although it is not always discussed, most listeners to popular music are likely aware of the "fundamental structuring force" of genre in the way that different styles of music influence how, where, and with whom people experience and make music.[24]

Many audience members and scholars may claim that certain genres began or ended with a specific text; however, John Frow claims that "genres have no transhistorical essence, only historically changing use values."[25] Gledhill makes a similar claim by insisting that genres go out of fashion in time and come back with similar elements or codes but a different cultural meaning or name, causing some scholars to prefer the term "cycle" over "genre."[26] Mittell addresses this as well, by contrasting the nature of genre development with biological evolution. In biology, it is possible to follow the evolution of a species through its genealogy; however, genres do not follow this same pattern of direct lineage, so, in order to make connections, a scholar must execute a very broad scan of texts in order to see connections.[27]

Just as with film and literary texts, musical texts remain stable while genres can shift around them.[28] Brackett discusses how many a musical genre was originally "comprehensible in contexts beyond those in which we imagine it might have begun," so it would be difficult to identify a specific moment of origin.[29] Holt argues that, unlike literature, "music is not referential," in that it "does not have the precision of iconic or indexical representation" and it is therefore almost impossible to theorize the development of musical genres.[30] Additionally, Brackett dismisses "the idea of authorial intention from an understanding of genre," since genres, he argues, are the accumulation of multiple authors, or "collective creativity," rather than developing from a single song or artist and a single point in time.[31]

Codes and conventions are the shaping force of genre. They are established through the repetition and citation of elements that make genres recognizable to audiences, based on comparison to other texts in the same genre. In addition to the elements that are repeated, texts also contribute to the evolution of genre as they introduce or adapt elements. Gledhill calls this "heteroglossia and dialogism"—an interaction between two or more voices—that work together repeating codes and conventions, while, at the same time, shifting to "maintain credibility with changing audiences by connecting with the signifiers of contemporary verisimilitude."[32] These codes rely on an audience's understanding, and, as Mittell argues, are sometimes the most obvious when two or more genres are mixing as "within more 'pure' generic texts, such conventions are often downplayed or unspoken to avoid appearances of formula or repetition."[33]

Rather than discussing generic elements, Franco Fabbri, one of the first popular musicologists to write about genre, defines musical genres as "a set of musical events (real or possible) whose course is governed by a definite set of socially accepted rules."[34] These rules include formal, semiotic behavior, ideological, and economical rules that are the standard for any discussion of musical genres.[35] Fabbri acknowledges that this guideline is incomplete, and offers a reminder that not all genres give equal weight to each rule.[36] Brackett makes an important contribution to the discussion of codes and conventions in genre with his idea of "legibility," meaning that, even if a song follows all the conventions of a genre, it may not be accepted as participating in that genre because the audience does not understand that it does so.[37] This issue of legibility becomes an issue in popular music when artists attempt to cross genres, and are sometimes accepted, such as when Taylor Swift transitioned from a country artist to a pop artist. But when Beyoncé, a pop and R&B artist, wrote "Daddy Lessons" using many country music conventions,[38] the country music community was not as accepting. Many country fans were disturbed when Beyoncé performed "Daddy Lessons" at the Country Music Awards, because they did not accept it as a country song, ostensibly due to Beyoncé's history as an R&B star.[39] The reaction was also likely due to Beyoncé being an African-American woman, when conventional country music stars are usually white men, with white female artists only taking approximately one-fifth of radio play and positions on the Billboard charts.[40] According to Jada Watson's research, women of color are virtually non-existent in popular country music, which could partly explain why country fans would not have seen Beyoncé's "Daddy Lessons" as a country song.[41]

Much discussion of genre uses the term "world" or "worldmaking," as Frow claims that "genres create effects of reality and truth which are central to the different ways the world is understood" within a text or group of texts.[42] Gledhill terms this as "generic verisimilitude," drawing the connection to "audience expectations of the world created by a text," although she makes it clear that "genres are fictional worlds, but they don't remain in fictional boundaries."[43] Discussions of genre happen in the "real world" all the time, as do discussions of the impact of these genre worlds through the way they shape audiences' understandings of their everyday lives.

This dichotomy between reality and fiction is clearer in the musical world. The fictional world consists of the musical elements that create a musical world presented through assumptions of a time and place, with a specific type of people creating and listening to this music. Contrastingly, the real world consists of who is actually performing the music and where the music is being performed, which may be quite different from what is assumed, especially for listeners with access to the internet who are now able to find music created all over the world, and targeted to a different audience.

Genres rely upon industry and cultural contexts to shape how they are presented and understood. Gledhill argues that genres exist in three contexts: (1) an "industrial mechanism," where texts are shaped to fit within a popular genre in order to be financially successful; (2) "aesthetic practice," which is the codes and conventions that allow texts to be understood through that genre; and (3) "an arena of cultural-critical discursivity," where consumers discuss the meaning and importance of a text.[44] Frow describes genres as culturally important in that they can include "information about the situation to which a text responds and in which it has a particular communicative point."[45] This intended cultural information, however, is not always how the texts are used by audiences. Mittell calls upon scholars to "look behind the wheel" of a genre and, rather than looking at how a genre functions, look instead at a genre's audiences and ask: why are they watching and how does their interaction with the text influence our understanding *in a particular cultural instance?*"[46]

While genres inform and reflect culture, they are also constrained by their industrial contexts. Brackett discusses the importance of genre classification for marketing music, as this affects how songs are promoted and charted,[47] in addition to the cultural purposes, which influence how critics and fans communicate about genres.[48] Gabriele Marino also addresses how the classification of genre names communicates important elements of the genre using terms such as descriptive, prescriptive, or locative.[49] She goes on to say that the names can represent "a precious key to understanding how communities understand and appropriate music, what they consider meaningful in it."[50] In the chapter entitled "Crossover Dreams" in *Categorizing Sound*, Brackett discusses how genres are also heavily influenced by cultural issues such as appropriation or genre crossover.[51] Appropriation can bring attention to new genres that were originally marginalized due to the race of the artists originally performing them, while genre crossovers have the reverse effect of bringing attention to marginalized artists only once they have transitioned to mainstream attention, as seen in the careers of artists such as Michael Jackson and Prince.[52]

Rather than existing as distinct entities with strict boundaries between differing genres, individual genres are understood to exist within a larger system. The texts that participate within this genre system are stable and may end up being categorized differently as the genre system evolves over time;[53] however, while genres are often described through their rules and conventions (as discussed above), they are also connected to other genres through understandings of how they are dissimilar.[54] While it could be argued that genre boundaries are becoming fuzzier as texts become more hybridized, Mittell and Gledhill both suggest that genre mixing helps to solidify the organizing principle of genre,[55] with Gledhill going as far as to say that those moments of interaction between different genres are important because "desire is generated at the boundaries, particularly where social identities—gender, class, ethnicity, sexuality—are shifting."[56]

The musical genre system is similar to literary genre systems in that, as Brackett argues, musical genres are "not static entities with stable boundaries."[57] Musical genres are constantly evolving as new music is being written and released. Due to the immense and complex nature of the musical genre system, it is impossible to have a complete understanding of all the ways in which genres interact. Brackett describes a "branching process" that could go on "indefinitely,"[58] and Marino discusses the attempts that people have made to understand music through visual representations of the genre system.[59] Such authors have attempted to organize genres by affinity, genealogy, synchronicity, or even topography, but are never fully successful in offering a complete picture.[60] Brackett states the importance of this genre system as it relies on a system of difference, in that "genres become meaningful only in relation to one another."[61] How genres are organized, and how they distinguish themselves from each other through the elements that they emphasize, reveal their priorities and values.

Each text that participates in a genre is both consumed and created by human subjects who carry cultural assumptions. Frow emphasizes the importance of not only "deciphering textually inscribed meanings," but of "understanding how those meanings are organized by high-level discursive structures such as those of genre."[62] According to Gledhill, genre enables us to look beyond what is presented in order to reveal the "cultural work of producing and knowing the texts,"[63] and Mittell argues that "genre categories emerge, change, and impact our broader cultural contexts."[64] Thus, not only are cultural understandings shaped by texts through genre, they are influenced by the creators, whose subjectivities are ever-present in their works.

Similarly, in the music industry, genres reveal important aspects of the people who create, produce, and listen to music. Within the field of popular musicology, Brackett explains that "the question of genre … is often inextricably tied to how people identify with different types of music, which, in turn, is bound up with basic forms of cultural identification in terms of categories such as race, gender, sexuality, religion, and nationality."[65] Brackett invokes Bakhtin's notion of addressivity to explore the way in which an artist imagines their audience and addresses them accordingly, stating that "the style of the utterance depend[s] on those to whom the utterance is addressed, [and] how the speaker (or writer) senses and imagines his addressees." He goes on to say that "each speech genre in each area of speech communication has its own typical conception of the addressee, and this defines it as a genre."[66] At the same time, however, persona theory, which I will discuss below, accounts for the ways in which, even while addressing an assumed audience, the artist reveals their own personality through their performance. These assumptions of both performer identity and audience identity are critical to an understanding of genre.

Since Fabbri's article in 1982 on popular music genres, the examination of genre in popular music studies has become more established; however, a genre-focused perspective is only recently emerging in the study of music videos. One early example is Rob Strachan's article "Music Video and Genre: Structure, Context, and Commerce."[67] In this article Strachan argues that "the structural elements of music video are inextricably linked to the ideological constructions and marketing processes of popular music," including genre.[68] Through an analysis of two music videos from different genres, Strachan shows how "the characteristics of music video are related to the structures of musical signification but are also grounded in the visual tropes and social conventions of individual genres."[69] He addresses all seven elements of genre that I have outlined earlier in this chapter, acknowledging that music videos participate in and shape genre; utilize and introduce conventions; create a fictional world; are produced and understood through industrial and cultural contexts; and take into consideration the identity of the performer and viewer. Yet, by only analyzing two videos, Strachan's work points to the need for a broader overview of each genre and the larger genre system.[70]

Music videos are often organized into visual or narrative categories, without considering musical genres. This includes Carol Vernallis's sliding scale of non-narrative to narrative videos[71]; Joe Gow's differentiation between conceptual and performance videos;[72] E. Ann Kaplan's categorization of music video into (1) romance, (2) social consciousness, (3) modernism, (4) opposition, and (5) nihilism;[73] and Diane Railton and Paul Watson's discussions of (1) pseudo-documentary, (2) staged performance, (3) art, and (4) narrative videos.[74] These scholars assume that music videos from different musical genres have more in common with each other than not. Railton and Watson acknowledge that very little work has been done to connect musical genre to music video, maintaining that a video's visual genre cannot easily match the song's musical genre.[75] Instead, they focus solely on visual styles, as listed above, that are used to promote the artist rather than the song. With the exception of Strachan,[76] what none of these authors state is that, while these categories may be helpful, videos from some musical genres will be more likely to use certain visual styles over others as they are also constrained by genre conventions and ideologies.

The lyric video as genre

Although lyric videos have not been discussed in terms of genre nearly as much as other, more established genres, they follow the seven genre elements by having their own codes and conventions, creating fictional worlds, participating in the larger genre system as well as industry and cultural contexts, and contributing to the subjectivities of the artists and the cultural assumptions of the viewers. The components of lyric videos can be organized into three discursive domains—music, lyrics, and images—that interact with each other in various ways to present and enhance the original song.

The first domain, "music," incorporates both the musical elements and lyrical content of the song, and addresses how these musical elements are depicted in the video by visually indicating the tempo and rhythmic feel, the formal structure and dynamic range, any musical riffs or hooks, as well as the subject or object of the lyrics; for example, who is singing, and who/what are they singing to/about? A way to think about this domain is that, based solely on the graphics (i.e., if the video was muted), would the viewer still be able to tell if the song was fast or slow, energetic or somber, static, or filled with contrasting sections. The second domain focuses on the key element of the genre, the "lyrics," and how they are presented as text. Here the focus is on the words as they appear and move throughout the video—do they seem to have agency or are they driven by another force, their placement and prominence on-screen, and the graphic design of the words themselves, including font, size, and color. Finally, the third domain encapsulates any other visual elements or images that are presented on-screen, and again traces their movement on-screen, narrative content, and subjects depicted.

Of course, it is important to note how these three elements in the video communicate as a whole. Are the music, lyrics, and background images completely distinct from one another, or do they interact? The two most common conventions for lyrical presentation in this genre are as follows: (1) "kinetic typography," which is defined as "the art of integrating movement with text … it attempts to engage a viewer's attention by forcing them to visually track words which move across, up or down the page. It also uses color, size and font selection to highlight particular words";[77] and (2) the placement of the lyrics as a line of text at the bottom of the video, to allow for more action in the rest of the video.

As the lyric video has evolved, the images supporting and often surrounding the words have revealed a number of emerging strategies, including featuring still images from the official music video, colorful or textured backgrounds, and live-action footage of the artist, other actors, or objects interacting with the words. Of course, the various ways in which the music, lyrics, and images are presented are limitless, as are the ways in which they interact with each other to create an engaging video. The period of rapid development of the lyric video beginning in 2010 revealed a number of rising and falling trends until around 2017, when some artists began to develop their own conventions; consequently, each of an individual artist's lyric videos began to bear closer stylistic resemblances to one another rather than to the lyric videos of other artists.

Through the conventional combinations of music, lyrics, and on-screen images, lyric videos create fictional worlds. The use of colors, textures, and movement offers artists the ability to create a physical world, imitate another world, or create an aesthetic world within the lyric video setting. Surrounding such internal aesthetics, however, are larger cultural and industrial contexts that shape how the lyric video is formulated and received. As a tool used to advertise a single, the lyric video is part of the song's promotional rollout, whether it appears before, on the day of, or after the release of the single. Additionally, as the genre has developed, the industry's attention to lyric videos has heightened, and, while earlier lyric videos did not list credits, it is common now to see a credited director, editor, and producer, with multiple other possibilities including graphic designers and animators. Lyric videos are also situated within popular culture more broadly; they have received considerable online attention over the years, even earning the aforementioned MTV VMA category in 2014. Furthermore, lyric videos often feature the artist or reference their public life, as well as cultural moments or viral trends. All of these strategies are mobilized by the artist to heighten the intended message of the video. By referencing other cultural moments, lyric videos are situated within the larger web of genre, where they interact with other visual genres, including official music videos, behind the scenes videos, performance videos, prosumer lyric videos, and innumerable others. Finally, as an additional text that an artist chooses to release in conjunction with a single, lyric videos are an important vehicle for the artist to express a personal message or social critique, by using the videos to shape their own persona, or to amplify the meaning of the lyrical content.[78]

"Wide Awake": Becoming aroused to the possibilities of a new genre

Official lyric videos entered the mainstream in 2010. Katy Perry can be seen as a frontrunner in this trend since she was not only an early adopter of the genre but, at the time of this study, had consistently released lyric videos for most of her singles over the past eight years. Over the course of seven years and sixteen lyric videos, Perry has experimented with all three elements of lyric video—music, lyrics, and images—and has also introduced innovative and influential practices to the genre.

To illustrate the elements of the lyric video genre, I have selected one of Katy Perry's lyric videos, "Wide Awake,"[79] from her 2012 album *Teenage Dream: The Complete Confection* (referred to hereafter as *TD:CC*). Although it is an early example of the genre, the video exemplifies many of the key genre elements that have remained constant throughout the development of the lyric video, while also revealing how this new genre encourages innovative narrative techniques.

"Wide Awake" is organized around a Facebook timeline from 2012. The timeline runs down the middle of the screen, with text bubbles emerging out of points on that line. The text bubbles alternate between the lyrics of "Wide Awake" and genuine posts from Perry's official Facebook page from 2010 to early 2012 (Figure 9.1).

This video constructs a fictional space by combining two worlds that are often separated: the internal emotions and thoughts as expressed in the lyrics and the public social media posts. These posts, drawn directly from Perry's official artist Facebook page, outline her professional success, by systematically highlighting and celebrating the promotion and triumphs of her last album, thus presenting an image of achievement and overall happiness. The lyrics, however, communicate a much more somber story of heartache and disillusionment. They appear word-by-word in time as they are sung. The pale blue font still manages to draw the viewer's eye from promotional posts due to the large block capital letters, which jump out as they appear in their own text boxes connected to the

Figure 9.1 "Wide Awake" title screen (0:03).

timeline (Figure 9.2). When interspersed with the Facebook posts, the combined effect creates a dichotomy between the internal voice of the lyrics, and what is now understood to be a false front concealing this turmoil. While social media is commonly assumed to be truthful, and song lyrics sometimes understood as fictional stories, this lyric video seems to suggest the opposite: that the social media posts do not reveal Perry's authentic reality, whereas the lyrics are honest about her real-life experiences. This innovative juxtaposition mobilizes the lyric video genre to explore a storyworld in which the line between private and public is blurred. The video requires the viewer to absorb the meaning of both the lyrics and the social media posts simultaneously as the timeline continuously "scrolls" up, imitating the never-ending social media loop that many people look at every day.

"Wide Awake" is transparently positioned within both industry patterns and cultural contexts. By setting the lyrics on a Facebook timeline, it situates itself within the world of social media, with which almost all viewers will be familiar. The timeline depicted in the lyric video is not a personal Facebook account, but rather a promotional site for Perry's public persona. It does not include many personal posts, but instead outlines her many successes as a pop artist and appearance as a guest actress on *How I Met Your Mother*. Her profile picture is the album cover for *TD:CC* rather than a candid photo (Figure 9.3). Owing to these stylistic choices, the lyric video for "Wide Awake" becomes not only promotion for the single, but also an advertisement for every other lyric video, music video, and public performance that she had released during that two-year period. Multiple times throughout the video viewers are invited to "watch the video below." While it is only a recreation of a Facebook feed and thus contains no active links to those videos, the content that is being promoted is real, and spectators can seek it out elsewhere if they want to.

Figure 9.2 "Wide Awake" lyrics mixed with promotional Facebook posts (1:49).

Figure 9.3 "Wide Awake" final screen revealing the Facebook profile (3:42).

Highly relevant to the cultural understanding of "Wide Awake" is the fact that, in the two years between the releases of *Teenage Dream* (2010) and *TD:CC* (2012), Perry married and divorced the well-known British comedian, Russell Brand. "Wide Awake" is largely received as a personal declaration of disappointment and grief following her short fourteen-month marriage.[80] Although their romantic relationship is never depicted in the lyric video and the lyrical content alludes to heartbreak in a broad sense, spectators who have followed her career and her personal life are able to understand that the song is about more than a general disillusionment—it is also specifically about a failed romantic relationship.

By depicting the intimate lyrics as an invitation into Perry's life, the final post in the video announces her upcoming documentary *KATY PERRY: PART OF ME* (2012), which offers her fans an even more intimate glance into her personal life, including moments revealing the disintegration of her marriage. Therefore, not only is this lyric video promoting "Wide Awake," it is promoting her earlier music videos, lyric videos, television appearances, albums, singles, and the upcoming film. By advertising so much content from different media types and genres in a single lyric video and imitating a social media feed, this video is an exemplary example of media convergence.[81] Perry additionally relies on the participatory culture of her fans to actively seek out that content through various media platforms.[82]

The overall message of disillusionment in the song can be summarized in its own lyrics: "everything you see / ain't always what it seems." Through the lyric video, Perry is visually able to "amplify" this meaning as it "introduces new meanings that do not conflict with the lyrics, but that add layers of meaning," thus offering a more in-depth message and visually illustrating a larger narrative than is suggested in the song alone by presenting three distinct façades in the video: (1) her personal heartbreak and disillusionment; (2) the false front of social media; and (3) her own artistic persona, which only reveals a small part of her identity.[83]

First, and most relevant to the song itself, is the dichotomy she presents between her public professional success and her personal anguish, previously concealed from the public. This is laid out clearly through the setting of the mournful lyrics against the positive promotional Facebook posts. By inserting the lyrics between the authentic social media posts, Perry reveals a dichotomy between what she was presenting to the public and what she was really experiencing during that period of time.

Second, using the style of the Facebook timeline to connect the two types of posts offers an additional interpretation: that social media can be a false front. Utilizing the promotional posts in contrast to the emotional lyrics offers a commentary, or critique, on how social media is often used. Here Perry is, perhaps, inviting her audience to realize that a person's social media life does not often reflect their reality and, while they may seem happy and fulfilled, there is often heartache that does not get posted online.

Finally, by acknowledging her own participation in this kind of mediated social media presence, and by lyrically referencing melancholy moments that were not shared through social media at the time, Perry's vulnerability and somber presentation broaden our understanding of her "performance persona," and how it was constructed through her songs and videos.[84] Up to this point, Perry's constructed person was a fun, quirky, energetic pop star whose most well-known songs were "Ur So Gay," "I Kissed a Girl," and "Teenage Dream." Due to the lyrical content in these songs, she was often seen as a superficial or juvenile starlet, who used her gender and sexuality to draw attention from fans and critics alike. The lyric video demonstrates this through the many Facebook posts and videos, where Perry is habitually surrounded by bright colors and candy, with her femininity and sexuality emphasized. Meanwhile, everything surrounding these social media posts contrasts with those images, through the plain, pale blue font, highlighting the somber and vulnerable aspects of her persona.

Drawing intertextual connections between the lyric video and the official music video reinforces themes of disillusionment and Perry's softer persona.[85] Although the two videos may seem drastically different on the surface, both videos for "Wide Awake" tell a complementary narrative of personal struggles being hidden behind public successes. As with the lyric video, the music video refers to specific events from Perry's professional history by depicting Perry filming the music video for "California Gurls" and emerging onstage to sing "Teenage Dream." Her journey between these two events is much more theatrical, as she journeys with her younger self through a dark maze, overcoming frightening obstacles and avoiding deceptive traps. The visual juxtaposition between the bright and energetic performance scenes and the dark scenes of her mythical journey mirrors the contrasts of the pale blue text with the colorful Facebook posts in the lyric video. By highlighting these different versions of Perry's persona, both videos insinuate that she is aware of the colorful construction of her public image; the lyric video in particular invites the viewers into her personal narrative. Of course, these videos, along with the documentary that the lyric video promotes, are carefully constructed to create this idea of maturity and genuineness.

Conclusion

Through this close reading of the "Wide Awake" lyric video, I have demonstrated how lyric videos can be used to convey a personal message, to offer a social critique through an amplification of the lyrical content, to shape an artist's persona, or to explore a range of audiovisual effects that are available within this new visual genre. My hope is that this chapter inspires academic attention to be given to the study of lyric video, and provides a foundation for future research. Incorporating lyric video analysis into popular music and digital media scholarship can provide additional insight into artistic performance, lyrical meaning, artistic persona, identity representations, and genre aesthetics.

Notes

1   Hugh McIntyre, "The MTV Video Music Awards Go for the Second Screen Experience," *Forbes*, August 21, 2014.

2   Kevin O'Keefe, "Where Did All These Lyric Videos Come From and Why Are We Giving Them Awards," *Atlantic*, August 14, 2014.

3   Katy Perry, "Katy Perry—Wide Awake (Lyric Video)," YouTube video (3:46), music video, posted by "Katy Perry," May 20, 2012, https://www.youtube.com/watch?w=-3D5FwwtNVM.

4   "Audio" videos typically feature a static image, and are used as a way to get the song on YouTube in an official capacity.

5   Simon Frith, *Performing Rites: On the Value of Popular Music* (Cambridge, MA: Harvard University Press, 1996); and Philip Auslander, "Performance Analysis and Popular Music: A Manifesto," *Contemporary Theatre Review*, 14, no. 1 (2004): 1–13.

6   Carol Vernallis, *Unruly Media: YouTube, Music Video, and the New Digital Cinema* (Oxford and New York: Oxford University Press, 2013), 207.

7   The emergence of the lyric video was also influenced by the nature of YouTube, which places official music videos released over the past fifty years alongside prosumer lyric videos for fans to watch, not to mention the infinite other genres of videos on YouTube, from which some lyric videos draw inspiration.

8   Guilia Gabrielli, "An Analysis of the Relation between Music and Image: The Contribution of Michel Gondry," in *Rewind/Play/Fast Forward: The Past, Present, and Future of the Music Video*, edited by Henry Keazor and Thorsten Wübbena (New Brunswick, NJ and London: Transaction Publishers, 2010), 92.

9   Other examples include R.E.M.'s "Fall on Me" (1986) and Talking Heads' "(Nothing But) Flowers" (1988), which both address environmental issues, and "Praying for Time" (1990) by George Michael, who did not want to be in the music video so as to not distract from the lyrics which discuss social issues and poverty.

10 Carol Vernallis defines a prosumer as "a consumer who does production. The work can be semi-professional" in "Music Video's Second Aesthetic?," in *The Oxford Handbook of New Audiovisual Aesthetics*, edited by John Richardson, Claudia Gorbman, and Carol Vernallis (Oxford and New York: Oxford University Press, 2013), 465.

11 There is no way of knowing when the first prosumer lyric video appeared online, and, due to the nature of copyright, it has likely been removed from the site; however, prosumer lyric videos continue to be uploaded frequently, with little evolution in style.

12 Examples are difficult to find because they often get removed or fixed quickly. This could also be due to an avoidance of copyright infringement.

13 For example, a lyric video for "Hello" by Adele, uploaded by the account "Lyrics and More," has several million views on YouTube and yet it is not Adele's official audio or vocals, but in fact an unmarked cover. No information is provided to show who the singer actually is.

14 A "view count" of "views" on YouTube connotes the amount of times that video has been watched. Each social media platform has its own way to count views. YouTube counts a view if the video has been clicked and watched for at least the first 30 seconds.

15 Henry Jenkins, *Convergence Culture: Where Old and New Media Collide* (New York: New York University Press, 2006), 2.

16 Ibid., 2.

17 Ibid., 2–4.

18 Gérard Genette, *Palimpsests: Literature to the Second Degree*, translated by Channa Newman and Claude Doubinsky (Lincoln, NE: University of Nebraska Press, 1997).

19 Jason Mittell, *Genre and Television: From Cop Shows to Cartoons in American Culture* (New York: Routledge, 2004), 1.

20 Christine Gledhill, "Rethinking Genre," in *Reinventing Film Studies*, edited by Christine Gledhill and Linda Williams (New York: Oxford University Press, 2000).

21 Ibid., 221.

22 Fabian Holt, *Genre in Popular Music* (Chicago, IL: Chicago University Press, 2007).

23 David Brackett, "Popular Music Genres: Aesthetics, Commerce and Identity," in *The SAGE Handbook of Popular Music*, edited by Andy Bennett and Steve Waksman (London: Sage, 2015), 190.

24 Holt, *Genre in Popular Music*, 2.

25 John Frow, *Genre* (London and New York: Routledge, 2015), 167.

26 Gledhill, "Rethinking Genre," 226.

27 Mittell, *Genre and Television*, 15.

28 We can see this especially as we look at popular music with genre labels such as "oldies," or "proto" genres. At the time that these songs were first performed, they were labeled as a different genre, but, while the songs themselves have not changed, they now fall under different genre categories.

29 Brackett, "Popular Music Genres," 195.

30 Holt, *Genre in Popular Music*, 5.

31 Brackett, "Popular Music Genres," 195.

32 Gledhill, "Rethinking Genre," 238.

33 Mittell, *Genre and Television*, 151.

34 Franco Fabbri, "A Theory of Musical Genres: Two Applications," in *Popular Music Perspectives: Papers from the First International Conference on Popular Music Research*, edited by David Horn and Philip Tagg (Gothenberg and Exeter: IASPM, 1982), 52.

35 Ibid., 55–59.

36 Ibid., 59.

37 Brackett, "Popular Music Genres," 195.

38 Examples of country music conventions in this song are: lyrics describing guns and the Bible, as well as the use of harmonica, fiddle, banjo, and washboard in the instrumentation.

39 Randall Roberts, "Conservative Country Music Fans Lash Out at CMA Performance by Beyoncé and the Dixie Chicks," *Los Angeles Times*, November 3, 2016.

40 Jada Watson, "'Girl on the Billboard': Changing Billboard Methodologies and Ecological Diversity in Hot Country Songs," paper presented at the annual conference of the International Association for the Study of Popular Music—US Branch, Nashville, TN, March 2018.

41 Ibid.

42 Frow, *Genre*, 20.

43 Gledhill, "Rethinking Genre," 235.

44 Ibid., 223.

45 Frow, *Genre*, 133.

46 Mittell, *Genre and Television*, 3–5 (original emphasis).

47 Brackett, "Popular Music Genres," 194.

48 David Brackett, *Categorizing Sound: Genre and Twentieth-Century Popular Music* (Oakland, CA: University of California Press, 2016), 16.

49 Gabriele Marino, "'What Kind of Genre Do You Think We Are?': Genre Theories, Genre Names and Classes within Music Intermedial Ecology," in *Music, Analysis, Experience: New Perspectives in Musical Semiotics*, edited by Maeder Costantino and Reybrouck Mark (Leuven: Leuven University Press, 2015).

50 Ibid., 251.

51 Brackett, *Categorizing Sound.*

52 Ibid.

53 Frow, *Genre*, 166.

54 Brackett, "Popular Music Genres," 193.

55 Mittell, *Genre and Television*, 151.

56 Gledhill, "Rethinking Genre," 237.

57 Brackett, "Popular Music Genres," 192.

58 Ibid., 193.

59 Marino, "What Kind of Genre," 240.

60 Ibid.

61 Brackett, "Popular Music Genres," 192.

62 Frow, *Genre*, 133.

63 Gledhill, "Rethinking Genre," 222.

64 Mittell, *Genre and Television*, 192.

65 Brackett, "Popular Music Genres," 190.

66 Mikhail Bakhtin, *Speech Genres and Other Late Essays* (Austin, TX: University of Texas Press, 1986), 95.

67 Robert Strachan, "Music Video and Genre: Structure, Context, and Commerce," in *Music and Manipulation: On the Social Uses and Social Control of Music*, edited by Steven Brown and Ulrik Volgsten (New York and Oxford: Berghahn Books, 2006).

68 Ibid., 187.

69 Ibid.

70 Other examples of genre study in popular music are: Lori Burns, "Multimodal Analysis of Popular Music Video: Genre, Discourse, and Narrative in Steven Wilson's 'Drive Home,'" in *Coming of Age: Teaching and Learning Popular Music in Academia*, edited by Carlos Xavier Rodrigues (Ann Arbor, MI: University of Michigan Press, 2017), 81–110; Lori Burns and Jada Watson, "Subjective Perspectives Through Word, Image, and Sound: Temporality, Narrative Agency and Embodiment in the Dixie Chicks Video 'Top of the World,'" *Music, Sound, and the Moving Image* 4, no. 1 (2010): 3–38; and Lori Burns and Jada Watson, "Spectacle and Intimacy in Live Concert Film: Lyrics, Music, Staging, and Film Mediation in P!nk's *Funhouse Tour* (2009)," *Music, Sound, and the Moving Image* 7, no. 2 (2013): 103–140.

71 Vernallis, Carol, *Experiencing Music Video: Aesthetics and Cultural Context* (New York: Columbia University Press, 2004), 4.

72 Joe Gow, "Making Sense of Music Video: Research During the Inaugural Decade," *Journal of American Culture* 15, no. 3 (1992): 35–43.

73 E. Ann Kaplan, *Rocking Around the Clock: Music Television, Postmodernism, and Consumer Culture* (London and New York: Routledge, 1987).

74 Diane Railton and Paul Watson, *Music and the Moving Image: Music Video and the Politics of Representation* (Edinburgh: Edinburgh University Press, 2011).

75 Ibid., 43.

76 Strachan, "Music Video and Genre."

77 Kerry Maxwell, "Kinetic Typography," in *Macmillan Dictionary*, https://www.macmillandictionary.com/dictionary/british/kinetic-typography.

78 For a more in-depth history of how lyric videos have developed, see Laura McLaren, "The Lyric Video as Genre: History, Definition and Katy Perry's Contribution," MA thesis

(University of Ottawa, 2018), where I show the larger evolution of trends of the genre, through sixteen of Katy Perry's lyric videos and several others by popular artists.

79 This lyric video can be viewed at http://www.youtube.com/watch?v=-3D5FwwtNVM.

80 As evidenced by the speculation in several articles published shortly after the song's release, such as: Metro World News, "Monday Gossip Roundup: Katy Perry's 'Wide Awake' is Definitely about Russel Brand," *Metro.us*, May 21, 2012; Gabrielle Chung, "Katy Perry's New Song 'Wide Awake': Is She Singing about Russell Brand? (Video)," *Celebuzz!*, May 20, 2012; "Russell Brand Speaks on Katy Perry's Break Up Single 'Wide Awake': It's a Nice Song," *Capital FM*, July 19, 2012.

81 Jenkins, *Convergence Culture*.

82 Ibid.

83 Andrew Goodwin, *Dancing in the Distraction Factory: Music Television and Popular Culture* (Minneapolis, MN: University of Minnesota Press, 1992), 86–87.

84 Auslander, "Performance Analysis," 11.

85 Many pop music scholars doing work on intertextuality and music video have laid the foundation for this type of analysis, cited throughout this chapter, including Serge Lacasse, Lori Burns, Alyssa Woods, Jada Watson, John Richardson, and others.

Part III

Mediations: Multimodality/ Intermediality/Transmediality

10

Dynamic Multimodality in Extreme Metal Performance Video: Dark Tranquillity's "Uniformity," Directed by Patric Ullaeus

Lori Burns

This chapter examines the dynamic integration of words, music, and images in the extreme metal performance video of Dark Tranquillity's "Uniformity," directed by Patric Ullaeus.[1] Originating from Gothenburg, Sweden, Dark Tranquillity have been active since 1989 and are known as forerunners in the extreme metal subgenre known as melodic death metal.[2] The song under examination is the third track from their tenth album, *Construct* (Century Media, 2013), an album characterized by heavy riffs, melodic guitar work, atmospheric keyboard, and both clean and harsh vocals. *Construct* was received as a change in direction as the band shifted focus from an abrasive toward a more atmospheric sonic palette.[3] "Uniformity," a moody, mid-tempo song with a lyrical focus on the forces of societal oppression, stands out on the album as an anthemic moment due to the dynamic contrasts, unusual formal structure, and slower tempo. It is considerably slower than the other tracks on *Construct*, and it is even a slow offering in the context of the band's larger work list. Given the unique styling of this song, it is interesting that Dark Tranquillity selected it as a promotional single and video for the album. With its release, the band introduced the video as follows:

> After the introspective "For broken words" and the up-tempo riffing of "The science of noise," it's time to showcase the more anthemic aspects of the new album with the song "Uniformity." In contrast to the more experimental promo videos we made last year, we wanted the "Uniformity" clip to be an intimate and genuine performance video. Nothing but the music itself and the band members playing in the rehearsal room. For this, we hired renowned director Patric Ullaeus, and we're very happy to share the result with you. Stand up and be counted![4]

Also from Gothenburg, Patric Ullaeus's heavy metal music videos are characterized by a dark yet energetic quality that renders a powerful portrayal of performance style and aesthetics. His videography, beginning in the early 1990s, reveals a strong interest in Scandinavian heavy metal, featuring bands such as Amorphis, Arch Enemy, Children of Bodom, Dark Tranquillity, Dimmu Borgir, Evergrey, and Sonata Arctica. Offering an intimate view of the band members during the song performance, he defines clearly the scope and unique arrangement of the performance space. His cinematic capture of spatial, temporal, and corporeal elements yields an evocative representation of extreme metal performance, enhancing the given artwork by providing the spectator with a sense of immediate engagement. Ullaeus draws the spectator into the dynamic workings of performance that comprise the genre conventions of song structure, expressive strategies, and discursive (worldbuilding) elements. His finely detailed visual aesthetics place the spectator "inside" the work, encouraging an acute awareness of the embodied sensibilities of the performance. As the spectator-listener engages with the interpretation of embodied subjectivity and cultural meaning, a number of questions can be posed about the multimodal expression:

- How does the performance video present bodies and materials?
- How do bodies move within space and time?
- How do the elements of structure and design shape the performance?
- How are the expressive strategies of the performers captured?
- What discursive values drive the artistic representations?

The challenge for the analyst lies in exploring such questions while doing interpretive justice to the expressive layers of lyrics, music, and images.

Multimodal expression: Theoretical and analytic perspectives

To begin, let's consider a basic definition of multimodality and a summary of the analytic approaches applied in this field of inquiry.[5] In the domain of media narratology, Marie-Laure Ryan and Jan-Noël Thon understand multimodality as the integration of signs from different expressive modes (e.g., moving images, spoken language, and music) within the same media text.[6] Taking this as a point of departure, I understand multimodality as the artistic integration of multiple expressive modes within one media artifact. For ease of reference, I will refer to these modes as "expressive channels" or "domains" and identify the pertinent channels for music video as the lyrical, musical, and visual realms, which I will summarize as word–music–image. None of the channels will be treated as the site of static representational content, but rather will be considered as dynamic, gesture-based modalities of expression. For instance, in my analysis of the lyrical realm I will consider word choice as well as narrative actions and subjectivity, the musical realm will include the contexts of genre as well as the expressive elements of musical performance, and the analysis of the visual realm will, as Sarie Mairs Slee advocates, "include both image (noun) and action (verb)."[7] Furthermore, the analysis of these individual expressive channels will be put into dialogue with one another, illuminating the intersections between and among the expressive domains.

With the rise of digital media, analysts have responded to the challenge of how to explore multimodal texts with a number of fascinating approaches. One of the primary analytic motivations has been to identify how *meanings* emerge in and through the multimodal medium. To address meanings in music video, Andrew Goodwin (1992) identifies three types of relationship that can exist between a song and its video: *illustration, amplification,* and *disjuncture.*[8] He activates these categories as he considers the narratives, lyrical messages, and performance qualities of music videos. In a similar vein, Nicholas Cook (1998) proposes three models for multimedia relations: *conformance, complementation,* and *contest.*[9] With their comparable approaches, both Goodwin and Cook operate at the level of semantics and semiotics to identify how two domains (e.g., music and word, or music and image) work to convey meaning. This approach encourages the analyst to look for agreement or disagreement in the symbolic codes that emerge through the individual expressive channels. As such, the lyrics of a song might appear to convey a particular meaning, while the musical support for those lyrics could set up an oppositional meaning.

In *Experiencing Music Video* (2004), Carol Vernallis also works at the level of semantics and semiotics to identify intersections between sound and image, by examining symbols, metaphors, and structures.[10] She explores the aesthetic attributes of the music video text by identifying a number of specific elements for sound-image relations, including motion, continuity, contour, form, shape, motive, phrase, lyrics, timbre, harmony, and rhythm.[11] For each of these elements, Vernallis illustrates how music and images can be understood to interrelate in music video examples. Her analysis of Madonna's "Cherish," for instance, invokes kinesthetic relationships between the movements of the figures and water in the visual field and the momentum of the bass line and harmonic motion of the music.[12]

Working in the field of comparative literature, Lars Elleström (2010) presents an original model for the analysis of intermedia relations. Instead of referring to the individual expressive channels (image, sound, etc.) as modalities, he defines modalities as the basic characteristics that all media share: material modality (based on bodies and materials), sensorial modality (based on the human senses), spatiotemporal modality (based on material, cognitive, and virtual manifestations of space and time), and semiotic modality (based on the interpretation of symbolic, iconic, and indexical signs).[13] These four modalities "constitute a sort of a skeleton upon which all media are built."[14] Elleström's model thus invites the spectator to analyze the characteristics of a medium according to the crosscutting parameters of *materiality, sensoriality, spatiotemporality,* and *semiotics.*[15] This framework—although not explicitly articulated as a framework for the study of embodied motion—opens the door for its consideration: gestures are articulated by bodies through time and space, thus materials, senses, and space/time modalities provide a framework through which we can analyze the expressive gestures of music video.

In her 2017 study of "Sonic Spaces in Movies," Kathrin Fahlenbrach also proposes a crosscutting approach, building a dynamic model for image and sound that focused on the "amodal" qualities of *duration, intensity,* and *position.* By invoking these expressive parameters, Fahlenbrach analyzes image-sound relationships to interpret the affective moods of a film as well as its narrative meanings.[16] She treats these expressive parameters as a vehicle for analyzing the embodied dimensions of meaning by focusing on how "complex cultural and narrative meanings are associated with bodily based audiovisual Gestalts."[17]

Certainly, the attribute of embodied motion or gesture is of paramount importance in the consideration of multimodal expression, emerging as a guiding point of inquiry in recent music video studies. Slee (2017) has summarized the writings on dance in music videos by exploring "the use of dance and embodied action in the constructed identity of the singer, the embodied experience of the song, and the methods in which video-makers support the spectator's potential to transition from passive to active."[18] Slee's approach offers a perspective on spectator engagement, specifically showing how the multimodal text can be designed to suggest motion. To that end, the concept of "dancefilm" (a term that is used interchangeably with "screendance") has emerged within a field of inquiry that aims to examine a range of creative and interpretive issues in the cinematic capture of dance and gesture. Erin Brannigan defines dancefilm "as a modality that appears across various types of films including the musical and experimental shorts and is characterized by a *filmic performance* dominated by choreographic strategies or effects."[19] In his monograph *Screendance: Inscribing the Ephemeral Image*, Douglas Rosenberg provides a foundational description of the process of capturing dance on film:

> The collaborators experiment with choreographic form as well as the formal structure of filmmaking itself, altering camera placement, shot composition, and visual space to find the most efficient and aesthetic methods of framing movement. Within this conceptual shift from live to mediatized representation, the "dance" is reduced to the smallest sum of its parts. A gesture is isolated and viewed for its innate characteristics, as if through a microscope, and there is a scientific precision involved in the reproduction of even fleeting sequences of movement … Dance in cinematic space is necessarily conceived as a product of individual parts, and as the screendance progresses from preproduction to production to postproduction, additional elements are constructed, added, or removed.[20]

In this creative process of screendance, one might locate several sites of common ground with the capture of a music video performance:

1   the videographer labors to design the visual space for the video, as well as plan the shot composition and camera placement in relation to the performers;
2   performance gestures are isolated for their essential attributes;
3   technological precision is required for the capture and editing of movement sequences;
4   the process of production involves several stages from preparation to postproduction.

These aspects of the visual production (spatial design, shot composition, isolation of performance gestures, and precision of editing and production processes) provide the analyst with valuable perspectives on the presentation of space, time, and bodies in music videos.

The third element in Rosenberg's account—the isolation of performance gestures—has particular relevance for the capture of extreme metal performance videos. The genre of metal relies upon the performance video to represent the work of a band, with such videos featuring not only live performances from actual venues, but also a range of more abstract performance spaces, including rehearsal halls, derelict buildings, theatrical spaces, and outdoor venues. The chosen space becomes a setting in which to feature the performance gestures, thus providing the spectator-listener with a dynamic view of the instrumental and vocal expression. As video production technology has advanced, the filming and processing of metal performance has become highly technical, with intense close-ups of the band members, edited in careful synchronization with the audio track. In this regard, I will borrow a notion from Brannigan, who, in dedicating a chapter of *Dancefilm* to the close-up, offers the following remarks about the strategy: "By both enlarging the object within the frame and bringing it closer to the viewer, however, the close-up also emphasizes the physical and appears tangible."[21]

In response to the foregoing conceptual pathway through a range of interpretive approaches, my interpretation of the selected video will engage with the following critical perspectives:

- *Discourse*: How does the multimodal expression embody and inscribe the values of the band's performance and the song? At the level of semiotics,[22] what symbolic, semantic, and/or other narrative devices emerge to communicate meaning?[23]
- *Cross-domain intersections*: How do the expressive qualities and characteristics of the words, music, and images intersect and interrelate?[24] For instance, the analyst could ask: how do the video images allow us to "see" the music in a different way and (conversely) how do the musical elements shed light upon the images; or how does the musical and visual content connect to the subjective perspectives of the lyrics?
- *Dynamic gestures and engagement*: How does the multimodal text constitute the embodied expression of the performers[25] and invite the spectator into that performance? In this regard, the capture of micro-choreography in dancefilm is comparable to the close-up shots of virtuosic instrumental performance in metal music videos.

With the aim of bringing the expressive qualities of this performance video into view, I propose a framework that distinguishes the *spatial, temporal,* and *corporeal* dimensions as these cut across the expressive composite of word–music–image.[26] This analytic approach yields multi-dimensional perspectives on the music video as the site of lyrical, musical, and visual expression, facilitating the analyst's exploration of how meanings are created in the audiovisual text. I shall first distinguish the individual expressive channels, in order to scrutinize the apparent strategies. Then, based on this analysis of the individual layers, I shall examine significant intersections between and among these channels.

Dark Tranquillity's "Uniformity," directed by Patric Ullaeus

Word

The lyrics of "Uniformity" offer a philosophical reflection on a social group that is striving to resist subjugation, ultimately illuminating a sense of hope for escape.[27] Verse 1, part 1 describes an ongoing ambition for the fulfillment of desire and ambition, even though failure seems inevitable; the second part of verse 1 identifies the "faceless" who have toiled for the cause. The instructions to recognize false assertions and discover autonomy build a resistant front against unreasonable constraints. In contrast to the effort of resistance, the chorus insists that "we" must admit defeat, with "uniformity" implying, in that context, conformance to dictated standards. Ambiguously, "Uniformity" also bears the implication of group solidarity. The bridge asks if it is possible to escape subjugation ("life in the distance?") and the final outro affirms this direction as the social group is "dared" to hold onto hope.

Spatial contexts (Table 10.1) are implied by the force of constraint upon the social group that is contained within a bleak circumference, occupied by fallacies and agony. Verse 1 offers a glimmer of open space that is suggested by a "never ending sky," although it is declared to be limited. The bridge does not return precisely to that image, but connects to it through the concept of a "beacon of light."

Temporal contexts emerge in the lyrics through words that connote the continuing actions of the freedom strivers: "always fail," "remember the hours," "come to terms," "endure," and "endless resistance." This is a sense of time that bears a burden and connotes a feeling of weight, with the human condition portrayed as a seemingly unending battle against suffering. The verb tenses and phrase structures in the verses connote ongoing actions, while the chorus offers a more direct statement in the present tense, to deliver the imperative: "admit we are defeated." The bridge, in posing its powerful question about life in the distance, invokes a sense of the future.

The *corporeal* content of these lyrics is only ever implicit in the invocation of the human collective: the subject speaks of and for his people, always in the first person plural ("we," "our," "us"). The embodied actions to emerge are those connected with subjugation (e.g., "fail," "endure"), as mentioned in relation to the temporal content. The statement of action that suggests a potentially empowering gesture is delivered with each statement of the chorus that invites the collective to "stand up and be counted."

Table 10.1 *Word*: Summary of spatial, temporal, and corporeal content in Dark Tranquillity's "Uniformity."

Spatial	The implicit force of constraint upon a people is juxtaposed with the image of the open sky
Temporal	Ongoing actions that strive for freedom
Corporeal	A sense of burden upon the bodies of the subjugated group

This brief attention to the contexts of space, time, and bodies in the lyrics reveals a narrative of struggle, although the subject anticipates freedom. The structural divisions of the lyrics (verse, chorus, bridge) serve significantly different narrative functions: the *verses* account for the experience of ongoing resistance; the *chorus* appears to give in and declare defeat, however, the ultimate statement is ambiguous and can be heard instead as organized opposition; and the *bridge* and *outro* offer hope for escape. With these lyrical contexts in view, I now turn to the music.

Music

Although analytically productive to separate spatial, temporal, and corporeal elements, such a task poses a challenge due to their musical interdependence: musical gestures occur in time, performed by bodies in musical space. During this discussion, I will endeavor to maintain the distinctions, although the overlapping of parameters will occasionally be evident. Table 10.2 maps the musical content, with the purpose of identifying, for each formal section, the *temporal* features (metric/hypermetric structure), *spatial* features (harmonic and melodic design), and *corporeal* features (instrumental/vocal timbres and gestures).

Table 10.2 *Music*: Temporal (metric/hypermetric structure), spatial (harmonic and melodic design), and corporeal parameters (instrumental and vocal timbres and gestures).

Intro (00:16)	
3.5 bars	*Keyboard*: dark, blended tone
Cm	Melody outlines C minor Establishes 100 BPM
Intro, part 2 (00:25)	
12 bars: 6-bar phrase × 2	*Guitar*: clean; chorus effect yields bright tone; E♭ major patterns
a – a – b	
Cm – A♭ – B♭	*Rhythm g.* and *bass*: deep register power chords; heavy distortion, low in mix
	Kit: strong downbeat/hard backbeat; 8th-note activity in sync with guitar
Verse 1, part 1 (00:54)	
8 bars: each lyric phrase = 2 bars	*Vocal*: deep, distorted growl; rhythms emphasize beat (group coherence)
Dm – D♭ – Cm – Dm – D♭*	*Guitar* doubled by *keyboard*: distorted tremolo melody follows harmonic progression
*elides to Cm in next section	*Rhythm g.* and *bass*: increase in distortion level from intro
	Kit: crash (compressed to darken) plays every quarter; floor tom fill in-between each quarter
Verse 1, part 2 (01:14)	
8 bars: 4-bar phrase × 2	*Vocal*: maintains distortion; intensification of rhythmic activity creates momentum
Cm – E♭ – D♭ – C♭*	*Guitar* doubles *bass*: darker "buzz-saw" tone
*elides to Cm in next section	*Rhythm g.* and *bass*: harmonic change on downbeat; distortion level reduces back to intro level
	Kit: standard rock beat; ride cymbal

Chorus (01:32)	

12 bars: 6-bar phrase x 2
a – a – b
 	
Cm – A♭– B♭
2nd statement moves to Dm of
    verse 2
	Vocal: clean baritone; outlines E♭; resolves to E♭ (over A♭);
	    descends F – E♭– D on "uniformity"; elides to verse 2
	Guitar: clean, bright tone, E♭ major
	Rhythm g. and *bass*: continue with distorted power
	    chords, despite clean tone in guitar and voice
	Kit: as in verse 1, but china cymbal replaces crash to
	    create an edgy beat

Bridge (02:20) (occurs between parts 1 and 2 of verse 2)	

13 bars: 3-bar phrase x 4, with final
    phrase extended to 4 bars
| – 3 – | Cm
| – 3 – | Cm – B♭– Cm
| – 3 – | Cm – B♭– A♭
| – 4 – | Cm – B♭– Cm – A♭
	Kit: sudden temporal shift to half time (bar is twice as long)
	Vocal: distorted; drawn-out rhythms not in sync with guitar
	    melody, but align for final cadence
	Guitar: new melody; distorted tone, sustaining in upper
	    register, enunciative role in manner of clock "chimes"
	Rhythm g. and *bass*: distorted power chords on downbeat

Outro (03:58)	

13 bars x 3, with fade-out during
    final statement (as in bridge)
	Instrumental content from bridge
	Kit: very active; crash on every downbeat, tom fills
	    throughout, snare and kick played with full force
	Solo during the 2nd full statement

Beginning with the *corporeal* attributes of the music, I consider the voice and instruments that are featured on the recorded mix, with special attention given to timbre and gesture.[28] It is evident that the corporeal parameter also has implications for musical *space*, since sounds are situated within a spatial context;[29] however, my emphasis here will be the instrumental and vocal qualities and actions. "Uniformity" features Mikael Stanne's baritone voice, Martin Henriksson on both bass and rhythm guitar, Niklas Sundin on lead guitar, Anders Jivarp on drums, and Martin Brändström on keyboard. The overall sound quality is dark, yet full across the range of registers: the mid-high melodic elements in lead guitar and keyboard, harmonic lines and heavy riffs in rhythm guitar and bass, combined with a deep-registered activity in the toms, leave space for Stanne's distorted low growl, which is given depth through reverb enhancement. In the stereo mix, the guitars are panned to the left and right, while the voice is centered, with bass and kick placed below, and the keyboard, snare, and toms in a higher mid-range position. The rhythm guitar and bass are notably pulled back in the mix, to the effect that, despite the heavy distortion, they do not overpower the mix.

The song opens with a repeated keyboard gesture characterized by a dark, blended tone. The rest of the instruments enter for the second part of the intro: the lead guitar presents a chorused melody with a clean and bright tone; the rhythm guitar and bass strike heavily distorted power chords in a slow harmonic rhythm; and the kit delivers a strong downbeat-backbeat pattern, with 8th-note activity in sync with the guitar melody. The verse introduces a distorted vocal and guitar tremolo and the band members are in gestural agreement as they build the phrase; the overall effect is one of heavy distortion, especially on the heels of the intro.[30] The tremolo guitar melody in part 1 of the verse is replaced by a "buzz-saw" distortion in part 2 and an increase in rhythmic activity builds momentum.[31]

In striking contrast, the chorus features Stanne's undistorted ("clean") vocal, which sits naturally in a baritone range, overdubbed and enhanced by reverb to create a warm and open vocal space. His clean vocal part is complemented by a similarly clean tone in the guitar. The contrast between clean tone and distortion is an emblematic contrast between verse and chorus. Another significant *corporeal* contrast occurs at the bridge section, where the guitar presents a new melody with a distorted, sustained treble tone that suggests the "chimes" of a clock tower.[32]

For this framework, I consider *musical space* to comprise the pitch space, realized as melodic and harmonic content. In this regard, it is important to note that, within the context of melodic death metal (melodeath)—a genre that can be dominated by melody—much of the melodic content on this track is minimalistic, serving more as accompaniment than lead. Emphasis is placed on the harmonic structure, with its unconventional usage and its workings within an unusual formal design.

Although the harmonic material of the song is C Aeolian, the tonal center is challenged by passages that introduce chromatic harmonies around C (D♭ and C♭) and others that suggest E♭. Harmony is thus a site through which musical *space* is negotiated: in the verse structure, the harmony explores chromatic movement, opening up potential directions to new spaces, as compared with the chorus, where the harmony directs to C. Although the chorus progression relies upon its own cyclic repetition for the resolution, any expectation is disrupted when the chorus is followed by the verse (0:54 and 2:01) and its striking commencement on D minor. The bridge also operates subversively by taking the progression from the chorus and reversing it; that is, instead of moving from A♭ through B♭ to C, the bridge moves from C to B♭ to A♭, tentatively at first, but ultimately in an emphatic gesture (and I will have more to say about this in the discussion of *temporality* below).

Space is also negotiated through the parameter of melody, which is an important expressive element of melodic death metal. That the melodic content of the verse follows the harmonic progressions can be considered as an enactment of unity or agreement. By contrast, the melodic content of the chorus creates an effect of disagreement: while the clean guitar accompaniment and vocal melody outline the E♭ triad, the harmonic progression is striving toward C minor. Although the vocal melody presents a major mode (in an undistorted timbre), it is only apparently in obedience with convention; in fact, in its actual context, it is running contrary to the established order. And that order is even further disrupted when melody and harmony both move to D at the start of the ensuing verse. The melodic descent to D in the voice is an overt indication of musical resistance, inviting the listener to reflect upon its significance. Here is a moment when we can appreciate the function of discourse analysis to understand the meaning of a musical gesture: in this case, the denial of the expected musical resolution signals disruption or defiance.

In the *temporal* parameter, the song follows a consistent tempo (a walking pace of 100 beats per minute [BPM]) and meter (4/4, with backbeat structure), however, the bridge section and outro stand out for their shift to half time, giving the illusion of expanded time. The parameter of temporality also includes the hypermetric (phrase-level) design. In this song, subtle manipulations of phrase conventions disrupt our sense of phrase regularity and predictability. To begin, the simple keyboard melody that introduces the song (0:16) might seem to begin on the downbeat, but that interpretation has to be revised when the next section begins, as it converts what we might have thought was beat 3 into the downbeat. It is a jarring moment, a moment of realization that the melody actually begins on beat 3.

The second part of the intro (0:25) subverts conventional phrasing in another way: the 12-bar section is subdivided into two 6-bar phrases with a 2-bar subphrase design in the pattern *a–a–b*, as the harmony holds on to C minor for the *a–a* material and then moves at a faster harmonic rhythm from A♭ to B♭ for the *b* subphrase. When the second statement of the 6-bar phrase begins, the return to the *a* material seems to function as the expected bars 7–8 of an 8-bar phrase, with the resolution to the tonic C minor. This might sound quite logical and conventional (*a–a–b–a*), however, it does not hold up in the continuation. Under that interpretation, the second phrase would then only comprise a statement *a–b*, followed by the surprising arrival on D-minor harmony. Thus, the listener is compelled to reconsider what was just heard, and revise their understanding to a contracted 6-bar phrase structure with an open harmonic form (*a–a–b*). When this material becomes the basis of the chorus, it is once again misleading by design.

By comparison with the intro and chorus, the verse delivers a straightforward 8-bar phrase in part 1 and two 4-bar phrases in part 2. Thus, the temporal parameter provides yet another site of negotiation: while the verse upholds hypermetric conventions, the intro and chorus serve to disrupt. The bridge section is arguably the main site for temporal disruption: first, the kit shifts the sense of meter to double the length of the bar (referred to as half time); the effect is one of slowing down or expansion, as we wait for the downbeat to occur or for the ominous thud of the backbeat. The bridge is not only unconventional for its framing—or disguising—between the two halves of the verse, but also for its internal structure. It comprises four statements of a 3-bar guitar melody, the fourth of which is extended temporally by one bar. I have already referred to this material in relation to the subversion of the expected harmonic progression; this is the section that reverses the pattern of the chorus so that the harmony moves strongly and emphatically to A♭, denying the previous progressions to C. The temporal design reinforces this progression, amplifying the effect of subversion. Furthermore, Stanne's vocal growl here is delivered in drawn-out rhythms that do not entrain to the "chimes" guitar melody, until the final cadence of the fourth statement. It is the final section of the song that mobilizes the disruptive content of the bridge, closing out the track with that material. Whereas the bridge—with its challenges to musical convention—is framed by the verse sections, the outro stands as the final statement, offering a conclusive gesture of defiance.

Image

How does Ullaeus build a visual world for this song? Inspired by the questions posed by Rosenberg for the field of screendance,[33] we can study the design of visual space, the isolation of performance gestures, the technological production, and the processes of post-production. These elements map quite effectively onto my proposed framework of *spatial, temporal*, and *corporeal* elements. Let's apply these now to the visual field, before interpreting how this expressive channel works in multimodal dialogue with the lyrics and music.

Spatial elements

Ullaeus filmed the musicians in a rehearsal hall, where they performed in close position. The images are captured with a short depth of field, with many shots taken from a low position (Table 10.3, figure a). A very hard spotlight, shining toward the spectator, makes it impossible to discern the back or sides of the space and the black floor contributes to the paradoxical effect of tight constraints juxtaposed with indiscernible borders. The majority of images are medium and close-up shots that focus on the performers. This is prepared immediately during the song intro, when a series of shots present the musical entries of the keyboardist (0:18), the drummer (0:25), the guitarist (0:25), and the rhythm guitarist (0:29). (The recorded track features the same musician on bass and rhythm guitar, thus he is not seen to be playing the bass in the music video.) Although the vocalist (Stanne) does not sing until the first verse (0:54), he is shown arriving on "stage" (0:20), much as he would do in a live performance. Ullaeus seldom provides an establishing shot with a full perspective of the space (Table 10.3, figure b). In these moments, a wide-angled lens (with no correction for lens aberration) yields a curved or distorted shot. Overhead camera work (Table 10.3, figure c) offers another perspective on the scenario, often focusing on Stanne who frequently looks upward when he sings, but also capturing the other musicians. Despite the constrained setting, Ullaeus manages to suggest other spaces in order to give the illusion of an escape from the rehearsal hall. He accomplishes this in a number of ways:

1 The use of black and white and/or film burn to create other colors as points of departure from the established performance (3:14).
2 The change of focus (pull focus, also to be discussed below as a temporal effect) from the performers to the surface of the camera lens—covered with specks of dust and other detritus—brings into view an abstract image that one might compare to a night sky with stars, thus an external space that connotes the outdoors (0:34, 1:20; 1:36, 2:06, 2:45, 4:09).
3 The placement of Stanne in a different setting for the chorus, standing alone against a wall on which the symbol associated with the album (a white circle, with a line through it) is projected (1:40).

Temporal elements

In his video treatment, Ullaeus creates a sense of constant motion. Although the space is cramped and the image capture very limited, he accomplishes the effects of movement through a number of techniques, achieved through both production and post-production. At the level of production, these are some of the movement effects: the camera pans across the bodies of the performers and instruments; the camera capture for the kit is likely on a slider, so that the image moves gradually around the instruments; shifts of focus are accomplished through focus pull (or rack focus), which is used to change the focus on a given performer; and the frequent use of light flare (Table 10.3, figure c), created when the light hits the lens while the camera is moving (which can also be added in post-production). At the level of post-production, movement is created by the following techniques: the rapid

Table 10.3 *Image*: Screenshots to illustrate spatial, temporal, and corporeal content (a. 1:04; b. 1:34; c. 1:23; d. 1:28; e. 1:29; f. 2:06).

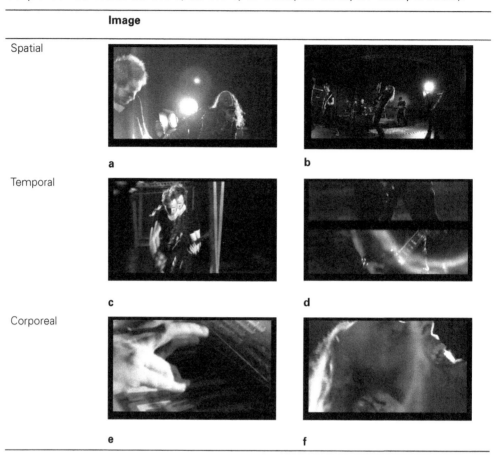

	Image	
Spatial		
	a	b
Temporal		
	c	d
Corporeal		
	e	f

pace of editing, as the image shifts from one performer to another, or from one angle of the same performer to another; the jumping of one frame to another, as if in an old film (Table 10.3, figure d), as well as the inclusion of dust and scratches on the film which flicker from one frame to the next; and the superposition (echo effects) of one moving image upon another, thus augmenting the gestures (Table 10.3, figures c and e).

Corporeal elements

As a metal performance video, the dynamic presentation of the performers and the instruments is vitally important. Ullaeus uses his techniques of capture and process described above to position the performers' bodies in full view. Compared to attending a live concert event, access to the performance is made intimate by extreme close-ups of the gestures that create the sounds. For instance, we have visual access to the hands of the keyboardist (Table 10.3, figure e), articulating the notes on the instrument; the guitarist's hands on the neck and on the strings; the sticks in contact with the drums; and the vocalist in a range of stances (Table 10.3, figure f). Furthermore, in his shot selection, Ullaeus is highly sensitive to the song, such that when an instrument delivers an important gesture or when the song lyrics are presented, the instrument or vocalist is in view. This approach showcases the song's structure at the front and center of the film. The techniques of movement, described in connection with the temporal elements, enhance and intensify the musical expression, for instance, when the flickering and echo effects work rhythmically in time with the music, suggesting a careful integration of the expressive channels.

Word–music intersections

To analyze the composite multimodal expression, I will begin with words and music, and then build upon that analytic foundation with the visual treatment. Dark Tranquillity's "Uniformity" communicates a strong message of resilience and resistance in the face of tyranny. The music intensifies the lyrics through the invocation of certain *corporeal* elements, including tone production (levels of distortion) and vocal-instrumental interactions, all of which create gestural agreement or opposition. These effects convey the sentiment of enduring struggle in the verses, with the ambiguous statement of defeat in the chorus contrarily suggesting an uprising and the hope for escape emerging in the bridge and outro. Distortion is activated as a vehicle for the expression of both opposition and anger in the face of tyranny: while the clean guitar melody and vocal tone during the chorus appear to submit to the imposed constraints, they are accompanied by heavily distorted power chords. The distortion levels reach a peak of intensity in the verses (i.e., increased distortion level in the power chords; distorted tremolo melody followed by "buzz-saw" melody in the lead guitar; and deep vocal distortion), establishing the role of distortion as a discursive symbol of unified resistance. In the bridge and outro, the guitar "chimes" melody (with distorted and sustained tone) serves as a melodic "call to arms," affirming the potential for escape.

The message that emerges from this *corporeal* interpretation of words and music seems consistent with the results of the *spatial* and *temporal* analysis. In the *spatial* realm (defined for this analysis as pitch content), the harmonic-melodic structure communicates a persuasive story about resistance to convention: the harmonic-melodic development of the verse is unconventional in its chromatic patterning; the chorus is then characterized by an apparent harmonic directionality toward C minor, which is thwarted by the shift to D minor—emphasized by the vocal turn to D—as the final chorus cadence elides with the verse. Ultimately, the bridge emphatically (and insubordinately) reverses the directional progression of the chorus. In the *temporal* realm, these effects are further enhanced: the verses present conventional 8-bar phrases with hypermetric coherence; the chorus is ambiguous in its phrase structure, as the contracted 6-bar phrase denies expectations; and the bridge, by contrast, expands temporality through the half-time effect and the four statements of a 3-bar phrase with the expansion of the fourth statement. The placement of the bridge is of tremendous discursive significance as it is "disguised" between the two halves of the verse, pointing again to the clandestine mobilization of resistance.

Word–music–image intersections

In his video treatment of this song, Ullaeus conveys a visual story that simultaneously captures the band in performance and upholds the lyrical and musical meanings. A performance video of this kind calls for a very different approach to videography as it does not include footage from external scenes that might expand our conception of the narrative. That is not to say that the video is lacking in narrative, but rather that the narrative emerges only in and through the shaping of the musical performance. As I mentioned in the theoretical introduction to this chapter, it is productive to borrow analytic values from screendance/dancefilm, especially in consideration of the performance space, the capture of micro-gestures, and the potential effects to be achieved by production and post-production.

Ullaeus sculpts the performance video with a deep respect for song content and expression, as evidenced by his intensification of the emergent meanings of the verse, chorus, and bridge sections. Let's begin with the *corporeal* attributes of distortion and gestural unity/disunity that emerged in my foregoing discussion of word–music intersections. Ullaeus translates the peak of distortion intensity (in the first part of the verse) into a feast of visual distortion: the band members are featured in close-up shots that change quickly from one to another, highlighting their individual gestures through contrasting camera angles and motion, pull-focus effects, and post-production echoes, light flares, and image flickering. Ullaeus also shows sensitivity to the subtle decrease of distortion in the second half of the verse when he similarly reduces the intensity of his visual effects to create a smoother, yet still distorted, presentation of the phrase. At the same time that we experience the visual distortion, we are also keenly aware of the gestural unity of the band members: each of the vocal-instrumental gestures is shown to contribute to the forward momentum of the phrase. Furthermore, Ullaeus provides an establishing shot at the cadence of the verse, to reinforce the band's sense of unity as a group.

Staying with the verse for the moment, let's consider how Ullaeus treats the *spatial* values of the music. The striking harmonic features of the verse comprise its point of origin on D minor and its chromaticism. The arrival on D minor (following the intro, which was directed toward C minor), is treated visually as a moment of spatial disruption: the image sequence includes, within the span of a few seconds, four different shots of the vocalist, featuring different angles, distances, levels of focus, and visual distortion, all of which combine to create a sense of destabilization. The second instance of the D minor arrival (at the start of verse 2) features a comparable disruption as the image shifts from Stanne, who was featured alone in the chorus, to even more extreme close-up shots of the band members. Again, the third instance (at the start of verse 3) is characterized by extreme close-ups and intense distortion effects.

Ullaeus's chorus treatment stands out for its presentation of Stanne alone. My earlier word–music analysis revealed the chorus as the moment when "uniformity" connotes both conformance and uprising ("stand up and be counted"). The visual representation of Stanne's body during the chorus scene suggests a speaker on a platform, in front of the flag that stands for the cause (1:40). While he is seen, as a leader, to deliver a persuasive, potentially coherent, statement, the visual distortion continues through the flickering and blurring of the image, the use of pull-focus, and the echo effects of his body and face. The visual echo of his face at the word "defeated" (supported by the A♭ harmony of the chorus progression) is particularly noteworthy for the augmentation of his duplicated (echoed) image (1:41), which bears a hopeful expression. The visual scene for the chorus thus affirms the sense of ambiguity that emerges in the lyrics and music: is he conveying a message for the oppressor or for the oppressed?

Perhaps the answer to this emerges in the second statement of the chorus. It is treated similarly to the first, with Stanne as the focus; however, there are some subtle differences that suggest a potential change in the discursive function. To begin, the second chorus opens (as did the first chorus) with a colorful moment of film burn, but this time the warm golden and red tones wash and flicker over Stanne's image, adding a layer—and potentially creating a new space—for his social platform. Not only do we have the color of the film burn, it is also remarkable that the footage in the second chorus is otherwise black and white, a color change that also signals a change in the discursive conditions. In addition, the final statement of "uniformity" is allowed, at the end of the second chorus, to cadence visually on his face, as compared with the interrupted visual cadence at the end of the first chorus (2:00) where the sonic attention to the guitar tremolo is matched by a visual shift of attention. The second chorus thus closes with more confidence, and this, occurring in the context of the new sense of space, tips the scale in the interpretation of how this material functions. I interpret this statement as confirmation that the chorus declaration ("stand up and be counted in uniformity") serves the oppressed more than the oppressor.

A similar shift in visual space occurs at the beginning of the outro, where Ullaeus again opts for a change to black and white color treatment. This change, in keeping with the previous chorus statement, once again symbolizes the opening of a new space that creates the potential for escape, in alignment with the lyrical-musical message.

In my analysis of the word–image intersections, I drew attention to the bridge section for its "disguised" placement in the middle of verse 2, and for its remarkable changes in musical form and expression, which signaled it as the site of greatest contestation: together, the metric shift to half time, the reversal of the harmonic order, and the distorted and sustained guitar "chimes" all serve to mobilize the group in a call to action. Visually, Ullaeus affirms the feeling of disrupted space and time as he implements a distortion of the establishing shot, appearing to bend the space at the word "light" (2:22). He also lingers over each band member, holding longer shots than in previous sections.

Conclusion

Reflecting on the complex process of analyzing the multimodal content of a performance video, I would like to conclude by highlighting a few of the methodological issues to have emerged during this study. First and foremost, in order to respect the performance attributes of the video treatment, my aim has been to develop an analytic model that would facilitate consideration of the embodied expression of the band members. Although an approach grounded in discourse analysis (which includes semiotic and semantic meanings) exposes the emergent cultural meanings, it seems inadequate to elucidate the embodied expression of this performance-based work. A discursive approach does well to uncover how the lyrical expression of resistance is channeled in and through a musical structure that works within, but also unsettles, conventions. In order to achieve a deeper understanding and appreciation for the subtle meanings that reside within the expressive channels of words, music, and images, however, it is important to expand the analytic approach to include the cross-domain relations that operate at the level of material embodiment. The framework parameters (*spatial, temporal,* and *corporeal*) therefore offer a productive focus for the analysis of the multimodal domains.

My overarching concern is that a multimodal analytic methodology should do justice to the individual expressive channels before attempting to draw interpretive multimodal conclusions. I would even go so far as to argue that it is in the peeling apart of the layers that the real multimodal analysis and interpretation take place. In my experience, it is the separation of the layers for rigorous consideration that leads to my most advanced understanding of a multimodal work. Ultimately, my analytic goal has been to employ a method for multimodal interpretation that will hold value for other analyst-spectators who wish to engage intimately with the embodied expression of performance videos.

Acknowledgments

The author wishes to acknowledge the Social Sciences and Humanities Research Council of Canada (SSHRC), for its support of a five-year program of research on music video (2013–2018). This study grows directly out of that research. A preliminary version of this chapter was presented at the Art of Record Production Conference in Huddersfield, United Kingdom (September 2019).

Notes

1   Patric Ullaeus of Gothenburg, Sweden is the founder of the *rEvolver Film Company* for music videos, commercials, and photography. His list of works and activities is described at www.revolver.se.

2   For an account of the early days of the band and the rise of the Gothenburg metal scene, see Century Media Records, "DARK TRANQUILITY—Out of Nothing—The DT Documentary," YouTube video, November 21, 2016, https://www.youtube.com/watch?v=vtWeRA-lbz0&t=3s.

3   See James Christopher Monger, "Construct Review," AllMusic.com, https://www.allmusic.com/album/construct-mw0002530325; and Kyle Ward, "Dark Tranquility: Construct," SputnikMusic.com, https://www.sputnikmusic.com/review/56961/Dark-Tranquillity-Construct.

4   "Dark Tranquillity: Premieres 'Uniformity' Music Video on Metal Hammer UK," CenturyMedia.com, May 13, 2013, http://www.centurymedia.com/newsdetailed.aspx?IdNews=12825&IdCompany=3.

5   For a summary of the developments in the field of multimodal studies, which had its origins in the discipline of linguistics, the interested reader is encouraged to consult Carey Jewitt, Jeff Bezemer, and Kay O'Halloran, *Introducing Multimodality* (Abingdon, Oxon: Routledge, 2016). See also Gunther Kress and Theo van Leeuwen, *Multimodal Discourse: The Modes and Media of Contemporary Communication* (London: Arnold, 2001); and David Machin, *Analysing Popular Music: Image, Sound, Text* (Thousand Oaks, CA: Sage, 2010). Machin promotes a semiotic approach to multimodal expression in popular music when he suggests that we "attempt to create an inventory, a code-book or phrase-book, of these meanings as they are found in the semiotic choices made throughout the music, lyrics, and look of the artist and in the soundscapes we find in video sequences" (212).

6   Marie-Laure Ryan and Jan-Noël Thon, eds., "Storyworlds Across Media," in *Storyworlds Across Media: Toward a Media-Conscious Narratology* (Lincoln, NE: University of Nebraska Press, 2014), 10–11.

7   Sarie Mairs Slee, "Moving the Music: Dance, Action, and Embodied Identity," in *Music/Video: History, Aesthetics, Media*, edited by Gina Arnold, Daniel Cookney, Kirsty Fairclough, and Michael Goddard (London: Bloomsbury, 2017), 149.

8   Andrew Goodwin, *Dancing in the Distraction Factory: Music Television and Popular Culture* (Minneapolis, MN: University of Minnesota Press, 1992), 86.

9   Nicholas Cook, *Analysing Musical Multimedia* (New York: Oxford University Press, 1998): 98–99. For a critical response to Cook's definition of multimedia, see Jamie Sexton, "Introduction," in *Music, Sound and Multimedia: From the Live to the Virtual*, edited by Jamie Sexton (Edinburgh: Edinburgh University Press, 2007), 2–3.

10 Carol Vernallis, *Experiencing Music Video: Aesthetics and Cultural Context* (New York: Columbia University Press, 2004), 183–194.

11 Ibid., 211–220.

12 Ibid., 211–212.

13 Lars Elleström, "The Modalities of Media: A Model for Understanding Intermedial Relations," in *Media Borders, Multimodality and Intermediality*, edited by Lars Elleström (Basingstoke: Palgrave Macmillan, 2010), 11–48.

14 Lars Elleström, "Transfer of Media Characteristics among Dissimilar Media," *Palabra Clave* 20, no. 3 (2017): 674.

15 My own approach to multimodality has much in common with Elleström's work in comparative literature (ibid.). Over the past decade, I have developed a variety of models that examine the expressive channels of word–music–image in and through a range of crosscutting parameters; see Lori Burns, Marc Lafrance, and Laura Hawley, "Embodied Subjectivities in the Lyrical and Musical Expression of PJ Harvey and Björk," *Music Theory Online* 14, no. 4 (2008); Marc Lafrance and Lori Burns, "Finding Love in Hopeless Places: Complex Relationality and Impossible Heterosexuality in Popular Music Videos by Pink and Rihanna," *Music Theory Online* 23, no. 2 (2017); Lori Burns, "Multimodal Analysis of Popular Music Video: Genre, Discourse, and Narrative in Steven Wilson's 'Drive Home,'" in *Coming of Age: Teaching and Learning Popular Music in Academia*, edited by Carlos Xavier Rodrigues (Ann Arbor, MI: University of Michigan Press, 2017), 81–110; and Lori Burns and Marc Lafrance, "Gender, Sexuality, and the Politics of Looking in Beyoncé's 'Video Phone' (featuring Lady Gaga)," in *The Routledge Research Companion to Popular*

Music and Gender, edited by Stan Hawkins (London and New York: Routledge, 2017), 120–134.

16   Kathrin Fahlenbrach, "Sonic Spaces in Movies: Audiovisual Metaphors and Embodied Meanings in Sound Design," in *Body, Sound and Space in Music and Beyond: Multimodal Explorations*, edited by Clemens Wöllner (Abingdon, Oxon: Routledge, 2017), 129.

17   Ibid.

18   Slee, "Moving the Music," 148.

19   Erin Brannigan, *Dancefilm: Choreography and the Moving Image* (New York: Oxford University Press, 2011), 7.

20   Douglas Rosenberg, *Screendance: Inscribing the Ephemeral Image* (New York: Oxford University Press, 2012), 1.

21   Brannigan, *Dancefilm*, 19.

22   Goodwin, *Dancing in the Distraction Factory*; Cook, *Analysing Musical Multimedia*.

23   For a music video analysis framework that incorporates discourse analysis, see Burns, "Multimodal Analysis."

24   Elleström, "The Modalities of Media"; Fahlenbrach, "Sonic Spaces in Movies."

25   Brannigan, *Dancefilm*; Rosenberg, *Screendance*; Slee, "Moving the Music."

26   The spatial, temporal, and corporeal parameters here relate to some of my recent models, however, the specific crosscutting parameters do change according to the attributes of the specific object of inquiry. Since the Dark Tranquillity video, directed by Ullaeus, privileges live performance capture, the identified parameters of space, time, and body are particularly relevant. It is also important to point out the connections here to Elleström's model, which is based on four modalities: material, sensorial, spatiotemporal, and semiotic (Elleström, "The Modalities of Media").

27   The lyrics to the song are available at: https://genius.com/Dark-tranquillity-uniformity-lyrics. For the video, see Dark Tranquillity, "Dark Tranquillity—Uniformity (Official Video)," YouTube video (5:43), directed by Patric Ullaeus, posted by "Century Media Records," May 10, 2013, https://www.youtube.com/watch?v=BolGeBNPK1w.

28   It is relevant here to reflect on Simon Frith's formulation of the voice as body in *Performing Rites: On the Value of Popular Music* (Cambridge, MA: Harvard University Press, 1996), 187.

29   Ruth Dockwray and Allan F. Moore, "Configuring the Sound-Box 1965–1972," *Popular Music* 29, no. 2 (2010): 181–197.

30   The distortion of the rhythm guitar increases at the start of the verse. According to Ciro Scotto's distortion scale, the distortion level of the rhythm guitar would be a 3.0 in the intro, but a 3.3 in the first part of verse 1. That level then falls back to 3.0 again for the second part of verse 2. See Ciro Scotto, "The Structural Role of Distortion in Hard Rock and Heavy Metal," *Music Theory Spectrum* 38, no. 2 (2017): 185.

31   This style of distortion was made popular in death metal through bands such as Entombed; see, for instance, their track "Drowned" on *Left Hand Path* (Earache, 1990). The effect is created by the prominent upper harmonic content of the distorted guitar in the 3.2 or 3.3 range of Scotto's distortion scale (ibid.).

32   Scotto would place the level of distortion on the guitar melody of the bridge at the 2.0 level (Scotto, "The Structural Role of Distortion"). A special thank you to Ciro Scotto for his consultation on the interpretation of these distortion levels.

33   Rosenberg, *Screendance*, 1.

11

Tying It All Together: Music Video and Transmedia Practice in Popular Music

Christofer Jost

Introduction

Popular music as we know it today is almost inconceivable without audiovisual media. Moving images have shaped the expectations of the visual appeal of popular music for generations, from the captivating film performances of the early (crooning) music stars—who were also movie stars—via the elaborate show arrangements of television entertainment to the postmodern video worlds of MTV. The vast potential of combining moving image and music is by no means exhausted, as evidenced by the many creations uploaded to video platforms and social media sites, mostly produced by people without a professional background. Scholars from different academic disciplines (popular music studies, cultural studies, film studies, and so on) have stressed the tremendous dynamism at the intersection of popular music and audiovisual media, indicating, on the one hand, the emergence of aesthetic conventions beyond the norms of cinematic art and, on the other hand, the reorientation of such conventions due to changing media environments.[1]

The music video still occupies a central place in the mediation of popular music. The "central" attribute is to be understood quite literally, since music videos—at least in the segment of global mainstream pop music—occupy a peculiar middle position in the spheres of producing and distributing popular music.[2] They usually come into existence *after* an album has been produced, promoting songs from an album as singles. Music videos are typically released *before* the artist or band goes on tour and/or plays festival gigs. Because of this intermediary position, they become a powerful producer of meanings; they prescribe a reading of the song (and of the artist's persona) due to the selection of images and the form of their presentation. Some artists have begun to produce visual albums (also in the mainstream segment, for instance, Beyoncé's *Lemonade*), thereby challenging the popular music distribution network and making the audiovisual product the official artwork.

Nevertheless, it remains to be seen whether such phenomena function as a violation of the rule (and derive their specific appeal from it) or whether a new rule will arise.

This chapter deals with the phenomena of the cross-media linking of popular music artifacts and characterizes these as manifestations of a transmedia practice. In order to clarify what the peculiarities of this practice are, I unveil first the theoretical implications of the term "transmediality" and then introduce a model that identifies three manifestations within transmedia popular music production. My aim is to create a tableau of comprehension categories that provide a common basis for discussion in the growing field of transmedia-oriented music research.[3] The field of transmedia music production calls for broad insights that allow an abstract understanding of its practical and structural conditions.

On the transmediality of popular music: Some theoretical considerations

The history of popular music and audiovisual media comprises several stages of development, genres, and creative practices, including concert films, television shows, and music videos, as well as widely forgotten formats such as soundies and scopitones.[4] In spite of such media diversity, it should not be forgotten that phonography—the primary mode of producing and presenting popular music—is also a media practice.[5] The live performance also must be addressed by reference to the concept of mediality: pop stages are complex apparatuses that fuse microphones, amplification, public address system, and image and video projections (or LED walls) into a functional whole and shape the aesthetic experience during a concert.[6]

The history of popular music reveals that there have always been musicians who have felt compelled to "tie together" the media-based outcome of their creative work. Once a particular topic or motif is brought into focus, a variety of links and cross-references emerges within the work of a musician or a band. Musical sound, audio-vision, and performance are brought into effect in a sequence of mutually dependent events. Consequently, producing music becomes tied to a conceptual approach. Such practices challenge the notion of popular music as being culturally determined by phonography.[7] Transmediality offers a framework to explore musical products within the complex interdependencies of cultural structures and practices. According to media theorist Irina O. Rajewsky, "transmediality" refers to the occurrence of a specific subject,[8] aesthetics, or discourse within various media types, without it being necessary or possible to identify a particular source medium.[9]

Transmediality is inextricably tied to the concept of transmedia storytelling, which focuses on filmic-narrative content and the transitions in the distribution of such content via different communication channels, stressing the equally conceptual and participatory character of this kind of media output.[10] With regard to popular music, this concept needs to be scrutinized for a number of reasons: (1) it is necessary to clarify to what extent music-based, transmedia products can be explained by certain narrative traditions and narratologies; (2) lyrics do not necessarily tell a story; and (3) narrative structures that constitute a story rarely extend beyond the individual song, except in the case of the concept album or one of its subtypes, the rock opera (see below).[11]

Rajewsky employs the term transmediality in line with the concepts of intramediality and intermediality. These three terms all address the hybridization of media production. Intramediality refers to media phenomena that involve only one medium (e.g., literature), in which textual references (e.g., text-to-text references) are conveyed. Intermediality addresses hybrid forms that include at least two media types.[12] Both terms are just as important for the analysis of the artifacts of popular culture as the concept of transmedia, however, the latter has the advantage that it is not limited to the aspects of media combination or media reference. Music can be analyzed as a process of aesthetic production by using different media types, the latter of course also being considered from an economic point of view, since artists and their creative staff are forced to renegotiate their appearance against the backdrop of various music-related media genres and an immeasurable range of musical products circulating in these genres.[13]

In sum, transmediality can play an important role in music analysis, since it implicates the overall phenomenological spectrum of popular music, including voice, image, gesture, or fashion. Such an analytic approach responds to the realities of popular music reception. The para-social relationships of fans with "their" music support the idea that the attractions of popular music need to be scrutinized in a holistic manner.[14]

Transmediality in practice: Three common manifestations

The phenomena underlying the model I provide below can be understood as hybrid aesthetic phenomena that unfold and interact in a cultural network of different media, domains of knowledge, and symbolic resources. My discussion is organized to explore the broader concepts that I find useful in my analytic considerations of transmedia music: aesthetic concepts, artification, and virtual stardom. I will discuss each and then illustrate the model with the example of U2's "The Fly."

Aesthetic concepts

Aesthetic concepts are powerful and applicable to a wide range of cultural phenomena.[15] Take the concept of trash, for example. The impression of the trashy can be conveyed when listening to a song or when watching a movie, and it is by no means clear whether aesthetic concepts like trash (or camp, retro, cool, or realness) can be ascribed to a particular source medium, so that an accurate impact history containing more or less clear causalities can be reconstructed. One can relate to such concepts as creative agents, without being brought into line with a particular art movement, style, or oeuvre. Aesthetic concepts are not only powerful, but also complex: a flawed object cannot automatically be considered "trash,"[16] an ironic performance "camp,"[17] or a casual pose "cool,"[18] and so on. Furthermore, aesthetic concepts presuppose a discursive process and can be determined along a narrow terminological framework (often by means of a single word). Aesthetic concepts emerge on the basis of past interpretations of objects. Such interpretations can assume the status of cultural knowledge: something is classified as "trash" in the present because something similar has been classified and communicated as "trash" in the past. Aesthetic concepts thus result from the interplay of several institutional and cultural agents (including consumers). Consequently, they cannot be launched (like products and brands) and their effectiveness depends on the extent to which knowledge about them is present in society.

Camp is an apt example of the importance of knowledge in the diffusion of aesthetic concepts. The fact that this expression is used today for labeling aesthetic products results to a great extent from an essay by Susan Sontag, which bears the simple title "Notes on 'Camp'" (first published in 1964 in the journal *Partisan Review*). A study of the impact of "campy" artifacts in popular culture is simply inconceivable without Sontag's work, because it deciphered a behavior toward aesthetic objects that was actually designed for exclusivity—Sontag characterizes it as an aristocratic taste predominantly homosexuals used for communication—thus creating a reference horizon for subsequent interpretations. Although Sontag's approach is quite nuanced, she extracts an "essence" of camp as "[the] love of the unnatural: of artifice and exaggeration."[19]

It took a while, however, for the "pleasures" of camp to find their way into mainstream popular music culture. Primarily female stars, such as Dusty Springfield, Grace Jones, Cher, and Madonna, began to pick up the aesthetic codes of camp (knowingly or unknowingly) and then feed them into new communication circuits. Camp cannot be determined by a series of more or less binding features; camp is rather identifiable as a style, yet treated as a question of attitude. The campiness of a performance is revealed in how an artist positions him/herself against the overflowing abundance of cultural utterances circulating at a given time and the prevailing social norms. According to this understanding, artists such as those mentioned above, who in musical-stylistic terms and with regard to the temporal embedding of their work can clearly be distinguished, can be assigned to the camp concept in segments of their artistic work. In the case of Dusty Springfield, "campiness," for example, is expressed in the combination of pompous love songs with dramatic string arrangements, a very glamorous look (consisting of bleached and mostly pinned-up hair, elegant evening gowns, and the highly visible use of mascara), and television appearances that were steeped in very lively and, in most cases, theatrical and dramatic gestures. Meanwhile, "campiness" in Madonna's work of the 1980s and early 1990s can be detected in her hyperbole and stylized glamor-prone music video personae (as in the clips for *Like a Virgin* or *Material Girl*) and the elaborately choreographed eroticism of revue shows citing live performances (see the *Blond Ambition Tour* in 1990). The most recent example of docking with the camp concept in the pop mainstream is Lady Gaga, who fulfills the requirement of the artificial at the level of audio production (by presenting an overdetermined mix of popular electro styles, especially in her early albums), as well as in her highly theatrical music videos and live performances.

These examples, and Sontag's essay, suggest that an analytical approach to the materializations of popular culture must consider the worlds of meaning that emerge in and through these materializations. In doing so, a veritable jungle of meanings comes to the fore that requires a broad range of analytical competencies from every researcher. For instance, is camp a tonal, pictorial, cinematic, or performative phenomenon? What about the concepts of trash, retro, or cool? The attribution of meaning to the social world occurs well beyond these boundaries, requiring a holistic approach.[20] It is the responsibility of the analyst to bring order to the immensity of meaningful ramifications in the social world. Detecting aesthetic concepts and analyzing their intertwined manifestations in different media is one way to fulfill this task.

Artification

The relationship between art and popular culture has been and is still widely discussed in society. While in academic research the opposition implied in this relationship has been extensively problematized and reconstructed as a result of social processes of appreciation (art) and devaluation (non-art), it remains highly relevant for both creative actors and recipients.[21]

With the increasing social visibility of a music-centered youth culture in the second half of the 1960s, its actors became aware of their own cultural significance. This certainly did not apply to all musical products in the same way, but did apply to those marked with the then new label "rock."[22] Indeed, in a segment of popular music production a dynamic of "artification" arose, revealing a substantive orientation toward art on both an ideational and aesthetic level.[23] This cultural dynamic can be reconstructed, among other things, by means of the so-called concept album, which, as the name implies, sought to present popular music with a "concept," suggesting a degree of sophistication.[24] While the concept albums produced at that time did not necessarily lead to transmedia modes of presentation (although the thematic coordination of artwork and music can most likely be interpreted as a transmedia approach), a variant of the concept album—the so-called rock opera—did result in transmedia development.[25]

At present, the rock opera, at least the re-creation of such works, does not seem to play a major role in global popular music. Nonetheless, it has enjoyed great commercial success in Western popular music and can be accredited with having greatly pushed the artistic boundaries of pop music. As an example, I will discuss The Who's *Quadrophenia* from 1973,[26] as the abundance of cross-media links that emerge in this work provide an insight into the creative challenges associated with a conceptual approach that integrates various media.

Quadrophenia was produced as a double album and eventually released in October 1973. A short text written in the style of an interior monologue portrays the everyday life of the protagonist, a young man called Jimmy. In addition to this, a total of thirty-two monochrome photographs illustrate different stages of the plot in the style of a photo novel. Apart from this, narrativity is constituted within the lyrics, which are printed in the booklet; they provide important perspectives on the protagonist's psyche and his perception of the world. On top of this, there is a fourth level of narration: environmental sounds. As in the case of radio plays, these sounds characterize different settings within the plot.

Six years after the album release, in 1979, *Quadrophenia* was produced as a feature movie (directed by Franc Roddam). The cinematic realization led to a multitude of changes in the plot, but the most striking difference was in how the musical material was reorganized. The songs were turned into a film score, leading to a number of interesting changes and atmospheric effects. The adaptation not only affected the songs' sequential order and selection (only ten out of the original seventeen songs of the album were included in the movie), but also the level of sound production. More specifically, some songs were reproduced during the course of the film production, with single audio tracks remixed in order to give them a punchier sound.[27]

In 1973 and 1974 *Quadrophenia* was performed for the first time in the course of a tour by The Who. The performances constituted a conventional rock show that focused on the idiosyncratic expressivity of the four band members, rather than the embodiment of the fictional characters outlined in the album storyline. The second staging of *Quadrophenia* took place in 1996 and 1997, during another tour, and featured guest appearances by three singers who embodied some of the fictional characters.[28] The stage design for that tour was dominated by a video screen on which either the live action on stage or film sequences—comprising historical imagery, extracts taken from the original movie, or newly produced material—were shown. The newly produced sequences played an important role in constituting a theatrical reality during the music performance. They appeared between the songs, depicting Jimmy, the protagonist, in various situations and poses. Due to their length, these clips influenced the flow of the concert, making it "more" narrative and consequently "more" theatrical.

The rock opera is a clear example of a transmedia approach that is based on the cross-media elaboration of a specific subject; however, artification can also refer to the *oeuvre* of an artist or a band. Popular music appears in this case as a *Gesamtkunstwerk* that extends over space and time. Kraftwerk—the German exponents of electronic pop music—have played a pioneering role in such manifestations of transmediality. Founded in 1970 by Ralf Hütter and Florian Schneider, Kraftwerk wanted to revive a specific German tradition concerning the world of art and design—a tradition that was disrupted by the hypertrophic neoclassicism of National Socialism. One major reference was the Bauhaus philosophy, which, as a core element, conveyed the idea of combining art, architecture, and technology.

Due to Kraftwerk's integration of these design aesthetics, the band's works carry a very strong visual appeal.[29] The creative vision of the band is closely linked to the idea of the man-machine, an entity based on the mutual relatedness of human conduct and technological devices. This is not only expressed with the help of album titles (*Autobahn, Radio-Aktivität, Trans Europa Express*), cover artwork, and lyrics, but is also conveyed *in* the music. At least until the early 1980s, most of the instrumental parts were performed in the studio, although programming tools were already available at the time.[30] This artistic approach results in a refined and crisp sound that can still be associated with the band. The interest in clear and concise forms is also revealed in Kraftwerk's music videos. In the video for "Trans Europa Express" (1977), the band members are shown as businessman-like passengers of the train of the same name, which was back then commonly regarded as a highly modern vehicle. "The Model" (1981) features their performances within the futuristic stage setup of the *Computerwelt* tour, combined with found footage depicting typical scenery of the fashion world. The video for "Showroom Dummies" (1982), in turn, presents the band as a group of androids who pose in a freeze position or move in a mechanical manner, and these gestures are enhanced by extremely minimalistic graphic material (colored stripes).

On stage, Kraftwerk's sonic and visual identity is transformed into the aesthetics of technological functionality. For instance, the stage from the band's 1981 *Computerwelt* tour looked like the control room of a factory or a power plant, and, furthermore, a set of dummies contributed to the show as the materialization of "the robots," which the band addressed in the song of the same name. An interesting point concerning a recent stage setup (as in the band's retrospectives in the MoMA or Tate Modern in 2012 and 2013) is that the equipment is reduced to table-like stands, and it is not clear what is actually inside those stands.[31] Instead of four musicians, singing and playing their instruments, the audience experiences four male persons standing almost motionless in front of four toolbars, invoking an everyday work routine. A video screen behind the musicians suggests the idea of functional minimalism: it is rectangularly shaped and marks the end of the stage.

Traces of the above-described manifestation of transmediality are likely to be found in the *oeuvres* of several pop artists, for instance, the adaptation of postmodern aesthetics in U2's work in the early 1990s (to be discussed below) or, more recently, the orientation toward sacral forms of representation in the visual aesthetics of Swedish heavy metal band Ghost.[32] But it must be added that a somewhat coordinated appearance in several media products—for example, the same look on an album cover and in a music video—does not necessarily coincide with the creation of a transmedia "Gesamtkunstwerk."

Virtual stardom

For my third aspect of transmedia development, I shall consider the concept of "virtual stardom." While it might be understood to overlap with the related concepts of persona or image,[33] it directs us to particular attributes of the phenomenon. To be specific, the adjective "virtual" has two meanings: (1) it refers to phenomena that are not real, but appear to be real, and (2) it suggests a potentiality, in other words, the capability of being something else.[34] Both meanings are highly relevant to the concept of virtual stardom. Accordingly, virtual pop stars can be understood as fictitious, non-physical, and quasi-personal entities, which are not tied to a particular media *dispositif*, but which provide the spectator with a "social" counterpart, albeit one whose being-in-the-world is unpredictable. The aspect of unpredictability distinguishes the addressed phenomena from the cultural technique of narration, which always refers to a series of events that have started and ended at a definite time, and thus, in other words, are determinable. Also, a distinction must be made from the concept of fiction, since the constructs in question are not located and do not operate in a world beyond that of the beholder. The virtual stars perform for "real" people and try, as indicated above, to enter into a kind of social interaction with them.

With respect to the apparent realness, it should be noted that the impression of the real requires a number of creative decisions and procedures that incite the viewer's imagination to ascribe an independent existence to the virtual stars. On the one hand, the viewer has to pay attention to a convincing design of forms (in the sense of *Gestalt*)—the personal entities conveyed must develop a certain appeal, which can be grounded in their exceptionality, their erotic aura, their novelty character, and much more. On the other hand, the virtual entities must understandably attach to existing value formations and social meaning structures, that is, they must have characteristics—personality traits, as it were—on the basis of which they are experienced as convincing and interesting counterparts.

Strictly speaking, my first example of virtual stardom is contentious, because Guy-Manuel de Homem Christo and Thomas Bangalter, who together make up Daft Punk, are undeniably human, and thus understood to be "real" rather than "virtual." And yet, Daft Punk is distinguished by its virtual presentation. After having had little success with their indie rock band Darlin', the duo switched to the house genre and disappeared behind robot masks. In doing so, they challenged a keystone of popular culture: the star concept. The film star of the classical Hollywood cinema of the 1940s and 1950s is an early example of how a "real" person repeatedly appears in the mass media, developing—in the course of their media presence—certain attributes that convey a special charm.[35] The shift of the artistic identity of Christo and Bangalter into the realm of the virtual breaks with well-established conventions of music presentation and reception. Daft Punk thus challenges the spectator's imagination: the audience is potentially carried off into a fantasy realm of friendly androids who bring pleasure to the people by producing dance music. According to Cora Palfy, it is most notably the dynamic tension between the artificial and the organic that constitutes the specific appeal and cultural value of Daft Punk's music. Palfy suggests that the duality of the robotic and the human signifies the larger relationship between technology and humanity, and she critiques how society at large understands and interprets such artistic utterances.[36] According to this view, Daft Punk acts in the spirit of Kraftwerk, whose work addresses the (possible) symbiosis of humanity and technology, contravening performance norms in popular music.

The case of a "completed" virtuality can be found in another band, Gorillaz, that has been in circulation since 1998 and consists of four "members": 2D, Murdoc Niccals, Noodle, and Russell Hobbs. The driving forces behind this project are Damon Albarn, mastermind of the Britpop veterans Blur, and Jamie Hewlett, a British comic-book artist (*Tank Girl*). The Gorillaz project conveys its cartoon image across all media channels of communication. Of course, the real people responsible for the music of the Gorillaz do not completely disappear; Damon Albarn gives interviews as the head of Gorillaz and performs the band's music on stage with fellow musicians. In contrast to Daft Punk, however, the Gorillaz team strives to construct identities that operate beyond human physicality.

Music videos are central to the virtual star construct of "Gorillaz." Through this medium, the stars are presented in different stories and settings, without a superordinate narrative concept relating the actions of the four protagonists. One can only assume that the fragmentary nature of their collective biography is intended. Similar to the real-life performance of people, the life of the Gorillaz is presented as a series of situations, which offers the production advantage that new accents and unforeseen twists can be effected with each new clip. It is worth noting that the clips do not always follow the precept of the "human," because the four characters, as in many cartoons, are relieved of the laws of physics. The possible occurrence of new accents and unforeseen twists correlates with the aforementioned second meaning of the word virtual: potentiality. A coherent narrative framework would place the entire "Gorillaz" product too close to literary and cinematic presentation logics and transform the virtual framework into conventional fictionality. The group exists in an "anywhere" (which can also be an "everywhere") and this state of indeterminacy may not be dismantled.[37]

The band's (fictitious) autobiography, *The Rise of the Ogre* (2006), plays a central role in identifying its members' personal characteristics. Autobiographical works are not typically central to the perception and understanding of a pop performance; they appear as a supplementary source for ardent fans who urge to know "everything" about their beloved stars. But in the case of the Gorillaz the prerequisites are different. Since there is no such thing as a personal identity of the band members that the fans can identify with, individual background stories fulfill an important function. Consequently, the book in question comprises the fictitious biographies of the four band members.

Furthermore, the transmedia conception of the Gorillaz is manifest on stage. The four protagonists appear in film sequences that are shown parallel to the performance of the real musicians or they are brought into effect as holographic projections.[38] Through these virtual characters, the Gorillaz seem to turn into old acquaintances whose quirkiness one knows too well.

I would like to close this section on virtual stardom with an example of participation-based transmediality. Known as Hatsune Miku, this artificial figure carved out a career with a synthetic singing voice that was developed in 2007 as a demonstration object for the software *Vocaloid2*, produced by the Japanese company Crypton Future Media. Since then, the software has been extended to include different voice effects, registers, and languages. The figure, a juvenile schoolgirl visualized in manga style, is provided with her own biography and now exploited as an independent brand, including live performances—where she appears as a hologram—and a Facebook entry. Over time, a fan base of considerable size has grown, as evidenced by concerts in well-filled large halls, now no longer only in Japan.[39] Crucial to the participatory nature of Hatsune Miku is that amateurs have the opportunity to produce songs for it. KarenT, the music label of Crypton Future Media, publishes these songs; particularly successful pieces are then distributed through iTunes and Amazon. In this new process, amateurs can create videos that are then presented through free websites (such as Nico Nico Douga).[40] The virtuality described here depends upon the communicative options offered by the internet or, more precisely, the so-called Web 2.0. Axel Bruns subsumes the dynamics of presenting and sharing self-produced products that were unfolded by Web 2.0 under the term "produsage" (a portmanteau of "production" and "usage").[41] The key requirements for such produsage comprise the provision of cost-neutral and easy-to-use web applications as well as the refinement of networking options through open programming interfaces.

In light of its internet transmission, Hatsune Miku might be seen to forecast future developments in music presentation and reception. It seems quite realistic to expect that participatory star constructs like Hatsune Miku, which very much depend on interactive media, will co-exist in the future with conventional forms of presentation alongside forms nobody has yet imagined.

A concise case study: U2's music video "The Fly" (1991)

"The Fly" was the first single and music video release for *Achtung Baby* (1991), U2's seventh studio album.[42] At the beginning of the 1990s, the band was working toward a new public image. The song "The Fly" and the persona of the same name were central to this undertaking. The music video incorporates various elements of the album, while anticipating elements that should play an important role in the following tour, *Zoo TV* (1992–1993). Taken together, the music video and the artistic products created during this time comprise a transmedia artification of popular music. The band and its production team drew on current trends and practices of the time that were understood to be manifestations of postmodernism and postmodern art, respectively. Although *artification* is the main theoretical point of reference in this case, the example also includes elements of artistic production that can only be interpreted thoroughly with reference to *aesthetic conceptuality* and *virtual stardom*.

The singer of U2, Bono, embodies "The Fly" persona, which is fashionably marked by a black leather jacket, greased hair, and a pair of dark, round sunglasses that evoke associations with a fly because of their oval shape. In the course of the video, Bono appears in various situations in which he reveals a behavior that can best be described as exalted, egocentric, and ostentatious. According to the band, the persona of "The Fly" is the epitome of egocentric exaggeration, a kind of barstool philosopher desperate for admiration, who serves as an artistic vehicle to disclose the contradictory state of postmodern society that promoted knowledge and ignorance at the same time.[43] In the music video, Bono adopts this persona to interact with passersby at London's Piccadilly Circus, who do not seem to be informed about his performance and react accordingly with surprise; the corresponding video passages subsequently evoke the impression of a filmed art performance. A crucial detail in the transmedia artwork is that this persona is already recognizable on the back cover of the album. Hence, the transmedia connection does not only refer to song and video, but also to artwork and video.[44]

The persona-centered approach does not end at this point, but rather is transferred to the realm of the virtual. This results from the music video for "Hold Me, Thrill Me, Kiss Me, Kill Me," a song featured in the film *Batman Forever* (1995). Here, the persona appears as a character in cartoon passages that seize on the setting (Gotham City) of the Batman narrative and are combined with scenes from the film. The persona thus breaks away from the personal identity of U2's singer Bono and is transformed into a quasi-personal entity whose future is indefinable, but which cannot be grasped physically. These features are in accordance with the parameters of virtual stardom, although only to a limited extent, since the virtual character does not have a real star career. After 1995, U2 turned to other projects and the persona/character was dropped.

Let us return to the indications of postmodern artification: the songs on *Achtung Baby* seem like an acoustic assemblage compared to the previous albums. For example, the love song, "So Cruel," precedes the noisy "The Fly," which is followed by the laid-back, groove-oriented "Tryin' to Throw Your Arms Around the World," which, in turn, is followed by the psychedelic "Mysterious Ways." The listener is taken from one affective style to another. In addition, sampling, percussion, wah-wah, voice distortion, and guitar fuzz effects are used—all of which are sonic elements that are not found on the previous albums. It seems as if U2 created a style mix that had no reference point in the band's own career.[45] Consequently, the song collection on *Achtung Baby* can be interpreted as an instance of sonic appropriation; "The Fly" especially, with its noisy lo-fi sound, supports this interpretation. The sonic context of lo-fi also indicates an orientation toward the aesthetic concept of trash. The sound texture of the song is mainly determined by the heavily distorted electric guitar. Along with the wah-wah pedal, the distortion produces a shrill sound at various points, and the larger sonic profile of the recording can be described as boisterous, giving the impression of a cheap and bumbling production. In the music video, this impression is created by strong contrasts between light and dark, extremely fast zooms, shaky hand camera, and a rough-grained image texture.[46]

The music video also takes up the concept of appropriation, which becomes apparent due to stacked television sets in the showcase of an electronics store. Here, the act of appropriating manifests itself—literally in the sense of appropriation art's premises—in the transformation of industrially manufactured everyday artifacts into fundamental elements of an artistic representation. This representation addresses the ambiguous set of meanings that are attributed to such artifacts by society.[47] The television sets would also be used during the tour as stylized projection screens. In addition, the tour revealed a close tie to appropriation art through the integration of chunky industrial headlights and East German "Trabant" cars.

Furthermore, the use of television sets indicates an orientation toward the techniques of media art practiced at that time (e.g., in the works of Nam June Paik).[48] Explicitly, the correlation with media art is expressed in the use of an oversized video wall on Piccadilly Circus. Deviating from its actual purpose, namely to place advertisements, it depicts short text messages written in capital letters (e.g., "Watch More TV"), including the name of the subsequent tour ("Zoo TV"). This means of representation reveals great similarity with the works of concept and media artists Barbara Kruger and Jenny Holzer; in a tour report, the band indicated that this similarity was intentional.[49] During the tour, the same messages were broadcast on the projection screens.

The brief analysis presented here establishes that—in certain cases—the meaning potentials and social effects of popular music videos can only be adequately understood with reference to the superordinate concept of transmediality. At the same time, I have indicated that music-centered transmediality requires a transdisciplinary, historically grounded, theoretical framework that uses individual terms—in this case, artification, aesthetic concepts, and virtual stardom—to reveal which strategies, procedures, and domains of knowledge are at the basis of aesthetic practices.

Conclusion

Popular music operates in the visual realm and is complex in its structuration. Not only is there an abundance of (historical) audiovisual genres, but also the aesthetic practices that organize the interplay of image and sound are highly differentiated. Since MTV, the music video has functioned as a media genre in its own right and is today the central platform for the further development of music-based audiovisual aesthetics. Nonetheless, the developments of the last three to four decades are characterized by strongly converging currents between and among media. Convergence generally suggests that formerly distinct systems start to develop common operational procedures, at least in certain areas of the system. With regard to popular music, this means that, until the 1960s, the media diversity of popular music was expressed in the fact that musicians produced records, performed their music on a stage, became visible on press pictures and record covers, and—only the most successful among them—acted in music films or television. Only from the late 1960s onwards were artistic products increasingly coordinated with each other, leading to the instance in which a narrative core could unite them, as in the "rock opera."

The music video, it can be argued, is a child of these convergent dynamics. Based on the symbolic links between image, body, and sound that emerged in media genres, such as music and concert film, television show, or promotional clip, it then developed new aesthetic accents, leading to the prevalence of the terms "(music) video aesthetics" and "clip culture." Although the music video seemed to dwarf everything in the heyday of MTV in the 1980s and 1990s, temporarily becoming the dominant medium of pop culture, the production of music videos has always been embedded in a network of factors that extend beyond the aesthetic codes of audiovisual media.

Transmedia phenomena emphasize the multidimensional contexts of music videos and provide insight into the levels of complexity that are now possible in music production. An analysis of popular music that considers the variety of media genres and intersections casts an important light upon the motives, strategies, and procedures adopted by pop musicians and their production teams to shape their musical aesthetics. Such production concerns must undoubtedly also be read against the background of cultural and economic factors, as transmediality is temporally constituted as a vehicle for achieving long-term attachment by the audience. Pop musicians tend to put everything in the balance to stay popular, which is not to be construed as a criticism per se. After all, this circumstance has given rise to aesthetic constructs that inspire, astonish, and confound spectators all around the world, which cannot be found in any other field of artistic production.

Notes

1   See Jean Burgess and Joshua Green, *YouTube—Online Video and Participatory Culture*, 2nd ed. (Cambridge: Polity Press, 2018), 32–44; Carol Vernallis, *Unruly Media: YouTube, Music Video, and the New Digital Cinema* (Oxford and New York: Oxford University Press, 2013), 3–29; Martin Herzberg, *Musik und Aufmerksamkeit im Internet. Musiker im Wettstreit um Publikum bei YouTube, Facebook & Co.* (Marburg: Tectum Wissenschaftsverlag, 2012), 91–120; and Carol Vernallis, *Experiencing Music Video: Aesthetics and Cultural Context* (New York: Columbia University Press, 2004), 3–26.

2   Of course, online-based distribution environments have exerted considerable influence on the music video. For one thing, globally acclaimed mainstream pop stars have become much more flexible in terms of when music videos are released, and for another, non-professional or semi-professional actors have established alternative distribution structures, some based on participatory procedures. See Mathias Bonde Korsgaard, "Music Video Transformed," in *The Oxford Handbook of New Audiovisual Aesthetics*, edited by John Richardson, Claudia Gorbman, and Carol Vernallis (Oxford and New York: Oxford University Press, 2013), 501–521.

3   See Paola Brembilla, "Transmedia Music: The Value of Music as a Transmedia Asset," in *The Routledge Companion to Transmedia Studies*, edited by Matthew Freeman and Renira Rampazzo (London and New York: Routledge, 2019), 82–89; Lori Burns, "Interpreting Transmedia and Multimodal Narratives: Steven Wilson's 'The Raven That Refused to Sing,'" in *The Routledge Companion to Popular Music Analysis: Expanding Approaches*, edited by Ciro Scotto, Kenneth Smith, and John Brackett (London and New York: Routledge, 2018), 95–112; and Alex Jeffery, "Marketing and Materiality in the Popular Music Transmedia of Gorillaz' 'Plastic Beach,'" *Revista Mediterránea de Comunicación* 8, no. 2 (2017): 67–80.

4   Henry Keazor and Thorsten Wübbena, *Video Thrills the Radio Star. Musikvideos: Geschichte, Themen, Analysen*, 2nd ed. (Bielefeld: Transcript, 2007), 55–77.

5   See Theodore Gracyk, *Rhythm and Noise: An Aesthetics of Rock* (London: I.B. Tauris, 1996), 73–75; and Serge Lacasse, "Toward a Model of Transphonography," in *The Pop Palimpsest: Intertextuality in Recorded Popular Music*, edited by Lori Burns and Serge Lacasse (Ann Arbor, MI: University of Michigan Press, 2018), 12.

6   See Christofer Jost, *Musik, Medien und Verkörperung. Transdisziplinäre Analyse Populärer Musik* (Baden-Baden: Nomos, 2012), 175–180; Christian Jooß-Bernau, *Das Pop-Konzert als Para-theatrale Form* (Berlin: De Gruyter, 2010), 13–43; Philip Auslander, *Liveness: Performance in a Mediatized Culture* (Abingdon, Oxon: Routledge, 1999), 23–38; Jamie Sexton, *Music, Sound and Multimedia: From the Live to the Virtual* (Edinburgh: Edinburgh University Press, 2007); and John Richardson, *An Eye for Music: Popular Music and the Audiovisual Surreal* (New York: Oxford University Press, 2012).

7   See Gracyk, *Rhythm*, 37–50.

8   The German-language source cites the term *Stoff*, which may be best defined—condensing the disparate definitional traditions—as basic narrative structure.

9   Irina O. Rajewsky, *Intermedialität* (Tübingen: A. Francke, 2002), 12.

10 Henry Jenkins, *Convergence Culture: Where Old and New Media Collide* (New York: New York University Press, 2006), 96.

11   Lori Burns, "The Concept Album as Visual-Sonic-Textual Spectacle: The Transmedial Storyworld of Coldplay's 'Mylo Xyloto,'" *iaspm@journal* 6, no. 2 (2016): 96–98; David Machin, *Analysing Popular Music: Image, Sound, Text* (Thousand Oaks, CA: Sage, 2010), 92–97.

12   Rajewsky, *Intermedialität*, 12–13.

13   See Brembilla, "Transmedia."

14   See Holger Schramm and Tilo Hartmann, "Identität durch Mediennutzung? Die Rolle von parasozialen Interaktionen und Beziehungen mit Medienfiguren," in *Mediensozialisationstheorien: Neue Modelle und Ansätze in der Diskussion*, edited by Dagmar Hoffmann and Lothar Mikos (Wiesbaden: VS Verlag für Sozialwissenschaften, 2007), 210–214.

15   The academic discourse on aesthetic conceptuality in popular culture is extremely disparate. In various disciplines (film studies, literary studies, popular music studies, etc.) one comes across works (sometimes monographs) that contextualize, describe, and interpret certain popular cultural phenomena with reference to an aesthetic concept. See Richard Keller Simon, *Trash Culture: Popular Culture and the Great Tradition* (Berkeley, CA: University of California Press, 1999). The international conference I hosted at the University of Freiburg, Germany, in May 2018 ("Cool Retro Camp Trash: Aesthetic Concepts in Popular Culture") will be documented in a collective volume (Münster and New York: Waxmann, forthcoming).

16   See Keyvan Sarkhosh and Winfried Menninghaus, "Enjoying Trash Films: Underlying Features, Viewing Stances, and Experiential Response Dimensions," *Poetics* 57 (2016): 40–54.

17   See Doris Leibetseder, *Queer Tracks: Subversive Strategies in Pop and Rock Music* (Abingdon, Oxon: Routledge, 2012), 59–80.

18   See Harsh V. Verma, "'Cool,' 'Brands' and Cool Brands," in *Brand Culture and Identity: Concepts, Methodologies, Tools, and Applications*, edited by Information Resources Management Association (Hershey, PA: IGI Global, 2018), 123–138.

19   Susan Sontag, "Notes on 'Camp,'" *Partisan Review* 31, no. 4 (1964): 515. For the scholarly discussion on camp see Fabio Cleto, ed., *Camp: Queer Aesthetics and the Performing Subject. A Reader* (Edinburgh: Edinburgh University Press, 1999); Stefanie Roenneke, *Camp als Konzept. Ästhetik, Popkultur, Queerness* (Moers: Posth Verlag, 2017); and, with regard to music, Christopher Moore and Philip Purvis, *Music and Camp* (Middletown, CT: Wesleyan University Press, 2018). As one might expect, Sontag's essay serves as a major reference in these works.

20   Thomas Luckmann, *Theorie des sozialen Handelns* (Berlin: Walter de Gruyter, 1992), 31–32. In popular music studies, the question of how to analyze popular music in its material, above all sonic, dimension in connection with its cultural contexts and social meanings has been discussed for quite some time. Quite recently, several contributions to this issue have been made, paying particular attention to the reflection upon aesthetic discourse; see Stan Hawkins, *Queerness in Pop Music: Aesthetics, Gender Norms, and Temporality* (New York: Routledge, 2016); Lori Burns and Jada Watson, "Spectacle and Intimacy in Live Concert Film: Lyrics, Music, Staging, and Film Mediation in P!nk's *Funhouse Tour* (2009)," *Music, Sound, and the Moving Image* 7, no. 2 (2013): 103–140; Richardson, *An Eye for Music*; and Freya Jarman-Ivens, "Notes on Musical Camp," in *The*

Ashgate Research Companion to Popular Musicology, edited by Derek B. Scott (Aldershot: Ashgate, 2009), 189–203.

21   See Derek B. Scott, "Policing the Boundaries of Art and Entertainment," in *Kulturkritik und das Populäre in der Musik*, edited by Fernand Hörner (Münster: Waxmann, 2016), 53–63.

22   Keir Keightley, "Reconsidering Rock," in *The Cambridge Companion to Pop and Rock*, edited by Simon Frith, Will Straw, and John Street (Cambridge: Cambridge University Press, 2001), 117.

23   See Simon Obert, "Die Artifizierung der Popmusik. Anfänge der Popkritik in US-amerikanischen Printmedien nach 1965," in *Populäre Musik, Mediale Musik? Transdisziplinäre Beiträge zu den Medien der Populären Musik*, edited by Christofer Jost, Daniel Klug, Axel Schmidt, and Klaus Neumann-Braun (Baden-Baden: Nomos, 2011), 115–127.

24   See Simon Obert, "Song Cycles, Operas, and a 'War on Singles': The Emergence of Concept Albums in the Late 1960s," in *Große Formen in der Populären Musik/Large-scale Forms in Popular Music*, edited by Gregor Herzfeld and Christofer Jost (Münster: Waxmann, 2019), 41–58.

25   It is critical to note that the term rock opera potentially leads to false interpretations. Most of the works that are said to be rock operas do not match the institutional and aesthetic criteria of the "classic" opera. In a manner of speaking, the term has a strong associative appeal, not least aiming at the grandeur and complexity of "classic" opera.

26   The Who [album], *Quadrophenia*, 2657 013 (Track Record LP, 1973).

27   John Atkins, *The Who on Record. A Critical History, 1963-1998* (Jefferson, NC: McFarland & Co., 2000), 249–250.

28   Another staging took place during a tour by The Who during the years 2012 and 2013, in which basically the film-centric approach of the 1996 performances was taken over.

29   See David Buckley, *Kraftwerk: Die unautorisierte Biografie* (Berlin: Metrolit, 2013), 36–45.

30   Ibid., 220.

31   See the various videos on YouTube that spectators of the MoMA and Tate Modern shows made with their mobile phones.

32   See Catherine Hoad, "'He can be whatever you want him to be': Identity and Intimacy in the Masked Performance of Ghost," *Popular Music* 37, no. 2 (2018): 175–192.

33   See Philip Auslander, "Musical Personae," *The Drama Review* 50, no. 1 (2006): 100–119; and Silkie Borgstedt, *Der Musik-Star. Vergleichende Imageanalysen von Alfred Brendel, Stefanie Hertel und Robbie Williams* (Bielefeld: Transcript, 2008).

34   The definition refers to common parlance. Both meanings can also be found in academic discourse, in which they are subject to theoretical conceptualizations and function—most commonly—as a semantic unit. See Brian Massumi, *Parables for the Virtual: Movement, Affect, Sensation* (Durham, NC: Duke University Press, 2002), 133–143.

35   See Richard Dyer, *Stars* (London: British Film Institute, 1979); and, with regard to popular music, Auslander, "Musical Personae."

36   Cora S. Palfy, "*Human After All*: Understanding Negotiations of Artistic Identity through the Music of Daft Punk," in *The Oxford Handbook of Music and Virtuality*, edited by Sheila Whiteley and Shara Rambarran (Oxford: Oxford University Press, 2016), 289.

37   Alex Jeffery addresses the trope of the "anywhere/everywhere" by examining aspects of materiality and fan-based practice. He states that, in addition to the official music videos,

a video was shot in stop-motion, using ready-made materials; this was supposed to pick up the do-it-yourself aesthetics of home-made web clips. Furthermore, a competition to design a new character was launched on the official band homepage (Jeffery, "Marketing and Materiality"). According to John Richardson, the fact that the Gorillaz somehow seem to diffuse into the social world is the consequence of a conscious decision by those responsible (especially Damon Albarn). By withdrawing from the public as "real" artists, they wanted to break away from "'manufactured' pop" and "the cult of personality" in the mainstream (Richardson, *An Eye for Music*, 203). Their critical (or subversive) attitude is linked to the desire to enable new modes of perceiving and dealing with cultural products.

38   This was the case during the 2016 Grammy Awards.

39   Janina Klassen, "Queere Stimmen, Vocal Cyborgs und (k)ein Genderdiskurs," in *Image—Performance—Empowerment. Weibliche Stars in der populären Musik von Claire Waldoff bis Lady Gaga*, edited by Michael Fischer, Christofer Jost, and Janina Klassen (Münster: Waxmann, 2018), 14.

40   Beate Flath, "Musik(wirtschafts)kulturen—eine Annäherung am Beispiel von Hatsune Miku," in *Lied und populäre Kultur/Song and Popular Culture. Jahrbuch des Zentrums für Populäre Kultur und Musik: Musik und Professionalität*, edited by K. Holtsträter and Michael Fischer (Münster: Waxmann, 2017), 232–240; see also Rafal Zaborowski, "Hatsune Miku and Japanese Virtual Idols," in *The Oxford Handbook of Music and Virtuality*, edited by Sheila Whiteley and Shara Rambarran (Oxford: Oxford University Press, 2016), 111–128.

41   See Axel Bruns, *Blogs, Wikipedia, Second Life, and Beyond: From Production to Produsage* (New York: Lang, 2008), 23–36.

42   U2 [album], *Achtung Baby*, 262 110 (Island Records CD, 1991). For the video, see U2, "U2—The Fly Official Video," YouTube video (4:52), directed by Jon Klein and Ritchie Smyth, posted by "U2Archive," July 29, 2011, https://www.youtube.com/watch?v=5Y1YFH9A3Bw.

43   David Fricke, "U2's Serious Fun," *Rolling Stone*, October 1, 1992, http://www.rollingstone.com:80/news/coverstory/u2s_serious_fun/page/6.

44   During the tour, Bono also embodied the Fly persona over long stretches of each performance, which reinforces the impression of the conceptual and makes the proximity to performance art even clearer. The persona-centered approach has been represented in performance art by artists such as Gilbert & George, Kim Jones, Joan Jonas, and Richard Gallo. It is also known to be part of the aesthetic spectrum of popular music performance since the late 1960s, with David Bowie being one of its most prominent exponents. With regard to the stage personae of popular music, it needs to be added that artification also derives from the theatrical impetus of onstage role-taking. Hence, the art status of institutionalized theater genres is inscribed in these performances. The term "rock opera" (see above) is emblematic of the latter, as it quite literally suggests the incorporation of a high-cultural theater genre ("opera") into the sphere of the popular. See also Gregor Herzfeld, "Die Rockoper. Genese, Verstetigung und Diversifikation eines Genres," *Musiktheorie* 30, no. 1 (2015): 43–60.

45   According to the band, this style mix was intended to stand in contrast to U2's history. U2 and Neil McCormick, *U2 by U2* (New York: HarperCollins, 2007), 272.

46 It must be added that "The Fly" is the only attempt on the album—with the exception of "Zoo Station"—to approach the "trash universe" and that, on top of that, the "trashy" elements only appear in stylized form. With regard to the latter, one needs to consider that the album (like its predecessors) resulted from a high-end production in which nothing was left to chance.

47 See Diane Waldman, *Collage, Assemblage, and the Found Object* (New York: Harry N. Abrams, 1992).

48 Yung Bin Kwak, "Mediating States of Media: Nam June Paik's Art of (Im)Mediation," in *NJP Reader 6*, edited by Kyunghwa Ahn (Yongin: Nam June Paik Art Center, 2016), 161–167.

49 Bill Flanagan, *U2 at the End of the World* (New York: Delta, 1996), 38.

12

The Palimpsestic Pop Music Video: Intermediality and Hypermedia

Jem Kelly

Current debates concerning popular music videos frequently center on notions of hybridity exploring how post-cinematic visual aesthetics develop from and enhance a pre-existing music soundtrack. With this chapter I propose the application of intermedia theory for the analysis of popular music videos because it centers on the conceptual, practical, and modal interrelations between and across different media. Lars Elleström (2010) notes that "intermediality has tended to be discussed without clarification of what a medium actually is."[1] This lack of clarification is what I shall address in this chapter, with the aim of interrogating notions of what a popular music video might be, as well as how it is informed by, or intersects with, other media. I will discuss the remediation of older media within video in an act of "multiplying mediation" known as "hypermediacy," specifically the creation of composite images using visual overlay or parallel dieges, such that discrete moments in time, alternative narrative spaces, and different technologies are represented and referenced through a process of palimpsest.[2]

Palimpsest depends upon composite images, superimpositions, and the "interaction of different temporal traces" so that the present is seen to be "haunted by a past" that is either made visible, or brought into view through montage.[3] Examining the ontology of the palimpsestic pop music video through examples by The White Stripes, Björk, and The Lotus Eaters, I will attempt to show how a variety of contexts of representation—film, DVD, internet, and installation—produce new meanings through assimilation and extension from one medium to another. These examples affirm the relevance of intermediality for examining new meanings afforded by popular music videos. Central to the chapter is my examination of *medienerkenntnis*, or media recognition that calls the spectator's attention to medial border-crossings and hybridization.[4] Indeed, intermediality depends to a great extent on the recognition of "media borders and medial specificities" within specific instances of "intermedial practices within the arts," for without such recognition the term would lose its potency and relevance.[5]

Intermediality and the pop music video

The pop music video is based upon pre-recorded music, the forms and structures of which inform or determine the video image sequence and have particular material, perceptual, semiotic, or conceptual properties. It is always already a hybrid medium, comprising audio and visual forms and structures that intersect and interrelate in ways that can be described as intermedial. Offering a theoretical approach to the analysis of media, the term intermedia was first coined by Dick Higgins of the Fluxus movement in 1966.[6] A notable feature of twenty-first-century intermediality is "the blurring of generic boundaries" between media and art forms, including film, video, animation, theater, live art, photography, typography, literature, and recorded music.[7] Intermediality refers to artworks that incorporate multiple media techniques, themes, or aesthetics typically found in one medium and displaying in another. I argue here that the pop music video is intermedial because it offers a dialogue between the recorded musical performance and a sequence of video images that are made afterwards. Just as a multi-track recording of popular music offers the listener the semblance of a singular, authentic musical performance, so too does the addition of video images appear to intersect in fundamental ways with the music that may appear literal (e.g., the performance video), but always function metaphorically. This consideration of the intermedia relationship between a song and its video leads me to pose the following questions:

- What are the connections between the recorded sound and the images we see?
- How are these images and sounds rooted in other media that existed before the video?
- What visual and auditory techniques and conventions are used that enable the viewer to comprehend or perceive the video?
- What new meanings do intermedia artworks enable performers, creators, and makers to communicate?

A key aspect of intermediality, then, is the concept that different media have discernible borders with clearly defined characteristics and operations that can be crossed or transgressed. Ágnes Pethő identifies the "crossing of media borders ... as one of the most persistent metaphors in the study of intermediality,"[8] making it a category of value and a productive starting point for analysis. Since the 1980s, pop music videos have challenged the borders and formal conventions of film—the principal medium that precedes video—and the techniques used in videos have been assimilated into contemporary film forms.[9] This cross-media fertilization is typical of remediation, an idea that stems from Marshall McLuhan's theories concerning media and the messages they convey. McLuhan was among the first theorists to comment on the cultural shift from written, printed, and other linguistic forms of expression to electronic modes of communication that emerged in mass media practices of the twentieth century. McLuhan observes that "ways of thinking implanted by electronic culture are very different from those fostered by print culture."[10] He creates a dialectic between the perceptual modes of literary, typographic forms, typified by their "*lineality*, a one-thing-at-a-time awareness," and those of "electronic media," identifiable by the "field of simultaneous relations" they produce.[11] Central to McLuhan's thinking is the idea that each medium is infused with forms and structures of earlier media practices, so that we never perceive the message of the medium alone without an awareness of both the medium and its progenitors: the medium is the message. In their book, *Remediation— Understanding New Media*, Jay David Bolter and Richard Grusin take this idea further and claim that the "process of remediation" is one in which "media (especially new media) become systematically dependent on each other and on prior media for their cultural significance."[12]

One form of remediation is the imbrication of an older medium with a newer one as a means by which "to express the way in which one medium is seen by our culture as reforming or improving upon another."[13] The Lotus Eaters' video for the song "It Hurts"[14] demonstrates both the simultaneous relations identified by McLuhan and the systematic dependence of contemporary and past media forms advocated by Bolter and Grusin. This video remediates scenes from G.W. Pabst's 1927 film, *Pandora's Box*, starring silent movie icon, Louise Brooks. In planning the video, it was decided that visual moments from the silent film should be identified and a storyboard produced that would enable semantic, graphical, and thematic links to be made with the band performing on a constructed studio set following an expressionistic design. The two discrete media—*Pandora's Box* (1927) and the video footage of the band—could then be brought together in the editing stage to allow the film and video footage to cohere and appear to interrelate. The video for "It Hurts" opens with Louise Brooks's character lifting a veil to reveal her face, cuts to a long shot of the castle, and then to a tracking shot of the band performing. The opening shots situate Brooks and the band within an establishing sequence as though both she and the band are part of the same general location: inside a castle. The camera tracks to a medium close-up of the guitarist, Jem Kelly, who is wearing a blindfold and appears in direct address to the camera (0:21).

Figure 12.1 shows a frame from the storyboard with Kelly blindfolded and depicted roughly in this position within the *mise en scène* of the video. Kelly begins to turn to his left as if looking toward something or someone (0:25), then the shot cuts (0:27) to a close-up of Louise Brooks on the last word of the verse line, "Let me feel, let me come and stare." Brooks's face is positioned to her right, enabling the viewer to construct an eye-line match as though she is looking in the direction toward Kelly, thereby creating an intermedia relation between the film footage and the pop music video. This is one of many techniques in which the film footage is re-formed so that meanings and visual similarities are brought to a state of coherent interplay. Bolter and Grusin refer to the "double-logic of remediation" as one of "immediacy and hypermediacy," a part technological/part cultural move that "wants both to multiply … media and to erase all traces of mediation."[15] In the "It Hurts" video, two discrete media—video and film—are brought together in a state of immediacy in which the mediating forms and structures appear to cohere seamlessly as part of the same storyworld. Despite the six decades that lay between *Pandora's Box* (1927) and "It Hurts" (1985), the video aspires to attain "the logic of immediacy" to the extent that the "medium itself" appears to "disappear" and

Figure 12.1 Storyboard image from The Lotus Eaters' "It Hurts" (1985), with guitarist Jem Kelly wearing a blindfold (0:21).

leave the viewer "in the presence of the thing represented": the band's performance in a specific, if imaginary, location with identifiable characters and actions that relate to the lyrical content of the song.[16]

Intersections of the lyrics and the recontextualized film images enable the otherwise disparate images to cohere, and they do so in a way that provides an example of palimpsest. Kattenbelt observes that intermediality interrogates "the mutual relations between materiality, mediality and aesthetic conventions of making and perceiving."[17] In Figure 12.2 we see Brook's character, Lulu, being offered a gun, while the lyrics at this point (0:43) proclaim: "All I need is the warmth of your gun, it's so cold when I haven't got one." Since we know that *Pandora's Box* is a silent film, the sound is non-diegetic in relation to the film, but for the purposes of the remediated images the sound also functions non-diegetically as it does not emanate from the *mise en scène* depicted, but as though from another location within the castle. This is an example of palimpsest as one medium (the contemporary sound) over-layered upon another, where the semantic link between what is sung ("gun ... one") coheres with the visual iconography in the film clip. This is also an example of palimpsestic memory, producing what Max Silverman refers to as a "Lazarean image" in which images "are drawn from a life after death" and the ability to distinguish between an imagined present and historical past (the film) is

Figure 12.2 Louise Brooks in *Pandora's Box* (1927): "All I need is the warmth of your gun" (0:43).

troubled.[18] The principal device allowing palimpsestic memory is the fact that the video footage is rendered in black and white. By pursuing the black and white visual aesthetic of *Pandora's Box*, and by the viewer forging links between the contemporary lyrics and performer action of the *mise en scène*, "It Hurts" was one of the first music videos to exploit the making and perceiving of silent movie conventions for the postmodern era and, in doing so, the present is "haunted by the past" and creates an "overlapping layering of time and space."[19]

Carol Vernallis claims that the pop music video has brought about a "new stylistic configuration," based upon "intensified audio-visual aesthetics,"[20] because it is a medium that has few limitations, no fixed conventions, and is a fertile site for experimentation. Castanheira contends that the emergent aesthetics of the pop music video are "characterised by camera work and editing strategies" that affect the viewer's perceptions in new ways as they develop "an intensely sensorial lexicon made possible by the sophistication of new technologies."[21] The use of black and white and palimpsest in "It Hurts" enables a form of narrative cohesion to be created to bridge a six-decade cultural gap of different media: film and video. But many pop music videos eschew narrative structure, preferring instead to "foreground unpredictable teleology and ambiguous endings."[22] Even when there is a discernible narrative structure in the video it is often accompanied by a self-referentiality that calls the viewer's attention to the processes of mediatization being employed as well as to medial borders being transgressed or, as Elleström puts it, "trespassed."[23] The pop music video frequently calls attention to "relations between media, to medial interactions and interferences,"[24] and this is evident in much of the work produced by French pop music video and film director, Michel Gondry.

Michel Gondry and The White Stripes: "The Hardest Button to Button" (2003)

Trained as a drummer, Michel Gondry preceded his career in film by making pop music videos for crossover artistes such as Björk and Beck, as well as more conventional rock acts such as The Rolling Stones and Foo Fighters, and mainstream pop acts such as Kylie Minogue. One technique that pop music video directors employ is to "turn to a song's structure to generate the image."[25] Michel Gondry takes this to an extraordinary level with his direction of American rock duo The White Stripes' video for "The Hardest Button to Button" (Figure 12.3).[26] Gondry's intention is to "create a visual echo" of the music "in camera by using a manipulation" of the band's "instruments,"[27] and by linking images to the song's rhythmical structure. The White Stripes comprises singer-songwriter guitarist Tom White and drummer Meg White. Gondry's intention in this video is to create a canonical effect in which multiple drum kits, guitar amplifiers, and microphones repeat within the *mise en scène* to the beat. In his reflections on this video, Gondry explains:

> Each time Meg hits one part of her drum kit, this part remains on the spot it was hit and Meg, in a cut, moves next to it. She hits the same part again and AGAIN remains at the same spot as she moves to the next spot and so on … So, she leaves behind a trail of drum kits wherever she plays.[28]

The viewer is presented with a sequence of composite images in which the rectilinear frame of the video is populated by repeated images of the drum kit, and later amplifiers

Figure 12.3 Storyboard ideas for "The Hardest Button to Button."

and microphones, in an additive way. The instruments form geometrical shapes that, on the one hand, appear and remain in the image to the logic of the beat, but, on the other, also attenuate the authenticity associated with live performance as the band replays the song. A convention of the performance video is to encourage the viewer to apprehend the band in its natural state, represented either as performing the song as if to a live audience or depicted performing the song in a specific location. Walter Benjamin, in his 1935 essay, "The Work of Art in the Age of Mechanical Reproducibility," points to our association with authenticity as a "unique existence in a particular place."[29] Transferring Benjamin's ideas to the interpretation of performance videos, we are given the illusion that the band is performing somewhere "in the here and now," as if the viewer is co-present in the performance and witnessing its "authenticity."[30] In "The Hardest Button to Button," the illusion of authenticity is destroyed through the visual motifs established by Gondry. There is something deeply satisfying and yet uncanny in seeing the proliferation of the instruments synchronized to the beat: our eyes see and continue to behold what our ears hear and have heard, all the while knowing that this is an impossible effect to create live. The disjunction of sound, action, and image, while the instruments remain in view, alludes to a past temporal moment in the song's structure so that we see simultaneously what the musicians are doing and what they have just done.

This strategy, based on repetition and mirroring, employs the technique known as *mise en abyme* in which the instruments—drums and guitar amplifiers—appear and are repeated in a ghostly, intermedia echo of the music.

> *Mise en abyme* presupposes the occurrence of at least two hierarchically different levels. It appears on a subordinate level by "mirroring" (content or formal) elements of a superior level … "Mirroring" can mean the repetition of the same, similarity or even to a certain extent contrast. The elements thus "mirrored" can refer to form (e.g. a painting is mirrored within a painting) or content (e.g. a theme occurring on different levels).[31]

In "The Hardest Button to Button," the subordinate level can be seen in the repetition of the instruments, but the higher level could refer to the musical text, itself constructed of repetitive elements: melodies and lyrical rhymes. In addition, as Gondry's focus is on a specific element—musical rhythm—we could say that the director is drawing upon his lived experience to create a meta-text that reflects upon its own construction and the recollected skill of the director as drummer. The viewer is presented with a palimpsestic memory in which the space of the *mise en scène* is structured by the geometry of the musical instruments appearing progressively in time to the beat. The mirroring of drum kits and guitar amplifiers calls our attention to the constructedness of the video image in the condition of "hypermediacy" in which "fragmentation, indeterminacy and heterogeneity … emphasises process or performance."[32] The repetition of the instruments troubles our perception of the simple, linear progression of time as it focuses on the rhythmical and melodic process of performance as the product of what has gone before. In a composite image we are reminded of what we have heard when we see multiple drum kits echoing back to the previous beats.

Bolter and Grusin define hypermediacy as "A style of visual representation whose goal is to remind the viewer of the medium," [33] and this self-reflexivity reminds us that video is an artificial assemblage of images. Instead of making an outright claim to immediacy—the representation of the real in illusory form—we are reminded of video's relation to film as a sequence of multiple frames per second and, in this case, the capturing of visual moments synchronized to the tempo of the song: 128 beats per minute. The visual repetition relates to the function of photographic images as captured moments in time because they remain in a palimpsestic, composite image as a "time-based mosaic of different shots."[34] This supports Rajewsky's claim regarding "media recognition" and the "formation of a given medium" as we are reminded that video, like film, comprises a sequence of individual shots.[35] Technologies of film enable the "persistence of vision" or "critical fusion factor" to trick the eye and the mind into perceiving "sequences of minutely variant" photographic images as continuous movement as opposed to individual frames.[36] Laura Mulvey describes the ability of films "to create the illusion of 'natural' movement" as being eroded in a contemporary cultural context that offers multiple platforms for the delivery and viewing of moving images.[37] Mulvey describes a move away from "moments of spectacle" that previously accounted for communicative structures of film and the new screen media, including pop music video, that instead produces "moments of narrative halt, hinting at the stillness of the single celluloid frame."[38] "The Hardest Button to Button" is intermedial precisely because it foregrounds the stillness of the frame and alludes to photographic images as representations of discrete moments in time, while allowing the passage of time to be seen to move forward and paradoxically to view the present as a product of the still visible past.

In its allusion to photography's ability to halt the flow of time, "The Hardest Button to Button" is exemplary of Rajewsky's second definition of intermediality as: "media combination (*Medienkombination*), which includes phenomena such as opera, film, theatre … Sound Art installations … multimedia, mixed-media and intermedia forms."[39] But this media combination, of video and photography, is not overtly referenced as it does not offer an homage to photographic forms, but it is a case of remediation, a kind of "complex borrowing, in which one medium is itself incorporated or represented in another medium."[40] This brings us into a field of intermedia relations in which we can see quite clearly that one medium, video, is made up of individual images combined in such a way that both immediacy and hypermediacy are constructed visually. A performance video at heart, "The Hardest Button to Button" nonetheless breaks the illusion of the band performing in a unique place, as we know that, in reality, Meg's drum kit cannot replicate as it does. We are presented with an example of "ontological montage" in which the coexistence of "ontologically incompatible elements within the same time and space" produce a jarring effect typical of hypermediacy.[41] From an ontological perspective, photography has become increasingly problematic to define owing to an array of platforms through which a still image can now be mediated. Digital photography has developed a long way from analog processes, defined as "a system of image making whereby light and chemicals create a negative," but share with analog photographs the ability to "produce an infinite number of positives."[42]

The introduction of photography as a medium in the nineteenth century reshaped our perceptions and expectations of what is possible with pictorial representation, but it has also been a fertile ground for exploring the limits of the medium and, to an extent, helping to determine possibilities for composite images in other art forms.

Figure 12.4 reproduces the work entitled *Woman Walking Downstairs*, a series of photographic images taken by Eadweard Muybridge depicting human locomotion.[43] The presentation of the individual shots within a single composite image produces an appearance of locomotion as successive moments, but it also moves away from the convention of the photograph as a single image. Instead, we are presented with a composite image in which the figures have been staged so that the camera can accurately depict the woman's moving body. This is another example of ontological montage, because the viewer has to connect the images in the sequence in order to imagine that the movement is continuous. Muybridge produces an "illusion of movement and of reality: not an analysis, but a spectacle."[44] This photographic illusion of physical movement became an inspiration for Marcel Duchamp, whose time-motion painting *Nude Descending a Staircase, No. 2* (1912) contains "all the phases and lines of movement ... pasts, presents and futures of a gait, flight, descent" that Muybridge represented sequentially.[45]

The geometrical shapes in Duchamp's work reflect Gondry's creative process in making "The Hardest Button to Button" video "more ... geometrical to reach an apotheosis of instrument shapes."[46] In focusing on the geometrical shapes, Gondry is privileging the video's formal qualities and creating an interplay of the visual and musical that is non-narrative and self-reflexive. The three different media—painting, photography, and video—demonstrate the notion of transmediality, or "the appearance of the same matter in a different medium."[47] In "The Hardest Button to Button," although Meg and Jack are not repeated, the motif of visual repetition occurs on a formal, aesthetic level that references

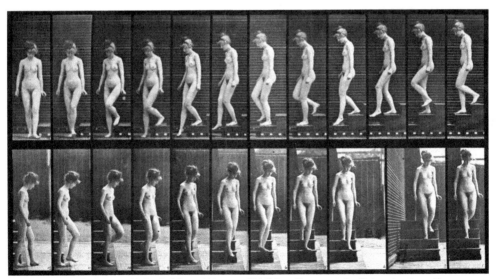

Figure 12.4 Eadweard Muybridge: *Woman Walking Downstairs* (late nineteenth century).

the early work in different media. Performance videos can follow a visual mode in which the performers and their instruments cohere and cohabit space and time, not just by playing instruments, but also operating within a narrative structure, which is what we will discuss next.

Michel Gondry and Björk's "Bachelorette" (1997)

As a hybrid form, the popular music video has been accused of "cultural cannibalization" on the basis that it has to borrow its content "from culturally 'higher' art forms such as literature and film by plundering them."[48] In the video to Björk's song, "Bachelorette,"[49] Michel Gondry constructs a transmedia narrative that elaborates the protagonist's story in and through an intermedia modality. The video offers an implicit homage to a variety of media, including silent film, literature, black and white photography, photo-roman, printing, typography, animation, theater, and video. Gondry revels in attempting to cram as many references to these different media within the telling of a story, while managing to sustain a coherent narrative. Therefore, remediation rather than cannibalization is a more appropriate way to consider this process of border-crossing between media. This transmedia video is exemplary of remediation, "the formal logic by which new media refashion prior media forms," because music and narrative forms provide semantic stability through combinations of music, melody, lyrics, and cause and effect.[50] This enables the various media to cohere and flow, rather than to confuse or interrupt the viewing experience of the story.

"Bachelorette" offers an extended version of Björk's song tailored to suit Gondry's vision. It begins with a music-driven prologue, which situates Bjork's character, the eponymous Bachelorette, as the protagonist located outside a hut in a sylvan glade digging a hole. This establishing scene (0:08–0:35) is shot in black and white, and offers a prologue to the story and a preface to the song, referencing silent movies as the first moving-image medium, signified in the video by a flickering vignette effect. In a sense, the narrative resonates with the journey from innocence, located in the countryside, to experience, located in the city, and back again. There is a somewhat tenuous symbolism of nature as Eden, from which the protagonist, as an Eve figure, is lured away, not by a snake, but by the arts, just as John Keat's protagonist, Lycius, is lured in his poem *Lamia* (1820) by artifice.[51] Björk and Gondry create a protagonist whose voice-over accompanies the musical introduction to the song and to the narrative. Both music and voice-over are non-diegetic because, as Bachelorette is seen silently digging the ground outside the hut with a spade, we hear her disembodied voice narrate: "One day I found a big book buried deep in the ground" (0:11–0:15). But, once the book is opened, it takes over as the narrator and, subsequent to the character announcing "Then, to my surprise, the book started writing itself," we hear Bachelorette reading as the alphabetic text appears on the blank pages of the book (0:22). This is an example of *ekphrasis*, in antiquity a "rhetorical device," but which film theorist

Agnes Pethó relates to intermediality as "the urge of an artist working in the medium of language to express whatever falls beyond the realm of language … and thus cross over into the domains of the visible."[52] This is suggestive both of the Holy Bible—"In the beginning was the word … and the word was God"[53]—and the omnipotence of the written word to extend out into and determine visual media following the process of *ekphrasis*.

The video "Bachelorette" illustrates the lyrical content of the song in abstract ways, through a condition of *ekphrasis* in which "one medium"—video—"becomes the mirror of the other"—the book that writes itself.[54] The video features many examples of *ekphrasis*, including when Bachelorette appears in a composite image walking in the forest within the pages of the book (0:29), in a position usually occupied by a photograph, her walking figure appearing beneath the written text. Another example is when she is on the train "reading about my journey, the narration being one step ahead of what was happening," words we see being written as a subtitle to a speeding train travelling in the same direction as the printed text, before cutting to an image of Bachelorette reading from the book inside the train (0:34–0:36). As the narrative progresses in black and white, we are presented with an "intermedial [*sic.*] *mise en abyme*," as first words relate the action, then the actions described in the alphabetic text are represented visually within the *mise en scène*.[55]

I interpret the conceit of this video to be that, through a combination of *ekphrasis* and intermedia *mise en abyme*, Gondry is able to tell a visual story that does not represent the song lyrics in a direct way, unlike the synchronization of lyrics and images examined in the video for The Lotus Eaters' "It Hurts." The book predicts the story of Bachelorette, but is told in a combination of past tense (visually on stage) and present tense (in the lyrics) by Bachelorette. The visual narrative is told not once, but four times, in a scripted repetition that resonates with the rhythms and repeated sections of the song. While the song lyrics contain many images, including the chorus refrain, "like a killer whale, trapped in a bay," the plot of the video does not reference the lyrics at all until the very last verse. The plot sees Bachelorette find the book and, at its behest, travel from the country to the city, where she meets and falls in love with a publisher. This first section of the story is represented through black and white *film*, then in a montage of photographs (photo-roman 0:53–0:59). We then experience a montage comprising black and white video footage, black and white film stock depicting a Warner's cinema (1:24), and photographic images during which the book is published and mass produced, and then she and the publisher, Clark, meet with a theatrical producer (1:17). It is only when Bachelorette performs the story for the first time on a theatrical stage that color video is used, which suggests that we are now in the present, if not co-present with her as we would be in an actual theater (1:28). There is now a sense of theatrical immediacy in what we see, even though the story represented belongs to the past, but with each of three tellings a change takes place.

From a visual perspective, each theatrical rendition of the story requires a smaller *mise en scène* and the repetition of set, props, and characters suggests attenuation of lived experience as it passes into memory. In each retelling of the story something essential to the first love story is being lost and the ability to represent it diminishing emotionally as well as in scale. Each scenographic element of the theatrical stage set is duplicated, forming a composite image in a *mise en abyme* suggestive of a Russian doll, as set artifacts are reduced in scale. Prior to the theatrical telling of Bachelorette's story, the video, photographic, and photo-roman forms that are used suggest that the story is being documented as it happens by an objective observer. In the theatrical versions, we are presented with a post-Brechtian, post-dramatic theatrical modality in which naturalistic illusion is eschewed on stage as there is no fourth wall: Bachelorette uses direct address (this is also typical of bands when they perform songs to live audiences). In the video the theatrical telling of the story also employs intermediality in the form of projected typography, which defamiliarizes the spectator by reminding them of theater as a construct. Hans-Thies Lehmann describes this post-dramatic modality as "a world open to its audience, an essentially possible world, pregnant with potentiality."[56] Ironically, the message of the narrative seems to be that love is cyclical and must return, like the story, to an inchoate state.

The final verse of the song lyrics enables auditory, semantic, visual, and narrative connections to be made with the video. As Bachelorette sings "I'm a tree that grows hearts" (4:16), she is framed by two-dimensional theatrical flats that resemble trees and represent the sylvan glade where the story began, thus connoting Bachelorette's affinity with nature. A few lines later, as Bachelorette sings "I'm the branch that you break," we see the first of the three publishers transform into a bush (4:22) and this shot cuts to a black and white montage of books beginning to unwrite themselves in the hands of their readers (4:24). By forging semiotic and semantic links that cross borders between auditory and different visual media, we observe what Rajewsky calls "*intra*compositional intermediality."[57] This is a state in which a variety of different media—video, animation (the bush, the unwriting pages), and music—participate in the meaning-making process while foregrounding their own medium specificity. For example, Bachelorette's book functions as a unifying visual motif, an object that is present in every scene and thereby functions to provide a semantic link with the original medium and location of the story. When she enters the publisher's office within the theatrical production for the fourth time (4:34), the publisher has become a bush in the shape of a man and Bachelorette turns the empty pages. What follows is a deconstruction of the story represented by the blank pages: the readership no longer immersed in the storyworld discard the book, and the principal characters apart from the protagonist become treeified. Gondry undertakes an *intra*compositional exercise as a range of different media participate in the untelling of the story, including black and white vignette film, treeification, and animation. The theatrical stage set is increasingly overgrown with tree tendrils and the book is overcome with branches—reabsorbed into nature with the implication that artistic birth, as with biological reproduction and perhaps human emotion, is cyclical. The video concludes with Bachelorette returning to the starting point of the story in the countryside, but in a scene that is fully color-saturated, reminiscent of early VHS videos. The narrative resolution depicts Bachelorette still wearing her stage costume, itself an ambivalent signifier as it is a full dress when seen from the front, but just an apron when seen from behind or the side: there are two sides to every story, an inner and an outer aspect to the psyche, a private and a public persona. Despite the *intra*compositional intermediality used to tell Bachelorette's story providing a perceptual effect that is, at times, jarring, it is apparent that the cyclical nature of love—like life—can be narrated in emotionally affective ways that are—like performance—ephemeral.

Conclusion

As I have argued, intermediality is a critical lens through which to interrogate the interactions of different media in the popular music video, and intermedia strategies for the conception and production of pop videos appear to be burgeoning. While the prevalence of digital media production tools offers a reason for why this might be, we have also considered that pop music video is a hybrid form—it is already intermedial—and in a sense its task is to erode borders between the pop music song and the medium of moving images used to promote it by finding new and innovative audiovisual connections between media. Pop music videos that reference other, or remediate older, media can bring new life and interest to forgotten cultural artifacts, such as is the case with *Pandora's Box*, scenes from which are intercut with video images in the Lotus Eaters' "It Hurts." But, if a central concern of the performance video is to represent an authentic image of a band playing, intermedia strategies that employ remediation tend to develop hypermediacy, which attenuates authenticity by reminding the viewer that the pop video is an artificial construct and not a document of live performance. The *mise en abyme* generated in "The Hardest Button to Button" is a device that references photography in an implicit way, while lending itself to a form of transmediation in an episode of The Simpsons in which the guitar amps, drum kits, and Meg and Jack are not videated, but subject to animation. The ease with which pop music video can transform itself across media suggests that media borders can be blurred, transgressed, or suspended, thereby locating the spaces in-between media as an emerging and fertile site for analysis. Gondry's direction of "Bachelorette" tests the limits of media borders, opening the way for a methodology in which different media are absorbed within each other in a process of cross-fertilization that produces new and vibrant perspectives on what the popular music video might be or become. With the rapid development of video creation and post-production technologies, it is likely that intermediality will be a useful tool in helping us to comprehend and analyze the new forms, structures, and methodologies that may emerge for some time to come.

Notes

1   Lars Elleström, ed., *Media Borders, Multimodaility and Intermediality* (Basingstoke: Palgrave Macmillan, 2010).
2   Jay David Bolter and Richard Grusin, *Remediation—Understanding New Media* (Cambridge, MA: MIT Press, 2000), 53.
3   Max Silverman, *Palimpsestic Memory—The Holocaust and Colonialism in French and Francophone Film and Fiction* (Oxford: Berghahn Books, 2015).
4   Irina O. Rajewsky, "Border Talks: The Problematic Status of Media Borders in the Current Debate about Intermediality," in Elleström, *Media Borders*, 51.
5   Ibid., 53.

6   Bernd Herzogenrath, ed., *Travels in Intermedia[lity]: Reblurring the Boundaries* (Hanover, NH: Dartmouth College Press, 2012), 168.

7   Freda Chapple and Chiel Kattenbelt, eds., *Intermediality in Theatre and Performance* (Amsterdam: International Federation for Theatre Research, 2007), 11.

8   Ágnes Pethó, "Approaches to Studying Intermediality in Contemporary Cinema," *Acta Universitatis Sapientiae, Film and Media Studies* 15 (2018): 167.

9   Carol Vernallis, *Unruly Media: YouTube, Music Video, and the New Digital Cinema* (Oxford and New York: Oxford University Press, 2013).

10 Marshall McLuhan, "The Agenbite of Outwit," in *Marshall McLuhan Essays: Media Research, Technology, Art Communication*, edited by Michel A. Moos (Amsterdam: Overseas Publishers Association, 1997), 123.

11 Ibid., 123.

12 Bolter and Grusin, *Remediation*, 56.

13 Ibid., 59.

14 The Lotus Eaters, "The Lotus Eaters—It Hurts," YouTube video (3:06), official music video, directed by Jem Kelly, posted by "TheLotusEatersVEVO," August 13, 2015, https://www.youtube.com/watch?v=nFxw02oNMTs.

15 Bolter and Grusin, *Remediation*, 5.

16 Ibid., 5–6.

17 Chiel Kattenbelt, "Intermediality in Theatre and Performance: Definitions, Perceptions and Medial Relationships," *Culture, Language and Representation* 6 (2008): 27.

18 Silverman, *Palimpsestic Memory*, 5.

19 Ibid., 5.

20 Vernallis, *Unruly Media*, 94.

21 José Cláudio Siqueira Castanheira, "Timeline Philosophy: Technological Hedonism and Formal Aspects of Films and Music Videos," in *Music/Video—Histories, Aesthetics, Media*, edited by Gina Arnold, Daniel Cookney, Kirsty Fairclough, and Michael Goddard (London: Bloomsbury, 2017), 217.

22 Vernallis, *Unruly Media*, 94.

23 Elleström, *Media Borders*, 27.

24 Rajewsky, "Border Talks," 51.

25 Vernallis, *Unruly Media*, 9.

26 The White Stripes, "The White Stripes—The Hardest Button to Button," YouTube video (3:34), official music video, directed by Michel Gondry, posted by "whitestripes," May 26, 2009, https://www.youtube.com/watch?v=K4dx42YzQCE. Figure 12.3 shows storyboard ideas for the White Stripes' video "The Hardest Button to Button." The storyboard is to be found in a short booklet accompanying a DVD of Gondry's pop music videos and is entitled "The Work of Director Michel Gondry" (2003). The booklet provides insights to Gondry's creative stimuli and childhood obsessions, but is structured in an ad-hoc manner, without page numbers.

27 *I've Been Twelve Forever* [film], directed by Michel Gondry (Sleeping Train Productions, 2003).

28 Ibid.

29 Walter Benjamin, "The Work of Art in the Age of Its Mechanical Reproducibility," in *Walter Benjamin—Selected Writings Volume 4 1938–1940*, edited by Howard Eiland and Michael W. Jennings, translated by Edmund Jephcott, Howard Eiland, and Gary Smith (London: Belknap Press of Harvard University Press, 2006), 253.

30   Ibid., 253.

31   Werner Wolf, *Metareference Across Media—Theory and Case Studies* (Amsterdam and New York: Rodopi, 2009), 45. See also William J. Mitchell, *The Reconfigured Eye: Visual Truth in the Post-Photographic Era* (Cambridge, MA: MIT Press, 1994), 8.

32   William J. Mitchell, *The Reconfigured Eye: Visual Truth in the Post-Photographic Era* (Cambridge, MA: MIT Press), 1994, quoted in David Jay Bolter and Richard Grusin *Remediation—Understanding New Media* (Cambridge, MA: MIT Press, 2000), 31.

33   Bolter and Grusin, *Remediation*, 272.

34   Lev Manovich, *The Language of New Media* (Cambridge, MA: MIT Press, 2001), 155.

35   Rajewsky, "Border Talks," 51.

36   Brian Winston, *Technologies of Seeing—Photography, Cinematography and Television* (London: British Film Institute, 1996), 11.

37   Laura Mulvey, *Death 24x a Second: Stillness and the Moving Image* (London: Reaktion Books Ltd., 2006), 7.

38   Ibid., 7.

39   Rajewsky, "Border Talks," 55.

40   Bolter and Grusin, *Remediation*, 45.

41   Manovich, *Language of New Media*, 159.

42   Winston, *Technologies of Seeing*, 12.

43   Eadweard Muybridge [series of photographs], *Woman Walking Downstairs* (late-nineteenth century), https://www.flickr.com/photos/desdetasmania/647788068/sizes/l/in/photostream.

44   Sam Rhodie, *Montage* (Manchester: Manchester University Press, 2012), 4.

45   Ibid., 111.

46   *I've Been Twelve Forever*.

47   Axel Englund, "Intermedial Topography and Metaphorical Interaction," in Elleström, *Media Borders*, 75.

48   Henry Keazor, "'I had the strangest week ever!' Metalepsis in Music Videos," in *Metalepsis in Popular Culture*, edited by Karin Kukkonen and Sonja Klimek (Berlin: Walter de Gruyter, 2011), 104.

49   Björk, "Björk—Bachelorette," YouTube video (5:17), official music video, directed by Michel Gondry, posted by "Björk," July 1, 2007, https://www.youtube.com/watch?v=XJnhaXwK86M.

50   Bolter and Grusin, *Remediation*, 273.

51   "Lamia," a poem by John Keats, relates the story of a snake-like creature who takes on human shape and deceives her lover, Lycius. The act of transformation can be taken as a metaphor for all artistic conceits. See https://www.gutenberg.org/files/2490/2490-h/2490-h.htm.

52   Ágnes Pethó, "Media in the Cinematic Imagination: Ekphrasis and the Poetics of the In-Between in Jean-Luc Godard's Cinema," in Elleström, *Media Borders*, 212.

53   Gospel According to St. John, https://www.biblica.com/bible/niv/john/1.

54   Pethó, "Media," 214.

55   Ibid., 215.

56   Hans-Thies Lehmann, *Postdramatic Theatre*, translated by Karen Jüers-Munby (London: Routledge, 2006), 12.

57   Rajewsky, "Border Talks," 57.

13

"How Does a Story Get Told from Fractured Bits?" Laurie Anderson's Transformative Repetition

John McGrath

Laurie Anderson traverses various media, offering fragmentary stories via multimodal outputs that involve image as well as sound: film, installation, live performance, and music video forms all oscillate around, and extend the traditional album format.[1] By drawing audiovisual ideas across platforms and through projects over four decades, she has continued to open up the idea of large-scale, expanded forms of the music video many years before the recent popularity of long-play video forms. Yet Anderson's expanded projects do not arise through the conventional means of "transmedia storytelling," whereby paratexts offer additional information to what Henry Jenkins has called "the mothership" work by enhancing the backstory of characters, offering parallel or alternative viewpoints, or fleshing out the general fictional world.[2] Instead, she offers a form of affective transmedia that arises through developing repetitions and re-combinations of both musical and visual material that fundamentally complicate the traditional idea of music video as a discrete audiovisual form. Despite her experimental approach to unfolding a story, however, narrative remains a fundamental concern of her work, as she explains during a discussion of her 2015 film *Heart of a Dog*:[3]

> It's a series of short stories about telling stories ... How do you tell a story? How does a story get told from fractured bits? What happens when you forget your story? What happens when you really remember your story? What happens when you repeat it too many times? What happens when somebody plasters their story onto you? It's not about me talking about who I am at all. It's a voice that kind of goes, what do you want? How do you see? Who am I? It's mostly questions and zero answers.[4]

Anderson has explored a myriad of media platforms ever since first arriving on the Downtown New York experimental music scene in the 1970s. A ravaged Manhattan provided affordable space and community for artists such as Lounge Lizards, Talking Heads, Rhys Chatham, Blondie, and John Zorn, as well as venues like the Knitting Factory, CBGB, and The Kitchen. What has become known as the Downtown Scene encapsulated a spirit of pushing boundaries and experimentalism. As Susan McClary writes of Anderson: "It is virtually impossible to separate out any one aspect of her pieces without violating her own insistent violation of the genre boundaries that organize the traditional art world."[5]

An avant-garde artist working on the experimental fringes of popular music, Anderson shared this transgressive character with her late spouse Lou Reed. His group, The Velvet Underground, achieved much in deconstructing supposed high/low dichotomies of classical and pop worlds—bringing together the minimalism of Downtown compatriot Philip Glass, the drones of La Monte Young (The Velvet Underground's John Cale famously was a member of the Theatre of Eternal Music), the NoWave of DNA and Arto Lindsay, and punk and Andy Warhol's Factory (the Velvets were a central part of *The Exploding Plastic Inevitable* and it was the place which inspired the lyrics to Reed's hit "Walk on the Wild Side" in 1972).

Working alongside such a broad range of progressive creativity, it is no surprise that Anderson's work is infused with experimental gestures similar to those propelling several contemporaneous art practices. Chiming most clearly with the work of New York's visual art scene was her consistent foregrounding of her often numerous forms of media, a trait that Clement Greenberg described as a key feature of avant-garde art:

> The history of avant-garde painting is that of a progressive surrender to the resistance of its medium; which resistance consists chiefly in the flat picture plane's denial of efforts to "hole through" it for realistic perspectival space … The motto of the Renaissance artist, *Ars est artem celare* [Art is the concealing of art], is exchanged for *Ars est artem demonstrare* [Art is the manifesting of art].[6]

Anderson's employment of technology—the "tools of electronic mediation"—affords a method of storytelling in "fractured bits" that is crucial to her unique form of cross-media storytelling.[7] McClary writes that Anderson "insists on and problematizes her mediation,"[8] critiquing the alienating influence of the media on human authenticity. By contrast, Philip Auslander defends Anderson's surprise commercial appeal in the 1980s—in light of contemporary critics' adherence to tired art vs. commercial and ideological presumptions. Discussing the Downtown Scene, he writes: "mass culture itself has emerged as a site of possible resistance to the mainstream."[9] Such an attempt to resist the mainstream via its own modes of discourse infuses many aspects of Anderson's work, which constantly pushes the use of innovative technology into the aesthetic foreground: "My work is expressed through technology," she explains.[10] Such expression has not only influenced her compositional process, but also has led to the invention of new instruments, such as the tape-bow violin, a talking stick that employs granular synthesis, and even an early incarnation of interactive musical clothing (a suit that activates drum pads). Most recently she has ventured into storytelling in virtual reality (VR) with *Chalkroom* (2017), a collaboration with Hsin-Chien Huang.[11]

Although Anderson frequently mixes media, three works in particular abound with a transmedia flow that seems to move fluidly back and forth across platforms, suggesting that the texts are not separate but rather form part of a much larger storyworld. The song "O

Superman (for Massenet)" (1981) and two works that appeared in 2015, *Heart of a Dog*—a film she wrote, directed, co-produced, and scored—and her installation at Park Avenue Armory entitled *Habeas Corpus*, a work that focuses on Chadian Guantánamo Bay prisoner Mohammed El Gharani, complement one another in transmedia ways.[12] The song explores the failures and dangers of modern technology through repetition and alienation; the film looks at death through the lens of personal fragments, technology, and meditations; and the installation invokes an exterior focus to address many of the same themes. As Anderson describes the 2015 pieces: "for me these two completely disparate projects aren't really that different ... They're both about how you tell stories, and what they mean, and how you create a world with them."[13] This chapter aims to explore how Anderson tells stories across media through her employment of discursive transformative repetition. I will undergo a case-study analysis of the record and music video for "O Superman"[14] before offering a theoretical exploration and analysis of multimodal and "transmedia storytelling"[15] in Anderson's work; investigating how material from the song and the album *Big Science* (1982) resonates in these 2015 works and suggests new forms of transmedia flow.[16]

Theoretical framework

Music videos are multimodal; they combine music, image, and text for the most part in addition to other forms such as dance choreography. Music, image, and text have continually interacted and informed one another, and with new media come new combinations and convergences.[17] Media combine to create layers of potential semiotic meanings and it is clear that artists who work with both film and music video (as Anderson does) often share a keen awareness of the possibilities of immediacy in music video aesthetics. They learn to foreground musical materials in conveying a message, while long-form film allows them to nurture an awareness of subtle leitmotifs and temporal development. An experience of both formats, in other words, imbues multimodal artists with an expanded and transmedia vocabulary.

Transmedia forms and devices are those that do not have an origin in one form, as Werner Wolf writes:

> Transmediality concerns phenomena which are non-specific to individual media and/or are under scrutiny in a comparative analysis of media in which the focus is not on one particular source medium. Being non-media specific, these phenomena appear in more than one medium. Transmediality as a quality of cultural signification can occur, for instance, on the level of content in myths which have become cultural scripts and have lost their relationship to an original text or medium (notably, if they have become reified and appear as a "slice" of [historical] reality). Transmediality also comprises ahistorical formal devices that can be traced in more than one medium, such as the repeated use of motifs, thematic variation, narrativity, descriptivity, or meta-referentiality.[18]

Transmedia storytelling describes a process of "worldbuilding," utilizing a multifaceted narrative universe. Jenkins's concept evokes a fractured "storyworld" in which multiple parts augment one another: "[a] transmedia story unfolds across multiple media platforms, with each new text making a distinctive and valuable contribution to the whole."[19] Jenkins gives the example of *The Matrix* (1999):

> [I]n *The Matrix* franchise, key bits of information are conveyed through three live action films, a series of animated shorts, two collections of comic book stories, and several video games. There is no one single source or ur-text where one can turn to gain all of the information needed to comprehend the *Matrix* universe.[20]

In a digital age of "collective intelligence" and, I would add, in light of our post-structural problematization of knowledge transfer from author to reader,[21] Jenkins posits transmedia storytelling as the "ideal aesthetic form":

> [T]ransmedia storytelling expands what can be known about a particular fictional world while dispersing that information, insuring that no one consumer knows everything and insure [*sic.*] that they must talk about the series with others (see, for example, the hundreds of different species featured in *Pokemon* or *Yu-Gi-O* [*sic.*]). Consumers become hunters and gatherers moving back across the various narratives trying to stitch together a coherent picture from the dispersed information.[22]

Jenkins further explains how the independent artist might be best placed to maintain such complex consistencies:

> Because transmedia storytelling requires a high degree of coordination across the different media sectors, it has so far worked best either in independent projects where the same artist shapes the story across all of the media involved or in projects where strong collaboration (or co-creation) is encouraged across the different divisions of the same company.[23]

In the current mainstream music industry, for instance, pop stars are increasingly becoming transmedia storytellers, creating a unified brand and developing and augmenting content across platforms: Instagram, Twitter, Spotify, Facebook, and so on. Taylor Swift even offers superfans a "tailor-made" gift, the individual's tastes being accommodated for in unique presentations.[24] Live performances, YouTube/ Facebook live-streams and crowd-sourcing platforms like Kickstarter all become part of "spreadable media."[25] How we interact and interpret these stories is less finite, unidirectional, and teleological than ever. As Jenkins writes: "In between opening and closing, the order in which we get story information is crucial to our experience of the story world … Facing multiple points of access, no two consumers are likely to encounter story information in the same order."[26] But while multiple points of access can lead us into a transmedia world, storytelling can also arise through numerous, incomplete, and fragmented forms. Resonances can add layers and new meanings can come to the surface, but what does this mean for music video and how does it complicate previous analytical methods and techniques? Lori Burns offers a way forward in her multimodal analysis of Coldplay's concept album, *Mylo Xyloto* (2011), focusing not just on the video or on the paraphonographic (Lacasse) elements, but on a wider cohesive gamut: comics, record, live performance spectacle, concert film, and music video. Burns investigates "the intersections of music, word, and image across these media to examine the central aesthetic and cultural conception of the work."[27] Perhaps the future of music video is a transmedia one, analytically speaking, but is it possible any longer to detach the music video from its role in the connected web of worldbuilding that has become the mainstay of the current pop music industry?

Repetition is a device that offers Laurie Anderson an innovative way of approaching two key themes that infuse her work: time and memory. Repetition is naturally transmedial, in the manner Wolf defined above: it is without a clear source medium and it is ubiquitous across media. That said, there are differences between types, such as local motivic repeats and large-scale architectonic formal repetitions.[28] Repetition theory is currently a flourishing field in musicology with scholars building on Deleuze's idea of repetition-as-change at the reception level, granting insight into the role of repetitions in modern music and the arts.[29] With this new flurry of analytical engagement with repetition in mind, we can interrogate that multimodal employment of transmedia repetition that begins in "O Superman" before spreading through various other projects. To do this, we can employ a taxonomy of repetition that I developed elsewhere for the analysis of literary texts and contemporary composition.[30] Although this taxonomy, consisting of four related but distinct forms of repeated material, can result from language or sound, it can also arise through image and, most significantly here, audiovisuality:

1 *Exact clothed repetitions:* these are recurrences of the "same" material, always with Deleuze's warnings of the importance of different successive contexts—hence the use of his word "clothed" rather than "naked" repetition—there is always an assimilation of meaning that snowballs with each exact repetition.[31]
2 *Local musematic repetitions:* after Middleton's "musematic"—these are local repeats often with minor variations; position and phonetics are of particular importance here.[32]
3 *Binary oppositional repetitions:* those used to emphasize contrasting themes, contradictions, and homonyms.
4 *Discursive repetitions:* again named after Middleton—these are repeats acting on a more architectonic, structural level, often recurring throughout an entire work, coming and going in almost leitmotivic fashion in that these combine and develop over time.[33]

In the analysis that follows, I will apply this framework to Anderson's "O Superman." Such an application of repetition theory will then be extended to the new contexts of transmediality in Anderson's work.

"O Superman (for Massenet)"

Music

Anderson's most famous work, "O Superman," first appeared as part of a large performance piece *United States* (1981), before being released as a single later that year. It became a surprise hit record and reached number 2 in the UK charts in 1981, having been picked up by John Peel. Anderson signed a subsequent major-label deal and the song went on to feature on her breakthrough album *Big Science* (1982).

An analysis of the track by McClary reveals several important contexts. McClary recognizes the correlation between Anderson's focus on multiple identities, tonal instability, and disparate perspectives in line with a reaction against the supposed hegemony of art music complexity, gender politics, and functional harmony. In particular, she notes that tonal instability and ambiguity are foregrounded in the two-chord progression (A♭/C–C minor) from a major triad, first inversion (C, E♭, A♭) to a root position C minor triad (C, E♭, G).[34] For McClary, this is a defining feature of the song; but compellingly, this instability floods beyond the confines of the song and in fact appears, before and after its iteration in "O Superman," elsewhere in Anderson's extended catalog. I shall discuss this discursive repetition later in more detail.

Over a steady looping C note, the "ha ha ha" clothed exact repetition, these chords act as a relative major to minor movement, a fluid texture without any tonal home. The unstable and uneasy feel evokes the insecure homeland presented in the lyrics. It is significant, however, that on iterations of the word "Mom"—the United States often portrayed as the motherland—Anderson consistently uses the major chord. The themes of homeland security and surveillance are persistent ones in Anderson's work from *United States* through *Big Science* to *Homeland* (2010) and *Habeas Corpus* (2015), as I shall discuss below.

The ostinato refrains in "O Superman" reference Anderson's Downtown compatriot Philip Glass's work, most notably the organ sound and minimal introduction to *Einstein on the Beach* (1975). The first ostinato refrain, a local musematic repeat, derives from the vocal melody line. An arpeggio based on the A♭ major chord beginning on the third (C) before including the 2nd (B♭) and 7th (G, the leading tone, which offers some direction here) degrees of the A♭ major scale in addition to the major triad. This light Glass-esque texture later returns for a second time in the track. The other ostinato in "O Superman" occurs toward the close, consisting of the first five notes of the C♮ minor scale in ascent (C, D, E♭, F, G). This rising musematic motif has an Aeolian feel (the 6th mode of the E♭ major scale, which is, in this case, C♮ minor). If Anderson was dealing with diatonic tonality and seeing A♭ major as the stable home key, then we would be hearing a Phrygian mode on C, and a D♭ rather than a D♮ in the rising melody. In the context of this motif we hear the major chord A♭/C further destabilized, already in first inversion but now with a melody motif cantering around C and the C Aeolian mode.

Lyrics

Anderson's lyrics[35] reveal a similar focus on the strategy of repetition. Of the 182 words in the lyrics, only ninety-six are unique, rendering a ratio of almost 2:1. Within its fifty sentences, the most common words after the definite article are as follows: you (ten statements); arms (nine); your (nine); mom (eight); hand (five); I (four); dad (four). Anderson does not choose to match the lyrics directly to musical repetitions, instead the musematic repetitions allow her the musical time and space to focus on the specific themes outlined. The binary oppositional thematic repetitions of human/machine, self/other, found throughout Anderson's work, operate to destabilize false dichotomies.[36] Nowhere is this more apparent than in "O Superman." The crash of a military rescue helicopter outside Tehran during the Iran hostage crisis in 1979–1980 becomes the starting point for a work that touches on many of Anderson's central threads—technology and its failures/dangers, surveillance, relationships, and loss. Other binary oppositional repeats are the playful "Smoking or Non-smoking"—an example of Anderson's persistent switching of subject perspective from dog to air steward, etc.

Anderson's classic spoken narration delivery has, at points, stylistic language references from the *Tao Te Ching* and the US Postal Service slogan/Herodotus. The title itself, as highlighted by Taruskin and Ross, is a play on Jules Massenet's aria "Ô Souverain, ô juge, ô père" [O Sovereign, O Judge, O Father] from the opera *Le Cid* (1885).[37] At the same time, the "O" recalls an opening Homeric call to the muses, while Anderson's Superman is as much comic-book character as historically-tarnished Nietzschean figure. Anderson switches persona and perspective as we shift to the narration of the mother—"hello this is your mother"—before switching persona again to deliver the "message" (2:02). The instability that we hear in the harmony is furthered by the lyrics in this manner.

Anderson employs a trio of exact clothed repeats: "This is the hand, the hand that takes. This is the hand, the hand that takes. This is the hand, the hand that takes." "Hand" is employed six times here alone. The additive compositional procedure of this musematic repetition *à la* Glass (the technique of adding a note or extra bar with progressive iterations, for instance) is employed as we turn to various types of "arms" toward the end: "Your military arms. In your electronic arms."[38] The exact clothed, musematic, and binary oppositional repetitions in the lyrics, then, further destabilize the fixed sense of identity and deconstruct the concept of stable resolution or home outlined in the harmony and musematic ostinato refrains of the music.

The video

Anderson employs the video to highlight key themes in the visual domain. Sometimes these instances are literal, such as the appearance of smoke at the point it appears in the lyric mentioned above. As the musematic ostinato refrains enter, the visuals move beyond the performer toward abstraction: in the first instance the picture dissolves, signaling the change of persona to come. Anderson's dry humor really comes across visually—for instance, the playful wave as she says "Hi Mom!" comments on the role of television in 1980s' culture. This resonates with screen culture today and the continued prevalence of "reality" television and newscast screen-bombers—those compulsively seeking to be recognized on the medium. Anderson's work, however, juxtaposes multiple identities and appears to seek a dissolution of the ego in the Buddhist tradition. The video begins with the sole image of a Moon-like circle, which later morphs into a globe and acts as a backdrop for musematic hand-shadow gestures throughout. Repeating musematic hand-shadow figures are the hand wave, fist, gun, and scales of balance. As Anderson enters the screen (0:35), she appears bottom-left (Figure 13.1).

Figure 13.1 "O Superman": Anderson first appears (0:35).

Her miming vocoder delivery sets the tone for a quintessential performance video, but one that sees her perform in various modes: American sign-language interpreter, singer, keyboardist, dancer, and hand-shadow artist. The use of red for the war themes plays on familiar martial semiotic codes and reinforces the lyrical signification. Anderson says "I've got a message," before the line "American planes" and the references to military aerial threat are raised. The keyboard acts as an altar table from which the message is to be delivered, as Anderson raises her arms in a priest-like fashion (Figure 13.2).

Anderson's performance is subtle yet theatrical, reflecting the fact that this song originated as part of a performance art work. Her directorial decision to focus on the musematic movement of her left arm focuses the eye toward reinforcing a powerful message. She plays on the homonym "arms"— meaning both the physical limbs employed in the choreography but also the military ammunition that the physical gestures of strength and force in the movement signify. The gun gestures (at 7:06) and the relinquishing and inevitable power of "military arms," echoed in the final flex of Anderson's arm as the closing image, exemplify such a message (Figure 13.3).

Anderson's immediate and cohesive union of image and music in this video continue to resonate with a contemporary audience through relevant references to current politics, government, and ethical debates around artificial intelligence (AI). The images work to parallel and reinforce the musical and lyrical material. A form of transmedia arises from this varied employment of repetition, developing a narrative not only laterally but also

Figure 13.2 "O Superman": Altar-like pose with keyboard (2:32).

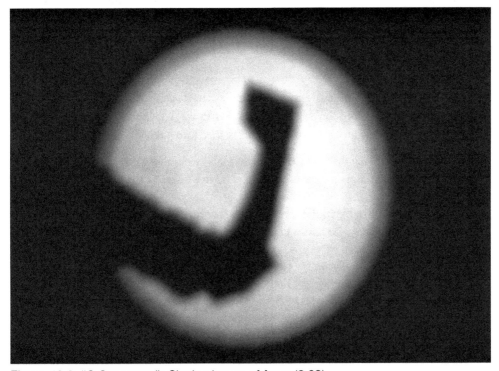

Figure 13.3 "O Superman": Closing image of force (8:23).

vertically and simultaneously. Most recently, "O Superman" made an appearance amid the innovative interactivity of the "Bandersnatch" film-length episode of *Black Mirror* (2018), finding an emotive relevance in an alternate reality of Netflix tech-satire, itself comprised of multiple and parallel storyworlds.[39] Significantly, Anderson's song appears in the story path that concerns a fatal journey the boy takes with the mother in the story. Anderson's difficult relationship with her own mother and the use of "mother" as an overpowering state metaphor is a theme I shall return to later. Post 9/11, Anderson returned to performing "O Superman," recognizing its ability to speak to a new audience, and it has remained a fixture in live shows. What we will now explore is how "O Superman" continues to add to and augment its story in semiosis from *Big Science* through *Heart of a Dog* to *Habeas Corpus*.

Heart of a Dog

Short-listed for "Best Documentary" (final fifteen films) at the eighty-eighth Academy Awards 2016, *Heart of a Dog* is a tour-de-force artistic work in which Anderson provides direction, narration, 8-millimeter home videos, mobile-capture videos, animations, and drawings, in addition to text and music. The soundtrack was subsequently released by Nonesuch, containing all sound, narration, and score material.[40] On the project's formation, Anderson explains:

> I was looking at stories you use to *represent* childhood. I probably think of ten or so such stories when someone asks, "What was your childhood like?" I tried to make this film about getting attached to those stories and realizing that they weren't necessarily true—particularly, in my case, that one about the hospital.[41]

The strained relationship between Anderson and her mother (whom Anderson says she couldn't love in the film) returns as a key theme as she meditates on other recent losses. The fallibility of memory and the erosion of meaning through excessive repetition return as themes as the verisimilitude of storytelling itself is called into question. Anderson elaborates:

> The film is about language, stories, and how you tell stories more than anything else. *Heart of a Dog* is disguised as a story about love, death, and dogs. At the center of the film is a story about the hospital, and remembering a story the way you want to. For me, that's the key, and the reason I put it in the film. There is a speech by my mother on her deathbed. She was a very proud person and waited until everyone was surrounding her, like a lot of dying people do. It [the speech] was almost like stepping up to a microphone and saying, "Thank you all for coming," and she would then get quite formal, and be distracted by all the animals she saw on the ceiling, and she would talk about that for a while, then go back to the microphone. I watched language falling apart, as her brain was shutting down. I thought, Whoa! This is really something: to still be conscious and use words as a way to show that you are. I would come back to that more than any other theme. My work is based in stories—how they get made, why, and what their usefulness is.[42]

In "O Superman," the images parallel the storytelling—acting as reinforcement of meaning for the most part rather than counterpointing or inviting cognitive dissonance. Attention is focused and directed toward visual cues that highlight perspectives. Many of the same themes return: narration of the story—parts of the whole that also work as individual tracks; her dog Lolabelle; death and loss; and temporality, the senses, military, surveillance, metastory/storytelling, and how our stories are controlled, forgotten, and mixed together or confused. For instance, in track 22, "A Story about a Story,"[43] Anderson ruminates on the fallibility of memory and the erosion of meaning through repetition: "every time you tell it you forget it more." There is a point at which repetition starts to break down meaning rather than reinforcing it. Elsewhere, I have referred to this process as enabling "semantic fluidity."[44]

A review of *Heart of a Dog* in *Bomb Magazine* by Gary M. Kramer stresses the film's breadth:

> to chronicle not just her life with Lolabelle, her rat terrier, but more generally how humans and animals communicate, their shared sense of companionship, and our processes of death, grief, and coping with trauma. That said, Anderson's film is essentially about storytelling—a theme the artist/filmmaker/musician has been exploring since the start of her long and storied career. Here, her voice carries us into a kaleidoscope of images, textures, and music that evoke both human and canine experiences of the world.[45]

There are a number of discursive repetitions in the music and leitmotif material that span Anderson's work—expanding and enhancing her storyworld. The samples of helicopters, trains, and crowd and animal sounds align with the recurring themes of military force, surveillance, love, and loss beside familiar string motifs, accordion solos, and ambient guitar figures. The very opening theme recalls the epizeuxis in the melody line "Love, Love, Love" from the Beatles' "All You Need is Love" (1967); this triple repeat (tricolon) on a theme of love may be subconscious but is apt nonetheless in a film about love and loss. We are asked to "recognize this?" six times in track 19, "The Bardo" (The Bardo being the forty-nine-day transition between death and rebirth in Tibetan Buddhism), as clocks have stopped, samples and musematic repetitions play in reverse, and the lyrics describe "everything you knew about time slipping repeating." Although far from explicit, *Heart of a Dog* echoes some political aspects of the novel with the same name by Bulgakov (1925), which invites reflection on soviet/authoritarian power.[46]

The Nonesuch Records website credits for *Heart of a Dog* signpost some reuse of former, and as yet unreleased (in 2015), materials from Anderson's discography: "The Lake" and "Flow" from *Homeland* (2010), "Beautiful Pea Green Boat"—most notably the accordion solo—from *Bright Red* (1994), "Rhumba Club" from *Life on a String* (2001), and excerpts from *Landfall* with the Kronos Quartet (2018).[47] What is hitherto undiscussed is the prevalence of other earlier materials in *Heart of a Dog*, musical materials with functional and semiotic significance.

Transmedia storytelling in Anderson's work

I mentioned earlier that the A♭/C–C minor progression is not limited to "O Superman." I would now like to explore briefly some of the transmedia occurrences of this material. Different meanings are revealed as new resonances augment and expand signification.

Fragmentary elements might also be added to some extent over time as themes are stitched together. Yes, the progression Ab/C–C minor (Ib–iii) is not particularly unusual in pop music, but these are the exact same chords (if indeed clothed in the Deleuzian sense[48]): Ab/C to C minor. What's more, there are also thematic coherences: the subject/protagonist is recognizing an aerial threat in all instances. There is another deeper layer here, a subterranean musically discursive layer. Within the album *Big Science*, on which "O Superman" was first released by a major label (Warner Brothers), this same chord progression (Ab/C–C minor) first appears toward the end of the first track on the album, "From the Air." This song takes the form of an address from the captain of a plane to passengers, with a similar vocoder loop effect to "O Superman," this time doubled by saxophone. The chords in question initially enter when the captain persona (Anderson) mentions that the plane is "going down." In *Heart of a Dog*, the motif of "From the Air" (Ab/C–C minor) appears again, in a *Twin Peaks*-esque leitmotivic fashion, signaling a familiar ominous tone.[49] It appears as Anderson recounts the episode where, while walking Lolabelle, hawks are "changing their plans" after realizing that the white dog is not a rabbit or more suitable and attainable prey. The track in question from *Heart of Dog* is also called "From the Air" and, while the title prepares the listener for the trajectory of the narrative, it is very different until this point. The piece switches to the dog's perspective as Lolabelle recognizes that she might be the hawk's prey and that the danger could be from above: "they could come from the air" and "it would be that way from now on." Anderson relates this loss of innocence to the 9/11 attacks and the terror from the skies that changed New Yorkers forever. The connection with "O Superman" is palpable. This is undoubtedly a case of transmedia storytelling; the theme of aerial threat is signaled and expanded upon with the transmedia use of the "From the Air" motif: Ab/C–C minor. Where initially it was a rescue helicopter in Tehran, then transformed into "American planes," now it signals the events at the World Trade Center. The motif finds new resonances as meanings snowball in fresh contexts through different forms, across the album to the music video and film soundtrack. The discursive repetitions transform meaning through transmedia semiosis.

While this progression of "From the Air" holds transmedia salience in Anderson's work, and in *Heart of a Dog*, another discursive musical repetition—what I forebodingly refer to as the "grief motif"—comprises an ambient guitar figure that is first heard on the track "World Without End" from the album *Bright Red* (1994). "World Without End" is a song that discusses the death of Anderson's father. When the grief motif recurs in *Heart of a Dog*, it is employed in the context of direct discussion of Lolabelle's death and the passing of Anderson's mother. Furthermore, Lou Reed emerges as a significant link here: Reed appeared on *Bright Red* and his death plays a major role in *Heart of a Dog*, where the closing image is of Lou with Lolabelle and the final track is Reed's (track 28, "Turning Time Around," which also relates to the temporal focus of the film). The film itself is dedicated to his memory. The motif resonates transmedially: the theme of death holds but is expanded in relation to the new subjects of Husband, Mother, and Dog (where it had previously attached to Father), and is developed in another media artifact (documentary/art film).

Another musical discursive repetition that is hitherto hidden is the re-employment of a motif from "My Right Eye" (heard at 2:42 in the song) on the album *Homeland*. This same motif reappears as the main theme that opens track 4, "From the Air," on *Heart of a Dog*. I mentioned earlier that the larger part of "From the Air" has little in common with its earlier namesake. It is an entirely new track but in fact much of its materials are taken from "My Right Eye." This motif consists of a violin ostinato, sustained synth drone, and electronic bass figure. A similar rhythmic electronic figure is also heard on the track "Dark Side" on *Landfall*.

"Rhumba Club" appears in track 23, "Facebook," on the *Heart of a Dog* soundtrack when Anderson considers "half-remembered songs." This discursive repetition is a playful nod to a track that was left off the official release of *Homeland*. The "dreamland" of the lyric is also apt in regard to the virtual construction of stories in social media. In this way, even minor playful discursive repetitions such as this "dreamland" can expand the storyworld with transmedia force.

Such discursive repetitions can be combined in a way that is similar to Wagnerian leitmotif treatment. In track 11 of *Heart of a Dog*, entitled "The Cloud," Anderson discusses how surveillance and data storage by government inevitably lead to confusion. As a citizen's story is constructed from fragments in a reverse order—a notion she relates to Kierkegaard's statement in track 10 ("life can only be understood backwards but it must be lived forwards")—Anderson posits that "the likelihood that your story is going to get mixed up with someone else's is extremely high." Significantly here, the motif from "My Right Eye" combines ("get[s] mixed up") with the accordion solo motif from "Beautiful Pea Green Coat," a track from the same album *Bright Red*.[50] Another layer of combination is the fact that a transposition (up a 5th) of the "From the Air" discursive motif itself (E♭/G–G minor) forms the harmony of "My Right Eye."

In the same year, 2015, we also see further transmedia recontextualization of material. The palpable resonances that augment the storyworld materials in semiosis render this more than intertextual reference. We see the storyworld of "O Superman" and the "From the Air" motif appear discursively again in *Habeas Corpus*, a collaboration with Mohammed El Gharani—the youngest detainee at Guantánamo Bay, who was imprisoned for eight years from the age of 14. Now free but unable to enter the United States, Anderson arranged for his telepresence, via live-stream from Africa, onto a 3D model of the Lincoln Memorial statue. On the occasion of the premiere of *Habeas Corpus*, Anderson chose to perform a single song from her back catalog: "O Superman." A review in *The Guardian* recognized the significance:

The continued resonance of that song's lyrics was much discussed on the occasion of Anderson's live shows directly following the 9/11 attacks. ("This is the hand, the hand that takes / Here come the planes / They're American planes / Made in America.") But on a night dedicated to Gharani's story, the words that hit hardest came toward the end: "Cause when love is gone, there's always justice. And when justice is gone, there's always force."[51]

Are the individual parts "complete" and intelligible in themselves? Are the other parts needed for "understanding"? Within layers of significance, resonances are manifest amid positive transformation and philosophical questioning. McClary recognized the multifaceted identities and their political dimension in Anderson's work early on.[52] I would go further and say that we often cannot separate her work over albums and projects beyond single album releases and installations.

"O Superman" itself is a transmedia work that operates across media and is not tethered to one form. Knowledge of its origins as part of a long-form performance art opera *United States* (later released as *United States Live* in 1984) is unnecessary for it to become a pop hit in adaptation. The multimodal employment of image (performance, setting, and gesture), music, and spoken/sung text in the music video take on new transmedia life as the work resonates in new social contexts and timeframes—post September 11, most notably. Returning with revitalized meaning, via a process of semiosis following the New York attack and political response, "O Superman" continues to resonate with citizens of a nation living under increased surveillance and scrutiny. These themes are further explored in *Heart of a Dog* and, significantly, as we've discussed, "O Superman" was the only song from Anderson's back catalog to be performed at the premiere of *Habeas Corpus*.

Anderson finds freedom in the ambiguity of calling herself a multimedia artist, as everyone is one nowadays: "it's meaningless but you won't get trapped," she posits.[53] She fights against being labelled and finds solace in the nebulous ubiquity of the term wherein artists do not need to "defend their territory." Instead, she affirms: "Don't put yourself in a box, just position yourself to be a really good observer."[54] In transmedia storytelling, parts and wholes become indivisible as one art form feeds into and augments another. Pop musicians should look beyond the corporate marketing potential of transmedia storytelling that dominates the industry. Instead, they should look to the aesthetic and artistic possibilities and freedoms afforded by transmedia storytelling as exemplified in the work of artists like Anderson.

Notes

1   In multimodality, different types of signs combine within the same media object; for example, moving image, spoken language, music, and sometimes text in film. See Gunther Kress and Theo van Leeuwen, *Multimodal Discourse: The Modes and Media of Contemporary Communication* (London: Arnold, 2001).
2   Henry Jenkins, *Convergence Culture: Where Old and New Media Collide* (New York: New York University Press, 2006).
3   *Heart of a Dog* [film], directed by Laurie Anderson (Canal Street Communications DVD, 2015).
4   Jenkins, *Convergence Culture*.
5   Susan McClary, "This Is Not a Story My People Tell: Musical Time and Space According to Laurie Anderson," *Discourse* 12, no. 1 (Fall–Winter 1989–1990, Special Issue on Music): 105.

6   Clement Greenberg (1940) quoted in Daniel Albright, *Untwisting the Serpent: Modernism in Music, Literature and Other Arts* (Chicago, IL and London: University of Chicago Press, 2000), 12.

7   McClary, "This Is Not a Story My People Tell," 109.

8   Ibid., 110.

9   Philip Auslander, "Going with the Flow: Performance Art and Mass Culture," *TDR* 33, no. 2 (1989): 123.

10 Laurie Anderson, quoted in McClary, "This Is Not a Story My People Tell," 110.

11 *Chalkroom* [VR installation], by Laurie Anderson and Hsin-Chien Huang (2017), various venues.

12 Laurie Anderson [single], "O Superman (for Massenet)," OTR 005 (One Ten Records, 1981); Laurie Anderson [album], *Big Science*, BSK 3674 (Warner Bros., 1982); *Habeas Corpus* [installation], by Laurie Anderson, October 2–4, 2015, Park Avenue Armory.

13 Laurie Anderson, quoted in Jon Pareles, "Laurie Anderson Is Telling Stories, Hers and Ours," *New York Times*, October 18, 2015, https://www.nytimes.com/2015/10/18/movies/laurie-anderson-is-telling-stories-hers-and-ours.html.

14 Laurie Anderson, "Laurie Anderson—O Superman," YouTube video (8:27), official music video, posted by "Nonesuch Records," May 20, 2016, https://www.youtube.com/watch?v=Vkfpi2H8tOE.

15 Jenkins, *Convergence Culture*.

16 Anderson, *Big Science*.

17 See Kress and van Leeuwen, *Multimodal Discourse*; John McGrath, *Samuel Beckett, Repetition and Modern Music* (London and New York: Routledge, 2018); and Marie-Laure Ryan and Jan-Noël Thon, eds., "Storyworlds Across Media," in *Storyworlds Across Media: Toward a Media-Conscious Narratology* (Lincoln, NE: University of Nebraska Press, 2014), 1–21.

18 Werner Wolf, "(Inter)mediality and the Study of Literature," in *CLCWeb: Comparative Literature and Culture* 13, no. 3 (2011). https://doi.org/10.7771/1481-4374.1789.

19 Jenkins, *Convergence Culture*, 95–96.

20 Henry Jenkins, "Transmedia Storytelling 101," *Henry Jenkins: Confessions of an Aca Fan*, March 21, 2007, http://henryjenkins.org/blog/2007/03/transmedia_storytelling_101.html.

21 Roland Barthes, *Image, Music, Text*, translated by Stephen Heath (London: Fontana, 1977); William K. Wimsatt Jr. and Monroe C. Beardsley, "The Intentional Fallacy," in *The Verbal Icon: Studies in the Meaning of Poetry*, by William K. Wimsatt (Lexington, KY: University of Kentucky Press, 1954), 3–20.

22 Jenkins, "Transmedia Storytelling."

23 Ibid.

24 The PR team seems to have missed a trick by not employing that pun, however, opting instead for "Tay-lurking" at "Swiftmas," https://www.youtube.com/watch?v=j3yyF31jbKo.

25 Henry Jenkins, Sam Ford, and Joshua Green, *Spreadable Media: Creating Meaning and Value in a Networked Culture* (New York: New York University Press, 2013).

26 Henry Jenkins, "The Aesthetics of Transmedia: In Response to David Bordwell (Part Three)," *Henry Jenkins: Confessions of an Aca Fan*, September 15, 2009, http://henryjenkins.org/blog/2009/09/the_aesthetics_of_transmedia_i_2.html.

27   Lori Burns, "The Concept Album as Visual-Sonic-Textual Spectacle: The Transmedial Storyworld of Coldplay's 'Mylo Xyloto,'" *iaspm@journal* 6, no. 2 (2016): 98.

28   There are also historical differences in tolerance thresholds for repetition among disparate art forms, see McGrath, *Samuel Beckett*.

29   Gilles Deleuze, *Difference and Repetition* (New York: Columbia University Press, 1994 [1968]). See also Elizabeth Hellmuth Margulis, *On Repeat: How Music Plays the Mind* (New York: Oxford University Press. 2014); Olivier Julien and Christophe Levaux, *Over and Over: Exploring Repetition in Popular Music* (London: Bloomsbury, 2018); McGrath, *Samuel Beckett*.

30   McGrath, *Samuel Beckett*.

31   Deleuze, *Difference and Repetition*.

32   The concept of "museme" features in Phil Tagg's popular music analysis; see Philip Tagg, "Kojak, 50 Seconds of Television Music: Towards the Analysis of Affect in Popular Music," PhD dissertation (Göteborg University, 1979).

33   McGrath, *Samuel Beckett*, 73.

34   McClary, "This Is Not a Story My People Tell," 115.

35   See Laurie Anderson, lyrics to "O Superman," https://genius.com/Laurie-anderson-o-superman-for-massenet-lyrics.

36   There are further resonances today with the polarized and sectarian politics of the Twittersphere.

37   Alex Ross, "O Souverain, O Superman," *Alex Ross: The Rest is Noise*, October 13, 2015, https://www.therestisnoise.com/2015/10/o-souverain-o-superman.html. Ross cites Richard Taruskin's analysis of "O Superman" in Chapter 10: Millennium's End of *The Oxford History of Western Music, Vol. 5: Music in the Late Twentieth Century* (Oxford: Oxford University Press, 2005).

38   For a full illustration, see Anderson, lyrics to "O Superman."

39   *Black Mirror: Bandersnatch* [film], directed by David Slade (Netflix, 2018).

40   Laurie Anderson [soundtrack], *Heart of a Dog*, 552027–2 (Nonesuch/Elektra Records, 2015).

41   Laurie Anderson, quoted in Gary M. Kramer, "Laurie Anderson," *Bomb Magazine*, October 21, 2015, https://bombmagazine.org/articles/laurie-anderson.

42   Ibid.

43   All subsequent track numbers refer to the *Heart of a Dog* soundtrack.

44   McGrath, *Samuel Beckett*.

45   Kramer, "Laurie Anderson."

46   Mikhail Bulgakov, *Heart of a Dog*, translated by Mirra Ginsburg (Chicago, IL: Avalon Travel Publishing, 1994 [1925]).

47   Nonesuch webpage: http://www.nonesuch.com/journal/laurie-anderson-heart-dog-italian-soundtrack-out-now-nonesuch-2016-09-09. Albums referred to here are: Laurie Anderson, *Bright Red*, 9 45534–2 (Warner Bros., 1994); *Life on a String*, 795392–2 (Nonesuch/Elektra Records, 2001); *Homeland*, 524055–2 (Nonesuch/Elektra Records, 2010); and (with Kronos Quartet) *Landfall*, 564164–1 (Nonesuch/Elektra Records, 2018).

48   Deleuze, *Difference and Repetition*.

49   There are similarities with "Laura Palmer's Theme" (A^b–C minor on a slow synth pad), see Angelo Badalamenti, "Laura Palmer's Theme," YouTube video, https://www.youtube.com/watch?v=khMlcTE7lw8.

50   This accordion motif also appears in tracks 1 and 6 on the *Heart of a Dog* soundtrack.
51   Seth Colter Walls, "Laurie Anderson's Habeas Corpus Review—A Rare and Direct Work," *Guardian*, October 3, 2015, https://www.theguardian.com/music/2015/oct/03/laurie-anderson-habeas-corpus-review-guantanamo-omar-souleyman.
52   McClary, "This Is Not a Story My People Tell," 105.
53   Laurie Anderson in Q&A DVD extras on *Heart of a Dog*.
54   Ibid.

Part IV

Aesthetics: Space/Place/Time/ Senses

14

How to Analyze Music Videos: Beyoncé's and Melina Matsoukas's "Pretty Hurts"

Carol Vernallis

Music videos lend themselves to analysis. They're rich, evocative, and short, and repeated viewings can bring new aspects of them to light. But there aren't many analytical models to draw upon. Scholarship on the genre is underdeveloped.

Over the last twenty years I've taught courses on music video, and I've sought ways to help students write analyses. The close readings I tend to appreciate attempt to account for both the soundtrack and the image, but a student needn't have musical training to explore audiovisual relations. Characterizing the song's elements in everyday terms (buzzy, bell-like) rather than specifically musical ones can be helpful, as can drawing on liner notes and reviews, and suggestions from musically-trained friends. I've provided tip sheets on ways to begin an analysis, as well as links to useful books and articles. Sharing my own process of doing close readings, I thought, might be helpful for readers. In this chapter I'll take "Pretty Hurts," a clip directed by Melina Matsoukas from Beyoncé's self-titled video album (2014), and see where it leads.

When I begin working with a music video I often ask: "why do I like it?" or "why does it puzzle me?" I hold this question in reserve with the hope that answers will emerge as I engage with the clip. In "Pretty Hurts," the *Beyoncé* album's first clip, the singer competes in a beauty pageant. The video seems to both celebrate and critique the fashion industry: it considers professionalism and authenticity, and what might enable collaboration and personal happiness. I'm particularly drawn to a moment in the song's chorus when Beyoncé waves from the podium amidst the rows of women (3:12), and I'll pay special attention to the question of how and why this moment moves me (see Figure 14.1).

Beginning an analysis, I watch the clip many times. I'll listen to the song alone, I'll watch the images silently, I'll read the lyrics apart from both, and I'll run the clip in my imagination. I'll take a single visual or aural parameter, and follow it through the clip's entirety: tracking the song sections, counting out the rhythm, tracing the melody, attending to the musical arrangement, following the figures in the frame, studying the editing, and

Figure 14.1 Beyoncé waves from the podium (3:12).

so on. Sometimes I feel I'm in a conversation with the video, querying it. "What about that odd spot of color?" "What about that chorus?" All the while I take copious notes. As I start learning the music and image, I'll note key moments of audiovisual synchronization, and my attention will follow predictable paths through the video—almost as if the video and I are dancing together. I'll follow these paths, but I'll also direct my attention in other ways. In this analysis I'll track a process in which insights emerge gradually and unpredictably. Readers might periodically refer to the clip. My goal here is to help others have a richer experience of a music video, to see and hear more, and to want to watch it many times.

The video for "Pretty Hurts" has a moment when Beyoncé waves while standing on stage with the other contestants. This happens at (3:11) in the song's first chorus. I wonder why this moment stirs me. So why not begin with the choruses? Music videos, like feature films, use many devices to achieve their ends, and leave other techniques aside. Since each video leans on certain techniques, and it's the chorus that draws me in, I might begin by asking whether the video breaks into strongly demarcated song sections. To follow this further I might ask: how much does this video highlight song sections? (Lyric sheets and tablature transcriptions can be useful for determining sections even when a student doesn't have musical training.) Often, especially in classic, commercial music videos, visual and song sections parallel one another. This is true of "Pretty Hurts." For the first two choruses, Beyoncé is on the podium. In the third chorus (following the bridge), she and the models appear on the stage again, but then the image shifts to their self-inflicted harm. In the verses, Beyoncé preps for her competition and, while someone or something twirls or circles, she tends to take one step up. Most of the painful techniques demanded by the beauty industry occur in the bridge, and Beyoncé looks frustrated and angry here. And that tells me something. In a pop song, the verses often discuss the everyday. The bridges provide another way of seeing things. The choruses often crystallize an idea—a view that can seem more timeless—and reflect a communal wish. That Beyoncé can't transcend her situation during the bridge suggests that hers is a real struggle. The third chorus's shift in focus intrigues me (4:38). Continuing to work on this, I'll make greater sense of the last chorus. But I don't know this yet. What question might we consider next? To analyze this video, let's consider its various parameters in turn.

The use of color and texture to convey music and story

The color scheme emphasizes browns and golds. The warmth of the home's wood paneling, shag carpet, and silky outfits suggests a cave or burrow. I hear the song as exceptionally warm, and I think the mellow colors and textures draw our attention to the song's capaciousness (see Figure 14.2). There are also isolated spots of blue. Blue latex-covered hands intrude in the frame, looking uncanny (5:10). There's also a violating syringe and the models swallowing cotton and vomiting. (Afterwards, when Beyoncé emerges from the toilet, her earrings have sharp edges, as if they'd assimilated the women's self-injurious routines. At the video's triumphant end, the earrings will form full, large circles, mimicking Beyoncé's own richer sense of self.) Alongside the warmth of Beyoncé's voice and the often lullaby-like-rocking supporting vocals and the percussion, I ask: is there anything in the music that has a little sharpness?

I turn to the musical arrangement. Halfway into the first verse, the hard and brittle sound of the drum slaps on beats 2 and 4 (what's known as the "backbeat," here possibly a processed

Figure 14.2 Warm, cozy settings (5:52).

hand clap with an enhanced snare) could be seen to press Beyoncé onward (2:25). Earlier, we had spied on the women pushing and shoving her, then turning away, perhaps setting her in motion (Beyoncé is very much alone in this video!). Perhaps this timbral/rhythmic detail carries weight. John Mowitt reminds us that drumming is a form of beating.[1] There's also a bit of a protrusion or rushing in the second verse's melody when Beyoncé sings: "is all that matters … bigger is better" (3:22; 3:28). These stand out from the smoother, constantly-articulating rhythm arrangement, overdubbed voices, and reverberant synthesizer. These melodic touches, the sharp accents on beats 2 and 4, Beyoncé's concluding full-throated singing of "When you find yourself alone," as well as the fragmented, speechifying "pretty hurts," may support Beyoncé's trashing of her trophies. (Imagine the video without these musical touches, the close is harder to imagine.) Aural and visual protrusions don't necessarily need to simultaneously match what we see and hear, I believe. If the visual or aural motif is catchy enough, it can still forge a connection from a temporal distance.

As I continue to analyze "Pretty Hurts" I'll discover more about color, but, for now, let's turn to another parameter. When analyzing a video, I'll often work on one parameter until I catch an idea, then turn to a second, or to several, to then return to parameters I've already considered. I sometimes find myself posing questions to the video several times, and I don't always get an answer! I simply wait.

The implied geography of the video

I'm interested in the gorgeous images of Beyoncé, so I ask about the implications of setting and space: how do the figures move and where are they placed in the frame? The longest and steepest trajectories move from Beyoncé on the podium to her drop into water, and from the podium to her lying, belly up, on the carpet. She also seems to step up toward and away from these locations. These points help to chart her struggle to achieve beauty and win the pageant. But they might also describe formal distances within the song, like how it moves from section to section. Against this, I notice the stage's columns appear to suspend space and objects in attractive proportions, as do the podium's tiered steps that firmly and generously support the women. The song's spare opening also reflects a sense of balance and stasis. Against this, I might want to consider internal movement: the women's cat-fighting for hair dryers, their brisk pushings aside and graceful balletic moves, and then the more archetypally womanly flowing gestures Beyoncé adopts. Sometimes, but not always, the contours of the melodies and bass line can be reflected by the placement of objects and movement of figures in a frame (see Figure 14.3).

So far this feels like what I would call a classic music video. It's attentive to the song and committed to showing off its musical features in a balanced way, especially since its song sections are so carefully articulated. Individual phrases too, are clearly shown: when the melody dips or a phrase ends, Beyoncé often glances down. At melodic high points, a woman's enormously tall hairdo, or a suspended hair dryer crests the top of the frame. In the opening, one woman buttoning a dress and another pinching flesh from her sides might reflect the isolated chords of the accompaniment. A camera's pan, or a figure tapping in the background,

Figure 14.3a–b Long, steep trajectories from the podium to a) the carpet (2:42) and b) the water (4:12).

elucidates the ways in which the sounds trail off. I see and hear these shapes, but, in these cases, I don't expect other viewers and listeners to necessarily hear and see this as I do.

The role of lyrics

The lyrics begin like this: "Mama said, 'You're a pretty girl. What's in your head, it doesn't matter.'" For me these lines are so emotionally resonant that they hover over the clip. We might consider how the mother's advice shapes the video's iconography. Beyoncé's furniture looks like it belongs to an older generation. She may still live with her parents (see Figure 14.3).

How might the line "When you find yourself alone" also shape the video? The moment when Beyoncé stalls for time, as she seeks an answer to the question: "What is your aspiration in life?," feels jarring (4:03). As she falls into water, the microphone comes up from silence and starts buzzing reverberantly and words, too, become garbled. Some of the sounds seem as if they had emanated from the opening chords' sustain and pedal, which also begins to warble and merge into microphone feedback. Earlier, in the song's arrangement proper, every eighth note had been filled in with insistent percussion fills, sometimes using tiny bell-like sounds. Song sections frequently end with buzzy distortion, and the choruses open with a high-pitched breathy-like whistle (probably filtered white noise). At this point it's worth noting the musical arrangement sometimes functions here as an *unhelpful* partner—its noisy internal chatter or a buzz of activity keeps Beyoncé apart from herself. The isolation and silence of the water provide Beyoncé with an opportunity to ask questions and for the pageant's horrors to emerge.

In general, the song's overdubbed backing vocals support Beyoncé's lead voice, but Beyoncé's fellow models do not. So does "Pretty Hurts" suggest another, more receptive audience? In verse 1 especially, Beyoncé's overdubs of "Pretty Hurts" move forward dramatically to the front of the mix, claiming our attention. At the song's end, the rejoining "Pretty Hurts" becomes increasingly emphatic. Does Beyoncé improve upon her parents' and colleagues' advice, counseling us on ways to nurture ourselves? Are we her intended audience?

The influence of rhythm on narrative flow

I first listen to the song alone. There's the hand-clap snare on the backbeat, and small articulations that might sound like flamenco steps—possibly played by a *güiro* (a gourd instrument with ridges, stroked with a stick)[2] or snare with brushes—taking up every eighth note. The bass drum is syncopated. In the choruses, the bass drum articulates a 4-on-the-floor (every quarter note is articulated), the backbeat drops out, and a thick synthesizer pad fills things in (this kind of synthesizer pad is often used in the chorus, in the recently popular songwriting technique of "the soar").[3] The chorus's arrangement is highly unusual. Perhaps the producer and arrangers (Ammo, Rob Sucheki, Derek Dixie, and Stuart White) wanted an insistent and dramatic shift without change of scale between the verse and chorus. I count off the measures as the video progresses. In the verses, I notice Beyoncé tapping the carpet with her fingertips (Beyoncé's hands before her crotch seem either vulnerable or powerful—it's hard to determine what her posture might signify). The opening's editing is slightly irregular against the pulse and becomes smoother as the video progresses, as if Beyoncé and the pageant have become more coordinated. Beyoncé's cycling and walking also establish a pulse. In the chorus, when the rhythm becomes a straight 4-on-the-floor, Beyoncé becomes less mobile. Does the pulse then become internalized as something more subjective, like a heartbeat? This would support other aspects of "Pretty

Hurts"—like Beyoncé's drop into water—that seem more like an allegory, dreamscape, or memory than a documentary of a recent event.

The foregrounding of continuity

Because music video images often aim to keep pace with and draw attention to the song's flow, they tend to draw on several devices to establish continuity from shot to shot. Match-cuts are unusually common. In "Pretty Hurts" the stage's blue spangled curtains draw back and Beyoncé's blue trophy ribbons tacked on the den's wall etch the same pattern. Beyoncé stands against a wall next to a hanging spangled beige dress that frames her as much as the curtains do. (The camera before her bathroom stall reveals one extra wall-as-frame as well.) During the song's break (4:11), the camera cross-cuts between Beyoncé submerged underwater and the contestants preparing in the green room. A large bunched-up green duffel bag matches, via shape and placement, Beyoncé's submerged body.[4] There's also a preponderance of repetitive material to create flow. Wigs and hair curlers, for example, dot the video. Extra crowns surface, too. It's also worth following the video's images of feet, especially those gangsta socks and the way one foot delicately articulates the beat (2:10). There's an absence of feet in general, except when Beyoncé steps on the scale, or her foot trembles in the bridge. When Beyoncé is submerged in water, rows of shoes seem to upbraid her. But that's one of the tricky parts of analyzing a music video. Such a heterogeneous unfolding of material competes for attention. One can be pulled away.

Melina Matsoukas's style influences

Watching a director's other work can help us to tease out themes that thread through her oeuvre. Melina Matsoukas's other clips reveal an engagement with a neglected and worn-down 1950s America. She also likes muted colors. The visual language of "Pretty Hurts" suggests that the pageant is regional, small, and working class: on the podium and in the green room, for example, sashes say "Miss Jersey Shore," "Miss South Bronx," "Miss Jamaica Queens," and "Miss Oak Cliff." Is the winner's title of "Miss Shaolin"[5] a sign of otherness I wonder? How might these visual touches help to create sentiment, even nostalgia? And do these touches make the video's primary message more palatable? The video wants us to recognize the damage inflicted by women competing against one another as well as the fashion industry's harmful practices.

   In another of Matsoukas's videos, Beyoncé's "Why Don't You Love Me," an American flag projected onto Beyoncé is so prominent it feels like a personal statement, so I look for similar symbols in "Pretty Hurts." Sure enough, when Beyoncé sings a cappella before the judges, she wears black stars against a white field, with blue spangles behind her, although we're missing red. The video seems from this moment on to seek its missing red element: it's smeared here and dotted there within the images, only finding its real weight at the video's close, when the master of ceremonies' (MC's) assistant, in a luridly red-sequined gown, hands off the crown to Beyoncé's competitor, while our diva-heroine looks on.

The use of props

Matsoukas states that, with "Pretty Hurts," she attempted to freshly capture unplanned moments.[6] Beyoncé's vomiting wasn't scripted. But I believe there must have been a great deal of preparation before shooting occurred. In the music video's well-budgeted heyday of the 1980s and 1990s, directors and their crews often arrived at a shoot with several truckloads of props. Laid out on set would be rows of shoes, earrings, plates, and underthings. Several alternatives might be filmed on the spot. The outfits and accessories in "Pretty Hurts" adopt an "arc" that seems more determined than spontaneously chosen, however. The jewelry alone suggests a path from beginning to end: from the gold bands around Beyoncé's ankles (like a ball and chain) to the earrings that become whole at the video's close. The appearance of porcelain animals and human figurines throughout also seem too concerted to be last-minute fortuitous decisions, especially since they appear to accrue meaning as the video unfolds. Most intriguing is a white porcelain figurine of two seated women, one embracing the other, on the coffee table in front of Beyoncé. Traditionally, this would be a pair of heterosexual lovers. Yet a close look reveals two women wearing dresses, embracing, with one holding up what one might assume to be a pageant sash. At the video's close Beyoncé molds herself into the shape of the supporting porcelain figure, as if providing strength and support for the woman who wins the award. The visually choreographed doubling of statuary and live performers could be understood as pro-feminist, homosocial, or homosexual. (Foreshadowing this, in the intro at (0:33), against the tender but stoic chords, a woman's hand momentarily reaches into the frame and gently strokes Beyoncé's shoulder as she stands among the women.[7]) The white porcelain cat also gains meaning. Early on, the cat is placed over Beyoncé's head, doubling her blonde-waved hair. At the video's end, Beyoncé crawls on all fours, stalking forward to the camera, as if a cat-like alter-ego had emerged from inside her, and now, as female aggressor, she's readying to pounce on that oily MC (6:36). The fierce porcelain tiger peering from behind the top of the couch resembles the beauty pageant winner, Ms. Shaolin (their faces and expressions are similar) (6:09). Both figures seem to shadow or haunt Beyoncé. On the shelves of the exercise room, there's also a jeweled crown and a zebra. (Note that items seem to have been carefully chosen and edited into the video—there's a match-cut between a pageant woman's yellow dress and the yellow magazines stacked in a shelf's corner.) It's hard for me to decide on the zebra's role (3:20). I might imagine that, with the predatory environment of the video (including that fierce porcelain tiger), the zebra suggests Beyoncé's vulnerability. But I could also imagine the animal was chosen because it rhymes with the striping on Beyoncé's gym clothes. Matsoukas, too, may be like the music video and film director Francis Lawrence, who says he always adds a lot of flora and fauna to enrich his videos.[8] I'm also tempted to wonder—but this may be too much of a stretch—whether this and other "Pretty Hurts" images might be linked to Africa or African-American culture: the antique lamp has a black figure holding it up; the gold anklets might resemble shackles. Again, perhaps this is a stretch, but at this point I'm taking it seriously. The white cat has one single blue eye (6:35)—less stereotypically Anglo-Saxon-looking models often opt to wear contacts to lighten their appearance.

The beginning and end

Just as in film, a music video's opening often foreshadows its end. I notice the deep jade-green and spangles returning (0:10; 6:22–6:44). Then I catch that Beyoncé's blue and silver shorts match the MC's silver jacket and blue curtains. There's even some dusting of silver over the periodically reappearing white porcelain cat (2:07). This video is both color-coordinated and patterned! Horizontal lines traverse the frame, including the bands of light on the shiny gold drapery.

What about the song as a whole? Music videos often close with ambiguous double endings that encourage a viewer to watch the clip again. Michael Jackson's "Thriller" famously does so, and "Pretty Hurts" does so as well. I count four ways of reading the end of the video. First, Beyoncé triumphs. Yes, she loses this pageant, but she's reflecting upon or fantasizing about moments when she competed as a child, so she's in many ways already a winner. We're aware that she's more beautiful than any of the other pageant contestants and "should" win. We viewers recognize her as the "real" Beyoncé, who has already achieved a top position in pop-music history, so we can feel she's already risen above the event. Second, Beyoncé is angry about the pageant. She breaks trophies, encourages women to rebel, and threatens her MC. A match-cut shows him fixing his bow tie followed by Beyoncé stalking forward on all fours as if she's going straight for his jugular. Good for her! Third, she's made peace with herself and with the pageant. Fourth, she absents the event and has encouraged the women to do so as well. (The "Pretty Hurts" sash remains slung across the chair.)

Gestures that cross media

I suspect that some of this video's actors heard the song so often during filming that their mannerisms picked up aspects of the song's musical materials. This gestural exchange among media gives music videos a certain density. Toward the second chorus, the MC seems to pause and share an empathetic moment with Beyoncé, saying "You've done a great job in the competition," but then he abruptly turns and exclaims, as if repressing his sentiment, "as have all our ladies!" The judges attentively listen, enraptured by Beyoncé's singing, but then look down quickly to note their scores. The models seem to be listening to Beyoncé, but then swiftly turn their backs. Beyoncé gingerly gazes up at her trainer, and then he brusquely shoos her away. The song proper does this too. Gentle "Aha, ahas" suddenly become drowned out by the verse's very busy musical arrangement.

The use of costuming to underscore music and story

Bea Åkerlund, the designer, apparently chose the wire Playboy-bunny ears because they lent Beyoncé a quality of innocence.[9] I seek other odd touches. The gangsta socks quickly suggest a different set of alliances and history. There's also the strange designer jumpsuit and white plastic shoes that suggest the 1980s. The jeweled blouse and white mink fur that Beyoncé wears for her Botox session strongly contrast with her other outfits. (Note the way this scene's star-studded, high-heeled sandals chime with her opening black-starred dress.) Matsoukas reports that Beyoncé wears a strait jacket beneath her mink, but even though I can see some of her straps, the outfit doesn't really resonate with me.[10] My knowledge of this detail, however, may help me to notice that the MC's accessories are ominously black. Instead of the traditional white or pink carnation, he wears a black, brittle, spiky brooch that resembles a sea urchin. It projects potential to harm—especially Beyoncé. She wears earrings with dangling, diamond-studded crosses (3:41–3:46).

The MC's black accessories (establishing a villain), along with Beyoncé's range of hairstyles, costumes, bodily dispositions, and expressions help to establish "Miss Third Ward" as a densely-textured character. I think the numbers attached near the hips of the models' pageant dresses reduce the women to packaged wind-up dolls or graphic logos from a Leger painting. I also think the opening mirrored dress Beyoncé wears resembles her outfit for "Partition," another clip from her *Beyoncé* video album. Many types of hairstyles, lipstick colors, and earrings come forward, looking clearly chosen by Åkerlund and Matsoukas. Beyoncé's lipstick becomes the color of her competitor's gown, as if she bequeathed some of herself to her. Additional audiovisual rhyming and promiscuous cross-media sharing include Beyoncé's home's teardrop-shaped lampshade that resembles her waved hairdo (Keitel's is similarly waved—do these shapes intimate weeping?). The models' pageant dresses are chosen to create match-cuts across shots. One woman's shiny black and gold striped dress presages the living-room's design scheme. The living room's gold modernist mirror (its beveled glass pieces resembling a sash) rhymes with the room's furniture and Beyoncé's gold earrings and anklets. Even the mirrors down the den's hallway remind me of Beyoncé's "Partition" dress. Beyoncé's earrings sway and the models wave their numbered paper sheets back and forth, all marking the rhythm. Standing at the end of the rehearsal line-up, a woman dressed in baby blue and pink doubles for Beyoncé's tyrannous coach.

The role of harmony

A pop song's chord changes can often be found through a Google search using the song's title and the word "tab" (for guitar chords tablature). Sheet music is also often available for purchase. The chord changes on "Pretty Hurts" are simple—(I–ii–vi–V–I)—with the verse, bridge, and choruses all using the same chord progression. (The bridge, however, begins its progression on ii, as if the system had encountered a slight hitch. It also has one chord that's new for this song—a bvii chord.) The song's harmonic scheme suits the video's theme of a largely repetitive cycle.

Depictions of race, class, gender, and sexuality

The *güiro* and syncopated rhythm of flamenco footsteps have Latin associations. (Glenn McDonald, principal engineer for Spotify and Echo's Nest, has said he was surprised to discover how much of Beyoncé's music can be categorized as Latin pop.)[11] These musical choices may provide grounds for the video's many contestants of color. Although one might argue that the regional setting has mostly a documentary value—it's not the kind of beauty pageant most people saw in the 1970s—this location may have been specifically chosen to speak to the music. The pageant's professionals—the MC, judges, plastic surgeon, and beautician—are predominantly white or male. The meanest contestants are white. The coach is albino, although he may be seen as lower in status, and therefore closer to the women. These race relations accurately represent the current state of the culture industries in Hollywood and beyond.[12] But, analytically, I'm not getting a lot here yet. I'll just have to keep watching and listening.

There comes a point in most analytical work when I feel I'm not making as much progress as I would like. I've often wondered how much a successful music video needs strong audiovisual relations. Is a visually acute, flashy director enough? Some videos seem driven by intimate audiovisual engagement, and such relationships can serve dramatic ends. "Pretty Hurts" both heightens our identification with and critiques the fashion industry. How can I be sure exactly how close these relations are? I can't. Relations that emerge in the process of analysis tend to feel apt, and it makes sense in this case that the director would use close relations to elicit the viewer's empathy and antipathy. I also intuit that the video shares features with classic videos like Madonna's "Like a Prayer" (1989). Both "Pretty Hurts" and "Like a Prayer" have close, rich, audiovisual relations: images and music that respect strongly demarcated song sections, with each section telling a different story; explorations of race and of musical performance, and a variety of vocal styles; the podium as a separate realm; and an interplay between models and characters.

I have not seen any studies that show whether viewers tend to perceive what I am describing. The reader might simply check if the description seems true for them. The most popular and critically-admired clips seem, I've found, to hold up well to this kind of close viewing. With YouTube, music video's generic borders have become blurry, so that many types of audiovisual relations seem to count as music videos. But well-funded commercial videos function much as they always have. They still tend to emerge from collaborations between record companies, musicians, and directors (as with "Pretty Hurts"). The visual track is designed to sell the song—and, as the first clip on the album, "Pretty Hurts" may have been specially bound to do so. Commercial videos tend to be short, and often can seem uncanny. They need to accomplish many things: highlight the star, showcase performances, draw attention to the lyrics, and underscore the music. To sell a song—to teach listeners what's memorable about it—the image might emphasize the movement from verse to chorus, or highlight an unusual timbre, melodic contour, or striking rhythm. The visual track might point to one or two musical features at a time, like a tour guide. For while the music envelops us, visual features more often momentarily focus our attention, especially if they're working in service of the song.

Moment-to-moment instances of audiovisual synchronization: Suturing the image to the music

I discover verse 1 of "Pretty Hurts" has many moment-to-moment instances of audiovisual synchronization:

- The melody's contour rises while strips of light playing on gold surfaces behind Beyoncé gradually rise in the frame—even though she gazes down and looks away from us (0:08–1:03; 2:02–2:21) (Figure 14.4).
- A *güiro* or snare with brushes makes a scratchy sound. Simultaneously, Beyoncé rips off the hair-removal strip adhering to her face. Soon, one of the models pulls something off the back of a competitor's dress, and I assume the gesture elicits the same sound (2:17; 2:23).
- The vocals arrangement then presents a gentle "aha," and Beyoncé delicately pats her sinuses in the mirror. Soon she'll lean forward, and her bunny ears will bounce softly against another "aha." The next melodic phrase begins a step higher, and Beyoncé will step up to the weighing scale. The song now seems brighter and she stands a step closer to us (2:04; 2:05).
- A ballerina in the back of the rehearsal space stretches upwards, and another dancer pirouettes. These gestures help to carry Beyoncé and us into the first chorus. (Without them we wouldn't have such a graceful sense of movement to convey us into the next song section) (2:26–2:38).
- A brush drags across a cymbal, giving a voice to the curtains as they swing open (2:41).
- The camera pans on an open vowel in the lyrics, like "hair" or "stage." In general, the camera pans gently, perhaps aligning itself more with the vocals than the rhythm arrangement (3:14–3:18; 3:31).

The images for verse 2 possess a stronger sense of continuous movement and flow than verse 1, and the song has a more foregrounded synth pad. The stationary bicycle's wheels spin. Beyoncé pumps her arms up and down. The needle on the scale oscillates without settling. Again Beyoncé steps up as the melody rises (3:15–3:45). In verse 2 the women turn around together on stage. Rotations have been performed before (including by a ballerina, and the women who turn away from Beyoncé). Finally it seems these gestures of isolation

Figure 14.4a–b Beyoncé's gaze and strips of light help to show off the melody's contour: a) 0:04 and b) 0:26.

or hostility have been harnessed into a coordinated structure. We might suddenly admire the competition and its models for qualities of discipline and grace (3:20–3:22).

In the song's break, simple piano chords reappear and the camera and the figures in the frame gently seek connection with them through contour—up one whole step, down a third, a glance up or a look down (4:10–4:40). Beyoncé heaves forward to vomit. We hear the chorus's main hook ("pretty hurts!"). Does this moment suggest some suddenly emergent latent content? Beyoncé's singing often seems immediately pleasurable, generous, and expressive. I wonder if she must sometimes deliver a performance that feels internally forced. Beyoncé is such a consummate performer, we'll never know (4:54).

In the images of the bridge, many of the shapes are horizontal. A doctor's hand enters the frame, straight across. Beyoncé spreads her arms directly out, and the tanning spray and the beautician's arm also project parallel to the ground. The voices overdubbed closely together seem to form a thick, flat, horizontal band above the song's rhythm arrangement (5:09–5:39).

Watching for synchronization leads me to follow subtle touches that jut out from the video, seemingly untethered to the music. There's the nauseating orange juice next to a red candle. I note Beyoncé's logo-stamped tracksuit, it makes things seem as if she'd been bought by a corporation. One of the judges has striped glasses, with blue light making him look ominous. I focus on the alternating beige and purple carpeting of Beyoncé's den. (It's so real, just like the bad carpeting I saw growing up!) Beyoncé, with arms spread, momentarily resembles the circulating post-Super Bowl internet pictures her rep requested be taken down (5:42).[13]

Returning to form

Perhaps considering song sections in light of narrative will help. I've mentioned that the MC's question to Beyoncé, and her watery plunge, grant her an instant of reflection and an internal reset. The third chorus can now reveal the models' most painful preparations, like the self-harm of swallowing cotton balls and vomiting in toilets (4:51–4:55). This chorus's revelation, along with the bridge's new focus on the fashion industry's mercenary practices, may provide enough insight for Beyoncé to choose to leave, hopefully along with her fellow competitors.

So perhaps I have a story, but it feels hypothetical. I wonder if turning to Beyoncé's singing and the song's musical arrangement will reveal more of where character change takes place. Perhaps the video's mystery and charm stem partly from the fact that the music of "Pretty Hurts," more than the video's image, accomplishes much. The opening singing of "aha" is tentative and traditionally feminine. At the song's outro, Beyoncé is belting out the question, almost as if it is a call to arms: "When you're alone all by yourself … Are you happy with yourself?," and the overdubbed voices behind her concur, fragmentedly declaring "Pretty hurts. Pretty hurts." The voice in particular seems to guide us from failure to success, from the dressing room to the stage, from the verse to the chorus. Empty spaces shadow the vocals, giving a sense of haltingness: they make you wait. But Beyoncé is also almost always heard as multiple, either harmonizing with herself or doubling her lead vocal. Marvin Gaye often surrounded his lead vocal with closely overdubbed vocal tracks, especially when he was singing about community. Here Beyoncé draws on 1970s' soul practices, singing about and for a community of women. The rhythm tracks are supersaturated: every sixteenth note is articulated. While the lilting melody seems to offer the characters some comfort, the rhythm arrangement encourages them on.

Musical moments lead us and cue what's important: the timpani rolls that open the bridge overshadow the cymbals that accompany the curtains drawing back, for example.

Figure 14.5 Beyoncé is placed between women of different skin tones (2:19).

Beyoncé's opening fanfare suggests that her angry and bluesy singing should carry weight. Verse 2 has a greater sense of flow and more of the synth than verse 1. The voice, however, sometimes appears singly, or in multiples. Here Beyoncé works to pull herself together, but we're still picking up momentum at this moment in the song. As the video progresses, her soloing and overdubs become increasingly florid and emphatic, until finally, at the clip's end, we might imagine that she has convinced her confederates to leave the pageant. Beyoncé's chair is empty, with only her "Pretty Hurts" sash (not "Miss Third Ward") crossing it. We didn't see or hear all this activity unfolding, but somehow, mysteriously, the change has taken place. Now we must watch the video again to see how it has happened.

Returning to gender, sexuality, race, and class

Matsoukas has noted that Beyoncé requested the winner of the pageant be albino.[14] This woman will most likely strike viewers as attractive, but no match for Beyoncé. The competition's models are also more racially diverse than we might expect from the era depicted in the clip. In the first chorus, shots reveal women with the same bone structure and facial features, looking nearly identical except for skin tone. When Beyoncé preps in the dressing room, she sits between one woman with very dark skin and another who is very pale: the video seems to suggest that beauty pageants oppress many races. These last three choices of skin color might also be said to shift the video away from the mode of documentary realism to a broader discussion about how we think about beauty. Perhaps they also reflect a personal dreamscape, allegory, or wish (see Figure 14.5).

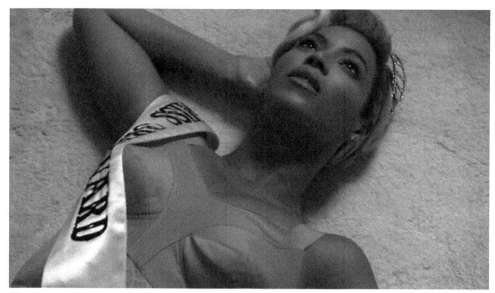

Figure 14.6 The carpeted floor is where power resides (6:17).

Returning to rhythm

The song is in 4/4. As in much funk, soul, and R&B, the "1" is dominant. Beat 3, coming up from behind, supports beat 1. Beats 2 and 4, the "backbeats," maintain the pulse, or, more often than the others, allow some slack. For the first two verses and choruses, Beyoncé is often highlighted on beat 3, as if she's a racehorse making a break for the lead. (Count the beats: you'll see her face or body appear there.) In the bridge, when the beauty industry obliterates the self, Beyoncé falls away from the beat. But in the last chorus and the out-chorus, she begins to take command of the rhythm. On beat 1, she crawls forward on all fours toward the camera; she also destroys her trophies on the downbeat. The winner of the pageant accepts her award on beat 3, while Beyoncé watches. Although the competitor has won first prize for "Miss Pretty USA," she's not a real winner. She has simply adopted Beyoncé's role as a struggler in a larger power structure. The last shot reveals a single close-up of Beyoncé that stretches across almost all four beats, as if she's broadened herself to fill in almost everything.

I listen again to the production of the "backbeat." I had described the articulations on 2 and 4 as beating, possibly pushing, Beyoncé on. Toward the end of the song, the backbeat's timbre changes, assimilating what sounds like a punch. (With her trophy slung over her shoulder, I could imagine Beyoncé decking her MC.)

Returning to timbre

The vocals are nasal and forward in the bridge—more aggressive. One could hear this nasality transposed down to the lowest vocal register in the out-chorus. Here, sonically,

Figure 14.7 The attractive choruses (3:08).

power and aggression come from below. Similarly, in the video, the floor is where the focus is. Count off every beat: even when Beyoncé lies on the carpet, she appears strong (see Figure 14.6). We can feel her and the other contestants weighted to the ground. Even though Beyoncé gives away the crown, she possesses poise.

Beyoncé has commented that the *Beyoncé* album embraces imperfection: not everything has to be prettified. In the third chorus, a harsh, striking, vocal fragment twice comes forward (an "Eeaow" at 5:58–5:59). It falls in the midst of moments when Beyoncé spreads out her arms and legs, looking ferocious or aggressively crawling forward. These moments wouldn't work as synergistically if Beyoncé wasn't someone to be reckoned with, and if the fragment wasn't so raw.[15]

Returning to shots, camera, and editing

I'm surprised that the average shot length of "Pretty Hurts" is low for a music video. (This is a stately clip!) Then I see it—part of the reason I'm drawn to the chorus—the color sweeps through the video, from the verses to these sections, from dull greens and tannish golds to a more viscerally vibrant setting containing bright lemon-yellow bathing suits, Beyoncé's shock of blonde hair, and a more saturated, deep sky blue, sequined curtain. Later, there will be glistening, primary-hued, multicolored dresses. So a color arc gradually builds, cycling through song sections to more heightened experiences in the choruses. The women are also more tightly organized and multiple in the chorus, a (potential) collective rather than the earlier isolated and scattered configurations. Of course the chorus is going to punch! These sections remind me of Spike Lee's *Bamboozled*. In Lee's film, the quotidian struggles of network producers and talent were shot on low-res video, and the television show proper—an objectionable valorization of minstrelsy—was filmed on gorgeous 35 millimeter. The minstrel numbers, which return cyclically like choruses, should evoke a sense of revulsion, but a viewer's response may be more mixed, because the image looks so strong. The African-American actors perform their roles with such wit, musicality, physical dexterity, and grace, one cannot help but admire them. "Pretty Hurts" works similarly (see Figure 14.7).

Reflections on the analytic discoveries

I think "Pretty Hurts" sets a hard task for itself—a task it succeeds at. Perhaps its closest kin is Martin Scorsese's *Raging Bull*, which aims at a critique of boxing's misogynistic, racist, and homophobic culture, but still moves many viewers as much with its stunning cinematography, editing, and sound. Some of Matsoukas's techniques make the pageant strikingly attractive, especially through the selection of beautiful women with their synchronized movements (like hand-waving), the warm textures and colors, and the sweeps that lead us from section to section. But many devices also work to critique the pageant, including the deployment of props and color, and the close attention to vocal performance, musical arrangement, and song structure.

"Pretty Hurts" starts in a traditionally feminine way and ends with a call to arms and a sense of community. For me, this is the video's most striking feature. Many details support this broad shift: the changes in Beyoncé's vocal style and the song's use of her overdubbed voice; the break's recasting of the rhythm arrangement as distraction; heralded by the bridge's opening timpani roll, Beyoncé's big statement that indicts the beauty industry; the singer's slow advance toward and eventual seizure of the downbeat; the role of props and costumes as markers of change—those earrings, of course! But I'm drawn to the white cat that enables Beyoncé's alter-ego to come forward. The video might even suggest a shadowy revenge narrative—Beyoncé, like Irena in *Cat People*, attacks and kills her MC. But at the same time, "Pretty Hurts" possesses a yearning and nostalgia for the fashion industry. Its historical turn and old-school musical touches are reassuring, including the Marvin Gaye vocal overdubs, the soft, cozy fabrics and the muted browns and golds. The video, shot at a high school, has a miniature quality. (These spaces are often scaled for adolescents.) Everything plays a role, including the smallest details: they work through contagion, substitution, expulsion, and reincorporation. Beyoncé shares her lipstick with the winner, who adopts Beyoncé's position on beat 3. Beyoncé's closing vocal fragment breaks into pieces and dissolves into the arrangement. It's a transmedia object linked to striking images of bulimia and anorexia. How well might the video work without these small details? I think they contribute much. The similarity between Matsoukas's, Beyoncé's, and Åkerlund's production and the contestant's preparations is worth considering. Fine visual choices lend the video a beautiful sheen with some dark touches. The contestants also produce themselves: Beyoncé applying Vaseline to her teeth for a bit more glisten—that's new to me.

"Pretty Hurts" and Madonna's "Like a Prayer" could be said to draw on the "backstage musical." We see not only the big stage productions, but also their behind-the-scenes preparation. We follow someone who, through talent and hard work, becomes a star.[16] Madonna's "Like a Prayer" puns off the star's name (Madonna plays a Madonna to Christ and closes out the show). Our protagonist in "Pretty Hurts" also draws on her star status outside the video. Our knowledge of Beyoncé's diligence and attention to detail inform our experience of Houston's Miss "Third Ward."

So now I've done the work of gathering together analytical material, which normally might be primarily notes at this point, and started putting it in an order. Next I'd sketch an outline, draft paragraphs, and reorder.[17] I won't do that now. Rather than a finished interpretation, I've opted instead to show the slow, unpredictable, and repetitive path music video analysis can take. Posing questions and taking notes can demand patience, but it can yield sudden insights. (When I'm successful, I feel like I've caught a fish!) It's an odd practice, one not everyone does.

I like to think of analysis as but one part of the film- and media-making process. Color-timers, sound-mixers, and post-production artists most likely engage with the work last, often adding touches that highlight or de-emphasize elements, thereby etching more deeply a particular path through the work. Although the critic doesn't alter the work directly, their insights suggest an affective stance that a viewer might take toward it (curious, affectionate, sardonic); by drawing attention to some features and not others, the critic, too, can direct a viewer's unfolding experience.

I've enjoyed writing this chapter. If I hadn't tried to document what I thought of as I engaged with the video, I wouldn't have seen as much. You may not see things as I do, but maybe you'll now find other things. Directors who know viewers are thinking about their work often become excited and push harder. Together we might build a shared cultural literacy and analytical practice.

Analyzing music videos calls for some boldness. The analyst must feel open to addressing the music, the image (including moving bodies, cinematography, and editing), the lyrics, and the relations among them. (This might include looking at a dance gesture against a harmonic shift and an edit, and asking how these might relate to one another.) But music video analysis is important, and we might care deeply about the genre for four reasons. First, it has a cultural centrality today. It remains among the most popular forms of moving media. It's also the most viewed content on YouTube; music videos are the most common way for audiences to consume popular music, more than through CDs, radio, iTunes, or blogs.[18] Second, its aesthetics have seeped into nearly every form of moving and visual media, from *Transformers* and *The Hunger Games*, to Bollywood, to television shows like *Game of Thrones*. Third, it's a genre with its own conventions and ways of carrying a narrative; eliciting emotions; deploying performers, settings, and props; and conveying space and time. It has unique ways of drawing relations between sound and image,[19] and it has unique ways of conveying brief states of bliss. It's dependent on ephemeralities of color, movement, and sound. Like popular music, music video possesses motifs, rhythms, grain, and fine details that carry weight. It resides somewhere between advertising and art. Fourth, it's a genre that's always in transition. It is but 35 years old, but it has shape-shifted countless times in response to dramatic technological, aesthetic, institutional, and audience pressures.

Stated in a more inclusive way, there's another reason to consider music video based on its relation to the larger culture and other media. Audiovisual aesthetics—the ways in which sound, image, and lyrics can be placed in relation—remains relatively unexplored. Short-form genres also remain under-examined, and they contain their own aesthetics. We participate in an audiovisually-intensified media landscape, and skills gained through interpreting music videos can help citizens become more discerning about Cambridge Analytica advertisements, Instagram teasers, blockbuster-film trailers, and Fox News segments. "Pretty Hurts" is a tale of empowerment, and we might take the lessons we've learned, partly through the bodily experiences we've gathered as we've encountered the video, to leave—like the characters in the clip—a more familiar space for a hopefully richer relationship with our communities.

Notes

1   John Mowitt, *Percussion: Drumming, Beating, Striking* (Durham, NC: Duke University Press, 2002), 3–5.
2   A *güiro* is a Latin-American percussion instrument consisting of a hollow, open-ended gourd with parallel notches cut into one side. A stick or tines run along the notches produce a ratchet-like sound.
3   "Pretty Hurts" was initially written for Katy Perry and then offered to Rihanna. Perry is famous for her use of "the soar" and her "Teenage Dream" provides an excellent example. The soar relies on a simple structure: a tiered chorus, which draws on principles of layering and textural "builds," long a staple of electronic dance music. The song's verse begins with a relatively sparse texture, then repeats a second time with added layers, along with a propulsive dance beat. A two-part chorus drives to a rapidly building textural crescendo. The verse scales back before the beginning of the pre-chorus, so it can make the buildup of the chorus even more dramatic. Many musicologists don't like the soar. They feel listeners are hectored into the ecstatic high of the chorus.
    "Pretty Hurts" does not possess all of the soar's elements. The verse tiers with "Just another stage, pageant the pain away. This time I'm gonna take the crown. Without falling down, down, down." One might even want to hear this as a pre-chorus. The rhythm arrangement also thickens here. There are striking silences between sections, but the chorus pulls back a bit as well. "Pretty Hurts" is not as anthemic as Katy Perry's "Roar" (it is in a minor key), but it did well on the dance floor, topping US Hot Dance Club Songs charts and peaking at number four of the year.
    Sia Furler and Ammo wrote the song—Sia sang backing vocals and Ammo oversaw production. Rob Suchecki and Derek Dixie engineered and recorded the song's instrumental and intro synthesizer. Stuart White recorded Beyoncé's vocals and mixed the song. "Pretty Hurts" was recorded in three studios: Kings Landing in Bridgehampton, and Jungle City Studios and Oven Studios in New York City. See http://en.wikipedia.org/wiki/Pretty_Hurts_%28song%29.
4   This body bag replacing Beyoncé could be seen as a deathly image. Her earrings, shaped as a spine or fish scales, may prepare us for this (4:06).

5 I Google later and find out that Matsoukas picked inner-city neighborhoods from across the country for the titles of the contestants' sashes. Is this a national inner-city beauty pageant? The video was shot in a little high school in Brooklyn, definitely not glamorous. See http://www.vulture.com/2013/12/beyonce-pretty-hurts-director-melina-matsoukas-interview.html.
"Shaolin" is urban slang for Staten Island. The term was popularized by The Wu-Tang Clan.

6 Patti Greco, "'Pretty Hurts' Director Melina Matsoukas on Beyoncé's Throw-up Scene and Casting Harvey Keitel," *Vulture*, December 16, 2013, www.vulture.com/2013/12/beyonce-pretty-hurts-director-melina-matsoukas-interview.html.

7 I've always seen the close-up of the contestant's face (at 1:00) as an object of tender desire. Might the hand that reaches out to Beyoncé (0:33) belong to this contestant, encouraging me to see it in this way?

8 Carol Vernallis, interview with Melina Matsoukas (2001).

9 Dan Crane, "What Would Beyoncé Wear? She Knows," *New York Times*, December 18, 2018, www.nytimes.com/2013/12/19/fashion/B-Akerlund-Stylist-Beyonce-Visual-Album-Fashion.html?pagewanted=all.

10 I usually don't Google until late into the analytic process—a personal choice. But doing so, I'm amused to discover some more details. I reassess other costume decisions. When Beyoncé sings *a cappella*, her white dress with black stars could be seen as built up from ace bandages that have been wrapped around her, like a mummy. The dress now looks to me overly confining. I like that what the star wears gives her very different kinds of movement and physical disposition: the high-heeled clogs, which she chunk-chunks in at the dress rehearsals; the traditional high heels in the chorus; the low-slung tennis shoes in verse 2; and her gangsta socks, which give her the greatest freedom. The high-school setting suggests an even dinkier and lower-budget location than I had imagined. See http://en.wikipedia.org/wiki/Pretty_Hurts_%28song%29#Charts.

11 Glenn McDonald, "The Genre Grinder's Song (What It's Like to Run a Machine for Sorting Music)," McGill Conference—Music and Genre: New Directions, September 27, 2014 (Montreal: McGill University).

12 See Sarah Baker, "Sex, Gender and Work Segregation in the Cultural Industries," in *Gender and Creative Labour*, edited by Bridget Conor, Rosalind Gill, and Stephanie Taylor (Malden, MA: Wiley-Blackwell, 2015), 23–36; see also the "2014 Hollywood Diversity Report: Making Sense of the Disconnect," Ralph J. Bunche Center for African American Studies at UCLA, https://bunchecenter.ucla.edu/2014/02/12/new-2014-hollywood-diversity-report-making-sense-of-the-disconnect.

13 Caity Weaver, "Beyoncé's Publicist Wants to Erase These Unflattering Photos from the Internet," Gawker.com, February 5, 2013, http://gawker.com/5981957/beyonces-publicist-wants-to-erase-these-six-unflattering-photos-from-the-internet;http://www.buzzfeed.com/buzzfeedceleb/the-unflattering-photos-beyonces-publicist-doesnt-want-you-t#.ihXzDYONDq; http://knowyourmeme.com/memes/unflattering-beyonce. I empathize with Beyoncé's and her management's desire to exert some control over her image. I wonder if, in surprising ways, the *Beyoncé* album, with its celebration of multiplicity and imperfection, was shaped by this experience of negotiation between the star, her management, and the press.

14 "Pretty Hurts (Song)," Wikipedia, Wikimedia Foundation, July 24, 2017, en.wikipedia.org/wiki/Pretty_Hurts_%28song%29.

15   A psychoanalyst might find this fragment interesting. It possesses some ululation and glottal fry, and sounds Arabic or African. Ululations are often long, wavering, high-pitched vocal sounds resembling a trilling howl. Women most often perform them during communal celebrations or grieving, for example, at weddings or funerals. The fragment may elicit some of these cultural connections. Isolated and projected, the fragment might connect with other ingested or evicted elements, like the swallowed cotton balls and the bulimic vomiting in the bathroom. The video seems to achieve some release through purging—the vocal occurrence, now healthy, cathartic, and incorporated. Finally the fragment seems to break apart or dissolve into the rhythm arrangement and Beyoncé's overdubs.

16   Jane Feuer, *The Hollywood Musical* (Bloomington, IN: Indiana University Press, 1993).

17   My video analyses often take the shape of a description by parameters, with what I perceive as the most striking or moving discussed first, and others related following close by. I'll also often include a description that tracks temporal flow.

18   Sean Michaels, "YouTube is Teens' First Choice for Music," *Guardian*, August 16, 2012, http://www.theguardian.com/music/2012/aug/16/youtube-teens-first-choice-music.

19   See Carol Vernallis, *Experiencing Music Video: Aesthetics and Cultural Context* (New York: Columbia University Press, 2004).

15

Rural-Urban Imagery in Country Music Videos: Identity, Space, and Place

Jada Watson

"Place" and "space" are important themes in Canadian alternative-country artist Corb Lund's music. Like many country musicians, Lund invokes place-based narratives to tell stories about working-class issues, to express hardships of growing up in a particular region, and to reflect nostalgically on a simpler way of life. Over the span of his more than twenty-year career as an alternative-country artist, Lund has continually turned to aspects of southern Alberta's heritage, culture, politics, landscape, and environment to inform his songwriting. While his discography is replete with both nostalgic, rough and tumbling cowboy songs about his beloved southern Alberta landscape, and characters that have touched his life, his music reveals the tensions that exist between rural and urban spaces. Lund's songs have become a powerful vehicle for social commentary on the conflicting socio-cultural and political values of these spaces. At the same time, his songs articulate a strong sense of relationship with rural spaces, and play a critical role in the construction of his artistic identity. While his songs draw on iconic imagery of both the country and the city, his music videos often unfold in the countryside—rendering the city as an implied "other" in the video narrative. When urban spaces do emerge, they are often presented as empty or shattered spaces, establishing an emotional distance between the cowboy and the city.

Drawing on scholarship from the fields of cultural geography, ecocriticism, and media studies, this chapter explores the role that place and space play in elaborating complex narratives about identity and belonging in music videos. The works of Yi-Fu Tuan, James Cantrill, Cheryll Glotfelty, and Murray Forman offer critical tools for considering how the contextual aesthetic domains of a music video setting define the geo-cultural elements of places, while also elaborating the relationship between individuals and their surrounding environment.[1] Forman's work, in particular, offers a conceptual framework for considering the ways in which the spatial terrains of a popular song's content and context—what he terms elements of text, genre, and geography—intersect in popular music narratives to articulate diverse conceptions of and relationships to place.[2] With this chapter, I seek to extend this discussion to include video narratives and examine their potential for elaborating an artistic identity intimately tied to the values and traditions of place—elements that would otherwise remain hidden, obscured, or overshadowed.[3] Providing an interesting case study, Corb Lund's song "September" (*Cabin Fever*, 2012) uses place and space to articulate complex narratives about relationships and identity in music videos. "September" explores the common country music trope of a broken relationship, developing a narrative that juxtaposes the subject's romantic conflict with a contrast between urban and rural lifestyles. The video employs montage editing to shift between past/present and reality/fantasy, where formal elements of lighting and setting, and cultural symbols, are invoked to articulate complex relationships with place and, by extension, define core elements of the singer-songwriter's artistic identity through a decidedly geo-cultural lens. I argue that the geographic locations become active participants in these narrative structures; the lyric and filmic representations of topographic features, cultural traditions, and socio-political and economic values impart character and identity to the urban and rural spaces. Following an exploration of the pertinent cultural geographic and media studies literature, I consider the complex roles that place and space play in music video narratives as setting, context, and participant. Through an analysis of the intersecting domains of text, genre, and geography, I examine how Lund mobilizes place and space to articulate strong senses of both identification with and opposition to rural and urban landscapes, lifestyles, and cultures.

Place, space, and narratives

Defining place and space

Cultural geographic discourses offer a rich understanding of the ways in which place and space are mobilized to elaborate complex narrative structures in music videos. While genre provides the musical context of an artist's style, sound, values, and traditions,[4] geography—both as a physical place and cultural space—establishes an additional contextual and narrative layer of identification. What emerges in this literature is a definition of *place* as a definite, physical, or geographic location, and *space* as a more abstract concept that refers to the material settings of a place's social relations and cultural traditions.[5] Place and space, as Tuan argues, have no inherent meaning; rather, individuals and communities ascribe or invest physical environments with meaning through their lived experiences.[6] The term "sense of place" emerges from this literature to describe the intangible and sometimes unconscious associations that individuals and communities feel about a particular geographic region. Eco-critical scholar Glotfelty argues that this connection is so intimate that individuals are inherently influenced by place and environment in a similar manner to gender, sexuality, race, and class. By elevating the role of place in shaping identity, she acknowledges the ways in which geo-cultural spaces shape how humans see, understand, define, and engage with the physical environment. These connections are magnified (as Cantrill argues) by the duration of tenure in a region and reliance on the natural world.[7] For these scholars (and indeed this case study), an individual's identity is expressed through both cultural membership and geographic affiliation, or what the political sciences has termed "geo-cultural" identity.[8]

Since the 1990s, cultural geographic studies have turned increasingly toward popular music to consider the ways in which lyrical and musical narratives define, respond to, and negotiate complex relationships between individuals, communities, and place. For example, Warren Gill and Ray Hudson have demonstrated how lyrical narratives and stylistic sounds often emerge as a response to local conditions and social tensions, while Colin McLeay and Blake Gumprecht have investigated how popular narratives serve to express ideas of regional and national identity.[9] Song narratives about geographic locations engage with place on a number of levels; they describe landscapes and topographic features, they relay stories that unfold in real and/or archetypal places, and they map out terrain in an effort to define the cultural and geographic environment that informs individuals, to name but a few narrative strategies. This body of work has influenced popular music scholarship, which has long been interested in examining the spaces in which music is experienced, produced, and consumed. As Andy Bennett states in the introduction to *Music, Space and Place*: "music plays an important role in the narrativization of place, that is, in the way in which people define their relationship to local, everyday surroundings."[10] This collection, co-edited with Sheila Whiteley and Stan Hawkins, explores how music works to articulate shared senses of community, identity, and belonging—especially as it relates to displaced peoples of the world's diasporic populations.[11]

Recent musicological scholarship has demonstrated how popular music communicates messages about place. The work of Adam Krims and Travis Stimeling has shown how musical codes and stylistic conventions mark out place, demonstrating music's potential for highlighting, embracing, and/or critiquing aspects of a place's environment as described in the lyrical narrative.[12] Drawing on the ideas put forth by these authors and those of the cultural geographers named above, my own work has focused on the ways in which country musicians draw on such musical codes and conventions to elaborate intimate connections to place, showing how an artist's geo-cultural origins form core elements of an artist's *persona*. Influenced by Simon Frith, Philip Auslander, Theodore Gracyk, and Pamela Fox, this work presents a framework for considering how country artists evoke *real* places in their biography, publicity, and songs in a conscious effort to tie their persona to specific geographic regions and cultural traditions.[13] These ideas are integral to the present study, which extends this line of inquiry to include music video narrative, to interrogate how images and related media contribute to messages about place and identity.

Place and space of music videos

Place and space are therefore critical aesthetic domains of music video narratives. At their most basic level, they provide the setting in which a video narrative unfolds, ranging from a live concert or rehearsal space, an archetypal location, or a specific geographic or cultural site. Carol Vernallis defines a video's settings as a function of musical genre, arguing that some place types have particular cultural resonance for musical communities (performers and audiences).[14] Each genre, she states, "develops a repertoire of settings," that advance musical ideas and make territorial claims.[15] In this way, Vernallis is interested in how videos work to reinforce or challenge generic conventions through their formal properties, including aesthetic appearance, placement in a song's structure, and visual narrative strategies. Influenced by Vernallis, recent scholarship has pushed beyond the boundaries of genre to consider more complex socio-cultural messages and geo-cultural relationships articulated in video narratives.

While video settings provide the context for a song's story, they also play an important role in conveying complex cultural messages. Influenced by Vernallis's work, Lori Burns and I co-authored a series of articles demonstrating the important role that a video's setting—architectural forms, interior design, and even color schemes—can play in defining the era or socio-cultural and political contexts of a video narrative.[16] For example, the Dixie Chicks' video for "Not Ready to Make Nice" created a symbolic setting of imprisonment through wardrobe, color schemes, and staging, "capturing the essence of a disciplinary society through references to a court trial … a punitive school system, and finally a macabre health institution, all of which work to contain the Dixie Chicks as a consequence" of their political beliefs in opposition to those strongly associated with the country genre.[17] In doing so, we show how a video's setting conveys important messages about narrative contexts and relationships between individuals and (in this case) the surrounding genre community—both linked to distinct geo-cultural beliefs, attitudes, and traditions.

Beyond their role as setting, place and space function as important markers of regional and individual identity. Drawing on the framework developed with Burns, my recent work considers how specific geographic regions and natural landscapes can be used to elaborate and animate local histories in music videos. Focusing on Corb Lund's musical responses to the fossil fuel energy industry in rural Alberta and Sarah Harmer's musical documentary about protecting the Niagara Escarpment, this work shows how the juxtaposition of contrasting landscapes, heavy machinery and tools, and activities associated with industrial activity highlights the tensions that exist in places "where residents have competing understanding of local history and where occupation and lifestyle result in varied relationships to place."[18] In this way, geographic places are not merely a *setting* for a music video, but also a defining element and even an *active participant* in complex narratives about a region's community, traditions, practices, and culture. Indeed, these studies demonstrate the ways in which video narratives impart character and identity to geographic settings, using filmic strategies in conjunction with lyrical metaphor to anthropomorphize geographic place and transform it into a living, breathing organism vulnerable to exploitative industrial practices.[19]

Underlying this discussion is the acknowledgment of the intimate relationship between person and place, and the role music videos play in articulating complex narratives about regional and individual identity. In his work on rap and hip-hop songs,

Forman demonstrates how the spatial terrains of text, genre, and geography intersect to communicate diverse concepts of and relationships to place.[20] For Forman, the *textual space* refers to the social mapping that unfolds in popular texts (song lyrics, musical setting) and related media (interviews, blogs, films, etc.)—a narrative space that defines place and space and relationships to them.[21] Industry space is re-defined here as *genre space*, which includes the organizational constructs, codes, conventions, and traditions of a musical genre.[22] Finally, *geographic space* considers the real, material space in which social practices and relationships are enacted—this includes both the actual location (on a map) and the socio-cultural traditions and practices of a region.[23] When mapped onto the lyrical, musical, and visual layering of music video narratives, this framework considers how the spatial dimension of the music video and related media (as *text*) are mobilized through a cultural lens of *genre* codes and conventions to make sense of and articulate lived *geo-cultural experiences* of popular musicians. In this way, music videos offer additional commentary about place-based relationships and allow an artist to consciously construct an artistic identity (or persona) that is intimately tied to a region's culture and traditions, which could not be elaborated in a lyrical narrative alone. The following analysis of Lund's "September" will demonstrate how place and space function as markers of identity in music video narratives.

Rural-urban imagery in country music videos: A case study

Narrative conventions

The concept of place is integral to country music, a genre conventionally associated with geographic regions, rural landscapes, and community values. While country music literature has defined the genre's connection to place in relation to the geography of its origins and prominent scenes,[24] there has been a growing scholarly interest in the place-themed songs that proliferate the genre.[25] The tradition of place songs is rooted in early hillbilly recordings, songs of the singing cowboy, Kentucky bluegrass, and western swing, where songwriters expressed nostalgia for the seemingly simpler places and times of their childhood. Not only do these narratives describe the landscape and culture of geographic regions, but also they define the relationship between individuals and their surrounding environment and community, unveiling elements of the artist's character, values, and beliefs.

One of the ways in which country artists have defined their relationship to place is through the juxtaposition of the city and country in lyrical narratives, which often articulate underlying tensions between conflicting religious/spiritual beliefs, lifestyles, and socio-cultural and political values.[26] Songs invoking such narrativity tend to draw, at least in part, on the stereotypical representations of rural and urban spaces in order to tell their story,[27] as Joli Jensen has observed:

A rural-urban tension underlies most country songs. Home is always portrayed as rural—green, welcoming, often with mother or girlfriend waiting. Yet home is inaccessible, because the protagonist has gone to the city and been tainted by it. He can long for home and remember it as he sits in his lonely room, or in a some-filled bar, but he can never truly return. Cities are portrayed as unfriendly, dehumanising places, full of temptations, greed and selfishness.[28]

The idea of companionship lies at the heart of Jensen's narrative paradigm. True companionship, as she explains, is only available to rural dwellers, in the form of a mother's welcoming arms and a girlfriend's loyal heart—or, in cowboy songs, in the form of a horse. Urban dwellers, then, can never truly attain true companionship: "he will seek them," Jensen states, but "he will never fully attain them."[29] Female characters are thus integral to understanding the song protagonist's relationship to place—and are often used to represent these contrasting spaces.

Yet, this relationship is not so easily generalized. Indeed, Williams argues that these contrasting places have been constructed through the imagination of individuals and community; the countryside often represents the past, old ways, and traditions, while the city may symbolize the future, modernization, and progress.[30] These ideas are further complicated, however, by the myriad ways in which individuals perceive and relate to open spaces and urban development. Any landscape can represent a geographic or cultural space that is at once welcoming and inhospitable, free and limiting, or peaceful and hostile; in short, "what may provide a sense of freedom for one individual may cause feelings of isolation for another."[31] The duality of these tensions often results in complex and contradictory responses and relationships to landscape in a song or video narrative. The way in which an individual describes landscape and their movement through the land is often reflective of deeper feelings toward a particular region, which are not easily defined.[32]

Corb Lund's Alberta

A fourth-generation rancher and rodeo rider, Corby "Corb" Clark Marinus Lund (b.1969) grew up on his family's ranch in Taber, Alberta, fully immersed in local, rural, cowboy culture. Lund's songs and music videos present an overwhelmingly rural portrait of southern Alberta, describing life, work, culture, and traditions of ranchers and rodeo cowboys from the region—not just their present, but also their past. The narrative of his songs unfolds in a variety of Alberta's bucolic landscapes, ranging from the horse corrals in the video for "We Used to Ride Em'," to the "Little Foothills Heaven" hideaway in the Rocky Mountains, to the fields and forests presented in "This Is My Prairie" (to name just a few). Lund honors these landscapes and fights to protect them; he even mourns the loss of those that he was too young to witness. Indeed, several of his songs reveal nostalgia for a terrain he has only heard about from his ancestors. The images that emerge from Lund's lyrics are those of a sacred or spiritual terrain, a paradise that disappeared before he could experience it, one that continues to erode as a result of urban sprawl and expanding industry.

For a ranching family nestled in the foothills of Alberta's Rocky Mountains (like Lund's), urban sprawl and general encroachment of industry on family land and rural landscape are significant issues in southern Alberta. Lund addresses them in three songs in his discography: "The Truth Comes Out" (2005), "This Is My Prairie" (2009), and "Gettin' Down on the Mountain" (2012). While "The Truth Comes Out" laments the loss of natural habitat for wild animals that have made the Rockies their home, the latter two songs reveal a growing concern with land ownership laws and the increased presence of oil and gas excavation projects in rural landscapes.[33] Together, these songs reveal the impact that the expansion of city limits and the growth of industry have had not just on families in rural communities, but also on the animals that have lived in the region for centuries. Yet the urban environments that loom in the lyrical narrative of these songs are largely absent from the video settings. Lund does not provide visual space for the urban "other" in "The Truth Comes Out" or "This Is My Prairie."[34] Instead, these two videos focus on the natural landscape of rural southern Alberta, showing the impact of urban encroachment and conveying a sense of despair over the potential loss of these sacred places. In contrast, "Gettin' Down on the Mountain" paints an apocalyptic vision of this same region, predicting a need for pioneering skills and social unrest that would follow the inevitable petroleum shortage. In this video, the city is depicted as an abandoned, grim space through images of shattered glass windows, a dangling telephone, an abandoned apartment building, and (presumably) empty commercial buildings.[35] These images establish tension between urban and rural ideals about the value of land, and hint at deeper concerns for the fate of humanity should these spaces be lost to industrial enterprise.

When towns and cities do emerge in Lund's narratives, they are often seen as places to go to for entertainment—but not to live. Despite the fact that Lund lived in the city of Edmonton for nearly two decades (and now resides near Calgary), his music and persona project an image of seeming to be unable to imagine living in the city, as the majority of his song narratives unfold in rural spaces. In "(Gonna) Shine Up My Boots" (2002), he describes preparing for an evening out on the town to meet a lady. But even in his lyrical daydreams, his song protagonist returns to the countryside: he sings about winning big in gambling and buying himself and his lady a ranch with a Palomino herd.[36] The video begins with a five-second clip of Lund shining his boots and getting into his truck to drive to town. The rest of the video (0:06–2:12) captures Lund in profile as he drives his truck, adding passengers in each section of the song. He never makes it to town in the video, which ends (as it began) with him driving alone down a rural road.

Even when songs reference events from his personal life, his more "idealized" artistic voice instinctively turns to the landscape of his youth, establishing a persona that inhabits the countryside. As Simon Frith notes, popular musicians are "involved in a process of *double enactment*: they enact both a star personality (their image) and a song personality, the role that each lyric requires, and the pop star's art is to keep both acts in play at once."[37] Frith's observations highlight three distinct yet intersecting layers of an artist's identity. Philip Auslander systematized this tripartition in popular music performance as (1) the *real person*, (2) the *performance persona* (i.e., the star personality/image), and (3) the *song* character.[38] Because all of these "identity levels" (as Lacasse calls them) can be present simultaneously, the distinction between real *person* and *persona*, and even between *persona* and song *character* can be ambiguous, even (as Auslander observes) in the case of an artist whose work is autobiographical.[39] For an artist like Lund, who draws heavily on autobiography in his music, performance, and related media, these layers seem to become, at times, indistinct. Indeed, "Lund the *person*" and "Lund the *persona*" seemingly collapse in upon one another, making it difficult to discern where one ends and the other begins. This is challenging precisely because Lund turns to his own life experiences to inform his songwriting. And while it would be easy to presume that Lund's song narratives are honest and accurate representations of his life and ideas—that they give us a true glimpse into his inner world—these narratives present the version of his world that he wants his audience to see. Thus, however faithful Lund may be in depicting his "reality," a level of "autobiographical" construction—what Serge Doubrovsky calls "autofiction"—remains in the image projected to his audience, as mediated through his songwriting practices.[40] Such a technique does not just create distance between Lund and his audience (allowing him to guard the intimate details of his real life), but it also allows him to further elaborate the aspects of his rancher/cowboy persona, one that is strongly connected to the countryside of southern Alberta. As we will now see, in "September" Lund uses the disintegration of his personal romantic relationship to further define his artistic identity and relationship to the land, painting cityscapes as uninviting.

"September" (2012)

In the lead single from his 2012 studio album *Cabin Fever*, Lund pleads with a summer love to stay with him through "September," instead of departing for New York City. He wrote "September" while visiting a friend in New York just before the album's recording sessions began.[41] Not surprisingly, the singer-songwriter comes to terms with this heartbreak through his relationship to, and understanding of, these contrasting places and spaces. "September" can be read as a reversal of Jensen's narrative paradigm: in Lund's narrative the female character leaves *him* behind in the Rocky Mountains. The revised narrative put forward in "September" suggests that the singer-songwriter used the situation to reinforce his connections to place and to the geographic and cultural spaces in which he feels most at home. Instead of being associated with a *female figure* (as per Jensen's paradigm), it is the *countryside* (and certainly his *horse*) that provides the comfort and security for Lund's solitary cowboy personal ambling through his pastoral Alberta life. The city, specifically New York, is then portrayed as foreign territory to the protagonist. While the overriding sentiment is that of a broken-hearted cowboy trying to make sense of the turn of events as he now prepares for a life of solitude in the foothills of the Rocky Mountains, the video articulates *human-like relationships* between Lund and the geographic settings in the song. Indeed, throughout the video the city emerges as an unfamiliar lover, while his rural home is portrayed as a comforting, almost maternal space—with her welcoming arms open wide for this brokenhearted cowboy.

Throughout the song's narrative, Lund compares the landscapes and lifestyles of the countryside and the city. Southern Alberta is presented as already exhibiting cold weather at night in September, with picturesque views of ranch land and mountains, and moving at a slow pace. Despite this pace, however, he reveals that he still had much to do in order to prepare for winter, notably selling off the cattle. In his description of New York, he draws on common stereotypes of living in large cities, including "starving in the city" and living in a tiny apartment, and situates his lost love on the Lower East Side of Manhattan. The timing of this break up is certainly important: September marks the end of the more carefree summer season, and the return to life's responsibilities. While the month often signifies the start of new adventures and life milestones (timed with the start of the North American academic year), for ranchers, September signals the end of a cattle season and the push to sell off stock and prepare property (buildings, livestock, and even crops) for the winter months. The protagonist admits that he understands that the lifestyle is not glamourous or exciting. His contrasting imagery of New York reveals that, while he does not really understand the allure of living in cramped quarters, he appreciates his lover's desire to explore life in a vibrant environment—admitting that the Rocky Mountains cannot compete with the experience. Yet even though he understands and supports her decision to leave, the lyrics display the protagonist's disbelief that anyone could part ways with the region and its natural beauty. At the close of the song, the listener is left with the image of a solitary cowboy preparing for yet another long and lonely winter. These sentiments are further elaborated in the musical setting and, especially, in the music video, which highlights the urban-rural tension driving the song's narrative.

The musical setting for the song conjures up country life through its simple arrangement of Lund's soft strumming of the acoustic guitar, Kurt Ciesla's plucking of the bass line, and Brady Valgardson's nearly whisper-quiet brush work on the snare drum. These instruments maintain the harmonic and rhythmic support for the musical conversation between Lund's vocal line and electric guitar played by Grant Siemens. The electric guitar has a twangy surf sound, harkening back to the up-tempo subgenre of 1960s' surf rock. The sound here is reminiscent of Chris Isaak's popular song "Wicked Game" (1990), which opens with the distinctive two-note motive of James Calvin Wilsey's electric guitar played through a spring reverb and uses a vibrato arm to bend pitches downward to create ethereal reverberant tones.[42] Using this technique, the long downward-moving pitch bends of the Siemens' guitar capture the sorrow of the lyrical narrative, while also evoking a sense of rurality through the twangy quality and the open space suggested by the long reverb. Throughout the song, Siemens imitates Lund's vocal line, inserts rising and falling gestures at the ends of phrases, or interjects with four- or five-note motives that weave around the melodic line. In the chorus, Lund sings his vowelized yodels—a musicalized gesture of crying—as Siemens plays arpeggiated or rolled chords.[43] This gesture from the electric guitar represents the fleeting relationship: the guitar dances through the musical setting, slipping away from the straight rhythmic and harmonic structure provided by the rest of the instruments. Although the pitch bends and twang of the electric guitar do evoke a twinge of sadness over the dissolution of the relationship, it continually ducks or dips away like a free spirit, unable or unwilling to be confined to the unglamorous rustic (musical) setting.

The video was shot entirely in southern Alberta. The countryside scenes were filmed at John's Swinging 7 Ranch and The Crow Ranch near Longview, AB.[44] This ranch is located in the foothills of southern Alberta, near the Alberta Provincial Highway 22, known affectionately as the "Cowboy Trail" because it passes through stunning ranch-land territory. It also boasts the remarkable backdrop of the Rocky Mountains—an important geographic marker in the song narrative. The signage and architecture captured in the "city" scenes point strongly to the shooting location of downtown Calgary. The narrative layer that captures Lund singing in an empty loft-style building was actually shot in the old Simmons Mattress Factory in Calgary. The scenes capturing Lund wandering through empty city streets were shot along 4th Avenue SW in Calgary. The glass and steel architecture of this area of Calgary underscores the cold and uninviting feeling of the urban landscape developed in the narrative.[45]

Lund worked with John Kerr and Trevor Smith to create the video for "September," which elaborates the inner turmoil surrounding the two geographic spaces and the demise of this summer fling.[46] Producer John Kerr revealed that they had "set out to create a distinctly Albertan and haunting Rocky Mountain vision of the solitary cowboy, broken-hearted, and preparing for a cold winter of solitude."[47] Lund plays the role of a narrating protagonist in the video, which captures the lonely cowboy's reflective moments as he speaks/sings to himself in an empty city loft and alone at his ranch (Figures 15.1a and 15.1b). Thus, he has a homodiegetic narrator role in the music video, capturing the double nature of Lund's role as both narrator and protagonist of the story.[48] As the protagonist undertakes the many ranching tasks to prepare his property and livestock for the winter, he has visions of alternate solutions to dissolving the relationship: he imagines himself living in New York or his former lover in his beloved foothills landscape. Neither image, however, lives up to the fantasy of the summer love. Lund does not belong in the urban landscape, since it feels alien, cold, and even more isolating than living alone in rural Alberta. Likewise, his summer lover seems restless in the foothills, and throughout the video she fades from his daydreams and leaves him behind to face September on his own. To establish this narrative layering, Kerr and Smith used montage-style editing and lighting effects to elaborate daydream sequences while the subject reflects on his breakup during daily ranching activities. In this way, the video shifts between reality and fantasy, blurring the lines between these two states and creating strong correspondences between the lyrics, music, and video images.

The video protagonist tries first to imagine himself living in the city. At the end of verse 3 and into the first chorus, the video features the protagonist walking around the city looking up at steel and glass high-rise buildings, or standing in front of them with his saddle and tackle on the ground beside him (Figures 15.2a, 15.2b, and 15.2c). Lund is dressed as a cowboy, hauling his saddle around the city streets where the sidewalks and streets are empty save for a few parked cars as he walks down the street. He looks lost and alone as he tries to find his way in this urban environment. Despite the fact that he is clearly surrounded by a number of impressive buildings, it is actually Lund who stands out in this setting: he clearly does not belong in this landscape. The narrative shifts back to the present tense, where images of Lund singing on the worn porch of the foothills cabin

Figure 15.1a "September": Lund singing in an abandoned warehouse.

Figure 15.1b "September": Lund singing on the ranch.

or riding his horse through an open field support the mention of the wide-open space and Rocky Mountains. The first chorus thus establishes Lund's relationship to these contrasting environments. He is portrayed as "at ease" in the countryside, while he appears out of place in the city. His movements, gestures, and awkward stance in the deserted streets suggest a sense of alienation. The visual representation of Lund being "out of place" is also articulated musically through his vowelized crying yodel, which appears in conjunction with the fragmented shots of street lights or buildings. The yodel here functions as his emotional response to the situation, as he drags his saddle along with him, trying to find a place in which he belongs. This visual-musical correspondence communicates a sense of discomfort with the urban environment, an inability to picture a life there, and the sense that he would not know how to function in this space.

Figures 15.2a–c "September": Lund wandering around empty city streets with his saddle.

Following the emotional release that emerges with the chorus yodel, the video's protagonist is presented in a fantasy sequence in the instrumental interlude. Although she first appeared in the instrumental introduction (the third image in the opening sequence [0:05–0:07] shows the back of his lover as she gazes off into the Rocky Mountains), his lover has a larger role starting in the daydream sequence of the instrumental interlude (2:44–3:00). The section opens with Lund riding his horse along a hill ridge, and then alternates between shots of his lover in the trees and the singer-songwriter on his horse. Although the characters are in the same geographic location, lighting helps to establish two different states: a darker, cloudy sky marks the protagonist's reality as he rides his horse through the landscape, while the bright beaming sun that provides backlight to the trees and the woman characterize the dream-like space. The electric guitar accompanies these images: shots of the lonesome cowboy in the darker lighting coincide with the guitar's long-held twangy pitch-bends at phrase beginnings, while shots of his lover in bright lighting that is filtered through the trees are paired with the faster-moving and seductive melodic gestures. Thus, these two individuals are not only defined visually through lighting, but also through musical gestures. The audience never sees the woman's face; she is, as Kerr reflects, "just a memory that never turns her face back to us—always leaving over the hill."[49] Images of this woman seem almost otherworldly, as bright beams of sunlight provide incredible backlighting that illuminates the landscape around her as she moves between the trees in the foothills (Figure 15.3). In some frames, the lighting causes a glowing effect on or around her body, emphasizing that these moments are not reality, but rather an illusion. She is never within reach for Lund: she is always a few steps ahead or off in the distance, slowly fading not just from view, but also from memory as she walks away at the video's end (Figures 15.4a and 15.4b). Yet this is all a dream. The transition to the final verse (2:54–3:18) marks the protagonist's return to reality and the realization that his lover has gone. He is alone in the foothills, singing the final chorus alongside his horse in an open field (3:18–3:32). In the two previous choruses, images of Lund in the foothills

Figure 15.3 "September": Fantasy image of love interest.

Figures 15.4a and 15.4b "September": Love interest walking off toward the horizon.

are juxtaposed with shots of him wandering aimlessly around the city while carrying his saddle. In this final chorus, the video captures him in his rural element, accompanied by his loyal horse companion with the Rocky Mountains looming in the background.

The saddle, like the Rocky Mountains, is an important cultural symbol throughout the video. Like a piece of clothing or even his guitar, the saddle goes everywhere with him. It emerges in the video narrative as a symbol of the safety and security of home. Perhaps more importantly, the saddle is a strong visual code that helps to define his relationship to place. The saddle clearly does not belong in the urban landscape: there are no fields, no horses, and no sign of companionship. While the singer-songwriter is on his own in the rural setting, he is never truly alone, as he has a horse by his side. The saddle, like Lund, has a purpose in this rural setting. Here, he does not wander aimlessly and wonder about what he would do in this environment; rather, in the foothills, he has land and property to maintain, livestock to care for, and a horse as his companion. While this video offers a seemingly straightforward description of the cowboy's sense of belonging and purpose on the ranch, the horse functions here as a metaphor for deeper questions concerning identity and relationships. Drawing on a long cowboy song tradition of invoking the animal as a metaphor for human relationships, the horse provides comfort and companionship to this heartbroken cowboy—the type of intimate relationship he apparently cannot find in the city.[50]

Conclusion

Lund's music video "September" highlights the complex ways in which individuals respond to contrasting cultural spaces, and, by extension, the profound impact that these spaces have on an individual's sense of being. Perhaps stereotypically, his narratives characterize the country as a cultural space that honors the past and the city as a place of progress and modernization. While the video presents both spaces as empty, the ways in which the protagonist moves through and relates to each space reveal much about his relationship to rural and urban spaces. He is presented as feeling most at "home" in the rural setting of southern Alberta: he has a role, he has purpose, and he is always in the company of his cattle and (most importantly) his horse. The urban environment is foreign and alien to this protagonist: he wanders aimlessly down the abandoned city streets, dragging his horseless saddle behind him. In fact, these places are characterized in human-like ways throughout the video, and come to represent human relationships. The city is portrayed as the cold and uninviting lover, while the foothills of the Rocky Mountains are depicted as an open and welcoming maternal figure for this lonesome cowboy.

The textual space of "September" expresses a sense of loss, further articulated in the musical setting through twangy pitch-bends and yodel breaks. But Lund breaks with genre convention, disrupting Jensen's narrative paradigm in which the narrative protagonist reflects nostalgically on rural spaces from a distance. In Lund's narrative, the protagonist remains firmly planted in the rural setting—the territory of his paternal and maternal ancestors. The music video demonstrates the protagonist's realization of what he would have had to give up to remain in this romantic relationship—the land, the cultural traditions of the region, and the generations of family heritage to which he is so intimately tied in this video (and indeed his entire discography). Leaving the beloved foothills region of southern Alberta is a sacrifice that the song protagonist seems unwilling to make. This is made all the more interesting by the fact that, in real life, he (the *real* Corb Lund) had been living in Edmonton for more than two decades at the time of writing and recording this song/video.[51] While this could simply be a case of a singer-songwriter drawing on and modifying a popular country music narrative device to tell a story, the fact that Lund admitted in his webisode for "September" that his love songs emerge from real experiences in his life—and that this is a setting to which he frequently returns in his songwriting/videos—suggests that this song reinforces his connection to place.[52] Instead of writing about the place (Edmonton) in which he actually resided at the time of this breakup, Lund instinctively returned to the foothills where he was raised, strongly pointing to the importance of this geographic and cultural space—so firmly embedded within his family history—and highlighting the importance of this geo-cultural space to his family history. In this way, Lund becomes the author of his autofictional persona, creating a musical, lyrical, and visual bridge between the *real* Lund and the *persona* Lund. He reimagines his life events as a form of auto-commentary—as a way to consciously construct his artistic identity. As with most of the songs in his discography, the figure of the cowboy and his relationship with the land emerge as a crucial way in which Lund negotiates his artistic persona as an identity intimately bound to the cultures and traditions of place. Even though the *real* Lund has lived in the city for most of his adult life, the *persona* (and *protagonist*) Lund inhabits rural spaces in his songs. Indeed, his *persona* seems to have never left the family ranch. His music and videos therefore demonstrate both his attachment to this rural southern Alberta landscape and a strong sense of identification with the traditions, values, lifestyle, and culture of the region.

Notes

1   Yi-Fu Tuan, *Sense of Place: The Perspective of Experience* (Minneapolis, MN: University of Minnesota Press, 1977); James Cantrill, "The Environmental Self and a Sense of Place: Communication Foundations for Regional Ecosystem Management," *Journal of Applied Communication Research* 26, no. 3 (1998): 301–318; Cheryll Glotfelty, "Introduction: Literary Studies in an Age of Environmental Crisis," in *The Ecocriticism Reader: Landmarks in Literary Ecology*, edited by Cheryll Glotfelty and Harold Fromm (Athens: University of Georgia Press, 1996), xv–xxxvii; and Murray Forman, *The 'Hood Comes First: Race, Space, and Place in Rap and Hip-Hop* (Middletown, CT: Wesleyan University Press, 2002).
2   Forman, *The 'Hood Comes First.*
3   Jada Watson, "The Dixie Chicks' 'Lubbock or Leave It': Negotiating Identity and Place in Country Song," *Journal of the Society for American Music* 8, no. 1 (2014): 52.
4   See John Frow, *Genre* (London and New York: Routledge, 2015); Fabian Holt, *Genre in Popular Music* (Chicago, IL: University of Chicago Press, 2007); and David Brackett, *Categorizing Sound: Genre and Twentieth-Century Popular Music* (Oakland, CA: University of California Press, 2016).
5   John Agnew, "Space and Place," in *The SAGE Handbook of Geographical Knowledge*, edited by John Agnew and David N. Livingstone (London: Sage, 2011).
6   Tuan, *Sense of Place*, 12.
7   Glotfelty, "Introduction"; Cantrill, "The Environmental Self."
8   Md. Munir Hossain Talukder, "In Defence of Geo-cultural Identity: An Argument Against Kymlicka's View of Multiculturalism and Minority Rights," *CEU Political Science Journal* 8, no. 4 (2013): 426.
9   Warren Gill, "Region, Agency, and Popular Music: The Northwest Sound, 1958–1966," *The Canadian Geographer* 37, no. 2 (1993): 120–131; Ray Hudson, "Regions and Place: Music, Identity and Place," *Progress in Human Geography* 30, no. 5 (2006): 626–634;

Colin McLeay "Popular Music and Expressions of National Identity," *New Zealand Journal of Geography* 103 (1997): 12–17; and Blake Gumprecht, "Lubbock on Everything: The Evocation of Place in Popular Music (a West Texas Example)," *Journal of Cultural Geography* 18, no. 1 (1998): 68–77.

10 Andy Bennett, "Introduction: Part 2: Music, Space and Place," in *Music, Space and Place: Popular Music and Cultural Identity*, edited by Sheila Whiteley, Andy Bennett, and Stan Hawkins (Farnham: Ashgate, 2005), 2.

11 Sheila Whiteley, Andy Bennett, and Stan Hawkins, eds., *Music, Space and Place: Popular Music and Cultural Identity* (Farnham: Ashgate, 2005).

12 See Adam Krims, *Music and Urban Geography* (New York: Routledge, 2007); and Travis D. Stimeling, "Music, Place, and Identity in the Central Appalachian Mountaintop Removal Mining Debate," *American Music* 30, no. 1 (2012): 1–29.

13 Drawing on the writings of Simon Frith, Philip Auslander, Theodore Gracyk, and Pamela Fox, my previous work developed a framework for considering how an artist's geo-cultural origins are used to construct elements of their artistic persona. See Jada Watson, "Country Music and Geography: Constructing 'Geo-cultural' Identities," in *The Oxford Handbook of Country Music*, edited by Travis D. Stimeling (New York: Oxford University Press, 2017), 95–116. For work on persona theory, see Simon Frith, *Performing Rites: On the Value of Popular Music* (Cambridge, MA: Harvard University Press, 1996); Philip Auslander, "Performance Analysis and Popular Music: A Manifesto," *Contemporary Theatre Review* 14, no. 1 (2004): 1–13; Theodore Gracyk, *I Wanna Be Me: Rock Music and the Politics of Identity* (Philadelphia, PA: Temple University Press, 2001), 35; and Pamela Fox, *Natural Acts: Gender, Race, and Rusticity in Country Music* (Ann Arbor, MI: University of Michigan Press, 2009), 114.

14 Carol Vernallis, *Experiencing Music Video: Aesthetics and Cultural Context* (New York: Columbia University Press, 2004), 83.

15 Ibid., 87.

16 Jada Watson and Lori Burns, "Resisting Exile and Asserting Musical Voice: The Dixie Chicks Are 'Not Ready to Make Nice,'" *Popular Music* 29, no. 3 (2010): 339–340; Lori Burns and Jada Watson, "Subjective Perspectives Through Word, Image, and Sound: Temporality, Narrative Agency and Embodiment in the Dixie Chicks Video 'Top of the World,'" *Music, Sound, and the Moving Image* 4, no. 1 (2010): 3–38.

17 Watson and Burns, "Resisting Exile," 340.

18 Jada Watson, "'This Is My Prairie': Corb Lund and the Fossil Fuel Energy Debate," *American Music* 34, no. 1 (2016): 46. See also Jada Watson, "'If They Blow a Hole in the Backbone': Sarah Harmer's Campaign to Protect the Niagara Escarpment," *MUSICultures* 44, no. 2 (2016): 81–108.

19 Both of these studies were influenced by Yi-Fu Tuan's work in his article "Language of Making a Place" (*Annals of the Association of American Geographers* 81, no. 4 (1991): 684–696), which theorizes the metaphorical and narrative-descriptive power of words to anthropomorphize objects and place by ascribing them human-like characteristics.

20 Forman, *The 'Hood Comes First*, 6–25.

21 Ibid., 14–18.

22 Ibid., 18–22. Forman's conception of industry space is broader and considers genre as an *institution*, linking it to commercial procedures and commercial interests in local, national, and international markets. Given the scope of this chapter encompassing

analytic frameworks for music video narratives, this aspect of the spatial layering will not be explored here.

23　Forman, *The 'Hood Comes First*, 22–25.

24　The seminal history of the genre remains Bill C. Malone's *Country Music U.S.A.* (Austin, TX: University of Texas Press, 1968; now in its fourth edition), which outlines the origins of the genre from its folk roots in the rural US South to the emergence of the genre now known as "country" music. This "southern" thesis has been actively challenged by several scholars, including Patrick Huber, *Linthead Stomp: The Creation of Country Music in the Piedmont South* (Chapel Hill, NC: University of North Carolina Press, 2008); Patrick Huber, "The New York Sound: Citybilly Recording Artists and the Creation of Hillbilly Music, 1924–1932," *Journal of American Folklore* 127, no. 504 (2014): 139–158; and Paul L. Tyler, "Hillbilly Music Re-imagined: Folk and Country Music in the Midwest," *Journal of American Folklore* 127, no. 504 (2014): 159–190. Geography also emerges as an important element in literature addressing the genre's various country music "scenes," including Nashville: Joli Jensen, *Nashville Sound: Authenticity, Commercialization, and Country Music* (Nashville, TN: Vanderbilt University Press and Country Music Foundation Press, 1998); Diane Pecknold, *The Selling Sound: The Rise of the Country Music Industry* (Durham, NC: Duke University Press, 2007); Barry Shank, *Dissonant Identities: The Rock 'n' Roll Scene in Austin, Texas* (Hanover, NH: Wesleyan University Press, 1994); Travis D. Stimeling, *Cosmic Cowboys and New Hicks: The Countercultural Sounds of Austin's Progressive Country Music Scene* (New York: Oxford University Press, 2011); and Barbara Ching, *Wrong's What I Do Best: Hard Country Music and Contemporary Culture* (New York: Oxford University Press, 2001).

25　For studies on how country lyrics describe or construct images of place, see Nicholas Dawidoff, "Lubbock or Leave It: Jimmie Dale Gilmore and The Flatlanders," in *In the Country of Country* (New York: First Vintage Books, 1998): 291–308; Gumprecht, "Lubbock on Everything," 68–77; Jada Watson, "Dust-blown Tractor Tunes: Representations of Environment in Butch Hancock's Songs About Farming in West Texas," *Canadian Folk Music* 45, no. 2 (2011): 10–18; Watson, "The Dixie Chicks' 'Lubbock or Leave It'"; Jada Watson "Region and Identity in Dolly Parton's Songwriting," in *The Cambridge Companion to the Singer-Songwriter*, edited by Justin A. Williams and Katherine Williams (Cambridge: Cambridge University Press, 2016), 120–130; Watson, "Country Music and Geography"; and Pamela Wilson, "Mountains of Contradictions: Gender, Class, and Region in the Star Image of Dolly Parton," in *Reading Country Music: Steel Guitars, Opry Stars, and Honky-Tonk Bars*, edited by Cecelia Tichi (Durham, NC: Duke University Press, 1998), 98–120. For a discussion of country music responses to regional environmental issues, see Stimeling, "Music, Place, and Identity"; Gillian Turnbull, "CoalDust Grins: The Conscious Creation of Western Canadian Mining Songs," conference paper (Lancaster, PA: Society for American Music, Lancaster Marriott, March 6, 2014); Watson, "This Is My Prairie"; and Watson, "If They Blow a Hole."

26　Watson, "The Dixie Chicks' 'Lubbock or Leave It,'" 51.

27　Popular examples of this narrative paradigm include Dolly Parton's "Down on Music Row" (1973), Mac Davis's "Texas in My Rearview Mirror" (1980), and Carrie Underwood's "Ain't in Checotah Anymore" (2005), to name just a few. For more discussion of this narrative paradigm, see Watson, "Dixie Chicks' 'Lubbock or Leave It,'" 49–75.

28 Jensen, *Nashville Sound*, 29–30.

29 Ibid., 29.

30 Raymond Williams, *The City and the Country* (New York: Oxford University Press, 1973), 291–297.

31 Watson, "The Dixie Chicks' 'Lubbock or Leave It,'" 50.

32 For further discussion of the role that place-based narratives play in shaping a country musician's identity, see Watson "Region and Identity," 120–130; and Watson, "Country Music and Geography."

33 For discussion of how Lund has used his videos to respond to Alberta's fossil fuel energy debate, see Watson, "This Is My Prairie," 43–86.

34 See Corb Lund, "The Truth Comes Out—Corb Lund," YouTube video (3:41), official music video, directed by Trevor Smith, posted by "Corb Lund," October 28, 2007, https://www.youtube.com/watch?v=EljkIvHAfWc; and Corb Lund, "This Is My Prairie—Corb Lund," YouTube video (3:45), official music video, directed by Fish Griwkowsky, posted by "Fish Griwkowsky," April 9, 2012, https://www.youtube.com/watch?v=AhAB6Wj0pGw.

35 Corb Lund, "Corb Lund—Gettin' Down on the Mountain (Online Exclusive)," YouTube video (3:28), official music video, directed by Fish Griwkowsky, posted by "Corb Lund," June 13, 2012, https://www.youtube.com/watch?v=5uASQgLwaIs.

36 Corb Lund, "(Gonna) Shine Up My Boots—Corb Lund," YouTube video (2:12), official music video, directed by Joel Stewart, posted by "Corb Lund," October 28, 2007, https://www.youtube.com/watch?v=fmdq2NrnGg0. Even in Lund's gambling song, "A Game in Town Like This" (2009), he expresses a preference for gambling in a small town rather than in Las Vegas. The lyrics can be viewed at http://www.cowboylyrics.com/lyrics/lund-corb/a-game-in-town-like-this-28822.html.

37 Frith, *Performing Rites*, 186, 212.

38 Auslander, "Performance Analysis," 6.

39 See Serge Lacasse, "Stratégies narratives dans 'Stan' d'Eminem: Le rôle de la voix et de la technologie dans l'articulation du récit phonographique," *Protée* 34, no. 2–3 (2006): 11–26; and Auslander, "Performance Analysis," 6–7.

40 French writer Serge Doubrovsky coined this term in 1977 to describe the narrative style of his novel, *Fils*, which recounts the events of his own life, but employs unconventional syntax, chronology, and perspective in order to (intentionally) disrupt the autobiographic narrative. Doubrovsky explained his term on the back cover of the novel. See Serge Doubrovsky, *Fils* (Paris: Gallimard, 1977), 10.

41 Corb Lund, "What That Song Means Now #7: 'September,'" YouTube video (7:57), Corb Lund video blog, posted by "Corb Lund," September 11, 2012, https://www.youtube.com/watch?v=Bf7wCk6i-mA.

42 Reviewer Steve Huey (of AllMusic.com) has described Isaak's opening motive as feeling "like the sonic equivalent of a brief but queasy zero-G drop in the pit of one's stomach, sliding just a bit further down than the ear expects before resolving onto stable ground." "September" and "Wicked Games" have strikingly similar arrangements which make use of acoustic guitar, bass (upright in the former, electric in the latter), brushes on snare drums, and lead electric guitar. See Steve Huey, "Wicked Game," AllMusic.com, http://www.allmusic.com/song/wicked-game-mt0010704597.

43   See Greg Urban, "Ritual Wailing in Amerindian Brazil," *American Anthropologist* 90, no. 2 (1988): 285–400.

44   Information about the "September" video shoot can be viewed on the Crowsnest Films Facebook page: https://www.facebook.com/media/set/?set=a.194764467320220.44284.162441410552526&type=3.

45   While the lyrical narrative points specifically to New York City, it seems likely that they chose to shoot in Calgary not just for legal ease, but to avoid having to deal with permissions and fees to shoot in the United States. It is possible that they also chose this location for its architecture and for the fact that they might be able to shut down the street for the shoot at a time that would not interrupt business.

46   Corb Lund, "September" Vimeo video (3:54), official music video filmed in 2012, produced by John Kerr, directed by Trevor Smith, posted by "John Kerr," 2012, https://vimeo.com/47201124.

47   John Kerr, "Corb Lund: SEPTEMBER," Vimeo video, 2014, http://vimeo.com/47201124.

48   In *Narrative Discourse*, Genette defines homodiegesis as a narrative in which the "narrator [is] present as a character in the story he tells." See Gérard Genette, *Narrative Discourse: An Essay in Method*, translated by Jane E. Lewin (Ithaca, NY: Cornell University Press, 1980), 244–245.

49   Kerr, "Corb Lund: SEPTEMBER."

50   For more on the tradition of using horses as metaphors for human relationships, see Michael Allen's work in *Rodeo Cowboys and the North American Imagination* (Reno, NV: University of Nevada Press, 1998) and "'I Just Want to Be a Cosmic Cowboy': Hippies, Cowboy Code, and the Culture of a Counterculture," *The Western Historical Quarterly* 36, no. 3 (2005): 275–299. See also Terrence Cox, "*Cowboyography*: Matter and Manner in the Songs of Ian Tyson," in *Slipper Pastimes: Reading the Popular in Canadian Culture*, edited by Joan Nicks and Jeannette Sloniowski (Waterloo, ON: Wilfrid Laurier University Press, 2002), 279–295.

51   One year following the release of "September," Lund put his Edmonton home up for sale so that he could move closer to his family. See Huffington Post, "Corb Lund's Edmonton House for Sale," *HuffPost Alberta*, October 16, 2013, http://www.huffingtonpost.ca/2013/10/17/corb-lund-house-for-sale_n_4116997.html.

52   Lund, "What That Song Means Now #7."

16

"More Solemn Than a Fading Star": David Bowie's Modernist Aesthetics of Ending

Tiffany Naiman

David Bowie, describing his creative process, once stated:

> I see the whole of what I do in terms of painting. I've always thought they were very close. A lot of the songs I've written are, for me, paintings in words. A lot of the more embellished pieces, the ones really loaded with sound, came from the idea of building up layers of paint so that you see something new each time.[1]

An excavation of the significative strata that define so much of Bowie's work is perhaps at the core of any attempt to appreciate or discuss his creative output. His musical works have always been accompanied by powerful visual components, whether carefully designed stage shows, eye-catching album covers, or videos that contribute additional meaning. Indeed, Bowie had been pairing his songs with the moving image since 1967, over a decade before MTV made it commonplace. This meant that he had been making music videos for nearly half a century by the time "Blackstar" was released on November 19, 2015.[2] The video contains a culturally diverse array of mythological symbols of life and death interspersed with mementos from Bowie's past. By utilizing these symbols in "Blackstar," Bowie worked to reconcile memory, death, and his own legacy, searching for meaning in the face of mortality. To effect this, he utilized an art form most often associated with postmodernism—the music video—but aligned himself with modernist traditions and values in the work itself.[3] These themes and methodology are discernable in his early work, but this kind of artistic formulation is much more palpable and clearer in the video for "Blackstar."

This chapter analyzes the song and video for "Blackstar," considering the ways in which Bowie weaves auditory and visual pieces from his own career with those from other artists, most notably modernists T.S. Eliot and Igor Stravinsky, across disciplines and eras to create a new modernist composition that asks the age-old question: is it possible to find meaning in death.[4] Bowie offers no clarity on what that meaning might be, if one exists. Rather, he points to all the ways in which powerful myths of various origins, including his own, are infused with that question. As I will show, the song fixates on death, sacrifice, and the hope of transcendence. Multiple strands of sacrificial ritual are layered upon each other in the video in a way that simulates and supports the song's musical texture. The visuals contribute to the interpretation of the song as a musical expression of Bowie's ongoing ruminations upon emptiness and its relationship to death and the afterlife, with a modernist belief in the transcendent power of art that persists even as religious certainties are doubted.

The song and visual component were simultaneously introduced to audiences, which speaks to the importance of the video to meaning creation for "Blackstar."[5] The assimilation of different forms of media lies at the heart of Bowie's creative pursuit. Lacasse and Burns state, in their introduction to *The Pop Palimpsest* (2018), that popular music is inherently intertextual.[6] Bowie is unique in the extent to which he references as well as the variety of referents he uses. Pieces and fragments of art, literature, music, children's television, and radio shows surface across his entire career. Both his musical and video productions show cultural references drawn from Surrealism, avant-garde mime, and flashy West End musicals, all the way to German Expressionism and Kabuki. With "Blackstar," the audience continually experiences separate worlds and epochs, blurring one's sense of time and place and allowing for the creation of variant meanings. The video performs multiple Bowie pasts, locations, and references through re-articulations, remediation, and reverberations expressed in song and image. Bowie layered "Blackstar" with images and referents specific to his personal history alongside those common to shared Western musical, historical, and popular culture. In so doing, the music video catalyzes a series of memories in the song's audience. Utilizing the performative nature of persistent and haunting traces, visual and sonic fragments engage with each other, linking the personal, cultural, and historical in reconfigurations of memory that allow for new meaning to be created with each encounter.

I have argued elsewhere that Bowie's music has a "pastiche nature" to it. As Kathryn Johnson notes: "Bowie's music is purposely porous; leaving listeners various points of entry—and exit—so that multiple forms of connection and meaning have room to proliferate."[7] Admitting "multiple readings," Bowie confers "creative agency on us, his audience."[8] But this does not automatically write the listener or critic a hermeneutic blank check. As Simon Frith warns: "Musical experiences always contain social meaning, are placed within a social context—we are not free to read anything we want into a song."[9] In light of this, it is incumbent on any interpreter to keep an open mind and approach a close reading with a great deal of caution and a reluctance to claiming truth (but that does not mean that one cannot present a strong argument for a particular reading). The analysis of Bowie's music videos provides further layers and allusions that point in a specific direction, although there are side roads to be taken all along the way.[10]

I posit that Bowie's juxtaposition of memorial traces from his own career and personal life, with allusions to artists, musicians, and symbols from disparate cultures and mythologies, serves to comment on the present and project into the future through retrospection.[11] Bowie's endeavor, therefore, is similar to the one detailed by T.S. Eliot in "Tradition and the Individual Talent" (1919), which describes Eliot's view of the relationship of the poet (although we can read "artist") to tradition. Eliot wrote of the absolute necessity of a knowledge of history to the artist, who must be aware of both the inaccessibility of the previous time and its bearing on the present. For Eliot, such knowledge could only be gained through active work and was what made an artist both traditional and alert to his own time.[12] Bowie, the inveterate student and consumer of culture, had done this labor.[13] Like the modernists, he grounded his work in his historical understanding while using reconfigurations to create something radically new. Eliot goes on to explain: "The poet's mind is in fact a receptacle for seizing and storing up numberless feelings, phrases, images, which remain there until all the particles which can unite to form a new compound are present together."[14] Bowie creates just such an amalgamation. Artifacts and objects within the "Blackstar" video trigger and allow for building a story, stitching over ellipses in the master narrative of the song itself. The characters, objects, and performed scenes in "Blackstar" constitute the present by making a new rendering by referencing the past. Ultimately, "Blackstar" provides multiple alternative narratives that intensify the awareness of anxiety, rather than attempting to obfuscate it.

Blackstar: One word, multiplicity of meanings

Bowie, who famously wrote the song "Sound and Vision" (1977), always included the visual as part of the experience of his music, whether sartorial choices in live performance, album artwork, or music videos. Indeed, one of Bowie's strengths as an artist throughout his career was his curatorial prowess and his ability to find partners able to collaborate with him on these components. In making the album *Blackstar* (2016), Bowie completed a final work that would survive long after he was gone; one that seemed quite special at the time, filled with mysteries and revelations that would continue to unfold. In the black on black vinyl artwork, there are special surprises, such as a galaxy that appears on the album cover when it is exposed to sunlight, or the album's star image, which turns a radiant blue under ultraviolet light.[15] Bowie was no stranger to the uses of moving images to complement music. He made the *Love You 'Til Tuesday* promo film in 1969 with songs from his self-titled album, although this was not released until 1984. He then worked with Mick Rock in 1972 on a series of promotional clips for "John I'm Only Dancing," "The Jean Genie," and "Space Oddity." He again worked with Rock in 1973 on the now famous, vibrant, yet stark "Life on Mars?" "Ashes to Ashes," his 1980 song from *Scary Monsters*, which saw Major Tom as a junkie Pierrot figure, was also made prior to MTV and would go on to influence the surrealist construction of New Wave videos of the 1980s. At the time, it was the most expensive music video ever made with a budget of $500,000.

Bowie released "Blackstar" on November 19, 2015, with no advance warning, as he had with "Where Are We Now?"[16] Also, as with "Where Are We Now?," "Blackstar" did not just arrive as a single, but came with a dramatic, not to say enigmatic, music video. It is appropriate, even necessary, to analyze the two together. The music video contains imagery that positions "Blackstar" as an avatar of modernist late style that evokes Theodor Adorno's and Edward Said's intransigence and difficulty—and, like many such late works, it looks pointedly toward posterity, a witness to Bowie's desire to be remembered like Eliot, Yeats, or Stravinsky.[17] I have argued elsewhere that Bowie was interested in being remembered not just as a postmodern gender-bending rocker and purveyor of pop plasticity, but that he had a desire for a kind of high art canonization. "Blackstar" is a continuation of that endeavor as he seemed "endlessly determined to insert himself into the canon of the great musical artists."[18] A vaunting ambition was revealed when he stated, in 2002: "I would like to feel what I did actually changed the fabric of music."[19]

"Blackstar," filled with a beautiful sonic tension and sense of dread, is a tightly constructed labyrinth, one that can lead the listener in many directions: from the real to the unreal, from the occult to the philosophical, from morbid humor to painful reality, from representations of life to those of death. There seems to be no end to the array of suggestive meanings just for the title and lyric "Blackstar." It could be the ancient Judaic term for the planet Saturn; a 2013 multimedia dystopian science-fiction creation *Blackstar* by novelist Josh Viola drawn from and enhanced by the music of Celldweller's album *Wish Upon a Blackstar* (2009); an anarchist group active in Greece at the turn of the millennium; amplification and effects pedal company based out of the United Kingdom; the means by which the starship Enterprise travels through time in the 1967 *Star Trek* episode *Tomorrow is Yesterday*; the symbol of Africa or more recently the country of Ghana; or a 1981 animated fantasy series about an astronaut, John Blackstar, who is stranded on an alien planet (conceivably Bowie's son, Duncan Jones, who later directed *Moon*, was a fan).[20] Finally, a few Bowie sleuths have pointed to the fact that some cancer lesions are called "black stars," although these tend to occur in patients with breast cancer.[21] Indeed, there are a few other possibilities that, I believe, are quite important when considering the multiplicity of artworks or theories that Bowie may have been directing his listeners toward with his concept of *blackstar*. First, the black star, part of semi-classical gravity theory, is a collapsing star like a black hole but with a difference—a black star has no singularity (the frightening lack that defines a black hole) and the star's in-falling matter is, instead, converted to a perpetual state of in-between, a constant source of vacuum energy. Thus, the black star is eternal and "its predicted interior is a realm in which space and time are subject to strange new laws."[22] Most poignantly, there is the obscure Elvis Presley song, "Black Star," recorded for a 1960 Western shot under the same title that also starred Presley. The song remains little known since, when the film's name was changed to *Flaming Star*, the song was dumped and it remained unreleased until the 1990s. It is a dark ditty about the desire to outrun death. Its chorus (featuring the line: "Black star don't shine on me, black star")[23] repeats three times, between the three verses. Bowie, like most kids of the 1950s, regarded Presley as a musical and cultural idol. He once said in an interview that "Elvis was a major hero of mine. And I was probably stupid enough to believe that having the same birthday as him actually meant something."[24] It did mean that Bowie wore suits, had hairdos, and danced like Presley at different points in his career. In the recent documentary, *The Last Five Years* (2017), Bowie's long-time pianist, Mike Garson, supports this claim:

You could feel that David wanted to be the greatest artist and the next Elvis Presley. You could feel it from every pore of his body. He would bring me up to his suite and we would watch Elvis Presley videos and Frank Sinatra, and we'd have discussions about it. He would do certain moves and would ask if it seemed right and natural. He set such icons as his goals.[25]

The last, and surely true, influence is T.S. Eliot's "The Hollow Men" (1925), which, like "Blackstar," contains sightless eyes and is a composite form that encourages multiple interpretations in which readers find both a "fading star" and a "valley of dying stars."[26] There is no singular message in Eliot's works such as "The Wasteland" (1922) or "The Hollow Men" (1925); rather, Eliot created works that proliferated unfixed and fluid meanings that circle around questions of disillusionment and death. "The Wasteland" is unusual in its form, combining traditional known legends, such as the Arthurian quest for the grail and manifold religious referents with contemporaneous elements of Eliot's world along with borrowings from Shakespeare and Spenser, creating an artwork the meaning of which is still being debated today. "The Hollow Men" is similar in feeling but "his [Eliot's] lyrical evocation of moods" feels more desperate and visceral.[27] Like Eliot's works, Bowie's "Blackstar" is filled with a multiplicity of formal, cinematic, and literary allusions, and is unhinged from place and time. It is filled with unrecognizable settings and sounds that, at the same time, feel familiar, creating a work that has no clear-cut interpretation—a deeply modernist move.

The visual intertextual style within "Blackstar"

With "Blackstar," Bowie, the well-known music video pioneer, with the help of director Johan Renck, created, from this fan's perspective, certainly one of his best videos. In this, his penultimate effort, Bowie creates a fascinating, elliptical, mysterious, and clever media object. It is quite beautiful, and its painterly lighting, sumptuous art direction, and fluid cinematography are indebted to Bowie's and Renck's shared interest in film directors such as Alejandro Jodorowsky, Aleski German, and Andrei Tarkovsky, as well as their mutual interest in the painted worlds of Hieronymus Bosch and Matthias Grünewald.

Some of the images are like nothing ever seen in a Bowie video, others are obvious allusions to his past. The music video begins with close-up shots of unidentifiable fabric, then a duct-taped boot, a helmet, a shoulder with a smiley-face patch, and suddenly—with the sound of Bowie's first vocal line, "In the Villa of Ormen"—the image cuts wide to a lunar night scene and we realize we have been seeing the crumpled form of a space suit. This space-suited body patched with duct tape, who just might be Major Tom, is lying lifeless in an alien landscape. One should notice the yellow smiley patch on the astronaut suit, which is most likely a nod to his son Duncan, whose man lost in space film, *Moon* (2009), starred the computer character GERTY, which had the same smiley emoji face as its user interface. The sky is dominated by an eclipsed sun: a black star, we might assume.

When we first hear a Coltranesque saxophone assert itself (1:45), a girl with a mousey tail arrives and lifts the starman's visor to reveal a bejeweled skull.[28] While the figure could still be Major Tom, the skull provides new fodder for alternate meanings. During Bowie's Tin Machine days, in the song "Goodbye Mr. Ed," he sings of "Andy's skull enshrined" and later in the video's narrative the mouse-tailed girl has said skull in a reliquary. Bowie also performed his "Cracked Actor" skull routine, which visually referenced the way Hamlet's soliloquy "To Be or Not To Be" has often been staged, on tour in 1974 and again on his *Serious Moonlight* tour in 1983. Returning to Major Tom one last time, Bowie had already used a skull motif in the space helmet on his 2003 *Reality* tour shirts (see Figure 16.1).

But the ornamented skull references more than Bowie's personal symbology. This adorned skull is not of the Damian Hirst fashion and is much more like the human skulls found in the Vajryana Buddhism of Tibet and Nepal.[29] Bowie's commitment to Buddhist thinking extended to his planning of his death in that he asked to be cremated "in accordance with the Buddhist rituals"[30] and his ashes scattered in Bali.[31] Rather than representing individual death or loss, in Tibetan Buddhism skulls serve as a symbol of the pivotal concept of emptiness (*sunyata*). In Buddhist ontology, emptiness is considered to be a quality of the universe. In a state of universal emptiness, experience has no inherent meaning by itself; rather, we attach meaning to what we experience, so that all events are neutral until we do something with them in our minds. This is how Bowie saw his own art as it appeared in the world. As the images of the astronaut are shown, we may decide Major Tom is in that space suit, or maybe Bowie himself, but, upon being revealed, what we find is emptiness. Bowie created figures that were empty enough for those who came into contact with his music to fill in what was needed in that moment. Because we thus have a personal relationship to his figures—in a sense created by us, his fans, not Bowie—they become important to us in a more deeply personal way.

Bowie's voice provides something solid and recognizable to cling to when it first appears in the song. The vocal part starts and stays on the pitch B, intoning "In the Villa of Orman / Stands a solitary candle."[32] Here is Bowie's own ostinato, simultaneously minimalist and liturgical. But what is this liturgy? *Orman* is the Norwegian word for serpent, a symbolic creature whose actions in Genesis catalyzed the entry of death and sin into the world, and figures prominently in the occult. The "solitary candle" that appears both on-screen and in the lyrics is an understandable metaphor. A lit candle has significance in nearly every world religion and occult practice, and is a common symbol for death, life, and the afterlife. During the 1970s, when Bowie presented himself as the Thin White Duke and largely survived on a diet of milk, red peppers, and cocaine, he was heavily inspired by the writings of occultist Aleister Crowley, a founding member of The Hermetic Order of the Golden Dawn, an organization devoted to the study and practice of magic, metaphysics, and paranormal activities during the late nineteenth and early twentieth centuries. One of the Golden Dawn's initiation ceremonies for neophytes was to be "secluded with but a single candle and a skull to meditate upon." The instructions continue: "Meditate upon your death. Keep your death always before your eyes. Knowledge of death should cause for honesty in life." "Quicksand," from Bowie's 1971 *Hunky Dory* album,[33] found him "closer to the Golden Dawn" and "immersed in Crowley's uniform of imagery";[34] in 2016, "your eyes"

Figure 16.1 Photo of author's David Bowie *Reality* tour T-shirt design by Rex Ray (2004).

had become a sung chant around the "solitary candle" within "Blackstar." As evidenced, we have many interpretations to choose from and the hermeneutic windows keep flinging open. To contextualize, we are only two minutes into a ten-minute video.

When Bowie first appears in the video, he is revealed as a man who seems to have bandages blindfolding him with buttons sown on for eyes. Bowie has played a blind believer more than once in his career. In 1985 this sort of character was found in the "Loving the Alien" video and was further brought to life during his rendition of the song on the *Glass Spider* tour in 1988, as well as again on the cover of *Heathen* (2002) and in the live performances of the title song during the tour of the same year. Behind him in the attic, two men and a woman jitter and shake, enacting a dance that first appeared in Bowie's 1980 video for "Fashion." Thirty-nine seconds into the video, Bowie sings about a "brand new dance" that is "big and … bland / full of tension and fear" and he does what I have always called the Bowie bunny bop.[35] His hands are bent at the wrists like rabbit paws and he does a little bounce in place. About twenty seconds later in the video, a group of people looking like they are doing aerobics execute a slightly less graceful and exaggerated version of the same dance. Finally, twenty seconds after that, an African-American man with a large mustache shakes convulsively along with this "bunny bop." This odd dance reappears in "Blackstar," most strikingly at 2:11. It is similar to the final man's dance in the "Fashion" video, but is performed even more vigorously and on screen is much longer, making it a somewhat nerve-wracking reminiscence of the agonal convulsions that accompany death, as nerves stop getting the oxygen they need, causing rapid muscular contractions. This is the nervous system going haywire as the body shuts down—the life force, if you believe in one, slipping away.[36]

This convulsive jerking dance references more than just Bowie's own past. It also draws on one of the most famous dances of death in Western art music history: the final "Sacrificial Dance," choreographed by Vaslav Nijinsky for Stravinsky's *The Rite of Spring* (1913). The spastic shaking dancers directly reference the movements of the participants in the opening tableau of *The Rite*, "Augurs of Spring." As the "Blackstar" video continues, the girl with the tail carries the skull in a reliquary through a deserted town to a group of women in an empty, sand-covered space. The allusion to *The Rite* is even more striking during scenes in "Blackstar" that feature this group of simply dressed young women. These sections were either shot with a red filter on the camera or an effect was added in post-production to give these scenes their soft-focused, blood-like tint. At 3:10, the girls move in a circle, with one young woman in the center, frozen, head bent downward—a clear reference to the "Mystic Circles of Young Girls" that determine the sacrificial victim in *The Rite*, as well as the stage picture during her subsequent "glorification." At 3:29, we see the young girls bounce-shaking in place, an obvious Nijinsky reference, and, at 3:44, they exit, peeling off from the circle with the same geometric precision as in Nijinsky's choreography. After their exit, nothing remains but their footprints in the dirt. Viewers are then given a quick glimpse of a field of wheat with the same red overtones as the ritual scenes with the young girls—the sacrifice has been successful, and the harvest has begun.

As the video moves to its middle section, viewers encounter Bowie in a new guise; gone are the bandages and the nervous twitch, replaced by a calm priestly serenity that is removed, righteous, and villainous. Indeed, he slightly resembles Robert Mitchum in the film *Night of the Hunter* (1955). Bowie holds a tattered book that looks like a bible but has a black star on the cover (another allusion to Mr. Crowley). The three dancers from the attic are now behind this preacher-like Bowie, with a blue-sky backdrop, as if posing for an Eastern European propaganda poster. The video's setting quickly shifts back to the attic, where Bowie presents a third persona: a huckster who seems to be purveying religion. Put in very simple terms, this character seems to represent another trajectory in Bowie's career in a critique of the certainties offered by the church and its hypocrisy.

The girls conducting the ritual of sacrifice are not seen on screen for another four minutes. Instead, their story begins to intertwine with another myth of sacrifice, that of Jesus and the two thieves with whom he was crucified. At 6:18 we are taken back to the field of which viewers only had a glimpse earlier, and, in a wide shot, three figures are revealed on crosses (see Figure 16.2).

The music shifts and Bowie's huckster voice takes over. Although the settings in the video vary, they have a dark, strange, otherworldly cohesion to them. What alters the scenes for the viewer and develops the narrative are the three very distinct vocal shifts that occur. Kevin Holm-Hudson calls these "vocal masks" and they perform different roles within the song: the mystic, the everyman, and the religious huckster.[37] As Frith once noted: "the voice ... may or may not be a key to someone's identity, but it is certainly a key to the ways in which we change identities, pretend to be something we're not, deceive people, lie."[38] Holm-Hudson describes how the use of the harmonizer, a pitch-shifting effect, helps Bowie to convey a mystic element, "adding a vocal layer a perfect fifth above Bowie's natural voice in the first section of the song, the organum-like connotations reinforcing the ritualistic implications of the lyrics" and assisting to reinforce the possibility of the occult through images that are flashing before viewers.[39] In "Blackstar," Bowie uses what Serge Lacasse calls "vocal staging" to alter the timbre of his voice in the case of the mystic and the huckster; in the case of the everyman vocal, it is sonically a very clean and clear signal with none of the kind of varied menace found in the other two.[40] Holm-Hudson has noted the fragility of the voice that I call the everyman: "The central section of 'Blackstar' strips away the layers of personae Bowie had accumulated over his career ... Without all these constructed images, all that remains is a fragile, wraithlike voice denoting Bowie's frailty as The Man Who Sold the World comes to grips with becoming The Man Who Left the World."[41]

Figure 16.2 Screenshot of straw men crucified in a field from the video "Blackstar" by David Bowie, directed by Johan Renck (2015) (6:18).

After the unnerving sonic trickster voice of the huckster ceases, the camera zooms into the field to reveal that the "people" on the crosses are actually straw men. Yet they are alive, moving, grinding, and making horrific faces. The video intercuts from one sacrifice to another as they continue to blend together. These straw men are a terrifying visual reference to T.S. Eliot's "The Hollow Men." As with many of Eliot's poems, it is overlapping, fragmentary, and, most importantly, it "[resounds] the poet's dread of death and dissolution."[42] Hope is slowly lost in "The Hollow Men" as they languish in their absolute lack of religious faith. It is not unlikely that, by depositing so much of "The Hollow Men" into "Blackstar," Bowie is pointing to his own life-long grappling with religion and what that means if one is still struggling for faith in the face of one's own death. "Blackstar" is in harmony with the "prevailing theme of Eliot's poems, which are about the emptiness of life without belief, an emptiness that finally resounds with a sickening fear and desperation in 'The Hollow Men.'"[43]

When the girls return, the scene is no longer drenched in red and a new woman enters, whose jewelry seems to be some type of religious vestment, marking her as distinct from the others. She carries the skull from the opening of the video and, as she displays it, the women shake and the chosen one bows in submission. She places the skull on the back of the girl who was once in the middle of the circle, who was also dancing in the attic with Bowie. The women hold their hands at their sides, move side to side with a slight tilt to their bodies, and then raise one arm straight into the air, with fists clenched tight, directly imitating the concluding moment of the *Rite*'s first tableau: the violent "Dance of the Earth." This punching up of one arm is a visual leitmotif of the ballet; it occurs in the "Glorification of the Chosen One" and in the "Sacrificial Dance" (see Figures 16.3 and 16.4).

The young women momentarily rise up on their toes and then drop to the ground on all fours, beginning to shake and swoop back and forth, arms extended.[44] In the end, they seem to have summoned some sort of god, monster, or creature, appearing first at 8:48 until it is more consistently cut into the video and is fully revealed at 8:54 as it heads toward the field with the straw men. The conjured entity's stamping and pawing motions evoke the bear-totem summoned by the Russian tribal dancers at the end of *The Rite*'s first tableau.[45] All these myths of ritual and sacrifice merge as the video concludes with quick edits of the creature, the crucified hollow men, the girls dancing in a circle, the skull, and Bowie as the button-eyed figure.

It is well documented that Bowie found Stravinsky to be a source of inspiration. On more than one occasion he suggested that his long-time keyboard player, Mike Garson, should do something in the vein of Stravinsky.[46] Further, when Bowie discussed his favorite records he named a 1960s' recording of *The Rite of Spring* as a piece of music "that changed his life."[47] Bowie might well have recognized the rock 'n' roll possibilities of the work as a result of the immense public celebration on its 100-year anniversary in 2013, reminding him of his admiration for this kindred creator. Richard Taruskin has described Stravinsky in terms that could easily be used to describe Bowie—as an artist who, untethered to a specific tradition, but having done the necessary labor, is therefore able to utilize many traditions. Taruskin further explained: "the same quality has been touted as presciently postmodern. But Stravinsky was no agent of cultural fragmentation. On the contrary,

Figure 16.3 Screenshot of "The Glorification of the Chosen One" from the Joffrey Ballet's production of *The Rite of Spring* (1987).

Figure 16.4 Screenshot of female dancers referencing *The Rite of Spring* from the video "Blackstar" by David Bowie, directed by Johan Renck (2015).

he was … one of music's great centripetal forces, the crystallizer and definer of an age" whose work maintained a constant quality unique to the artist "that could accommodate an endless variety of surfaces."[48] Although much has been made of Bowie's drive for change and utilization of multiple personae and musical styles, his work always exhibits that "rare authenticity and constancy."[49]

Regardless of his admiration for Stravinsky, Bowie may have chosen to reference *The Rite of Spring* because of its connection to musical embodiment, sacrifice, and religious ritual. The ballet depicts a sacramental sacrifice in which a young girl is chosen to dance herself to death supposedly to ensure spring's arrival. The girl's selection is completely random: she happens to stumble as the group of girls play a simple dance game in a circle, which makes her "the chosen one." It is a fate that to any modern audience is cruel and unnecessary, since we know that without her death spring still would have arrived. The premiere of *The Rite of Spring* in 1913 is still one of the most mythologized episodes in twentieth-century modernism, with the ballet's riotous opening a harbinger of things to come, including the horrors of World War I, during which millions of young men would similarly sacrifice their lives at the command of their elders. In the ballet, as in trench warfare, the individual's death serves no purpose, even when it is culturally construed as meaningful and necessary.[50] In "Blackstar" and its accompanying video, Bowie may be asking whether it is possible to find meaning in death, a meaning that does not prove false. Bowie offers no clarity on what that meaning might be, if one exists. Rather, he points to all the ways in which really powerful myths of various origins, even fragments of his own rock and roll mythology, are interpenetrated with that question. As he created the video with Renck, he may certainly have been thinking about the arbitrary timing of one's own passing.

The art of ending

Through multiple listenings to "Blackstar" and viewings of the video, I have continually been reminded of "Under Ben Bulben" by another modernist, William Butler Yeats. The poem has traditionally been understood as Yeats's self-eulogy, and the video for "Blackstar," created after Bowie knew he was terminally ill, arguably could be taking on a similar role. Bowie, like Yeats, utilized various styles from diverse historical periods and particular practitioners he admired. Both works assert that art has meaning for the living, even in the face of death. Bowie is "pointing towards the argument that even in our final stages or when confronting ourselves in our darkest hours, we remain creatures who require poetic narratives."[51] But, where Yeats seems sure that art could help usher in souls to God, Bowie has no such certainty. Indeed, his work does less to answer questions than it does to prompt the audience to reflect on the questions themselves; however, his belief in the affective power of art and the value of attempting self-expression remains unshakeable, with "Blackstar" the result and an expression of that belief.

Bowie actively strove to create layered works that allowed for multiple readings. Referencing Bertolt Brecht, Bowie once said that artists must "portray emotion symbolically. You don't try to draw the audience into the emotional content of what you are doing, but give them something to create their own dialogue about what you're portraying."[52] Eliot also addressed emotion in art, describing the most potent iteration as that which has life in the work, not in an artist's personal history or personality. "The emotion of art is impersonal," Eliot wrote, "and the poet cannot reach this impersonality without surrendering himself wholly to the work to be done. And he is not likely to know what is to be done unless he lives in what is not merely the present, but the present moment of the past."[53] Although music videos and even the analysis of such works could be classified as postmodern, pieces like Bowie's "Blackstar" work to remind us of the modernist potentiality of the use of historical knowledge in creating radical newness.

Notes

1   Nicholas Pegg, *The Complete David Bowie* (London: Titan Books, 2016), 55.
2   David Bowie, "David Bowie—Blackstar (Video)," YouTube video (10:00), posted by "David Bowie," November 19, 2015, https://www.youtube.com/watch?v=kszLwBaC4Sw.
3   I argue here that "Blackstar" is a work more informed by modernism than postmodernism because of the way that (1) Bowie engages with the past to create new forms, (2) the video makes a statement about art's role, and (3) it makes multiple allusions to some of the most important modernist works by artists such as T.S. Eliot, William Butler Yeats, and Igor Stravinsky. Much of the scholarship on Bowie discusses him only as a postmodern artist, often largely due to his performance of gender in his early work. No artist whose career spans decades is necessarily only ever one of the two. The ways in which I configure the designations modernism and postmodernism are not based solely on the era during which a work was created. I do not subscribe to the idea that modernism came to an abrupt end in the 1960s. Free from a definition of these categories that relies on time period alone, both modernism and postmodernism can be evident in a single artist's *oeuvre*. As I have stated elsewhere in my work on Bowie, we must always emphasize the context in which we consider what "post" really means. I have found Wendy Brown's definition of post to be useful in thinking about both Bowie's relationship to Berlin and the post-Berlin era of his music making. See Tiffany Naiman, "When Are We Now?: Walls and Memory in David Bowie's Berlins," in *Enchanting David Bowie: Space/Time/Body/Memory*, edited by Toija Cinque, Christopher Moore, and Sean Redmond (New York: Bloomsbury, 2015), 310. For Wendy Brown, "'post' signifies a formation that is temporally after but not over that to which it is affixed. 'Post' indicates a very particular condition of afterness in which what is past is not left behind, but, on the contrary, relentlessly conditions, even dominates a present that nevertheless also breaks in some way with the past. In other words, we use the term 'post' only for a present whose past continues to capture and structure it." Wendy Brown, *Walled States. Waning Sovereignty* (Brooklyn, NY: Zone Books, 2010), 21. Because of this, it can often be difficult to determine what is modernist and what is postmodernist, but I believe that, for this work especially, Bowie is aligned with the modernists and actively works to draw on that lineage. It is a disservice to Bowie not to acknowledge the level to which he educated himself and consumed a broad range of art. We must, therefore, interpret the informed references he chose to utilize as an alliance with a specific lineage.
4   Some portions of this chapter that consider death, temporality, and lateness are drawn from my dissertation, "Singing at Death's Door: Late Style, Disability, and the Temporality of Illness in Popular Music," PhD dissertation (UCLA, 2017), as well as the various talks I have given at conferences for the International Association for the Study of Popular Music (IASPM) and the Film and Media Studies department at Stanford's symposium "Pieces."

5   "Blackstar" is not the first time that Bowie released a song and video simultaneously. He similarly released "When Are We Now?," the first single off his previous album, in the very same way. For one of many interviews of Bowie where he explains how he considers the visual component integral to the song rather than supplementary, see David Bowie, "David Bowie: Rare & Uncut Interview from 1997," YouTube video (21:12), posted by "TheBestOfVoxPop," March 11, 2013, https://www.youtube.com/watch?v=IhaRvqI0nHk. Bowie did not just consider his creativity to be confined to music and these videos are one iteration of his broad range of artistic expression.

6   Lori Burns and Serge Lacasse, eds., *The Pop Palimpsest: Intertextuality in Recorded Popular Music* (Ann Arbor, MI: University of Michigan Press, 2018).

7   Tiffany Naiman, "Art's Filthy Lesson," in *David Bowie: Critical Perspectives*, edited by Eoin Devereux, Aileen Dillane, and Martin J. Power (New York: Routledge, 2015), 185.

8   Kathryn Johnson, "David Bowie Is," in *David Bowie: Critical Perspectives*, edited by Eoin Devereux, Aileen Dillane, and Martin J. Power (New York: Routledge, 2015), 3.

9   Simon Frith, *Taking Popular Music Seriously: Selected Essays* (London and New York: Routledge, 2017), 36.

10 This is very much in line with modernists' construction of the artwork, be it T.S. Eliot's *The Wasteland* or James Joyce's *Stephen Hero*.

11 In her writing on T.S. Eliot and high modernism, Jewel Spears Brooker is most concerned with what she sees as a "defining characteristic of high modernism, namely, the tendency to move forward by spiraling back and refiguring the past." Jewel Spears Brooker, "Transcendence and Return: T.S. Eliot and the Dialectic of Modernism," *South Atlantic Review* 59, no. 2 (May 1994): 54.

12 T.S. Eliot writes: "Tradition is a matter of much wider significance. It cannot be inherited, and if you want it you must obtain it by great labour … This historical sense, which is a sense of the timeless as well as of the temporal and of the timeless and of the temporal together, is what makes a writer traditional. And it is at the same time what makes a writer most acutely conscious of his place in time, of his contemporaneity." T.S. Eliot, "Tradition and the Individual Talent (1919)," in *The Sacred Wood and Major Early Essays*, edited by Frank Kermode (Mineola, NY: Dover Publications, 1998), 28.

13 Throughout his entire career Bowie discussed the amount of popular, and more occult parts of, culture and society he took in and thus helped to create his artistic output. In a 1973 interview with Russell Harty, while discussing his ability to "take on the guises of different people," he explained his consumption of the people and the world around him through the lens of being a collector: "I've always found that I collect. I'm a collector, and I've always just seemed to collect personalities and ideas." (See https://rockscenemagazine.com/yesterday/david-bowie-russell-harty.) This collecting, consuming, and refashioning falls in line with Eliot's thoughts on the necessity of work needed for artistry. Furthermore, almost thirty years later during an interview with Bob Guccione Jr. in "David Bowie on 9/11 and God," Bowie stated: "I read voraciously. Every book I ever bought, I have." See Bob Guccione Jr., "David Bowie on 9/11 and God," *Daily Beast*, January 16, 2016, https://www.thedailybeast.com/david-bowie-on-911-and-god?ref=scroll.

14 Eliot, "Tradition."

15 The font used on the back cover to give the duration of the songs is "Terminal."

16   It was known that David Bowie was creating music in some sense, as a brief snippet of an earlier version of "Blackstar" was used for the opening credits of *The Last Panthers* (2015) by Johan Renck, and was previewed on the internet on October 6, 2015.

17   For a more in-depth discussion of late style and how it can be applied to "Blackstar," see Naiman, "Singing at Death's Door."

18   For a discussion of David Bowie's concern with his legacy within the Western arts canon, see Naiman, "Art's Filthy Lesson."

19   David Bowie in Michael Apted's documentary *Inspirations* (Argo Films, 1997).

20   For longer lists of possible "Blackstar" meanings, see Pegg, *The Complete David Bowie*, 41; Jude Rogers, "The Final Mysteries of David Bowie's Blackstar—Elvis, Crowley and 'The Villa of Ormen,'" *Guardian*, January 21, 2016, https://www.theguardian.com/music/2016/jan/21/final-mysteries-david-bowie-blackstar-elvis-crowley-villa-of-ormen; or simply look at the Wikipedia page for Black Star.

21   Tibor Tot, "Subgross Morphology, the Sick Lobe Hypothesis, and the Success of Breast Conservation," *International Journal of Breast Cancer* (2011): 634021.

22   Pegg, *The Complete David Bowie*, 42.

23   Elvis Presley, "Black Star," written by Sherman Edwards and Sid Wayne (1960).

24   David Cavanagh, "Changesfiftybowie," David Bowie interview, *Q Magazine*, February 1997, 53.

25   Mike Garson, in Francis Whately [documentary], *David Bowie: The Last Five Years* (HBO, 2017).

26   T.S. Eliot, *Collected Poems: T.S. Eliot* (London: Faber & Faber, 1964), 79.

27   David Ellis, "Modernism and T. S. Eliot," *Cambridge Quarterly* 47, no. 1 (March 1, 2018): 55.

28   As pointed out in Naiman, "Singing at Death's Door," 121, John Coltrane influenced Bowie's musical thinking. In "Blackstar," Coltrane's rhythmic pattern from "Olé" emerges in full force, bringing to the fore a dark, Andalusian cadence of flamenco. The flamenco and the esoteric and funky sounds of the North African Moors, who once ruled the Iberian Peninsula, were cross-pollenated with Western tonality by Coltrane for "Olé." This collage of sound Coltrane enacted is marked as a modernist work. Richard Brody noted that this freedom with blending historical sonic influences meant that "the politics of free jazz were inseparable from its aesthetic transformation of jazz into overt and self-conscious modernism." Coltrane is yet another modernist who is part of Bowie's repertoire of references. See Richard Brody, "Coltrane's Free Jazz Wasn't Just 'A Lot of Noise,'" *New Yorker*, November 10, 2014, https://www.newyorker.com/culture/richard-brody/coltranes-free-jazz-awesome.

29   Bowie made reference to visual artist Damien Hirst, known as one of the famed Young British Artists of the 1990s, a number of times in interviews prior to 2000 and he is also referred to in the notes on *1. Outside*. See Naiman, "Art's Filthy Lesson," for more on that relationship.

30   James Barron, "David Bowie's Will Splits Estate Said to Be Worth $100 Million," *New York Times*, January 29, 2016, https://www.nytimes.com/2016/01/30/nyregion/david-bowies-will-splits-estate-said-to-be-worth-100-million.html.

31   David Bowie discovered Buddhism early in his life. He recalled in a1997 interview with MTV News: "When I was about eighteen I studied Tibetan Buddhism for about two–three years, and I had a teacher named Chimi Tulku Rinpoche." He went on to say that he

"was within a month of having my head shaved, taking my vows, and becoming a monk." See http://www.mtv.com/video-clips/pxgwj1/mtv-news-david-bowie-spirituality.

32 David Bowie [song], "Blackstar," on the album *Blackstar* (ISO/Columbia CD, 2016).

33 David Bowie [song], "Quicksand," on the album *Hunky Dory*, LSP-4623 (RCA Victor, 1971).

34 Israel Regardie, *The Golden Dawn: The Original Account of the Teaching, Rites, and Ceremonies of the Hermetic Order*, edited by John Michael Greer (Woodbury, MN: Llewellyn Publications, 2015), 55.

35 David Bowie, "David Bowie—Fashion (Official Video)," YouTube video (3:25), posted by "David Bowie," July 10, 2018, https://www.youtube.com/watch?v=F-z6u5hFgPk.

36 It would be remiss of me not to note that Johan Renck, the director of the video, has said that David Bowie sent him a clip of an old *Popeye* cartoon and said he'd "like something like this," referring to the jerky motions of the background characters in the clips. See Jon Blistein and Kory Grow, "David Bowie Plays Doomed, Blind Prophet in Haunting 'Blackstar' Video," *Rolling Stone*, November 19, 2015, https://www.rollingstone.com/music/music-news/david-bowie-plays-doomed-blind-prophet-in-haunting-blackstar-video-61585.

37 Kevin Holm-Hudson, "'Who Can I Be Now?': David Bowie's Vocal Personae," *Contemporary Music Review*, 37, no. 3 (2018): 217.

38 Simon Frith, *Performing Rites: On the Value of Popular Music* (Cambridge, MA: Harvard University Press, 1996), 197.

39 Holm-Hudson, "Who Can I Be Now," 228.

40 Lacasse states that vocal staging is a "deliberate practice whose aim is to enhance a vocal sound, alter its timbre, or present it in a given spatial and temporal configuration with the help of any mechanical or electrical process, presumably in order to produce some effect on potential or actual listeners." See Serge Lacasse, "Interpretation of Vocal Staging by Popular Music Listeners: A Reception Test," *Psychomusicology* 17, no. 1–2 (2001): 56.

41 Holm-Hudson, "Who Can I Be Now," 228.

42 Francis Otto Matthiessen, *The Achievement of T.S. Eliot: An Essay on the Nature of Poetry* (London: Oxford University Press, 1965), 118.

43 Ibid.

44 The 1987 Joffrey Ballet version of *The Rite of Spring* is available on YouTube, see https://www.youtube.com/watch?v=iH1t0pCchxM, and anyone who chooses to watch it can immediately see the physical allusions to it in the "Blackstar" video.

45 This can be seen clearly in the Joffrey Ballet performance in 1987 at 5:21 (ibid.).

46 The story goes that, in creating the incredible piano break in "Battle for Britain" on *Earthling*, Bowie challenged Mike Garson to play based on the idea inspired by a piece Stravinsky wrote called "Ragtime for Eleven Instruments." See J.D. Considine, "Fi Interview: David Bowie," *Fi: The Magazine of Music & Sound*, October 2, 1997: 37.

47 David Bowie, "David Bowie's Favorite Albums," *Vanity Fair*, November 20, 2003: 293.

48 Richard Taruskin, *Stravinsky and the Russian Traditions, Volume II* (Berkeley and Los Angeles, CA: University of California Press, 1996), 1975.

49 Ibid.

50 See Tamara Levitz, "The Chosen One's Choice," in *Beyond Structural Listening?: Postmodern Modes of Hearing*, edited by Andrew Dell'Antonio (Berkeley and Los Angeles, CA: University of California Press, 2004), 70–108. Levitz does an extraordinary

job of arguing for the multisensory construction of musical meaning when attending to Nijinsky's choreography of the "Sacrificial Dance" and interpreting it as a "physical expression of a critical spirit of opposition" (72). Her work in this essay has significantly informed my readings of Bowie's work, as he was a musical artist who was also heavily invested in bodily gesture and the visual aspect of meaning-making with sound.

51 Nick Stevenson, "David Bowie Now and Then: Questions of Fandom and Late Style," in *David Bowie: Critical Perspectives*, edited by Eoin Devereux, Aileen Dillane, and Martin J. Power (New York: Routledge, 2015), 289.
52 Joe Gore, "New Digital Stimulation from David Bowie & Reeves Gabrels," David Bowie interview, *Guitar Player* (issue 330) 31, no. 6 (June 1997): 29–35.
53 Eliot, "Tradition," 28.

Part V

Subjectivities and Discourses: Gender, Sexuality, Race, and Religion

17

Justin Timberlake's "Man of the Woods": Lumbersexuality, Nature, and Larking Around

Stan Hawkins and Tore Størvold

The trailer for Justin Timberlake's concept album *Man of the Woods* (2018) prepared his fans for something quite different from his previous releases. At 36, finally a "man's man," he could pride himself on fatherhood, a beautiful wife, superstar status, and immense wealth. Not unlike the Marlboro Man, he would be framed against the sweeping landscapes of Montana as pensive, sincere, and rugged, a veritable coding of the masculinized North American stereotype (see Figure 17.1). At the same time, there was a sensibility in the trailer, underscored by the solitude and beauty of his new surroundings, establishing the ideal setting for seeming to live happily ever after. In no uncertain terms, the nostalgia that besets the cowboy role continues boldly into the twenty-first century, and it is as if Timberlake would choose the road of self-appeasement, intertwining personal concepts of nature, manhood, and clean living. His self-positioning in the trailer, among the mountains, lakes, and forests, provided a platform for impressions of mythical constructs and hipsterism. Furthermore, it demonstrated not only a fascination on his part, but a mythologization of the wilderness and the white male. Through ecocritical and musicological readings, this study attempts to unpick some of the paradoxes of the lumbersexual—a complicated exercise in itself—which yoke subjectivities within a pop-oriented environment. In our search for understanding the constructs of masculinity in contemporary pop music audiovisuality, we explore the critical discourses of nature and gender, pointing out the ways in which they intersect in the music video "Man of the Woods."[1] The gendering process tied to Timberlake's specific constitution of the construct of nature, we have observed, has much in common with archetypes found in cinema, cartoons, folklore rituals, and literature, all under the aegis of freedom, tranquility, and hunting.

Personas exhibited in videos can be interpreted through a layering of texts, and to consider this we draw on various theories that map gender against race, class, and culture.[2] A prime objective of our narrative approach and close reading is to examine the strategies of a white male pop star who reinvents himself within a new context, with the powerful aid of the music video. The interdisciplinary task of successful audiovisual analysis lies in identifying

Figure 17.1 Justin Timberlake roaming free in the trailer video for his album *Man of the Woods* (2018).

both the visual and sonic aspects that comprise the performance, with specific emphasis on audiovisual structures and the narrative. Table 17.1 offers a summary of the audiovisual narrative, broken down according to the song form, as well as an emblematic screenshot from each section. The reader is encouraged to consult this as the analysis proceeds. From the outset, we are compelled to stress that the lyrics contribute significantly to the video's narrative, reinforcing many of the tactics employed. In particular, Timberlake regulates the body on display through a repertoire of gestures and verbal utterances that prompt us to evaluate male representational politics. Dwelling on his attitude and accompanying gestures, we contemplate the tactics aligned to specific conceptions of nature. Inevitably, how masculinity is aestheticized underpins our consideration of musical agency.[3] The framing of the shots, the aesthetics of the video production, and the gendered codes support a personal narrative that is imported into the protagonist's persona. Timberlake's message in the song's hook comes across crystal clear: "I brag about you to anyone outside / But I'm a man of the woods, it's my pride." In sum, our framework for this video analysis draws on a range of methods that aim to provide a critical perspective on Timberlake's take on himself through the establishment of a persona that is accommodated within a well-worn genre.

Audiovisual excursions

The "Man of the Woods" video is a blend of slapstick cartoon-type figurations and slickly choreographed stage performances. As the video begins, the viewer encounters Timberlake standing in a field, surrounded by outdoor hiking gear displayed on nearby boulders. Centrally positioned in the foreground of the shot, the artist, filmed in a woodland stage

Table 17.1 Audiovisual synopsis.

Form	Narrative	Musical codes	Visual codes
Pre-song (0:00–0:05)	• JT perched in a forest meadow • Camping gear and a mule deer flank the pop star clad in flannel shirt and jeans	• Environmental sound and the chittering of birds • A high-pitched, repeated gesture on the electric guitar—resembling a warning siren—sets the song in motion	• Opening titles announce the video in cinematic style • The camera stages JT centrally in the shot
Chorus (0:06–0:27)	• JT scouts the area with his binoculars • Unpacks a treasure-hunt-style map	• Vocals layered with back-up vocals • Sparse texture of pitched 808-style percussion, open chords on the electric guitar, sliding licks on the pedal steel	• Camera zooms in on the cartoon-like map, filling the screen
Verse 1 (0:28–0:45)	• JT uses exaggerated and playful gestures as he half walks, half dances through the woods, continuously locking eyes with the camera	• The bass enters, expanding the texture in the lower end • Upper register is kept open and sparse, leaving JT's voice unhindered	• Camera follows JT's movements in a sideways, continuous shot
Pre-chorus (0:46–1:04)	• JT grabs a fishing rod that catapults him into a tree house • Jumps onto a zip-line and slides back down over the trees	• A second electric guitar fills out the middle register with a funk-style rhythmic accompaniment	• A dramatic zoom to a close shot simulates looking through binoculars

Table 17.1 (*Continued*)

Form	Narrative	Musical codes	Visual codes
Chorus (1:05–1:24)	• JT walks past lumberjacks cutting and sawing wood in stylized, parodic gestures	• Musical texture largely identical to the first chorus • More presence in the synthesized bass	• Sideways tracking shot continues, the camera movement masking any cuts
Verse 2 (1:25–1:43)	• JT enters a tiny tent with an oversized sign proclaiming "Camp" • The interior is house-sized and containing vintage, designer items	• A break occurs where JT sings in close, parallel harmony with back-up voices	• Camera faces the mirror; this reveals that the camera's lens is equated with the gaze of JT's wife, Jessica Biel
Pre-chorus (1:44–2:02)	• JT motions to the viewer/his wife to follow him into a rowing boat • We arrive at the timber tavern	• Vocal delivery and lyrics identical to first pre-chorus • Percussive, whistle-like sound on the off-beat	• Camera is hand-held, suggestive of first-person movements as the viewer/Biel follows JT into the boat
Chorus (2:03–2:21)	• JT walks through crowds of denim-clad lumberjacks • Passes a beer to a bearded man	• Musical texture is identical to the previous choruses	• JT occupies the center of a carefully choreographed shot with actors passing by in the foreground and background

Form	Narrative	Musical codes	Visual codes
Bridge (2:22–2:59)	• JT extends his arm to the camera, prompting Biel to emerge and take his hand • They dance a traditional ballroom dance on the floor of the tavern, gazing into each other's eyes	• Chorus of backing vocals enters together with a piano, forming a ballad-like instrumentation • Percussion emphasizes half-time rhythm, producing the effect of slowing downBacking vocals repeat the line "me and you" • Backing vocals repeat the line "me and you"	• Realistic lighting transforms to spotlights • The dramatic lights coalesce on JT and Biel as the camera moves close-up on the dancing couple
Chorus (3:00–3:18)	• Four cloned Justin Timberlakes, each dressed in different outfits, perform the chorus *a cappella* on the tavern stage	• The lush instrumentation trails off, leaving only a four-part *a cappella* vocal group • "Barbershop" style, with characteristic finger snaps on the third beat of each bar	• A sequence of static shots • Each shot framing one of the Timberlake clones
Outro chorus (3:19–4:04)	• JT performs dance choreography with a large group of dancers onstage • Takes the hand of his wife and walks off with her into the woods	• The melody and vocal delivery is now more R&B-like in its quick pacing and rhythmic accentuations in the high end of JT's tenor register	• Creative editing blends interior and exterior: JT walks off the stage, and is suddenly outside in morning daylight • Camera frames JT and Biel, with a black screen encircling the two

set, has his look enhanced by the deployment of countless props and gestures. Embarking on a hike through the woods, his movements are captured by tracking shots that are well above average for a pop music video (12.2 seconds). Notably, the opening scene, lasting 26 seconds, is followed by a minute of camera movement, where the cross-cuts and transitions create an impression of one continuous shot extending into the second verse (1:27).

Corollaries to the visual style can be found in indie film director Wes Anderson's work; for instance, in the eye-catching typography in the opening shot (0:00–0:04) and the construction of a flat space and geometrically ordered *mise en scène*. Camera techniques involve wide shots with symmetrical features, long sideways tracking shots, snap-zooms (with rapid in or out zooms), and the "binocular view" (0:56), a trademark of Anderson's *oeuvre* (for instance, in *Moonrise Kingdom*, 2012). The "looney tunes" moment occurs when Timberlake bounces up into the tree house (0:52) with a similar surreal humor encountered in Anderson's films.[4] In particular, traces of Anderson's *Moonrise Kingdom* are discernible in the several visual tropes that are directly imported into the "Man of the Woods" video; these comprise an over-stylized tree house, a hand-drawn map, as well as outdoor gear and items (tents, binoculars, boots, hunting knives, etc.).[5] Undoubtedly, Anderson's stylistic influence has a hipster quality to it,[6] and as James MacDowell posits, his work is central to the quirky sensibility found in recent US indie cinema.[7] Such quirkiness is on display through most of "Man of the Woods," at least until the culmination in the barn dance bridge section, which we will return to later in the chapter. In the main, the overall artificiality of the visual narrative is highlighted by a cartoon-like wooden signpost bearing the word "camp" made visible as Timberlake enters the tent (1:26). Depending on how one chooses to interpret "camp," this term and its concept form a potent signifier in the context of any popular cultural text.[8]

Indeed, the sheer shape and display of the wooden camp signpost bring to mind Jean Baudrillard's theory of simulacrum, insofar as the relationship between the sign and the real collapses into hyperreality.[9] In addition, the imagery of the map, a central feature at the commencement of the video (0:20–0:25), serves to blur the distinction between signifier and reality. Drawing on Jorge Luis Borges's fable, Baudrillard employed the analogy of an empire that seeks to map its territory.[10] Eventually, after many attempts to represent the map as accurately as possible, cartologists ended up with a map that was as large as the empire itself, covering the exact territory that it depicted. This is what defines the simulacrum—the artifact that precedes the reality it claims to simulate by becoming real. Exemplifying this in the opening shot of "Man of the Woods," Timberlake unrolls a hand-drawn map, holding it up to the camera. In what seems like a crude representation of the landscape, the path in the woods leads to the designated "X" of the timber tavern. Yet, such a cartographic representation symbolizes another set of symbols (the stylized woods of the video) that are just as removed from any actual sense of "real nature." Accordingly, the video assumes the form of an amusement park ride, hyperbolized by the rapid, continuous camera movements that track Timberlake on his adventures through the woods.

Arguably, based upon a Disneyland aesthetic, the visual narrative is rife with action gimmicks, such as Timberlake being catapulted high up into the tree house to the accompaniment of comic gestures in the music. Notably, the melody in the pre-chorus section (Example 17.1) harks back to the well-known novelty song "Itsy Bitsy Teenie Weenie Yellow Polkadot Bikini." "Itsy Bitsy," a fun-loving song in a "bubblegum pop style," written by Paul Vance and Lee Pockriss, reached number one in the Billboard charts in 1960 in a version sung by Brian Hyland.[11] Closely following the steady rhythm of the text, the chorus tune of "Itsy Bitsy" possesses a singsong quality, and, in the pre-chorus of "Man of the Woods," the same effect occurs with lyrics that are full of innuendo. As with the original "Itsy Bitsy," the melody is composed around a repeated figure that straddles the interval of a 4th. Through this stylistic lineage, then, the music assumes a comic and banal quality, aided by the harmonic, melodic, and rhythmic material. Such aspects in the music underscore the slapstick qualities of the visual narrative, as Timberlake is catapulted up into the tree house.

Harmony has a major role in capturing the southern feel of the track: the chords are straightforward in a major key, predominantly centered on the tonic, subdominant, and dominant (I–IV–V in C). It is only in the bridge section that a notable key shift occurs, coupled with the introduction of a new chord progression (in E♭: IV–I–V), constituting the form of elevated modulation that literally heightens the mood of the song (Example 17.2). This passage is rendered romantic and intimate by soft vocal backings, lush pad effects, and Timberlake's gentle crooning on five phrases that all end with *me and you*. In the video this is marked by a sense of stark poignancy as Timberlake and his wife, Jessica Biel, engage in a barn dance with other couples moving in the background. Transporting a real-life situation into his own star text, Timberlake knowingly blurs his staged persona with his real-life situation. On completion of this sequence there is a

Example 17.1 Melodic material and visual comedy in the pre-chorus section (0:46–1:04).

Example 17.2 Harmonic and melodic features of the bridge section (2:22–2:59).

return to the home key of C major, where symbolically, he is cloned into four differently dressed lumberjacks, emulating a barbershop *a cappella*. Not unexpectedly, his wife is absent from this scene.

Throughout the song the employment of instrumental timbres and musical gestures evokes notions of the urban and rural, through their associations with styles and genres. These are delivered in different registers: in the low range there are percussive bass notes, reminiscent of late-1980s drum machines, a signature of producer Timbaland and his major role in defining the sonic template of mainstream hip-hop and R&B during the last two decades. Superimposed over the bass are arpeggiated chords within mid-register and played by a "clean" electric guitar alongside the occasional slide on a pedal steel guitar, such instrumental timbres evoke impressions of rural country music. In particular, the rhythm guitar idiom (0:48) is reminiscent of guitarist John Mayer, whose blues and funk influences are subsumed in harmonic and melodic structures coming from white country and pop genres. Although the guitar articulates a common funk pattern, in this tempo (100 beats per minute) and half-time groove there is little sense of syncopated rhythmic elements, hence rendering the overall effect rather bland.

Musical traits expose a blending of irony, banality, and sincerity. For instance, the exaggerated vocalizations used during the *a cappella* chorus in "barbershop quartet" style (3:00–3:18) come across as humorous in intent.[12] Such usage in the context of a contemporary pop track—a stylistic anachronism—might well be interpreted as ironic. Then, featured more prominently at the culmination of the heightened intensity of the bridge section, blatant hints of barbershop also offer a degree of ironic detachment.[13]

Throughout the video, camera techniques work cleverly in tandem with musical features, including optical effects that underpin the politics of looking. Upon Timberlake entering the tent (1:35), the camera focuses on a mirror, revealing Biel. From this moment onwards, the direction of the camera (and hence the viewer) tracks Biel while simultaneously harnessing Timberlake's gaze. As he assuredly escorts her (and us) through the woods, optical technologies position the viewer subordinately on a par with the female. Continuously, the camera is positioned slightly lower than Timberlake, enabling him to address the viewer from above. Importantly, it is the male's control of the camera that dominates and captures the viewer's attention, the only exception being in the bridge where the focus shifts onto the female subject. Ultimately, the ploy of eye contact with the spectator emphasizes Timberlake's motions, beckoning us into his neck of the woods with his wife on his arm.

Into the woods we go …

Somewhat impishly, "Man of the Woods" draws on myths of the frontier and the wilderness to then reverse them in a fake-take on the North American pastoral tradition. The woods are unashamedly garish—an ideal setting for larking around—indeed, they suggest a cardboard cut-out parody of the American Midwest, where the great outdoors emerges Disney-fied. Toying with notions of the American pastoral, the video nonetheless succumbs to its own cultural entrapments and discourse on heteronormativity. Right at the end, as Timberlake and Biel walk off into a sunset, hand in hand, the Montana woods are portrayed as a nostalgia-laden utopia. All this poses critical questions ranging from: how does one evaluate the narratives of nature in the video, to what type of ecocritical perspectives are evoked?

Historically, the Midwestern heartland has essential notions of North American landscape: the place where the virtues of wholesome labor and rugged individualism prosper under the open sky. Myths of the wild frontier, with their narrative motifs of escape and spiritual retreat, are endemic to American identity.[14] Such tropes of New World pastoralism reached their apotheosis in the figure of poet and philosopher, Henry David Thoreau (1817–1862), American literature's foremost man of the woods. In his book *Walden; or, Life in the Woods* (1854), he recounted his experiences of living self-sufficiently in a small cabin in the Massachusetts wilderness.[15] Part memoir and part spiritual quest, *Walden* turned Thoreau into an icon of American environmentalism. Alongside disciples, such as John Muir, he has been regarded as largely responsible for establishing a spiritual notion of the wilderness as a touchstone of American cultural identity—an ideological basis for conservation efforts.

In recent decades, however, the foregrounding of the American landscape as an untamed wilderness has been critiqued for its emphases on masculine colonial aggression, not least directed against women, Native Americans, and the land itself.[16] Underlying the ideologies of the wilderness is an aesthetic of purity and the "undisturbed," sanctified by the creation of the US national parks in the late-nineteenth century. Yet, ideals of purity are only achievable by erasing the local human history. In the case of Yosemite, both the Ahwaneechee Indians and the white miners who lived and worked there were forcibly expelled.[17] In William Cronon's words: "the removal of Indians to create an 'uninhabited wilderness' reminds us just how invented, just how constructed, the American wilderness really is."[18] Cronon's critique assumes the form of a warning: "nature"—that most natural of things—is ideologically malleable so as to serve political purposes.

Contemporary American history abounds with men in their woods, and music has vividly illustrated this. Variations of the *Walden* narrative crop up in figures such as Pulitzer prize-winning composer John Luther Adams and the indie rock artist Bon Iver (artist name of Justin Vernon). Bon Iver's debut album, entitled *For Emma, Forever Ago* (2007), resulted from a period of self-imposed seclusion in his family's cabin in remote Wisconsin. This small biographical detail was latched onto by the music media and fashioned into a myth about the creative artist, who, in becoming tired of urban living, retreats into the woods to fully immerse himself in his art. Although Iver has indicated that journalists were largely responsible for the creation of this narrative of seclusion surrounding the production of his debut album, his career as a rock artist is strongly grounded in the authenticity of a perceived closeness to nature. During the late 2000s, Iver emerged as one of the leading figures in the indie rock world, his iconography an obvious point of reference for Timberlake's own lumberjack construction.[19]

In stark contrast to Iver, however, "Man of the Woods" aspires to a different constructedness of the North American wilderness. Presenting a postmodern take on the woods, the music video acknowledges its own sense of history by becoming a playful representation of the *representations* of the New World frontier. For Timberlake and his fans, the "real" frontier (that's if it ever existed!) becomes lost somewhere in the mesh of Disneyland reproductions, resulting in a hyperreality comprising symbols that refer back to other symbols. For example, depictions of lumberjacks sawing timber in the background of Timberlake's leisurely trail are nothing more than caricatures. Replete with obligatory beards and bulky builds, their mechanical movements hark back to the animatronic lumberjacks often featured in the classic log rides in American amusement parks. Similarly, the mule deer standing next to Timberlake in the opening scene is irrevocably bound up in the Disney character Bambi, its calm disposition juxtaposed with a human being having very little to do with the reality of this shy species.

The postmodern pastoral, as theorized by Scott Hess,[20] champions the pursuit of happiness through leisure in a secular and sensual utopia. In this sense, it caricatures a clean and air-brushed depiction of nature that is refracted through the omnipresent media technologies. Hess's critique references television advertisements, such as those for SUV cars, which utilize a visual style not entirely unrelated to the "Man of the Woods" video. Here, the pastoral mode is mobilized to underscore our current capitalist social order as "natural," turning nature into a kitsch supermarket that is centered knowingly around the individual consumer.[21] As a result, the depiction of nature in "Man of the Woods" is nothing less than a leisure center, crammed with amenities, such as the bar from which Timberlake serves Biel a drink in the tent. Arguably, pastoral semiotics are employed to mask the complex social and environmental systems upon which our lifestyles depend. As such, Timberlake's persona is based on a lifestyle of consumerism that is dubious in spite of him wishing to appear in harmony with nature.

A long lineage in US popular culture has appropriated natural imagery to mask suppressive practices and societal structures as seemingly "natural." Timberlake draws on a tradition that includes Western films and country music, cultural forms that operate to naturalize identities by framing them in a free-range habitat. Other forms of appropriation are obvious within a landscape that serves the purposes of the white male. Rooted in the *vaqueros* of northern Mexico, the American cowboy is part of the body of men who worked the midwest ranges after the American Civil War; however, this also included a significant number of African-American freedmen, with cowboy ballads demonstrating a degree of multicultural exchange.[22] By the end of the nineteenth century, such diversity had been predominantly written out, and, with the aid of Hollywood, the cowboy now emerged as exclusively white, embodying masculine virtues of self-reliance and individual freedom. By the 1930s, the visual costuming of white singing cowboy acts, such as those highlighted by Gene Autry and Roy Rogers, seemed a far cry from the realities of cattle herding.[23] Thus, when Timberlake invokes the Montana wilderness in his album trailer, as we have discussed above, he draws on a landscape that is literally whitewashed by Hollywood and the popular culture industries.[24]

An ecocritical approach therefore necessitates an inquiry into how such cowboy imagery might—or might not—orient us toward our environment in sustainable ways. In a time of global ecological crisis, it would seem pertinent to excavate the narratives that structure what we imagine to be "nature" and what kinds of values we attach to it. Hence, when faced with the "Man of the Woods" video, we might well ask what are the ethics that underpin this in the twenty-first century in the namesake of entertainment? If intended as a travesty of traditional representations of the wilderness, the video might well succeed in exposing the fakeness of its foundational myths; however, in terms of environmental ethics, it could also signal a cul-de-sac. The superficiality of the visual composition of "Man of the Woods" lies in its deployment of nature as a glossy backdrop. Hyperbolically, it presents a non-urban United States as a playground, where white men are free to roam and play in exactly the way they wish and on their own terms. In reality, however, the woods are more than a backdrop: they are complex ecosystems consisting of hundreds of species of trees, plants, animals, birds, and insects under threat of extinction precisely *because of* nature being posited as a prop; woods and forests are not amusement parks (nor are they the romantic sanctuary of Thoreau), but rather living, breathing, and tangible spaces for the planet's survival.

Timberlake's ventures into the woods idealize white masculinity and patriarchal control. Consider the first line of the first verse, and its address to the female: "Hey sugar plum, look at where we are, so tonight if I take it too far, it's okay." It is as if the wilderness ("look at where we are") justifies his maleness ("so tonight if I take it too far"). Ecofeminist Carolyn Merchant claims that dominant images and metaphors of nature as female have functioned historically to reinforce male domination of both women and the land.[25] In "Man of the Woods," Biel is rendered ephemeral, almost merging into the woods. When she appears, she is dressed in white, never speaking, and always gazing at her husband: a forest nymph waiting to be won-over by the contemporary rugged lumbersexual.[26]

And, out of the woods *the man* doth come ...

Etymologically, lumbersexuality denotes a cross between the lumberjack and the metrosexual, designating a specific form of gender performativity that is found predominantly in groups of young males at the beginning of the twenty-first century. Directed toward a male who is stylized, pensive, and bent on being manly, lumbersexuality also authenticates a version of hipster masculinity. At the time of conducting this research, lumbersexuals are primarily in their 20s and 30s and loom large in gentrified spaces and places on a global scale. Willa Brown has traced their historic roots:

> This particular brand of bearded flannel-wearer is a modern take on the deeply-rooted historical image of Paul Bunyan, the ax-wielding but amiable giant, whose stomping grounds were the North Woods of the upper Midwest. Paul and his brethren emerged as icons in American pop culture a little over a century ago. What links the mythic lumberjack to his modern-day incarnations is a pervasive sense—in his time and ours—that masculinity is "in crisis."[27]

Distinguishable by habitat, as much as crisis, the Bunyan derivative involves picking and mixing styles willy-nilly. In particular, where one comes from and then chooses to live helps to authenticate the lumbersexual; places of habitation can range from gentrified urban neighborhoods to log cabins. More often urban than rural, lumbersexuals tend to pride themselves on good taste and looking good, often deriding those who pander to mainstream culture. Top of the range products in high-end boutiques and stores are meticulously sought out, with an emphasis on quality and costly materials: plaid flannel shirts, cuffed jeans, woolen leather jackets and leather gloves, belts, watches, and glasses. A calculated degree of gender bending in attire is often permitted, evident in florals ranging from shirts to half-sleeve tattoos. When it comes to physical appearance, manscaping—the meticulous grooming of hair—reveals a dominant trait of vanity. Opting for carefully sculpted unkempt beards or mustaches rather than stubble, the lumbersexual fastidiously shirks a clean-shaven appearance, which is entirely at odds with the desired casual, down-to-earth scruffy image. Underpinning this is a verification of "heteronormative manliness" (regardless of one's personal orientation), complemented by just the right gear and backpack.

As already stated, millennial lumbersexuals are ubiquitous and "Man of the Woods" might be read as a spoof on the traditions that privilege dominant white males in the United States. For sure, lumbersexuality is more deceptive than meets the eye. Accessing the outdoor aesthetic, where environmentalism and rebellion against office jobs prevail, the plight of the lumbersexual is in one sense inauthentic, often nothing more than a token gesture—countless websites, online catalogs, product ratings, and accessories testify to this. Such fashioning of masculinity is charged with a conscious working out of what it is to be a man and an acute awareness of gender stereotypes and concepts of attractive white masculinity. Certainly, a wry sense of self-irony has steered Timberlake's trailblazing pop career since the 1990s, with him modeling himself on Michael Jackson and numerous other African-American male artists. Staging his personas in diverse ways has provided him with the necessary leverage to gain a foothold in the pop industry. From the outset, his status as a Mickey Mouse Club child-star conditioned him for his 20s, where attention to style, image, and attitude were highly influenced by close alliances to Pharrell Williams, Timbaland, and the Neptunes. Cunningly, the ambience of *Man of the Woods* is varied, with Timberlake's personas by no means solely relegated to the lumbersexual, as he works this through a range of idioms and styles. The underlying message (based on the cover art work, the album's teaser documentaries, and countless interviews) is that he has matured and turned a corner. All in all, then, a sense of detachment and sophistication in the trailer for the album release frames his look against shots of the vast open Wild West, merging into the mini-drama of the video "Man of the Woods." In many ways, Timberlake's brand of lumbersexuality seems a far cry from his roots in the south in Tennessee, with a sense that he is reaching out to white America in the new reality era of Trump, fetishizing a place of escape in the big-sky outback. Cynically, this can be perceived as a set change rather than a tangible move to the Wild West. After all, easing into the luxury surrounds of a multi-millionaire residential estate—Yellowstone Club in Montana—his lifestyle could not be further removed from lumberjacks and ranchers, such as Bunyan and his followers.

Above all, male iconography in "Man of the Woods" denotes gentrification, as much as the plight of the hipster, with the pop star situated anachronistically in the woods. Timberlake's image is epitomized by the "manscaped" oiled beard, the flannel, the beanie, the layering of work shirts, and the fur-lined jacket. Turning to stereotypes of a down-to-earth Southern style, his musical journey slots into a genealogy of famous films, musicals, and series: *Bonanza, Annie Get Your Gun, Gone With the Wind*, and *Oklahoma*. Posing as a modern-day cowboy, or for that matter a "fake Bunyan," he delivers his lyrics with a good deal of humor and panache. Teasingly, this affords him the opportunity to access the more serious matters of hard-working male exigency, whiteness, and heteronormative privilege. That such a Wild West spoof targets a mainstream audience is in little doubt, as it processes the pop hero's colonization of the once savage space, where lighting campfires, chopping wood, and skillfully throwing the ax take on conservative values of Americana. Musically, Timberlake's vocal style complements the pseudo-romantic haze of the barn dance. In particular, the details of his singing lock into the child-like folksy, country style of the musical expression with a flexibility that is as animated as the images themselves. One might argue that this bolsters the white privilege of the cis-male via a prime objective to show off his wife, emblazoned by contentment. Intentional or not, his overly sentimental disposition in the middle-section sequence resonates loud and clear.

Foolery aside, immersing oneself in lumbersexuality in the "last best place to dwell" in the United States might be perceived as more than a tactic for reinforcing male norms. The desire to return to an imaginary and secure place also provides an opening for men to experiment with the fantasy of being real men. In this sense, the video yields a portal for enacting a special breed of masculinity that is in diametric opposition to the landscapes of New York, Los Angeles, and Tennessee. Moreover, it works as a buffer to the teaser trailer, where images of "real" nature (as opposed to the technicolored sets in "Man of the Woods") illustrate the "real" Timberlake, offstage, in a minute's duration of forty-nine shots:[28] the visual semiotics of mountain sweeps, glittering fresh water, snowy fields, long grass, expansive skies, and rows of corn form a striking background for Timberlake, shirtless, clasping a small child in front of a bonfire. Peering into the distance, now offstage, he is natural, pensive, and sincere. The double-codedness of such a representation is intended to market not only the album, but his new self as harnessed by the juxtaposition of the documentary trailer and the video of "Man of the Woods." In the end it might well be that the trailer serves as a disclaimer for the pop video in its attempt to authenticate who the artist really wants to be—its mission is to give us a sober insight behind the personas and the scenes.

Conclusion

In our reading, Timberlake signals a homecoming to a conservative base camp (where in fact he actually never sprung from). Chronologically, this is rooted in the Trump era, where white, hetero-patriarchal values flourish at the expense of others. Compelling in the music video is the mix of signifiers detected in the style, the vocals, the Disney-like set, and the codes of lumbersexuality, all of which stem from the high-street trends in young male fashion. As we have been keen to stress, an air of ambivalence permeates the images, gestures, and mannerisms that complement his musical expression. In turn, these get us to ponder over the wider questions that underpin the complex layout of fun-loving pop videos. Even if Timberlake's fantasy of nature is palpable to the majority of his fans, we still need to question the ramifications of this. Fusing the real to the fantasy, the technologies of animation rely on ideals of race, nature, generation, nationality, and gender. In this sense, Timberlake's very take on these categories implies a deliberate sense of larking around that is entertaining and yet a lot more than this. Positioning himself in the Wild West is a bold yet contentious move in itself, encoding and empowering a logic of expression that works on his own premises.

The intermeshing of gender with ecopolitical concerns in mainstream pop videos needs to be comprehended in terms of its full social impact. On the whole, the quirkiness of Timberlake's agency arises from narratives inherent within the history of music videos. After all, the prime markers of mainstream pop are harnessed by the artist's own market value and negotiated in terms of musical and non-musical operations. Timberlake demonstrates commercial survival as he continues to maintain a position as one of the best-selling male artists worldwide. There is little doubt that the source of his success resides in the relationships he has with his fans and his appeal to groups with varying national, geographic, class, and cultural backgrounds. As we have pointed out, the video "Man of the Woods" evinces a new point of departure that conflates and reinvents Timberlake in quite remarkable ways. By turning to a lumbersexual landscape he valorizes stark impressions of male identity always on his terms, and it is the overtly heteronormative narrative of the video that drives a performance that is emotionally charged. In our analysis we have indicated that the romantic sentiments and sexuality exhibited in the video are unequivocally straight, where the depiction of "real manhood" nullifies any sense of transgression. Yet, his vocality is hardly hypermasculine: there are still hints of queering the pitch that are well in line with pop and rock celebrities, such as Prince, Michael Jackson, Robbie Williams, and Jay Kay.[29]

Representations of nature in "Man of the Woods" are configured in relationship to the gendered body. With the surfacing of the lumbersexual in popular culture, a focus falls on the problematics of masculinity and its fashioning and prized standing in hipster culture at a point in time when our natural environment is in great peril. In recent years, scholars increasingly have recognized the convergence of popular music structures with perceptions of the environment.[30] Emerging theories have begun to advocate new approaches for interconnecting cultural scripts of nature to the environment and reframing issues of gender, race, and class according to the constellations of ecosystems. Consequently, "Man of the Woods" gets us to rethink pop audiovisuality, its joins, overlaps, and disruptions that function across a range of layers. Given that music is about politics, discussions of how we are entertained seem central to making sense of a common future. Positioned in the woods for the first time in his career, Timberlake offers up a beguiling opportunity to reflect on the politics of communication, gender, and issues that relate to how we live our lives. Certainly, this video reminds us that it does matter how we inscribe sound and vision in the everyday contexts of existence.

Finally, we return again to the extended bridge section in the video of "Man of the Woods," featuring the dance between Timberlake and his wife (2:21–3:00). Dwelling on this sequence raises the question of function—structurally and narratively—and the cause of the diversion the music and images take in order to reinforce the goal orientation of the song as a whole. The move to A♭ tonality from C major has significant ramifications for the type of elevated effect in mood, which ultimately entices the listener in. The unexpected change, albeit a common device in all genres of Western music, contains a tender expressiveness that simultaneously marks the song's inventiveness and poignancy. In his application of the concept, "elevated modulation," Dai Griffiths refers to examples in Western popular music where such harmonic devices function as an integral part of compositional techniques.[31] Although the more standard modulation is by a semitone or tone, Timberlake opts for a rare I–♭VI key shift. With the home tonality based solely around the white keys of the keyboard, the jump to the black keys in A♭ major gives cause to pause, think, and react. What defines this bridge section, however, is not only an elevated modulation and melodic alteration, but also several other elaborations. Deftly, the video maximizes this musical innovation by emerging as a self-contained narrative within a larger narrative as Timberlake's voice holds the clue to the ways in which the subject negotiates a sense of desirable embodiment through normative aesthetics. The presumed norm is the male-female heteronormative dyad— the dance sequence is good-natured, jovial, and stable, with the celebrity's sweetheart on his arm—the hipster-naturalist portrayal of manliness in the form of a ballad does the trick. Yet, while beards and flannel might look (and even sound) good on set, it is the bluff that has to be of concern. Larking around by sending up the North American lumberjack, Timberlake's act overflows with pretense. There is no denying the patriarchal coding of this performance; it is decisive and exhibits the dominant role of masculinity commonly found in the majority of pop songs. Vividly, the visuals of this bridge section highlight the controlling function of Timberlake by centralizing his ego in a variety of guises. Ultimately, the ideal of the lumbersexual is affirmed in an excess of expression that is adroitly produced and packaged, all of which leaves us wondering if parody might well be the hallmark of something more cynical.

Notes

1   Justin Timberlake, "Justin Timberlake—Man of the Woods," YouTube video, official music video, directed by Paul Hunter, posted by "Justin Timberlake," February 1, 2018, https://www.youtube.com/watch?v=baj6llvgpWA.

2   See Raewyn Connell, *Gender and Power: Society, the Person and Sexual Politics* (Cambridge: Polity Press, 1987); bell hooks, *We Real Cool: Black Men and Masculinity* (New York: Routledge, 2004); Matthew Bannister, *White Boys, White Noise: Masculinities and 1980s Indie Guitar Rock* (Aldershot: Ashgate, 2006); Freya Jarman-Ivens, *Oh Boy! Masculinities and Popular Music* (New York: Routledge, 2007); Michael S. Kimmel and Michael A. Messner, *Men's Lives*, 9th ed. (Boston, MA: Pearson, 2013); Jacqueline Warwick, "Singing Style and White Masculinity," in *The Ashgate Research Companion to Popular Musicology*, edited by Derek B. Scott (Aldershot: Ashgate, 2009); Stan Hawkins, *The British Pop Dandy: Masculinity, Popular Music and Culture* (Farnham: Ashgate, 2009); and Lori Burns, Alyssa Woods, and Marc Lafrance, "Sampling and Storytelling: Kanye West's Vocal and Sonic Narratives," in *The Cambridge Companion to the Singer-Songwriter*, edited by Katherine Williams and Justin A. Williams (Cambridge: Cambridge University Press, 2016).

3   This study builds on the gender theories of scholars including Lori Burns and Marc Lafrance, "Gender, Sexuality, and the Politics of Looking in Beyoncé's 'Video Phone' (Featuring Lady Gaga)," in *The Routledge Research Companion to Popular Music and Gender*, edited by Stan Hawkins (London and New York: Routledge, 2017); Stan Hawkins, "On Male Queering in Mainstream Pop," in *Queering the Popular Pitch*, edited by Sheila Whiteley and Jennifer Rycenga (London: Routledge, 2006); Sheila Whiteley, ed., *Sexing the Groove: Popular Music and Gender* (London: Routledge, 1997); bell hooks, *Black Looks: Race and Representation* (Boston, MA: South End Press, 1992); Laura Mulvey, *Visual and Other Pleasures*, 2nd ed. (Basingstoke: Palgrave, 2009); and E. Ann Kaplan, *Women and Film: Both Sides of the Camera* (New York: Methuen, 1983).

4   For instance, this is found in the exaggerated fake shark that features in the climactic scene of *The Life Aquatic* (2005).

5   Several of the visual tropes used in the "Man of the Woods" music video can be viewed in the trailer for Anderson's *Moonrise Kingdom*, including the map (at 0:27), the binocular view (0:33), and a similarly surreal tree house (1:09). See "Moonrise Kingdom—Official Trailer [HD]," YouTube video, official movie trailer, posted by "Universal Pictures Ireland," April 14, 2012, https://www.youtube.com/watch?v=_eOI3AamSm8.

6   Anderson is an icon of hipster culture and an important figure in American indie cinema from the last decade. See Peter C. Kunze, ed., *The Films of Wes Anderson: Critical Essays on an Indiewood Icon* (New York: Palgrave MacMillan, 2014), 1–4.

7   This is defined by a range of aesthetic conventions, as noted in James MacDowell, "Notes on Quirky," *Movie: A Journal of Film Criticism* 1 (2010): 1–16. The "quirky" is particularly productive for making sense of the audiovisual style of "Man of the Woods." MacDowell defines it as a contemporary comedic sensibility characterized by "a fastidious artificiality" and "a tone which balances ironic detachment with sincere engagement" (1).

8   In many pop videos, camp is a main ingredient, which warrants close scholarly attention. For studies on camp in popular music, see Freya Jarman-Ivens, "Notes on Musical

Camp," in *The Ashgate Research Companion to Popular Musicology*, edited by Derek B. Scott (Aldershot: Ashgate, 2009); Hawkins, *The British Pop Dandy*; John Richardson, "Intertextuality and Pop Camp Identity Politics in Finland: The Crash's Music Video 'Still Alive,'" *Popular Musicology Online* 2 (2006); and Christopher Moore and Philip Purvis, eds., *Music and Camp* (Middletown, CT: Wesleyan University Press, 2018).

9   Jean Baudrillard, *Simulacra and Simulation*, translated by Sheila Faria Glaser (Ann Arbor, MI: University of Michigan Press, 1994).

10 Ibid., 1.

11 "Bubblegum pop" denotes a genre of American music that flourished during the late 1960s and early 1970s, exemplified by a light, "airy" pop style and often specifically engineered by producers to appeal to the pre-teen market. See Kim Cooper and David Smay, eds., *Bubblegum Music is the Naked Truth: The Dark History of Prepubescent Pop, from the Banana Splits to Britney Spears* (Port Townsend, WA: Feral House, 2001). Terms such as "bubblegum" may appear derogatory, a problem that is addressed in Stan Hawkins, ed., *Pop Music and Easy Listening* (London: Routledge, 2011).

12 Gage Averill comments that barbershop (originally a style of four-part harmony, now a genre) involves a commitment to a repertoire of popular songs roughly from the period 1890–1930s, and symbolizing "a utopian Main Street, U.S.A., long ago." See Gage Averill, *Four Parts, No Waiting: A Social History of American Barbershop Quartet* (Oxford: Oxford University Press, 2003), 3.

13 Stan Hawkins has theorized the act of interpreting ironic intent in popular music texts in *Settling the Pop Score: Pop Texts and Identity Politics* (London and New York: Routledge, 2002), 19–21. For a recent collection on irony in pop music, see Katherine L. Turner, ed., *This Is the Sound of Irony. Music, Politics and Popular Culture* (New York: Routledge, 2016). A recent study that grapples with irony, specifically in relation to interpreting artists' personas constituted through the aesthetics of music videos, is found in Kai Arne Hansen's, "Holding on for Dear Life: Gender, Celebrity Status, and Vulnerability-on-Display in Sia's 'Chandelier,'" in *The Routledge Research Companion to Popular Music and Gender*, edited by Stan Hawkins (London and New York: Routledge, 2016).

14 Lawrence Buell, *The Environmental Imagination: Thoreau, Nature Writing, and the Formation of American Culture* (Cambridge, MA: Harvard University Press, 1995).

15 Henry David Thoreau, *Walden* (Princeton, NJ: Princeton University Press, 1971).

16 Greg Garrard, *Ecocriticism*, 2nd ed. (London: Routledge, 2012), 54.

17 Ibid., 77.

18 William Cronon, "The Trouble with Wilderness; or, Getting Back to the Wrong Nature," in *Uncommon Ground: Rethinking the Human Place in Nature*, edited by William Cronon (New York: W.W. Norton & Co., 1995), 79.

19 Bon Iver is a central figure in a branch of post-2000 indie rock music that features folk revival idioms in acoustic instrumentation, including the bands Fleet Foxes, Arcade Fire, as well as Sufjan Stevens on the concept album *Michigan*. This "indie folk" style is a dominant reference here, signaled more by Timberlake's apparel (flannel shirt) than by musical codes. But, on certain tracks on *Man of the Woods* ("Flannel" and "Livin' Off the Land"), he incorporates layered vocal choruses that are derivative of Bon Iver. This is a fitting example of how mainstream pop appropriates the subcultural codes of hipster culture.

20   Scott Hess, "Postmodern Pastoral, Advertising, and the Masque of Technology," *Interdisciplinary Studies in Literature and the Environment* 11, no. 1 (2004): 71–100.

21   Ibid., 72.

22   Alan Lomax's collections exemplify this. See David Ingram, *The Jukebox in the Garden: Ecocriticism and American Popular Music Since 1960* (New York: Editions Rodopi B.V., 2010), 89.

23   Although these icons defined the popular cowboy image and were the forerunners of the country music recording industry. Ibid., 90–92.

24   Alan Lomax originally collected "Home on the Range" (as made famous by John Denver) not from a white cowboy, but from a black cook who had worked on a chuck wagon on a Texas cattle trail. Robert Cantwell, *When We Were Good: The Folk Revival* (Cambridge, MA: Harvard University Press, 1996), 72.

25   Carolyn Merchant, *The Death of Nature: Women, Ecology, and the Scientific Revolution* (New York: Harper & Row, 1982).

26   The white-dressed female in the woods is a common fairy-tale trope, which is similarly employed in Kanye West's music video for the song "Coldest Winter" (2010). An interesting fact in this context is that the Kanye West track "Lost in the World," from the album *My Beautiful Dark Twisted Fantasy* (2012), features Bon Iver, who is referenced by Timberlake on *Man of the Woods*. Thanks to Lori Burns for these intertextual observations.

27   Willa Brown, "Lumbersexuality and Its Discontents," *Atlantic*, December 10, 2014, https://www.theatlantic.com/national/archive/2014/12/lumbersexuality-and-its-discontents/383563.

28   The trailer video for the album can be viewed online. See Justin Timberlake, "Justin Timberlake—INTRODUCING MAN OF THE WOODS (Teaser)," YouTube video, posted by "Justin Timberlake," January 2, 2018, https://www.youtube.com/watch?v=bVU-MmJZFFA.

29   Numerous scholars have addressed the phenomenon of high register by male vocalists, with an emphasis on gender and sexuality. See Barbara Bradby, "Growing Up to Be a Rapper? Justin Bieber's Duet with Ludacris as Transcultural Practice," in *The Routledge Research Companion to Popular Music and Gender*, edited by Stan Hawkins (London and New York: Routledge, 2017); Richard Middleton, "'Last Night a DJ Saved My Life': Avians, Cyborgs and Siren Bodies in the Era of Phonographic Technology," *Radical Musicology* 1 (2006); Hawkins, "On Male Queering" and "[Un]*Justified*: Gestures of Straight-Talk in Justin Timberlake's Songs," in *Oh Boy! Masculinities and Popular Music*, edited by Freya Jarman-Ivens (London: Routledge, 2007); Sheila Whiteley, *Women and Popular Music: Sexuality, Identity, and Subjectivity* (New York: Routledge, 2000); and Simon Frith, *Performing Rites: On the Value of Popular Music* (Cambridge, MA: Harvard University Press, 1996).

30   Nancy Guy, "Flowing Down Taiwan's Tamsui River: Towards an Ecomusicology of the Environmental Imagination," *Ethnomusicology* 53, no. 2 (2009): 218–248; Ingram, *The Jukebox in the Garden*; James Edwards, "Silence by My Noise: An Ecocritical Aesthetic of Noise in Japanese Traditional Sound Culture and the Sound Art of Akita Masami," *Green Letters: Studies in Ecocriticism* 15, no. 1 (2011): 89–102; William Echard, "Psychedelia, Musical Semiotics, and Environmental Unconscious," *Green Letters: Studies in Ecocriticism* 15, no. 1 (2011): 61–75; Mark Pedelty, *Ecomusicology: Rock, Folk, and*

the Environment (Philadelphia, PA: Temple University Press, 2012); Travis D. Stimeling, "Music, Place, and Identity in the Central Appalachian Mountaintop Removal Mining Debate," *American Music* 30, no. 1 (2012): 1–29; Aaron S. Allen and Kevin Dawe, eds., *Current Directions in Ecomusicology: Music, Culture, Nature* (London and New York: Routledge, 2016); and Tore Størvold, "Music and the Kárahnjúkar Hydropower Plant: Style, Aesthetics, and Environmental Politics in Iceland," *Popular Music and Society*, July 20, 2018: 1–24.

31 Dai Griffiths, "Elevating Form and Elevating Modulation," *Popular Music* 34, no. 1 (2014): 22–44.

18

Gangsta Crisis, Catharsis, and Conversion: Coming to God in Hip-Hop Video Narratives

Alyssa Woods and Robert Michael Edwards

Religious experience and expression comprise an ever-present, and increasingly prevalent, factor in hip-hop. Historically, rap artists have incorporated their faith in ways that reinforced the norms of hip-hop culture. For example, the narratives constructed by Christian rappers are often centered around symbols of prosperity (bling, the Jesus-piece, etc.), while Black Muslim rappers have adopted a more socially conscious, urban perspective. The success of Kanye West's "Jesus Walks" (2004) drew mainstream attention to the issue of religious expression in hip-hop videos. Prior to this, the hip-hop world witnessed such iconic figures as Joseph "Run" Simmons (of Run-DMC) and MC Hammer become ordained as Christian ministers.

In contrast to the aforementioned artists, who were already associated with an organized religious tradition, there is also a growing trend of "finding God" within hip-hop. The ever-growing list of rappers who have undergone an experience of religious conversion includes: The Game, Snoop Dogg, Loon, Doug E. Fresh, Shyne, and Kendrick Lamar. Interestingly, there is not one singular path to conversion in the hip-hop sphere. The Game underwent Christian baptism before releasing his album *Jesus Piece* (2012); Snoop Dogg converted to Rastafarianism and reimagined his brand; Loon converted to Islam before leaving the music industry; Doug E. Fresh became a follower of Scientology; and Shyne followed the path of Hasidic Judaism. What becomes apparent through the visual, lyrical, and musical analysis of the work produced pre- and post-conversion is that there is a tension between industry norms and expectations (concerning masculinity, wealth, power, and gender dynamics) and the post-conversion idealized public expression of faith (actions, interviews, lyrics, videos, and promotional materials). In effect, we see these artists struggling to live in two worlds: that of commercial viability, and that of their post-conversion convictions.

This chapter explores the history of conversion in hip-hop as illustrated through the lens of music videos. We contextualize our discussion within the broader landscape of religious imagery in hip-hop videos, focusing on the negotiation of meaning on the part of rappers who have undergone conversion experiences. The second part of this chapter engages with the work and religious journey of Kendrick Lamar. Drawing on theories of religious conversion[1] and the development of African-American freedom movements,[2] we analyze Lamar's engagement with religious symbolism in the production of his music videos. The concept album *DAMN.* (2017) and the accompanying videos act as a sonic and visual exploration of the crisis and catharsis that characterize religious conversion.[3] From a methodological standpoint, we approach the study of religion in hip-hop videos through a lens that intersects religious studies and music analytic perspectives. Taken together, we examine the videos under discussion as examples of multimodal texts wherein music, lyrics, and image function together as a communicative whole in the transmission of meaning.[4] Our multimodal analysis (images, lyrics, and music) illuminates how Lamar portrays and problematizes his association with a particular worldview and religious community. Ultimately, this chapter illustrates the tensions that exist between mainstream hip-hop norms and religious imagery in relation to the audiovisual expression of artists' identity and socio-political positioning.

Situating religious expression in hip-hop music videos

Although becoming more prevalent in hip-hop music, the use of religious imagery and lyrics has developed virtually concurrently with the history of mainstream hip-hop. Five Percent Nation (FPN) discourse was incorporated into the rhetoric of groups such as The World's Famous Supreme Team in the early 1980s. Throughout the later 1980s and 1990s, there were a number of significant hip-hop artists who were adherents to the Nation of Gods and Earths (FPN), including Rakim of Eric B. and Rakim, Poor Righteous Teachers, Big Daddy Kane, Brand Nubian, and Wu-Tang Clan.[5] Stephen Wiley's album *Bible Break* (1985) is cited as the first commercial release of a gospel-inspired hip-hop album.[6] Christian hip-hop developed further in the late 1980s and 1990s with artists such as T-Bone, P.I.D. (Preachers in Disguise), TobyMac, and MC Hammer with the 1990 release of "Pray."

As noted in the introduction, there is a growing movement (post-2000) of artists who have not only "found God," but have also used their position as a platform for the expression of their newfound faith and, in some cases, even for proselytism. This continues the rich history of religious imagery in hip-hop music, lyrics, videos, performances, interviews, and promotional materials. While, in some cases, the exploration or invocation of religious symbols and ideas will only occur in the song lyrics or music video, most often the message is crafted into the full sonic, lyrical, and visual package that comprises a given song. Even so, in light of the varied nature of the music industry, some of the following examples, while relevant to the question of religious expression and conversion, will not necessarily have a corresponding video.

Hip-hop is a complex system of interconnected cultures with varying codes and cues. This stems from variables including geography, gender, politics, and religion. As an organizational tool we have developed the following categories to classify the varying forms of religious affiliation and expression in hip-hop. These categories should be understood as representing a starting point for continuing discussion, rather than as a list of rigidly introduced typologies.

Type 1: Religious hip-hop

The overt expression of religious themes, affiliation, proselytism, and praise by rappers who self-identify as either religious/spiritual or part of a defined religious group. This includes:

- Christian hip-hop (e.g., Lecrae, MC Hammer);
- FPN (e.g., Rakim, Wise Intelligent of Poor Righteous Teachers, Masta Killa of the Wu-Tang Clan);
- Judaism/Hebrew Israelites (e.g., Chingy);
- Rastafarianism (e.g., Damian Marley, Snoop Lion[7]).

Type 2: In-group use of religious imagery

Rappers who invoke the imagery (via music—sampling and references, lyrics, promotional artwork, videos, etc.) as a symbol of their faith or upbringing, but in the context of songs that are otherwise non-religious (or where the religious message may not be overt):

- Lupe Fiasco calling out "God is great" at the opening of "Audubon Ballroom" (2013);
- Mos Def, "Fear Not of Man" (1999), opens with the phrase "Bismallah ir Rahman ir Rahim" ["In the name of God, the most beneficent and the most merciful"].

Type 3: Secular use

The overt use of religious language and imagery outside of a faith-based/spiritual context to accomplish aims other than worship or in-group self-identification; for example:

- Claims of status wherein the language and imagery refer to the artists themselves to underscore or increase their credibility. This includes acts of self-aggrandizement and braggadocio. Among more-established figures this can also include a process of autobiographical mythmaking.[8] Examples include:
  - Eminem, "Rap God" (2013);
  - Kanye West, "I am a God" (2013).

- Use of imagery that denotes a connection with a familial or cultural background by an artist who is not known to actively engage with the faith in question:[9]
  - Meek Mill feat. Drake "Amen" (2012);
  - Jay-Z feat. Justin Timberlake "Holy Grail" (2013).

Type 4: Religious seekers

Musicians who appear to explore different faiths as expressed in their public and musical identity; for example:

- Nas (Christianity, FPN);
- Kendrick Lamar (Christianity, Hebrew Israelites).

Religious expression in hip-hop culture is not a one-dimensional construct. Instead, it acts as a microcosm wherein the larger forces of religious expression are distilled through the common tropes of hip-hop norms and subcultural cues.

Contextualizing conversion in hip-hop videos (post-2000)

Examining religious conversion in hip-hop presents some methodological challenges. Lewis R. Rambo and Charles E. Farhadian emphasize that there is no single theory of conversion experience and that the differing theories are influenced by numerous factors, including the field of study that the particular scholar works within.[10] For this study, we have adopted a basic working definition of conversion experience that is largely based on the process theory developed by Rambo.[11] Conversion experience is characterized by a new, renewed, or strengthened association with a religious movement, group, or conviction.[12] This point of adoption or renewal is also understood to follow a period wherein the subject acts as a religious seeker. Conversion experiences are also often associated with periods of crisis (spiritual, personal, emotional, or physical) that lead to the subject questioning their ontological security and attempting to rationalize their worldview. Conversion is a process that occurs over an extended period of time.

It is important to note that the reporting of conversion experience is not necessarily consistent and can encompass a range of perceived processes and outcomes.[13] Christina Zanfagna notes that "Religious conversion was a seismic event in the lives of gospel rappers—an event that sometimes struck suddenly like an earthquake or built up over time as repeated rumblings and aftershocks."[14] While it is true that the classic concept of conversion—Saul on the road to Damascus in Acts of the Apostles chapters 9 and 22—is often understood as a spontaneous event, in reality, there is little to no evidence to suggest this. Instead, as Rambo notes, conversion is consistently a process that may include some form of dramatic event the new believer might point to as a point of conversion.[15]

Quantifying conversion experience is difficult as the data is subjective and relies almost exclusively on self-reporting. As a consequence, it is not possible to state with absolute certainty that someone claiming a conversion experience has actually undergone said experience. A notable example illustrating these difficulties can be found in the figure of Snoop Dogg, who came out with a public claim of conversion to Rastafarianism in 2012.

His conversion was questioned within the Rastafarian community, in particular by Bunny Wailer, an original member of Bob Marley's band The Wailers. In an interview with TMZ, Wailer claimed that the conversion was not genuine, but instead was being used to market a documentary film.[16] Snoop Dogg's recent release of *Bible of Love* (2018), his first gospel album, and recent interviews wherein he self-reports as a born-again Christian would seem to call his conversion to Rastafarianism into question.[17] In addition to the question of conversion, the case of Snoop Dogg also exemplifies the difficulties associated with creating a typology to classify religious phenomena. While it is true that we cannot fully quantify claims of conversion, Snoop Dogg's movement between in-group identification and the serial adoption of cultural cues and practices is representative of the larger notion of interaction with the religious economy/marketplace.[18]

In the following section we present three brief examples that illustrate how rappers have expressed their experience of religious conversion. Although not exhaustive, they provide a range of experiences within the previously mentioned typologies. In addition, they help to frame Kendrick Lamar's recent work within the context of religious imagery and conversion in hip-hop.

DMX's "Lord Give Me a Sign" (2006)

DMX's "Lord Give Me a Sign" is an overt example of religious hip-hop that publicly affirms his beliefs and acts as a tool for the spread of his faith (type 1 above). Looking at the combination of his religious beliefs and personal background, DMX represents the tensions existent in the lives of many hip-hop artists who also have strong faith-based convictions.[19] DMX is known to have fathered fifteen children, many of whom were conceived through extra-marital affairs. In addition, he has had legal troubles throughout his career, having spent time in jail on a number of occasions for convictions ranging from animal cruelty to drug possession and theft.[20] In contrast to this, DMX is currently a Christian deacon and has stated that he has received the call to become a pastor.[21] In relation to the tensions that would seem to exist between his lifestyle and his beliefs, he has said that his time in jail has brought him closer "to realising, to actualising my true calling in life, which is to be a pastor."[22]

"Lord Give Me a Sign" is the second single from the 2006 album *Year of the Dog ... Again*, with a video directed by Marc Klasfield. DMX refers to the song as a conversation with the lord: "I've had a gospel song and a conversation with the Lord on every album."[23] The song begins with an invocation of Jesus ("In the name of Jesus," 0:08), followed immediately by the recitation of a quote from the book of Isaiah 54:17 (0:10).[24] Interspersed throughout the quote of Isaiah, DMX repeatedly says "Preach" in a tone that leaves the listener unclear as to whether he is commanding or being commanded to do so. The interjection of "Preach" is similar to the Black Christian practices of "shouting in the spirit" (on the part of members of the congregation), or "whooping" (a practice whereby the pastor uses various vocal practices to generate excitement).[25] The invective "Preach" then, delivered between lines of DMX's "sermon," is likely best understood as a call and response pattern wherein the artist is acting as both the preacher and the congregation. The call and response format is further reinforced by a live performance from the 2006 BET Awards, during which the DJ performing with DMX acts as a "hype man" engaging in the receptive end of the call and response while also reinforcing the vocals to create a more emphatic tone.[26]

The song opens with staccato 16th notes repeating on a single pitch. The rapid pace and consistency create a sense of urgency, reinforced by the entrance of the vocal line (0:08) with the aforementioned invocation of the name of Jesus, framing the narrative within the context of apostolic/evangelical Christianity, and indicating that what follows is based on the authority of a higher power. The invocation seems to signal the beginning of a process of healing/exorcism wherein Jesus acts in an intercessory capacity. The imagery corresponds directly to the quotation from Isaiah, a messianic text written during the period of the captivity of the Hebrew people in Babylon (586–538 BCE).[27] It is likely being invoked to show an identification between contemporary African-American experiences and the historical oppression of the Hebrews.[28] The video is set "in the wilderness," alluding to the forty years during which the Hebrews wandered following the exodus, prior to reaching the promised land.[29] In a Christian context, DMX also references Matthew 4:1–11, which shows Jesus wandering in the wilderness for forty days and nights and being tempted by Satan, before beginning his ministry. While the connections to the African-American struggle are apparent, identification with Jesus and the struggle with Satan might also signify DMX's own personal and spiritual struggles.

As the video progresses, shots of DMX in the wilderness give way to people wandering on the highway, leaving New Orleans during Hurricane Katrina. These shots are then interspersed with images of a child that has died of AIDS, attack helicopters, flooding, and soldiers in the Middle East. These "signs of the times" illustrate the eschatological worldview adopted by DMX as his faith has strengthened. Hurricane Katrina is seen as a form of domestic tribulation, given the same significance as conflicts overseas and epidemics, to show that he sees himself as living in the end times.[30]

The final section of the song (2:25) features the addition of a gospel choir. The choir first backs DMX's vocals in a new sung passage and is then featured prominently in the texture (at 2:47) singing "ahhh" to accompany DMX's repetition of the passage from Isaiah. The addition of the choir, along with DMX's more urgent lyrical delivery, seems to signify that events, and the need for faith and action, are accelerating. The quote from Isaiah is repeated at the end of the song, now possibly signifying a sense of hope.

From a typological standpoint, DMX falls into the category of religious hip-hop (type 1 above), with the overt expression of religious themes as an in-group participant. From the standpoint of conversion, DMX has not migrated between traditions, but instead has gone through a period (in prison) where he saw his faith strengthened, which is effectively equivalent to conversion experience. We should also note that DMX, while expressing a faith-based identity, exemplifies the tensions faced by hip-hop artists—arrests, drug use, etc.—who are attempting to live within the mores of their faith.

Nas's "Just a Moment" (2004)

"Just a Moment" is the third single from *Street's Disciple* (2004).[31] This song is illustrative of Nas as an artist who is known for exploring spirituality and faith, but without an expressed focus within one religious group. Zanfagna notes that Nas "has stood at multiple religious crossroads. His music evokes the names of Jesus, Jah, and Allah as he positions himself simultaneously as both saint and sinner."[32] While not necessarily an example of religious hip-hop, the album *Street's Disciple* contains imagery overtly related to both Christianity and Islam. The album artwork depicts Nas in a tableau recreating Da Vinci's fifteenth-century painting *The Last Supper*. In this setting, Nas is shown in the role of Jesus, creating the impression that he sees his role as being prophetic or salvific. We see further evidence of both Christian and Islamic influence on several of the album's tracks. Examples of religious imagery on the album include: "Nazareth Savage," a reference to the locale in which Jesus, who Nas associates himself with on the album cover, was raised; "U.B.R. (Unauthorized Biography of Rakim)" recounts the life of Rakim, a member of FPN, which Nas is known to have been associated with at various points in his life; and, "Disciple," which opens with a hook that includes the repeated command to "Prophesy," an ecstatic form of religious expression often observed in African-American evangelical churches. In a 2004 interview, Nas, when asked about his religious background, replied: "I was surrounded by Christians … my grandmothers, all my family was from the South, Baptist. As I got older I got into the 5 Percent Nation, and then that pushed me toward Islam. But I'm not any religion … I know there's a higher power."[33] In this way, much as we will see with Lamar, Nas is best described as a religious seeker who interrogates societal norms and transgressions within his work (type 4 above).

The opening scene of the video for "Just a Moment" shows Nas driving with the radio playing in the background, in the middle of which he calls for a moment of silence. This moment of silence is intended for those close to him who have died, but also expands throughout the track to include rappers who have died through violence or illness, members of the armed forces who will not be returning to their families, and someone passing away in a hospital bed. Throughout, the lyrics, music, and visual images work in unison to evoke a sense of loss and reaction that is openly religious but vague in affiliation. This level of inclusivity is underscored by featured artist Quan, with the line: "Can we please have a moment of peace? For every G that fell for his flag in the streets … Or just for poor righteous teachin'" (1:05). While asking for peace, Quan problematizes gang violence while also referencing the Poor Righteous Teachers, a hip-hop group affiliated with FPN.

The musical underpinning contributes to the atmosphere of remembrance and reflection. The sampled moderate-tempo disco production and lush arrangement of Chic's "Will You Cry (When You Hear This Song)" (1979) is significant in reference to the song's title. It is looped consistently throughout the song and set to a prominent beat while the crackle of the needle finding its groove on a record is featured in homage to old-school hip-hop remembrance and tradition.

Unlike DMX's "Lord Give Me a Sign," the lyrics are not overtly religious, with the exception of references to the Poor Righteous Teachers in verse 1, prayer in verse 2, and verse 3 where Nas raps: "We all fall victims, we all call Christian. Or Islamic faith, to restore our faith" (3:05). Instead, the overarching theme is mourning, remembrance, and respect for those who have died. Even so, the song should be understood within the album as a whole (Last Supper image, other tracks: "Nazareth Savage," etc.) and the imagery employed in the music video. The forms of religious expression portrayed in the video are familiar to the context of urban tragedy. At 0:14, Nas is shown driving past a cemetery where the majority of the headstones are topped with crosses. Following this, the image shifts to a makeshift memorial of the type that is often spontaneously erected at the site of a tragic event (0:21).[34] The acts of mourning continue where Quan raps "Can we please pour out some liquor," while the video shows the act of pouring liquor onto the ground (0:33). Much like the items left at the makeshift shrine, this act of pouring libations is an offering to the deceased and can be interpreted as a form of ancestor worship. In verse 3, Nas mentions both Christians and the Islamic faith, while the scene shifts to a group of men kneeling around a photograph, with their hands clasped in prayer (3:07).

The imagery in the video, with the exception of the cemetery scene, is not specific to any one faith tradition. Instead, the video explores the universal themes of mourning and loss, from a perspective that is inclusive of the common humanity experienced among adherents of different faiths. As such, particularly when viewed within the context of the album, the video reinforces Nas's identity as a religious seeker.

The Game's "Holy Water" (2012)

The Game's album *Jesus Piece* (2012) reflects the tensions that exist in post-conversion rap narratives.[35] Released following his Christian baptism, the concept album pairs religious imagery with mainstream hip-hop norms (guns, strippers, drugs, and material wealth). The Game said of the album: "Jesus Piece gives me an opportunity to speak about situations that people like me who love God but are still street and still wanna remain themselves … You can still have your Ciroc in the club, it's just a faith thing and making sure you try to do right."[36] The album cover features an enthroned image of The Game based on a stained glass image of the Sacred Heart of Jesus.[37] In this image, The Game/Jesus is depicted holding the sacred heart, wearing a red bandana over his face associating him with the Piru Crips and a blinged out Jesus Piece around his neck. In addition to the signs of wealth and gang cred, the other major alteration to the original image is the insertion of two circular panels above his head showing, on the left, a palm tree with a city-scape in the background, and, on the right, a palm tree with an ocean background, both of which situate the image within the context of the US west coast, particularly Los Angeles.

The song "Holy Water" illustrates the thematic approach taken on *Jesus Piece*. The song dropped on November 4, 2012 as part of The Game's weekly online "Sunday Service" series, to promote the album release.[38] It opens with a sampled vocalization of dubstep artist Mala's song "Changes" (2007), which creates an ethereal atmosphere. Solo male and female voices alternate with the sustained vocable "ah," which is treated to a high level of both echo and reverb. The effect mimics the aural impression of a large space, possibly a church.

The song lyrics are rife with religious imagery but reinterpreted within the context of hypermasculine hip-hop norms.[39] We see this immediately with the opening of the chorus and the lines: "My phantom so mean / Like I washed that motherfucker every Sunday in Holy Water" (0:14). The lyrical intersection of hood and religious imagery continues throughout the track. The same juxtaposition is played out in the video, perfectly capturing the tension and The Game's intention to marry the public expression of his beliefs and the portrayal of his lifestyle. The imagery includes washing his Rolls Royce (0:15), repeated shots of the Jesus piece (0:05), and focus on a woman's explicitly displayed glutes being "baptized" in "holy water" (0:31).

"Holy Water" and the album *Jesus Piece* exemplify the tensions that exist between hip-hop's accepted norms and the adopted mores of religious converts. The Game has stated that the album is meant to express how he negotiates his faith within the context of his lifestyle and career. From a typological standpoint, "Holy Water" presents a problematic case as it does not, at first reading (due to the overt use of sexual imagery, etc.), appear to fit cleanly into the categories presented. Keeping in mind that religious devotion is subjective, and individual expression is not necessarily a rigid construct, we would argue that this song and video should be classified as religious hip-hop (type 1), showing a clear intention on the part of The Game to create an expression of his faith.

The three case studies discussed represent a very small part of the broad landscape of religious affiliation and expression in hip-hop. The examples cited show a divide in public and personal life, and in the manner in which artists negotiate that tension in their work while also employing imagery associated with their faith. Nas and DMX explore socially conscious themes—Nas with subtle references to Christian and Muslim practices and DMX with an overt call to worship—in their music while balancing hip-hop norms and religious mores in their personal lives. In contrast, The Game confronts these tensions, acknowledging that he is living in two different worlds with competing behavioral expectations.

We now turn to a case study of religious themes on Kendrick Lamar's 2017 album *DAMN.*, with particular focus on the music video "HUMBLE." While a comprehensive album study is beyond our current scope, an overview of the central lyrical, visual, and musical themes on the album will situate Lamar's position within our typological framework. This will illustrate how Lamar and his collaborator Dave Free (The Little Homies) have used the music video as a medium to engage in societal-level commentary while expressing and exploring Lamar's identity as a religious seeker.

Kendrick Lamar: Call of the Prophet

Kendrick Lamar gained mainstream attention with his 2012 album *good kid, m.A.A.d city*.[40] He has been praised for innovative flows, lyrical mastery, his musical revival of "vintage" hip-hop, mainstream revival of conscious hip-hop, and interrogation of racial politics.[41] In particular, *To Pimp a Butterfly* (2015)[42] contained highly charged messages about racial politics, and the song "Alright" was adopted as an anthem of the Black Lives Matter movement.[43] Lamar's work has consistently engaged with religious themes. The song "Faith" (2009), the use of the "Sinner's prayer" to open *good kid, m.A.A.d city* (2012), and the song "I" from *To Pimp a Butterfly* (2015) all exemplify Lamar's identification with spirituality and belief in God. Expressions of faith have also become part of his public persona, including announcing his baptism during Kanye West's Yeezus tour,[44] and dressing as Jesus Christ for Halloween in 2014, stating: "If I want to idolize somebody ... I'm gonna idolize the Master."[45]

Followers have liberally applied the terms savior and messiah to Lamar based on his skill, innovation, and contributions to the genre.[46] Beyond this, we suggest that neither term accurately describes the product of Lamar's mythic identity. Instead, considering his interrogation of societal transgressions, concern for social justice, subjectively ascetic image, and overt and systematic use of religious imagery, we suggest that Lamar's identity within the hip-hop community is that of a prophet. Our understanding of Lamar's prophetic identity is based on his place in hip-hop lineage as well as the biblical understanding of the prophet's role. The Hebrew word for a prophet ("navi") is derived from a Semitic word meaning to call. A prophet is one who is both called by God and calls out. The role of the prophet is not necessarily to predict future events, but instead to act as a messenger and to interrogate contemporary political and religious events and transgressions.[47] A common trope throughout prophetic narratives (beginning with Moses)[48] is that the would-be prophet struggles with their calling prior to accepting their role. Lamar's struggles as a religious seeker, and possible convert, embody a contemporary journey that is akin to that of the prophets of Israel. While publicly exploring his faith, Lamar has self-identified as being called, either by God, or to spread the word of God. Concerning the album *DAMN.*, he says:

> I feel it's my calling to share the joy of God, but with exclamation, more so, the FEAR OF GOD ... I love when artists sing about what makes Him happy. My balance is to tell you what will make Him extinguish you ... I briefly touched on it in this album, but when he tells me to react, I will take deeper action.[49]

Lamar's quote about bringing not only the joy of God, but also His righteous condemnation, shows an embodiment of the classical prophetic archetype whose role was not so much to interpret or prophecy concerning future events, but to interrogate the contemporary political or religious climate.[50]

These themes are interrogated throughout the concept album *DAMN.*, wherein Lamar grapples with personal and societal demons while constructing a cycle of sin, redemption, and prophecy. Because of the very deliberate design of the album's message, it is imperative that the analysis of any one song or video is not performed in isolation, but rather in dialogue with the other tracks. Even before being exposed to the lyrics and visual imagery, the audience is confronted by the rhetoric of sin and redemption in the titles and ordering of the tracks. The conceptual framework of the tracks can be expressed as *transgressions* ("BLOOD," "PRIDE," "LUST," and "FEAR"), *virtues* ("LOYALTY" and "LOVE"), and *lineage and religious/prophetic identity* ("DNA," "YAH," "GOD," "DUCKWORTH," "ELEMENT,"

"FEEL," and "XXX"). Overall, *DAMN.* leads us through an introspective cycle expressing Lamar's struggles as a religious seeker. The vices (blood, pride, lust, and fear) represent those elements of personal or societal crisis that Lamar appears to be confronting. The confrontation and condemnation come in the form of heavy pronouncements of both judgment and redemption in the songs "LOYALTY" and "LOVE." Finally, the cycle of sin and redemption (largely informed by Deuteronomy 28) is guided by Lamar's own continuing quest of identity formation.

Hebrew Israelite influence on *DAMN.*

DAMN. was released on April 14, 2017 (Good Friday), coinciding with Passover. As a life event, the release of *DAMN.* represents a possible turning point for Lamar, who has become increasingly associated with the Israelites United in Christ (IUIC), part of the Hebrew Israelite movement. This organization is an African-American revival movement founded on the belief that the true descendants of the twelve tribes of Israel are the African-Americans, Latinos, and Native Americans. They are part of a larger trend of African-American religious movements that have distanced themselves from participation in "mainstream" Christian worship, due to elements of belief that they see as inconsistent or contradictory. Evolving in a context of systematic oppression and institutionally reinforced racism in the United States, these movements rebelled against the idea that, in some circumstances, Christianity could justify slavery.

Many of these movements understand their own circumstances in light of the books of Exodus and Deuteronomy, respectively describing, first the captivity and release of the Israelites (Exodus), and then the condemnation of the Israelites for being unfaithful and sinning (Deuteronomy). Ultimately, the Hebrew Israelite movement is a syncretic religion, blending elements of Judaism and Christianity with a fundamental group identity that is formed through the direct identification with another historically oppressed people.[51] What we see on the album *DAMN.* appears to be expressive of Lamar's struggle in coming to terms with some type of conversion experience, likely guided, at least in part, by his cousin Carl Duckworth, a member of IUIC who has spoken publicly about teaching Lamar.[52] The most frequently cited lyrical connection to the Hebrew Israelites can be found on the track "YAH." The name of the track is derived from the Hebrew name for God, a similar form of which, "Jah," is used in Rastafarian tradition. The chorus of "YAH" features the repeated calling out of the name of God, while verse 2 refers directly to his cousin and the book of Deuteronomy: "My cousin called, my cousin Carl Duckworth. Said know my worth. And Deuteronomy say that we all been cursed." The inclusion of these elements, wherein Lamar identifies himself as having contact with the IUIC, while exhibiting familiarity with their interpretation of Deuteronomy, would be indicative of contact or dialogue with the ideas of the movement, but not necessarily conclusive evidence of conversion. Most striking, however, is Lamar's direct statement earlier in verse 2 ("I'm an Israelite, don't call me black no more),", which, in the context of the album, and knowing Lamar's history as a religious seeker, likely speaks of a turning point in his self-conception.[53]

Religious imagery in "HUMBLE" (2017)

"HUMBLE," the first single released from the album (March 30, 2017), was met with immediate success, becoming Lamar's first solo track to reach #1 on the Billboard *Hot 100*. The video is rife with religious imagery and is representative of the complex intertextual network that Lamar weaves on the concept album.[54] While the song's title is in itself explicitly suggestive of the religiously charged virtue of humility, there are a number of other prominent themes, both sacred and secular, pervading the lyrical and visual content. Lyrical themes include: a claim to status (skill and wealth); starting out poor and working his way to the top; and a warning to other rappers to be humble about their own accomplishments and status. Musically, "HUMBLE" opens with a solo record scratch before launching into a driving, distorted riff that then settles into a hypnotic trap-style beat featuring a low-end piano riff. The visual imagery employed is complementary to the lyrical and musical message. Throughout the video (directed by Dave Meyers and the Little Homies), Lamar engages with a combination of recognizable religious images and themes that are broadly related to the landscape of African-American belief and experience.[55] Given that the musical, lyrical, and visual elements of the audiovisual text work together to convey meanings, we will discuss key elements of the song and video as they unfold (rather than presenting a separate analysis of music, lyrics, and images).

The video opens with the ultimate representation of institutional religious imagery in the form of Lamar appearing in pope-like robes (Figure 18.1). Lamar takes the form of the highest earthly authority, a position in which he is conspicuously alone. He stands, at first

Figure 18.1 Opening scene of Kendrick Lamar's "HUMBLE" (0:00).

with his head bowed, in a large space with high ceilings and ornate doors, where a shaft of light is seen entering through the windows, signifying contact with the divine.[56] The picture presented is one in which Lamar receives some form of divine inspiration. We see Lamar standing with his head bowed as the opening title and credits appear on the screen. The silence is broken with the screech of a record scratching (0:06), punctuated by an accented open 5th (A♭ and E♭). The distorted pitches are accented on the first two quarter notes of the bar (set in common time), and are featured prominently in the texture, alternating as Lamar delivers a vocal call, playing a total of four times before the full backing texture enters (0:14). This opening line is delivered as a call to prayer or worship: "Wicked or weakness / You gotta see this."[57] The repeated interrogation of wickedness and weakness on the album could be a simple question of why he (or others) indulge in the various vices that are explored across the concept album. We might also consider it in relation to his potential conversion to the IUIC faith and Lamar's own interpretation of biblical prophecy, in particular the book of Revelations.[58] Regardless, this opening visual, musical, and lyrical sequence frames the video in a religious context.

Another significant moment that draws on visuals, music, and lyrics in the representation of religious themes occurs leading into the song's chorus (0:58). Lamar is featured in the center of a congregation of bald men dressed in identical black clothing (Figure 18.2). By placing himself in the center, in the same garb as the others, Lamar underscores his own humility and identifies as one of the people. The image of Lamar in the midst of this "congregation" coincides with the catchy hook, featuring repeated iterations of the phrase "Sit down bitch, be humble." The delivery of the hook is where we see differentiation between Lamar and the other men as he leads the call and response. At the start of this section, Lamar is the only one with his head up while the others are all standing in a posture of humility with their eyes lowered. Upon completing the phrase "There's levels to

Figure 18.2 Lamar amidst his congregation (0:59).

it, you and I know" and as he repeats "Bitch, be humble," he lowers his gaze to match the humble posture of his fellows while others in the crowd take turns raising their heads as they respond with "hol' up" (1:05). Musically, the call and response works with the visual imagery to create an association with African-American religious traditions and practices while not necessarily claiming a direct connection to any single tradition.[59]

At 1:14 we see the image of the congregation shift to Lamar and his "disciples" recreating Da Vinci's iconic painting, *The Last Supper*, with Lamar in the center telling the figure to his left to sit down and be humble (Figure 18.3). While there are only six apostles represented in the video (versus the twelve in Da Vinci's painting), the figure being addressed by Lamar might be understood as a conflation of the apostles Thomas (the doubting Thomas of the Gospel of John 20:24–29) and James the son of Zebedee (who asks to be enthroned next to Jesus in the Gospel of Mark 10:35–45), both of whom are rebuked by Jesus in the biblical narratives for a lack of humility. This identification underscores the idea that nobody is above a lesson in humility, even those possessing fame and status.

The directed commandment of humility begins in the final line of verse 1 with a reference to Meek Mill's song "Levels" ("It's levels to it, you and I know"). This is followed by the repeated line "Sit down … be humble," an intertextual reference to Big Sean with whom Lamar has shared some public animosity. Lamar stirred up controversy with his verse on Big Sean's "Control" (2013), in which he called out eleven other rappers (including Big Sean) and stated: "I got love for you all, but I'm trying to murder you niggas."[60] Lamar and Big Sean have continued to make jabs at one another through their song lyrics, including the promotional single for *DAMN.*, entitled "The Heart Part 4," which appears to reference their animosity. Fans and critics made note of the line: "And crush ya whole lil' shit / I'll Big Pun ya punk-ass, you a scared lil' bitch."[61] "Lil' bitch" is considered to be Big Sean's signature ad-lib, occurring on many of his tracks.[62] This reference, combined with Lamar's

Figure 18.3 Recreation of the Last Supper (1:17).

repeated "Sit down, lil' bitch" in the chorus of "HUMBLE," provides a potential target for Lamar's message of humility.

The intertextual connection between the chorus and the work of Big Sean is further reinforced by the backing singers' repetition of "hol' up, hol' up." Big Sean's "Marvin and Chardonnay" (2011) features an almost identical rhythmic repetition of "hol' up," which, combined with the use of the signature phrase "Lil' bitch," underscores the conclusion that Lamar is referring to Big Sean while offering a more general comment on humility within hip-hop culture. The musical elements then, taken with the lyrical content, imply that Lamar's prophetic interdictions and critiques are intentionally targeted at his peers and contemporaries.

The larger visual landscape of the video displays an overt reflection on different spheres of religious and political influence. These include: *institutional/hierarchical* imagery, *iconic* imagery, and *grassroots or revivalist* imagery. In addition to the already discussed use of *institutional* (Lamar dressed in the cope in the "cathedral") and *iconic* imagery (Da Vinci's Last Supper), the video also uses *grassroots and revivalist* imagery to tie together the various spheres of influence that Lamar, as a successful hip-hop artist and media personality, operates within.

From a *grassroots* perspective, the video includes a combination of protest and preaching. At 1:30, immediately following the Last Supper, the scene shifts to Lamar wearing a white hooded sweatshirt that says "Dreamer" surrounded by figures in black whose heads are covered in rope (Figure 18.4). They are shown in front of a series of shipping containers from which a similarly attired audience observes the proceedings. In this frame, Lamar and his "disciples" have their heads engulfed in flames but are not being burned.[63] There are several possible interpretations for this imagery. Politically, the flames may signify the many people worldwide who have self-immolated to protest against foreign occupation of their countries.[64] From a religious standpoint, and continuing the theme of humility, the flames may indicate divine inspiration (halos), and following the Last Supper scene,

Figure 18.4 Flames of divine inspiration (1:41).

be meant to show Lamar and his followers experiencing the descent of the holy spirit, emulating one of the foundational events of Christianity.[65] In addition, the image is abstract enough that it could also be intended to inclusively signify divine inspiration, a motif that has historically been depicted through the illustration of flames surrounding the head of the enlightened individual.[66]

In addition to imagery that is overtly religious, the video for "HUMBLE" contains numerous congregational scenes (*grassroots/revivalist*). These images include the aforementioned scene of call and response (0:58), two cyphers (flaming heads at 1:30, under the bridge dressed as Steve Jobs at 1:56), and finally, a crowd of men gathered on the stairs of what appears to be a church or temple (Figure 18.5). The figures depicted are male and dressed formally in black suits and ties. While many interpretations are possible, we suggest that the image is meant to depict a congregation, likely a group associated with the Nation of Islam. The imagery used in the video for "ELEMENT," from the same album, reinforces this assertion. "ELEMENT," directed by Jonas Lindstroem and the Little Homies, takes inspiration from the iconic civil rights era photography of Gordon Parks. Throughout the video, viewers are confronted with recreations of Parks's photographs, often in the same setting, but sometimes with minor stylistic and politically motivated variations. Of note is that the video contains congregational images depicting members of the Nation of Islam at 0:46 (a group of women, dressed all in white, featuring Elijah Muhammad's daughter Ethel Sharrieff, also at 2:57) and 1:41 (Nation of Islam, Fruit of Islam training). With this context in mind, the group on the steps in the "HUMBLE" video is reminiscent of Gordon Parks's photograph, *Black Muslims Rally* from 1963.[67]

What contributes to the effectiveness of the religious imagery, and the congregational images in particular, is that they are vague enough that they can be interpreted as representative of a number of traditions, including Nation of Islam, Five Percent Nation, Hebrew Israelites, or black Protestant Christianity. The album and imagery have been strongly informed by the Hebrew Israelite tradition. Even so, the imagery in the video

Figure 18.5 One of the congregational scenes from "HUMBLE" (2:27).

does not lead to identification (through mode of dress, religious symbols, gathering place, etc.) with any one group. Instead, the visual imagery shows engagement with the African-American community as a whole, interrogating political, economic, and religious questions and concerns in which they find common ground. In this way, Lamar is portrayed, not only as being engaged, but also in a guiding role for his community. This is reinforced through the repeated references to Deuteronomy 28, which inform the listener of two key issues: first, the contemporary African-American experience in the United States as being akin to the Israelites wandering in the desert post-exodus (but pre-arrival in the promised land), and that if need be God will keep his people in the desert; and second, that Lamar is engaging with the Hebrew Israelite movement on the level of their scriptural beliefs, not necessarily implying conversion, but still showing a direct influence of the movement on his work.

This brief exploration of Lamar's album *DAMN.* provides insight into how the artist has made use of various mediums (music, lyrics, video, and interviews) to reinforce his positioning in a prophetic or messianic role (attributed to him by others), while also publicly working through his own struggles with faith, identity, and worldview.

Conclusion

Lamar's use of religious imagery and themes, as well as his (possible) experience of religious conversion, are not unique among hip-hop artists. Even so, there is a range of variation concerning how and why artists employ the language, imagery, and symbols of faith in their work. In the case studies explored above, the videos of both DMX and The Game have the common purpose of professing and promoting their engaged devotion to Christianity. In this way they both fall under the classification of religious hip-hop (type 1), while engaging with the expectations and mores of their faith traditions in an absolutely divergent fashion: DMX is apocalyptic, calling attention to societal ills; The Game explores the intersection of Christian faith and the hip-hop lifestyle. The case study of Nas's "Just a Moment" moves into the realm of conscious hip-hop, with limited and subtle references to religious movements that have significance within an African-American urban context. By engaging with more than one religious group, Nas reinforces his role as a religious seeker (type 4), someone who holds to a form of faith or belief without publicly professing their personal association with any one group.

The aforementioned artists have all undergone some form of religious transformation that is then put on display in the form of song lyrics and music videos for the general public to consume and comment on. As we have discussed, religious expression and conversion experience in hip-hop culture are not anomalous. There is a long tradition in rap that invokes a confession of faith (Lecrae, Poor Righteous Teachers, etc.) as well as the use of religious symbols (the Jesus Piece and the FPN medallion) that act as both expressions of devotion and identity, as well as symbols of status. What becomes unique with each artist is how they choose to negotiate meaning within their faith tradition while also mitigating the tension between the competing elements of vice and virtue in their lives.

Notes

1   Lewis R. Rambo, *Understanding Religious Conversions* (Newhaven, CT: Yale University Press, 1993); Lewis R. Rambo and Charles E. Farhadian, "Conversion," in *Encyclopedia of Religion*, 2nd ed., vol. 3., edited by Nicholas Jones (Detroit, MI: Macmillan Reference, 2005); Christina Zanfagna, *Holy Hip Hop in the City of Angels* (Oakland, CA: University of California Press, 2017); Ines W. Jindra, *A New Model of Religious Conversion: Beyond Network Theory and Social Construction* (Leiden: Brill, 2014).

2   Anthony B. Pinn, *The African American Religious Experience in America* (Westport, CT: Greenwood Press, 2006); Anthony B. Pinn, *Varieties of African American Religious Experience: Toward a Comparative Black Theology* (Minneapolis, MN: Fortress Press, 2017); Andre E. Key, "Toward a Typology of Black Hebrew Religious Thought and Practice," *Journal of Africana Religions* 2, no. 1 (2014): 31–66; Merrill Singer, "Symbolic Identity Formation in an African American Religious Sect: The Black Hebrew Israelites," in *Black Zion: African American Religious Encounters with Judaism*, edited by Yvonne Patricia Chireau and Nathaniel Deutsch (New York: Oxford University Press, 2000), 55–72.

3   Kendrick Lamar [album], *DAMN.*, B0026716-02 (Top Dawg Entertainment, Aftermath Entertainment, Interscope Records, 2017).

4   We understand music videos as multimodal texts, where "the individual domains of words, music, and images work together—in mutually reinforcing ways—to be culturally productive and constitutive of the social realm." Lori Burns, "Multimodal Analysis of Popular Music Video: Genre, Discourse, and Narrative in Steven Wilson's 'Drive Home,'" in *Coming of Age: Teaching and Learning Popular Music in Academia*, edited by Carlos Xavier Rodriguez (Ann Arbor, MI: University of Michigan Press, 2017), 82.

5   See Felicia Miyakawa, *Five Percenter Rap: God Hop's Music, Message, and Black Muslim Mission* (Bloomington, IN: Indiana University Press, 2005).

6   Zanfagna, *Holy Hip Hop*, 9.

7   We have listed Snoop Dogg as Rastafarian due to his self-reported conversion experience and the expression of this identity on the album *Reincarnated* (2012). He has since come out as a born-again Christian, identifying with his reported faith on the album *Bible of Love* (2018).

8   For a discussion of autobiographical mythmaking in hip-hop see Lori Burns and Alyssa Woods, "Rap Gods and Monsters: Words, Music, and Images in the Hip-Hop Intertexts of Eminem, Jay-Z, and Kanye West," in *The Pop Palimpsest: Intertextuality in Recorded Popular Music*, edited by Lori Burns and Serge Lacasse (Ann Arbor, MI: University of Michigan Press, 2018), 215–251. For a discussion of Jay-Z's negotiation of religious themes see Michael Eric Dyson, "God Complex, Complex Gods, or God's Complex: Jay-Z, Poor Black Youth, and Making 'The Struggle' Divine," in *Religion in Hip Hop: Mapping the New Terrain in the US*, edited by Monica R. Miller, Anthony B. Pinn, and Bernard "Bun B" Freeman (New York: Bloomsbury, 2015), 54–68.

9   Monica Miller observes that there "are definitely cultural expressions that are of familial inheritance of particular aspects of religion … They use the language that they are at home with to make certain points about their own human interests." Cited in Vincent Funaro, "Religion in Hip-Hop: Reconciling Rap and

Religion," *Christian Post*, October 26, 2012, https://www.christianpost.com/news/religion-in-hip-hop-reconciling-rap-and-the-gospel-83980.

10 Rambo and Farhadian, "Conversion." For an overview of the possible limitations of previous theories on conversion experience see Jindra, *A New Model*, 7–10.

11 Rambo lays out a seven-stage sequential process of religious conversion as follows: (1) context, (2) crisis, (3) quest, (4) encounter, (5) interaction, (6) commitment, and (7) consequences. See Rambo, *Understanding Religious Conversions*, 16–18. While our working definition is very close in scope to that of Rambo, it would be useful to take into account the work of Jindra who defines "conversions as changes in a person's religious beliefs that can happen suddenly or gradually. These changes are accompanied by an alternate view of reality and of self, and in general also entail a 'reconstruction of one's biography.'" Jindra, *A New Model*, 10.

12 Jindra, *A New Model*, 10.

13 Ibid., 10–11.

14 Zanfagna, *Holy Hip Hop*, 4.

15 Rambo, *Understanding Religious Conversions*, 5.

16 TMZ, "Snoop Lion Rejected by Bunny Wailer & Rastas," TMZ.com, January 23, 2013, http://www.tmz.com/2013/01/23/snoop-lion-snoop-dogg-rejected-bunny-wailer-rastarians-reincarnated.

17 Lisa Bowman, "Snoop Dogg Responds to Critics Slating His Move into Gospel Music," *NME*, March 31, 2018, https://www.nme.com/news/music/snoop-dogg-responds-slating-move-gospel-music-stellar-awards-2277514.

18 Rodney Stark, "Economics of Religion," in *The Blackwell Companion to the Study of Religion*, edited by Robert Alan Segal (Malden, MA: Blackwell, 2006), 47–67.

19 Robert Tinajero observes that DMX has "openly and discursively embodied a struggle between a 'gangsta' lifestyle and a life of spirituality." Robert Tinajero, "Hip Hop and Religion: Gangsta Rap's Christian Rhetoric," *Journal of Religion and Popular Culture* 25, no. 3 (Fall 2013): 326.

20 Katherine Weber, "Rapper DMX Reads Bible Verses to Struggling Fan on Los Angeles Street," *Christian Post*, October 14, 2013, https://www.christianpost.com/news/rapper-dmx-reads-bible-verses-to-struggling-fan-on-los-angeles-street-video-106611.

21 DMX, "Interview with KSAZ-TV," Fox Phoenix, 2009, https://www.dailymotion.com/video/x818gf.

22 Ibid.; Eric Young, "Rapper DMX Says Life Calling Is to Be a Pastor," *Christian Today*, January 19, 2009, https://www.christiantoday.com/article/rapper.dmx.says.life.calling.is.to.be.a.pastor/22333.htm.

23 DMX [album], *Year of the Dog … Again*, 82876 87866 2 (BMG, 2006). DMX, interview with Dr. Phil, *Dr. Phil Show*, Oprah Winfrey Network, March 19, 2013, https://www.youtube.com/watch?time_continue=16&v=9s1BMAVLGS8.

24 "'No weapon formed against you shall prosper / And every tongue which rises against you in judgment / You shall condemn. This is the heritage of the servants of the Lord / And their righteousness is from Me,' Says the Lord." Isaiah 54:17 New King James Version (NKJV).

25 For insight into the development and purpose of African-American preaching style, see Grace Sims Holt, "Stylin' Outta the Pulpit," in *Signifyin', Sanctifyin', and Slam Dunking: A Reader in African-American Expressive Culture*, edited by Gena Dagel Caponi (Amherst,

MA: University of Massachusetts Press, 1999 [1972]), 331–347; and Erica R. Britt, "Talking Black in Public Spaces: An Investigation of Identity and the Use of Preaching Style in Black Public Speech," PhD dissertation (University of Illinois at Urbana Champaign, 2011).

26   DMX, "Lord Give Me a Sign (Live)," Facebook, February 28, 2016, https://www.facebook.com/dmx/videos/1090625524347200.

27   Ben Witherington III, *Isaiah Old and New: Exegesis, Intertextuality, and Hermeneutics* (Minneapolis, MN: Fortress Press, 2017); John J. Collins, *Introduction to the Hebrew Bible* (Minneapolis, MN: Fortress Press, 2014), 325–344.

28   A useful discussion of Isaiah and its interpretation within a Christian context can be found in Witherington, *Isaiah Old and New*, particularly chapters 4 and 5 which discuss the eschatological context.

29   During the Babylonian Exile, the Hebrew people developed a concept of "exile and return" and a cyclical understanding of history wherein their contemporary struggles were understood in light of the bondage in Egypt and the exodus event. There was the expectation that God would send a Messiah to act as an intercessory figure and free them from captivity.

30   The identification between the contemporary African-American experience and the tribes of Israel will be explored further in relation to the Hebrew Israelite movement and Kendrick Lamar.

31   Nas [album], *Street's Disciple*, C2K 92065 (Columbia, 2004).

32   Zanfagna, *Holy Hip Hop*, 133.

33   The Associated Press, "Nas: The Mature Voice of Hip-Hop," *Today*, January 4, 2005, https://www.today.com/popculture/nas-mature-voice-hip-hop-wbna6786474. This interview is also remarked upon by Zanfagna, *Holy Hip Hop*, 133.

34   While there is no imagery in this scene locating the shrine within a particular religious tradition, the shrine includes candles and a picture. These devotional items are generally used in conjunction with prayer for the salvation of the soul of the deceased in a Christian context.

35   The Game [album], *Jesus Piece*, B0017791-02 (DGC Records, Interscope Records, 2012).

36   John Kennedy, "V Exclusive! Game Catches The Holy Ghost With New Album Title," *VIBE Magazine*, August 12, 2012, https://www.vibe.com/2012/08/v-exclusive-game-catches-holy-ghost-new-album-title.

37   The image by artist Mike Saputo is based on the Sacred Heart of Jesus imagery that is often associated with the Society of Jesus (Jesuits).

38   "Holy Water" was a leftover track that was not originally included on the album.

39   For further discussion of hypermasculine hip-hop norms, see Marc Lafrance, Lori Burns, and Alyssa Woods, "Doing Hip-Hop Masculinity Differently: Exploring Kanye West's '808s & Heartbreak' Through Word, Sound and Image," in *The Routledge Research Companion to Popular Music and Gender*, edited by Stan Hawkins (London and New York: Routledge, 2017), 285–299. For further discussion of gangsta rap narratives, see Eithne Quinn, *Nuthin' But a "G" Thang: The Culture and Commerce of Gangsta Rap* (New York: Columbia University Press, 2005).

40   Kendrick Lamar [album], *good kid, m.A.A.d city*, B0017534-02 (Aftermath Entertainment, Interscope Records, 2012).

41   See Christopher R. Weingarten, "Review: Kendrick Lamar Moves from Uplift to Beast
Mode on Dazzling 'Damn.,'" *Rolling Stone*, April 18, 2017, http://www.rollingstone.
com/music/albumreviews/review-kendrick-lamar-damn-album-w477376; and Maura
Johnston, "Kendrick Lamar's *DAMN*. Proves He's the Most Important Rapper in
America," *Time*, April 17, 2017, http://time.com/4741238/kendrick-lamar-damn-review
for representative reviews of the album.

42   Kendrick Lamar [album], *To Pimp a Butterfly*, B0022958-02 (Top Dawg Entertainment,
Aftermath Entertainment, Interscope Records, 2015).

43   A widely circulated image of Lamar performing "Alright" at the BET Awards on June 28,
2015 in Los Angeles reflects the politics of the album. Atop a police cruiser, he raps: "And
we hate Popo, wanna kill us dead in the street for sure." Molly Beauchemin, "Kendrick
Lamar Performs 'Alright' at the BET Awards," *Pichfork*, June 28, 2015, https://pitchfork.
com/news/60163-kendrick-lamar-performs-alright-at-the-bet-awards.

44   Lamar has undergone "two baptisms, the first at 16 and 'again in my 20s'—just for that
reassurance and belief in God." Lisa Robinson, "The Gospel According to Kendrick
Lamar," *Vanity Fair*, June 28, 2018, https://www.vanityfair.com/style/2018/06/
kendrick-lamar-cover-story.

45   Maud Deitch, "Exclusive: Kendrick Lamar Sings Taylor Swift's 'Shake It
Off,'" *Fader*, November 4, 2014, http://www.thefader.com/2014/11/04/
kendrick-lamar-interview-halloween-taylor-swift.

46   For example, Jessica Hopper, "Kendrick Lamar: Not Your Average Everyday Rap Saviour,"
Spin Magazine, October 9, 2012, https://www.spin.com/2012/10/kendrick-lamar-not-
your-average-everyday-rap-savior; and Caspian Kang, "Notes on the Hip-Hop Messiah,"
New York Times, March 24, 2015, https://www.nytimes.com/2015/03/24/magazine/notes-
on-the-hip-hop-messiah.html.

47   Examples of prophets being called in biblical narratives include: Isaiah 6:40, Jeremiah 1,
Ezekiel 1–3, and Amos 7. These passages provide examples of the personal convictions
that motivated the prophets of Israel.

48   As Moses is called by God in Exodus 3 and 4, he repeatedly questions his worth as
a leader to bring the Hebrew people out of Egypt. This resistance to being called is a
common theme in prophetic narratives.

49   Brian "Z" Zisook, "Kendrick Lamar Responded to Our Article About
His Fear of God," *DJBooth*, April 28, 2017, https://djbooth.net/
features/2017-04-28-kendrick-lamar-god-response.

50   See Collins's discussion of Isaiah, Micah, Nahum, and Zephaniah in *Introduction to the
Hebrew Bible*, 325–347.

51   For further discussion of the Black Hebrew Israelite movement see Key, "Toward a
Typology." On the larger context of African-American religious expression see Pinn, *The
African American Religious Experience*, 20.

52   Duckworth has posted updates to this effect on both Twitter and Facebook. There is also
a video posted on YouTube by the IUIC wherein Duckworth discusses teaching Lamar:
Jewelz Malachi, "The Israelites: Cousin Carl Duckworth Breaks the Silence on Kendrick
Lamar," posted May 20, 2017, https://www.youtube.com/watch?v=0gN2f3Mi96k.

53   We see a foreshadowing of Lamar's possible conversion on DJ Khaled's 2016 track "Holy
Key" where he raps "I don't wear crosses no more, Yeshua's coming back."

54   For example, see Althea Legaspi, "Watch Kendrick Lamar's Richly Symbolic New 'Humble' Video," *Rolling Stone*, March 31, 2017, https://www.rollingstone.com/music/music-news/watch-kendrick-lamars-richly-symbolic-new-humble-video-109039; and Brad Wete, "Kendrick Lamar Exposes the Fake to Encourage the Real in 'Humble' Video," Billboard, March 31, 2017, https://www.billboard.com/articles/columns/hip-hop/7744412/kendrick-lamar-humble-video-exposes-fake-encourage-the-real.

55   This would include reactions to the US history of slavery and oppression, and the evolution of movements such as Black Protestant Christianity, Nation of Islam, FPN, and the Hebrew Israelite movement.

56   The video was filmed in Los Angeles' famous Park Plaza Hotel (now known as The MacArthur).

57   The words "wickedness or weakness" are significant in the context of the concept album, as they are the opening lines sung by guest artist Bēkon on the album's first track "BLOOD." The opening lyrics of the "HUMBLE" video are altered from the album: "Nobody pray for me / It's been that day for me."

58   In a 2015 interview, Lamar references the *Book of Revelation*, chapters 7 and 8, stating: "This is the Rapture. This is God comin' back and you're hearin' the horns and the skies crackin' open." Gabriel Alvarez, "Kendrick Lamar: The Rapture," interview with Kendrick Lamar, *Mass Appeal*, April 28, 2015, http://archive.massappeal.com/mass-appeal-issue-56-cover-story-kendrick-lamar. While this quote predates the release of "HUMBLE," one might interpret the silence, followed by the open 5ths, as representing the silence in the wake of the opening of the seventh seal in Revelation 8:1, which is followed with thunder, lightning, and an earthquake (Revelation 8:5), before the seven angels blow the trumpets that bring about the destruction of the earth.

59   Call and response is a common trope within various forms of religious expression that fall under the umbrella category of Black Protestant Christianity. For further discussion see Gillian R. Richards-Greaves, "'Say Hallelujah, Somebody' and 'I Will Call Upon the Lord': An Examination of Call-and-Response in the Black Church," *The Western Journal of Black Studies* 40, no. 3 (2016): 192–204.

60   Earlier in the verse, Lamar made the bold claim: "I'm Makaveli's offspring, I'm the king of New York / King of the Coast, one hand, I juggle them both," before calling out many of his contemporaries, including Drake and Big Sean. While this type of braggadocio is common in hip-hop, the reaction to his verse led to an ongoing feud with Big Sean.

61   See Khal, "How Kendrick Lamar and Big Sean's Relationship Went Wrong," *Complex*, March 25, 2017, https://www.complex.com/music/2017/03/big-sean-kendrick-lamar-relationship-timelinefor a discussion of Lamar's and Big Sean's interactions.

62   It can be heard, for example, at the beginning of Big Sean's track "I Don't Fuck with You" (2015), and in Big Sean's verse on Lil' Wayne's "My Homies Still" (2013).

63   In hip-hop culture, the scene depicted would be a cypher (spontaneous delivery of rapped verse, without a backing track, in a group setting). At 1:57 we see another cypher, this time under a bridge. In this case, Lamar is engaging with a different type of worship, wearing a black turtleneck and adopting poses that mimic Apple co-founder Steve Jobs. This may be a commentary on the mythical status and cult-like following that Jobs had during his lifetime.

64   The Buddhist practice of self-immolation as a form of protest began in 1963 with the martyrdom of Thich Quang Duc, a Buddhist monk who burned himself to death in

the middle of a busy street in Saigon. He did this to protest against the persecution of Buddhists on the part of the South Vietnamese government. In the intervening years, approximately two-dozen Buddhist monks in Tibet have self-immolated in a similar manner. May 2018 also saw the self-immolation of a Palestinian protester in Gaza.

65 The Pentecost event is related in the Acts of the Apostles, chapter 2, where the spirit is said to descend on the apostles like tongues of fire (Acts 2:3), and is understood as the missionary foundation point for many Christian denominations. Mike Martinez S.J., writing for the *Jesuit Post*, refers to the scene as "resembling some dystopic Pentecost." Mike Martinez S.J., "Taking a 'Long, Loving Look' at Kendrick Lamar's Disturbingly 'Humble' Hip-Hop," *Jesuit Post*, April 14, 2017, https://thejesuitpost.org/2017/04/taking-a-long-loving-look-at-kendrick-lamars-disturbingly-humble-hip-hop/#fn-16632-6. Special thanks to Dr. Sally Hickson for pointing out the resemblance to the painting by El Greco entitled Pentecost (*c*.1600), wherein the apostles are portrayed with flames above their heads, representing divine inspiration.

66 There are a number of Persian illuminated manuscripts depicting the Prophet Muhammad as being either engulfed in flames or with the flame of divine inspiration surrounding his head. A prime example is the medieval Persian illustration of Muhammad leading the earlier prophets in prayer. See Barbara Hanawalt, *The Middle Ages: An Illustrated History* (New York: Oxford University Press, 1998), 36. We also see depictions of the Buddha with his head surrounded by flames in reference to his "fire miracles."

67 The Gordon Parks Foundation [photograph], *Black Muslims Rally* (New York, 1963), http://www.gordonparksfoundation.org/archive/black-muslims-1963.

19

Nicki Minaj's "Anaconda": Intersectional Feminist Fat Studies, Sexuality, and Embodiment

Anna-Elena Pääkkölä

In this chapter I employ approaches from audiovisual studies of music videos and feminist popular music studies to examine Nicki Minaj's music video "Anaconda" (2014).[1] This video, in combination with the cover art for the "Anaconda" single release, sparked public debate over a number of critical issues in contemporary society. Critics found her attire too lewd or pornographic, with the main objection being the visual prominence of her buttocks. In her Twitter feed, Minaj responded by posting images of similarly attired white women from the cover art of the glossy periodical *Sports Illustrated*, along with the comment, "Angelic. Acceptable. LOL." She then compared these images to her cover art with the text "UNACCEPTABLE" all in capital letters.[2] One of my goals with this study is to examine this perceived double standard more closely and to ask how it is connected to a cluster of attitudes and prejudices about women of color and their bodies in popular culture today.

In recent years, "Anaconda" has become a prime object of study in popular music studies and gender studies, especially in light of its potential for intersectional analysis.[3] More specifically, Minaj's video invites commentary on the following intersectional issues, implying that each of these issues influences the others, and the construction of socio-cultural meanings depend on their mutuality: the negotiation of womanhood, femininity, and sexuality in an era of third-wave feminism when expressive actions can be subjected to harsh scrutiny and contested in relation to "progressive" content; ideals of beauty and appropriate behavior as constrained by racially demarcated norms; and, hitherto largely neglected, questions about the relation of body size, especially fat bodies, to both of these issues in the context of audiovisual popular performances. With these priorities in mind, the music video and its reception raise critical questions about how body size is equated with sexual desirability, and how ideas of "proper" femininity vary greatly when applied to white and black female bodies. Precisely because it addresses so many elaborately intertwined critical questions, "Anaconda" has been the subject of several scholarly studies. Stan Hawkins approaches the video in terms of the spectacle it affords from a queer musicological angle;[4] Lori Burns and Alyssa Woods discuss it as an instance of self-empowering feminist parody;[5] Barbara Bradby approaches the song as an example of "phallic girl pop" that mixes attributes of feminine and masculine sexualities;[6] while Katariina Kyrölä's interpretation draws on approaches from the field of media studies to situate the video as a statement of black feminist pride.[7] In my analysis, I seek to extend these existing discussions, while also responding to the controversy surrounding the music video by demonstrating the pertinence of intersectional feminist thinking in scholarly discussions of this video. "Anaconda" shines a spotlight on popular culture's (and popular music's) current obsession with female bodies, (constructed) blackness, sexualized performance, and "fat asses," as they are knowingly called in the song's lyrics, issues that reverberate deeply in everyday social interactions, as evidenced by the social media attention that surrounded the video's release. My primary concerns are distilled in the following questions:

- How might intersectional feminist issues be discussed in reference to Nicki Minaj's sexualized performance in "Anaconda"?
- How do Nicki Minaj's actions in the music video, together with those of her creative team, articulate sexual agency?[8]
- How does the song and music video reproduce and respond to existing interventions to do with "black pride" and "fat pride"?

In seeking answers to these questions, I draw on critical perspectives from queer musicology,[9] research on audiovisuality,[10] black feminist studies,[11] and critical fat studies.[12] This particular combination of approaches, especially a fat studies perspective on popular music studies, extends existing debates in ways that should be of value to future critical inquiry. Such a discursively rich music video, I would argue, calls for an equally multifaceted reading that is capable of revealing intricacies and apparent contradictions. This is best achieved by using a broadly interdisciplinary approach. My analysis of Minaj's music video attends to music, lyrics, and corresponding visual images, which are understood in reference to ongoing debates in popular culture and critical scholarly research.[13] In order to shed light on the significance of Nicki Minaj's body in "Anaconda," I will introduce several perspectives on the song and video text.

Intersections of gender, sexuality, race, and body in Minaj's "Anaconda"

I begin with a close reading of the post-chorus of "Anaconda," which is a direct quotation from Sir Mix-a-Lot's music video for "Baby Got Back" (1992), as this section of the song and video crystallizes many of the issues that are the main focus of my analysis. Already here, the entanglement of race and body is expressed as a central theme in the song's lyrics;

the prominent line is spoken rather than sung and rhythmically accentuated (1:18–1:33; see Table 19.1). A female voice repeats the line: "Oh my gosh, look at her butt," but altered with each repetition by pitch shifting and the manipulation of formants to give the impression of a distorted masculine voice and a piercing feminine voice that both castigate Minaj. This section of the song (the post-chorus) references the "Baby Got Back" music video's prologue, which features two conservatively dressed white women who express dismay at the spectacle of an amply endowed black woman who sways in time with the music in a manner that emphasizes both her blackness (a spotlight effect on her bright yellow dress contrasts sharply with the darkness of her dimly lit legs and shining black hair) and her exaggerated feminine sexiness (her crouching position, hip movement, the tightness of the dress, and a low camera angle all accentuate her curves). In this influential example of hip-hop expression featuring a leading black rapper—Sir Mix-a-Lot—the audioviewer is encouraged to consider race as a factor in the white women's contempt for the black woman's body. Body shape and size are also significant factors here, as evidenced by the intentional focus on the dancer's "butt" in the lyrics and in the music video treatment. In Minaj's variation on this theme of disparaging white commentary, instead of just one body participating in fetishizing display, Minaj positions herself and four dancers in a formation

Table 19.1 Song structure of Nicki Minaj's "Anaconda."

Song part	First lyrics	"Baby Got Back" bass riff	"Anaconda" riff	Rapping speed	Key instrument
Intro	My Anaconda don't		x	Follows riff	Synthesizer
A	Boy toy named Troy	x		Lax	Bass
B	Btw, what he say	x		Quick	Clapping rhythm
Chorus	My Anaconda don't		x	Follows riff	Synthesizer
Post-chorus	Oh my gosh			Follows beat	Boom bass
A	This dude named Michael	x		Lax	Bass
B	Btw, what he say	x		Quick	Clapping rhythm
Chorus	My Anaconda don't		x	Follows riff	Synthesizer
Post-chorus	Oh my gosh			Follows beat	Boom bass
Extended post-chorus	Little in the middle			Rhythmic	Synthesizer
Chorus	My Anaconda don't		x	Follows riff	Synthesizer
Post-chorus	Oh my gosh			Follows beat	Boom bass
Bridge	Yeah he love this fat ass	x		Free to rhythmic	Bass
Chorus 2	I got a big fat ass		x	Follows riff	Synthesizer
Outro	(Instrumental)	x		None	Rhythm section

suggesting black female solidarity rather than a spectacle of otherness. Her dancers are dressed in baby-doll style: pink and white matching items with torn and faded denim shorts, bright colored sneakers, and cheap-looking plastic jewelry. The dancers alternate in their movements between putting on airs and provocative twerking, inviting onlookers to watch their performance of sexualized dancing that is rife with countercultural meanings, while confronting the gaze in direct address, head on—a point I shall return to later. The combination of white chairs and an entirely white floor and background combine with post-production techniques to make the dancers' bodies appear noticeably whiter than in the video's other scenes, suggesting parodic whiteness, but also the strategy of inserting black bodies into a traditionally white setting (see Figure 19.1).[14] This strategy is familiar from Minaj's earlier work, where she explicitly parodies white femininity using similar visual means.[15]

The entanglement of racialized images of women with depictions of heightened sexuality is longstanding in the West, but more specific questions are raised by the depiction of black women as sexual agents and/or objects. The stereotyping of black women is pervasive, with many feminists—black and white alike—expressing misgivings about media images of the sexualized black female body,[16] which can become "controlling images"[17] that serve to restrict the public visibility of black women. It is precisely the sort of sexualized display found in "Baby Got Back" that is held to be the most damaging in this respect, with critics arguing that it regulates not only black but also white female sexuality. Diane Railton and Paul Watson discuss the black female "butt" as it emerged in Victorian health discourses, where the sizeable posterior was held to be a trait distinguishing black women from white women, and situating the former as sexually available objects while branding, oppositionally, the latter as sexually subdued, coy, and in need of protection.[18] Are performances of black female sexuality that emphasize large bottoms inevitably "pre-racialized," and does such positioning invariably reproduce harmful binary stereotypes? Or is there room for feminist positioning and agency in representations of black sexuality? These questions, posed by Railton and Watson, are at the heart of my discussion here.

Figure 19.1 Post-chorus of "Anaconda" showing Minaj and four dancers in their "white" attire (1:19).

Much of the third-wave black feminist writing is critical of the assumption that black women have internalized, and are now simply regurgitating, white people's racist historical imagination in their sexualized actions. For Aph Ko, this implies that, supposedly, "there is no imagination outside of the white imagination … [and] black women can't envision themselves beyond the constructions that white people created."[19] Wendy Burns-Ardolino, for her part, makes a case for understanding female big buttocks as a sign of pride and self-assertion rather than abjection, while calling for the de-stigmatization of the negative connotations.[20] This area of theory opens up new possibilities for understanding Minaj in a different light, which is the starting point for my reading that pays close attention to the details of the video and their entanglement with the critical issues I have hitherto identified. Minaj's goal appears to be to celebrate her body as sexually empowered, while firing back at critics, whose voices are projected onto the "white girls" in the video's parodic staging of whiteness. This parodic treatment extends to the music in the references that are made to Sir Mix-a-Lot's song.

Let's return to the post-chorus of "Anaconda" (1:18–1:33) to consider some expressive elements in the musical domain. The track is dominated by a booming bass sound that extends to sub-bass depths. The looped sample of the "white girl" phrases from "Baby Got Back" is repeated three times, with distorted and pitch-shifted layers added to the original on the second repeat. This pushes the original voice higher, transposing it to a register that does not conceal its technological construction. The last bars of the post-chorus simply repeat the looped line "Look at her butt" twice, the first of which drops the melody by a distorted, low-register octave. This pushes the text into the domain of parody, implying "dual consciousness of the listener"[21]—consciousness both of the original and its new setting in Minaj's song. Recalling the judgmental white gaze of the original song and the confusion voiced by the two white women when confronted by the spectacle of black female sexual embodiment, Minaj uses the discrepancy between the two texts—borrowed and new—to position herself as a pro-sexuality black feminist. I interpret the song's auditory treatment of the incorporated spoken text as a means of stripping the "white voice" of its authority, rendering it unnatural and non-human. It is not accidental that Minaj manipulates the pitch of the original sample, as voice pitch is richly invested with social connotations, ranging from dominance and submissiveness to authority, politeness, and deference.[22] By pitch-shifting elements of the original song, the terms of the original are reconfigured, resulting in a remix of "Baby Got Back" that "take[s] pre-existing material and make[s] it different while also trying to keep the spectacular aura of the original in order to attain allegorical legitimation."[23] The pitch-shifting is not necessarily intended as gender-bending or queering,[24] but rather it is a means of making the voice a strange one,[25] and, at the same time, stealing authenticity from the original voice, denying its gender role, and depicting its subjects as grotesque, possibly also comical, "non-women." As the material is manipulated, its lyrical content becomes abstract, the pitch-shifted vocals and engulfing sub-bass turning the music into a form of auditory spectacle, which essentially erases the linguistic content of the spoken passage in "Baby Got Back," making it invalid and meaningless. Minaj and her dancers are performing their choreography in a wide-angle shot, with Minaj positioned closest, in the center, maintaining eye contact with the camera and using her chair as a prop while leering at viewers with an attitude of apparent boredom or just going through the motions—as in a dance rehearsal. Her performed "white voice space" is stripped of authority and, by extension, the ideals of white femininity are rendered invalid.[26]

Fat studies and sexuality in music videos

In the field of critical fat studies,[27] scholars have raised questions about the fat body, discourses of acceptable and unacceptable bodies, and the social repercussions of these attitudes. These scholars are currently formulating new ways of thinking about fat bodies that have nothing to do with the more familiar notions of equating thinness with health, success, and happiness, and fatness with illness, failure, and unhappiness. While excessive skinniness may be frowned upon, fat bodies are constantly branded as undesirable and unaesthetic in the public imagination.[28] Fat studies scholars start from the premise that images of bodies create complex fields of power that circulate and regulate social and cultural values about shape, size, and weight; as Deborah Lupton argues, "the human body is a complex admixture of biology, society and culture."[29] Fat studies scholars aim to disentangle and dismantle the connections between fatness and the presuppositions that are often attached to this category in order to allow fat people to function better in society. Because obesity is commonly associated with failure and social ostracism, fat people are commonly excluded, snubbed, and discriminated against.[30] Extending this discussion in an intersectional direction, multiple studies have shown that body size has a greater impact on women's bodies than men's, because fat men are still privileged as men, and women's appearance and body policing have a stronger impact on their social and personal lives.[31]

Fatness is more readily associated with black women's bodies than white women's bodies in the mainstream popular imagination, to the point that African-American women in the United States report fewer experiences of body oppression and confess to preferring the aesthetic of a larger body size.[32] But, if fatness is culturally constructed as a failure of lifestyle choice, as over-indulgence, or as a lack of self-control, then an extension of fat phobia to black women reveals a deep-seated social construct (perhaps mostly dictated by white discourses of the body) that reaffirms racist stereotypes. According to Kwate and Threadcraft: "moral panic around body size is likely to be particularly acute for Black women, who are already stereotyped as excessive, slothful and dependent on the state."[33] Body size, in this view, is indeed a contributing factor in the production of controlling images, which depict black women as different and inferior to white women.[34] Paradoxically, body size is seen as both desexualizing and hypersexualizing black female bodies.[35] Hypersexualization can shape the stereotype of black female sexuality as insatiable and being an uncontrollable threat to white men; since the lazy (because fat) black body is not keen on working, to sell this body for sexual favors becomes a sign both of the compliant black woman's "moral bankruptcy" and her "moral degeneracy."[36] Furthermore, for black females, "[media] depictions of fatness are not only common, but are central to whom characters are constructed to be."[37]

In short, fat black women represent a threefold lack: they are not men, they are not quite as desirable in their femininity as white women, and they are certainly not as desirable as thin women. Fat black women concretize "excess," but, at the same time, they symbolize "lack" when compared to dominant ideals of white femininity.[38]

Numerous examples from popular media show how black and Latino women construct counter-narratives that resist white ideologies of body shape.[39] It could be argued that Minaj in "Anaconda" negotiates the "excess/lack" continuum through her own hypervisibility, which Nicole Fleetwood describes as "conceptualizations of blackness as simultaneously invisible and always visible, as underexposed and always exposed."[40] Minaj's hypervisual performance in the music video articulates the excessive performance of fleshiness as "a performative that doubles visibility: to see the codes of visuality operating on the (hyper) visible body that is its object."[41] Furthermore, Minaj unabashedly valorizes her own posterior in parts of the video, revealing dominant social constructs while, at the same time, reveling in a display of black fatness that turns into a twerking extravaganza. Hansen and Hawkins perceive the sexualized performance of black female artists in music videos as "reappropriat[ing] sexual images" in order to claim space and regain control of their sexuality through a specific strategy of hyperembodiment.[42] Minaj's body and its fetishistic mediation provide support for the idea that, as Hansen and Hawkins put it, "the black female body is always troubling to dominant visual culture and its troubling presence can productively *trouble* the field of vision."[43] The prevalent view in dominant discourses of body size ideals is that thin bodies are more easily thought of as embodying containable, and therefore also culturally appropriate, expressions of sexiness, while other bodies seem to fall outside of this category in varying degrees, depending on their intersectional statuses (skin color, but also age, health, and disability). Sexual performances by fat bodies therefore "reveal … their fleshy materiality" as well as being "revealing of contemporary discourse about embodiment."[44] When discussing fat burlesque performers, D. Lacy Asbill claims that these go against the popular demand for the thin, sexual body: "burlesque performance redefines the fat body as an object of sexual desire and as a home to a desiring sexual subject."[45] "Anaconda" casts Minaj and her dancers as slithering snake-like around a jungle set[46] in an erotic display of their bodies, but with continuous signs of agency and skill. Setting aside for a moment the obvious phallic association of the male sex organ with the song's "anaconda," female bodies and snakes have a long shared history in audiovisual representations. Clips in early cinema's "cinema of attractions" frequently show female bodies gesturing and undulating when performing "snake dances," thereby conflating female bodies, female sexuality, exoticism, and bestiality.[47] This primitivism and the bestial nature of (especially black) female sexuality are then flaunted in Minaj's music video to such an extent that the imagery becomes kitsch.[48] I would further argue the video turns the kitschyness of its setting into a suspended arena of impossibility, the uncanny,[49] and fat pride.

In the sonic realm, Minaj develops a dialectic space; in addition to the "white voice" sample from "Baby Got Back," we hear instances of "auditory excess" that could include Minaj's use of her chest voice, fast rapping, and—of special significance—her raucous laughter (3:27–3:30).[50] While Minaj's body is present in a variety of shots in the song's

B section, concomitant with the lyrics "I'm missing no meals" followed by "he love my sex appeal" (0:56–1:10), the overall intensity of both the rapping and the visual editing grows. The bass riff[51] continues but is drowned out by added percussion, accentuating the beat on strong beats, and female shouts of "hey!" on the backbeat (an 8th note before the downbeat). Minaj's solo twerking on "missing no meals" is intensified by the use of a handheld camera shaking along with her buttocks, accentuating the physical gesture and contributing to "visceral feelings of sensuality" that are often encountered in pop videos.[52] The twerking of Minaj and her dancers intensifies along with the beat, and girl-on-girl eroticism is suggested through grinding movements while the lyrics tell of heterosexual mating rituals. A skull with a speaker in its mouth watches on,[53] implying an emasculated voyeuristic presence, while the girls line up to grab each other's buttocks and arch their backs in sync with Minaj's "dum-du-du-dum-dum du-du-dum-dum." This is perhaps the singer's indirect take on Emilíana Torríni's "Jungle Drum" (2009), in this instance not coyly assigning the jungle drum to the heart ("My heart is beating like a jungle drum, ba-da-dum du-dum du-dum du-du-dum dum"), but to the ample bottom (Figure 19.2), becoming a significant point of reference also later in the song (to be discussed below).

After the B section, a rhythmic drop-out leaves room for the chorus featuring a sample from Sir Mix-a-Lot's "Baby Got Back," with the vocals re-recorded by the original artist: "My Anaconda don't … buns, hun." As the beat stops and a synthesizer mimics the rhythms of Sir Mix-a-Lot's rapping, the on-screen images become rhythmically more subdued, but visual effects implying movement have been added in post-production. On a downbeat, we see a bottom shaking upwards ("don't," 1:12); a quickly revolving zoom-in and zoom-out centered on Minaj is synchronized with a whiplash sound on the fourth beat (1:13–1:14). Minaj lip-syncs to "don't want none" as the girl-on-girl eroticism is again played out, and a visual segue to the next section starts with a dancer throwing herself into the splits. The final sound of the chorus is an alarm sound, synced to start with the upward movement of another twerking backside, which remains suspended impossibly in midair, only descending with the resumption of the following section (1:17–1:18).

Figure 19.2 Minaj (second from the left) and her three dancers (1:07).

The suspension of the buttocks in mid-motion upwards is of particular interest in light of what follows—the "white girl" voice appropriation, which disdains the big (black) "butt." In a way, the spectacle not only of twerking fat buttocks, but of never-descending ones, produces an uncanny effect: the posterior assumes an impossible, elevated state of being, while also becoming a visual spectacle that invites horrified glances from the weight-intolerant, fat-phobic gaze. As fat bodies are usually kept out of sight and made invisible, the scene emphasizes the "over-visibility" of fat: when visible, fat invokes a state of "too much" embodiment, sexuality, space, and encourages affective reactions.[54] What makes the spectacle uncanny is the fat phobia of the onlooker: arguably, the twerking releases the wobble of the fat bottom, and at the moment when the fat-phobic's attention is drawn to what they fear, it is left suspended, unruly, and ungoverned by gravity. The fat booty remains for a while in its liberated, agentic, uplifted state. Similarly, the lyrics of the chorus toy with this fleshy spectacle, stating "don't want *none*," but presumably, "prefer too much over none." Minaj's lip-syncing of this particular lyric is worth attending to: while she adopts Sir Mix-a-Lot's voice, toying with gender roles,[55] she also disavows the "no-*thing*-ness" ("don't want none") of skinny body ideals and the supposed lack of "excess" body fat in favor of "*some*-thing-ness" ("buns, hun"): the fleshy, excessive spectacle of her own body. Black body pride is asserted before white female criticism is permitted to express its disapproval.

Auditory excess: Sounding the butt

As a sexual object, the posterior is possibly one of the most profane due to its associative connotations with non-mainstream, non-reproductive sex practices. Fabrício Silveira[56] reads Minaj's music video as "anal terrorism,"[57] based on the philosophical formulation of Beatriz Preciano, according to which the anus is "the damned and stigmatized organ," a primarily privatized bodily sphere, the overt exhibiting of which is considered to "display … a lack of politeness and good manners."[58] Silveira uses a string of pejorative terms, calling her music performances in the music video "lascivious dance," "gaudy," "self-annulation," "unappealing," and "overflowing."[59] Silveira's reading exemplifies prevalent cultural notions apropos the bottom; the "booty," let us not forget, is most closely aligned with fat, black (and Latina) bodies. Viewed through a discursively white lens, this sexualized body part can easily become hyperbolic: "the more protruding a woman's butt is, the more hypersexualized she becomes."[60] In this way, the black and sexualized "protruding butt" crosses a discursive line into inappropriateness, sexual excess, and hence, profanity: a disgusting "too much" or state of bodily "excess" that is easily dismissed as "unappealing." Inseparable from this are questions of class: the "hip-hop booty" is discursively rooted in working class sensibilities—those of ("ghetto") black women especially—which stigmatize the booty as "classless" and "nasty."[61]

Hip-hop's appreciation of the sizeable body is equated with authenticity: a fat body is a strong, formidable one. Joan Gross writes of the fat/phat bodies of hip-hop artists, mostly men, as acceptable and respectable, but the back-up dancers, mostly women, are less often encouraged to be fat.[62] But the big "booty" can function as a symbol of authentic black femininity in hip-hop texts.[63] Closer attention must be drawn to twerking, or the isolated movement of the hips in a mock-erotic way. Kyra Gaunt has written of twerking performed by young black girls on YouTube as "context collapse," implying competing discourses of black and white understandings of twerking, its meaning and history overlapping in a loose virtual community where "stigmatized and stereotypical views of musical blackness, childhood adolescence, and black girls' sexuality can overshadow first-hand local means of twerking. It is far easier to generalize all black girls who twerk by stigmatizing their social play as too 'black' or 'ghetto,' as 'ratchet' or 'thots' (*them hos over there*), and falling back on the stereotype about rap music as unsophisticated, egocentric nonsense, or a fad."[64]

Minaj's twerking is about more than a gesture to "stir the anaconda"; it is a practice with deep historical roots extending back to African dance cultures, not to mention a two-decade history in hip-hop culture.[65] Twerking and the "big butt" in motion are therefore densely packed with cultural significance. Twerking represents an embodied skill and "kinetic orality" that are closely intertwined with the rhythmic texture of the music.[66] Gaunt describes twerking as "auto-sexuality,"[67] a self-expressive form of erotic display in which the dancer's own viewing and kinesthetic pleasure are paramount. As such, twerking is as much about sexual embodiment, autonomy, and subjectivity as it is about erotic display (see Figure 19.3). But, since twerking implies context collapse between its black cultural meanings and narrower and more stereotyped white misconceptions, it actively participates in reproducing racial and gender ideology, extending to slut-shaming and racist commentary, as evidenced in the reception of "Anaconda" following its release.[68] Jennifer Nash critiques readings of sexualized black performances as "always-already" negative and racist.[69] Instead of thinking in terms of injury and wound, Nash interprets black women in pornography through queer theorist José Muñoz's term "ecstasy,"[70] which prioritizes possibilities and pleasure, while indicating separation from the self and temporality. Nash claims that ecstasy, with its connotations of Lacanian *jouissance*, provides an alternative way to interpret racially marked sexual imagery.[71] Seen through this lens,

Figure 19.3 The spectacle of twerking as auto-sexuality (0:23).

Minaj's auto-eroticized twerking becomes the will to oppose standardized (male/white) concepts of feminine beauty and sexuality. Minaj's music video thereby becomes a vehicle for carnivalized performance, a state of queer ecstasy where the possibility of experiencing pleasure in your own body, outside the demands of a fat-phobic and racist society, is brought to the fore: breaking expectations, laughing at stereotypes by exaggerating them to the point of ridicule, and, to top it all, celebrating who and what you are.

Minaj expresses *jouissance* not only through the visual spectacle of the moving "butt," but through an intricate web of audiovisual factors to do with embodiment and auto-eroticism. The multiple close-ups of Minaj and the dancers twerking emphasize "the surface of ... object[s] rather than (plunging) into ... depth," encouraging viewers to discern texture more than form.[72] They are not there simply to provoke male desire or disgust in the paranoid eye of fat-phobics. Paired up with other shots and framings, the close-ups toy with intimacy and eroticism as well as hypervisuality and "excess." Furthermore, close-ups of the twerking are edited into unnatural rhythms to synchronize with the beat of the music, accelerating to sixteenth notes in a sudden gesture. Natural fleshy movements could not keep up with the music, but with edited twerking movements this is possible. Editing trickery emphasizes the dancing aspect of the twerking gesture, but also differentiates it from the other visuals, making it more visible and audible. Editing the rhythm of the "jiggle" to the music attracts the gaze, but also dismantles the possibility of pure fetishization, because the visible flesh moves in time with an abnormal rhythm. It is Minaj and the dancers (and the video's editors) who decide on the rhythm and the movements of the buttocks to conform to the formal qualities of the music, and not the "natural" rhythm of the body, emphasizing agency and pleasure through motion that is synchronized with music.

The final scene of the video treats the bridge and outro of the song to a markedly different setting: Minaj dances in a blue-lit room for Drake, in what I think of as an extended lap-dance sequence (see Figure 19.4). Of particular interest here is the superimposed drum rhythm, which syncopates over the top of the regular four-on-the-floor beat while Minaj performs to an admiring male onlooker. It is here that the embodied feel of the

Figure 19.4 Minaj performing lap-dance choreography with Drake (3:43).

bouncing bottom is audiovisually accentuated—this time not in fetishizing close-up, but from a distance adjacent to the male viewer (Drake), with his eyes fixated on the motion. The added drum pattern could be understood as a take on "the booty clap,"[73] originally a snare sound in trap hip-hop, which was designed to mimic the sound of a stripper's buttocks slapping against each other or on the ground. Justin Adams Burton calls the booty clap, usually placed on the second and fourth beats, "an instrumental element that signals heteronormative hyper-masculinity."[74] In "Anaconda," however, the booty clap is treated as a form of sonic parody and appropriation, emphasizing Minaj's agency and pleasure rather than those of the drooling onlooker. Instead of a steady on-the-beat event, the playful syncopation of the drum dismantles any hypermasculinity that could be attached to the beat,[75] and by extension, Drake's leering presence. The tight bounce of the added drum sound in particular creates a sonic impression of firmness, bounciness, and resonance, which when combined with images of the buttocks in motion, turns the twerking "butt" into a drum itself.[76] Minaj's earlier "dum-du-du-dum-dum" resounds here in the music, emphasizing the influence of Torríni's "Jungle Drum": its beating, and the beating of the heart, become Burton's booty slap. Sonic reference is made to sexual pleasure: just as you strike a drum, you might also strike the bottom in playful spanking. The drum sound even suggests what this spanking might feel like: your hand would bounce off Minaj's butt while producing the sound of a beating drum (as in the "Mickey Mousing" effects used in classic cartoons).[77] This playful spank is precisely what Drake attempts to do, but he is immediately thwarted by Minaj as she pushes his hand and exclaims "hey!," suggesting a final important point about agency. The only person to play this drum, or slap this booty, is Minaj herself, which reinforces Gaunt's point of twerking being a form of "autosexuality,"[78] or Asbill's claim about fat burlesque redefining the fat body as a sexual subject.[79] It is precisely these intermodal effects that construct the music and the images as fleshy.

"My Anaconda don't": Closing remarks

The controversy surrounding Nicki Minaj's "Anaconda" is exemplary of many interrelated points of tension that still circulate in current discourses on popular music and culture: namely, misogyny, racism, fat shaming, and the policing of women's sexuality. But we might also see Minaj's song and music video as articulating a state of ecstasy, bravely confronting the aforementioned issues in the music world and society at large. The music video in this instance becomes a safe space where outside criticism cannot be heard, or where it is heard only to the extent that it is mediated or re-voiced with an attitude of contempt; it is a rampant jungle of embodied pleasures that include sexualized encounters and toys with queer desire.

The recognition of "Anaconda" as an empowering black feminist performance may not be quite so straightforward, however, mostly because of the video's enormous erotic and soft-porn appeal to a mainstream audience that crossed boundaries of "race" and ethnicity, resulting in "Anaconda" becoming one of the most viewed videos of all time on YouTube.[80] The story of events that took place at the Las Vegas Madame Tussauds gallery is telling. Here a wax figure that portrayed Minaj on her knees, dressed in the clothes she wore in "Anaconda," was continually violated by members of the public, with men performing gestures of fellatio or penetration on the wax doll.[81] Whenever sexuality is performed in an explicit way, even when the actions are obviously performative and intended to afford emancipatory meanings, these intentions will always be lost on certain members of the public, whose position of privilege in varied contexts of reception remains unchallenged. From publicly shaming her bottom to dry humping a replica of it, from the standpoint of a position of privilege, the default corresponding position for black (and white) women in the public eye still remains one of "public ownership."[82] The mistreatment of the Madame Tussauds wax doll evidences the fact that Minaj is walking a thin line, in danger of "becom[ing] fetishized to the extent that she has become devoid of her own meaning and filled with the dominant culture's desire for the mythical, spicy, exotic other."[83] This highlights the need for more nuanced discussions of this subject that are prepared to look beyond the "noisy" themes of moral outrage and incendiary commentary that have characterized some discussions both in the popular media and academic debates. Minaj's self-reflexive agency, underlined both in the video and her unabashed promotion of her music on social media platforms, seems often to be overlooked in academic discussions. Assumptions that female sexual display automatically signals female sexual availability need to be refuted once and for all, and the answer is not to limit the range of actions available to female performers—who otherwise demonstrate control and agency—by ruling out overtly sexual actions, simply because these might be interpreted as objectifying by certain viewers.

Minaj's video incited a number of feminists and academics to comment on the display of black female sexuality. bell hooks called Minaj's video "boring,"[84] implying that she was disappointed at the regurgitation of images of black female sexuality, which for her offered nothing that was new. Silveira similarly ruminates on the wasted potential of Minaj's display of her buttocks, in which she did nothing so risky that it could be thought of as transgression.[85] In his view, the video is a "risky exercise of empowerment" based on "self-deprecation" and "not leaving one's own allocated place, not offering overt alternatives." Silveira observes an "epistemic mistrust"[86] in the music video: while the artist and the music video claim to be empowering and feminist, they manage only to reformulate a phallocentric order of feminist empowerment, based on hypersexuality, (neo)capitalism, and hyperfeminization.[87] The context of hip-hop, a stereotypically masculine genre, heightens the probability of reading the video as catering to male expectations about black female sexuality.[88] Reiland Rabaka admits that the close connection of hip-hop feminism with sexist imagery is problematic, and looks for more subtle hues of feminist discourse in hip-hop texts, which I consider to be present in Minaj's song: "By critically studying and participating in hip hop culture, hip hop feminists bring their intimate knowledge of hip hop to bear on the ways in which patriarchy plays itself out within the world of hip hop and the wider sociocultural world. Contradictory and controversial … hip hop feminism challenges both hip hop *and* feminism."[89]

The challenge presented by Minaj to bell hooks and her other critics is, simply, that of the power femme; by demonstrating humor and laughter[90] as strategies for black and fat feminist empowerment; or, as Hansen and Hawkins so aptly put it, "through a flamboyancy that is subversive and teasing, intended to delight and revolt."[91] Self-determination is another relevant factor. A student pointed out to me that all of the above readings are, in fact, "hogwash," as Minaj "isn't really fat." What my otherwise observant student failed to recognize, however, is that I am not the one calling Minaj fat. What makes the field of fat studies a valid area of study is the fact that Minaj not only calls her "butt" fat, but she knowingly makes it a site of spectacle while doing so. A quote from Sarah Ahmed might be helpful here: "When you become a feminist, you find out very quickly: what you aim to bring to an end some do not recognize as existing."[92] To deny that Minaj's body is "fat" is to unknowingly demonstrate how deeply ingrained fat phobia is. Not unlike claiming that gender or race do not matter, to debate what a fat body *really is* in these circumstances is tantamount to making the fat body invisible, as opposed to openly discussing fat bodies and the discourses surrounding them in the public eye. Aside from answering specific questions relating to Minaj's music video and its cultural context, a goal here has been to show the value of approaches from critical fat studies, combined with intersectional feminist theory, when it comes to discussing music videos that foreground themes of embodiment and sexuality.

Notes

1   Nicki Minaj, "Nicki Minaj—Anaconda," YouTube video (4:51), official music video, directed by Colin Tilley, posted by "Nicki Minaj," August 19, 2014, https://www.youtube.com/watch?v=LDZX4ooRsWs.

2   See Derrick Clifton, "5 Important Lessons about Sexism from the Slut-Shaming of Nicki Minaj's NSFW Artwork," mic.com, July 2014, https://mic.com/articles/95268/5-important-lessons-about-sexism-from-the-slut-shaming-of-nicki-minaj-s-nsfw-artwork#.Nu6uZ7ShX.

3   Intersectional feminism focuses on how different axes of signification "shape power differentials, normativities and identity formations and co-produce inequalities." Noortje van Amsterdam, "Big Fat Inequalities, Thin Privilege: An Intersectional Perspective on 'Body Size,'" *European Journal of Women's Studies* 20, no. 2 (2013): 158. See also Patricia Hill Collins and Sirma Bilge, *Intersectionality* (Cambridge: Polity Press, 2016).

4   Stan Hawkins, *Queerness in Pop Music: Aesthetics, Gender Norms, and Temporality* (New York: Routledge, 2016), 112–123.

5   Lori Burns and Alyssa Woods, "Humor in the 'Booty Video': Female Artists Talk Back Through the Hip-Hop Intertext," in *The Routledge Companion to Popular Music and Humor*, edited by Nicolas Baxter-Moore and Tom Kitts (London and New York: Routledge, 2019), 310–320.

6   Barbara Bradby, "Phallic Girls of Pop: Nicki Minaj's Sampled Anaconda and the Semiotics of Contradiction," *PopScriptum—Sound, Sex und Sexismus* 12 (2016), https://www2.hu-berlin.de/fpm/popscrip/themen/pst12/pst12_bradby.html#1.

7   Katariina Kyrölä, "Music Videos as Black Feminist Thought—From Nicki Minaj's Anaconda to Beyoncé's Formation," *Feminist Encounters: A Journal of Critical Studies in Culture and Politics* 1, no. 1 (October 2017): 1–13.

8   Minaj, "Anaconda." Music and lyrics by Onika Maraj, Jamal Jones, Jonathan Solone-Myvett, Ernest Clarc, Marcos Palacios, and Anthony Ray. From Nicki Minaj [studio album], *The Pinkprint* (Young Money Entertainment, Cash Money Records, Republic Records, 2014).

9   See Hawkins, *Queerness*, esp. 3–4; Sheila Whiteley and Jennifer Rycenga, eds., *Queering the Popular Pitch* (New York: Routledge, 2006); Freya Jarman-Ivens, *Queer Voices: Technologies, Vocalities, and the Musical Flaw* (New York: Palgrave Macmillan, 2011).

10 See John Richardson, "Ecological Close Reading of Music in Digital Culture," in *Embracing Restlessness: Cultural Musicology*, edited by Birgit Abels, Göttingen Studies in Musicology, vol. 6 (Hildesheim: Olms, 2016), 111–142; Carol Vernallis, *Unruly Media: YouTube, Music Video, and the New Digital Cinema* (Oxford and New York: Oxford University Press, 2013); Stan Hawkins and John Richardson, "Remodeling Britney Spears: Matters of Intoxication and Mediation," *Popular Music and Society* 30, no. 5 (2007): 605–629.

11 See Sara Ahmed, *Living a Feminist Life* (Durham, NC: Duke University Press, 2017 [Kindle edition]); Jennifer C. Nash, *The Black Body in Ecstasy: Reading Race, Reading Pornography* (London: Duke University Press, 2014); Nicole R. Fleetwood, *Troubling Vision: Performance, Visuality, and Blackness* (Chicago, IL: University of Chicago Press, 2011); Collins and Bilge, *Intersectionality*.

12 See Deborah Lupton, *Fat* (New York: Routledge, 2018 [2013]); Esther Rothblum and Sondra Solovay, eds., *The Fat Studies Reader* (New York: New York University Press, 2009); van Amsterdam, "Big Fat Inequalities."

13 By drawing so extensively on interdisciplinary research, I hope to compensate to some extent for the limitations of my subject position as a researcher working in a predominantly white and, in some other respects also, relatively privileged cultural setting. Other aspects of this study are closer to home, but I hope to balance these out— the unfamiliar and the painfully familiar—with a reflexive attitude, deference to relevant research, and, as far as possible, carefully grounded and argued observations.

14 This strategy was famously in use in a later Beyoncé music video "Formation" (2016). See Mari E. Ramler, "Beyoncé's Performance of Identification as a Diamond: Reclaiming Bodies and Voices in 'Formation,'" *Constellations: A Cultural Rhetorics Publishing Space*, May 2018, http://constell8cr.com/issue-1/beyonces-performance-of-identification-as-a-diamond-reclaiming-bodies-and-voices-in-formation. See also Kyrölä, "Music Videos."

15 See Kyrölä, "Music Videos"; Bradby, "Phallic Girls."

16 bell hooks, *Black Looks: Race and Representation* (Boston, MA: South End Press, 1992), 4; Patricia Hill Collins, *Black Sexual Politics: African Americans, Gender, and the New Racism* (New York: Routledge, 2004), 26–28; Theresa Renee White, "Missy 'Misdemeanor' Elliott and Nicki Minaj: Fashionistin' Black Female Sexuality in Hip-Hop Culture—Girl Power or Overpowered?," *Journal of Black Studies* 44, no. 6 (2013): 607–626; Dayna Chatman, "Pregnancy, Then It's 'Back to Business': Beyoncé, Black Femininity, and the Politics of a Post-Feminist Gender Regime," *Feminist Media Studies* 15, no. 6 (2015): 926–941.

17   Patricia Hill Collins's term; see, for example, Julia S. Jordan-Zachery, *Black Women, Cultural Images, and Social Policy* (New York: Routledge, 2010), 13; Margaret L. Hunter, *Race, Gender, and the Politics of Skin Tone* (New York: Routledge, 2005), 29–31.

18   Diane Railton and Paul Watson, *Music and the Moving Image: Music Video and the Politics of Representation* (Edinburgh: Edinburgh University Press, 2011), 91–92. See also Kai Arne Hansen and Stan Hawkins, "Azealia Banks: 'Chasing Time,' Erotics, and Body Politics," *Popular Music* 37, no. 2 (2018): 167.

19   Aph Ko, "The Baartman Effect: Nicki Minaj, Gail Dines, and Chuck Creekmur," *Naturalhairmag*, July 30, 2014, http://www.naturalhairmag.com/baartman-effect-nicki-minaj-gail-dines-chuck-creekmur.

20   Wendy Burns-Ardolino, "Jiggle in My Walk: The Iconic Power of the Big Butt in American Popular Culture," in *The Fat Studies Reader*, edited by Esther Rothblum and Sondra Solovay (New York: New York University Press, 2009), 276–278.

21   Linda Hutcheon, *Theory of Parody: The Teachings of Twentieth-Century Art Forms* (New York: Routledge, 1985), 22.

22   Daniel Shanahan and David Huron, "Heroes and Villains: The Relationship between Pitch Tessitura and Sociability of Operatic Characters," *Empirical Musicology Review* 9, no. 2 (2014), http://emusicology.org/article/view/4441/4182.

23   Eduardo Navas, *Remix Theory: The Aesthetics of Sampling* (Vienna: Springer-Verlag, 2012), 116.

24   Unlike, for example, the Finnish singer Alma's song "Dye My Hair" from 2017; see Hanna-Mari Riihimäki and Anna-Elena Pääkkölä, "Alternative Femininities, Monstrous Voices, and Queer Body Politics in Alma's 'Dye My Hair,'" in *Made in Finland: Studies in Popular Music*, edited by Toni-Matti Karjalainen and Kimi Kärki (New York: Routledge, forthcoming).

25   John Richardson, "Between Speech, Music, and Sound: The Voice, Flow, and the Aestheticizing Impulse in Audiovisual Media," in *The Oxford Handbook of Sound and Image in Western Art*, edited by Yael Kaduri (Oxford: Oxford University Press, 2016), 493.

26   See also Burns and Woods, "Humor."

27   As I have suggested previously, fat studies as a field is ripe for musicological inquiry. For example, hip-hop seems to be one of the most prevalent platforms for valorizing fat bodies. As far as "fat booty" songs are concerned, in addition to Sir Mix-a-Lot's "Baby Got Back" (1992), I might mention Beastie Boys' "Shake Your Rump" (1989), LL Cool J's "Big Ole Butt" (1989), Sisqo's "Thong Song" (1999), Mos Def's "Ms. Fat Booty" (1999), and (arguably) The Black Eyed Peas' "My Humps" (2005). We should not, however, consider hip-hop the sole musical platform where fat bodies are discussed and valorized. Queen guitarist Brian May wrote an anthem for "Fat Bottomed Girls" (1979), and Meghan Trainor soared to the charts in 2014 with "All About the Bass." Reggae music has also discussed fat bodies in Carl Malcolm's "Hey Fatty Bum Bum"; while Finnish reggae artist Jukka Poika wrote a song "Pläski" (Phat) in 2007. See Anna-Elena Pääkkölä, "Mahtava Peräsin ja Pulleat Purjeet: Lihavuus, Naiskuva ja Seksuaalisuus Kolmessa Suomalaisessa Populaarimusiikkikappaleessa" ["Fatness, Womanhood, and Sexuality in Three Finnish Popular Music Songs"], *Etnomusikologinen vuosikirja* 29 (2017): 1–19.

28   See, for example, Lupton, *Fat*, 4–6; Katariina Kyrölä, *The Weight of Images: Affect, Body Image and Fat in the Media* (Farnham: Ashgate, 2014), 4; Deborah Harris-Moore, *Media and the Rhetoric of Body Perfection: Cosmetic Surgery, Weight Loss and Beauty in Popular Culture. The Cultural Politics of Media and Popular Culture* (Farnham: Ashgate, 2014),

128; Amy E. Farrell, *Fat Shame: Stigma and the Fat Body in American Culture* (New York: New York University Press, 2011), 6–7.

29 Lupton, *Fat*, 7–8. See also Kyrölä, *The Weight of Images*, 2.

30 Ariane Prohaska and Jeannine A. Gailey, "Theorizing Fat Oppression: Intersectional Approaches and Methodological Innovations," *Fat Studies: An Interdisciplinary Journal of Body Weight and Society* 8, no. 1 (October 2018), 1–9; Niall Richardson, *Transgressive Bodies: Representations in Film and Popular Culture* (Farnham: Ashgate, 2010), 75, 81; Kyrölä, *The Weight of Images*, 2.

31 van Amsterdam, "Big Fat Inequalities," 158–159; Apryl A. Williams, "Fat People of Color: Emergent Intersectional Discourse Online," *Social Sciences* 6, no. 15 (February 2017): 4. Critical fat studies are increasingly addressing intersectional questions, as is apparent from a forthcoming monograph by Sabrina Strings, *Fearing the Black Body: The Racial Origins of Fat Phobia* (New York: New York University Press, 2019 [forthcoming]).

32 van Amsterdam, "Big Fat Inequalities," 161; Williams, "Fat People of Color," 5–6, 8.

33 Naa Oyo A. Kwate and Shatema Threadcraft, "Perceiving the Black Female Body: Race and Gender in Police Constructions of Body Weight," *Race Social Problems* 7, no. 3 (September 2015): 213–226, https://www.ncbi.nlm.nih.gov/pmc/articles/PMC4606888.

34 See also Nina Cartier, "Black Women On-screen as Future Texts: A New Look at Black Pop Culture Representations," *Cinema Journal* 53, no. 4 (Summer 2014): 152.

35 Desexualization through the "Mammy" stereotype; see Gina Masullo Chen, Sherri Williams, Nicole Hendrickson, and Li Chen, "Male Mammies: A Social-Comparison Perspective on How Exaggeratedly Overweight Media Portrayals of Madea, Rasputia, and Big Momma Affect How Black Women Feel About Themselves," *Mass Communication and Society* 15, no 1 (2012): 116; van Amsterdam, "Big Fat Inequalities," 162. Hypersexualization through the historical image of the "Hottentot Venus"; see Sander L. Gilman, "Black Bodies, White Bodies: Toward an Iconography of Female Sexuality in Late Nineteenth-Century Art, Medicine, and Literature," *Critical Inquiry* 12, no. 1 (1985); Nash, *The Black Body*, 35–38; Burns-Ardolino, "Jiggle," 273; Ko, "The Baartman Effect"; Bradby, "Phallic Girls."

36 Kwate and Threadcraft, "Perceiving."

37 Ibid., 216.

38 See Fleetwood, *Troubling Vision*, 110–111; Hansen and Hawkins, "Azealia Banks," 167; Railton and Watson, *Music Video*, 108; Kyrölä, "Music Videos."

39 See, for a brief selection, van Amsterdam, "Big Fat Inequalities," 161.

40 Fleetwood, *Troubling Vision*, 111.

41 Ibid., 112. I have omitted the emphasis of the original.

42 Hansen and Hawkins, "Azealia Banks," 169.

43 Ibid., 113. Emphasis in the original.

44 D. Lacy Asbill, "'I'm Allowed to Be a Sexual Being': The Distinctive Social Conditions of the Fat Burlesque Stage," in *The Fat Studies Reader*, edited by Esther Rothblum and Sondra Solovay (New York: New York University Press, 2009), 299.

45 Ibid., 300.

46 See Hawkins, *Queerness*, 117.

47 See Maureen Turim, "Women Singing, Women Gesturing: Music Videos," in *Body Politics and the Fictional Double*, edited by Debra Walker King (Bloomington, IN: Indiana University Press, 2000), 134. See also Bradby, "Phallic Girls."

48   Hawkins, *Queerness*, 77.

49   Sigmund Freud, "The Uncanny," in *The Uncanny*, translated by David McLintock (Suffolk: Penguin Books, 2003 [1919]), 121–162.

50   Burns and Woods refer to this gesture as "a witch-like cackle." See Burns and Woods, "Humor," 315.

51   See Hawkins, *Queerness*, 117.

52   Hansen and Hawkins, "Azealia Banks," 168.

53   This moment of product placement may deserve its own discussion elsewhere about the close connections of hip-hop feminism and neocapitalism.

54   Kyrölä, *The Weight of Images*, 10; compare to "hypervisuality" of the black female body and its "excessive flesh" in Fleetwood, *Troubling Vision*, 111–113.

55   See Justin Adams Burton, *Posthuman Rap* (Oxford: Oxford University Press, 2017), 119–121; Lauren Michelle Jackson, "The Rapper Laughs, Herself: Nicki Minaj's Sonic Disturbances," *Feminist Media Studies* 17, no. 1 (2017): 128.

56   Fabrício Silveira, "Anal Terrorism in Nicki Minaj's 'Anaconda,'" in *Music/Video: Histories, Aesthetics, Media*, edited by Gina Arnold, Daniel Cookney, Kristy Fairclough, and Michael Goddard (London: Bloomsbury, 2017), 133.

57   Note also a similarity to bell hooks's description of Beyoncé as a "terrorist." The logic is similar for both these writers: terrorism depends in some measure on affective spectacle that is employed to sway public opinion. Once the inflammatory rhetoric is removed from hooks's and Silveira's arguments, their main objections seem to be that the examples they discuss are forms of embodied spectacle employing questionable means and purposes of representation. See bell hooks, "Moving Beyond Pain," bellhooksinstitute. com, May 9, 2016, http://www.bellhooksinstitute.com/blog/2016/5/9/moving-beyond-pain; and bell hooks, "Femme Feminista," bellhooksinstitute.com, May 11, 2016, http:// www.bellhooksinstitute.com/blog/femme-feminista.

58   Silveira, "Anal Terrorism," 133.

59   Ibid., 134, 136.

60   Burns-Ardolino, "Jiggle," 275.

61   Aisha Durham, "'Check On It': Beyoncé, Southern Booty, and Black Femininities in Music Video," *Feminist Media Studies* 12, no. 1 (2012): 41.

62   Joan Gross, "Phat," in *Fat: The Anthropology of an Obsession*, edited by Tom Kulick and Anne Meleney (London: Penguin Books, 2005), 66–68.

63   Durham, "Check On It," 43.

64   Kyra D. Gaunt, "YouTube, Twerking & You: Context Collapse and the Handheld Co-Presence of Black Girls and Miley Cyrus," *Journal of Popular Music Studies* 27 no. 3 (2015): 247. See also Bradby, "Phallic Girls," for a discussion of the stigmatization of the dancing black booty in the jazz era of the early 1900s.

65   Gaunt, "YouTube," 245, 247, 253.

66   Ibid., 248.

67   Ibid., 249. See also Fleetwood, *Troubling Vision*, 133.

68   Gaunt, "YouTube," 249.

69   Nash, *The Black Body*, 6–7.

70   José Muñoz, *Cruising Utopia: The Then and There of Queer Futurity* (New York: New York University Press, 2009), 186.

71   Nash, *The Black Body*, 2–3.

72 Laura U. Marks, *Touch: Sensuous Theory and Multisensory Media* (Minneapolis, MN: University of Minnesota Press, 2002), 8.

73 Burton, *Posthuman Rap*, 115.

74 Ibid. Compare to McClary's "phallic backbeat"; Susan McClary, *Feminine Endings: Music, Gender and Sexuality* (Minnesota, MN: University of Minnesota Press, 2002), 154.

75 Burton, *Posthuman Rap*, 115: "The booty clap is the sound of misogyny turned up in the mix."

76 In comparison, Burton demonstrates in *Posthuman Rap*, 120–121, how Minaj utilizes the "booty clap" as a sign of feminine empowerment in an otherwise masculine music video, Rae Sremmurd's "Throw Sum Mo."

77 "Mickey Mousing" is a technique originating in cartoons but prevalent in classic Hollywood films where music is very closely synchronized to visual actions and sound effects. Michel Chion, *Audio-Vision: Sound on Screen*, edited and translated by Claudia Gorbman (New York: Columbia University Press, 1994), 121–122.

78 Gaunt, "YouTube," 249.

79 Asbill, "I'm Allowed," 300.

80 At the beginning of February 2019, the video had nearly 840,000,000 views on YouTube.

81 Amanda Holpuch, "Madame Tussauds Rethinks Nicki Minaj Waxwork Display over Saucy Fan Photos," *Guardian*, August 19, 2015, https://www.theguardian.com/music/2015/aug/19/madame-tussauds-nicki-minaj-display-waxwork.

82 See Hansen and Hawkins, "Azealia Banks," 169.

83 Burns-Ardolino, "Jiggle," 275.

84 Victoria Uwumarogie, "'I Was Like, This S**t Is Boring': bell hooks on Nicki Minaj's 'Anaconda' Video, Beyoncé and the Female Body in Pop Culture," madamenoire.com, October 14, 2014, https://madamenoire.com/477942/like-st-boring-bell-hooks-nicki-minajs-anaconda-video-beyonce-female-body-pop-culture.

85 Silveira, "Anal Terrorism," 139.

86 Ibid., 137; see also bell hooks, "Moving Beyond Pain" and "Femme Feminista."

87 Silveira, "Anal Terrorism," 139.

88 Hansen and Hawkins, "Azealia Banks," 166.

89 Reiland Rabaka, *Hip Hop's Inheritance: From the Harlem Renaissance to the Hip Hop Feminist Movement* (New York: Lexington Books, 2001), 166.

90 "Laughter is, in some feminist traditions, the starting point for feminist critique; it presents a possibility to liberate and overturn patriarchal norms and thinking, but also the thought of feminist theory as serious, high brow and humorless." Jackson, "The Rapper Laughs," 126.

91 Hansen and Hawkins, "Azealia Banks," 166.

92 Ahmed, *Living a Feminist Life*, 162.

20

Going Too Far: Representations of Violence against Men in Pink's "Please Don't Leave Me"

Marc Lafrance

Introduction

Written and performed by the Grammy award-winning artist Pink, the album *Funhouse*[1] was released in 2008 and quickly reached the #2 spot on Billboard's Top 200 charts.[2] Pink described the album as her most vulnerable to date, stating that many of its songs are about the heartbreak that followed her separation from her husband, Carey Hart.[3] But the album is not just a break-up album. Many of the songs are about break ups, but as Pink put it in an interview with the *Chicago Media Guide*: "there is fun happening too, which is why I named it *Funhouse* in the end."[4]

Despite her insistence on fun and the important role it plays on the album, Pink acknowledged over the course of the interview that funhouses are often frightening. "Clowns are supposed to be happy," she explained, "but they are really scary. Carnivals are supposed to be fun, but really they are kind of creepy. But, we go and we buy cotton candy and we force our laughter and we get on rides and we strap ourselves in and we do it. And that's like life to me, and love."[5] Pink went on to emphasize "the funhouse mirrors that make [us] look so distorted that [we] don't recognize [ourselves]" and how they can make us ask: "How did [we] get here? How do [we] get out of here?"[6] With its uncanny contradictions and disquieting distortions, the funhouse is Pink's metaphor of choice for a "nervy power pop" album characterized by what some critics have called "emotional bloodletting."[7]

One of the best-known songs on the album, "Please Don't Leave Me" charted in over two dozen countries around the world including Australia,[8] Germany,[9] and the United Kingdom.[10] In the United States, it reached the #2 spot on the Billboard *Adult Pop Songs* chart,[11] the #7 spot on the Billboard *Adult Contemporary* chart,[12] and the #6 spot on the Billboard *Pop Songs* chart.[13] Ultimately, the song reached the #18 spot on the Billboard *Hot 100* chart, making it Pink's sixth Top 20 hit at the time of its release.[14]

Context

Released in 2009, the music video for "Please Don't Leave Me" features parodic intertextual allusions to a number of Stephen King's novels-turned-films—such as *The Shining, Cujo,* and *Misery*[15]—and contains graphic scenes of violence against an intimate partner. Interpreted by many as a dark comedy, the video met with favorable reviews from critics. For instance, Billboard's Patrick Crowley rated Pink's ten best music videos and gave the number one spot to "Please Don't Leave Me,"[16] describing it as "hilarious, irreverent, and a cinematic masterpiece."[17] Similarly, *Digital Spy*'s Nick Levine referred to her video as "entertaining" and claimed that "it makes you realize a song is better than you thought."[18] That said, not all of the reviews were favorable. In a blog written for *The Huffington Post,* Shelby Knox argued that the video goes "a little too far" and is a "disturbing depiction of the lengths [Pink] would have gone to keep [her partner] from walking away."[19] Knox goes on to draw parallels between Pink's video for "Please Don't Leave Me" and Lady Gaga's video for "Telephone," maintaining that "Pink seems to buy into the idea that domestic violence perpetrated by women is ok, even funny, even deserved."[20] In the end, she suggests that Pink's video is harmful to those who view it since "anyone watching will come away with the idea that true love is worth fighting for, to the point of inflicting serious physical harm on your partner."[21]

While the claim that "Please Don't Leave Me" goes too far is open to debate, there can be no denying that the video makes a mockery of intimate partner violence (hereafter referred to as IPV) against men in the context of heterosexual relationships. Despite the fact that it contains three graphic scenes of aggravated assault and is defined by its ongoing depictions of forced confinement, many of those who have watched the video have found it funny. Like Crowley[22] and Levine,[23] thousands of online viewers have said that the video made them laugh. Yet neither the critics nor the online viewers have been unanimous. Other critics, like Knox,[24] have been open about the fact that they have serious reservations about the video, and many online viewers have done the same.[25] Here, then, attitudes toward the video are divided in much the same way as attitudes toward IPV against men.

Given the divisive nature of the matters at hand, it is important to be clear about what I do and do not set out to do in the current chapter. To start, I do not set out to take a position on either the frequency or the severity of IPV against men in present-day Western societies. To do so would be to become embroiled in a decades-long debate that has polarized scholars across the social sciences and remains, in many ways, unresolved. Indeed, some scholars associated with family violence studies argue that men and women are equally likely to perpetrate IPV,[26] whereas other scholars associated with feminist studies argue that IPV is perpetrated mainly by men against women.[27] The research by both family studies scholars and feminist scholars is worthy of further debate by those studying violence in intimate partnerships, but it is not my object of analysis.

That said, my analysis is guided by a number of assumptions about my object that are worth noting here. Most importantly, I assume that IPV against men is neither the same as nor equivalent to IPV against women. The latter is structural and systemic in ways the former is not, making the two phenomena different in kind.[28] Similarly, I assume that, because the two phenomena are different in kind, they require different responses. For instance, IPV against women demands a more wide-ranging strategy on the part of the state and its apparatuses than IPV against men.[29] At the same time, however, I reject the claim that IPV against men does not matter. Instead, I argue that it matters for at least three reasons: first, because the violation of male persons is every bit as important as the violation of female persons; second, because the violation of male persons is inextricably linked to the violation of female persons; and third, because violence in intimate partnerships—regardless of whether it is perpetrated by men or by women—is bound up with dominant norms of gender in ways that should concern us if we wish to do away with it. Similarly, I reject the claim that examining violence committed by women against men in the context of intimate partnerships is incompatible with feminism's overall objectives. Problematizing prevailing stereotypes of men's so-called natural tendency toward aggression and women's so-called natural tendency toward passivity is crucial because these stereotypes are essentialist and essentialism is the engine of patriarchy.

While it would go beyond the scope of this chapter to comment further on these matters, it suffices to say that my goal is not to show that IPV against men is more important, less important, or just as important as IPV against women. Instead, my goal is to think critically about how IPV against men is constructed in and through the cultural imaginary. After all, this imaginary is a crystallization of our most common and, in many cases, complex fears and fantasies.[30] Simply put, making sense of these fears and fantasies as they relate to representations of IPV is what I seek to do throughout the chapter.

To access the cultural imaginary, I take the popular music video as my object of analysis. A preliminary search of the videos made over the course of the last fifteen years reveals that a surprisingly large number of them represent IPV against men. Made by commercially successful artists, both male and female, these videos include, but are not limited to, examples such as: "Goodbye Earl" by The Dixie Chicks (2009); "It's My Life" by No Doubt (2009); "Before He Cheats" by Carrie Underwood (2009); "Paparazzi" by Lady Gaga (2009); "Telephone" by Lady Gaga featuring Beyoncé (2010); "Misery" by Maroon 5 (2010); "Your Body" by Christina Aguilera (2012); "Where You Stand" by Travis (2013); "Magnets" by Disclosure featuring Lorde (2015); and "Close" by Rae Sremmurd featuring Travis Scott (2018).[31] While all of these examples make for telling case studies, I have chosen Pink's "Please Don't Leave Me" for three reasons: first, because its representations of IPV are among the most graphic; second, because its production strategies are unusually sophisticated; and third, because Pink has been claimed by many as a "feminist hero."[32] With these reasons in view, my case study seeks to answer two key research questions: first, how does "Please Don't Leave Me" construct male victims and female aggressors? And second, how are these constructions bound up with dominant norms of masculinity and femininity?

Theory and method

To answer my research questions, I approach Pink's video as a cultural critic. Like much cultural criticism, my approach is transdisciplinary in nature and aims to make the contextual specificities of the video's form and content more intelligible—and, indeed, more meaningful—to those interested in making sense of the popular media.[33] As some scholars have put it, cultural criticism is best understood as an activity rather than a framework: that is, while it almost always focuses on how its objects shape and are shaped by specific social conditions and the power relations that pervade them, its overall approach is more free-floating than other approaches.[34] Cultural criticism is not, in other words, associated with "a specific methodology or a discrete area of interest: its approach tends to be needs-based, meaning that it applies theory according to the case at hand."[35]

Cultural criticism may be defined in broad terms, but that does not mean that it cannot be rigorous and systematic. To arrive at an analysis that is both the former and the latter, it is important that I be clear about my theoretical and methodological commitments. On a theoretical level, my analysis is informed by three key fields: first, gender and sexuality studies; second, critical disability studies; and third, popular music studies. With respect to the first field, my analysis is informed by scholarship on dominant norms of masculinity, femininity, and heterosexuality;[36] with respect to the second field, my analysis is informed by scholarship on the social construction of ability and disability;[37] and, with respect to the third field, my analysis is informed by scholarship on the implications of parody and intertextuality in popular music.[38]

On a methodological level, my approach is organized around three relational components that are themselves organized around three relational sub-components. More specifically, the first component pertains to the video's *normative content* and considers the category of gender as it intersects with the categories of sexuality and ability; the second component pertains to the video's *expressive form* and considers the intersections of word, sound, and image; and the third component pertains to the video's *thematic structure* and considers the intersecting themes that I identify in the following analysis: namely, circularity, temporal ambiguity, and funhouse frivolity.

Analysis

Introduction (0:00–0:06)

The song opens with Pink singing *a cappella*. There are no lyrics at this early point in the song; instead what we hear is her vocalizing a sequence on the syllable "da." Paralleling a progression that we will later hear on the rhythm guitar, these vocalizations have heavy reverb on them and make Pink sound as though she is in a large enclosed space. The vocalized sequence is combined with a fast-moving montage of two visual images: first, a circular white home shot from the outside at what could be either dawn or dusk; and second, a dimly-lit entrance shot from the inside, filled with a carousel horse, a clown, and other artifacts associated with amusement parks. Taken together, these images—and the reverberating vocalizations that accompany them—can be seen to establish circularity, temporal ambiguity, and funhouse frivolity as three of the video's key themes. And these themes, it is worth noting, are mutually constitutive and reinforcing: carousel horses turn in circles; clowns never change; and amusement parks feature big-tent-like structures in which voices ring as though in an echo chamber.

Verse 1 (0:06–0:47)

At the beginning of the first verse, the instrumental arrangement is introduced while the video cuts to the bedroom. The room is lit by lamps and overhead spotlights, and the natural daylight is blocked out by the mostly-drawn curtains. The set is filled with props that recall the funhouse theme established earlier, such as pink and black burlesque lampshades and a ghoulish self-portrait of Pink characterized by a similar burlesque color scheme. The ghoulishness of the self-portrait, combined with a passing shot of handcuffs hanging above the bed, suggest that Pink's funhouse might not be so fun after all. What once appeared to be magical and mysterious now seems as though it might be coercive and constraining.

In the bedroom, we see Pink arguing with a man whom we assume is her boyfriend. Her facial gestures convey desperation and remorse, and her body language, innocence and vulnerability. Her skin is flawless and slightly tanned, her make-up conventional and understated, and her hair is brushed softly to the side, its synthetic whiteness shimmering under the warm, flattering lights. Clutching her boyfriend's clothes as he attempts to leave with them, she delivers the first line of the song with her signature rasp: "I don't know if I can yell any louder," her plaintive question reminding us of the echo-chamber-like *a cappella* vocals we heard at the beginning of the song. She then refers to the number of times she has insulted him, or kicked him out of her home, and as she does so her vocal tone is rugged and forceful—not unlike the stripped-down rhythm guitar that drives the song from start to finish.

The first two lines of the verse suggest that the couple's relationship is characterized by a circular pattern of conflict initiated, first and foremost, by her. Yet if the circularity of this pattern is made immediately obvious in the lyrics, then the same cannot be said of the images. In fact, when the couple's argument is first represented visually, it appears to unfold in a linear manner: Pink's boyfriend tries to leave, and she tries to stop him; he grabs his golf clubs, and she tries to pull them away from him; he straps his golf clubs onto his back, and she tries to claim some of his other possessions; he reclaims his other possessions, walks out of the door and heads toward the stairs. Here the visual imagery indicates that the argument has a beginning and an ending. But the ending we see at this point in the video is, in fact, not one. For instance, the struggle over who gets to keep the golf clubs—which are, without a doubt, phallic symbols—is a circular one that makes itself felt on a number of occasions throughout the video. These phallic objects—objects that are linked not only to her boyfriend's masculinity but also to his agency and autonomy—are later appropriated by Pink precisely for the purposes of incapacitating and imprisoning him.

The narrative intensifies after the boyfriend has left the bedroom and is heading toward the stairs. Pink still appears vulnerable and almost childlike in her *naïveté*, but there is little question at this point that she is upping the ante. In fact, she states plainly that she can be mean and menacing where he is concerned. She is, by her own admission, capable of just about anything when her "heart is breaking" and this includes "[cutting him] into pieces." Here Pink's creepy confession prefigures the disorienting combination of violent intimidation and overblown affection that is to come. And while her boyfriend does not know what she has in store for him, his facial gestures—especially his incredulous utterance of the word "what" followed by his furrowed brow—make clear that he is unconvinced and, ultimately, unmoved by Pink's plea for sympathy. He turns to leave but, as he does so, he slips on a set of marbles spread out across the floor and crashes down the stairs. Ultimately, the cause of the boyfriend's crash down the stairs foreshadows what we will later come to very clearly comprehend: Pink has, quite literally, lost her marbles.

Chorus 1 (0:47–1:15)

The boyfriend's ill-fated descent down the stairs marks a number of shifts with respect to both the video's form and content.[39] In terms of form and, more specifically, lyrical form, the descent marks the point at which the song moves from the verse's reproachful self-reflection to the chorus's more forceful demand. Pink makes this demand twice before she admits that it is circular in nature: that is, while she may claim not to need him, she always ends up asking him to come back to her.

The chorus marks a shift in musical form as well. The minimal arrangement that characterizes the verse—during which we hear only the lead and background vocals, rhythm guitar, bass, shaker, and drum kit—multiplies in the chorus. The lead vocals are strengthened by being stacked in unison, split, and panned; the rhythm guitars are layered one on top of the other, their subtle differences coming together to create a richer and more robust texture; the bass travels further up and down the scale, playing a more prominent role in the mix; and the percussion is pumped up, as it were, by the addition of the hi-hat and the more regular cymbal crashes.

Like the formal elements associated with the lyrics and the music, those associated with the images change during the chorus. Characterized by a soft-focus lens and generous lighting, these images are—like those of the verse—reminiscent of the aesthetics of a network soap opera. Gradually, however, the images get blurrier as it becomes increasingly obvious that the gaze of the camera has shifted. We are no longer seeing the world through Pink's eyes but through those of her boyfriend. And in keeping with one of the video's key themes, the world seen through his eyes is temporally ambiguous: Pink is there one moment but gone the next. The screen goes black, then lights back up, then goes black again and stays that way for a sustained period of time. The visual imagery leaves us, like the banged-up boyfriend, unsure of what is happening now or what will happen next. In doing so, it leaves him in a disoriented state—the sort of state in which one might find oneself after having ridden a carousel horse too quickly, and for far too long.

The formal elements outlined above, be they lyrical, musical, or visual, are full of anticipatory metaphors that lay the foundations for the violence that pervades the rest of the video. These metaphors, and how they make themselves felt during the chorus, are particularly telling where Pink is concerned: lyrically, she goes from plaintive pleas to insistent demands; musically, from stripped down vulnerability to souped-up strength; and visually, from the weakened object of the gaze to the more powerful subject of the gaze. And, of course, these metaphors of form travel in tandem with metaphors of content. Just as the video's form suggests a redistribution of power from man to woman—that is, a proportional increase in her strength and his weakness—so too does its content.

The content of the chorus raises the issue of control, asking the viewer to consider who had it then—that is, in the verse—and who has it now. If, up to this point, the camera work has emphasized Pink's out-of-control emotionality, then here it is the boyfriend's out of control physicality that is at the center of the visual imagery. Pink starts off weak on the inside, but now her boyfriend is weak on the outside. And the boyfriend's golf clubs—once a symbol of both his ability to make his own choices and his gendered normativity—do nothing but compound the injuries he sustains as he tumbles down the stairs.

The issue of control is played out not only through the camera work but through the character blocking as well. For instance, in the verse, Pink finds herself looking up at her taller and more physically imposing boyfriend. But, by the end of the chorus, when her boyfriend hits the bottom of the stairs, it is he who is looking up at her. Pink cocks her head as she registers the role reversal that has taken place between them, and the expression on her face goes from pleading to plotting (see Figure 20.1). His immobile body is, for her, a great opportunity: a chance to force him to participate in what will soon become an unadulterated drama of mental and physical abuse.

Figure 20.1 Pink looks down at her boyfriend as he lies at the foot of the stairs.

Verse 2 (1:15–1:50)

As the chorus ends and the second verse begins, we see a very different version of Pink's boyfriend. Once able-bodied, agential, and autonomous—not to mention white and apparently affluent—his previous claim to gendered normativity is no more. In fact, his fall from the top of the stairs symbolizes a more far-reaching fall where gender norms are concerned: he has gone from what appears to be a socially dominant man—that is, a man who enjoys the privileges that go along with being at the top of the hierarchy of masculinities—to a socially subordinated one. Indeed, if stereotypical ideals of masculinity tend to be characterized by bravery, invulnerability, strength, self-sufficiency, and stoicism, then his physical state—and particularly his physically disabled state as it is represented over the course of the video—disqualifies him from them in no uncertain terms.

The second verse begins with the boyfriend waking up in Pink's bedroom after having blacked out at the end of his fall down the stairs. Now, however, he looks considerably worse than he did then. His right eye is badly bruised and bulging, which we can only assume is Pink's doing. This bulging bruise is the first in a long series of Pink's assaults against her boyfriend, and the fact that it is directed at his eye is not insignificant: these assaults are, for Pink, assaults to which she is entitled under the law of retaliation. They are, in other words, her own special version of the Old Testament's "an eye for an eye."[40]

Two more attacks follow on from the one on the boyfriend's eye, taking us through to the end of the verse. The first consists of an unanaesthetized surgical stitching on his left forearm, which he resists in vain; and the second consists of a blunt blow to his leg (Figure 20.2), which leaves him with what appears to be a broken tibia bone. Both attacks are brought into being through parodic intertextual allusions to Stephen King's *Misery*, and both must be considered lyrically, musically, and visually if we hope to achieve a deeper understanding of how they do the meaning-making work that they do.

Figure 20.2 Pink prepares to hit her boyfriend's leg with a golf club.

Lyrically, the second verse is more overtly aggressive than the first. Gone is the vulnerability that characterizes Pink's statements about her broken heart; now what we hear about are her "obnoxious" habits and "nasty" tendencies. There is, moreover, a shift in responsibility at this point in the song. In the first verse, Pink takes most—if not all—of the blame for the failure of the relationship. But, in the second verse, everything is her boyfriend's fault; there are, as she puts it, things about him that make her behave as she does. The sentimentality that characterizes the first verse is replaced by a callous combativity; relationships are nothing more than a contest and, as Pink sees it, the winner will be the one who "hits the hardest." Interestingly, this lyrical moment coincides with two other important moments, one musical and one visual; first, a background vocal is layered onto the lead vocal when Pink sings "hits the hardest" and this is the only time, in either verse, that this layering takes place; and second, the video portrays Pink hitting her boyfriend's leg with the golf club just as the line in question is sung. Here, then, the lyrics become more tightly intertwined with the music and images than they do at any other point in the song, creating a powerful portrayal of physical abuse. The physical abuse, however, does not operate in isolation; in fact, the last part of the verse brings mental abuse to bear on this portrayal as well. That is, while she is hitting her boyfriend's leg with the golf club, she explains that she does not mean to cause him any harm. But her explanation changes a split second later when she exclaims: "I mean it, I promise." Not only do the lyrics capture the emotional gas-lighting often experienced by victims of IPV, but they also connect to the video's key themes through their allusions to circularity; in this case, the well-known circularity of abusive relationship patterns.

While the music is not as aggressive as the lyrics, it is, nevertheless, bigger and more muscular. For instance, the lead vocal is belted out, as it were, and has none of the breathiness that it did in the first verse. In addition, the second verse is generally wordier than the first, giving the lead vocal a more prominent place in the arrangement. The guitars, too, take up more space in the second verse than they do in the first; not only do they maintain the rich and robust texture they had in the chorus, but they are also filled out by an additional guitar, played close to the bridge, that takes the sound to the top of the pitch register. And finally, the drum kit is more present than it was in the first verse, keeping the hi-hat and the more frequent cymbal crashes that characterized it in the chorus.

If the lyrics and the music intensify the video's overarching narrative in the second verse, then the images do so even more. Indeed, unlike the conventional aesthetics that characterized it in the first verse, the bedroom is now an over-the-top tribute to burlesque iconography, campy artifacts, and amusement park aesthetics. The set is bursting at the seams, making it difficult to visually register everything on the screen. This assault on our vision is not unlike the one the boyfriend experiences as he struggles to "come to" after his fall down the stairs. We see him trying to make sense of the sick infirmary in which he has now been confined, like a circus animal, in Barnum and Bailey striped pajamas. Neither he, nor we, can believe our eyes.

Pink is dressed suggestively, in a nurse's outfit taken right out of the pornographic imagination, and appears to be doing a low-level pole dance with the golf club she has now won after having lost it earlier in the video.[41] Here, again, the circular return of the golf club indexes who is in control and who is not; or, put differently, who gets to wield phallic power and who does not. The question of who gets to be in control is asked and, ultimately, answered through a series of contradictory juxtapositions: her smiling playfulness and his fearful suffering; her extreme agency and his pitiless passivity; and, perhaps most interestingly, her sexualized femininity and his abject masculinity. It might be tempting to think that normative notions of both femininity and masculinity are subverted through these juxtapositions, but a closer inspection suggests otherwise.

In some ways, the representations of the feminine that characterize the second verse are, indeed, subversive. And they are subversive, at least in part, because they make use of sexist stereotypes of caregiving, nurturing, and physical attractiveness while transforming them through a logic of specifically feminine strength. But Pink's strength—represented, first and foremost, through her total authority over her boyfriend and whether he lives or dies—comes at a price. Rather than being gained through a progressive collective politics, Pink's strength is gained through the appropriation of a phallic masculinity that harms through its capacity to penetrate her boyfriend's body by means of surgical interventions and the breaking of bones. In this way, Pink's strength is neither the cause nor the effect of an empowering emancipation from dominant gender norms; it is, instead, a mere turning of the tables that does little to change the status quo. What is more, Pink's power as it is portrayed here is not what we might call a healthy kind of power. It is sadistically weaponized and, perhaps most importantly, persistently pathologized. Far from subverting dominant gender norms, Pink's performance of femininity at this point in the video is characterized by the most conventional notions of the harmfully phallic masculine and the pathologically powerful feminine.

Characteristic of the zero-sum-game symbolism that runs through the video, Pink gains power as her boyfriend loses it. No longer in a position to get up and leave, or even to make a phone call, the boyfriend's body becomes more dependent as Pink's becomes more independent. And these representations of the boyfriend's dependence are bound up with a number of other non-normative representations of masculinity that must be unpacked if they are to be fully understood. To start, the boyfriend is portrayed as the opposite of stoic. The pain to which he is subjected is so crushing that it cannot be concealed, leaving him visibly weak and vulnerable. Similarly, the boyfriend is portrayed as the opposite of heroic. His good does not triumph over her evil—at least not at this point in the video— and he is in no position to perform feats of superhuman strength to get himself out of the predicament in which he finds himself. What we are left with, then, is a stark image of the boyfriend splayed on the bed, desperate and defenseless, screaming in agony as Pink breaks his leg with the phallic object that he has lost and she has gained.

The non-normative representations of masculinity that we see over the course of the second verse rely on a number of symbolic equations; that is, the boyfriend's dependence is equated with weakness and vulnerability, which is, in turn, equated with a failure of masculinity. As a result, the video's visual imagery suggests that disability—particularly when it is defined by dependence—is not a viable state for a "real" man. Here, disabled masculinity comes to equal failed masculinity, and it is for this reason that the video can be seen to reproduce dominant norms of not only gender but ability as well. In other words, the video offers us nothing that subverts stereotypes of men, as it reinforces the belief that they must be strong, stoic, and self-determining in order to lay claim to a normative category of masculinity. Similarly, the video does nothing to subvert stereotypes of ability—or, rather, disability—as its representations of the boyfriend's disabled body are put in the service of making Pink's abled body appear as though it is the generic ideal.

Chorus 2 (1:50–2:16)

After we see the patriarchal *cliché* of the naughty nurse in the bedroom, we see that of the unhinged housewife in the kitchen. The second chorus is now in full swing, and while the lyrics and the music are for the most part the same as they were in the first chorus, the images change. In fact, they appear to accelerate, giving the video a frantic and foreboding feel. For instance, the speed with which Pink chops the vegetables for her salad is strangely fast and seems to suggest that her grip on reality is slipping still more. Wielding a long, sharp knife, she cuts the vegetables—and especially the penis-like carrots—"into pieces" in a way that recalls the lyrics in the last part of the first verse.[42] All of this unfolds in a space traditionally associated with women's work and, by extension, women's oppression. Yet, in the context of the second chorus, this space is transformed from a space of women's oppression into a space of women's aggression. It is fitting, therefore, that she appropriates yet another phallic object—that is, an oversized kitchen knife—to effect such a transformation.[43]

As she is preparing the salad for the romantic dinner she hopes to have with her boyfriend, he is creeping down the stairs on one leg in an effort to escape from her sordid funhouse. He reaches the door, but as he opens it, he is viciously attacked by an enormous dog. Making use of a parodic intertextual allusion to Stephen King's *Cujo*, the visual imagery in this scene is just as, if not more, graphic than it was in the scene that preceded it. The boyfriend's body is ravaged by the dog, his face clearly communicating his excruciating pain. But unlike the earlier scene, this one unfolds very quickly; the shots of the boyfriend's face are fast and fleeting, and even his arm appears to flail at great speed. Pink, meanwhile, watches the entire episode from a safe distance (Figure 20.3) with a "blame the victim"-type

Figure 20.3 Pink watches as her boyfriend is attacked by a dog.

expression on her face: if he had behaved as she had wanted him to, it would never have—as she puts it in the second to last line of the chorus—"come right back to this."

Bridge (2:16–2:46)

In keeping with the video's emphasis on both circularity and temporal ambiguity, the boyfriend blacks out after the end of the second chorus just as he did after the end of the first. The accelerated pace of the images that characterizes the second chorus continues into the bridge, at which point a series of brutal acts are inflicted on the boyfriend. Here the video's dark drama escalates on all levels: lyrically, musically, and visually. Lyrically, Pink's abusive ambivalence toward her boyfriend is expressed more explicitly in the bridge than it is elsewhere. The first line sounds full of regret as she realizes that she has never really told him how "beautiful" he really is. But this regretful statement is quickly replaced by the guiltless avowal that she loves him, first and foremost, so that she can abuse him. Here Pink refers to her boyfriend as a "perfect little punching bag" while, at the same time, declaring her ongoing need for him. Indeed, Pink's ambivalence is articulated right from the beginning to the end of the bridge, for even as she claims with great conviction that she likes to abuse him, she apologizes.

The music, too, intensifies in the bridge as the guitars go from background to foreground. Now the most audible among them are performing the same note sequence as Pink, supporting her melodic lyrical phrasing. The guitars sing along with her, so to speak, doubling and redoubling her vocal performance. Pink's lyrics over the course of the bridge are, therefore, bolstered by her own guitar-driven battalion, and this makes them—and her—sound stronger and more powerful.

While the lyrics and the music contribute in no small way to the dramatic escalation that characterizes the bridge, it is the imagery that takes the overarching narrative of the video to the next level. Pink's boyfriend awakens to find himself seated in and bound to a wheelchair. Once again, he struggles to see her clearly in his injury-induced state. Pink's physical appearance has none of the sumptuous soap-opera aesthetics that it had heretofore; instead, she now looks like a cross between a circus master and a burlesque dancer. With her whitened complexion, she looks more like a scary joker from an evil magician's deck of cards than a daytime celebrity.

Pink paints her boyfriend's face against his will, as though she is preparing him to perform as a circus act (Figure 20.4). The face-paint feminizes his facial features, and he now looks as though he is wearing eye shadow, mascara, rouge, and lipstick. His face, too, is whitened, although the whitening does not make him look as frighteningly formidable as it does Pink; instead, he looks like a mutilated and, indeed, humiliated doll. The visual imagery makes clear that this is exactly what he is to her: one doll among the many that line her living room.

The mutilation and humiliation continue, as Pink spins him around as though on a merry-go-round in a wheelchair that looks like it belongs in a curiosity shop. Here the bridge culminates in another moment of circularity: he crashes down the stairs yet again.

Figure 20.4 Pink applies make-up to her boyfriend's face after having bound him to a wheelchair.

This time, however, Pink pushes him while applauding approvingly as he tumbles onto a red velvet cinema-like chair.[44] He is surrounded by dolls, the most prominent of which is a male doll that serves as a metaphor for Pink's boyfriend and the role he plays in her life. Pushed up against the chair, the boyfriend is very visibly in distress. But still Pink presses herself against his back, worsening his pain as she smothers him with cloying affection.

Rather than contest dominant norms of femininity and masculinity, the bridge consolidates them. For instance, Pink is portrayed as abusively ambivalent toward her boyfriend, and this portrayal reinforces sexist stereotypes of women as at once controlling and controlled in their relationships with men. The problem is not just that Pink's control over her boyfriend is formulated through feelings of both love and hate; it is that she is, herself, controlled by these feelings. In fact, the power she has in this relationship is not, strictly speaking, empowering; it is, instead, characterized by a dysfunctional cycle of overpowering her boyfriend and being overpowered by him. Similarly, the fact that she is overpowered by her boyfriend or, more specifically, by her feelings for him, makes her seem almost immature. This immaturity is revealed for the first time in the first verse, during which she demonstrates an almost child-like *naïveté*. And it is revealed yet again over the course of the bridge, when Pink's ostensible obsession with face-painting and dolls makes her seem like the girl who cannot and will not grow up. After all, hers is a world of play—perverse play, to be sure, but play nonetheless.

Like its representations of the feminine, the video's representations of the masculine over the course of the bridge tend to support rather than subvert dominant gender norms. They pick up where those of the second verse leave off, continuing and, at times, compounding the symbolic equations associated with them. More specifically, in the second verse, the boyfriend's disability is equated with dependence, which is equated with weakness and vulnerability, which is then equated with a failure of masculinity. All of these equations are carried over, almost without adjustment, to the bridge. But if, in the second verse, the failure of the boyfriend's masculinity is expressed by his bedridden state and his lost golf club, then over the course of the bridge it is expressed by his confinement in the wheelchair and his face make-up. Even more than in the second verse, the representations that characterize the bridge suggest that, the more disabled the man, the more feminine, and the more feminine, the more failed.

If the bridge's representations reinforce rather than resist dominant norms of gender, then it is precisely because they intersect with dominant norms of ability. Consider, for instance, the scene during which the boyfriend is struggling to free himself from his wheelchair while she skips and jumps merrily around him before gripping the wheelchair's handles and pushing him down the stairs. When juxtaposed with his body, her body comes across as not only abled but hyper-abled: unlike her boyfriend, Pink can move freely and easily and, even more importantly, has the power to take control of him and determine whether he lives or dies. Similarly, consider the scenes during which Pink spins her boyfriend around in the wheelchair and then later applauds his tumultuous tumble down the stairs. In both scenes, Pink treats her boyfriend like he is a freak who can be made to engage in dangerous, degrading, and dehumanizing acts. In doing so, she turns his disabled body—with its innumerable injuries, its open wounds, and its kitschy make-up—into an exploitative spectacle. And while exploitative spectacles are consistent with the circus theme that we see throughout the video, they are also part of why the circus—at least in its most traditional forms—has fallen out of favor and is now associated with a legacy of cruelty and ethical maltreatment.

Chorus 3 and 4 (2:46–3:52)

The end of the video is characterized by two consecutive choruses, during which the lyrics, music, and images come together to both continue and conclude the video's narrative. The lyrics, for instance, do not differ from what we have already heard, but they are important insofar as their central demand is repeated until the song draws to a close. This repetition makes the demand sound less insistent and more desperate than it did in the first and second choruses, thereby contributing to the sense of urgency that pervades the last part of the video.

Musically, the vocals are more complex in the third and fourth choruses than they are at any other point in the song and this, as we will soon see, serves as a compelling counterpart to the increased complexity of the images. That is, in the same way that the repetitive lyrics deepen the desperation that characterizes the chorus's central demand, so too does the broader and more diverse range of background vocals. Like the repetitive lyrics, this broader and more diverse range of background vocals heightens the tension associated with the last part of the video. The harmonies layered onto the lead vocals, combined with short supporting statements such as "no don't leave" and "I always say," emphasize the themes that we have seen throughout the video and, in doing so, contribute to their dramatic effect.

Visually, the images are—like the vocals—more intricate in terms of how they are made to mean in the context of the video's overarching narrative. The beginning of the third chorus sees Pink waking up after having fallen asleep on her boyfriend's back. She is shocked and appalled to find that he has managed to sneak out from under her. We see the boyfriend moving toward the door on one leg, trying to escape yet again. Like the narrative itself, the funhouse seems to go around in circles—like a carousel at an amusement park—and has no obvious exit. The boyfriend is frantic, but Pink is confident and full of conviction. In what is clearly an intertextual allusion to *The Shining*, she heads for the garage, takes a large woodsman's ax down from the wall, and begins to pursue her fleeing boyfriend.

Pink marches through the house with a crazed look on her face (Figure 20.5). Even more than it was in the second verse, her physical appearance is mean and menacing: her hair is standing straight up and, most importantly, her eyes have been darkened by large quantities of make-up. From a narrative perspective, the change in her eye make-up is not insignificant. Indeed, as we have already seen, eyes tell stories in this video: in the second verse, the boyfriend's bruised and bulging eye tells the story of a vengeful act of violence on the part of his intimate partner, while, over the course of the bridge, his made-up eyes tell the story of his ongoing humiliation by her. Similarly, Pink's eyes get more ominously black as the video proceeds, and, as they do, they tell the story of both her increasingly sadistic disposition and her mounting mental decomposition. The video's changing eye-related representations, therefore, can be seen to serve as metaphors for the amoral darkness into which one descends when one lives by the law of retaliation, not to mention the inevitably injurious implications of doing so.

With Pink closing in on him, the boyfriend reaches the bathroom and shuts the door. She is breaking down the door, bit by bit, with the ax's forbidding blade. Here we see Pink

Figure 20.5 Pink chases her boyfriend around the house with an ax.

appropriating yet another phallic object and this one, even more than the other two, is inextricably linked to a highly traditional and inherently destructive masculinity.[45] As the blade of her ax penetrates the door and creates a small opening through which she can see him, she once again implores him not to leave her. Panicked, he grabs an aerosol can from the bathroom vanity and sprays it into her eyes. The aerosol spray proves to be too much for her: she stumbles backwards, slips on the same mislaid marbles that we saw at the beginning of the first chorus, flies over the railing, and falls to the floor where she will stay for the rest of the video. The final scene of the video shows the boyfriend being wheeled away on a stretcher, while Pink lies immobile and continues—in yet another circular act—to plead with him to stay. The video closes with Pink coming out from behind the fourth wall, raising her hand to her mouth and blowing the audience a kiss. Her theatrical appeal to those watching the video suggests that what they have just seen was nothing more, and indeed nothing less, than a performance.

The images that accompany the fourth chorus resolve a number of the video's overarching narrative problems: first, the victim escapes the aggressor and we now know that he will survive; second, the aggressor is injured in much the same way as the victim was at the beginning of the video and, as a result, she gets the punishment we feel she deserves; and third, we are relieved of any concern we might have had for the victim given that we have now been told that the violence visited upon him never really happened. These resolutions are, admittedly, fairly standard and provide predictable forms of relief from the dramatic tension that had been building over the course of the video. It is, however, precisely their standard and predictable nature that makes them so problematic. In fact, neither the first resolution nor the second calls into question dominant norms of femininity or masculinity, and this is, at least in part, because the third actively maintains them. Put succinctly, the video makes a circus out of IPV against men, while, at the same time, asking us to deny that we ever witnessed any of it.

It would, however, be a mistake to claim that there is nothing about the final scenes of the video that calls into question dominant norms of femininity and masculinity. While Pink wields objects associated with masculinity throughout the video, it is ultimately an object associated with femininity—in this case, an aerosol can that resembles what could be a can of mace or pepper spray—that ends up being the most powerful one of all. Here we see a man defending himself in the way a woman would have to if she were to be attacked by someone she could not overpower.[46] If there is a moment of genuine subversion in this video where gender is concerned, then it is this one: that is, the one where the boyfriend appropriates a tool typically associated with women's self-defense—a tool of the oppressed rather than of the oppressor—to save himself. The subversive value of the video does not, therefore, lie in Pink wielding golf clubs, or large kitchen knives, or axes in order to retaliate for the violence men have visited upon women. That, in the words of Audre Lorde, would be to try to use the master's tools to dismantle the master's house.[47] Instead, what makes the boyfriend's hard-won freedom so meaningful here is that it is gained not through patriarchal tactics and strategies but against them.

Conclusion

Drawing on my analysis of the video's normative content, expressive form, and thematic structure, I argue that "Please Don't Leave Me" tends to confirm rather than contest prevailing stereotypes of gender, sexuality, and ability. With respect to its normative content, for example, I have shown that the video makes use of traditional tropes of the unhinged woman and the defenseless man. What is more, I have demonstrated that the video sets up symbolic equations that associate agency and autonomy with psychopathology in the case of Pink, and disability with feminization and failure in the case of the boyfriend. So, while "Please Don't Leave Me" may appear to disrupt dominant norms of masculinity and femininity, heterosexuality, and disability, I maintain that it does exactly the opposite: not only are agential women represented as dangerous and disturbed women, but disabled men are represented as feminized, and, most importantly, feminized men are represented as failed men. Far from being an empowered woman whose strength and determination allow her to define herself independently of her romantic attachments, Pink is portrayed as a deeply disturbed one whose attachments enslave others while, quite crucially, making her a slave to them. And as for the boyfriend, his enslavement to Pink and all of the degrading and dehumanizing things of which that consists are depicted in comedic terms: male victims of IPV are to be laughed at, and the spectacle of their victimization is to be excused and, ultimately, enjoyed.

Like its normative content, the video's expressive forms are a key part of what allows it to do the meaning-making work it does. More specifically, my analysis shows that word, sound, and image are mutually constitutive and reinforcing in Pink's "Please Don't Leave Me" as they work together to create an emotionally-charged and sensorially-intense multimedia experience. And, of course, the video's normative content and expressive forms are themselves inextricably linked to the video's thematic structure. Characterized by circularity, temporal ambiguity, and funhouse frivolity, the video's key themes both shape and are shaped by the stories it tells and how it tells them. That said, the video's key themes are not just derived from funhouse aesthetics; they are also, quite crucially, derived from the parodic intertexts that run through the entire video.

If the findings of my analysis suggest that the video's representations of gender, sexuality, and ability are for the most part conservative, then we might ask how its parodic intertextuality is implicated in this conservatism. Of course, some critical scholars show that the use of parody[48] and intertextuality[49] can allow artists to resist oppressive stereotypes through a variety of popular media forms. My analysis, however, demonstrates that this is not the case in the context of Pink's video. In fact, my analysis indicates that the video's so-called comedic allusions to *The Shining*, *Cujo*, and *Misery* are associated with a number of important implications that reinforce rather than resist oppressive stereotypes. More specifically, the video's parodic intertextuality invites viewers to occupy themselves with making comparisons between the source text and the intertext, thereby leading them to be less concerned by the nature of what they see before them. Similarly, the video's use of parodic intertextuality encourages viewers to excuse and, in some cases, embrace the intertext due to its references to and reliance on the source text. And finally, the video's parodic intertextuality allows viewers to let the creators of the intertext "off the hook," as it were, for they are not the creators of the source text and, therefore, are not seen as the source of the problems that the intertext might pose. Taken together, the operations and effects of parodic intertextuality—at least in the context of the video of interest to us here— are of considerable cultural consequence. On the one hand, they are such that male victims of IPV are not taken seriously; and, on the other hand, they are such that those who create and disseminate videos like "Please Don't Leave Me"—that is, videos that poke fun at male victims of IPV—do so with relative impunity.

Some might argue that the video's parodic intertextuality is best read as a critical commentary on the violence done to women by men in intimate partnerships.[50] And this reading might well be a plausible one. But, as my analysis shows, even if the video is read as a critical commentary of men's violence against women, it is nevertheless bound up in the patriarchal politics of gender, sexuality, and ability. And insofar as it is bound up in these politics, we must ask whether it can be put in the service of social justice. We must, in other words, consider the consequences of linking autonomous women to transgressive strength and mental pathology while linking vulnerable men to feminization and feminization to failure. Ultimately, my analysis shows that the video stages good gendered subjects as normative gendered subjects and, insofar as it does so, it cannot be taken seriously as counter-cultural critique.

Acknowledgments

I am grateful to the editors of the volume for their supportive feedback as well as to the Social Sciences and Humanities Research Council of Canada for funding my research on popular music videos. I am, moreover, indebted to the incredible cast of graduate students who helped me to bring the current chapter to fruition: Jamilah Dei-Sharpe, Pauline Hoebanx, Samantha Ilacqua, Jay Manicom, and Melissa McCullagh. And finally, I am appreciative of Zara Saeidzadeh for her ongoing feedback; Sam de Boise for his insightful suggestions; and all of those who participated in the Critical Feminist Studies and Media and Communications Studies seminars at Örebro University over the course of Fall 2018.

Notes

1   Pink [studio album], *Funhouse*, 88697406492 (LaFace Records CD, 2008).
2   Billboard, "The Week of November 15, 2008," *Billboard 200*, November 15, 2008, https://www.billboard.com/charts/billboard-200/2008-11-15.
3   Jonathan Keefe, "Review: Pink, Funhouse," *Slant Magazine*, October 26, 2008, https://www.slantmagazine.com/music/pink-funhouse.

4 Cara Carriveau, "Pink Interview," *Chicago Media Guide*, May 14, 2009, https://chicagomusicguide.com/interview-with-pink.

5 Ibid.

6 Ibid.

7 Keefe, "Review: Pink, Funhouse."

8 Australian Recording Industry Association, "Pink—Please Don't Leave Me Song," *ARIA Top 50 Singles*, 2009, https://australian-charts.com/showitem.asp?interpret=P!nk&titel=Please±Don%27t±Leave±Me&cat=s.

9 Offizielle Deutsch Charts, "Pink: Please Don't Leave Me (Single)," *Top 10 Singles Charts*, 2009, https://www.offiziellecharts.de/titel-details-523080.

10 Official Charts, "3 May 2009–9 May 2009," *Official Singles Chart Top 100*, 2009, https://www.officialcharts.com/charts/singles-chart/20090503/7501.

11 Billboard, "The Week of August 22, 2009," *Adult Pop Songs*, August 22, 2009, https://www.billboard.com/charts/adult-pop-songs/2009-08-22.

12 Billboard, "The Week of November 7, 2009," *Adult Contemporary*, November 7, 2009, https://www.billboard.com/charts/adult-contemporary/2009-11-07.

13 Billboard, "The Week of July 25, 2009," *Pop Songs*, July 25, 2009, https://www.billboard.com/charts/pop-songs/2009-07-25.

14 Billboard, "The Week of July 11, 2009," *The Hot 100*, July 11, 2009, https://www.billboard.com/charts/hot-100/2009-07-11.

15 Stephen King, *The Shining* (New York: Doubleday, 1977); *The Shining* [film], directed by Stanley Kubrick, 146 minutes (Warner Brothers, 1980); Stephen King, *Cujo* (Toronto: Viking, 1981); *Cujo* [film], directed by Lewis Teague, 93 minutes (Warner Brothers, 1983); Stephen King, *Misery* (Toronto: Viking, 1987); *Misery* [film], directed by Rob Reiner, 107 minutes (Columbia Pictures, 1990).

16 Pink, "Please Don't Leave Me," YouTube video (3:52), directed by Dave Meyers, posted by "PinkVideoVault," October 25, 2009, https://www.youtube.com/watch?v=eocCPDxKq1o.

17 Patrick Crowley, "Pink's 10 Best Music Videos: Critic's Picks," Billboard, August 17, 2017, https://www.billboard.com/articles/news/7933280/pink-music-videos-best-ranking.

18 Nick Levine, "Pink: Please Don't Leave Me," *Digital Spy*, April 14, 2009, https://www.digitalspy.com/music/single-reviews/a152654/pink-please-dont-leave-me-152654.

19 Shelby Knox, "Pink's New Video Goes a 'Little' Too Far," *HuffPost*, November 8, 2010, https://www.huffingtonpost.com/shelby-knox/pinks-new-video-goes-a-li_b_678010.html.

20 For a scholarly reflection on representations of violence against men in music videos, see Lori Burns and Marc Lafrance, "Celebrity, Spectacle and Surveillance: Understanding Lady Gaga's 'Paparazzi' and 'Telephone' Through Music, Image and Movement," in *Lady Gaga and Popular Music: Performing Gender, Fashion and Culture*, edited by Martin Iddon and Melanie Marshall (London: Routledge, 2013), 117–147; as well as Marc Lafrance and Lori Burns, "The Dark Side of Camp: Violence Against Men in Christina Aguilera's 'Your Body,'" in *Music and Camp*, edited by Christopher Moore and Philip Purvis (Middletown, CT: Wesleyan University Press, 2018), 220–240.

21 Due to what Patricia Louie has described as the video's disturbing depictions of "gender-based violence" (see "Gender-Based Violence in Pink's 'Please Don't Leave Me,'" *The Sociological Cinema*, February 10, 2014, https://www.thesociologicalcinema.com/videos/gender-based-violence-in-pinks-please-dont-leave-me), a censored version of it was

made and released shortly after the original version. The censored version does not contain some of the more graphic scenes of aggravated assault, such as the one in which Pink brings the golf club down on her boyfriend's leg and the one in which the boyfriend is viciously attacked by the dog. The censored version does not appear to be available on either YouTube or in major online music retail stores such as iTunes, however, so I have had to rely on the video's Wikipedia (2019) page for details. It is, moreover, worth noting that Pink made an entirely different version of the video, which she called the "Funhouse" version. This video was released in 2010 and featured Pink and Hart after they had reconciled. Shot in black and white, the video features Pink as a "giantess" and Hart as a "little person" in a sideshow tent. Just as I argue in my analysis of the original version, Knox ("Pink's New Video Goes a 'Little' Too Far") argues in her analysis of the funhouse version that the video is characterized by a variety of representations that reinforce the normativity of those with abled bodies and the non-normativity of those with disabled bodies. Once again, the "Funhouse" version of the video appears not to be available online or in music retail stores.

22 Crowley, "Pink's 10 Best Music Videos."

23 Levine, "Pink: Please Don't Leave Me."

24 Knox, "Pink's New Video Goes a 'Little' Too Far."

25 Melissa McCullagh and Marc Lafrance's statistical study of YouTube viewer comments relating to music videos that contain scenes of violence against men is relevant here ("A Thematic Analysis of YouTube Comments on Music Videos Featuring Violence Against Men by Women," forthcoming). The study shows that, of the 2,866 comments pertaining to "Please Don't Leave Me," 902 of them suggest that the video's representations of violence against men are humorous. The "violence against men is humorous" category, which comprised 31.5 percent of our sample, was the most common comment category in our study. Overall, the study indicates that 1,494 (52.1 percent) of the comments imply that violence against men is acceptable, while 827 (28.9 percent) of them imply that it is unacceptable.

26 See Richard Gelles, Donileen Loseke, and Mary Cavanaugh, eds., *Current Controversies on Family Violence* (Thousand Oaks, CA: Sage, 2005).

27 See Walter Dekeseredy, *Violence Against Women: Myths, Facts, Controversies* (Toronto, ON: University of Toronto Press, 2011); and Michael Kimmel, "Gender Symmetry in Domestic Violence," in *Misframing Men: The Politics of Contemporary Masculinities*, edited by Michael Kimmel (New Brunswick, NJ: Rutgers University Press, 2010), 99–121.

28 United Nations General Assembly, *In-Depth Study on All Forms of Violence Against Women: Report of the Secretary General* (New York: United Nations, 2006), http://www.un.org/womenwatch/daw/vaw/v-sg-study.htm; World Health Organization, *Promoting Gender Equality to Prevent Violence Against Women: Series of Briefings on Violence Prevention: The Evidence—Overview* (Geneva: World Health Organization, 2009), http://whqlibdoc.who.int/publications/2009/9789241597883_eng.pdf.

29 Government of Canada, *A Year in Review: Canada's Strategy to Prevent and Address Gender-Based Violence* (Ottawa, ON: Status of Women, 2018); Government of the United States of America, *The Violence Against Women Act* (Washington, DC: US Government Publishing Office, 2018); Her Majesty's Government, *Ending Violence Against Women and Girls: Strategy 2016–2020* (London: National Archives, 2006).

30 Douglas Kellner, *Media Spectacle* (London: Routledge, 2003); Rhonda Hammer and Douglas Kellner, *Media/Cultural Studies: Critical Approaches* (New York: Peter Lang, 2009).

31 The Dixie Chicks, "Goodbye Earl," YouTube video (4:17), official music video, directed by Evan Bernard, posted by "dixiechicks," October 2, 2009, https://www.youtube.com/watch?v=Gw7gNf_9njs; No Doubt feat. Christina Aguilera, "It's My Life," YouTube video (3:50), official music video, directed by David LaChapelle, posted by "NoDoubtTV," October 5, 2009, https://www.youtube.com/watch?v=ubvV498pyIM; Carrie Underwood, "Before He Cheats," YouTube video (3:18), official music video, directed by Roman White, posted by "Carrie Underwood," October 2, 2009, https://www.youtube.com/watch?v=WaSy8yy-mr8; Lady Gaga, "Paparazzi," YouTube video (7:10), official music video, directed by Jonas Åkerlund, posted by "Lady Gaga," November 25, 2009, https://www.youtube.com/watch?v=d2smz_1L2_0; Lady Gaga feat. Beyoncé, "Telephone," YouTube video (9:30), official music video, directed by Jonas Åkerlund, posted by "Lady Gaga," March 15, 2010, https://www.youtube.com/watch?v=EVBsypHzF3U; Maroon 5, "Misery," YouTube video (3:30), official music video, directed by Joseph Kahn, posted by "Maroon 5," June 30, 2010, https://www.youtube.com/watch?v=6g6g2mvItp4; Christina Aguilera, "Your Body," YouTube video (4:40), official music video, directed by Melina Matsoukas, posted by "Christina Aguilera," September 28, 2012, https://www.youtube.com/watch?v=6cfCgLgiFDM; Travis, "Where You Stand," YouTube video (3:44), official music video, directed by Blair Young and Fran Healy, posted by "Travis," April 30, 2013, https://www.youtube.com/watch?v=W-ZT2Hgonwc; Disclosure feat. Lorde, "Magnets," YouTube video (3:34), official music video, directed by Ryan Hope, posted by "OfficialDisclosure," September 29, 2015, https://www.youtube.com/watch?v=b_KfnGBtVeA; Rae Sremmurd feat. Travis Scott, "Close," YouTube video (3:24), official music video, directed by Mike Piscitelli, posted by "Rae Sremmurd," April 25, 2018, https://www.youtube.com/watch?v=-wo8HsrmYvU.

32 Olivia Truffaut-Wong, "7 Pink Moments That You Didn't Realize Were Super Feminist," *Bustle*, August 24, 2017, https://www.bustle.com/p/7-pink-moments-that-you-didnt-realize-were-super-feminist-78726.

33 Valda Blundell, John Shepherd, and Ian Taylor, eds., *Relocating Cultural Studies: Developments in Theory and Research* (New York: Routledge, 1993); Simon During, ed., *The Cultural Studies Reader* (London and New York: Routledge, 1993).

34 Arthur Asa Berger, *Cultural Criticism: A Primer of Key Concepts* (London: Sage, 1995).

35 Ian Buchanan, "Cultural Studies," in *A Dictionary of Critical Theory* (Oxford: University of Oxford Press, 2010), http://www.oxfordreference.com/view/10.1093/acref/9780199532919.001.0001/acref-9780199532919-e-153.

36 Chris Beasley, Heather Brook, and Mary Holmes, *Heterosexuality in Theory and Practice* (New York: Routledge, 2012); Judith Butler, *Gender Trouble: Feminism and the Subversion of Identity* (London: Routledge, 1990); Judith Butler, *Bodies that Matter: On the Discursive Limits of Sex* (London: Routledge, 1993); Raewyn W. Connell, *Gender and Power: Society, the Person and Sexual Politics* (Palo Alto: Stanford University Press, 1987); R.W. Connell, *Masculinities* (Cambridge: Polity Press, 1995); Chrys Ingraham, ed., *Thinking Straight: The Promise, the Power and Paradox of Heterosexuality* (New York: Routledge, 2005); Stevi Jackson and Sue Scott, *Theorizing Sexuality* (New York: McGraw-Hill Open University Press, 2010).

37 See Rosemarie Garland Thomson, *Extraordinary Bodies: Figuring Physical Disability in American Culture and Literature* (New York: Columbia University Press, 1997); Rosemarie Garland Thomson, ed., *Freakery: Cultural Spectacles of the Extraordinary Body* (New York: New York University Press, 1996); and Margrit Shildrick, *Embodying the Monster: Encounters with the Vulnerable Self* (London: Sage, 2002).

38 Lori Burns and Serge Lacasse, eds., *The Pop Palimpsest: Intertextuality in Recorded Popular Music* (Ann Arbor, MI: University of Michigan Press, 2018); Lori Burns, Alyssa Woods, and Marc Lafrance, "The Genealogy of a Song: Lady Gaga's Intertexts on The Fame Monster (2009)," *Twentieth-Century Music* 12, no. 1 (2015): 3–35; Kurt Mosser, "Cover Songs," in *Music in American Life: An Encyclopedia of the Songs, Styles, Stars, and Stories That Shaped Our Culture*, edited by Jacqueline Edmondson (Santa Barbara, CA: ABC-CLIO, 2013), 310–312.

39 The video's parodic intertextuality spans beyond the work of Stephen King. Consider, for instance, the iconic staircase scene in the film *Gone With the Wind*, directed by Victor Fleming (221 minutes [Selznick International Pictures and Metro-Goldwyn Meyer, 1939]). The scene consists of Scarlett O'Hara trailing down a huge red stairwell from the darkness above and ends with her being carried back up the stairwell by her drunken husband Rhett Butler (Brad Williams, "28 Classic Movie Scenes Involving Stairs," *WhatCulture*, February 19, 2013, http://whatculture.com/film/28-classic-movie-scenes-involving-stairs). As with "Please Don't Leave Me," the characters' ascents and descents symbolize shifting relations of power in the relationships they share. See http://www.youtube.com/watch?v=_36zsAP-Wh0.

40 I thank Jamilah Dei-Sharpe for suggesting that I consider the law of retaliation in videos that represent violence against men by women.

41 My previous and ongoing research suggests that most of the commercially successful videos that represent IPV against men are characterized by hypersexualized female characters. I explore the implications of this hypersexualization at more length in my work with Lori Burns on representations of gender and sexuality in Christina Aguilera's video for "Your Body" (Lafrance and Burns, "The Dark Side of Camp," 223–224).

42 I thank Pauline Hoebanx for drawing my attention to the symbolic significance of the carrots in this scene.

43 For another parodic intertextual allusion, see the kitchen fight that features the psychotically-obsessed female character, Alex Forrest, wielding an enormous kitchen knife against male character, Dan Gallagher, in *Fatal Attraction*: https://www.youtube.com/watch?v=mPxz5iCekro.

44 I thank Jeff Hearn for pointing out the aesthetic similarities between the chair onto which the boyfriend falls and the chairs typically found in a movie theatre.

45 Here I am alluding to the figure of the lumberjack and the destruction of the natural world with which this figure is traditionally associated.

46 In *The Shining*, it is the female character (Wendy Torrance) who is trapped in the bathroom as she tries to fight off the deranged male character (Jack Torrance). In "Please Don't Leave Me," however, it is the male character who is trapped in the bathroom as he tries to fight off the female character. This intertextual inversion supports the claim I make below: namely, that Pink's boyfriend is being staged as the female character, and she the male character, at this point in the video. I thank Pauline Hoebanx for bringing the intertextual implications of the bathroom scene to my attention.

47 Audre Lorde, "The Master's Tools Will Never Dismantle the Master's House," in *Sister Outsider: Essays and Speeches* (Berkeley, CA: Crossing Press, 1984), 110–114.

48 Butler, *Gender Trouble*; Sara Salih, "On Judith Butler and Performativity," in *Sexuality and Communications in Everyday Life: A Reader*, edited by Karen E. Lovaas and Mercilee M. Jenkins (London: Sage, 2006), 55–68; Helene Shugart, "Parody as Subversive Performance: Denaturalizing Gender and Reconstituting Desire in *Ellen*," *Text and Performance Quarterly* 21, no. 2 (2001): 95–113.

49 Lori Burns and Alyssa Woods, "Humor in the 'Booty Video': Female Artists Talk Back Through the Hip-Hop Intertext," in *The Routledge Companion to Popular Music and Humor*, edited by Nicolas Baxter-Moore and Tom Kitts (London and New York: Routledge, 2019 [forthcoming]).

50 I thank Sofia Strid for inviting me to consider the video's violence against men as a critique of men's violence against women.

Bibliography

Adams, Tony E., Stacy Holman Jones, and Carolyn Ellis. *Autoethnography: Understanding Qualitative Research*. New York: Oxford University Press, 2015.

Agnew, John. "Space and Place." In *The SAGE Handbook of Geographical Knowledge*, edited by John Agnew and David N. Livingstone. London: Sage, 2011.

Ahmed, Sara. *Living a Feminist Life*. Durham, NC: Duke University Press, 2017. Kindle edition.

Ahn. "Frozen Grand Central." Thesociologicalcinema.com. June 23, 2011. https://www.thesociologicalcinema.com/videos/frozen-grand-central.

Albright, Daniel. *Untwisting the Serpent: Modernism in Music, Literature and Other Arts*. Chicago, IL, and London: University of Chicago Press, 2000.

Albright, Deron. "Tales of the City: Applying Situationist Practices to the Analysis of the Urban Drama." *Criticism* 45, no. 1 (2003): 89–108.

Allen, Aaron S., and Kevin Dawe, eds. *Current Directions in Ecomusicology: Music, Culture Nature*. London and New York: Routledge, 2016.

Allen, Graham. *Intertextuality: The New Critical Idiom*. London: Routledge, 2000.

Allen, Michael. *Rodeo Cowboys and the North American Imagination*. Reno, NV: University of Nevada Press, 1998.

Allen, Michael. "'I Just Want to Be a Cosmic Cowboy': Hippies, Cowboy Code, and the Culture of a Counterculture." *The Western Historical Quarterly* 36, no. 3 (2005): 275–299.

Althusser, Louis. "Ideology and Ideological State Apparatuses." In *Lenin and Philosophy and Other Essays*, translated by Ben Brewster, 127–188. New York: Monthly Review Press, 1971.

Alvarez, Gabriel. "Kendrick Lamar: The Rapture." *Mass Appeal*. April 28, 2015. http://archive.massappeal.com/mass-appeal-issue-56-cover-story-kendrick-lamar.

Anderson, Jack. "Don't Say You're a Dancer: Choreographer David Winters Won't Settle for Typecasting." *Dance Magazine* 2 (1965): 49.

Anderson, Tim. "The Melodramatic Mode of Sofia Coppola." In *Popular Music and the New Auteur: Visionary Filmmakers After MTV*, edited by Arved Ashby. New York: Oxford University Press, 2013.

Annesley, James. "Being Spike Jonze: Intertextuality and Convergence in Film, Music Video and Advertising." *New Cinemas: Journal of Contemporary Film* 11, no. 1 (2013): 23–37.

Ardrey, Caroline. "Dialogism and Song: Intertextuality, Heteroglossia and Collaboration in Augusta Holmès's Setting of Catulle Mendès's 'Chanson.'" *Australian Journal of French Studies* 54, no. 2–3 (2017): 235–252.

Arlander, Annette. "Artistic Research and/as Interdisciplinarity." In *Artistic Research Does #1*, edited by Catarina Almeida and André Alves, 1–27. Porto: i2ADS, 2016.

Arnold, Gina, Daniel Cookley, Kirsty Fairclough-Isaacs, and Michael Goddard, eds. *Music/Video: Histories, Aesthetics, Media*. New York: Bloomsbury, 2017.

Asbill, D. Lacy. "'I'm Allowed to Be a Sexual Being': The Distinctive Social Conditions of the Fat Burlesque Stage." In *The Fat Studies Reader*, edited by Esther Rothblum and Sondra Solovay, 299–304. New York: New York University Press, 2009.

Atkins, John. *The Who on Record. A Critical History, 1963-1998*. Jefferson, NC: McFarland & Co., 2000.

Aufderheide, Pat. "Music Videos: The Look of the Sound." *Journal of Communication* 36, no. 1 (1986): 57–78.

Auslander, Philip. "Going with the Flow: Performance Art and Mass Culture." *TDR* 33, no. 2 (1989): 119–136.

Auslander, Philip. *Liveness. Performance in a Mediatized Culture*. Abingdon, Oxon: Routledge, 1999.

Auslander, Philip. "Performance Analysis and Popular Music: A Manifesto." *Contemporary Theatre Review* 14, no. 1 (2004): 1–13.

Auslander, Philip. "Musical Personae." *The Drama Review* 50, no. 1 (2006): 100–119.

Auslander, Philip. *Performing Glam Rock: Gender and Theatricality in Popular Music*. Ann Arbor, MI: University of Michigan Press, 2006.

Auslander, Philip. "Music as Performance: The Disciplinary Dilemma Revisited." In *Sound und Performance*, edited by Wolf-Dieter Ernst, 527–540. Würzburg: Verlag Königshausen & Neumann, 2015.

Auslander, Philip. "On the Concept of Persona in Performance." *Kunstlicht* 36, no. 3 (2015): 62–79.

Auslander, Philip. "'Musical Personae' Revisited." In *Investigating Musical Performance: Theoretical Models and Intersection*, edited by Gianmario Borio, Alessandro Cecchi, Giovanni Giuriati, and Marco Lutzu. London: Routledge [forthcoming].

Auslander, Philip, and Ian Inglis. "Nothing Is Real: The Beatles as Virtual Performers." In *The Oxford Handbook of Music and Virtuality*, edited by Sheila Whiteley and Shara Rambarran, 35–51. Oxford: Oxford University Press, 2016.

Austen, Jake. *TV-a-Go-Go: Rock on TV from American Bandstand to American Idol*. Chicago, IL: Chicago Review Press, 2005.

Austerlitz, Saul. *Money for Nothing: A History of the Music Video from the Beatles to the White Stripes*. London and New York: Continuum, 2007.

Australian Recording Industry Association. "Pink—Please Don't Leave Me Song." *ARIA Top 50 Singles*. 2009. https://australian-charts.com/ showitem.asp?interpret=P!nk&titel=Please+Don%27t+Leave+Me&cat=s.

Averill, Gage. *Four Parts, No Waiting: A Social History of American Barbershop Quartet*. Oxford: Oxford University Press, 2003.

Baker, Sarah. "Sex, Gender and Work Segregation in the Cultural Industries." In *Gender and Creative Labour*, edited by Bridget Conor, Rosalind Gill, and Stephanie Taylor, 23–36. Malden, MA: Wiley-Blackwell, 2015.

Bakhtin, Mikhail. *Speech Genres and Other Late Essays*. Austin, TX: University of Texas Press, 1986.

Bakhtin, Mikhail. "Discourse in the Novel." In *The Dialogic Imagination: Four Essays*, edited by Michael Holquist, translated by Caryl Emerson and Michael Holquist. Austin, TX: University of Texas Press, 1981.

Bakhtin, Mikhail. *Art and Answerability: Early Philosophical Essays*, edited by Michael Holquist and Vadim Liapunov. Austin, TX: University of Texas Press, 1990.

Bal, Mieke. *Traveling Concepts in the Humanities: A Rough Guide*. Toronto, ON: University of Toronto Press, 2002.

Banks, Jack. *Monopoly Television: MTV's Quest to Control the Music*. Boulder, CO and Oxford: Westview Press, 1996.

Bannister, Matthew. *White Boys, White Noise: Masculinities and 1980s Indie Guitar Rock*. Aldershot: Ashgate, 2006.

Barron, James. "David Bowie's Will Splits Estate Said to Be Worth $100 Million." *New York Times*. January 29, 2016. https://www.nytimes.com/2016/01/30/nyregion/david-bowies-will-splits-estate-said-to-be-worth-100-million.html.

Barthes, Roland. *Image, Music, Text*, translated by Stephen Heath. London: Fontana, 1977.

Bateson, Gregory. *Steps to an Ecology of Mind*. Northvale, NJ: Jason Aronson, 1972.

Baudrillard, Jean. *Simulacra and Simulation*, translated by Sheila Faria Glaser. Ann Arbor, MI: University of Michigan Press, 1994.

Beasley, Chris, Heather Brook, and Mary Holmes. *Heterosexuality in Theory and Practice*. New York: Routledge, 2012.

Beauchemin, Molly. "Kendrick Lamar Performs 'Alright' at the BET Awards." *Pichfork*. June 28, 2015. https://pitchfork.com/news/60163-kendrick-lamar-performs-alright-at-the-bet-awards.

Beebe, Roger, and Jason Middleton, eds. *Medium Cool: Music Videos from Soundies to Cellphones*. Durham, NC: Duke University Press, 2007.

Bennett, Andy. "Introduction: Part 2: Music, Space and Place." In *Music, Space and Place: Popular Music and Cultural Identity*, edited by Sheila Whiteley, Andy Bennett, and Stan Hawkins, 2–7. Farnham: Ashgate, 2005.

Bennett, Andy, and Ian Rogers. "Popular Music and Materiality: Memorabilia and Memory Traces." *Popular Music and Society* 23 (2015): 28–42.

Benjamin, Walter. "The Work of Art in the Age of Its Mechanical Reproducibility." In *Walter Benjamin—Selected Writings Volume 4 1938–1940*, edited by Howard Eiland and Michael W. Jennings, translated by Edmund Jephcott, Howard Eiland, and Gary Smith. London: Belknap Press of Harvard University Press: 2006.

Berman, Judy. "'This Is America': 8 Things to Read About Childish Gambino's New Music Video." *New York Times*. May 8, 2018. https://www.nytimes.com/2018/05/08/arts/music/childish-gambino-this-is-america-roundup.html.

Billboard. "The Week of November 15, 2008." *Billboard 200*. November 15, 2008. https://www.billboard.com/charts/billboard-200/2008-11-15.

Billboard. "The Week of July 11, 2009." *The Hot 100*. July 11, 2009. https://www.billboard.com/charts/hot-100/2009-07-11.

Billboard. "The Week of July 25, 2009." *Pop Songs*. July 25, 2009. https://www.billboard.com/charts/pop-songs/2009-07-25.

Billboard. "The Week of August 22, 2009." *Adult Pop Songs*. August 22, 2009. https://www.billboard.com/charts/adult-pop-songs/2009-08-22.

Billboard. "The Week of November 7, 2009." *Adult Contemporary*. November 7, 2009. https://www.billboard.com/charts/adult-contemporary/2009-11-07.

Binder, Steve. "The Interviews: Steve Binder, Creator/Producer/Director." Television Academy. March 4, 2004. https://interviews.televisionacademy.com/interviews/steve-binder#interview-clips.

Birdsall, Carolyn. "Earwitnessing: Sound Memories of the Nazi Period." In *Sound Souvenirs: Audio Technologies, Memory and Cultural Practices*, edited by Karin Bijsterveld & José van Dijck, 169–181. Amsterdam: University of Amsterdam Press, 2009.

Blake, David. "Timbre as Differentiation in Indie Music." *Music Theory Online* 18, no. 2 (2012). http://mtosmt.org/issues/mto.12.18.2/mto.12.18.2.blake.html.

Blistein, Jon, and Kory Grow. "David Bowie Plays Doomed, Blind Prophet in Haunting 'Blackstar' Video." *Rolling Stone*. November 19, 2015. https://www.rollingstone.com/music/music-news/david-bowie-plays-doomed-blind-prophet-in-haunting-blackstar-video-61585.

Blundell, Valda, John Shepherd, and Ian Taylor, eds. *Relocating Cultural Studies: Developments in Theory and Research*. New York: Routledge, 1993.

Bodroghkozy, Aniko. *Equal Time: Television and the Civil Rights Movement*. Urbana, IL: University of Illinois Press, 2012.

Bodroghkozy, Aniko, ed. *A Companion to the History of American Broadcasting*. Hoboken, NJ: John Wiley & Sons, 2018.

Bolter, David Jay, and Richard Grusin. *Remediation—Understanding New Media*. Cambridge, MA: MIT Press, 2000.

Borgstedt, Silke. *Der Musik-Star. Vergleichende Imageanalysen von Alfred Brendel, Stefanie Hertel und Robbie Williams*. Bielefeld: Transcript, 2008.

Bourdieu, Pierre, "The Forms of Capital." Reprinted in *Handbook of Theory and Research for the Sociology of Education*, edited by John G. Richardson, 241–258. Westport, CT: Greenwood, 1986.

Bourdieu, Pierre. *In Other Words: Essays Towards a Reflexive Sociology*, translated by Matthew Adamson. Stanford, CA: Stanford University Press, 1990.

Bourdieu, Pierre. *The Field of Cultural Production: Essays on Art and Literature*, translated and edited by Randal Johnson. New York: Columbia University Press, 1993.

Bowie, David. "David Bowie's Favorite Albums." *Vanity Fair*. November 20, 2003. https://www.vanityfair.com/culture/2016/04/david-bowie-favorite-albums.

Bowman, Lisa. "Snoop Dogg Responds to Critics Slating His Move into Gospel Music." *NME*. March 31, 2018. https://www.nme.com/news/music/snoop-dogg-responds-slating-move-gospel-music-stellar-awards-2277514.

Brackett, David. "Popular Music Genres: Aesthetics, Commerce and Identity." In *The SAGE Handbook of Popular Music*, edited by Andy Bennett and Steve Waksman. London: Sage, 2015.

Brackett, David. *Categorizing Sound: Genre and Twentieth-Century Popular Music*. Oakland, CA: University of California Press, 2016.

Bradby, Barbara. "Phallic Girls of Pop: Nicki Minaj's Sampled Anaconda and the Semiotics of Contradiction." *PopScriptum—Sound, Sex und Sexismus* 12 (2016). https://www2.hu-berlin.de/fpm/popscrip/themen/pst12/pst12_bradby.html#1.

Bradby, Barbara. "Growing Up to Be a Rapper? Justin Bieber's Duet with Ludacris as Transcultural Practice." In *The Routledge Research Companion to Popular Music and Gender*, edited by Stan Hawkins, 15–34. London and New York: Routledge, 2017.

Brannigan, Erin. *Dancefilm: Choreography and the Moving Image*. New York: Oxford University Press, 2011.

Brembilla, Paola. "Transmedia Music: The Value of Music as a Transmedia Asset." In *The Routledge Companion to Transmedia Studies*, edited by Matthew Freeman and Renira Rampazzo, 82–89. Abingdon, Oxon: Routledge, 2019.

Britt, Erica R. "Talking Black in Public Spaces: An Investigation of Identity and the Use of Preaching Style in Black Public Speech." PhD dissertation. University of Illinois at Urbana Champaign, 2011.

Brody, Richard. "Coltrane's Free Jazz Wasn't Just 'A Lot of Noise.'" *New Yorker*. November 10, 2014. https://www.newyorker.com/culture/richard-brody/coltranes-free-jazz-awesome.

Brooker, Jewel Spears. "Transcendence and Return: T.S. Eliot and the Dialectic of Modernism." *South Atlantic Review* 59, no. 2 (May 1994): 53–74.

Brougher, Kerry. "Visual-Music Culture." In *Visual Music: Synaesthesia in Art and Music Since 1900*, edited by Kerry Brougher, Jeremy Strick, Ari Wiseman, and Judith Zilcer, 88–179. London: Thames & Hudson, 2007.

Brown, Wendy. *Walled States, Waning Sovereignty*. Brooklyn, NY: Zone Books, 2010.

Brown, Willa. "Lumbersexuality and Its Discontents." *Atlantic*. December 10, 2014. https://www.theatlantic.com/national/archive/2014/12/lumbersexuality-and-its-discontents/383563.

Bruno, Giuliana. *Surface: Matters of Aesthetics, Materiality, and Media*. Chicago, IL: University of Chicago Press, 2014.

Bruns, Axel. *Blogs, Wikipedia, Second Life, and Beyond: From Production to Produsage*. New York: Lang, 2008.

Buchanan, Ian. "Cultural Studies." In *A Dictionary of Critical Theory*. Oxford: University of Oxford Press, 2010. http://www.oxfordreference.com/view/10.1093/acref/9780199532919.001.0001/acref-9780199532919-e-153.

Buckley, David. *Kraftwerk: Die unautorisierte Biografie*. Berlin: Metrolit, 2013.

Buell, Lawrence. *The Environmental Imagination: Thoreau, Nature Writing, and the Formation of American Culture*. Cambridge, MA: Harvard University Press, 1995.

Bulgakov, Mikhail. *Heart of a Dog*, translated by Mirra Ginsburg. Chicago, IL: Avalon Travel Publishing, 1994 [1925].

Bull, Stephen. "'Digital Photography Never Looked So Analogue': Retro Camera Apps, Nostalgia and the Hauntological Photograph." *Photoworks* 18 (Spring/Summer 2012). https://photoworks.org.uk/digital-photography-never-looked-so-analogue.

Berger, Arthur Asa. *Cultural Criticism: A Primer of Key Concepts*. London: Sage, 1995.

Burgess, Jean, and Joshua Green. *YouTube—Online Video and Participatory Culture*. 2nd ed. Cambridge: Polity Press, 2018.

Burke, Daniel. "Why Did Snoop Dogg Change His Name When He Became a Rasta?" *Washington Post*. August 3, 2013. https://www.washingtonpost.com/national/on-faith/why-did-snoop-dogg-change-his-name-when-he-became-a-rasta/2012/08/02/gJQA9OMfSX_story.html?noredirect=on&utm_term=.7e0d48c98673.

Burns, Lori. "The Concept Album as Visual-Sonic-Textual Spectacle: The Transmedial Storyworld of Coldplay's *Mylo Xyloto*." *iaspm@journal* 6, no. 2 (2016): 91–116.

Burns, Lori. "Multimodal Analysis of Popular Music Video: Genre, Discourse, and Narrative in Steven Wilson's 'Drive Home.'" In *Coming of Age: Teaching and Learning Popular Music in Academia*, edited by Carlos Xavier Rodrigues, 81–110. Ann Arbor, MI: University of Michigan Press, 2017.

Burns, Lori. "Interpreting Transmedia and Multimodal Narratives: Steven Wilson's 'The Raven That Refused to Sing.'" In *The Routledge Companion to Popular Music Analysis: Expanding Approaches*, edited by Ciro Scotto, Kenneth Smith, and John Brackett, 95–113. London and New York: Routledge, 2018.

Burns, Lori, and Serge Lacasse, eds. *The Pop Palimpsest: Intertextuality in Recorded Popular Music*. Ann Arbor, MI: University of Michigan Press, 2018.

Burns, Lori, and Marc Lafrance. "Celebrity, Spectacle and Surveillance: Understanding Lady Gaga's 'Paparazzi' and 'Telephone' Through Music, Image and Movement." In *Lady Gaga and Popular Music: Performing Gender, Fashion and Culture*, edited by Martin Iddon and Melanie Marshall, 117–147. London: Routledge, 2013.

Burns, Lori, and Marc Lafrance. "Gender, Sexuality, and the Politics of Looking in Beyoncé's 'Video Phone' (featuring Lady Gaga)." In *The Routledge Research Companion to Popular Music and Gender*, edited by Stan Hawkins, 102–116. London and New York: Routledge, 2017.

Burns, Lori, Marc Lafrance, and Laura Hawley. "Embodied Subjectivities in the Lyrical and Musical Expression of PJ Harvey and Björk." *Music Theory Online* 14, no. 4 (2008). http://www.mtosmt.org/issues/mto.08.14.4/mto.08.14.4.burns_lafrance_hawley.html.

Burns, Lori, and Jada Watson. "Spectacle and Intimacy in Live Concert Film: Lyrics, Music, Staging, and Film Mediation in P!nk's *Funhouse Tour* (2009)." *Music, Sound, and the Moving Image* 7, no. 2 (2013): 103–140.

Burns, Lori, and Jada Watson. "Subjective Perspectives Through Word, Image, and Sound: Temporality, Narrative Agency and Embodiment in the Dixie Chicks Video 'Top of the World.'" *Music, Sound, and the Moving Image* 4, no. 1 (2010): 3–38.

Burns, Lori, and Alyssa Woods. "Rap Gods and Monsters: Words, Music, and Images in the Hip-Hop Intertexts of Eminem, Jay-Z, and Kanye West." In *The Pop Palimpsest: Intertextuality in Recorded Popular Music*, edited by Lori Burns and Serge Lacasse, 215–251. Ann Arbor, MI: University of Michigan Press, 2018.

Burns, Lori, and Alyssa Woods. "Humor in the 'Booty Video': Female Artists Talk Back Through the Hip-Hop Intertext." In *The Routledge Companion to Popular Music and Humor*, edited by Nicolas Baxter-Moore and Tom Kitts, 310–320. London and New York: Routledge, 2019 [forthcoming].

Burns, Lori, Alyssa Woods, and Marc Lafrance. "The Genealogy of a Song: Lady Gaga's Intertexts on The Fame Monster (2009)." *Twentieth-Century Music* 12, no. 1 (2015): 3–35.

Burns, Lori, Alyssa Woods, and Marc Lafrance. "Sampling and Storytelling: Kanye West's Vocal and Sonic Narratives." In *The Cambridge Companion to the Singer-Songwriter*, edited by Katherine Williams and Justin A. Williams, 159–170. Cambridge: Cambridge University Press, 2016.

Burns-Ardolino, Wendy. "Jiggle in My Walk: The Iconic Power of the Big Butt in American Popular Culture." In *The Fat Studies Reader*, edited by Esther Rothblum and Sondra Solovay, 271–279. New York: New York University Press, 2009.

Burton, Justin Adams. *Posthuman Rap*. Oxford: Oxford University Press, 2017.

Butler, Judith. *Gender Trouble: Feminism and the Subversion of Identity*. London: Routledge, 1990.

Butler, Judith. *Bodies that Matter: On the Discursive Limits of Sex*. London: Routledge, 1993.

Candy, Linda. "Practice Based Research: A Guide." *CCS Report* 1.0 (November 2006): 1–19.

Cantrill, James. "The Environmental Self and a Sense of Place: Communication Foundations for Regional Ecosystem Management." *Journal of Applied Communication Research* 26, no. 3 (1998): 301–318.

Cantwell, Robert. *When We Were Good: The Folk Revival*. Cambridge, MA: Harvard University Press, 1996.

Carol Vernallis, Holly Rogers, and Lisa Perrott, eds. *Transmedia Directors: Artistry, Industry, and New Audiovisual Aesthetics*. New York and London: Bloomsbury, 2019.

Carriveau, Cara. "Pink Interview." *Chicago Media Guide*. May 14, 2009. https://chicagomusicguide.com/interview-with-pink.

Carroll, Noel. *Theorizing the Moving Image*. Cambridge: Cambridge University Press, 1996.

Cartier, Nina. "Black Women On-screen as Future Texts: A New Look at Black Pop Culture Representations." *Cinema Journal* 53, no. 4 (Summer 2014): 150–157.

Castanheira, José Cláudio Siqueira. "Timeline Philosophy: Technological Hedonism and Formal Aspects of Films and Music Videos." In *Music/Video—Histories, Aesthetics, Media*, edited by Gina Arnold, Daniel Cookney, Kirsty Fairclough, and Michael Goddard, 215–230. London: Bloomsbury, 2017.

Caston, Emily. "Not Another Article on the Author! God and Auteurs in Moving Image Analysis: Last Call for a Long Overdue Paradigm Shift." *Music, Sound, and the Moving Image* 9, no. 2 (2015): 145–162.

Cavanagh, David. "Changesfiftybowie." *Q Magazine*, February 1997: 52–59.

Chalko, Rosa. "Musical Meaning on the Screen: An Approach to Semiotics for Music in Cinema." In *Reinventing Sound: Music and Audiovisual Culture*, edited by Enrique Encabo, 102–116. Newcastle upon Tyne: Cambridge Scholars Publishing, 2015.

Chang, Heewon. *Autoethnography as Method*. Walnut Creek, CA: Left Coast Press, 2008.

Chang, Heewon, Faith Ngunjiri, and Kathy-Ann C. Hernandez. *Collaborative Autoethnography*. London: Routledge, 2013.

Chapple, Freda, and Chiel Kattenbelt, eds. *Intermediality in Theatre and Performance*. Amsterdam: International Federation for Theatre Research, 2007.

Chatman, Dayna. "Pregnancy, Then It's 'Back to Business': Beyoncé, Black Femininity, and the Politics of a Post-Feminist Gender Regime." *Feminist Media Studies* 15, no. 6 (2015): 926–941.

Chen, Gina Masullo, Sherri Williams, Nicole Hendrickson, and Li Chen. "Male Mammies: A Social-Comparison Perspective on How Exaggeratedly Overweight Media Portrayals of Madea, Rasputia, and Big Momma Affect How Black Women Feel About Themselves." *Mass Communication and Society* 15, no. 1 (2012): 115–135.

Ching, Barbara. *Wrong's What I Do Best: Hard Country Music and Contemporary Culture*. New York: Oxford University Press, 2001.

Chion, Michel. *Audio-Vision: Sound on Screen*. Edited and translated by Claudia Gorbman. New York: Columbia University Press, 1994 [1990].

Chivers, Emily Yochim. *Skate Life: Re-imagining White Masculinity*. Ann Arbor, MI: University of Michigan Press, 2010.

Chopra-Gant, Mike. "Pictures or It Didn't Happen: Photo-nostalgia, iPhoneography and the Representation of Everyday Life." *Photography & Culture* 9, no. 2 (July 2016): 121–128.

Chung, Gabrielle. "Katy Perry's New Song 'Wide Awake': Is She Singing about Russell Brand? (Video)." *Celebuzz!* May 20, 2012.

Cleto, Fabio, ed. *Camp: Queer Aesthetics and the Performing Subject. A Reader*. Edinburgh: Edinburgh University Press, 1999.

Clifton, Derrick. "5 Important Lessons about Sexism from the Slut-Shaming of Nicki Minaj's NSFW Artwork." Mic.com. July 2014. https://mic.com/articles/95268/5-important-lessons-about-sexism-from-the-slut-shaming-of-nicki-minaj-s-nsfw-artwork#.Nu6uZ7ShX.

Coates, Norma. "Excitement Is Made, Not Born: Jack Good, Television, and Rock and Roll." *Journal of Popular Music Studies* 25, no. 3 (September 2013): 301–325.

Coates, Norma. "Television Music." In *A Companion to the History of American Broadcasting*, edited by Aniko Bodroghkozy, 321–345. Hoboken, NJ: John Wiley & Sons, 2018.

Collins, John J. *Introduction to the Hebrew Bible*. Minneapolis, MN: Fortress Press, 2014.

Collins, Patricia Hill. *Black Sexual Politics: African Americans, Gender, and the New Racism*. New York: Routledge, 2004.

Collins, Patricia Hill. *From Black Power to Hip Hop: Racism, Nationalism and Feminism*. Philadelphia, PA: Temple University Press, 2006.

Collins, Patricia Hill, and Sirma Bilge. *Intersectionality*. Cambridge: Polity Press, 2016.

Comino, Jo. "Underground Film-Making: British Super 8 in the 1980s." In *The Routledge Companion to British Cinema History*, edited by I.Q. Hunter, Laraine Porter, and Justin Smith, 306–316. London: Routledge, 2017.

Confino, Alon. "Collective Memory and Cultural History." *The American Historical Review* 102, no. 5 (1997): 1386.

Connell, John, and Chris Gibson. *Sound Tracks: Popular Music, Identity and Place*. New York: Routledge, 2003.

Connell, Raewyn. *Gender and Power: Society, the Person and Sexual Politics*. Palo Alto: Stanford University Press, 1987.

Connell, Raewyn *Masculinities*. Cambridge: Polity Press, 1995.

Considine, J.D. "Fi Interview: David Bowie." *Fi: The Magazine of Music & Sound*. October 2, 1997: 36–41.

Cook, Nicholas. *Analysing Musical Multimedia*. New York: Oxford University Press, 1998.

Cooper, Kim, and David Smay, eds. *Bubblegum Music Is the Naked Truth: The Dark History of Prepubescent Pop, from the Banana Splits to Britney Spears*. Port Townsend, WA: Feral House, 2001.

Coscarelli, Joe. "Kendrick Lamar on His New Album and the Weight of Clarity." *New York Times*. March 16, 2015. https://www.nytimes.com/2015/03/22/arts/music/kendrick-lamar-on-his-new-album-and-the-weight-of-clarity.html.

Cox, Terrence. "*Cowboyography*: Matter and Manner in the Songs of Ian Tyson." In *Slipper Pastimes: Reading the Popular in Canadian Culture*, edited by Joan Nicks and Jeannette Sloniowski, 279–295. Waterloo, ON: Wilfrid Laurier University Press, 2002.

Crane, Dan. "What Would Beyoncé Wear? She Knows." *New York Times*. December 18, 2018. www.nytimes.com/2013/12/19/fashion/B-Akerlund-Stylist-Beyonce-Visual-Album-Fashion.html?pagewanted=all.

Cronon, William. "The Trouble with Wilderness; or, Getting Back to the Wrong Nature." In *Uncommon Ground: Rethinking the Human Place in Nature*, edited by William Cronon, 69–90. New York: W.W. Norton & Co., 1995.

Crowley, Patrick. "Pink's 10 Best Music Videos: Critic's Picks." Billboard. August 17, 2017. https://www.billboard.com/articles/news/7933280/pink-music-videos-best-ranking.

Cuevas, Efrén. "Change of Scale: Home Movies as Microhistory in Documentary Films." In *Amateur Filmmaking: The Home Movie, the Archive, the Web*, edited by Laura Rascaroli, Gwenda Young, and Barry Monahan, 139–152. New York and London: Bloomsbury, 2014.

Cush, Andy. "These Are All of the Secrets David Bowie Fans Have Found in the Blackstar Artwork." *Spin*. November 15, 2016. https://www.spin.com/2016/11/these-are-all-of-the-secrets-david-bowie-fans-have-found-in-the-blackstar-artwork.

Dabek, Ryszard. "Immaterial/Materiality." *Journal of Asia-Pacific Pop Culture* 2, no. 2 (2017): 220–237.

D'Acci, Julie. "Nobody's Woman? *Honey West* and the New Sexuality." In *The Revolution Wasn't Televised: Sixties Television and Social Conflict*, edited by Lynn Spigel and Michael Curtin, 73–94. New York: Routledge, 1997.

Dante, Alighieri. *The Divine Comedy of Dante Alighieri: Inferno, Purgatory, Paradise*. Reprinted. New York: Union Library Association, 1935.

Dawidoff, Nicholas. "Lubbock or Leave It: Jimmie Dale Gilmore and The Flatlanders." In *In the Country of Country*, edited by Nicholas Dawidoff, 291–308. New York: First Vintage Books, 1998.

Debord, Guy. *The Society of the Spectacle*, translated and annotated by Ken Knabb. Berkeley, CA: Bureau of Public Secrets, 2014. [Originally published as *La Société du Spectacle*. Paris: Buchet-Chastel, 1967.]

Debord, Guy. *Comments on the Society of the Spectacle*, translated by Malcolm Imrie. London: Verso, 1998. [Originally published as *Commentaires sur la société du spectacle*. Paris: Editions Gérard Lébovici, 1988.]

Debord, Guy. *Complete Cinematic Works: Scripts, Stills, Documents*, translated and edited by Ken Knabb. Oakland, CA: AK Press, 2003.

Deitch, Maud. "Exclusive: Kendrick Lamar Sings Taylor Swift's 'Shake It Off.'" *Fader*. November 4, 2014. http://www.thefader.com/2014/11/04/kendrick-lamar-interview-halloween-taylor-swift.

Dekeseredy, Walter S. *Violence Against Women: Myths, Facts, Controversies*. Toronto, ON: University of Toronto Press, 2011.

Deleuze, Gilles. *Difference and Repetition*. New York: Columbia University Press, 1994 [1968].

Deleuze, Gilles. *The Fold: Leibniz and the Baroque*, translated by Tom Conley. London and New York: Continuum, 2006.

Demopoulos, Maria. "Blink of an Eye: Filmmaking in the Age of Bullet Time." *Film Comment* 36, no. 3 (May/June, 2000): 34–39.

Demos, T.J. "Moving Images of Globalization." *Grey Room* 37 (2009): 6–29.

Denisoff, R. Serge. *Inside MTV*. New Brunswick, NJ and Oxford: Transaction Books, 1988.

Dettmar, Kevin J.H. *Is Rock Dead?* New York: Routledge, 2006.

Dockwray, Ruth, and Allan F. Moore. "Configuring the Sound-Box 1965–1972." *Popular Music* 29, no. 2 (2010): 181–197.

Doubrovsky, Serge. *Fils*. Paris: Gallimard, 1977.

Douglas, Susan J. *Where the Girls Are: Growing Up Female with the Mass Media*. New York: Times Books, 1994.

Dowd, A.A. "Interview: Avey Tare of Animal Collective Programs a Uniquely Trippy Movie Marathon." *AV Club*. November 14, 2014. https://film.avclub.com/avey-tare-of-animal-collective-programs-a-uniquely-trip-1798267797.

Draaisma, Douwe. *Metaphors of Memory: A History of Ideas about the Mind*. Cambridge: Cambridge University Press, 2000.

Durham, Aisha. "'Check On It': Beyoncé, Southern Booty, and Black Femininities in Music Video." *Feminist Media Studies* 12, no. 1 (2012): 35–49.

During, Simon, ed. *The Cultural Studies Reader*. London and New York: Routledge, 1993.

Dyer, Richard. *Stars*. London: British Film Institute, 1979.

Dyson, Michael Eric. "God Complex, Complex Gods, or God's Complex: Jay-Z, Poor Black Youth, and Making 'The Struggle' Divine." In *Religion in Hip Hop: Mapping the New Terrain in the US*, edited by Monica R. Miller, Anthony B. Pinn, and Bernard "Bun B" Freeman, 54–68. New York: Bloomsbury, 2015.

Echard, William. "Psychedelia, Musical Semiotics, and Environmental Unconscious." *Green Letters: Studies in Ecocriticism* 15, no. 1 (2011): 61–75.

Eckenroth, Lindsey. "Once Again. On the Music of Laurie Anderson's 'O Superman (for Massenet).'" *American Music Review* 43, no. 2 (2014).

Edmond, Maura. "Here We Go Again: Music Videos After YouTube." *Television and New Media* 15, no. 4 (2014): 305–320.

Edwards, Gavin. "Billboard Cover: Kendrick Lamar on Ferguson, Leaving Iggy Azalea Alone and Why 'We're in the Last Days.'" Billboard. January 9, 2015. https://www.billboard.com/articles/news/6436268/kendrick-lamar-billboard-cover-story-on-new-album-iggy-azalea-police-violence-the-rapture.

Edwards, James. "Silence by My Noise: An Ecocritical Aesthetic of Noise in Japanese Traditional Sound Culture and the Sound Art of Akita Masami." *Green Letters: Studies in Ecocriticism* 15, no. 1 (2011): 89–102.

Eisenstein, Sergei. *Towards a Theory of Montage: Sergei Eisenstein Selected Works*, vol. 2, edited by Michael Glenny and Richard Taylor, translated by Michael Glenny. New York: I.B. Tauris, 1991.

Elleström, Lars, ed. *Media Borders, Multimodality and Intermediality*. Basingstoke: Palgrave Macmillan, 2010.

Elleström, Lars. "The Modalities of Media: A Model for Understanding Intermedial Relations." In *Media Borders, Multimodality and Intermediality*, edited by Lars Elleström, 11–48. Basingstoke: Palgrave Macmillan, 2010.

Elleström, Lars. "Transfer of Media Characteristics among Dissimilar Media." *Palabra Clave* 20, no. 3 (2017): 663–685.

Eliot, T.S. "Tradition and the Individual Talent (1919)." In *The Sacred Wood and Major Early Essays*, edited by Frank Kermode, 27–33. Mineola, NY: Dover Publications, 1998.

Eliot, T.S. *Collected Poems: T.S. Eliot*. London: Faber & Faber, 1964.

Ellis, Carolyn. *Music Autoethnographies: Making Autoethnography Sing/Making Music Personal*. Bowen Hills: Australian Academic Press, 2009.

Ellis, David. "Modernism and T.S. Eliot." *Cambridge Quarterly* 47, no. 1 (March 1, 2018): 53–64.

Ellis, Jim. "The Erotics of Citizenship in Derek Jarman's *Jubilee* and Isaac Julien's *Young Soul Rebels*." *Southern Quarterly* 39, no. 4 (2001): 148–160.

Ellis, Jim. *Derek Jarman's Angelic Conversations*. Minneapolis, MN: University of Minnesota Press, 2009.

Encabo, Enrique, ed. *Reinventing Sound: Music and Audiovisual Culture*. Newcastle upon Tyne: Cambridge Scholars Publishing, 2015.

Englund, Axel. "Intermedial Topography and Metaphorical Interaction." In *Media Borders, Multimodality and Intermediality*, edited by Lars Elleström, 69–81. Basingstoke: Palgrave Macmillan, 2010.

Espinoza, Joshua. "People Think Kendrick Lamar Is Dissing Big Sean Again on 'Humble.'" *Complex*. March 30, 2017. https://www.complex.com/music/2017/03/people-think-kendrick-lamar-is-dissing-big-sean-on-humble.

Evers, Clifton. "'The Point': Surfing, Geography and a Sensual Life of Men and Masculinity on the Gold Coast, Australia." *Social & Cultural Geography* 10, no. 8 (2009): 893–908.

Fabbri, Franco. "A Theory of Musical Genres: Two Applications." In *Popular Music Perspectives: Papers from the First International Conference on Popular Music Research*, edited by David Horn and Philip Tagg, 52–81. Gothenberg and Exeter: IASPM, 1982.

Fahlenbrach, Kathrin. "Sonic Spaces in Movies: Audiovisual Metaphors and Embodied Meanings in Sound Design." In *Body, Sound and Space in Music and Beyond: Multimodal Explorations*, edited by Clemens Wöllner, 129–149. Abingdon, Oxon: Routledge, 2017.

Faiers, Jonathan. *Tartan: Textiles that Changed the World*. Oxford: Berg Publishers, 2008.

Farrell, Amy E. *Fat Shame: Stigma and the Fat Body in American Culture*. New York: New York University Press, 2011.

Fenster, Mark. "Genre and Form: The Development of the Country Music Video." In *Sound and Vision: The Music Video Reader*, edited by Simon Frith, Andrew Goodwin, and Lawrence Grossberg, 94–110. London and New York: Routledge, 1993.

Feuer, Jane. *The Hollywood Musical*. Bloomington, IN: Indiana University Press, 1993.

Fisher, Mark. *The Weird and the Eerie*. London: Repeater Books, 2016.

Fiske, John. "MTV: Post-Structural, Post-Modern." *Journal of Communication Enquiry* 10, no. 1 (1986): 74–79.

Flanagan, Bill. *U2 at the End of the World*. New York: Delta, 1996.

Flath, Beate. "Musik(wirtschafts)kulturen—eine Annäherung am Beispiel von Hatsune Miku." In *Lied und populäre Kultur/Song and Popular Culture. Jahrbuch des Zentrums für Populäre Kultur und Musik: Musik und Professionalität*, edited by K. Holtsträter and Michael Fischer, 225–240. Münster: Waxmann, 2017.

Fleetwood, Nicole R. *Troubling Vision: Performance, Visuality, and Blackness*. Chicago, IL: University of Chicago Press, 2011.

Forman, Murray. *The 'Hood Comes First: Race, Space, and Place in Rap and Hip-Hop*. Middletown, CT: Wesleyan University Press, 2002.

Fowler, William. "The Occult Roots of MTV: British Music Video and Underground Film-Making in the 1980s." *Music, Sound, and the Moving Image* 11, no. 1 (2017): 63–77.

Fox, Pamela. *Natural Acts: Gender, Race, and Rusticity in Country Music*. Ann Arbor, MI: University of Michigan Press, 2009.

Freud, Sigmund. "The Uncanny." In *The Uncanny*, by Sigmund Freud, translated by David McLintock, 121–162. Suffolk: Penguin Books, 2003 [1919].

Fricke, David. "U2's Serious Fun." *Rolling Stone*. October 1, 1992. http://www.rollingstone.com:80/news/coverstory/u2s_serious_fun/page/6.

Fricke, David. "Bitter Prophet: Thom Yorke on 'Hail to the Thief.'" *Rolling Stone*. June 26, 2003. https://www.rollingstone.com/music/music-news/bitter-prophet-thom-yorke-on-hail-to-the-thief-87869.

Frith, Simon. *Performing Rites: On the Value of Popular Music*. Cambridge, MA: Harvard University Press, 1996.

Frith, Simon. "Look! Hear! The Uneasy Relationship of Music and Television." *Popular Music* 21, no. 3 (October 2002): 277–290.

Frith, Simon. *Taking Popular Music Seriously: Selected Essays*. Aldershot: Ashgate, 2007/London and New York: Routledge, 2017.

Frith, Simon, and Howard Horne. *Art into Pop*. London: Methuen, 1987.

Frith, Simon, Andrew Goodwin, and Lawrence Grossberg, eds. *Sound and Vision: The Music Video Reader*. London: Routledge, 1993.

Frow, John. *Genre*. London and New York: Routledge, 2015.

Funaro, Vincent. "Religion in Hip-Hop: Reconciling Rap and Religion." *Christian Post*. October 26, 2012. https://www.christianpost.com/news/religion-in-hip-hop-reconciling -rap-and-the-gospel-83980.

Gaar, Gillian. *Return of the King: Elvis Presley's Great Comeback*. London: Jawbone Press, 2010.

Gabrielli, Guilia. "An Analysis of the Relation between Music and Image: The Contribution of Michel Gondry." In *Rewind/Play/Fast Forward: The Past, Present, and Future of the Music Video*, edited by Henry Keazor and Thorsten Wübbena, 89–110. New Brunswick, NJ and London: Transaction Publishers, 2010.

Garland Thomson, Rosemarie, ed. *Freakery: Cultural Spectacles of the Extraordinary Body*. New York: New York University Press, 1996.

Garland Thomson, Rosemarie. *Extraordinary Bodies: Figuring Physical Disability in American Culture and Literature*. New York: Columbia University Press, 1997.

Garrard, Greg. *Ecocriticism*. 2nd ed. London: Routledge, 2012.

Garritano, Carmela. "The Materiality of Genre: Analog and Digital Ghosts in Video Movies from Ghana." *Cambridge Journal of Postcolonial Literary Inquiry* 4, no. 2 (2017): 191–206.

Gaunt, Kyra D. "YouTube, Twerking & You: Context Collapse and the Handheld Co-presence of Black Girls and Miley Cyrus." *Journal of Popular Music Studies* 27, no. 3 (2015): 244–273.

Gelles, Richard J., Donileen R. Loseke, and Mary M. Cavanaugh, eds. *Current Controversies on Family Violence*. Thousand Oaks, CA: Sage, 2005.

Genette, Gérard. *Narrative Discourse: An Essay in Method*, translated by Jane E. Lewin. Ithaca, NY: Cornell University Press, 1980.

Genette, Gérard. *Palimpsests: Literature to the Second Degree*, translated by Channa Newman and Claude Doubinsky. Lincoln, NE: University of Nebraska Press, 1997.

Geslani, Michelle. "Thom Yorke Uses Radiohead's 'Burn the Witch' to Comment on the Ill-fated 2016 election." *CoS News*. November 10, 2016. https://consequenceofsound.net/2016/11/ thom-yorke-uses-radioheads-burn-the-witch-to-comment-on-the-ill-fated-2016-election.

Gildal, Peter. *Structural Film Anthology*. London: BFI, 1976.

Gill, Warren. "Region, Agency, and Popular Music: The Northwest Sound, 1958–1966." *The Canadian Geographer* 37, no. 2 (1993): 120–131.

Gilman, Sander L. "Black Bodies, White Bodies: Toward an Iconography of Female Sexuality in Late Nineteenth-Century Art, Medicine, and Literature." *Critical Inquiry* 12, no. 1 (1985): 204–242.

Gitelman, Lisa. "'Materiality Has Always Been in Play': An Interview with N. Katherine Hayles." *Iowa Journal of Cultural Studies* 2 (2002): 7–12.

Gledhill, Christine. "Rethinking Genre." In *Reinventing Film Studies*, edited by Christine Gledhill and Linda Williams. New York: Oxford University Press, 2000.

Glotfelty, Cheryll. "Introduction: Literary Studies in an Age of Environmental Crisis." In *The Ecocriticism Reader: Landmarks in Literary Ecology*, edited by Cheryll Glotfelty and Harold Fromm, xv–xxxvii. Athens: University of Georgia Press, 1996.

Goffman, Erving. *The Presentation of Self in Everyday Life*. New York: Anchor, 1959.

Goffman, Erving. *Frame Analysis: An Essay on the Organization of Experience*. Boston, MA: Northeastern University Press, 1986 [1974].

Goldmark, Daniel. "Before *Willie*: Reconsidering Music and the Animated Cartoon of the 1920s." In *Beyond the Soundtrack: Representing Music in Cinema*, edited by Daniel Goldmark, Lawrence Kramer, and Richard Leppert, 232–234. Oakland, CA: University of California Press, 2017.

Goodwin, Andrew. *Dancing in the Distraction Factory: Music Television and Popular Culture*. Minneapolis, MN: University of Minnesota Press, 1992.

Gorbman, Claudia. *Unheard Melodies: Narrative Film Music*. Bloomington, IN: Indiana University Press, 1987.

Gore, Joe. "New Digital Stimulation from David Bowie & Reeves Gabrels." *Guitar Player* (issue 330) 31, no. 6 (June 1997): 29–35.

Government of Canada. *A Year in Review: Canada's Strategy to Prevent and Address Gender-Based Violence*. Ottawa, ON: Status of Women, 2018.

Government of the United States of America. *The Violence Against Women Act*. Washington, DC: US Government Publishing Office, 2018.

Gow, Joe. "Making Sense of Music Video: Research During the Inaugural Decade." *Journal of American Culture* 15, no. 3 (1992): 35–43.

Gracyk, Theodore. *Rhythm and Noise: An Aesthetics of Rock*. London: I.B. Tauris, 1996.

Gracyk, Theodore. *I Wanna Be Me: Rock Music and the Politics of Identity*. Philadelphia, PA: Temple University Press, 2001.

Greco, Patti. "'Pretty Hurts' Director Melina Matsoukas on Beyoncé's Throw-up Scene and Casting Harvey Keitel." *Vulture*. December 16, 2013. www.vulture.com/2013/12/beyonce-pretty-hurts-director-melina-matsoukas-interview.html.

Greenberg, Clement. "Towards a Newer Laocoon." *Partisan Review* 7, no. 4 (1940): 296–310.

Griffiths, Dai. "Elevating Form and Elevating Modulation." *Popular Music* 34, no. 1 (2014): 22–44.

Gross, Joan. "Phat." In *Fat: The Anthropology of an Obsession*, edited by Tom Kulick and Anne Meleney, 63–76. London: Penguin Books, 2005.

Guccione, Bob, Jr. "David Bowie on 9/11 and God." *Daily Beast*. January 16, 2016. https://www.thedailybeast.com/david-bowie-on-911-and-god?ref=scroll.

Guesdon, Maël, and Philippe Le Guem. "Retromania: Crisis of the Progressive Ideal and Pop Music Spectrality." In *Media and Nostalgia*, edited by Katharina Niemeyer, 73–75. London: Palgrave Macmillan, 2014.

Gumprecht, Blake. "Lubbock on Everything: The Evocation of Place in Popular Music (a West Texas Example)." *Journal of Cultural Geography* 18, no. 1 (1998): 68–77.

Guralnick, Peter. *Careless Love: The Unmaking of Elvis Presley*. Boston, MA: Little, Brown and Co., 1997.

Guy, Nancy. "Flowing Down Taiwan's Tamsui River: Towards an Ecomusicology of the Environmental Imagination." *Ethnomusicology* 53, no. 2. (2009): 218–248.

Haenfler, Ross. *Subcultures: The Basics*. London: Routledge, 2014.

Halberstam, Judith. *The Queer Art of Failure*. Durham, NC: Duke University Press, 2011.

Hammer, Rhonda, and Douglas Kellner. *Media/Cultural Studies: Critical Approaches*. New York: Peter Lang, 2009.

Hanawalt, Barbara. *The Middle Ages: An Illustrated History*. New York: Oxford University Press, 1998.

Hansen, Kai Arne. "Holding on for Dear Life: Gender, Celebrity Status, and Vulnerability-on-Display in Sia's 'Chandelier.'" In *The Routledge Research Companion to Popular Music and Gender*, edited by Stan Hawkins, 89–101. London and New York: Routledge, 2016.

Hansen, Kai Arne, and Stan Hawkins. "Azealia Banks: 'Chasing Time,' Erotics, and Body Politics." *Popular Music* 37, no. 2 (2018): 157–174.

Harper, Graeme, Ruth Doughty, and Jochen Eisentraut, eds. *Sound and Music in Film and Visual Media*. New York: Continuum, 2009.

Harris-Moore, Deborah. *Media and the Rhetoric of Body Perfection: Cosmetic Surgery, Weight Loss and Beauty in Popular Culture. The Cultural Politics of Media and Popular Culture.* Farnham: Ashgate, 2014.

Harrow, Kenneth W. *Trash: African Cinema from Below*. Bloomington, IN: University of Indiana Press, 2013.

Hauke, Christopher. "'A Cinema of Small Gestures': Derek Jarman's Super 8—Image, Alchemy, Individuation." *International Journal of Jungian Studies* 6, no. 2 (May 2014): 159–164.

Hawkins, Stan. "Musical Excess and Postmodern Identity in Björk's Video 'It's Oh So Quiet.'" *Musiikin Suunta* 2 (1999): 43–54.

Hawkins, Stan. *Settling the Pop Score: Pop Texts and Identity Politics*. London and New York: Routledge, 2002.

Hawkins, Stan. "On Male Queering in Mainstream Pop". In *Queering the Popular Pitch*, edited by Sheila Whiteley and Jennifer Rycenga, 279–294. London: Routledge, 2006.

Hawkins, Stan. "Aphex Twin: Monstrous Hermaphrodites, Madness and the Strain of Independent Dance Music." In *Essays on Sound and Vision*, edited by John Richardson and Stan Hawkins, 27–53. Helsinki: Helsinki University Press, 2007.

Hawkins, Stan. "[Un]*Justified:* Gestures of Straight-Talk in Justin Timberlake's Songs." In *Oh Boy! Masculinities and Popular Music*, edited by Freya Jarman-Ivens, 197–212. London: Routledge, 2007.

Hawkins, Stan. *The British Pop Dandy: Masculinity, Popular Music and Culture*. Farnham: Ashgate, 2009.

Hawkins, Stan, ed. *Pop Music and Easy Listening*. London: Routledge, 2011.

Hawkins, Stan. *Queerness in Pop Music: Aesthetics, Gender Norms, and Temporality*. New York: Routledge, 2016.

Hawkins, Stan, and John Richardson. "Remodeling Britney Spears: Matters of Intoxication and Mediation." *Popular Music and Society* 30, no. 5 (2007): 605–629.

Hebdige, Dick. *Subculture: The Meaning of Style*. London: Methuen, 1979.

Hellman, Jack. "Television's Accent on Youth as New Faces Pop Up Everywhere." *Variety*. July 28, 1965. ProQuest Entertainment Industry Magazine Archive.

Her Majesty's Government. *Ending Violence Against Women and Girls: Strategy 2016–2020*. London: National Archives, 2006.

Herman, David. *Basic Elements of Narrative*. Hoboken, NJ: Wiley, 2009.

Herzberg, Martin. *Musik und Aufmerksamkeit im Internet. Musiker im Wettstreit um Publikum bei YouTube, Facebook & Co*. Marburg: Tectum Wissenschaftsverlag, 2012.

Herzfeld, Gregor. "Die Rockoper. Genese, Verstetigung und Diversifikation eines Genres." *Musiktheorie* 30, no. 1 (2015): 43–60.

Herzogenrath, Bernd, ed. *Travels in Intermedia[lity]: Reblurring the Boundaries*. Hanover, NH: Dartmouth College Press, 2012.

Hesmondhalgh, David. "Indie: The Institutional Politics and Aesthetics of a Popular Music Genre." *Cultural Studies* 13, no. 1 (1999): 34–61.

Hess, Scott. "Postmodern Pastoral, Advertising, and the Masque of Technology." *Interdisciplinary Studies in Literature and the Environment* 11, no. 1 (2004): 71–100.

Hibbett, Ryan. "'What Is Indie Rock?' *Popular Music and Society* 28, no. 1 (2005): 55–77.

Higgins, Robert. "Kicking Up Her Own *Hullabaloo.*" *TV Guide.* January 15, 1966: 22–24.

Hilmes, Michele. *Only Connect: A Cultural History of American Broadcasting.* Belmont, CA: Wadsworth Publishing, 2002.

Hoad, Catherine. "'He Can Be Whatever You Want Him to Be': Identity and Intimacy in the Masked Performance of Ghost." *Popular Music* 37, no. 2 (2018): 175–192.

Hoggatt, John. "Go-Go Finds New Twists to Keep Fad Go-Ing." *Variety.* October 16, 1965. ProQuest Entertainment Industry Magazine Archive.

Holland, Michael, and Oli Wilson. "Technostalgia in New Recording Projects by the 1980s 'Dunedin Sound' Band The Chills." *Journal on the Art of Record Production*, no. 9 (April 2015). https://arpjournal.com/asarpwp/ technostalgia-in-new-recording-projects-by-the-1980s-dunedin-sound-band-the-chills.

Holm-Hudson, Kevin. "'Who Can I Be Now?': David Bowie's Vocal Personae." *Contemporary Music Review* 37, no. 3 (2018): 214–234.

Holpuch, Amanda. "Madame Tussauds Rethinks Nicki Minaj Waxwork Display over Saucy Fan Photos." *Guardian.* August 19, 2015. https://www.theguardian.com/music/2015/ aug/19/madame-tussauds-nicki-minaj-display-waxwork.

Holt, Fabian. *Genre in Popular Music.* Chicago, IL: University of Chicago Press, 2007.

Holt, Fabian. "Is Music Becoming More Visual? Online Video Content in the Music Industry." *Visual Studies* 26, no. 1 (2011): 50–61.

Holt, Grace Sims. "Stylin' Outta the Pulpit." In *Signifyin', Sanctifyin', and Slam Dunking: A Reader in African-American Expressive Culture*, edited by Gena Dagel Caponi, 331–347. Amherst, MA: University of Massachusetts Press, 1999 [1972].

hooks, bell. *Black Looks: Race and Representation.* Boston, MA: South End Press, 1992.

hooks, bell. *We Real Cool: Black Men and Masculinity.* New York: Routledge, 2004.

hooks, bell. "Moving Beyond Pain." bellhooksinstitute.com. May 9, 2016. http://www.bellhooksinstitute.com/blog/2016/5/9/moving-beyond-pain.

hooks, bell. "Femme Feminista." bellhooksinstitute.com. May 11, 2016. http://www.bellhooksinstitute.com/blog/femme-feminista.

Hopper, Jessica. "Kendrick Lamar: Not Your Average Everyday Rap Saviour." *Spin Magazine.* October 9, 2012. https://www.spin.com/2012/10/kendrick-lamar-not-your-average -everyday-rap-savior.

Huber, Patrick. *Linthead Stomp: The Creation of Country Music in the Piedmont South.* Chapel Hill, NC: University of North Carolina Press, 2008.

Huber, Patrick. "The New York Sound: Citybilly Recording Artists and the Creation of Hillbilly Music, 1924–1932." *Journal of American Folklore* 127, no. 504 (2014): 139–158.

Hudson, Ray. "Regions and Place: Music, Identity and Place." *Progress in Human Geography* 30, no. 5 (2006): 626–634.

Huey, Steve. "Wicked Game." AllMusic.com. http://www.allmusic.com/song/ wicked-game-mt0010704597.

Huffington Post. "Corb Lund's Edmonton House for Sale." *HuffPost Alberta.* October 16, 2013. http://www.huffingtonpost.ca/2013/10/17/corb-lund-house-for-sale_n_4116997. html.

Hughes, Charles L. *Country Soul: Making Music and Making Race in the American South.* Chapel Hill, NC: University of North Carolina Press, 2015.

Hughes, Michael. "Country Music as Impression Management: A Meditation on Fabricating Authenticity." *Poetics* 28 (2000): 185–205.

Huizinga, Johan H. *Homo Ludens: A Study of the Play-Element in Culture*. London: Routledge & Kegan Paul, 1949.

Hunter, Margaret L. *Race, Gender, and the Politics of Skin Tone*. New York: Routledge, 2005.

Hutcheon, Linda. *Theory of Parody: The Teachings of Twentieth-Century Art Forms*. New York: Routledge, 1985.

Huxley, David. "Ever Get the Feeling You've Been Cheated?: Anarchy and Control in the Great Rock 'n' Roll Swindle." In *Punk Rock, So What? The Cultural Legacy of Punk*, edited by Roger Sabin, 81–99. London: Routledge, 1999.

Inglis, Ian. "The Road Not Taken. Elvis Presley: Comeback Special, NBC TV Studios, Hollywood, December 3, 1968." In *Performance and Popular Music: History, Place and Time*, edited by Ian Inglis, 41–51. Aldershot: Ashgate, 2006.

Ingraham, Chrys. *White Weddings: Romancing Heterosexuality in Popular Culture*. New York: Routledge, 1999.

Ingraham, Chrys, ed. *Thinking Straight: The Promise, the Power and Paradox of Heterosexuality*. New York: Routledge, 2005.

Ingram, David. *The Jukebox in the Garden: Ecocriticism and American Popular Music Since 1960*. New York: Editions Rodopi B.V., 2010.

Jackson, Lauren Michelle. "The Rapper Laughs, Herself: Nicki Minaj's Sonic Disturbances." *Feminist Media Studies* 17, no. 1 (2017): 126–129.

Jackson, Stevi, and Sue Scott. *Theorizing Sexuality*. New York: McGraw-Hill Open University Press, 2010.

Jarman-Ivens, Freya, ed. *Oh Boy! Masculinities and Popular Music*. New York: Routledge, 2007.

Jarman-Ivens, Freya. "Notes on Musical Camp." In *The Ashgate Research Companion to Popular Musicology*, edited by Derek B. Scott, 189–204. Aldershot: Ashgate, 2009.

Jarman-Ivens, Freya. *Queer Voices: Technologies, Vocalities, and the Musical Flaw*. New York: Palgrave Macmillan, 2011.

Jarre, Renee. "Louis Althusser: Hailing, Interpellation and the Subject of Mass Media." Ezine@rticles. June 27, 2007. http://ezinearticles.com/?Louis-Althusser:-Hailing,-Interpellation,-and-the-Subject-of-Mass-Media&id=614657.

Jeffery, Alex. "Marketing and Materiality in the Popular Music Transmedia of Gorillaz' 'Plastic Beach.'" *Revista Mediterránea de Comunicación* 8, no. 2 (2017): 67–80.

Jenkins, Henry. *Convergence Culture: Where Old and New Media Collide*. New York: New York University Press, 2006.

Jenkins, Henry. "Searching for the Origami Unicorn—The Matrix and Transmedia Storytelling." In *Convergence Culture—Where Old and New Media Collide*, 93–130. New York: New York University Press, 2006.

Jenkins, Henry. "Transmedia Storytelling 101." *Henry Jenkins: Confessions of an Aca Fan.* March 21, 2007. http://henryjenkins.org/blog/2007/03/transmedia_storytelling_101.html.

Jenkins, Henry. "The Aesthetics of Transmedia: In Response to David Bordwell (Part Three)." *Henry Jenkins: Confessions of an Aca Fan.* September 15, 2009. http://henryjenkins.org/blog/2009/09/the_aesthetics_of_transmedia_i_2.html.

Jenkins, Henry. "'Layers of Meaning': Fan Music Videos and the Poetics of Poaching." In *Textual Poachers: Television Fans and Participatory Culture*, 223–249. New York: Routledge, 2012.

Jenkins, Henry, Sam Ford, and Joshua Green. *Spreadable Media: Creating Meaning and Value in a Networked Culture*. New York: New York University Press, 2013.

Jensen, Joli. *Nashville Sound: Authenticity, Commercialization, and Country Music.* Nashville, TN: Vanderbilt University Press and Country Music Foundation Press, 1998.

Jensenius, Alexander. "Action-Sound: Developing Methods and Tools to Study Music-Related Body Movement." PhD dissertation. University of Oslo, 2007.

Jewitt, Carey, Jeff Bezemer, and Kay O'Halloran. *Introducing Multimodality.* Abingdon, Oxon: Routledge, 2016.

Jindra, Ines W. *A New Model of Religious Conversion: Beyond Network Theory and Social Construction.* Leiden: Brill, 2014.

Johnson, Kathryn. "David Bowie Is." In *David Bowie: Critical Perspectives,* edited by Eoin Devereux, Aileen Dillane, and Martin J. Power, 1–18. New York: Routledge, 2015.

Johnston, Maura. "Kendrick Lamar's *DAMN.* Proves He's the Most Important Rapper in America." *Time.* April 17, 2017. http://time.com/4741238/kendrick-lamar-damn-review.

Jones, Brian. "Signifying DIY: Process-Orientated Aesthetics in 1990s Alternative Rock and Hip-Hop." PhD dissertation. University of North Carolina at Chapel Hill, 2014.

Jooß-Bernau, Christian. *Das Pop-Konzert als Para-theatrale Form.* Berlin: De Gruyter, 2010.

Jordan-Zachery, Julia S. *Black Women, Cultural Images, and Social Policy.* New York: Routledge, 2010.

Jost, Christofer. *Musik, Medien und Verkörperung. Transdisziplinäre Analyse Populärer Musik.* Baden-Baden: Nomos, 2012.

Joyce, James, and Theodore Spencer. *Stephen Hero.* London: Triad Grafton, 1986.

Julien, Olivier, and Christophe Levaux. *Over and Over: Exploring Repetition in Popular Music.* London: Bloomsbury, 2018.

Kaiser, Marc, ed. "Watching Music: Music Video Cultures." Special issue of *Volume! The French Journal of Popular Music Studies* 14, no. 2 (2017): 1–6.

Kamp, David. "Live at the Whisky." *Vanity Fair.* November 2000. https://www.vanityfair.com/culture/2000/11/live-at-the-whisky-david-kamp.

Kang, Caspian. "Notes on the Hip-Hop Messiah." *New York Times.* March 24, 2015. https://www.nytimes.com/2015/03/24/magazine/notes-on-the-hip-hop-messiah.html.

Kaplan, E. Ann. *Women and Film: Both Sides of the Camera.* New York: Methuen, 1983.

Kaplan, E. Ann. *Rocking Around the Clock: Music Television, Postmodernism, and Consumer Culture.* London and New York: Routledge, 1987.

Karpovich, Angelina. "Reframing Fan Videos." In *Music Sound and Multimedia,* edited by Jamie Sexton, 17–28. Edinburgh: Edinburgh University Press, 2007.

Kattenbelt, Chiel. "Intermediality in Theatre and Performance: Definitions, Perceptions and Medial Relationships." *Culture, Language and Representation* 6 (2008): 19–29.

Katz, Mark. *Capturing Sound: How Technology Has Changed Music.* Berkeley, CA: University of California Press, 2004.

Keazor, Henry. "'I Had the Strangest Week Ever!' Metalepsis in Music Videos." In *Metalepsis in Popular Culture (Narratalogia; 28),* edited by Karin Kukkonen and Sonja Klimek, 104–126. Berlin: Walter de Gruyter, 2011.

Keazor, Henry, and Thorsten Wübbena. *Video Thrills the Radio Star. Musikvideos: Geschichte, Themen, Analysen.* 2nd ed. Bielefeld: Transcript Verlag, 2007.

Keazor, Henry, and Thorsten Wübbena, eds. *Rewind, Play, Fast Forward: The Past, Present and Future of the Music Video.* Bielefeld: Transcript Verlag, 2010.

Keefe, Jonathan. "Review: Pink, Funhouse." *Slant Magazine.* October 26, 2008. https://www.slantmagazine.com/music/pink-funhouse.

Keightley, Keir. "Reconsidering Rock." In *The Cambridge Companion to Pop and Rock*, edited by Simon Frith, Will Straw, and John Street, 109–142. Cambridge: Cambridge University Press, 2001.

Kellner, Douglas. "Cultural Studies, Multiculturalism, and Media Culture." In *Gender, Race, and Class in Media: A Critical Reader*, edited by Gail Dines and Jean M. Humez, 7–19. London: Sage, 2011.

Kennedy, John. "V Exclusive! Game Catches The Holy Ghost With New Album Title." *VIBE Magazine*. August 12, 2012. https://www.vibe.com/2012/08/ v-exclusive-game -catches-holy-ghost-new-album-title.

Kellner, Douglas. *Media Spectacle*. London: Routledge, 2003.

Key, Andre E. "Toward a Typology of Black Hebrew Religious Thought and Practice." *Journal of Africana Religions* 2, no. 1 (2014): 31–66.

Khabeer, Su'ad Abdul. *Muslim Cool: Religion, and Hip Hop in the United States*. New York: New York University Press, 2016.

Khal. "How Kendrick Lamar and Big Sean's Relationship Went Wrong." *Complex*. March 25, 2017. https://www.complex.com/music/2017/03/big-sean-kendrick-lamar-relationship-timeline.

Kimmel, Michael S. "Gender Symmetry in Domestic Violence." In *Misframing Men: The Politics of Contemporary Masculinities*, edited by Michael Kimmel, 99–121. New Brunswick, NJ: Rutgers University Press, 2010.

Kimmel, Michael S., and Michael A. Messner. *Men's Lives*. 9th ed. Boston, MA: Pearson, 2013

King, Geoff. *Indiewood USA: Where Hollywood Meets Independent Cinema*. London: I.B. Tauris, 2009.

King, Stephen. *The Shining*. New York: Doubleday, 1977.

King, Stephen. *Cujo*. Toronto, ON: Viking, 1981

King, Stephen. *Misery*. Toronto, ON: Viking, 1987.

Klassen, Janina. "Queere Stimmen, Vocal Cyborgs und (k)ein Genderdiskurs." In *Image— Performance—Empowerment. Weibliche Stars in der populären Musik von Claire Waldoff bis Lady Gaga*, edited by Michael Fischer, Christofer Jost, and Janina Klassen, 11–15. Münster: Waxmann, 2018.

Klastrup, Lisbeth, and Susana Tosca. "Transmedial Worlds. Rethinking Cyberworld Design." In *Proceedings of the 2004 International Conference on Cyberworlds*, edited by Masayuki Nakajima, Yoshinori Hatori, and Alexei Sourin, 409–416. Los Alamitos, CA: IEEE Computer Society, 2004.

Klein, Bethany. *As Heard on TV: Popular Music in Advertising*. Farnham: Ashgate, 2009.

Knox, Shelby. "Pink's New Video Goes a 'Little' Too Far." *HuffPost*. November 8, 2010. https:// www.huffingtonpost.com/shelby-knox/pinks-new-video-goes-a-li_b_678010.html.

Ko, Aph. "The Baartman Effect: Nicki Minaj, Gail Dines, and Chuck Creekmur." *Naturalhairmag*. July 30, 2014. https://www.naturalhairmag.com/ baartman-effect-nicki-minaj-gail-dines-chuck-creekmur.

Korsgaard, Mathias Bonde. "Music Video Transformed." In *The Oxford Handbook of New Audiovisual Aesthetics*, edited by John Richardson, Claudia Gorbman, and Carol Vernallis, 501–521. Oxford and New York: Oxford University Press, 2013.

Korsgaard, Mathias Bonde. *Music Video After MTV: Audiovisual Studies, New Media, and Popular Music*. London: Routledge, 2017.

Korsgaard, Mathias Bonde, and Tomáš Jirsa. "The Music Video in Transformation." *Music, Sound, and the Moving Image* 13, no. 2 (2019) [forthcoming].

Kramer, Gary M. "Laurie Anderson." *Bomb Magazine*. October 21, 2015. https:// bombmagazine.org/articles/laurie-anderson.

Kress, Gunther, and Theo van Leeuwen. *Multimodal Discourse: The Modes and Media of Contemporary Communication*. London: Arnold, 2001.

Krims, Adam. *Music and Urban Geography*. New York: Routledge, 2007.

Kristeva, Julia. "The Bounded Text." In *Desire in Language*, edited by Leon Roudiez, 36–63. New York: Columbia University Press, 1980.

Kunze, Peter C., ed. *The Films of Wes Anderson: Critical Essays on an Indiewood Icon*. New York: Palgrave MacMillan, 2014.

Kwak, Yung Bin. "Mediating States of Media: Nam June Paik's Art of (Im)Mediation." In *NJP Reader 6*, edited by Kyunghwa Ahn, 161–167. Yongin: Nam June Paik Art Center, 2016.

Kwate, Naa Oyo A., and Shatema Threadcraft. "Perceiving the Black Female Body: Race and Gender in Police Constructions of Body Weight." *Race Social Problems* 7, no. 3 (September 2015): 213–226.

Kyrölä, Katariina. *The Weight of Images: Affect, Body Image and Fat in the Media*. Farnham: Ashgate, 2014.

Kyrölä, Katariina. "Music Videos as Black Feminist Thought—From Nicki Minaj's Anaconda to Beyoncé's Formation." *Feminist Encounters: A Journal of Critical Studies in Culture and Politics* 1, no. 1 (October 2017): 1–13.

Kärjä, Antti-Ville. "Arty Adverts, Puffy Pictures? Finnish Music Videos in Cinema." *Musiikin Suunta: Special Issue in English on Music Videos* 21, no. 2 (1999): 33–42.

Lacasse, Serge. "Stratégies narratives dans 'Stan' d'Eminem: Le rôle de la voix et de la technologie dans l'articulation du récit phonographique." *Protée* 34, no. 2–3 (2006): 11–26.

Lacasse, Serge. "Interpretation of Vocal Staging by Popular Music Listeners: A Reception Test." *Psychomusicology* 17, no. 1–2 (2001): 56–76.

Lacasse, Serge. "Toward a Model of Transphonography." In *The Pop Palimpsest: Intertextuality in Recorded Popular Music*, edited by Lori Burns and Serge Lacasse, 9–60. Ann Arbor, MI: University of Michigan Press, 2018.

Lafrance, Marc, and Lori Burns. "Finding Love in Hopeless Places: Complex Relationality and Impossible Heterosexuality in Popular Music Videos by Pink and Rihanna." *Music Theory Online* 23, no. 2 (2017). http://mtosmt.org/issues/mto.17.23.2/mto.17.23.2.lafrance_burns. html.

Lafrance, Marc, and Lori Burns. "The Dark Side of Camp: Violence Against Men in Christina Aguilera's 'Your Body.'" In *Music and Camp*, edited by Christopher Moore and Philip Purvis, 220–240. Middletown, CT: Wesleyan University Press, 2018.

Lafrance, Marc, Lori Burns, and Alyssa Woods. "Doing Hip-Hop Masculinity Differently: Exploring Kanye West's '808s & Heartbreak' Through Word, Sound and Image." In *The Routledge Research Companion to Popular Music and Gender*, edited by Stan Hawkins, 285–299. London and New York: Routledge, 2017.

Lardine, Bob. "Teen Dances: Are They Indecent?" *New York Daily News*. June 27, 1965.

Larkin, Brian. *Signal and Noise: Media, Infrastructure, and Urban Culture in Nigeria*. Durham, NC: Duke University Press, 2008.

Lee, Susanne. "Punk 'Noir': Anarchy in Two Idioms." *Yale French Studies* 108 (2005): 177–188.

Legaspi, Althea. "Watch Kendrick Lamar's Richly Symbolic New 'Humble' Video." *Rolling Stone*. March 31, 2017. https://www.rollingstone.com/music/music-news/ watch-kendrick-lamars-richly-symbolic-new-humble-video-109039.

Lehmann, Hans-Thies. *Postdramatic Theatre*, translated by Karen Jüers-Munby. London: Routledge, 2006.

Leib, Kristin. *Gender, Branding, and the Modern Music Industry*. London: Routledge, 2017.

Leibetseder, Doris. *Queer Tracks: Subversive Strategies in Pop and Rock Music*. Abingdon, Oxon: Routledge, 2012.

Leonard, Marion. *Gender in the Music Industry: Rock, Discourse and Girl Power*. Aldershot: Ashgate, 2007.

Levin, Thomas Y. "Dismantling the Spectacle: The Cinema of Guy Debord." In *On the Passage of a Few People Through a Rather Brief Moment in Time: The Situationist International 1957–1972*, edited by Elizabeth Sussman, 72–123. Cambridge, MA: MIT Press, 1989.

Levine, Nick. "Pink: Please Don't Leave Me." *Digital Spy*. April 14, 2009. https://www.digitalspy.com/music/single-reviews/a152654/pink-please-dont-leave-me-152654.

Levitz, Tamara. "The Chosen One's Choice." In *Beyond Structural Listening?: Postmodern Modes of Hearing*, edited by Andrew Dell'Antonio, 70–108. Berkeley and Los Angeles, CA: University of California Press, 2004.

Lewis, Lisa. *Gender Politics and MTV: Voicing the Difference*. Philadelphia, PA: Temple University Press, 1990.

Literat, Ioana. "The Work of Art in the Age of Mediated Participation: Crowdsourced Art and Collective Creativity." *International Journal of Communication* 6 (2012): 2962–2984.

Long, Geoffrey. "Creating Worlds in Which to Play: Using Transmedia Aesthetics to Grow Stories into Storyworlds." In *The Rise of Transtexts: Challenges and Opportunities*, edited by Benjamin Derhy Kurtz and Mélanie Bourdaa, 139–152. New York: Routledge, 2016.

Lorde, Audre. "The Master's Tools Will Never Dismantle the Master's House." In *Sister Outsider: Essays and Speeches*, by Audre Lorde, 110–114. Berkeley, CA: Crossing Press, 1984.

Lotz, Amanda. *The Television Will Be Revolutionized*. New York: New York University Press, 2007.

Louie, Patricia. "Gender-Based Violence in Pink's 'Please Don't Leave Me.'" *The Sociological Cinema*. February 10, 2014. https://www.thesociologicalcinema.com/videos/gender-based-violence-in-pinks-please-dont-leave-me.

Loveless, Natalie. "Introduction, Short Statements on Research-Creation." *Polemics* 1 (2015): 41–54.

Luckett, Moya. "Sensuous Women and Single Girls: Reclaiming the Female Body on 1960s Television." In *Swinging Single: Representing Sexuality in the 1960s*, edited by Hilary Radner and Moya Luckett, 277–300. Minneapolis, MN: University of Minnesota Press, 1999.

Luckmann, Thomas. *Theorie des sozialen Handelns*. Berlin: Walter de Gruyter, 1992.

Lund, Corb. "Biography." Corblund.com. http://corblund.com/press.

Lupton, Deborah. *Fat*. New York: Routledge, 2018 [2013].

MacDowell, James. "Notes on Quirky." *Movie: A Journal of Film Criticism* 1 (2010): 1–16.

MacDowell, James. "Wes Anderson, Tone and the Quirky Sensibility." *New Review of Film and Television Studies* 10, no. 1 (2012): 6–27.

Macfarlane, Malcolm, and Ken Crossland. *Perry Como: A Biography and Complete Career Record*. Jefferson, NC: McFarland & Co., 1999.

Machin, David. *Analysing Popular Music: Image, Sound, Text*. Thousand Oaks, CA: Sage, 2010.

Mack, Edward. "The Surprising Origins of 'Wagon Wheel,' One of the Most Popular Country Songs Ever." Wideopencountry.com. 2015. https://www.wideopencountry.com/song-day-wagon-wheel.

Mahoney, Billie. "Jazz Dance." In *The International Encyclopedia of Dance*, edited by Selma Jeanne Cohen and Dance Perspectives Foundation. New York: Oxford University Press, 2005 [ebook].

Mallett, Shelley. "Understanding Home: A Critical Review of the Literature." *The Sociological Review* 52, no. 1 (2004): 63–89.

Malone, Bill C. *Country Music U.S.A.* Austin, TX: University of Texas Press, 1968.

Mann, Geoff. "Why Does Country Music Sound White? Race and the Voice of Nostalgia." *Ethnic and Racial Studies* 31, no. 1 (2008): 73–100.

Manovich, Lev. *The Language of New Media*. Cambridge, MA: MIT Press, 2001.

Marcus, Greil. *Lipstick Traces: A Secret History of the Twentieth Century*. Cambridge, MA: Harvard University Press, 1989.

Margulis, Elizabeth Hellmuth. *On Repeat: How Music Plays the Mind*. New York: Oxford University Press, 2014.

Marino, Gabriele. "'What Kind of Genre Do You Think We Are?': Genre Theories, Genre Names and Classes Within Music Intermedial Ecology." In *Music, Analysis, Experience: New Perspectives in Musical Semiotics*, edited by Maeder Costantino and Reybrouck Mark, 239–254. Leuven: Leuven University Press, 2015.

Mariet, Monique. "*Hullabaloo* Producer Calls a Challenge." *Chicago Tribune*. February 14, 1965. ProQuest Historical Newspapers.

Marks, Craig, and Rob Tannenbaum. *I Want My MTV: The Uncensored Story of the Music Video Revolution*. New York: Dutton, 2011.

Marks, Laura U. *Touch: Sensuous Theory and Multisensory Media*. Minneapolis, MN: University of Minnesota Press, 2002.

Martinez, Mike, S.J. "Taking a 'Long, Loving Look' at Kendrick Lamar's Disturbingly 'Humble' Hip-Hop." *Jesuit Post*. April 14, 2017. https://thejesuitpost.org/2017/04/taking-a-long-loving-look-at-kendrick-lamars-disturbingly-humble-hip-hop/#fn-16632-6.

Massumi, Brian. *Parables for the Virtual: Movement, Affect, Sensation*. Durham, NC: Duke University Press, 2002.

Matharoo, Sean. "'A Weird Creature That's Operating in the Theater': Cult, Synaesthesia and the Ethico-Politics of Horror in Danny Perez and Animal Collective's *ODDSAC*." *Horror Studies* 7, no. 2 (2016): 275–291.

Matthiessen, Francis Otto. *The Achievement of T.S. Eliot: An Essay on the Nature of Poetry*. London: Oxford University Press, 1965.

Maxwell, Kerry. "Kinetic Typography." In *Macmillan Dictionary*. https://www.macmillandictionary.com/dictionary/british/kinetic-typography.

McClary, Susan. "This Is Not a Story My People Tell: Musical Time and Space According to Laurie Anderson." *Discourse* 12, no. 1 (Fall–Winter 1989–1990, Special Issue on Music): 104–128.

McClary, Susan. *Feminine Endings: Music, Gender and Sexuality*. Minneapolis, MN: University of Minnesota Press, 2002.

McCullagh, Melissa, and Marc Lafrance. "A Thematic Analysis of YouTube Comments on Music Videos Featuring Violence Against Men by Women" [MS in preparation].

McDonald, Glenn. "The Genre Grinder's Song (What It's Like to Run a Machine for Sorting Music)." *McGill Conference—Music and Genre: New Directions*. September 27, 2014. Montreal, QC: McGill University.

McGrath, John. *Samuel Beckett, Repetition and Modern Music*. London and New York: Routledge, 2018.

McGrath, Tom. *MTV: The Making of a Revolution*. Philadelphia, PA and London: Running Press, 1996.

McIntosh, Heather. "Vevo and the Business of Online Music Video Distribution." *Popular Music and Society* 39, no. 5 (2016): 487–500.

McIntyre, Hugh. "The MTV Video Music Awards Go for the Second Screen Experience." *Forbes*. August 21, 2014.

McKenzie, Jon. "Laurie Anderson for Dummies." *TDR* 1, no. 2 (1997): 30–50.

McLaren, Laura. "The Lyric Video as Genre: History, Definition and Katy Perry's Contribution." MA thesis. University of Ottawa, 2018.

McLeay, Colin. "Popular Music and Expressions of National Identity." *New Zealand Journal of Geography* 103 (1997): 12–17.

McLuhan, Marshall. "The Agenbite of Outwit." In *Marshall McLuhan Essays: Media Research, Technology, Art Communication*, edited by Michel A. Moos. Amsterdam: Overseas Publishers Association, 1997.

McQuinn, Julie, ed. *Popular Music and Multimedia*. Burlington, VT: Ashgate, 2011.

Merchant, Carolyn. *The Death of Nature: Women, Ecology, and the Scientific Revolution*. New York: Harper & Row, 1982.

Merleau-Ponty, Maurice. *The Invisible and the Invisible*, translated by Alphonso Lingis. Evanston, IL: Northwestern University Press, 1968.

Michaels, Sean. "Radiohead Quadruple Aniboom Winners." *Guardian*. August 12, 2008. https://www.theguardian.com/music/2008/aug/12/radiohead.animation.pop.rock.news.

Michaels, Sean. "YouTube is Teens' First Choice for Music." *Guardian*. August 16, 2012. http://www.theguardian.com/music/2012/aug/16/youtube-teens-first-choice-music.

Middleton, Richard. "'Last Night a DJ Saved My Life': Avians, Cyborgs and Siren Bodies in the Era of Phonographic Technology." *Radical Musicology* 1 (2006). http://www.radical-musicology.org.uk/2006/Middleton.htm.

Miller, Monica R. *Religion and Hip Hop*. New York: Routledge, 2013.

Mishkin, Leo. "Those Teen-Agers Must Be Served—*Hullabaloo*." *New York Morning Telegraph*. January 15, 1965.

Mitchell, William J. *The Reconfigured Eye: Visual Truth in the Post-Photographic Era*. Cambridge, MA: MIT Press, 1994.

Mittell, Jason. *Genre and Television: From Cop Shows to Cartoons in American Culture*. New York: Routledge, 2004.

Miyakawa, Felicia. *Five Percenter Rap: God Hop's Music, Message, and Black Muslim Mission*. Bloomington, IN: Indiana University Press, 2005.

Mollaghan, Aimee. *The Visual Music Film*. Basingstoke: Palgrave Macmillan, 2015.

Monger, James Christopher. "Construct Review." AllMusic.com. https://www.allmusic.com/album/construct-mw0002530325.

Moore, Christopher, and Philip Purvis, eds. *Music and Camp*. Middletown, CT: Wesleyan University Press, 2018.

Mosser, Kurt. "Cover Songs." In *Music in American Life: An Encyclopedia of the Songs, Styles, Stars, and Stories That Shaped Our Culture*, edited by Jacqueline Edmondson, 310–312. Santa Barbara, CA: ABC-CLIO, 2013.

Mowitt, John. *Percussion: Drumming, Beating, Striking*. Durham, NC: Duke University Press, 2002.

Mulvey, Laura. "Visual Pleasure and Narrative Cinema." *Screen* 16, no. 3 (1975): 6–18.

Mulvey, Laura. *Visual and Other Pleasures*, 2nd ed. Basingstoke: Palgrave, 2009.

Mulvey, Laura. *Death 24 x a Second: Stillness and the Moving Image*. London: Raektion Books, 2006.

Muñoz, José. *Cruising Utopia: The Then and There of Queer Futurity*. New York: New York University Press, 2009.

Murch, Walter. *In the Blink of an Eye: A Perspective on Editing*. 2nd ed. Hollywood, CA: Silman James Press, 2001.

Naiman, Tiffany. "Art's Filthy Lesson." In *David Bowie: Critical Perspectives*, edited by Eoin Devereux, Aileen Dillane, and Martin J. Power, 178–195. New York: Routledge, 2015.

Naiman, Tiffany. "When Are We Now?: Walls and Memory in David Bowie's Berlins." In *Enchanting David Bowie: Space/Time/Body/Memory*, edited by Toija Cinque, Christopher Moore, and Sean Redmond, 305–322. New York: Bloomsbury, 2015.

Naiman, Tiffany. "Singing at Death's Door: Late Style, Disability, and the Temporality of Illness in Popular Music." PhD dissertation. UCLA, 2017.

Nash, Jennifer C. *The Black Body in Ecstasy: Reading Race, Reading Pornography*. London: Duke University Press, 2014.

Navas, Eduardo. *Remix Theory: The Aesthetics of Sampling*. Vienna: Springer-Verlag, 2012.

Nembhard, Candice. "8 Things You May Have Missed in Childish Gambino's 'This Is America' Video." *Highsnobiety*. May 7, 2018. https://www.highsnobiety.com/p/childish-gambino-this-is-america-recap.

Neumann-Braun, Klaus. *Viva MTV! Popmusik im Fernsehen*. Frankfurt am Main: Suhrkamp Verlag, 1999.

Newman, David, and Robert Benton. "'Hullabaloo'—It's Real GONE." *TV Guide*. June 26, 1965: 24–27.

Newman, Michael Z. *Video Revolutions: On the History of a Medium*. New York. Columbia University Press, 2014.

Ngai, Sianne. *Our Aesthetic Categories: Zany, Cute, Interesting*. Cambridge, MA: Harvard University Press, 2012.

Obert, Simon. "Die Artifizierung der Popmusik. Anfänge der Popkritik in US-amerikanischen Printmedien nach 1965." In *Populäre Musik, Mediale Musik? Transdisziplinäre Beiträge zu den Medien der Populären Musik*, edited by Christofer Jost, Daniel Klug, Axel Schmidt, and Klaus Neumann-Braun, 115–127. Baden-Baden: Nomos, 2011.

Obert, Simon. "Song Cycles, Operas, and a 'War on Singles.' The Emergence of Concept Albums in the Late 1960s." In *Große Formen in der Populären Musik/Large-Scale Forms in Popular Music*, edited by Gregor Herzfeld and Christofer Jost, 43–58. Münster: Waxmann, 2019.

Official Charts. "3 May 2009–9 May 2009." *Official Singles Chart Top 100*. 2009. https://www.officialcharts.com/charts/singles-chart/20090503/7501.

Offizielle Deutsch Charts. "Pink: Please Don't Leave Me (Single)." *Top 10 Singles Charts*. 2009. https://www.offiziellecharts.de/titel-details-523080.

O'Keefe, Kevin. "Where Did All These Lyric Videos Come From and Why Are We Giving Them Awards." *Atlantic*. August 14, 2014.

Ortiz, Edwin. "Kendrick Lamar Drops Video for New Single 'Humble.'" *Complex*. March 30, 2017. https://www.complex.com/music/2017/03/kendrick-lamar-humble-video.

Orwell, George. *Animal Farm*. Harcourt, NY: Brace and Co., 1946.

Orwell, George. *Nineteen Eighty-Four*. London: Secker & Warburg, 1949.

Otto, John S., and Augustus M. Burns. "Black and White Cultural Interaction in the Early Twentieth Century South: Race and Hillbilly Music." *Phylon* 35, no. 4 (1974): 407–417.

Oware, Matthew. "Brotherly Love: Homosociality and Black Masculinity in Gangsta Rap Music." *Journal of African American Studies* 15, no. 1 (2011): 22–39.

Palfy, Cora. S. "*Human After All:* Understanding Negotiations of Artistic Identity Through the Music of Daft Punk." In *The Oxford Handbook of Music and Virtuality*, edited by Sheila Whiteley and Shara Rambarran, 282–305. Oxford: Oxford University Press, 2016.

Pareles, Jon. "Laurie Anderson Is Telling Stories, Hers and Ours." *New York Times.* October 18, 2015. https://www.nytimes.com/2015/10/18/movies/laurie-anderson-is-telling-stories -hers-and-ours.html.

Pearson, Kent. "Conflict, Stereotypes and Masculinity in Australian and New Zealand Surfing." *Australia and New Zealand Journal of Sociology* 18, no. 2 (1982): 117–135.

Pecknold, Diane. *The Selling Sound: The Rise of the Country Music Industry.* Durham, NC: Duke University Press, 2007.

Pedelty, Mark. *Ecomusicology: Rock, Folk, and the Environment.* Philadelphia, PA: Temple University Press, 2012.

Pegg, Nicholas. *The Complete David Bowie.* London: Titan Books, 2016.

Pegley, Kip. *Coming to You Wherever You Are: MuchMusic, MTV, and Youth Audiences.* Middletown, CT: Wesleyan University Press, 2008.

Perren, Alisa. "Rethinking Distribution for the Future of Media Industry Studies." *Cinema Journal* 52, no. 3 (2013): 165–171.

Perrott, Lisa. "Music Video's Performing Bodies: Floria Sigismondi as Gestural Animator and Puppeteer." *Animation: An Interdisciplinary Journal* 10, no. 2 (2015): 119–140.

Perrott, Lisa. "Radiohead's Tonal Complexity: Animation: Creeping the Pop Out of Popular Music." Conference paper presented at *Mixing Pop & Politics: Subversion, Resistance and Reconciliation in Popular Music.* Wellington, New Zealand: IASPM-ANZ Conference, 2017.

Perry, Imani. *Prophets of the Hood: Politics and Poetics in Hip-Hop.* Durham, NC: Duke University Press, 2004.

Pethő, Ágnes. "Media in the Cinematic Imagination: Ekphrasis and the Poetics of the In-between in Jean-Luc Godard's Cinema." In *Media Borders, Multimodality and Intermediality*, edited by Lars Elleström, 211–223. London: Palgrave Macmillan, 2010.

Pethő, Ágnes. "Approaches to Studying Intermediality in Contemporary Cinema." *Acta. Universitatis Sapientiae, Film and Media Studies* 15 (2018): 165–187.

Phillips, Casey. "Bringing It Back: MTV, VH1, CMT Feature 12 Hours of All-Music Programming Today." *Times Free Press.* July 4, 2013. https://www.timesfreepress.com/news/ life/entertainment/story/2013/jul/04/bringing-it-back-mtv-vh1-cmt-feature-12/112397.

Pinch, Trevor, and David Reinecke. "Technostalgia: How Old Gear Lives on in New Music." In *Sound Souvenirs: Audio Technologies, Memory and Cultural Practices*, edited by Karin Bijsterveld and José van Dijck, 152–167. Amsterdam: University of Amsterdam Press, 2009.

Pinkus, Karen. "Self-Representation in Futurism and Punk." *South-Central Review* 13, no. 2–3 (1996): 180–193.

Pinn, Anthony B. *The African American Religious Experience in America.* Westport, CT: Greenwood Press, 2006.

Pinn, Anthony B. *Varieties of African American Religious Experience: Toward a Comparative Black Theology*. Minneapolis, MN: Fortress Press, 2017.

Prohaska, Ariane, and Jeannine A. Gailey. "Theorizing Fat Oppression: Intersectional Approaches and Methodological Innovations." *Fat Studies: An Interdisciplinary Journal of Body Weight and Society* 8, no. 1 (October 2018): 1–9.

Puckett, Kent. *War Pictures: Cinema, History, and Violence in Britain, 1939–1945*. New York: Fordham University Press, 2017.

Pääkkölä, Anna-Elena. "Mahtava Peräsin ja Pulleat Purjeet: Lihavuus, Naiskuva ja Seksuaalisuus Kolmessa Suomalaisessa Populaarimusiikkikappaleessa" ["Fatness, Womanhood, and Sexuality in Three Finnish Popular Music Songs"]. *Etnomusikologinen vuosikirja* 29 (2017): 1–19.

Quinn, Eithne. *Nuthin' but a "G" Thang: The Culture and Commerce of Gangsta Rap*. New York: Columbia University Press, 2005.

Rabaka, Reiland. *Hip Hop's Inheritance: From the Harlem Renaissance to the Hip Hop Feminist Movement*. New York: Lexington Books, 2001.

Radner, Hilary, and Moya Luckett, eds. *Swinging Single: Representing Sexuality in the 1960s*. Minneapolis, MN: University of Minnesota Press, 1999.

Railton, Diane, and Paul Watson. *Music and the Moving Image: Music Video and the Politics of Representation*. Edinburgh: Edinburgh University Press, 2011.

Rajewsky, Irina O. *Intermedialität*. Tübingen: A. Francke, 2002.

Rajewsky, Irina O. "Intermediality, Intertextuality, and Remediation: A Literary Perspective on Intermediality." *Intermédialités*, no. 6 (2005): 43–65.

Rajewsky, Irina O. "Border Talks: The Problematic Status of Media Borders in the Current Debate About Intermediality." In *Media Borders, Multimodality and Intermediality*, edited by Lars Elleström, 51–68. Basingstoke: Palgrave Macmillan, 2010.

Rambo, Lewis R. *Understanding Religious Conversions*. Newhaven, CT: Yale University Press, 1993.

Rambo, Lewis R., and Charles E. Farhadian. "Conversion." In *Encyclopedia of Religion*, vol. 3, 2nd ed., edited by Nicholas Jones. Detroit, MI: Macmillan Reference, 2005.

Ramler, Mari E. "Beyoncé's Performance of Identification as a Diamond: Reclaiming Bodies and Voices in 'Formation.'" *Constellations: A Cultural Rhetorics Publishing Space*. May 2018. http://constell8cr.com/issue-1/beyonces-performance-of-identification-as-a-diamond-reclaiming-bodies-and-voices-in-formation.

Regardie, Israel. *The Golden Dawn: The Original Account of the Teaching, Rites, and Ceremonies of the Hermetic Order*, edited by John Michael Greer. Woodbury, MN: Llewellyn Publications, 2015.

Reiss, Steve, and Neil Feineman. *Thirty Frames Per Second: The Visionary Art of the Music Video*. New York: Abrams, 2001.

Reynolds, Simon. *Blissed Out: The Raptures of Rock*. London: Serpent's Tail, 1990.

Reynolds, Simon. *Bring the Noise: 20 Years of Writing About Hip Rock and Hip-Hop*. London: Faber & Faber, 2007.

Reynolds, Simon. *Retromania: Pop Culture's Addiction to Its Own Past*. London: Faber & Faber, 2011.

Rhodie, Sam. *Montage*. Manchester: Manchester University Press, 2012.

Richards-Greaves, Gillian R. "'Say Hallelujah, Somebody' and 'I Will Call Upon the Lord': An Examination of Call-and-Response in the Black Church." *The Western Journal of Black Studies* 40, no. 3 (2016): 192–204.

Richardson, John. "Intertextuality and Pop Camp Identity Politics in Finland: The Crash's Music Video 'Still Alive.'" *Popular Musicology Online* 2 (2006). http://www.popular-musicology-online.com/issues/02/richardson-01.html.

Richardson, John. "Double-Voiced Discourse and Bodily Pleasures in Contemporary Finnish Rock: The Case of Maija Vilkkumaa." In *Essays on Sound and Vision*, edited by John Richardson and Stan Hawkins, 401–441. Helsinki: Helsinki University Press, 2007.

Richardson, John. "Resisting the Sublime: Loose Synchronisation in *La Belle et la Bête* and *The Dark Side of Oz*." In *Musicological Identities: Essays in Honour of Susan McClary*, edited by Steven Baur, Raymond Knapp, and Jacqueline Warwick, 135–148. Aldershot: Ashgate, 2008.

Richardson, John. "Plasticine Music: Surrealism in Peter Gabriel's 'Sledgehammer.'" In *Peter Gabriel, From Genesis to Growing Up*, edited by Michael Drewett, Sarah Hill, and Kimi Kärki, 195–210. Farnham: Ashgate, 2010.

Richardson, John. *An Eye for Music: Popular Music and the Audiovisual Surreal*. New York: Oxford University Press, 2012 [2011].

Richardson, John. "Music Videos." In *The Grove Dictionary of American Music*, 2nd ed., edited by H. Wiley Hitchcock and Stanley Sadie, revised from an original text by Alf Björnberg. New York: Oxford University Press, 2013.

Richardson, John. "Between Speech, Music, and Sound: The Voice, Flow, and the Aestheticizing Impulse in Audiovisual Media." In *The Oxford Handbook of Sound and Image in Western Art*, edited by Yael Kaduri, 479–501. Oxford: Oxford University Press, 2016.

Richardson, John. "Closer Reading and Framing in Ecocritical Music Research." In *Music Moves: Musical Dynamics of Relation, Knowledge and Transformation*, edited by Charissa Granger, Friedlind Riedel, Eva-Maria van Straaten, and Gerlinde Feller, 157–193. *Göttingen Studies in Musicology*, vol. 7. Hildesheim: Olms, 2016.

Richardson, John. "Ecological Close Reading of Music in Digital Culture." In *Embracing Restlessness: Cultural Musicology*, edited by Birgit Abels, 111–142. *Göttingen Studies in Musicology*, vol. 6. Hildesheim: Olms, 2016.

Richardson, John. "Surrealism in Icelandic Popular Music." In *Sounds Icelandic: Essays on Icelandic Music in the 20th and 21st Centuries*, edited by Þorbjörg Daphne Hall, Nicola Dibben, Árni Heimir Ingólfsson, and Tony Mitchell, 172–193. Sheffield: Equinox, 2019.

Richardson, John, and Stan Hawkins. *Essays on Sound and Vision*. Helsinki: Helsinki University Press, 2007.

Richardson, John, Claudia Gorbman, and Carol Vernallis, eds. *The Oxford Handbook of New Audiovisual Aesthetics*. Oxford and New York: Oxford University Press, 2013.

Richardson, Niall. *Transgressive Bodies: Representations in Film and Popular Culture*. Farnham: Ashgate, 2010.

Riihimäki, Hanna-Mari, and Anna-Elena Pääkkölä. "Alternative Femininities, Monstrous Voices and Queer Body Politics in Alma's 'Dye My Hair.'" In *Made in Finland: Studies in Popular Music. Routledge Global Popular Music Series*, edited by Toni-Matti Karjalainen and Kimi Kärki. New York: Routledge [forthcoming].

Riotta, Chris. "Radiohead Just Chose an Extraordinary Winner for Their 'Daydreaming' Short Film Contest." *Mic*. September 12, 2016. https://mic.com/articles/153936/radiohead-just-chose-an-extraordinary-winner-for-their-daydreaming-short-film-contest#.srM2wyQNA.

Roberts, Randall. "Conservative Country Music Fans Lash Out at CMA Performance by Beyoncé and the Dixie Chicks." *Los Angeles Times*. November 3, 2016.

Robinson, Lisa. "The Gospel According to Kendrick Lamar." *Vanity Fair*. June 28, 2018. https://www.vanityfair.com/style/2018/06/kendrick-lamar-cover-story.

Roenneke, Stefanie. *Camp als Konzept. Ästhetik, Popkultur, Queerness*. Moers: Posth Verlag, 2017.

Rogers, Jude. "The Final Mysteries of David Bowie's Blackstar—Elvis, Crowley, and 'The Villa of Ormen.'" *Guardian*. January 21, 2016. https://www.theguardian.com/music/2016/jan/21/final-mysteries-david-bowie-blackstar-elvis-crowley-villa-of-ormen.

Rook, Jean. "Waiting for Bowie—and Finding a Genius Who Insists He's Really a Clown." In *The Bowie Companion*, edited by Elizabeth Thomson and David Gutman, 133–135. New York: Da Capo Press, 1996.

Rose, Brian G. *Directing for Television: Conversations with American TV Directors*. Lanham, MD: Scarecrow Press, 1999.

Rose, Gillian. *Visual Methodologies: An Introduction to Researching with Visual Materials*. Los Angeles, CA: Sage, 2016.

Rosenberg, Douglas. *Screendance: Inscribing the Ephemeral Image*. New York: Oxford University Press, 2012.

Ross, Alex. "O Souverain, O Superman." *Alex Ross: The Rest is Noise*. October 13, 2015. https://www.therestisnoise.com/2015/10/o-souverain-o-superman.html.

Rothblum, Esther, and Sondra Solovay, eds. *The Fat Studies Reader*. New York: New York University Press, 2009.

Ryan, Marie-Laure. "Story/Worlds/Media: Tuning the Instruments of a Media-Conscious Narratology." In *Storyworlds Across Media: Toward a Media-Conscious Narratology*, edited by Marie-Laure Ryan and Jan-Noël Thon, 25–49. Lincoln, NE: University of Nebraska Press, 2014.

Ryan, Marie-Laure, and Jan-Noël Thon, eds. "Storyworlds Across Media." In *Storyworlds Across Media: Toward a Media-Conscious Narratology*, 1–21. Lincoln, NE: University of Nebraska Press, 2014.

Salih, Sara. "On Judith Butler and Performativity." In *Sexuality and Communications in Everyday Life: A Reader*, edited by Karen E. Lovaas and Mercilee M. Jenkins, 55–68. London: Sage, 2006.

Sangild, Torben. "Noise: Three Musical Gestures—Expressionist, Introvert and Minimal Noise." *The Journal of Music and Meaning* 2, no. 1 (2004). http://www.musicandmeaning.net/issues/showArticle.php?artID=2.4.

Sarkhosh, Keyvan, and Winfried Menninghaus. "Enjoying Trash Films: Underlying Features, Viewing Stances, and Experiential Response Dimensions." *Poetics* 57 (2016): 40–54.

Schaff, Adam. "Marxist Dialectics and the Principle of Contradiction." *The Journal of Philosophy* 57, no. 7 (1960): 241–250.

Schmidt, Axel. "Sound and Vision Go MTV—die Geschichte des Musiksenders bis heute." In *Viva MTV! Popmusik im Fernsehen*, edited by Klaus Neumann-Braun, 93–131. Frankfurt am Main: Suhrkamp Verlag, 1999.

Schott, Gareth, and Karen Barbour. "Filmic Resonance and Dispersed Authorship in Sigur Rós' Transmedial *Valtari Mystery Film Experiment*." In *Transmedia Directors: Artistry, Industry, and New Audiovisual Aesthetics*, edited by Carol Vernallis, Holly Rogers, and Lisa Perrott. New York: Bloomsbury, 2019 [forthcoming].

Schramm, Holger, and Tilo Hartmann. "Identität durch Mediennutzung? Die Rolle von parasozialen Interaktionen und Beziehungen mit Medienfiguren." In

Mediensozialisationstheorien: Neue Modelle und Ansätze in der Diskussion, edited by Dagmar Hoffmann and Lothar Mikos, 201–219. Wiesbaden: VS Verlag für Sozialwissenschaften, 2007.

Scott, Derek B. "Policing the Boundaries of Art and Entertainment." In *Kulturkritik und das Populäre in der Musik*, edited by Fernand Hörner, 53–63. Münster: Waxmann, 2016.

Scotto, Ciro. "The Structural Role of Distortion in Hard Rock and Heavy Metal." *Music Theory Spectrum* 38, no. 2 (2017): 178–199.

Service, Tom. "When Poles Collide: Jonny Greenwood's Collaboration with Krzysztof Penderecki." *Guardian*. February 23, 2012. https://www.theguardian.com/music/2012/feb/23/poles-collide-jonny-greenwood-penderecki.

Sexton, Jamie, ed. *Music, Sound and Multimedia: From the Live to the Virtual*. Edinburgh: Edinburgh University Press, 2007.

Sexton, Jamie. "Independent Intersections: Indie Music Cultures and Independent Cinema." In *A Companion to American Independent Film*, edited by Geoff King, 106–128. Malden, MA: Wiley-Blackwell, 2016.

Shakespeare, Torn, and Nicholas Watson. "The Social Model of Disability: An Outdated Ideology?" *Research in Social Science and Disability* 2 (2001): 9–28.

Shamsian, Jacob. "24 Things You May Have Missed in Childish Gambino's 'This Is America' Music Video." *Insider*. May 9, 2018. https://www.thisisinsider.com/this-is-america-music-video-meaning-references-childish-gambino-donald-glover-2018-5.

Shank, Barry. *Dissonant Identities: The Rock 'n' Roll Scene in Austin, Texas*. Hanover, NH: Wesleyan University Press, 1994.

Shaviro, Steven. *Digital Music Videos*. New Brunswick, NJ: Rutgers University Press, 2017.

Shanahan, Daniel, and David Huron. "Heroes and Villains: The Relationship Between Pitch Tessitura and Sociability of Operatic Characters." *Empirical Musicology Review* 9, no. 2 (2014). http://emusicology.org/article/view/4441/4182.

Shildrick, Margrit. *Embodying the Monster: Encounters with the Vulnerable Self*. London: Sage, 2002.

Shore, Michael. *The Rolling Stone Book of Rock Video. The Definitive Look at Visual Music from Elvis Presley—and Before—to Michael Jackson—and Beyond*. London: Sidgwick & Jackson, 1985.

Shugart, Helene. "Parody as Subversive Performance: Denaturalizing Gender and Reconstituting Desire in *Ellen*." *Text and Performance Quarterly* 21, no. 2 (2001): 95–113.

Shumway, David R. *Rock Star: The Making of Musical Icons from Elvis to Springsteen*. Baltimore, MD: Johns Hopkins University Press, 2014.

Silveira, Fabrício. "Anal Terrorism in Nicki Minaj's 'Anaconda.'" In *Music/Video: Histories, Aesthetics, Media*, edited by Gina Arnold, Daniel Cookney, Kristy Fairclough, and Michael Goddard, 133–140. London: Bloomsbury, 2017.

Silverman, Max. *Palimpsestic Memory—The Holocaust and Colonialism in French and Francophone Film and Fiction*. Oxford: Berghahn Books, 2015.

Simon, Richard Keller. *Trash Culture: Popular Culture and the Great Tradition*. Berkeley, CA: University of California Press, 1999.

Singer, Merrill. "Symbolic Identity Formation in an African American Religious Sect: The Black Hebrew Israelites." In *Black Zion: African American Religious Encounters with Judaism*, edited by Yvonne Patricia Chireau and Nathaniel Deutsch, 55–72. New York: Oxford University Press, 2000.

Sitney, P. Adams. *Visionary Film: The American Avant-Garde*. New York: Oxford University Press, 1974.

Slee, Sarie Mairs. "Moving the Music: Dance, Action, and Embodied Identity." In *Music/Video: History, Aesthetics, Media*, edited by Gina Arnold, Daniel Cookney, Kirsty Fairclough, and Michael Goddard, 147–162. London: Bloomsbury, 2017.

Smalley, Dennis. "Spectromorphology: Explaining Sound-Shapes." *Organized Sound* 2, no. 2 (1997): 107–126.

Smith, Iain, ed. "Cultural Borrowings: Appropriation, Reworking, Transformation." *Scope: An Online Journal of Film and Television Studies* 15 (2009): 1–224.

Sontag, Susan. "Notes on 'Camp.'" *Partisan Review* 31, no. 4 (1964): 515–530.

Spigel, Lynn, and Michael Curtin, eds. *The Revolution Wasn't Televised: Sixties Television and Social Conflict*. New York: Routledge, 1997.

Stark, Rodney. "Economics of Religion." in *The Blackwell Companion to the Study of Religion*, edited by Robert Alan Segal, 47–67. Malden, MA: Blackwell, 2006.

Stein, Louisa, and Kristina Busse. "Limit Play: Fan Authorship Between Source Text, Intertext, and Context." *Popular Communication* 7, no. 4 (2009): 192–207.

Stern, Harold. "Producer Thinks Young, Hopes for 'Hullabaloo.'" *Hartford Courant*. January 10, 1965. ProQuest Entertainment Industry Magazine Archive.

Stern, Barbara B. "Historical and Personal Nostalgia in Advertising Text: The Fin de Siècle Effect." *Journal of Advertising* 21, no. 4 (1992): 11–22.

Sterne, Jonathan. *The Audible Past: Cultural Origins of Sound Production*. London: Duke University Press, 2006.

Sterne, Jonathan. "The Preservation Paradox in Digital Audio." In *Sound Souvenirs: Audio Technologies, Memory and Cultural Practices*, edited by Karin Bijsterveld and José van Dijck, 55–68. Amsterdam: University of Amsterdam Press, 2009.

Stévance, Sophie, and Serge Lacasse. "Research-Creation in Music as a Collaborative Space." *Journal of the New Media Caucus*. 2015. http://median.newmediacaucus.org/research-creation-explorations/research-creation-in-music-as-a-collaborative-space.

Stevenson, Nick. "David Bowie Now and Then: Questions of Fandom and Late Style." In *David Bowie: Critical Perspectives*, edited by Eoin Devereux, Aileen Dillane, and Martin J. Power, 280–294. Routledge Studies in Popular Music. New York: Routledge, 2015.

Stimeling, Travis D. *Cosmic Cowboys and New Hicks: The Countercultural Sounds of Austin's Progressive Country Music Scene*. New York: Oxford University Press, 2011.

Stimeling, Travis D. "Music, Place, and Identity in the Central Appalachian Mountaintop Removal Mining Debate." *American Music* 30, no. 1 (2012): 1–29.

Strachan, Robert. "Do-It-Yourself: Industry, Ideology, Aesthetics and Micro Independent Record Labels in the UK." PhD dissertation. University of Liverpool, 2003.

Strachan, Robert. "Music Video and Genre: Structure, Context, and Commerce." In *Music and Manipulation: On the Social Uses and Social Control of Music*, edited by Steven Brown and Ulrik Volgsten, 187–206. New York and Oxford: Berghahn Books, 2006.

Strachan, Robert. *Sonic Technologies: Popular Music, Digital Culture and the Creative Process*. New York: Bloomsbury, 2017.

Straus, Murray A. "Why the Overwhelming Evidence on Partner Physical Violence by Women Has Not Been Perceived and Is Often Denied." *Journal of Aggression, Maltreatment & Trauma* 18, no. 6 (2009): 552–571.

Strings, Sabrina. *Fearing the Black Body: The Racial Origins of Fat Phobia*. New York: New York University Press, 2019 [forthcoming].

Størvold, Tore. "Music and the Kárahnjúkar Hydropower Plant: Style, Aesthetics, and Environmental Politics in Iceland." *Popular Music and Society*. July 20, 2018: 1–24.

Tagg, Philip. "Kojak, 50 Seconds of Television Music: Towards the Analysis of Affect in Popular Music." PhD dissertation. Göteborg University, 1979.

Talukder, Md. Munir Hossain. "In Defence of Geo-Cultural Identity: An Argument Against Kymlicka's View of Multiculturalism and Minority Rights." *CEU Political Science Journal* 8, no. 4: (2013): 405–426.

Taruskin, Richard. *Stravinsky and the Russian Traditions, Volume II*. Berkeley and Los Angeles, CA: University of California Press, 1996.

Taruskin, Richard. *The Oxford History of Western Music, vol. 5: Music in the Late Twentieth Century*. Oxford: Oxford University Press, 2005.

Tate, Joseph. *The Music and Art of Radiohead*. Aldershot and Burlington, VT: Ashgate, 2012.

Taylor, Timothy D. *Strange Sounds: Music, Technology and Culture*. London: Routledge, 2001.

Temporal, Ray Paul. *The Branding of MTV: Will Internet Kill the Video Star?* New York: John Wiley & Sons, 2008.

The Art Story. "Young British Artists." Theartstory.org. https://www.theartstory.org/movement-young-british-artists.htm.

The Associated Press. "Nas: The Mature Voice of Hip-Hop." *Today*. January 4, 2005. https://www.today.com/popculture/nas-mature-voice-hip-hop-wbna6786474.

Théberge, Paul. "'The End of the World as We Know It': The Changing Role of the Studio in the Age of the Internet." In *The Art of Record Production*, edited by Simon Zagorski-Thomas and Simon Frith, 77–90. Farnham: Ashgate, 2012.

Thompson, Stacy. "Punk Cinema." *Cinema Journal* 43, no. 2 (2004): 47–66.

Thoreau, Henry David. *Walden*. Princeton, NJ: Princeton University Press, 1971.

Thornton, Sarah. *Club Cultures: Music, Media, and Subcultural Capital*. Hanover, NH: Wesleyan University Press, 1996.

Tinajero, Robert. "Hip Hop and Religion: Gangsta Rap's Christian Rhetoric." *Journal of Religion and Popular Culture* 25, no. 3 (Fall 2013): 315–332.

TMZ. "Snoop Lion Rejected by Bunny Wailer & Rastas." TMZ.com. January 23, 2013. http://www.tmz.com/2013/01/23/snoop-lion-snoop-dogg-rejected-bunny-wailer-rastarians-reincarnated.

Tot, Tibor. "Subgross Morphology, the Sick Lobe Hypothesis, and the Success of Breast Conservation." *International Journal of Breast Cancer* (2011): 1–8.

Trier, James. "Guy Debord's 'The Society of the Spectacle.'" *Journal of Adolescent and Adult Literacy* 51, no. 1 (2007): 68–73.

Trouillot, Michel-Rolph. *Silencing the Past: Power and the Production of History*. Boston, MA: Beacon Press, 1995.

Truffaut-Wong, Olivia. "7 Pink Moments That You Didn't Realize Were Super Feminist." *Bustle*. August 24, 2017. https://www.bustle.com/p/7-pink-moments-that-you-didnt-realize-were-super-feminist-78726.

Tuan, Yi-Fu. *Sense of Place: The Perspective of Experience*. Minneapolis, MN: University of Minnesota Press, 1977.

Tuan, Yi-Fu. "Language of Making a Place." *Annals of the Association of American Geographers* 81, no. 4 (1991): 684–696.

Turim, Maureen. "Women Singing, Women Gesturing: Music Videos." In *Body Politics and the Fictional Double*, edited by Debra Walker King, 131–151. Bloomington, IN: Indiana University Press, 2000.

Turim, Maureen. "Art/Music/Video.com." In *Medium Cool: Music Videos From Soundies to Cellphones*, edited by Jason Middleton and Roger Beebe, 83–110. Durham, NC: Duke University Press, 2007.

Turnbull, Gillian. "CoalDust Grins: The Conscious Creation of Western Canadian Mining Songs." Conference paper. Lancaster, PA: Society for American Music, March 6, 2014.

Turner, Katherine L., ed. *This Is the Sound of Irony. Music, Politics and Popular Culture*. New York: Routledge, 2016.

Turner, Victor. "Frame, Flow, and Reflection: Ritual and Drama as Public Liminality." *Japanese Journal of Religious Studies* 6, no. 4 (December 1979): 465–499.

Tyler, Paul L. "Hillbilly Music Re-Imagined: Folk and Country Music in the Midwest." *Journal of American Folklore* 127, no. 504 (2014): 159–190.

United Nations General Assembly. *In-Depth Study on All Forms of Violence Against Women: Report of the Secretary General*. New York: United Nations, 2006. http://www.un.org/womenwatch/daw/vaw/v-sg-study.htm.

Urban, Greg. "Ritual Wailing in Amerindian Brazil." *American Anthropologist* 90, no. 2 (1988): 285–400.

Uwumarogie, Victoria. "'I Was Like, This S**t Is Boring': bell hooks on Nicki Minaj's 'Anaconda' Video, Beyoncé and the Female Body in Pop Culture." Madamenoire. October 14, 2014. https://madamenoire.com/477942/like-st-boring-bell-hooks-nicki-minajs-anaconda-video-beyonce-female-body-pop-culture.

U2 and Neil McCormick. *U2 by U2*. New York: HarperCollins, 2007.

Van Amsterdam, Noortje. "Big Fat Inequalities, Thin Privilege: An Intersectional Perspective on "Body Size."" *European Journal of Women's Studies* 20, no. 2 (2013): 155–169.

Van Dijck, José. "Users Like You? Theorizing Agency in User-Generated Content." *Media Culture Society* 31, no. 1 (2009): 41–58.

Verma, Harsh V. "'Cool,' 'Brands' and Cool Brands." In *Brand Culture and Identity: Concepts, Methodologies, Tools, and Applications*, edited by Information Resources Management Association, 123–138. Hershey, PA: IGI Global, 2018.

Vernallis, Carol. *Experiencing Music Video: Aesthetics and Cultural Context*. New York: Columbia University Press, 2004.

Vernallis, Carol. "Strange People, Weird Objects: The Nature of Narrativity, Character and Editing in Music Videos." In *Medium Cool: Music Videos From Soundies to Cellphones*, edited by Jason Middleton and Roger Beebe, 111–151. Durham, NC and London: Duke University Press, 2007.

Vernallis, Carol. "Music Video's Second Aesthetic?" In *The Oxford Handbook of New Audiovisual Aesthetics*, edited by John Richardson, Claudia Gorbman, and Carol Vernallis, 437–465. Oxford and New York: Oxford University Press, 2013.

Vernallis, Carol. *Unruly Media: YouTube, Music Video, and the New Digital Cinema*. Oxford and New York: Oxford University Press, 2013.

Vernallis, Carol, Amy Herzog, and John Richardson, eds. *The Oxford Handbook of Sound and Image in Digital Media*. Oxford: Oxford University Press, 2013.

Viénet, René. "The Situationists and the New Forms of Action Against Politics and Art." In *Guy Debord and the Situationist International: Texts and Documents*, edited by Tom McDonough, 181–186. Cambridge, MA: MIT Press, 2002.

Viénet, René. "The Practice of Theory: Cinema and Revolution." In *Guy Debord and the Situationist International: Texts and Documents*, edited by Tom McDonough, 187–212. Cambridge, MA: MIT Press, 2002 [1969].

Waldman, Diane. *Collage, Assemblage, and the Found Object*. New York: Harry N. Abrams, 1992.

Walls, Seth Colter. "Laurie Anderson's Habeas Corpus Review—A Rare and Direct Work." *Guardian*. October 3, 2015. https://www.theguardian.com/music/2015/oct/03/laurie-anderson-habeas-corpus-review-guantanamo-omar-souleyman.

Ward, Kyle. "Dark Tranquility: Construct." Sputnikmusic.com. May 22, 2013. https://www.sputnikmusic.com/review/56961/Dark-Tranquillity-Construct.

Warwick, Jacqueline. 2009. "Singing Style and White Masculinity." In *The Ashgate Research Companion to Popular Musicology*, edited by Derek B. Scott, 349–364. Aldershot: Ashgate, 2009.

Watson, Jada. "Dust-blown Tractor Tunes: Representations of Environment in Butch Hancock's Songs About Farming in West Texas." *Canadian Folk Music* 45, no. 2 (2011): 10–18.

Watson, Jada. "The Dixie Chicks' 'Lubbock or Leave It': Negotiating Identity and Place in Country Song." *Journal of the Society for American Music* 8, no. 1 (2014): 49–75.

Watson, Jada. "'If They Blow a Hole in the Backbone': Sarah Harmer's Campaign to Protect the Niagara Escarpment." *MUSICultures* 44, no. 2 (2016): 81–108.

Watson, Jada. "Region and Identity in Dolly Parton's Songwriting." In *The Cambridge Companion to the Singer-Songwriter*, edited by Justin A. Williams and Katherine Williams, 12–30. Cambridge: Cambridge University Press, 2016.

Watson, Jada. "'This Is My Prairie': Corb Lund and the Fossil Fuel Energy Debate." *American Music* 34, no. 1 (2016): 43–86.

Watson, Jada. "Country Music and Geography: Constructing 'Geo-Cultural' Identities." In *The Oxford Handbook of Country Music*, edited by Travis D. Stimeling, 95–116. New York: Oxford University Press, 2017.

Watson, Jada. "'Girl on the Billboard': Changing Billboard Methodologies and Ecological Diversity in Hot Country Songs." Paper presented at the annual conference of the International Association for the Study of Popular Music—US Branch. Nashville, TN: International Association for the Study of Popular Music, March 2018.

Watson, Jada, and Lori Burns. "Resisting Exile and Asserting Musical Voice: The Dixie Chicks Are 'Not Ready to Make Nice.'" *Popular Music* 29, no. 3 (2010): 339–340.

Way, Lyndon, and Simon McKerrell, eds. *Music as Multimodal Discourse: Semiotics, Power, and Protest*. London and New York: Bloomsbury, 2017.

Weaver, Caity. "Beyoncé's Publicist Wants to Erase These Unflattering Photos from the Internet." Gawker.com. February 5, 2013. http://gawker.com/5981957/beyonces-publicist-wants-to-erase-these-six-unflattering-photos-from-the-internet; http://www.buzzfeed.com/buzzfeedceleb/the-unflattering-photos-beyonces-publicist-doesnt-want-you-t#.ihXzDYONDq; http://knowyourmeme.com/memes/unflattering-beyonce.

Webb, Michael. "Re Viewing Listening: 'Clip Culture' and Cross-Modal Learning in the Music Classroom." *International Journal of Music Education* 28, no. 4 (2010): 313–340.

Weber, Katherine. "Rapper DMX Reads Bible Verses to Struggling Fan on Los Angeles Street." *Christian Post*. October 14, 2013. https://www.christianpost.com/news/rapper-dmx-reads-bible-verses-to-struggling-fan-on-los-angeles-street-video-106611.

Weingarten, Christopher R. "Review: Kendrick Lamar Moves From Uplift to Beast Mode on Dazzling 'Damn.'" *Rolling Stone*. April 18, 2017. http://www.rollingstone.com/music/albumreviews/review-kendrick-lamar-damn-album-w477376.

Weingarten, Marc. *Station to Station: The History of Rock 'n' Roll on Television*. New York: Pocket Books, 2000.

Wenders, W. "Lights, Camera, Achtung Baby! Interview mit U2." In *Sound and Vision: Musikvideo und Filmkunst*, edited by Deutsches Filmmuseum, 66–71. Frankfurt am Main: Deutsches Filmmuseum, 1993.

Wete, Brad. "Kendrick Lamar Exposes the Fake to Encourage the Real in 'Humble' Video." Billboard. March 31, 2017. https://www.billboard.com/articles/columns/hip-hop/7744412/kendrick-lamar-humble-video-exposes-fake-encourage-the-real.

White, Theresa Renee. "Missy 'Misdemeanor' Elliott and Nicki Minaj: Fashionistin' Black Female Sexuality in Hip-Hop Culture—Girl Power or Overpowered?," *Journal of Black Studies* 44, no. 6 (2013): 607–626.

Whiteley, Sheila. "Progressive Rock and Psychedelic Coding in the Work of Jimi Hendrix." *Popular Music* 9, no. 1 (1990): 37–60.

Whiteley, Sheila, ed. *Sexing the Groove. Popular Music and Gender*. London: Routledge, 1997.

Whiteley, Sheila. *Women and Popular Music: Sexuality, Identity, and Subjectivity*. New York: Routledge, 2000.

Whiteley, Sheila, Andy Bennett, and Stan Hawkins, eds. *Music, Space and Place: Popular Music and Cultural Identity*. Farnham: Ashgate, 2005.

Whiteley, Sheila, and Jennifer Rycenga, eds. *Queering the Popular Pitch*. New York: Routledge, 2006.

Wicke, Peter. "Sound-Technologien und Körper-Metamorphosen. Das Populäre in der Musik des 20. Jahrhunderts." In *Rock- und Popmusik. Handbuch der Musik im 20. Jahrhundert*, vol. 8, edited by Peter Wicke, 11–60. Laaber: Laaber, 2001.

Wikstrom, Patrik. *The Music Industry: Music in the Cloud*. Cambridge: Polity Press, 2009.

Williams, Apryl A. "Fat People of Color: Emergent Intersectional Discourse Online." *Social Sciences* 6, no. 15 (February 2017): 1–16.

Williams, Brad. "28 Classic Movie Scenes Involving Stairs." Whatculture. February 19, 2013. http://whatculture.com/film/28-classic-movie-scenes-involving-stairs.

Williams, Justin A. "Intertextuality and Lineage in The Game's 'We Ain't' (2005) and Kendrick Lamar's Good Kid, 'm.A.A.d. City' (2012)." In *The Pop Palimpsest: Intertextuality in Recorded Popular Music*, edited by Lori Burns and Serge Lacasse, 291–312. Ann Arbor, MI: University of Michigan Press, 2018.

Williams, Raymond. *The City and the Country*. New York: Oxford University Press, 1973.

Wilson, Pamela. "Mountains of Contradictions: Gender, Class, and Region in the Star Image of Dolly Parton." In *Reading Country Music: Steel Guitars, Opry Stars, and Honky-Tonk Bars*, edited by Cecelia Tichi, 98–120. Durham, NC: Duke University Press, 1998.

Wimsatt, William K., Jr., and Monroe C. Beardsley. "The Intentional Fallacy." In *The Verbal Icon: Studies in the Meaning of Poetry*, by William K. Wimsatt, 3–20. Lexington, KY: University of Kentucky Press, 1954.

Winston, Brian. *Technologies of Seeing—Photography, Cinematography and Television*. London: British Film Institute, 1996.

Witherington, Ben, III. *Isaiah Old and New: Exegesis, Intertextuality, and Hermeneutics.* Minneapolis, MN: Fortress Press, 2017.

Wodtke, Larissa. "The Child's Place in Pop Music." *Jeunesse: Young People, Texts, Cultures* 10, no. 2 (2018): 173–191.

Wood, Aylish. "Re-animating Space." *Animation: An Interdisciplinary Journal* 1, no. 2 (2006): 133–152.

Wolf, Mark. *Building Imaginary Worlds: The Theory and History of Subcreation.* New York: Routledge, 2012.

Wolf, Werner. *Metareference Across Media—Theory and Case Studies.* Amsterdam and New York: Rodopi, 2009.

Wolf, Werner. "(Inter)mediality and the Study of Literature." *CLCWeb: Comparative Literature and Culture* 13, no. 3 (2011). https://doi.org/10.7771/1481-4374.1789.

Wolf, Werner. "Literature and Music: Theory." In *Handbook of Intermediality. Literature—Image—Sound—Music,* edited by Gabriele Rippl, 459–474. Berlin: Walter de Gruyter, 2015.

World Health Organization. *Promoting Gender Equality to Prevent Violence Against Women: Series of Briefings on Violence Prevention: The Evidence—Overview.* Geneva: World Health Organization, 2009. http://whqlibdoc.who.int/publications/2009/9789241597883_eng.pdf.

Yeats, W.B. "Under Ben Bulben." *The Collected Poems of W.B. Yeats.* New York: Macmillan, 1959.

Young, Alex. "New Music: Game Feat. Scarface and Kendrick Lamar—'Murder.'" *Consequence of Sound.* December 9, 2012. https://consequenceofsound.net/2012/12/new-music-game-feat-scarface-and-kendrick-lamar-murder.

Young, Eric. "Rapper DMX Says Life Calling Is To Be a Pastor." *Christian Today.* January 19, 2009. https://www.christiantoday.com/article/rapper.dmx.says.life.calling.is.to.be.a.pastor/22333.htm.

Zaborowski, Rafal. "Hatsune Miku and Japanese Virtual Idols." In *The Oxford Handbook of Music and Virtuality,* edited by Sheila Whiteley and Shara Rambarran, 111–128. Oxford: Oxford University Press, 2016.

Zak, Albin. *The Poetics of Rock: Cutting Tracks, Making Records.* Berkeley, CA: University of California Press, 2001.

Zanfagna, Christina. *Holy Hip Hop in the City of Angels.* Oakland, CA: University of California Press, 2017.

Zisook, Brian "Z". "Kendrick Lamar Responded to Our Article About His Fear of God." DJBooth. April 28, 2017. https://djbooth.net/features/2017-04-28-kendrick-lamar-god-response.

Index